Teaching Children and Adolescents with Special Needs

Judy L. Olson and Jennifer M. Platt
University of Central Florida

Merrill, an imprint of
Macmillan Publishing Company
New York

Maxwell Macmillan Canada
Toronto

Maxwell Macmillan International
New York   Oxford   Singapore   Sydney

Editor: Ann Castel
Production Editors: Jan Mauer and Linda H. Bayma
Art Coordinator: Vincent A. Smith
Production Buyer: Pamela D. Bennett

This book was set in Galliard by Carlisle Communications, Ltd. and was printed and bound by Book Press, Inc., a Quebecor America Book Group Company. The cover was printed by New England Book Components.

Macmillan Publishing Company
866 Third Avenue
New York, NY 10022

Macmillan Publishing Company is part of the
Maxwell Communication Group of Companies.

Maxwell Macmillan Canada, Inc.
1200 Eglinton Avenue East, Suite 200
Don Mills, Ontario M3C 3N1

Library of Congress Cataloging-in-Publication Data

Olson, Judy L.
    Teaching children and adolescents with special needs / Judy L.
  Olson and Jennifer M. Platt.
        p.   cm.
    Includes bibliographical references (p.   ) and indexes.
    ISBN 0–675–21230–8
    1. Special education. 2. Teaching. 3. Classroom management.
  I. Platt, Jennifer M.   II. Title.
  LC3969.047   1992
  371.9 — dc20
                                                                    91–39910
                                                                    CIP

Printing: 2 3 4 5 6 7 8 9   Year: 3 4 5

Photo Credits: All photos copyrighted by individuals or companies listed. All photos by Donna Janeczko.

To Larry R. Olson,
To the memory of Virginia F. Cox,
and
To our students, who inspired the writing of this text:
Those we have worked with in the past, those we are
currently teaching, and those still to come.

Preface

This text is based on a personal philosophy that has evolved from the literature in special and regular education and from our professional experiences. The teacher effectiveness research in both special and regular education provides many exemplary teaching practices that we include in this text. Our professional experiences include teaching both elementary and secondary students in regular and special education settings, supervising student teachers, training preservice and in-service teachers, and continuing participation as learners in professional development activities involving effective teaching practices.

The basic philosophy that keeps us actively involved in the profession after more than 20 years is that as teachers, we can "make a difference" in the lives of our students. When the preservice and in-service teachers we work with express concern about not affecting the lives of each of their students to the degree they wish, we remind them of the following story of a young boy walking along the beach. To paraphrase:

> That morning the tide had brought in thousands of starfish and scattered them on the hot, dry, sandy beach. A little boy was walking along the beach, tossing starfish back into the cool, blue water. As he was doing this, an older man approached him. The older man looked at what the young boy was doing and said, "Why are you doing that? Don't you see it's impossible? Look at the thousands of starfish. You can't possibly make a difference." The young boy slowly looked up at the man, picked up another starfish and threw it back into the water, saying, "It makes a difference to this one." (author unknown)

We hope you find ideas and suggestions in this text to make a difference in your students' lives. You have the power to make a difference, for you have chosen to teach.

Features of the Text

We use an informal, personal tone in writing this text. Our students, with whom we have field-tested several of the chapters, have commented that they like the style because it sounds as if we are sitting and talking with them. They have also commented favorably about our frequent use of practical information. Additionally, we structure and organize the text to include recommendations of teacher effectiveness research, including the following effective teaching practices:

Advance Organizers and Postorganizers

We begin each chapter with an advance organizer by providing an outline that highlights the major points. Each chapter closes with a postorganizer, a summary designed to pull together the information in the chapter.

v

Reviewing/Checking for Understanding/Monitoring Progress

We build into each chapter several checkpoints so that you can monitor your progress as you read. These checkpoints take the form of "Important Points" sections.

Active Involvement

We provide opportunities for you to become actively involved by placing activity sections in each of the chapters. They are interspersed throughout each chapter to give you ample practice. Remember the Chinese proverb: "I hear and I forget, I see and I remember, I do and I understand."

Visual Aids

We include tables, figures, diagrams, photographs, and illustrations throughout the text. We hope you use them to clarify concepts and to increase your interest.

Organization of the Text

This textbook is organized into three parts: "Foundations for Instruction," "Instructional Techniques," and "Factors Affecting Instruction." In Chapter 1, "Teaching Students with Special Needs," we discuss student characteristics, cultural diversity of students, generic instructional techniques, delivery systems, and the Regular Education Initiative. In Chapter 2, "Beginning-of-the-Year Planning," we suggest ways to get to know your students and plan an effective start to the school year. We provide suggestions for organizing the classroom, scheduling your students' activities, grouping your pupils for instruction, and using the Individualized Education Program (IEP). Chapter 3, "Informal Assessment for Initial Planning," is designed to help you assess your students before you plan instruction. The chapter emphasizes the use of curriculum-based measurement, precision teaching, and other informal techniques for initial assessment and planning purposes.

Chapter 4, "Informal Assessment for Monitoring Student Progress and Intervention Effectiveness," addresses the important topic of monitoring student performance as part of daily classroom procedures. We present practical, efficient strategies such as charting, graphing, goal setting, and self-monitoring techniques. In Chapter 5, "Instructional Materials," we focus on teacher-made and commercially produced instructional materials. You learn how to analyze, select, develop, modify, and adapt instructional materials and learning centers for elementary and secondary students with special needs. In Chapter 6, "Communication and Collaborative Consultation," we describe consultation-based programming and the essential ingredients for effective collaborative consultation. We also suggest techniques for working with paraprofessionals and parents.

In the second part of the text, we include Chapter 7, "General Instructional Techniques," in which we show you how to develop lessons and deliver instruction by using instructional techniques identified in the teacher effectiveness research. We present the features of a lesson: presentation, guided practice, feedback, and independent practice. Additionally, we emphasize the use of effective questioning and suggest strategies for ensuring active involvement/participation of students. In Chapter 8, "Teacher-Directed Content Instruction," we describe teacher-directed methods and examine explicit skill instructional techniques such as Direct Instruction and unit teaching. In Chapter 9, "Teacher-Directed Strategy Instruction," we concentrate on teacher-directed methods for teaching implicit skills. These include metacognition, reciprocal teaching, and strategy instruction. In Chapter 10, "Teacher-Directed Instruction Study Skills," we address study skills and strategies to help students acquire, organize, and express information. In Chapter 11, "Student-Directed Instruction," we focus on teaching methods that are more student-directed, such as peer tutoring, cooperative learning, and whole language.

The final part "Factors Affecting Instruction," contains the last three chapters of the text, In Chapter 12, "Computer Technology for Teaching and Learning," we explore the uses of computers by students and teachers. We present ideas for instruction, practice, and reinforcement, and suggestions concerning effective software. We include Chapter 13, "Transition Skills: Career Education and Related Social Skills," because of the importance of these areas of preparing students for transition to various school, work, and life situations. In this chapter, we provide suggestions and implications for both assessment and instruction. We conclude the text with Chapter 14, "Identifying and Managing Teacher Stress." In this chapter, we first identify the stress-producing factors such as paperwork and time demands, behavior problems, and lack of support or recognition, and then suggest strategies for managing them.

As teacher educators we have heard students comment about the texts they have used in their classes (e.g., "I didn't get anything out of the book for that course" or "I didn't read the book—it had nothing to do with what goes on in school with kids"). We have written a textbook that students **will** get something out of—practical, research-based teaching strategies—and that **does** relate to what goes on in schools—motivating, experience-based activities for you and your students. We hope you enjoy reading it as much as we enjoyed writing it.

Acknowledgments

We wish to acknowledge the contributions of all those people who assisted us in the completion of this text. Thanks to Kathy Anderson, Kathy Dillard, Connie Kouchalokas, and Susan Yopp, who demonstrated exemplary teaching practices, and to the parents and their children who allowed us to capture these practices in photographs. We are indebted to Donna Janeczko for her photographic contributions and to Harry

Dangel, Georgia State University; Robert A. Gable, Old Dominion University; Sheila K. Hollander, Adelphi University; Jack Hourcade, Boise State University; Walter H. Kimball, University of Southern Maine; Beth Lasky, California State University at Northridge; Melinda Lindsey, Boise State University; Paula J. Smith, Illinois State University; and James Yanok, Ohio University, who reviewed our manuscript.

We appreciate the friendship, support, research, and editing contributions of Al Pearce in helping us complete this text, the assistance of Judith Corrales for her help on the text, the help of Rose Corso in duplicating the manuscript, the support of Barbara Huckabay in typing some of the manuscript, and the expertise of Eileen Pracek in the development of the "Software for Survival" appendix. The members of the Florida Diagnostic Learning Resource System (FDLRS) East and Action deserve special mention for their assistance.

We also offer our thanks to Donna Baumbach, who wrote Chapter 12, "Computer Technology for Teaching and Learning," and to Warren J. White and Linda P. Thurston, who wrote Chapter 13, "Transition Skills: Career Education and Related Social Skills." To Ann Castel, Jan Mauer, Linda Bayma, Vince Smith, and all the Macmillan staff, we express our gratitude for making our dream a reality.

A special thanks goes to Larry Olson, whose patience with and support of a part-time wife during this process is deeply appreciated. Gratitude and appreciation are given to Chris Platt for his advice, support, and concern during the completion of the text and to the memory of Virginia Cox, who shared so many valuable suggestions with her daughter.

Without the input of our students at the University of Central Florida in the field testing of chapters and the support and encouragement of our families and friends, we would not have had an opportunity to make a difference in the lives of students with special needs. We are deeply grateful for these many contributions.

Contents

Chapter 3
Informal Assessment for Initial Planning

Chapter 4
Informal Assessment for Monitoring Student Progress
and Intervention Effectiveness

Chapter 5
Instructional Materials

121

Chapter 6
Communication and Collaborative Consultation

153

Part II
Instructional Techniques

Chapter 13
Transition Skills: Career Education and Related Social Skills

---

Chapter 14
Identifying and Managing Teacher Stress

Appendix A
Ethnic Groups

Appendix B
Software for Survival

References

Author Index

Subject Index

Part I

Foundations for Instruction

1

Teaching Students with
Special Needs

Key Topics

The needs and characteristics of children and adolescents with learning and behavior problems are varied. This variation requires you as a teacher to be knowledgeable about and make decisions in a variety of areas, including student characteristics, planning, effective teaching techniques, monitoring and evaluation, types of service delivery, and research-based trends in special education.

Being knowledgeable about student characteristics means that you know your students' academic levels, can identify the skills they bring with them to the learning situation, and understand their cultural backgrounds. In planning, you should focus on the academic levels of your students as you decide upon your instructional arrangements, materials, subject matter, and scheduling techniques.

Children and adolescents with special needs often exhibit problems with academic and social skills that make it difficult for them to meet the demands of school, home, and community. For optimum learning to occur, it is important that you use teaching strategies found to be effective, such as those documented in teacher effectiveness research (Berliner, 1984; Rosenshine & Stevens, 1986).

Monitoring and evaluation are essential parts of instructional decision making. Your monitoring and evaluation techniques may include teacher monitoring, student self-monitoring, feedback, grading, and record keeping. You must also be aware of services available for students with special needs, and you should base your instructional decisions on the needs and characteristics of your students.

Student Characteristics

Students with special needs often have problems in academic areas, social interactions, motivation, and transition to adult roles. In many school districts, such students are referred to as having learning disabilities (specific learning disabilities), mental handicaps (mentally retarded, educable mentally retarded), or emotional handicaps (emotionally disturbed, behavior disorders).

Even though educational practice frequently categorizes children and adolescents into these three distinct groups, researchers document many similarities in the characteristics of these groups. Wilson, Cone, Bradley, and Reese (1986) found similarities in IQ scores, perceptual–motor performance, and achievement levels of students with learning disabilities and those with emotional disturbances. These researchers also found similarities in the classroom behaviors of students with learning disabilities and those with mental handicaps. On the *Stanford Achievement Test,* Scruggs and Mastropieri (1986) found no academic differences in the performance of 619 primary-aged students with learning disabilities and 863 with behavior disorders. Gajar (1977) analyzed intellectual achievement and behavioral data for 155 students who were learning disabled, 122 who were emotionally handicapped, and 121 who were mentally handicapped and found that all three groups performed similarly on reading and math assessments. Thus, it appears that there are more similarities than differences among these groups of students.

Students with special needs often display one or more of the following characteristics:

- *Inadequate academic achievement.* Often, such students are 2 or more years behind their grade-level peers in reading, mathematics, spelling, written expression, and oral language skills.
- *Inappropriate school behaviors.* Many times, such students are physically or verbally aggressive. They are easily frustrated or unable to cope with the demands of the school environment. Other signs of inappropriate school behavior include noncompliance with teacher directions and instructions and lack of teacher-pleasing behaviors, such as being prepared for class, maintaining eye contact, and raising hands for teacher recognition.
- *Poor attending behaviors.* Students with special needs often have trouble following teacher directions and instructions. They seem to have difficulty attending to the relevant information in a message and are frequently unable to concentrate on an assignment or task.
- *Poor memory.* Being unable to remember information from one week to the next or one day to the next is another characteristic common to students with special needs. Such students frequently have problems re-

membering spelling words, basic math facts, and two or more directions.
- *Inadequate organizational skills.* Students who have special needs may have problems organizing their materials to prepare for an exam or to write a report. Frequently, their desks are cluttered and their materials are lost or misplaced.
- *Poor self-concept.* For many of these students, school is not a comfortable, rewarding place. Instead, it is a place where they often fail to meet the standards for success.

Cultural Diversity

Within the population of students with special needs, are subgroups of students who are not members of the Anglo-American culture. These students are from Native American, Asian, Hispanic, African-American, or other cultures. Students from these groups are disproportionately represented in special education classes (see Table 1.1). In 1988 minority students comprised 38.6% of the total school-age population and 41% of the total population of individuals in the categories specified in Table 1.1 (DBS Corporation, 1988). It is projected that by the turn of the century 40% of the students in public schools will be from ethnically diverse backgrounds, with the percentage higher in many states (Ramirez, 1988). As can be seen from the 1988 figures, many of these children will need special education services.

Although the children in the schools are from various cultures, the school culture frequently reflects the values of the Anglo-American culture (Turnbull & Turnbull, 1986). These values, which are often at odds with those of other cultures, include a belief in competition versus cooperation, individual autonomy and independence, an achievement orientation, a future orientation, and an informal classroom atmosphere (Briganti, 1989; Grossman, 1990; McGill & Pearce, 1982; Turnbull & Turnbull, 1986).

Table 1.1
Minority Representation in Special Education

Enrollment	Native American	Asian	Hispanic	African-American	Minority	White	Total
Number	225345	778904	2809909	4735003	8549161	13542922	22092083
Percent	1.0	3.5	12.7	21.4	38.7	61.3	100.0
Educable Mentally Retarded:							
Number	2413	2258	23538	100771	128980	113032	242012
% of Total	1.0	0.9	9.7	41.6	53.3	46.7	100.0
Trainable Mentally Retarded:							
Number	644	2064	22814	39677	65199	38360	103559
% of Total	0.6	2.0	22.0	38.3	63.0	37.0	100.0
Seriously Emotionally Disturbed:							
Number	1323	902	9276	40724	52225	92274	144499
% of Total	0.9	0.6	6.4	28.2	36.1	63.9	100.0
Specific Learning Disabled:							
Number	13226	10684	109614	206841	340365	601977	942342
% of Total	1.4	1.1	11.6	21.9	36.1	63.9	100.0

Note. Adapted from *Elementary and Secondary School Civil Rights Survey, National Summary of Reported Data of 40,020 Schools* by the Department of Education, Office of Civil Rights, Washington, D.C., 1988.

Competition Versus Cooperation

School culture tends to promote competition over cooperation (Turnbull & Turnbull, 1986). The Hispanic culture emphasizes working together for the good of the group (Briganti, 1989; Grossman, 1990) and values cooperation over competition (Castaneda, 1976; Grossman, 1990). In the Native American culture, the needs of the family and the tribe are given priority over the needs of individuals (Johnson, 1987). The African-American culture also tends to be social, and it endorses working with others (Gitter, Black, & Mostofsky, 1972; Hillard, 1976; Shade, 1979).

Individual Autonomy and Independence

Anglo-American families tend to promote adult-like behaviors early in their children (Chinn &

Plata, 1987). In a study of maternal care, Oberg, Murret-Wagstaff, Moore, and Cummings (1983) found that mothers of Caucasian children prodded their children more often toward a goal or accomplishment and showed more disappointment when their children failed to reach their expectations than did mothers from other racial groups.

The Hispanic culture expects children to be dependent on parents and to seek their approval (Briganti, 1989). For example, parents help children dress and tie their shoes longer than do parents in the Anglo-American culture (Briganti, 1989). Likewise, the Asian culture does not rush children into becoming adults (Chinn & Plata, 1987). Until the preschool years, when children are given more responsibility for their behavior, Asian parents are more tolerant and permissive than are parents in Western cultures

(S. Chan, 1987). In the African-American culture, many children are taught to seek approval, guidance, and feedback from others (Grossman, 1990; Hale, 1981). Children who were raised in this manner may find it difficult to form their own opinions and may require assistance to function independently (Grossman, 1984; Grossman, 1990).

Achievement Orientation

In the school culture, high achievement is a goal that generates emphasis (Grossman, 1990). Although the Asian-American culture places a high value on educational achievement (Chan & Kitano, 1987; Kitano, 1987), this is not the rule of many of the other non-Anglo-American cultures. The Hispanic culture endorses the goal of developing a child's personality, not the highest potential to achieve, as in the Anglo-American culture (Briganti, 1989). Moreover, many Hispanics are taught that it is bad manners to excel over others in a group in an attempt to be recognized for individual achievement (Grossman, 1984).

In the African-American culture, the goal of school achievement is integrated into mental, emotional, and physical achievement. Wilson (1989) attributes the success of Project Interface, a preparatory math and science program for black junior high students, to the fact that both the achievement and behavior needs of the students are considered.

In a successful program of teaching high-risk Native American students, Uthe-Reyno incorporates self-esteem exercises into the curriculum (Uthe-Reyno & McKinnon, 1989). Affective or behavioral objectives are found on the individualized education programs of many special students.

Future Orientation

In both the Hispanic and African-American cultures, motivation is often connected to immediate needs, with very little planning or waiting for the future (Brown, 1986). Lack of a future emphasis promotes the importance of living to the fullest now, instead of delaying for the future. As

noted by Turnbull and Turnbull (1986), lack of emphasis on future goals may result in a reluctance of parents to think about future independent living for their children with special needs.

Informal Classroom Atmosphere

The informality of the typical school classroom is alien to many students from non-Anglo-American cultures. In the Vietnamese school culture, students are expected to learn by listening, watching, and imitating the teacher (Wei, 1980). Answering questions or speaking up in class is not valued in the Asian culture, which teaches deference toward authority figures (Briganti, 1989; Chinn & Plata, 1987; Grossman, 1990). The Hispanic culture also promotes a formal, respectful relationship with adults (Grossman, 1984).

Individual Differences

As you can see, some students have problems because their culture is in conflict with the school culture. However, there is an inherent danger of stereotyping when group characteristics are applied to individuals. Obviously, many students do not fit the group descriptions. Students from cultures other than the Anglo-American frequently adopt the Anglo-American culture and become acculturated, or Americanized (Leung, 1989). The degree of acculturation depends on such variables as proximity, age, birthplace, and time (Leung, 1989). Immigrants who live in ethnic centers in metropolitan areas have less opportunity to socialize with other ethnic groups, so they tend to retain their ethnic identity longer. Young people usually adapt more readily than do older people, and those born in the country usually adapt more readily than do those born in another country. Succeeding generations are less steeped in ethnic traditions than are the first.

Because of individual differences and the acculturation process, the previous descriptions may not apply to Juan or Latasha. Information concerning cultural differences should be only the first step in your selection of a teaching strategy. As soon as possible, you should begin to

---

☐ Important Points

1. Students with special needs often display one or more of the following characteristics: inadequate academic achievement, inappropriate school behaviors, poor attending behaviors, poor memory, inadequate organizational skills, and poor self-concept.

2. The school culture focuses on the values of the Anglo-American culture, even though students come from a variety of cultures.

3. The Anglo-American values, often at odds with those of other cultures, are a belief in competition versus cooperation, individual autonomy and independence, achievement orientation, future orientation, and an informal classroom atmosphere.

4. Some students from other cultures adopt the Anglo-American culture and become acculturated.

5. Cultural factors and individual differences should influence the selection of instructional techniques.

---

collect data and monitor the progress of individual students. For example, you may decide to place Juan with a peer to practice reading basic sight words to capitalize on the cooperative emphasis of the Hispanic culture as an initial instructional technique. However, if your monitoring shows that Juan is making little progress, you should change the strategy. More background information of the various cultures in addition to sources of information on multicultural issues may be found in Appendix A.

■ ■ Activity
Look back at the section on cultural diversity of students. Discuss how you would use the information about cultural differences in your work with students. (Answers for this and other activities are found in the Instructor's Manual.) ■ ■

General Instructional Strategies

General instructional strategies involve the teaching of explicit and implicit skills (Rosenshine, 1990). Explicit skills are basic, well-structured skills, while implicit skills are less-structured, higher-order skills. Explicit skills may be taught in a step-by-step manner. Explicit skills include learning math facts, decoding words, memorizing science terms, and following the rules for capitalization. Implicit skills do not follow a set of steps and often have more than one acceptable answer. Implicit skills include interpreting an author's message, summarizing a passage, and writing a theme. Rosenshine (1990) distinguishes between explicit and implicit skills in stating, "Before, we were asking students questions. Now we see we need to teach students how to ask questions" (p. 5). Educators in the field of special education teach both explicit and implicit skills; explicit, when they teach basic skills and well-structured content or tasks (e.g., reconciling a checkbook) and implicit, when they teach strategies and less-structured content or tasks (e.g., comprehension-monitoring).

Explicit Skills
Historically, special educators have concentrated on teaching explicit skills. Rosenshine and Stevens (1986) report several elements that have emerged from teacher effectiveness research.

The following elements are applicable in the teaching of explicit skills: (a) beginning lessons with a review and a goal statement, such as "Today, I will show you how to reduce fractions;" (b) giving clear directions and proceeding in small steps; (c) providing active, guided practice; (d) checking for student understanding, such as "Bruno, tell us the steps in long division;" (e) providing feedback with statements, such as "Elena, you are correct. That is the subject of the sentence;" and (f) monitoring student progress. In a review of instructional effectiveness for students with special needs, Christenson, Thurlow, and Ysseldyke (1987) identified the most efficient process for teaching a clearly defined skill as consisting of the three steps: "(a) demonstration of the skill or presentation of the rule or general principle, (b) student practice of each of the component parts of the skill with the teacher providing prompts and corrections, (c) independent student practice with teacher monitoring for a high student success rate" (p. 7). These steps are followed in specific instructional procedures, such as direct instruction, which is exemplified in the Reading Mastery programs.

Implicit Skills

Certain elements that are emerging may prove useful in teaching less-structured, implicit skills (Rosenshine, 1990). The first is the use of procedural facilitators (Scardamalia & Bereiter, 1985), or clues that support students as they learn a skill, such as identifying stop points in text. (Stop points are places at which students stop and ask themselves questions about what they read.) Procedural facilitators, such as prompting by the teacher, provide temporary support to students during learning. Second, new skills may be presented through (a) modeling (stopping in reading at premarked stop points); (b) thinking aloud (asking yourself what you read); and (c) anticipating difficulties ("This is hard to read. I need to stop often to ask myself questions about it."). Third, implicit skills may be taught by having students practice with easy materials and problems and then gradually increasing the level of difficulty. Fourth, practice may be enhanced by giving students partially completed problems to solve (e.g., "Write the ending to this story") and cue cards, prompt cards, or cards with questions to remind students how to paraphrase what they just read. Fifth, students may be taught self-checking to show them how to monitor their performance. A checklist may help students evaluate their work (e.g., "Does my paragraph have a topic sentence, detail sentences, and a clincher sentence?"). Sixth, students may be given independent practice that emphasizes application to new examples to facilitate generalization of the skills (e.g., "Now that I have learned how to proofread my schoolwork, I can use the same strategy to proofread job applications, forms, and letters").

In applying the instructional strategies involved in the teaching of implicit skills to the teaching of adolescents who were low achieving and had mild learning disabilities, Deshler and Schumaker (1988) focused on teaching the students how to meet the academic demands of the school setting. Investigations have shown that students who have learning disabilities and are low achieving can master learning strategies and successfully apply them (Deshler & Schumaker, 1986; Harris & Graham, 1985). Strategies for teaching implicit skills are easy to generalize across age levels and content areas and empower students to manage their own learning (Archer & Isaacson, 1990).

As you may have noticed, a basic structure is present in the teaching of both explicit and implicit skills. This structure includes the variables of planning, presentation, guided practice, feedback, independent practice, and evaluation. We organize these elements into a framework that you may use in making decisions concerning the teaching of explicit and implicit skills to children and adolescents with special needs (see Figure 1.1).

☐ Important Points

1. Explicit skills are basic, well-structured skills that may be taught in a step-by-step manner.
2. Explicit skills include learning math facts, decoding words, memorizing science terms, and following the rules of capitalization.
3. Implicit skills are less-structured, higher-order skills that do not follow a set of steps and that may have more than one acceptable answer.
4. Implicit skills include interpreting an author's message, summarizing a passage, and writing a theme.
5. Elements applicable in the teaching of explicit skills include (a) beginning lessons with a review and goal; (b) giving clear directions and proceeding in small steps; (c) providing active, guided practice; (d) checking for understanding; (e) providing feedback; and (f) monitoring student progress.
6. Three steps for teaching a clearly defined skill are (a) demonstrate the rule or principle, (b) prompt and correct as students practice, and (c) monitor during independent practice for a high success rate.
7. Elements applicable in the teaching of implicit skills include (a) using procedural facilitators, or clues; (b) modeling, thinking aloud, and anticipating difficulties; (c) regulating the difficulty of materials and problems; (d) giving partially completed problems and using cue, or prompt, cards; (e) teaching self-checking; and (f) providing independent practice with new examples.
8. The basic structure present in the teaching of explicit and implicit skills includes the variables of planning, presentation, guided practice, feedback, independent practice, and evaluation.

■ ■ Activity

Decide whether the following are explicit skills or implicit skills:

1. Locating the main idea in a sentence.
2. Adding fractions with common denominators.
3. Writing a research paper.
4. Counting from 1 to 10 in Spanish.
5. Identifying the parts of the digestive system.
6. Writing a business letter.
7. Critiquing an author's writing style. ■ ■

Planning

Presentation

Guided Practice

Feedback

Independent Practice

Evaluation

Figure 1.1
Structure for Teaching Explicit and Implicit Skills

Program Alternatives

Students with special needs are found in a variety of placements (Bos & Vaughn, 1988; Mercer & Mercer, 1991; Polloway, Patton, Payne, & Payne, 1989). These placements are arranged on a continuum and offer a range of service options to meet the needs of students. In Figure 1.2, the program alternatives are arranged from the least restrictive to the most restrictive. The term *least restrictive* means that "special education students

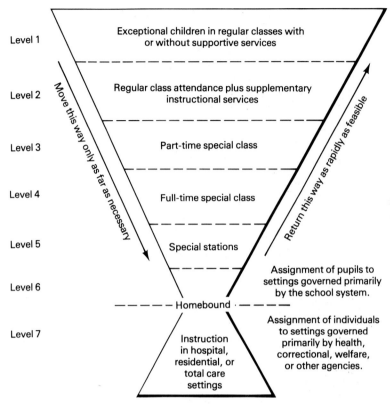

Figure 1.2

Deno's Cascade System of Special Education Services

Note. Original model from "Special Education as Developmental Capital" by E. Deno, 1970, *Exceptional Children, 37,* pp. 229–237. Adapted figure from *Introduction to Special Education,* 2nd ed. (p. 268) by J. E. Ysseldyke and B. Algozzine, 1990, Boston: Houghton Mifflin. Reprinted by permission of Houghton Mifflin.

should be educated in environments that are as much like normal—least restrictive—as possible" (Ysseldyke & Algozzine, 1990, p. 25). Notice that the model is wide at the top and eventually becomes narrower to reflect the differences in numbers served at the different levels.

Some students who have special needs attend regular classes with or without supportive services. Ysseldyke and Algozzine (1990) report this to be the largest number of students with special needs. (See level 1 of the model.) For example, Wally attends a sixth grade class in which his teacher modifies assignments and adapts materials when necessary. Sometimes, the special education teacher collaborates with the sixth grade teacher about Wally's assignments.

Other students receive assistance primarily from a regular classroom teacher, but they also receive some instruction from a special education teacher within the regular classroom. The regular classroom teacher may receive consultative services from a special education teacher, too. Carilla, an eighth grade student, works with both her seventh grade science teacher and the special education teacher as the two co-teach some of the science classes. This is level 2 in the model. The teachers have developed supplementary materials to facilitate understanding of the text.

Other students with special needs attend a pull-out program referred to as a resource room, or a part-time special class. These students spend most of the day in the regular classroom and leave for just part of the day to attend a resource room for instruction in specific skills and strategies or content areas. For example, Randy, a tenth grader, is scheduled in regular content classes for most of his school subjects. However, he attends one class in which a special education teacher teaches him strategies in test-taking and note-taking. This is level 3 in the model.

In some instances, students with special needs are served in full-time special class placements, which may be referred to as self-contained, or separate, classes. Students who attend these classrooms are frequently mainstreamed, that is, placed in regular classrooms with nonhandicapped students for part of the school day. For example, Luwanda attends a self-contained classroom, but she goes to a fourth grade class for math, music, physical education, and art. This is identified as level 4 in the model.

Some students who require more intensive services are enrolled in a special school within the school system, referred to as special stations (level 5). Mark attends Pineland School and receives special education services, speech therapy, physical therapy, and counseling.

The other two placements in the model, homebound (level 6) and hospital, residential, and total care settings (level 7), are appropriate for students who receive services outside the school system. These placements may involve instruction at home, in residential settings, detention centers, or hospitals. For example, Jamie receives special education and related services in the Polter Home for Boys.

The students with learning and behavior problems whom we address in this text may be served in regular classrooms, through the consultative model, in resource rooms, or in self-contained settings at one time or another, depending upon their individual academic and socioemotional needs. Placement decisions should be made on the basis of the needs, strengths, and weaknesses of individual students. In the rest of this text, we do not refer to levels 5, 6, and 7. Instead, we concentrate on

reporting research, providing examples, and making suggestions for the population of students with special needs who are being served in the first four levels.

The Regular Education Initiative

Currently, an initiative is being suggested by the federal government to change significantly the way in which educators provide services to students with mild to moderate disabilities and to other students with special needs (Teacher Education Division, Council for Exceptional Children, 1987). This initiative, or movement to place fewer students with disabilities in pull-out programs and instead educate them in regular education settings, is called the Regular Education Initiative (REI). This proposed partnership between regular and special education in serving students with special needs has received mixed reactions from professionals in the field of special education. The proposal to restructure regular and special education was made by Madeleine Will, Assistant Secretary for the United States Office of Special Education and Rehabilitative Services, at a conference in 1985. At that time, Will advocated a responsibility and commitment shared between regular and special education and the use of effective special education techniques "beyond" the special class setting (Will, 1986).

Many states place students in pull-out programs according to their identified category (mental, emotional, and learning disabilities). Will (1986) recommends that building-level administrators organize the personnel and resources necessary to produce appropriate services for all students, based on their educational needs rather than on the fact that they qualify for categorical programs. She recommends the use of trials in a number of states and school districts. These trials would incorporate approaches such as (a) utilization of effective intervention strategies in regular classrooms to prevent identification of students as disabled, (b) use of curriculum-based assessment, (c) application of effective teaching methods, (d) delegation of control and responsibility to school administrators for coordinating services to students with disabilities in the regular setting, and (e) provision of support to teachers, including school-based support groups. The federal government has funded six universities and six school districts to develop models for educating students with disabilities in regular education settings (Ysseldyke & Algozzine, 1990).

The Regular Education Initiative represents fundamental changes in current practice in educating students with mild to moderate disabilities, as well as students with other special needs (Hallahan, Kauffman, Lloyd, & McKinney, 1988). The initiative would significantly change the roles of service providers, especially regular and special education teachers.

Support for the Regular Education Initiative

A variety of reasons have been suggested for merging regular and special education. These reasons include inadequacy of conventional methods, problems with categorical programs, and the disjointedness of current efforts and programs.

Inadequacy of Conventional Education Methods

An increasing number of students in the schools are unable to learn adequately in the regular education system through conventional education methods (Will, 1986). In fact, Will estimates that of the school-aged population, approximately 30% of the students are having difficulty in school. Therefore, teachers need instructional techniques appropriate for working with student populations who are not progressing under the current system. The Regular Education Initiative provides an excellent opportunity for regular and special education teachers to work collectively toward this goal (Algozzine, Maheady, Sacca, O'Shea, & O'Shea, 1990).

Problems with Categorical Programs

The use of categories, for students with mild handicaps has been criticized (Reynolds, Wang, & Walberg, 1987). Will (1986) indicates that many students who need extra services are ineligible under the current categorical system. Wang, Reynolds, and Walberg (1986) state that categorical programs in special education may overlap with migrant programs and bilingual education programs, leading to confusion about where to place students who show evidence of low achievement but who do not meet eligibility criteria. They propose integrated programs in general education to include students with disabilities, and students from other special programs. Wang, Reynolds, and Walberg point out the ineffectiveness of the current classification system and the added burdens of administering, teaching, and funding. Additionally, students who are categorized, segregated from nonhandicapped peers, and labeled are frequently stigmatized.

Disjointedness of Current Efforts and Programs

Proponents of the Regular Education Initiative say that regular and special education programs seem to be operating as two separate and distinct systems, with little coordination of effort. They say that special educators tend to assume responsibility for students with disabilities. The roles of regular educators and building administrators in that regard tend to be weak and detached (Jenkins, Pious, & Jewell, 1990). Wang, Reynolds, and Walberg (1986) state, "The pull-out approach is driven by the fallacy that poor school adjustment and performance are attributable solely to the student, rather than to the quality of the learning environment" (p. 290). Lilly (1987) voices concern that the instruction delivered in pull-out programs may be implemented without regard to the instructional systems being utilized in the regular setting.

Concerns with the Regular Education Initiative

A number of important issues, concerns, and questions that are raised by professionals must be effectively addressed before the proposed merger between regular and special education can be considered. These concerns include attribution of students' failures to the school or teacher, the ability of students who are mildly handicapped or low achieving to succeed under the proposed initiative, the ability of regular teachers to cope with the demands under the proposed initiative, and the effects of wholesale mainstreaming.

Attribution of Students' Failures to the School or Teacher

Those who support the Regular Education Initiative allege that responsibility for failure in school should be removed from students and placed on teachers (Biklen & Zollers, 1986). However, placing the blame for students' failures on either students or teachers is probably a gross injustice. Just consider the complexity of instruction–learning transactions (Kauffman, Gerber, & Semmel, 1988). Schumaker and Deshler (1988) state that attributing failure in school to teachers without considering differences in organizational structures, curricula, learner characteristics, and setting demands oversimplifies a complex problem.

Ability of Students Who Are Mildly Handicapped and Low Achieving to Succeed Under the Proposed Initiative

Although some advocates of the Regular Education Initiative suggest that students with mild handicaps report feeling stigmatized as failures (Biklen & Zollers, 1986), apparently because they have been labeled and pulled out of regular classrooms for special services, others (Kauffman, Gerber, & Semmel, 1988) question how the performance of these students, if left in regular classrooms, will lose its stigma. Kauffman, Gerber, and Semmel (1988) argue that with more effective instruction in regular classrooms, students who ordinarily perform well will do even better and the differences between these students and students with learning and behavior problems will be just as obvious. Thus, the stigma may continue. Chisholm (1988) shares the concern that students who are low achieving may be "left in the lurch" (p. 488) when educators direct attention toward promoting higher mean achievement scores. In regard to the stigma that some claim results from pulling students out of regular classrooms for instruction, research on the effects of mainstreaming does not indicate that mildly handicapped students placed in regular classrooms, experience improved self-esteem (Coleman, Pullis, & Minnett, 1987).

Ability of Regular Education Teachers to Cope with the Demands Under the Proposed Initiative

Advocates of the Regular Education Initiative appear to believe that retraining of regular education teachers through programs like the Adaptive Learning Environments Model (Wang & Reynolds, 1985) will enable regular education teachers to meet the needs of all or most students assigned to them. They suggest that regular education teachers will be able to apply instructional techniques to students as effectively in the regular setting as do teachers in the special setting and will welcome "difficult to teach" students into their classrooms (Biklen & Zollers, 1986; Pugach, 1987; Teacher Education Division, Council for Exceptional Children, 1987). However, many demands are already placed on regular education teachers, and such teachers may not be able to implement the level of instruction necessary if categorical program placements are eliminated (Chisholm, 1988).

Success with the Regular Education Initiative will require the support and collaboration of regular and special educators. Has anyone asked regular classroom teachers their opinions about their proposed roles and responsibilities? Do they even want to be involved in the Regular

Education Initiative? If not, proponents of the initiative are similar to Lieberman's (1985) description of the eager, overly zealous bridegroom who plans the wedding but neglects to ask the bride.

Effects of Wholesale Mainstreaming

The changes proposed in regard to the Regular Education Initiative, "if implemented nationally, would have profound effects on every aspect of education from classroom instruction to the preparation of beginning teachers" (McKinney & Hocutt, 1988, p. 17). Since the passage of PL 94–142, educators have placed students with special needs in regular classrooms to the extent appropriate, offering assistance to facilitate the success of mainstreamed students. The Regular Education Initiative proposals appear to advocate wholesale mainstreaming of students with mild handicaps and students in compensatory programs (McKinney & Hocutt, 1988). Hallahan, Keller, McKinney, Lloyd, and Bryan (1988) state that instead of providing only one service delivery model for all students in the higher prevalence categories of special education, it is more logical to have a variety of service options available, as illustrated in Deno's Cascade System of Special Education Services (see Figure 1.2).

Points of Agreement

As you can see, there are a variety of perspectives in regard to the Regular Education Initiative. We include these divergent views not to discourage you, but to encourage you about a field that can boast of professionals who are committed to the continued improvement of educational programs and services for students with disabilities. Points of agreement about the Regular Education Initiative include:

1. Both advocates and critics of the initiative agree that there is dissatisfaction with existing regular and special education systems.
2. Both groups appear to advocate change or reform in education.

3. Proponents and critics are calling for an examination of strengths and weaknesses in current practices through analysis of efficacy research.
4. Advocates and critics view the Regular Education Initiative as an opportunity for regular and special educators to work together to develop effective instructional options for working with diverse student populations.

Conclusions and Recommendations

Although professionals agree that there are problems with current practices, they vary in their recommendations for improving instructional programs and educational services. We hope this discussion helps prepare you to participate in a field in transition and makes you aware of the changing roles in regular and special education. We believe that effective communication, problem solving, and collaborative consultation may facilitate a partnership between regular and special educators that will ultimately result in improved performance of students with handicaps (see Chapter 6). According to Fullan (1982):

> Our reach should exceed our grasp, but not by such a margin that we fall flat on our face. Instead of being discouraged by all that remains to be done, be encouraged by what has been accomplished by way of improvement resulting from your actions. (p. 97)

■ ■ Activity

Obtain a copy of the *Journal of Learning Disabilities 21*(1) (January 1988), an issue devoted to the Regular Education Initiative. Use the articles in this journal along with the information presented in this section on the Regular Education Initiative to complete the following activities.

Part 1. Interview a regular classroom teacher, a special education teacher, one of your professors, a principal, or the parent of a student with a mild disability about the Regular Education Initiative. Share your responses in class.

Part 2. Form two panels, one with members who will speak in favor of the Regular Education Initiative and the other with members who will speak against it. Arrange to have a debate in class. (*Suggestion:* Appoint a moderator to keep order.) ■ ■

Professional Commitment

Among the many important aspects of working in special education, one that we hope you will give careful thought to is that of professional commitment. The field of special education carries with it many professional responsibilities, which were organized into a Code of Ethics by the Council for Exceptional Children Delegate Assembly in 1983. The code consists of eight principles that form the basis for professional conduct:

1. Special education professionals are committed to developing the highest educational and quality of life potential of exceptional individuals.
2. Special education professionals promote and maintain a high level of competence and integrity in practicing their profession.
3. Special education professionals engage in professional activities which benefit exceptional individuals, their families, other colleagues, students, or research subjects.
4. Special education professionals exercise objective professional judgment in the practice of their profession.
5. Special education professionals strive to advance their knowledge

and skills regarding the education of exceptional individuals.
6. Special education professionals work within the standards and policies of their profession.
7. Special education professionals seek to uphold and improve where necessary the laws, regulations, and policies governing the delivery of special education and related services and the practice of their profession.
8. Special education professionals do not condone or participate in unethical or illegal acts, nor violate professional standards adopted by the Delegate Assembly of CEC. (p. 8)

With your acceptance of these responsibilities, you make a commitment to exceptional students, employers, and the teaching profession. Your behavior and conduct as a professional can help you view teaching as important and worthwhile.

What We Believe

Our text is centered around two beliefs:

1. There are generic, research-based instructional techniques that all teachers of students with special needs should know how to apply.
2. These generic, research-based techniques may be used in the teaching of various content areas and for various ages and levels of students.

Due to the importance of the use of generic techniques as documented in the teacher effectiveness research, in this text, we focus on providing you with a "solid foundation in effective generic methodologies" (Pugach, 1987, p. 310). We feel that special educators need to know both

☐ Important Points

1. Students may receive special education services in a variety of placements arranged on a continuum from least restrictive to most restrictive.
2. The term *least restrictive* means that students who have disabilities should be educated with nondisabled students to the extent appropriate.
3. Students may receive special education services in regular classrooms; through the consultative model; in resource rooms; in self-contained settings; in special schools; and in homebound, hospital, residential, and total care settings.
4. The Regular Education Initiative (REI) is a movement to place fewer disabled students in pull-out programs and educate them in regular settings instead.
5. Will's recommendations to restructure regular and special education include (a) utilization of effective intervention strategies in regular classrooms to prevent identification of students as disabled, (b) use of curriculum-based assessment, (c) application of effective teaching methods, (d) delegation of control to school administrators, and (e) school-based support for teachers.
6. Proponents of the Regular Education Initiative are critical of categorical programs that pull students out of regular education classrooms.
7. Critics of the Regular Education Initiative reject the idea that placing students with handicaps in the regular setting will help those students succeed.
8. Critics are concerned that regular education teachers may not be prepared to teach students with handicaps in regular settings and suggest providing a variety of service options as opposed to wholesale mainstreaming or one system for all.
9. Points of agreement include (a) dissatisfaction with existing regular and special education systems, (b) a need for change or reform in education, (c) the need to examine the strengths and weaknesses in current practices through analysis of efficacy research, and (d) the opportunity for regular and special education to work together to develop effective instructional options for working with diverse student populations.
10. The field of special education carries with it many responsibilities that are stated in its professional code of ethics.
11. In this text, we focus on research-based instructional techniques that may be used in the teaching of various content areas and for various levels of students.

content and teaching techniques. Currently, many texts focus on math, reading, and other content areas. Instead, we thoroughly discuss research-based instructional techniques and apply them with examples from various levels, settings, and content areas. We agree with Pugach (1987) in her recommendation that preservice and in-service teachers need a solid foundation in effective generic methodologies, and we believe that our text fulfills this need.

Summary

In this chapter, we introduced you to the students we discuss throughout our text. They include children and adolescents who exhibit one or more of the following characteristics: inadequate academic achievement, inappropriate school behaviors, poor attending behaviors, poor memory, inadequate organizational skills, and poor self-concept. They are children and adolescents with special needs who are often classified into the separate categories of learning disabilities (specific learning disabilities), mental handicaps (mentally retarded, educable mentally retarded), or emotional handicaps (emotionally disturbed, behavior disorders).

Many cultures are as rich in tradition as the Anglo-American culture, but the school culture focuses on the Anglo-American culture and may be at odds with the values of other cultures in terms of competition versus cooperation, individual autonomy and independence, achievement orientation, future orientation, and classroom atmosphere.

We presented general instructional strategies for the teaching of explicit and implicit skills. Explicit skills are basic, well-structured skills that may be taught in a step-by-step manner. Explicit skills include learning math facts and following the rules of capitalization. Implicit skills are less-structured, higher-order skills that do not follow a set of steps and that may have more than one acceptable answer. Implicit skills include summarizing a passage and writing a theme. Techniques for teaching explicit skills include reviewing, giving clear directions, providing guided practice, checking for understanding, providing feedback, and monitoring

progress. Techniques for teaching implicit skills include modeling, thinking aloud, anticipating difficulties, regulating the difficulty of problems and materials, providing prompts, teaching self-checking, and providing independent practice. A basic structure that may be followed in teaching both explicit and implicit skills includes the elements of planning, presentation, guided practice, feedback, independent practice, and evaluation.

We also included a discussion of different program alternatives as presented in Deno's (1970) Cascade System of Special Education Services. These settings consist of regular classrooms; the consultative model; resource rooms; self-contained settings; special schools; and homebound, hospital, residential, and total care settings. We presented a discussion of the Regular Education Initiative (REI), its impact on how educators provide services to students, descriptions of the support and criticism the REI has received, and points of agreement among professionals.

We concluded the chapter with the special education code of ethics and the beliefs around which our text is centered: That there are generic, research-based teaching strategies, and they may be used in the teaching of various content areas and for various levels of students.

2

Beginning-of-the-Year Planning

Key Topics

The procedures that teachers follow and the decisions that they make prior to and during the first week of school establish the climate and set the tone for the rest of the school year. In observations of teachers at the beginning of the school year, Moskowitz and Hayman (1976) found that the first day was crucial in setting the stage for the rest of the year. In a study of how effective teachers performed during the first weeks of school, Emmer, Evertson, and Anderson (1980) found that effective teachers (a) managed class time well by using a consistent daily schedule of activities; (b) established clear rules and procedures; (c) monitored progress effectively; (d) described objectives clearly; (e) had a variety of effective materials on hand; (f) gave clear, specific directions for activities; and (g) designed activities with an obvious purpose. It would appear that taking a proactive approach at the start of the school year, quickly establishing systems and routines, and clearly communicating expectations to students minimize the likelihood of the occurrence of problems later in the year. In this chapter, we focus on what you should do prior to and during the first week of school as you set up your classroom, orient your students, review individualized education programs (IEPs), plan, and schedule.

Setting Up the Classroom

Due to the varied and complex demands placed upon special education teachers (e.g., implementing the goals and objectives of IEPs and planning for the provision of direct and indirect services), many tasks must be accomplished before the start of the academic year. Careful attention to these tasks greatly facilitates the transitions that students experience as they return to school in the fall. One of the challenges teachers face as they begin the year is that of setting up the classroom environment. This may include organizing and storing equipment, materials, files, and records, and developing procedures for providing feedback, giving grades, and keeping records.

Equipment, Materials, and Files

Prior to the start of the school year, you should select and set up the equipment you will need. The classroom should have both desks and tables, so that individual work, group work, peer tutoring, and cooperative learning may take place. You may want to plan to have at least one study carrel, because some students benefit from separate work areas. Teachers who do not have wooden study carrels may check with school supply companies that sell devices made from sturdy cardboard and that can be easily assembled and placed on top of a student's desk. Because a study carrel has three sides, it eliminates visual stimuli, cuts down on auditory distractions, and provides an area that can be used for uninterrupted study similar to office areas. In using carrels or cubicles, you should emphasize their positive points and not use them for punishment.

Teachers who are not assigned to one classroom, but float from classroom to classroom or co-teach (such as when special and regular education teachers work together to jointly teach students in regular settings) may need to set up equipment and supplies on a cart to make their materials mobile. Some teachers use file boxes to organize and store their instructional activities, student folders, games, tape recorders, manipulatives, and worksheets. For example, Mrs. Nestrada used a three-tiered cart with two boxes on each shelf to teach six different classes. Although she stored additional materials elsewhere, the cart enabled her to keep the essential materials with her to use in her classes.

Dividers and Displays

You may want to section off your classroom into different instructional areas, or performance zones, for routine activities and tasks (Berdine & Cegelka, 1980; Mercer & Mercer, 1989). One way to accomplish this is to use dividers. Dividers may be used to create rooms within rooms, to display work, schedules, or rules. Dividers may be constructed from sturdy cardboard, such as that from refrigerator boxes. Natural dividers present in many classrooms are file cabinets and portable chalkboards. Special education teachers who are working collaboratively with regular classroom teachers may find dividers useful when working with separate groups in a regular classroom.

Displays or organizers may be designed by tacking shoebags to the wall. These displays may be used to store supplies, such as, pencils, scissors, clips, and markers, or to hold student schedules and assignments.

Storage Compartments

In some classrooms, teachers are faced with the dilemma of inadequate storage space for students' materials. There may be more students than desks. Ice cream cartons may be used to store lighter materials, such as worksheets, pencils, crayons, workbooks, paperback books, and students' journals. The ice cream cartons can be covered with contact paper and labeled with the students' names. Plastic dishpans may accommodate workbooks, books, and papers.

In secondary classrooms, students do not usually have desks in which to store materials. They may be seated at chairs with arms that are used as the writing surface or they may sit at tables. Teachers often set up folders in which to keep student work and sometimes code the folders by color for each class or period. Students usually store their books in lockers and are responsible for bringing them to class. Therefore, storage of students' materials may not be a problem in secondary classrooms.

Instructional Materials and Files

Prior to the first week of school, teachers should organize their files and set them up so that they are easily accessible. For example, many commercial cassette tape and worksheet programs are available to teach listening skills, phonics, and math. Set up a file with folders labeled with the name and number of each lesson from one of these programs. Store worksheets that correspond to each lesson in the folders for easy retrieval at a later date. Use a shoebox for the accompanying audiotapes. Insert index cards between tapes in the box with the appropriate name and number of each lesson written on them. By preparing such files ahead of time, you avoid having to find tapes and prepare worksheets each day before class. With this type of organization, it is possible to teach students to use the file to retrieve each day's lesson.

When teaching in an elementary resource setting, one of the authors trained two student assistants from the regular sixth grade to set up all of the tapes and worksheets for each day's lessons. After consulting each student's schedule, these students selected tapes and worksheets from the files and placed them in the assigned space or cubbyhole. You can use this type of system to organize other materials to make them accessible to teachers and students.

Teachers who are well organized and who plan ahead are more likely to begin instruction promptly instead of making students wait while they assemble materials. For example, Ms. Ortega, a special education teacher working in a secondary setting, prepared a set of videotapes illustrating work-related behaviors to use in her employability skills class. She organized them into a file with accompanying role-play activities. Each packet contained a videotape, a card explaining the role play, and handouts to accompany the activity.

Feedback Systems

During the first week of school, tell students how they will receive feedback regarding their performance. Therefore, you should have some systems already in place. "In" and "out" boxes meet this need. Students may be instructed to place finished work in the "in" box and pick it up later after you have checked it and provided written feedback, in the "out" box.

To provide immediate feedback, set up a checking station. Some classwork can be easily checked and scored by students themselves. Set up an area complete with answer keys for students to use upon completion of an assignment. This is workable when clear-cut answers are possible, such as with some types of math problems. When the students go to the checking station, they use a special pen to put a correct mark by each response that is accurate. They put a dot by each incorrect response. Then, they return to their desks. After they make their corrections, they mark "OK" by each dot. The teacher may choose to give a grade for the initial work and another for the corrections. The advantage of using a checking station is that students can receive immediate feedback. Carefully monitor

checking stations while in use and reinforce students for using it correctly.

An additional way of providing immediate feedback is with self-correcting materials. Many of the most common instructional tools contain self-correcting features (Lewis & Doorlag, 1991). These include textbooks, workbooks, games, and worksheets. In addition, Mercer and Mercer (1989) suggest using spelling tapes. Students listen to a word, a sentence using the word, a pause, a beep, and the correct spelling of the word. The students may stop the recorder at the pause, write the word, then restart the tape to self-check.

Grading and Record-Keeping Procedures

At the beginning of the school year, decide how you are going to grade student work, monitor progress, and keep records of student performance, and communicate these procedures to your students. Do this verbally, in writing, as part of the classroom rules, or in all three ways.

Grading

Grading is the most common system used to communicate student evaluation (Bigge, 1988). In regular education, report cards, midterm grades, progress reports, and parent conferences are the major reporting systems (Butler, Magliocca, Torres, & Lee, 1984). In the special education setting, you may be responsible for assigning grades, you may not assign grades at all, or you may assign grades in collaboration with the classroom teacher. If you are responsible for the assignment of grades, be certain to check district procedures and to inform parents of the grading procedures.

General techniques, such as assigning multiple grades, contracting for grades, basing grades on a variety of assignments, and establishing criteria for grades based on the individualized education program (IEP), have been found to be effective in grading students with special needs (Bender, 1984; Bigge, 1988; Butler, Magliocca, Torres, &

Lee, 1984; Cohen, 1983; Kinnison, Hayes, & Accord, 1981; Tiedt & Tiedt, 1986). In addition, Cohen (1983) suggests the use of descriptive notations as well as quantitative scores on the standard report card.

Many assignments may be evaluated with multiple grades. For example, you may assign two grades for a report—one for content and one for mechanics. Giving two grades takes into consideration the ideas (content) as separate from the mechanical aspects (punctuation, spelling, grammar), which provide stumbling blocks for many students with special needs. You may also want to consider effort, achievement, and ability.

Sometimes, instead of multiple grades, levels are assigned to the subject areas; that is, whether the student is below, on, or above grade level. Thus, an A given to a student on grade level does not mean the same as an A given to a student below grade level. These two students are not dealing with the same skills or content.

In addition, you may want to assign grades based on a variety of assignments, as opposed to just an exam. For example, "40% of the final grade may be based on tests; 20%, on reports; 10%, on attendance; 30%, on other assignments mutually agreed upon by the teacher and student" (Kinnison, Hayes, & Accord, 1981, p. 99).

Contracting with students for grades based on a certain level of proficiency on IEP objectives is another suggestion (Bender, 1984; Butler, Magliocca, Torres, & Lee, 1984). In this grading procedure, discuss the short-term objectives with the students and agree on the level of proficiency to be reached by the end of each grading period. Reaching the level results in a higher grade than not reaching it. With this procedure, if you select 80% as the mastery goal, then 80% should translate to the letter grade of A.

In addition to percentages, always make your criteria clear for the grades you give (Tiedt & Tiedt, 1986). May an A paper have spelling errors? Discuss with the students the characteristics of outstanding work, average work, and

poor work, and show them examples. For example, Mr. Lucas taught several students how to take notes so that they could improve their performance in their history class. As part of his teaching procedure, he showed them examples of good and poor notes. He specified his criteria for grading notes: for the content (key points of the lecture) and the technique (accurate use of a note-taking strategy).

One of the most troublesome questions for you as a teacher is whether students with special needs should fail in classes for which you have the responsibility of assigning grades. Special education teachers are supposed to provide students with an appropriate education plan. If a student is failing, the teacher should ask questions like, Did I design an appropriate education plan? Is there something else I might do? Should I add other motivations? We feel that students should not fail in a special education setting if they truly have been provided with an individualized education program.

Record Keeping

Teachers should keep careful, written records on a daily basis regarding student performance. Record-keeping systems may be designed prior to the start of the school year. Charts, graphs, checklists, and other forms may be developed to accompany the activities and materials that students will use in the classroom. In some cases, the record-keeping system is visible to everyone, as in Mrs. Murphy's fourth grade, with the posting of the names of the books each student has read. In other cases, the record is kept in folders, as in Mr. Russo's class, where his high school students are concentrating on work-related skills. A systematic record of knowledge of vocabulary, interviewing skills, and social skills is stapled inside each student's folder, where it is updated on a daily basis.

Other record-keeping systems can be developed by recording the date and score for listening center activities, computer activities, audiotape lessons, learning center activities, drill and practice activities, and progress toward master-

☐ Important Points

1. The procedures that teachers follow at the beginning of the school year set the tone for the rest of the year.
2. During the first week of school, effective teachers use a consistent daily schedule of activities, provide clear rules, monitor progress, give clear objectives, use a variety of materials, give clear directions, and make activities purposeful.
3. In setting up special education classrooms at the beginning of the year, teachers may identify furniture needs, secure or make dividers and display areas, and provide ways for students to store their work and supplies.
4. Teachers who float from class to class or work collaboratively with regular classroom teachers may prepare supplies and equipment on a cart to make materials mobile.
5. Systems for providing feedback to students include the use of "in" and "out" boxes, checking stations, and self-correcting materials.
6. Effective grading techniques include assigning multiple grades, contracting level of performance, basing grades on a variety of assignments, and establishing criteria based on the individualized education program (IEP).
7. Record-keeping procedures include the use of charts, graphs, and checklists to record student progress on listening center, computer, and audiotape activities.
8. Records of student performance may be used to plan, modify, and evaluate instruction and to motivate students to greater achievement.

---

ing specific skills. For example, Ms. Bonasso developed a chart to record her students' recognition of lowercase manuscript letters. She used it each day to show the students their progress, writing each letter along the top of the chart and the date down the left side of the chart. She placed an *x* in the box under each letter and next to the day's date each time a student responded correctly.

Students may be responsible for some of their own record keeping. Mercer and Mercer (1989) suggest using self-correction tapes to provide feedback to students about their math seatwork. After using such tapes, students may fill out their math record for the day (see Figure 2.1). Notice how this record keeping on the part of students may provide them with immediate awareness of their performance and lead to application of strategies to improve that performance.

Whatever grading and record-keeping procedures you develop, be certain they reflect the instructional objectives and level of performance designated for each student in each area of the academic and social skills curriculum. Records of student performance may be used to plan, modify, and evaluate instruction and to motivate students to greater achievement.

■ ■ Activity
Work with a partner to devise two ways of keeping records on individual students. For example, you could keep a daily record of the progress of individual students on their multiplication tables or their sight words. (Answers for this and other activities are found in the Instructor's Manual) ■ ■

Physical Arrangement
Although the design of a classroom is secondary to instructional methodology and curriculum,

```
Name _____

Today I listened to tape _____

My first score was _____

My score after corrections was _____
```

Figure 2.1
Math Record

evidence indicates that the physical setting may influence student behavior and attitudes (Weinstein, 1981). Furthermore, the physical arrangement of the classroom may affect the teacher's ability to implement each student's IEP (Walker, 1981). You may be working with students who have difficulty learning, attending, remembering, getting along, and being organized. You may have students who possess different preferences for the arrangement of the classroom. Students may vary in their desire to work alone, work with others, use a study carrel, sit at a table or a desk, or work in a learning center. Decisions about the classroom arrangement do not have to be totally teacher-made. You may want to actively involve your students in making decisions, using forms or checklists that allow them to provide input.

Also, consider cultural differences in setting up the classroom. Students from cultures that are people-oriented or that endorse working together for the good of the group may benefit from cooperative learning activities, group projects, and other collaborative activities. For example, Lewis and Doorlag (1991) report that the Native American culture emphasizes cooperation and group achievement and that Native American students may show a preference for actions as opposed to words. Teachers may want

to consider including physical arrangements and activities to complement these cultural emphases. Such physical arrangements include tables, peer tutoring areas, and activity areas.

In order to meet the needs of individual students with learning and behavior problems, provide a variety of options in terms of spatial arrangements, scheduling techniques, and learning activities. In doing this, you demonstrate that you view the classroom environment as a variable to be developed as carefully as any other aspect of learning.

As you physically design and organize your classroom, consider two important points. First, the physical setting does not teach; however, it can facilitate the occurrence of certain student behaviors (Weinstein, 1981). For example, if you want students to interact in solving a problem, facilitate interaction by seating students at a table as opposed to seating them at individual desks in rows. Second, not all students need the same physical setting (Polloway, Patton, Payne, and Payne, 1989). Therefore, include a variety of options. Some students require a high degree of structure, while others operate effectively with more freedom, less structure, and less guidance. The following general suggestions will help you get started in setting up your elementary or secondary physical setting.

Physical Variables

Some of the physical variables that affect the way classrooms are organized are the size of the room, the number of electrical outlets, and the storage needs; the acoustics (D'Alonzo, D'Alonzo, & Mauser, 1979); the furniture (Lewis & Doorlag, 1991); the equipment; the type of facility (e.g., portable building; classroom within the school); and whether the classroom has to be shared with another teacher. Again, consider cultural differences in planning the physical arrangement of the class. Arrange seating to avoid overcrowding and to provide for adequate personal space.

Student Variables

Student variables that affect classroom organization include the number of students in the class, the age and grade levels, the learning levels, cultural and language differences, and related problems that students have (mobility, language, behavior, etc.).

For example, one of Mr. Moore's new students, Kahn, is Vietnamese. Last year, Charles, another Vietnamese student was scheduled into Mr. Moore's resource room for an hour a day. Mr. Moore decided to seat the two students together in class to help Kahn adjust to a new culture and language. This may be an effective way to ease a student's transition into a new environment. Kitano (1987) states that few Asians participate freely in group discussions. This fact would be important for Mr. Moore to know as he plans instructional activities. In that way, Mr. Moore would not be likely to judge limited participation as lack of ability. Instead, he would attribute it to cultural or language differences.

Environmental Variables

Many important components may assist you in designing an effective instructional environment. Following are several for your consideration.

Learning Centers. Learning centers that include activities to accommodate many different levels of functioning and interest may be strategically placed around the room to provide the opportunity for students to work independently with materials on their own levels. In co-teaching situations, you may need to set up learning centers that are collapsible or mobile.

Listening Centers. Set up areas in quiet sections of the classroom to emphasize listening skills. Prompt students to follow the rules posted in these centers, and limit or restrict traffic in areas that require a high degree of listening and concentration.

Free-Time Areas. You may designate a specific area of the classroom as the free-time area. Provide activities within this area that are both enjoyable and educational. For example, provide structured choices for students who have earned free time. Give students the choice of completing a puzzle, solving some problems with a calculator, reading a book, or playing a game.

Storage Areas. Allocate specific areas of the room for the storage of equipment and audiovisual aids. Carefully label these areas so that teachers, students, substitutes, and teaching assistants can find equipment and supplies. This is especially helpful in small classrooms. To eliminate cluttered, crowded conditions, only the equipment that is currently being utilized should be out in the room. Items that are used only occasionally or that are not currently being used should be stored in a convenient location.

Instructional Materials. Materials should be readily available for students to use. When appropriate, they should be visible to students. For example, store games in see-through plastic containers so that students can find and retrieve them easily. Set up a system so that students know what materials they can use and how to access them.

Books and Other Reading Materials. Set up one area of the classroom to display books and other reading materials, possibly in the free-time area. Having the materials within easy reach should encourage students to interact with them. Some teachers like to arrange reading materials by readability level. It is also motivating to assemble reading materials that you know are of interest to your students, such as mysteries, sports and adventure stories, magazines, newspapers, books with accompanying tapes, books and stories that students have written, predictable books, and series books (e.g., Sweet Valley High Series, Pascal, 1983–89).

Teacher's Desk and Supplies. When teachers put their desks off to the side, in the back, or out of the central area of the class, they tend to sit at them less, are more mobile, and circulate more freely around the room to monitor student progress. This helps to eliminate a long line by the side of the desk as students seek assistance. In addition, by circulating, teachers can use proximity control to keep students on task, actively involved, and alert. By moving around the room to check on students, teachers become proactive—able to anticipate and prevent problems before they occur—instead of having to react after something has happened. In situations in which teachers float from class to class or co-teach in a regular setting, they may set up their supplies in another teacher's classroom or in a work area off to the side of the room.

Weinstein (1981) reports the results of four investigations examining the influence of the physical environment on young children. The following general principles emerged from the studies: (a) interest areas should be clearly defined; (b) areas should be located within easy access of any external requirements (water, electrical outlets, quiet); (c) incompatible activities should be separated (creative dramatics and listening centers); (d) areas should be clearly labeled and easy to see; (e) aisles and pathways should be clear and should not pass through work areas; (f) large, open spaces that may invite inappropriate physical activities should be avoided; (g) the teacher's desk should be located out of the way to encourage the teacher's movement around the room; (h) instructional materials should be accessible and easily retrieved; and (i) classrooms should contain options for students—quiet work areas, group interaction areas, and whole-class discussion areas. According-

ing to this research, adherence to these principles for organizing the physical environment should positively affect the ways that students acquire and express information in the classroom.

Bulletin Boards. Bulletin boards are classroom displays that can serve specific purposes in special education settings at both the elementary and secondary levels. Hayes (1985) suggests four types of bulletin boards: decorative, motivational, instructional, and manipulative. Hannah (1982) recommends a fifth category, informational. A sixth type of bulletin board displays students' work.

Decorative bulletin boards are designed to brighten and improve the appearance of a classroom. An example of a decorative bulletin board is one that says, "Hello" or "Welcome" in several different languages. This may encourage students to share more of their native language and perhaps some customs with the rest of the class. Charles, a Vietnamese student, was thrilled to see evidence of his culture in the classroom and immediately taught the other students several words and phrases. Middle school, junior high, and high school students enjoy the use of posters on bulletin boards. Teachers can purchase decorative posters with themes that are of interest to adolescents.

Motivational bulletin boards are used to recognize student efforts and progress. For example, teachers may post charts and graphs showing student progress in mastering a particular skill. Some teachers like to post student goals or progress toward a specific goal. Motivational bulletin boards may be most effective when students try to advance their own scores or progress. For example, Mr. Reczek posted his level system on the bulletin board in his middle school class. The students were able to view their progress through the level system toward the goals of gaining classroom privileges and attending mainstream classes.

Instructional bulletin boards are usually subject specific. They are related to the curriculum and used for instruction. For example, Ms. Stew-

☐ Important Points

1. Although the physical arrangement of a classroom is secondary to instructional methodology and curriculum, it may influence student behavior.
2. Factors to consider in setting up the classroom include physical, student, and environmental variables.
3. Physical variables include the size of the room, number of electrical outlets, storage needs, acoustics, furniture, equipment, type of facility, and whether the classroom is shared.
4. Student variables include the number of students in the class, the age and grade levels, the learning levels, cultural and language differences, and related problems, such as behavior.
5. Environmental variables include learning centers, listening centers, free-time areas, storage areas, instructional materials, books and other reading materials, and the teacher's desk and supplies.
6. Bulletin boards in a classroom may be decorative, motivational, instructional, manipulative, or informational, or they may display student work.

art posted the steps to an error monitoring strategy (Schumaker, Nolan, & Deshler, 1985) and taught it to her students directly from the bulletin board. Later, the bulletin board served as a cue to students as they practiced using the strategy, because it was constantly available as a reference.

Manipulative bulletin boards can be thought of as an enlarged version of a worksheet to be completed by actually attaching things (Hayes, 1985). For example, in Ms. Hall's elementary classroom, students were asked to pin a leaf containing a word with a specific vowel sound to a tree that has the same vowel sound printed on it. Students in a middle school or junior high may enjoy tracking the progress of a rocket or satellite in space by moving a pin or marker on a map of the world to show its location.

Informational bulletin boards are used to convey information to students. They can be used for announcements, for current events, or for communication between students. Teachers may also post the dates of tests and deadlines for projects. For both elementary and secondary students, one of the most effective uses of informational bulletin boards is to post the classroom rules and consequences.

Work display bulletin boards are used to display samples of students' work. These should be a regular part of the classroom and should be updated and changed frequently. Students may enjoy displaying their spelling tests, math papers, stories, themes, and products they have developed at learning centers. Special education teachers involved in consulting or co-teaching with regular classroom teachers may set up instructional or manipulative bulletin boards in the regular classroom. Teachers who float from class to class may carry a small bulletin board with them.

■ ■ Activity

Collect a picture file of men, women, adolescents, and children who represent a variety of cultural backgrounds and who are engaged in both common and unusual activities. Decide how you would use these pictures to construct either a decorative or an instructional bulletin board. ■ ■

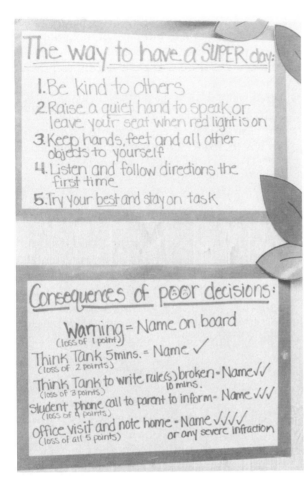

Post classroom rules and consequences on a bulletin board.

Instructional Grouping Arrangements

Instruction may be provided in a variety of ways: large groups, small groups, one-to-one, with peers, and independently. Individualization of instruction may be achieved by using any of these instructional arrangements. As Christenson, Thurlow, and Ysseldyke (1987) point out, individualization does not limit the grouping arrangement to situations in which a student works alone or in a one-to-one arrangement with a teacher. Individualization refers to "help-

ing students succeed, to achieve a high percentage of correct responses and to become confident in his/her competence" (p. 6).

Factors influencing decisions about how to provide instruction include the characteristics and needs of the students, the learning planned—whether the teacher is teaching a skill for the first time (acquisition learning) or whether students are practicing and maintaining a skill that has already been taught (proficiency and maintenance learning), and the activity (e.g., steps in long division, job interviewing, building a model of the digestive system, or writing in journals). Teachers should choose instructional arrangements that meet students' needs as documented in their IEPs and that address characteristics such as cultural and linguistic diversity or problems with memory, organization, or self-concept.

Large-Group Instruction

If the material is appropriate for all of the students, then teaching to the whole class is an effective way to present new material (Brophy & Good, 1986). For example, use large-group instruction to introduce a strategy for taking notes. Lewis and Doorlag (1991) suggest providing guided practice for the whole class at once. Have the students practice taking notes by watching a videotape while you circulate around the room to monitor use of the note-taking strategy. Other appropriate uses of whole-class instruction include the viewing of films or videotapes; large group discussions of science, social studies, history, and current events topics; and demonstrations.

Large-group instruction is used extensively in regular classroom settings. Experience in large groups may be helpful to students as they make the transition from special to regular settings (Bos & Vaughn, 1988). In addition, teachers who co-teach in the regular classroom may share the responsibility with regular classroom teachers for providing instruction to the whole class.

When providing instruction to the entire group, many teachers arrange the desks in rows. This may be appropriate when you are lecturing and making presentations through directive teaching. It may also be effective when students are viewing films, slides, or videotapes. When utilizing this type of arrangement, it is particularly helpful to move around the room and to direct comments and questions to students seated in the back of the room (Weinstein, 1981).

Small-Group Instruction

Small-group instruction is appropriate when teachers present different material to different students (Lewis & Doorlag, 1991). Small groups are frequently used in acquisition learning, to teach a specific skill (Polloway, Patton, Payne, & Payne, 1989). Groups should be flexible, meaning that Sondra, Tim, Rahji, and Bertha may be grouped for instruction in math and be part of other groups for spelling, or that if Bertha progresses more rapidly than the others, she is moved to another, more appropriate group.

Small-group instruction usually consists of groups of two to five students and is used when teachers want to work closely with students and provide frequent feedback (Bos & Vaughn, 1988). Small groups may also be used in cooperative teaching situations to divide the class into different skill groups. Brophy and Good (1986) suggest the use of small groups in classes that are highly heterogeneous. Small groups are used frequently in regular settings by regular classroom teachers because of the heterogeneity of the population. Students may be grouped for reading, math, spelling, or other academic skills.

Small-group arrangements are particularly effective for teaching academic skills. Reading instruction is frequently taught in small groups. Small-group arrangements are also useful for cooperative learning activities (activities in which students work together and teach each other), role playing, and for drill, practice, and review. Weinstein (1981) suggests that teachers arrange the seating within groups so that group leaders are accessible to all members of the group, and less vocal students are seated across from the more vocal leaders. For this reason, you should consider having some tables in your classroom to facilitate group work. When working with a group, some teachers prefer to seat students in a semicircle facing them in order to provide optimum feedback and attention. Small-group instruction may be appealing to students who have language differences because they may feel more comfortable asking for clarification in a small group and because they may have more opportunity to participate.

Small-group arrangements also facilitate maintenance learning, providing students with opportunities to practice or extend a skill that was presented through direct instruction. Group projects, such as interviewing someone, writing an article for the school newspaper, or developing a budget, may be assigned to groups as extension activities to prompt maintenance and generalization of skills taught.

Individual (One-to-One) Instruction

Working on a one-to-one basis with the teacher allows students to ask questions, receive corrective feedback, and interact directly with the teacher. Individual instruction is appropriate for students who are working on skills different from those of the rest of the class, or for students who are working on acquisition learning, having difficulty learning in a small-group setting, or needing assistance with specific aspects of assignments (Polloway, Patton, Payne, & Payne, 1989). The disadvantage of this arrangement is that the teacher's time and attention can be focused on only one student at a time.

Teachers using one-to-one instruction must plan for the rest of the class, perhaps by including cooperative learning activities and peer tutoring. Some teachers utilize the skills of paraprofessionals or volunteers to provide individual instruction to students. Other teachers ask paraprofessionals or volunteers to monitor the rest of

☐ Important Points

1. Instruction may be provided in a variety of ways: large groups, small groups, individually (one-to-one), with peers, and independently.
2. Factors influencing the decisions about how to provide instruction include attention to the needs of the students, the learning planned—acquisition learning or proficiency and maintenance learning, and the activity.
3. Large-group instruction is appropriate for guided practice activities, the viewing of films, discussions, and demonstrations.
4. Small-group instruction is effective in presenting different material to different students, acquisition learning, the teaching of academic skills, and maintenance learning.

5. Arrangements in which teachers and students work together on a one-to-one basis are appropriate for students who are working on skills that differ from those for the rest of the class, working on acquisition learning, having difficulty in a small-group setting, or needing assistance with specific aspects of assignments.
6. Peer tutoring is effective for proficiency and maintenance learning, monitoring progress, providing feedback, and teaching and reteaching specific skills to students who need extra help.
7. Independent learning is appropriate when students have acquired a skill and need opportunities for practice.

the class while they work with individual students. Teachers may want to set up tables or desks away from the rest of the class for one-to-one instruction.

Peer Tutoring

In peer tutoring, one student receives instruction from another after demonstration and under supervision of the teacher. Peer tutoring is effective for proficiency and maintenance learning, such as practicing math facts and spelling words. Tutors may also check answers to end-of-chapter questions, provide positive reinforcement and corrective feedback, and teach or reteach specific skills to other students who need extra help. When instruction is provided through tutorial arrangements, you may want to arrange areas in the classroom for peer tutors by putting two desks together or by providing small tables set aside from the rest of the class. Peer tutoring is often combined with other instructional options, such as large- and small-group arrangements.

Independent Learning

Students may work independently when they have acquired a skill and need opportunities for practice. Independent practice may include completing an activity at a listening center, using the language master, viewing a filmstrip or slide presentation, playing a game, or using self-correcting materials. It is helpful to include a self-correction component in independent work. The independent learning arrangement does not require the teacher's presence, so teachers should select activities that students can complete with minimal assistance (Bos & Vaughn, 1988). In that way, while some students are engaged in independent work, others work individually or in small groups with the teacher.

Classrooms may be set up to contain individual work areas, perhaps some in study carrels, where students can work quietly and independently. Students may also work independently at a table, listening to a tape, or at a computer. The challenge for teachers is to place the individual work areas away from the more active areas of the classroom.

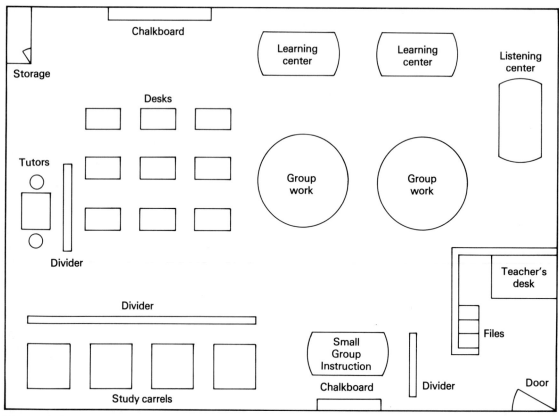

Figure 2.2
Combination Arrangement

There are a variety of ways to arrange the classroom for instruction. You may use any of the previously described arrangements or a combination of one or more (see Figure 2.2). It clearly depends upon your instructional purpose(s) along with the needs and characteristics of your students. Flexible grouping arrangements allow you to individualize instruction in a variety of ways.

■ ■ **Activity**
Choose an elementary, middle school, or high school setting and prepare a sketch of the classroom. Assume that you will have students who are involved in acquisition learning and proficiency and maintenance learning. Be sure to include evidence of the instructional arrangements (large-group, small-group, individual) you would use, as well as ideas from the section of the chapter called "Physical Arrangement" (learning centers, listening centers, free-time areas, bulletin boards, etc.). Make sure you have a rationale for each item you include. ■ ■

Planning

Planning guides teachers for the year, the 9 weeks, the day, or the lesson. It requires identification of goals and objectives, materials, instructional strategies, learner needs, and evaluation. Effective planning may prevent behavior problems and may make teaching more enjoyable. It is a "source of confidence, security, and direction for the teacher" (Florida Performance Measurement System, 1983, p. 3). Similar to the saying found on a greeting card, "It's not the mountains ahead that wear you down, but the grain of sand in your shoe," lack of planning may be your downfall.

Resources for planning include curriculum guides, textbooks, and individualized education programs. Many school districts and state departments of education produce curriculum guides that present the scope and sequence of skills for instruction so that all important competencies are covered without repetition. The curriculum for exceptional students may consist of a modification of the regular education curriculum, or alternative strands (Goldstein, 1986). Textbooks and curriculum programs such as *Reading Mastery:* (Englemann et al.), *Corrective Reading Program* (Englemann et al.), and the *Learning Strategies Curriculum* (Deshler et al.) present teachers with guides to follow. The teacher's manuals for *Reading Mastery, Corrective Reading Program,* and *Learning Strategies Curriculum* are so structured that teachers are told what to say and what correction procedures to use. Many regular classroom materials have accompanying teacher's manuals that identify objectives, activities, and even questions for teachers to ask.

Teachers in special education have an advantage in planning due to the requirement of the individualized education program. The individualized education program is a plan developed in consultation with input from parents and other professionals and based on information gathered from assessment.

Individualized Education Program

One of the most essential tasks at the beginning of the year is becoming thoroughly familiar with each student's individualized education program (IEP). The IEP is the road map for special education instruction. It tells where students are going and how they are going to get there.

IEP forms vary from state to state, school district to school district, and sometimes from exceptional category to exceptional category within the same district. However, all must contain seven components (see Figure 2.3). Section 4(a)(4)(19) of PL 94–142 requires that statements be written concerning (a) the student's present level of educational performance; (b) goals that the student is expected to attain by the end of the year; (c) short-term objectives, which are the intermediate steps leading to the attainment of the annual goal; (d) a description of special education and related services; (e) the amount of time that the student spends in a regular program; (f) projected dates for initiation and duration of special services; and (g) evaluation procedures and schedules for determining mastery of short-term objectives on an annual basis at least. Although a list of materials and techniques to reach the short-term objectives is not required by law, they often appear on the IEP.

Present Level of Performance and Annual Goals

The student's present level of educational performance and the annual goals are usually based on results from both formal and informal measures, whereas the short-term objectives are usually identified through informal measures. Formal assessment measures contain specific rules for administration, scoring, and interpretation. They are usually based on the comparison of the performance of students of the same age and grade level (i.e., they are norm referenced). Informal measures do not contain rigid rules for administration, scoring, and interpretation. They may consist of inventories, observations, or criterion-referenced tests. In examining the sample IEP in Figure 2.3, notice that both formal tests, such as the *Peabody Individual Achievement Test—Revised (PIAT—R)* (Markwardt, 1989), and informal measures, such as the *Brigance Diagnostic Inventory of Basic Skills* (Brigance,

Jimmy Smith	10-5-79
Student Name	DOB
32809	3
Student ID	Ethnic Code
Super middle school	6th
School	Grade
Littletown, USA	
Address	

Parent Notification (if not attending meeting) _____			
Date	Type of Attempt	By Whom	Results

(a) Performance Levels

Area	Source	Date	Scores
Reading Recog	PIAT-R, WRAT-R	11-1-91/10-25-91	5.9 / 6.0
Reading Comp	PIAT-R, Brigance	11-1-91/11-6-91	2.0 / 2.0
Math	WRAT-R	10-25-91	2.0
Addition- whole Numbers	Probe	11-6-91	10 correct / 5 wrong in 1 min.
Subtraction Facts (0-9)	Probe	11-6-91	8 correct / 5 wrong in 1 min
Vocabulary (context clues)	Brigance	11-6-91	1.0

(d) Exceptional Education & Related Services

Program or Service	Hours	(f) Initiation Date	Duration	Person/Program Responsible
Varying Exec. Resource	5 hours a week	12/10/91	12 months	VE Teacher

IEP Developers Teacher(s) — Ms. Peabody	
Parent/Guardian Ms. Smith	
LBA Rep. Mr. Rancid	

IEP Date	12-9-91
IEP Review	12-9-92
(e) Regular Education Hours	25 hours a week

Name:

Annual Goals Plus Short-term Objectives (g) Evaluation

		Teaching Methods & Materials	Criteria	Method	Date Started	Date Met
(b)	Goal Improve math skills to level commensurate with ability					
(c)	a. Obj Calculate subtraction facts	Demonstration Lang Master	10cc/2CE per min for 3 days	Probe	1-16	
	b. Obj Add two digits plus two with reg.	Direct Inst.	80% for 3 days	Teacher test	12-10	
	Goal Improve reading Comp. skills, commensurate with ability					
	a. Obj Paraphrase main idea of paragraph	High interest Low level texts	95%	Teacher observation	12-10	
	b. Obj Identify the meaning of two new words a week	Lang. Exp. Stories	100%	Checklist	12-10	

Figure 2.3
Sample IEP

1977), were administered to determine the current level of educational performance and the annual goals. Turnbull, Strickland, and Brantley (1982) recommend that there be three or four goals for each subject area needing remediation and that these goals be broad enough to take a year or more to accomplish. Examples of annual goals appropriate for students with special needs are:

1. Master basic computation facts at the first grade level.
2. Read the 220 Dolch words.
3. Apply note-taking techniques in content area classrooms.

Many school districts require the identification of two short-term objectives for each annual goal.

Short-Term Objectives

Informal measures, such as the *Brigance Diagnostic Inventory of Basic Skills* (Brigance, 1977), and curriculum-based measures may be used to identify and evaluate the attainment of short-term objectives. According to Turnbull, Strickland, and Brantley (1982), PL 94–142 requires that short-term objectives be stated in instructional or behavioral terms. For example, "Lucy is hyperactive" is not written in behavioral terms, whereas "Lucy got out of her seat 32 times during her 25-minute music class" is written in behavioral terms. A behavioral objective includes four components: the learner, the target behavior, the condition, and the criterion. The target behavior identifies what the learner is asked to do. It should be observable and specific so it can be measured. Following are some sample target behaviors frequently found in the IEPs of students with special needs. Notice that the target behaviors are observable and measurable.

1. Write the answer to subtraction facts.
2. Rephrase the main idea of a paragraph.
3. State the three expectations of an employer.

The condition of a behavioral objective usually relates the circumstances under which the behavior will occur. It frequently tells when or how. Following are examples of conditions:

1. Given a worksheet . . .
2. When asked to begin . . .
3. Without the use of a dictionary . . .

The criterion of a behavioral objective is the goal. It describes the minimum level of performance for mastery of the target behavior. The criterion may be expressed in terms of the following:

1. Accuracy—90%, or 15 correct.
2. Rate—15 correct in 1 minute.
3. Time—10 minutes.

Academic behaviors are usually measured in terms of accuracy or rate. To ensure mastery of an objective, an overlearning measure is frequently suggested (Alberto & Troutman, 1990). The overlearning measure requires that the student perform this behavior more than one time. Examples of overlearning measures include the following:

1. Three days.
2. Four sessions.
3. Five attempts.

Now, putting all four components of a behavioral objective together, the following represent examples of behavioral objectives appropriate for students with special needs:

1. Upon request, Jerome will apply the steps of the test-taking strategy to a practice test within 40 minutes for three sessions.
2. Without prompting, Matt will say the subjects and verbs of sentences with 90% accuracy on three assignments.
3. When asked, Penny will read a passage at 150 correct words per minute with two or fewer errors for 3 days.

In most cases, all of these components do not appear in one short-term objective on an IEP.

Instead, they are described in various sections of the IEP. For example, the behavioral objective of "Given a teacher-designed test of forty addition problems, Jimmy will add two digits plus two digits with regrouping with 80% accuracy for 3 days" is found in various sections of Jimmy's IEP (see Figure 2.3). The identification of the learner (student's name) is located on the first line of the IEP. The target behavior, "add two digits plus two digits with regrouping," is listed under the short-term objective (c). The criterion, "80% accuracy for 3 days," appears in the "Criteria" column under Evaluation (g). The condition, "given a teacher-designed test of forty addition problems," appears in the "Method" column under Evaluation (g).

Description of Services

Special education and related services appropriate for each student must be indicated in the IEP. Special education services may include either direct or indirect services. Direct services are those provided by a special education teacher to the student either in a self-contained, resource, or co-teaching situation, while indirect services are those provided by a special education teacher to the regular education teacher. Special education teachers may provide these indirect services by helping regular education teachers identify effective instructional techniques and adapt materials. Related services, provided by specialists, include counseling, social work, adapted physical education, psychological testing, and transportation. The roles, responsibilities, and amount of time allocated for special education and related services must be clearly stated in the IEP.

Initiation and Duration of Services

The projected dates for the initiation and duration of services must be indicated on the IEP. For example, Figure 2.3 shows that Jimmy will spend 1 hour a day in a varying exceptionalities class beginning 12/10/91 (initiation of services) for 12 months (duration of services).

Evaluation Procedures

Progress toward goals and objectives may be assessed by using the IEP as a tool to monitor students' progress. Teachers must specify the method, the criteria of acceptable performance, and the schedule for evaluation. When teachers use IEPs as working plans for their students, they can truly monitor their student's mastery of objectives.

■ ■ Activity

Concetta, a sixth grader, has been recommended for placement in a resource setting to work on spelling. Based on the following information, identify Concetta's present level of educational performance and write one annual goal and two short-term objectives for the IEP. Be sure to include evaluation procedures to determine how each short-term objective will be measured:

> On the *Peabody Individual Achievement Test—Revised,* Concetta had difficulty spelling words and scored on a third grade level on the spelling subtest. When her misspellings were examined, it appeared that she had the most difficulty with vowel combinations such as ea and silent letters such as *gh* in *high.* On an informal measure (a criterion-referenced test), Concetta again performed more like a third grader in spelling. An error analysis of her responses revealed that she had problems with the *ea, oa, ou,* and *ei* combinations. She also misspelled words that contained *gh, ph,* and *ght.* ■ ■

Weekly and Daily Plans

In addition to the IEP required by national law, weekly planning is required by principals. Often, teachers turn in plan books on Friday for their principal's approval of the next week's lessons. Usually, the weekly planning books do not leave much room for detail, which may be a problem

☐ Important Points

1. Resources for planning include curriculum guides, textbooks, and individualized education programs.
2. An individualized education program (IEP) is a written plan of instruction for the student, mandated by PL 94–142, and is the road map for special education instruction.
3. The components of an IEP describe (a) the student's present level of educational performance, (b) annual goals, (c) short-term objectives, (d) special education and related services, (e) the amount of time spent in regular education, (f) projected dates for initiation and duration of services, and (g) evaluation procedures for determining mastery of each short-term objective.
4. Information from both formal and informal assessment becomes part of an IEP.
5. Weekly and daily plans are based on information from IEPs, curriculum guides, and textbooks.

if there are five students working on different objectives or if a beginning teacher needs more detailed plans. For example, Mrs. Britz writes her overall plans for the week in a plan book (see Table 2.1). Notice that she includes times, materials, and page numbers. In the last column on the right, she lists the levels of the students in each of the curriculum materials used in the class and identifies the times, subjects, and names of students who are mainstreamed and the names of those who receive related services. She also provides each student with a daily assignment sheet that shows the objectives planned for the day. This careful planning helps her monitor completion of assignments (see Table 2.2). Notice that students take the daily assignment sheet home at the end of the day to share with their parents.

Scheduling

Scheduling is an essential part of effective teaching for special education teachers. Schedules provide structure and organization and allow teachers to accomplish the goals and objectives that they have planned for their students. Students with learning problems can benefit from the routine that systematic scheduling provides (Mercer & Mercer, 1989). Teachers should let students know what activities they are to accomplish and when they should complete them. Thus, the use of systematic scheduling may increase self-directedness and independence among students by eliminating the need to check with the teacher about each assignment.

Daily Schedules

Polloway, Patton, Payne, and Payne (1989) underscore the importance of daily schedules as the foundation for the learning that takes place in classrooms. Following are some of the general scheduling guidelines suggested by Gallagher (1988). These techniques are appropriate for scheduling in both resource and self-contained settings.

1. Alternate highly preferred and less preferred activities.
2. Provide time cues.
3. Require students to complete one assignment before they begin another.
4. Include feedback on a student's daily schedule.

It is important for students to complete their activities in the order assigned. A difficult task

Table 2.1

Plan Book

Subject or Section	MONDAY	TUESDAY	WEDNESDAY
8:00 – 8:10 8:10 – 8:50	Opening Exercises Decoding B - Lesson 28 Book 6 - T109-111 Lesson 35, Student Resource Booklet 24 Reader p. 204 - 216 SQRRR	Decoding B - Lesson 29 Book 6 - Reader Cont. Lesson 36 p. 299 Response p. 34-35	Decoding B - Lesson 30 Book 6 - T 117-119 Lesson 38 p. 302 Resource p. 26-27
8:50 – 9:30 9:30 – 9:40 9:40 – 10:10	Individualized Daily Assignment Sheets (Language) Activities Restroom Break Decoding A - Lesson 59 Book 3 - Student Response Booklet p. 30	Decoding A - Lesson 60 Book 3 Reader p. 159-177	Decoding B - Lesson 1 Book 3 Resource p. 23
10:10 – 10:40	T 107-109 Lesson 28 p 288 Student Resource Booklet 22 Book 5 T99-106 Lesson 31 p 328 Student Resource Booklet 21-22	Response 31 Lesson 29 p 289 Book 5 - Reader p 169-176 Lesson 32 p 329 Response 31-32	Response p. 32 Reader p. 178 T11 Book 5 - T113-114 Lesson 34 p. 332 Resource 23
10:40 – 11:20	Book 4 - T97-99 Lesson 33 p. 271 Student Resource Booklet p. 23-24	Book 4 - Reader p 191- 206	Book 4 - Reader Cont. Response 31-32
11:26 – 11:51 11:51 – 12:05 12:05 – 12:15 12:15 – 12:45 12:45 – 1:15	Lunch Recess Restroom Break Reading: Charlotte's Web by E.B. White Process Writing theme - Accepting Challenges		
1:15 – 1:45 1:45 – 2:15	Social Studies Resources p 61-65 Review Science Lesson 1 what's a tree to me?	Social Studies To help you remember p. 65 Class together written Science Lesson II Living in a "Hot House"	Social Studies Workbook p. 12 Science Lesson III The temperature's Rising
2:15 – 2:30	Plant a tree p. 5 Collage on Tree products Sign off Daily Assignment sheets	* Copy Greenhouse Effect	
2:30	Discuss		

Note. From Shauna Britz, special education teacher, Satellite Beach, FL. Copyright 1990 by Shawna Britz. Reprinted by permission.

Table 2.1

Continued

	THURSDAY	FRIDAY	NOTES
	Decoding B-Lesson 31 Book 6 - Reader 217-230	8:15 "Punchy" Drug Prevention Robot Spelling Test and Sentence Dictation Decoding B-Lesson 32 Book 6 Reader Cont. Response 37-38	Reading - Houghton Mifflin Book 6 - Jayson, Raymond Book 5 - Lisa, Kristina, Matt Book 4 - Paul, David, Michael Book 3 - Omar, Karl, Catisha, Ronny, Maria, Rashida, Juan
	Arts and Math, Decoding B-Lesson 2 Book 3 - T-113-114	Decoding B-Lesson 3 Book 3 - Reader p. 180-187	SRA Decoding A - Maria, Rashida, Juan Decoding B - Omar math Level 6 - Raymond, Antonio Level 5 - Jayson, Paul, Matt, Michael, Kristina
	Lesson 30 p. 292 Resource 24 Book 5 - Reader p 177-186 Response 34-35	Lesson 31 p. 293 Response p. 34 Book 5 T 121 - 125 Lesson 36 p. 334 Resource 24-25	Level 14 - Lisa, David, Latisha Level 13 - Omar, Maria, Karl, Ronny, Rashida Spelling Level 5 - Lisa, Kristina, Jayson, Matt
	Book 4 - Response 33	Book 4 - T 103-105 Lesson 35 p. 276 Resource p. 25-26	Level 4 - Raymond, David, Paul, Antonio Level 3 - Omar, Latisha, Maria, Karl Level 2 - Michael, Rashida, Ronny, Juan Language
		15 min Silent Sustained Reading	Level 5 - Raymond, Jayson, Matt, Kristina, Lisa Level 4 - Paul, David, Antonio Level 3 - Michael, Omar, Karl, Ronny, Latisha, Juan Level 2 - Maria, Rashida, Juan
	Science Lesson IV Keeping it Cool	1:00 - 1:30 Mrs. Baker Sunshine Books Science Finish Tree Products Collage	Mainstreaming Raymond 9:30-10:00 math Juan 10:15 - 10:50 Kristina ⎱ 8:10-8:50 Matthew ⎰ math
	Play Lotto type game	2:00 Library	Speech Maria T, TH 2:00 Rashida, M,T, TH Paul, Juan 8:15

Table 2.2
Daily Assignment Sheet

DAILY ASSIGNMENT SHEET	PARENT'S SIGNATURE:
DATE: 2/23 - Monday	NAME: Juan

TEACHER OR PARENT COMMENTS:

Juan completed all of his work today quickly and accurately. He scored 100% on his student Response Booklet lesson. He scored 90% on his Math quiz in Mr. Wong's class.

HOMEWORK:

Study spelling words

READING:

objectives: 5.0, 5.1

Houghton Mifflin book	Book 3
Reader	Lesson 28
Student resource booklet	p. 22
Student response booklet	p. 30
Literature reader	
Literature journal	

objective: 7.3

SRA decoding A, B	A
Explode the code 3	Lesson 59
Specific skill series	
Reading comp series	
Vowel sounds game	
Decoding B game	

MATH:

Addison Wesley book	
Math workbook	
Worksheet	
Multiplication flashcards	
Mainstreamed	Mr. Wong

SPELLING: objectives: 4.2, 4.3

Book 3 Lesson 14

Skills Page	p. 28
Spelling tape	#10
Write words	3 times
Dictionary definitions	
Alphabetical order	
Environmental alphabet	
Spelling test	

LANGUAGE:

objective: 3.5

HBJ language book	
HBJ workbook	
Extra practice master	
Process writing	Accepting Challenges
Apple II E computer	

WRITING:

Writing ditto	
Chalkboard	

SCIENCE: objectives: 9.6, 9.7, 9.8
- Read "What's a tree to Me"
- Make Collage on tree products

SOCIAL STUDIES: objectives: 5.3, 5.4
Review pages 61-65

8:15

COMPUTER LAB   PE   MUSIC   ART   LIBRARY   PROGRAM   (Speech)

Note. From Shauna Britz, special education teacher, Satellite Beach, FL. Copyright 1990 by Shawna Britz. Reprinted by permission.

should be followed by a less difficult and more highly preferred task to ensure completion of the first task. For example, Jeff disliked doing written math problems but loved practicing his math facts with some teacher-made games and other devices in the math center. His schedule indicated that as soon as he completed his written work and made any necessary corrections, he could go to the math center.

For students who have problems managing their time, it is helpful to provide time cues. Most daily schedules are developed with the times of activities listed on the schedules. Some teachers draw clock faces on schedules for young students to remind them when they should complete an activity. Other teachers set kitchen timers to cue students to start the next assignment. Students with learning or behavior problems may have difficulty finishing their work and staying with a task until it is completed. Daily schedules may provide a means of focusing attention on one task at a time until it is completed.

It is important to let students know how well they are performing the activities planned for them on their daily schedules. In writing directly on your students' schedules, you may note reinforcing comments, grades, progress toward mastering an objective, and happy faces. Alternately, you may provide verbal and written comments in their folders or on their work. Other suggestions for scheduling include:

1. Group students by level, interests, and needs.
2. Schedule opportunities for active involvement, cooperative learning, independent work, guided practice, teacher-directed instruction, and peer tutoring.
3. Stress goals and objectives.
4. Emphasize the connection between what is done in the special education setting and its application to regular classes.
5. Allot time in your schedule to visit regular classrooms, consult with teachers, and meet with other members of the educational team (counselors, school psycholo-

gists, administrators, teachers, and other specialists).

Special education teachers vary in the amount of time they spend providing direct services (working with students) and indirect services (working with other professionals). Some also plan time for assessment of students as part of their schedule. Thus, your assigned roles and responsibilities affect your schedule and the schedules of your students.

Scheduling in Elementary Schools

As teachers develop schedules in elementary schools, they should utilize the following information in making instructional decisions: (a) each student's needs, which can be prioritized and taken from the IEP; (b) the amount of time the student is supposed to work in the special education setting; (c) the amount of time the student is scheduled in other settings; and (d) the schedules of mainstream teachers.

Consultative Services in Regular Classrooms

Many students who have special needs are capable of functioning in regular classrooms with modifications and adjustments made by their teachers. These modifications and adjustments are accomplished through collaborative consultation between special and regular educators. Special education teachers provide indirect services by helping regular classroom teachers modify the curriculum, develop and adapt materials, and assess student behavior. At other times, special education teachers are called upon to provide direct services in the mainstream setting. These services may involve co-teaching, or working with the regular education teachers to teach students in regular classrooms. Additionally, special education teachers may provide consultative services outside regular classrooms through participation in school-based assistance teams. All of these functions are considered in developing the schedules of special education teachers.

Resource Rooms

Elementary resource rooms may be set up to accommodate primary grades, intermediate grades, or both. Scheduling is accomplished in cooperation with regular classroom teachers. Students attend the resource room for part of the day to work on specific academic and social behaviors identified in their IEPs. Because students attend resource programs for varying amounts of time, resource teachers are faced with many challenges in scheduling students for instruction. For example:

1. Students may range in age from six to twelve or fourteen.
2. Students may have varied and specific needs.
3. Students may be functioning on many different levels.
4. Regular classroom teachers may have preferred times for sending students to the resource room.
5. Communication with many regular classroom teachers may be difficult and time consuming.
6. Locating materials appropriate for many levels, ages, and interests may be challenging.

Despite the difficulties in scheduling students in the resource room, special education teachers may develop effective schedules by following a few guidelines:

1. Collect the schedules of all teachers who have exceptional students assigned to their regular classes.
2. List the academic and social skill areas with which students need help.
3. Group students by area of need, making an effort to keep primary and intermediate students separated.
4. Plan individual and group times to keep class size reasonable and instruction workable.
5. Revise the original schedule until it works.

There is no one way of setting up a resource room schedule. In addition to providing direct services to students within the resource setting, you may also need to consult with regular classroom teachers. This is important because of the responsibility for students that is shared between special education and regular education teachers. Finally, resource room teachers may be required to assess students and participate in school-based problem-solving committees that work with student referrals. All of these roles and responsibilities must be taken into consideration when setting up a resource room schedule. Table 2.3 is an example of an elementary resource room schedule.

Self-Contained Classrooms

Scheduling in a self-contained setting may be accomplished by first surveying the objectives of the IEPs to determine what activities may be taught in large groups, small groups, and individually. In addition, examining objectives allows teachers to determine which students may be grouped together for instruction as part of cooperative learning groups or as part of peer tutoring arrangements.

Teachers can set up schedules in elementary self-contained classrooms in many ways because they have the flexibility of establishing blocks of time that meet the needs of their students. They have to be concerned about the schedules of others only when they are integrating students into regular classes for instruction. Students may be scheduled into special activities, such as physical education, art, and music as a whole class, or individual students may participate in these special activities in regular classrooms (see Table 2.4).

Most schedules in self-contained classrooms contain blocks of time for opening and closing exercises. These time periods provide excellent opportunities for developing language and self-expression. Polloway, Patton, Payne, and Payne (1989) suggest using opening exercises to establish a learning set for the day's activities. Closing exercises may provide effective ways to evaluate progress, set goals for the next day, review the day's activities, and apply what has been learned to other situations.

Table 2.3
Elementary Resource Schedule (One Week)

	Monday	Tuesday	Wednesday	Thursday	Friday
8:00–8:30	Problem-solving committee meeting	Consult with classroom teachers	Consult with classroom teachers	Consult with classroom teachers	Consult with classroom teachers
8:30–9:30	Work with 1st, 2nd, + 3rd grade students (Teacher-directed instruction in reading)	(Learning Centers)	(Teacher-directed instruction in comprehension)	(Process writing)	(Teacher-directed instruction in comprehension)
9:30–10:30	Work with 4th + 5th grade students (Listening)	(Comprehension monitoring)	(Summarization)	(Comprehension monitoring)	(Paraphrasing)
10:30–11:15	Co-teach in 3rd grade	Co-teach in 4th grade	Co-teach in 5th grade	Co-teach in 1st grade	Co-teach in 2nd grade
11:15–12:00	Assessment	Adapt materials	Assessment	Adapt materials	Assessment
12:00–12:30	Lunch	Lunch	Lunch	Lunch	Lunch
12:30–1:00	Work with 4th + 5th grade students in math (Small group)	(Small group)	(Computer)	(Learning center)	(Small group)
1:00–1:30	Work with 2nd + 3rd grade students in language arts (Small group)	(Games)	(Small group & self-correcting materials)	(Computers)	(Small group)
1:30–2:30	Assist in regular classrooms on "as needs" basis in content area subjects (science, social studies, health)				
2:30–3:00	Planning / Consulting				
3:00	Dismissal	Dismissal	Dismissal	Dismissal	Dismissal

Scheduling in Secondary Schools

At the secondary level (middle school, junior high school, and high school), special education teachers may serve as consulting teachers in regular classrooms. Alternately, they may provide instruction in a resource room or a self-contained classroom.

Consultative Services in Regular Classrooms

Special education teachers at the secondary level fulfill the roles of consulting teachers in the same ways elementary special education teachers do. Services to students with special needs may be both direct and indirect. However, secondary schools are usually larger, which means there are more teachers to work with, more schedules to work around, and more subject area classes to deal with. Special education teachers may co-teach with regular education teachers in regular classrooms. For example, Mr. Jessup taught an outlining strategy to a science class to help the students organize the content that Mrs. Lange presented in science. He also worked with her in adapting some of the material in the textbook. Table 2.5 provides an example of a middle school teacher's schedule. Notice that the teacher works with students in and out of regular classes, co-teaches and consults with classroom teachers, plans, and conducts assessment.

Table 2.4

Elementary Self-contained Schedule (One Week)

Time				
8:00 – 8:15	Set up classroom, assemble materials, plan with paraprofessional or teaching assistant →→→			
8:15 – 8:30	Opening exercises →→→			
8:30 – 9:00	Group 1 Teacher-directed instruction in reading (with teacher)	Group 2 - Learning Centers - Listening Centers - Language Centers	Group 3 Review, drill, practice sight words with para-professional/using games	Group 4 Independent practice in folders and with self-correcting materials
9:00 – 9:30	- Learning centers - Listening centers - Language master	- Review, drill, practice sight words with para-professional using games	Independent practice in folders and with self-correcting materials	Teacher-directed instruction in reading (with teacher)
9:30 – 10:00	Review, drill, practice sight words with para-professional using games	Independent practice in folders, and with self-correcting materials	Teacher-directed instruction in reading (with teacher)	- Learning centers - Listening centers - Language master
10:00 – 10:30	Independent practice in folders and with self-correcting materials	Teacher-directed instruction in reading (with teacher)	- Learning centers - Listening centers - Language masters	- Review, drill, practice sight words with para-professional using games
10:30 – 11:00	Recess →→→			
10:50 – 11:00	Write in journals →→→			
11:00 – 11:30	Three students attend 3rd grade class for math; paraprofessional assists 3rd grade teacher; teacher teaches math to remaining students			
11:30 – 11:45	Students visit math centers, play math games, spend extra time with teachers, use computer, or work with peer tutor			
11:45 – 12:30	Lunch and recess →→→			
12:30 – 12:45	Silent, sustained reading →→→			
12:45 – 1:15	Spelling groups (teacher and paraprofessional) →→→			
1:15 – 1:45	P.E. (Mon.), music (Tues.), art (Wed.), social skills (Thurs. and Fri.)			
1:45 – 2:15	Social studies - large group (Mon., Wed., Fri.) cooperative learning (Tues. + Thurs.)			
2:15 – 2:45	Science - large group (Mon.), lab (Tues.), field trip (Wed.), large group (Thurs.) cooperative learning (Fri.)			
2:45 – 3:00	Closing activities →→→			
3:00	Dismissal →→→			

Resource Rooms

Students at the secondary level may attend resource rooms for assistance in academic skills, social skills, job-seeking skills, learning strategies, and leisure skills (Schumaker & Deshler, 1988). Resource teachers at the secondary level are responsible for providing direct services to students in the resource room and may also be responsible for assessment of students. In addition, they may have consulting responsibilities, such as working with teachers to adapt materials and instruction. They often work with guidance counselors to schedule students into their classes and into select regular classes.

Secondary schools operate with fixed class periods that are approximately 50 minutes long.

Good and Brophy (1984) suggest that the first 8 minutes of class be used for review, 20 minutes for teacher presentation and controlled practice, and 15 minutes for independent practice.

Mrs. Hefter used the first 5 minutes of class for attendance, general directions, orientation to the day's activities, and a brief review. She spent the next 20 minutes teaching her students how to monitor errors in their written work and providing guided practice. Then, the students spent 15 minutes in independent practice with feedback. The next 10 minutes were allocated to addressing pressing individual student needs, such as clarification of an assignment from a regular class, organization of notes and materials from a content area classroom, or a quick review for a

Table 2.5
Middle School Teacher's Schedule—Consultative Services in a Regular Classroom

	Monday	Tuesday	Wednesday	Thursday	Friday
7:45-8:30	School-based assistance-team meeting	Meet with science teachers	Meet with guidance counselor	Meet with English teachers	Attend IEP staffing
8:30-9:15	Preview science activity with 6th graders	Teach reference skills to 8th graders	Preview science activity with 7th graders	Teach reference skills to 8th graders	Review for science test with 6th graders
9:20-10:05	Co-teach in 6th grade science class	Co-teach with history teacher; monitor use of reference skills	Co-teach in 7th grade science class	Co-teach with history teacher; monitor use of reference skills	Consult with math teachers
10:10-10:45	Teach learning strategies class to 7th graders	→	→	→	→
10:50-11:35	Monitor use of outlining in selected 7th grade content classes (English)	(social studies)	(science)	(English)	(social studies)
11:40-12:25	Observe and assist in math classes	→	→	→	→
12:30-1:00	Lunch	→	→	→	→
1:00-1:45	Planning and/or assessment	Adapt materials for content teachers	Evaluate and select software	Adapt materials for content teachers	Planning and/or assessment
1:50-2:35	Teach math to 6th graders	→	→	→	→
2:40-3:25	Teach personal/social skills to 8th graders	→	→	→	→
3:30	Dismissal	→	→	→	→

test or report from a regular classroom. These final few minutes of class were also spent giving a post organizer, such as previewing the next day's class schedule; reinforcing work completed; reporting progress toward class or individual student goals; and announcing schedule changes. By scheduling in this way, Mrs. Hefter has effectively utilized all of the class time in a productive manner and has met her objectives and curricular responsibilities while providing time for individual student needs (see Table 2.6).

Mr. Fletcher, who teaches employability skills in a high school, used the first 5 minutes of class to explain the day's schedule to students. The schedule was posted on the wall of the class-room. He spent the next 15 minutes of class providing direct instruction to students. The next 20 minutes were devoted to small-groups, where students worked cooperatively in groups to complete assignments. The final 10 minutes of class were used for whole-class discussion in which students reported the results of their group work.

Many secondary teachers of exceptional students use a folder system. Students come into their classrooms, get their folders, and examine the schedule in the folder. This gives them a preview of the activities for the class period. While some students are receiving teacher-directed instruction, others complete work in their folders or work with a partner or small group. Some

Table 2.6
Secondary Schedule—Learning Strategies Class (One Class Period)

7:10 - 7:15	- Attendance - Announce next week's exam schedule - Explain class period's activities
7:15 - 7:35	- Review previous lesson in error-monitoring - Teach students how to detect and correct punctuation errors in paragraphs - Use overhead projector and handouts (cue cards) - Have students take turns practicing on overhead projector and orally as a group.
7:35 - 7:50	- Hand out paragraph worksheets. - Have students work independently to detect and correct punctuation errors - Circulate to monitor and check work
7:50 - 8:00	- Check with students on regular class assignments, homework, etc - Recap day's activities and preview tomorrow's lesson on detecting and correcting spelling errors
8:00	- Dismissal

teachers rotate students in and out of learning centers or cooperative learning activities. When not involved with other instruction, the teacher circulates around the room, providing instruction to individuals and groups, monitoring progress, and giving feedback and reinforcement. Notice that all of these teachers used techniques for structuring a class: (a) presentation, (b) guided practice, (c) feedback, and (d) independent practice.

Like resource teachers at the elementary level, resource teachers at the secondary level wear many hats. They must fulfill consulting responsibilities with regular classroom teachers, be curriculum and materials specialists, have knowledge of secondary diploma options and the courses students must have to graduate, possess good public relations skills, and be prepared to help students make the transition from school to work and life.

Self-Contained Classrooms
In some cases, students who have special needs because of the nature of their learning or behavior problems need instruction in self-contained settings. This means that instead of attending a math, English, or science class in a regular setting, they receive instruction in that subject from a special education teacher in a separate setting. Currently, materials are available to present the same subject matter for a course but do so with less emphasis on reading by modifying the for-

mat of the materials and the assignments to be completed (consult D'Alonzo, 1983, for a detailed description). A 50-minute class period could be set up in much the same way as a resource class.

Whatever type of scheduling teachers choose to employ at the secondary level, they should consider some general suggestions in setting up their schedules:

1. Develop schedules within schedules, or minischedules, that contain brief opening and closing exercises (Polloway, Patton, Payne, & Payne 1989).
2. In selecting activities for students, consider curriculum requirements, the amount of time the students have left in school, and what the students are going to do after graduation, and prioritize instruction accordingly.
3. In scheduling daily activities, consider the student's transition to the world of work by incorporating academic skills, problem-solving procedures, survival skills, social skill strategies, and career and vocational skills.

Efficient Use of Time

The National Committee on Excellence in Education (1983) included efficient use of time as one of its five primary recommendations for improved schools. In observation of 230 elementary students who were mildly handicapped Rich and Ross (1989) found that noninstructional time, such as transitions, wait time, free time, snacks, and housekeeping, accounted for almost 3 hours of the school day. An examination of fifty-two high school resource rooms of students who were learning disabled and mildly mentally handicapped indicated that the students spent an average of 24% of the time involved in nonacademic activities (Rieth, Polsgrove, Okolo, Bahr, & Eckert, 1987). Since research shows that time spent in academic learning tasks increases achievement, you should schedule the day to maximize student involvement in direct learning activities. As a teacher,

you can control the time dimensions of housekeeping, transition, and allocated time by the way you schedule.

Housekeeping Time

Housekeeping time is the time spent in performing such routine chores as taking attendance, passing out papers, and writing on the board. If well organized, these activities make a class run smoothly. However, if not managed correctly, these activities can cause behavior problems and loss of valuable teaching time. Housekeeping questions that need to be solved include the ways in which students are to turn in work, sharpen pencils, and get permission for restroom breaks and drinks. If you spend time planning routines, you will spend less time on housekeeping activities during class, thus maximizing instructional time.

Transition Time

Transition time involves changing from one activity to another or from one setting to another. Again, valuable teaching time may be lost without smooth transitions. For young students, role playing transition times, such as moving from the desk to the reading group, is helpful. Posted schedules help make both secondary and elementary students aware of subject changes. Teachers who circulate throughout the room to answer questions and monitor student behavior promote more on-task behavior during transition times (Englert & Thomas, 1982). Frequently, much time is lost in transition from the regular classroom to the resource setting. Incentives are often necessary to motivate students to arrive on time. Extra points, public posting of the names of on-time students, and on-time clubs with special privileges are effective solutions for late arrivals.

Allocated Time

Allocated time is the amount of time assigned to various instructional activities, such as reading groups, independent work, and noninstructional activities like completion of IEPs and consultations with classroom teachers. Effective schools

Important Points

1. Schedules provide structure and organization.

2. Gallagher provides guidelines for teachers to use in scheduling: (a) alternate highly preferred and less preferred activities, (b) provide time cues, (c) require students to complete one assignment before starting another, and (d) include feedback on a student's daily schedule.

3. Other considerations in scheduling include (a) group students by level, interests, and needs; (b) provide opportunities for active involvement, cooperative learning, independent work, guided practice, teacher-directed instruction, and peer tutoring; (c) stress goals and objectives; (d) emphasize the connection between special and regular settings; and (e) allot time for consultative work.

4. Consultative services at the elementary level may include indirect services (working with teachers) and direct services (working with students) in the mainstream setting.

5. Tips in scheduling in the elementary school include (a) identifying students' needs, (b) attending to the amount of time that students should spend in regular and special education, and (c) examining the schedules of classroom teachers.

6. Resource room scheduling at the elementary level requires attention to regular classroom schedules, the needs of students, grouping arrangements, and flexibility.

7. Self-contained scheduling at the elementary level involves planning instructional grouping arrangements and establishing blocks of time that meet student needs.

8. General aspects of scheduling at the secondary level include (a) developing schedules within schedules, (b) meeting curriculum requirements, and (c) providing transition to the world of work.

9. Housekeeping time refers to the time spent taking attendance, passing out papers, and writing on the board.

10. Transition time is the time spent changing from one activity or setting to another.

11. Allocated time refers to the amount of time assigned to various instructional activities, such as group work, independent work, completion of IEPs, and consultative services. Most of teachers' time should be allocated to direct instruction.

---

allocate more of their time to learning tasks than do ineffective schools (Thurlow, Christenson, & Ysseldyke, 1987).

Sargent (1981) collected data for 60 days on thirty resource room teachers serving mildly handicapped pupils in five different states and found that most of the time was allocated for and spent on direct instruction (51.48%) and preparing for instruction (16.38%). A number of studies found that time spent in teacher-directed instruction is the best single predictor of achievement (Leinhardt, Zigmond, & Cooley, 1981; Sindelar, Smith, Harriman, Hale, & Wilson, 1986; Stallings, 1980). Achievement is low when students are assigned much seatwork to do totally independently (Medley, 1979) or are taught with curriculum packages (Squires, Huitt, & Segars, 1983). In fact, time spent in independent instructional activities, such as silent reading, was unrelated to achievement for elementary students with mental disabilities and those with learning disabilities (Sindelar, Smith, Harriman, Hale, & Wilson, 1986). Secondary and elementary students achieve more when at least 50% of the school day is spent in direct instruction (Stallings, 1980). Thus, you need to schedule your day so that most of the time is allocated to direct instruction.

■ ■ Activity

Brainstorm with three other people to come up with more time-saving ideas dealing with housekeeping time, transition time, and allocated time. ■ ■

First-Week Bag of Tricks

It is important during the first week of school to get to know your students. To help build rapport and contribute to more effective classroom management, you should learn their names quickly. The first week of school is the ideal time to orient students to the class schedule, grading procedures, and classroom rules. This is the optimal time to establish the operating guidelines of the class, to communicate expectations, and to establish structure and routines.

Getting-to-Know-You Activities

In numerous ways, teachers may get to know their students at the beginning of the school year. Following are several ideas that may help teachers of students with special needs at the elementary and secondary levels. The activities are appropriate in both special and regular education settings.

Autobiographical and Biographical Activities

You may use autobiographical report forms to find out about students and involve them in a writing exercise. Following is a sample of questions that you may include. Adapt the items for different age groups.

- My name is _____ .
- I am _____ years old.
- My birthday is on _____ .
- My favorite television show is _____ .
- In my free time, I like to _____
  _____ .
- My favorite thing to do after school is ___
  _____ .
- One thing I can do well is
  _____ .

- My favorite sport, game, or activity is ____
  _____ .
- This year, I am looking forward to
  _____ .

Secondary students, in particular, enjoy interviewing another student in the class to collect biographical information. Give the students 10 to 15 minutes to talk with a partner. Have the students develop two headlines that can be put up on a bulletin board. One headline should be a school-related achievement and the other a personal accomplishment. Then, have the students present their information. For example, Manny Owens introduced another senior, Jerard Collins, with the school-related headline "Collins Makes Honor Roll at End of Junior Year" and the personal headline "High School Senior Lands Summer Job at Burger King."

Many students enjoy constructing a time line of their personal and school-related activities. Have the students draw a horizontal line and write in major events in their lives at the appropriate places along the line. (This is also an excellent sequencing activity.) Have the students begin with the time of their birth and continue to the present. Let the students present their time lines orally in class or transfer them to a bulletin board.

Students may create a "This Is Your Life" scrapbook to tell about themselves. Using construction paper, markers, photographs, and magazines, students make a large book to describe themselves to the rest of the class. They may include such topics as their hobbies, interests, goals, families, favorite music group, sports hero, movie star, and greatest accomplishment. Scrapbooks may be made with 12-inch by 18-inch pieces of construction paper as the pages, and wallpaper as the cover. Young students may call this book "All About Me" and draw pictures of themselves, their families, pets, things they like and dislike, favorite food, and what they want to be when they grow up.

Games

After students introduce themselves to the rest of the class, collect cards on which the students have written introductions. As you read what it says on each card, such as hobbies and favorite food, let the rest of the class guess which student is being described. You may also include a card for yourself.

Incorporate the first and last names of students into reading, writing, and spelling activities during the first week of school. Show the students flash cards during reading to see if they can say each student's name. In writing lessons, include practice exercises with sentences, paragraphs, or short stories about students in the class. Use a fill-in-the-blank format during a writing lesson. For spelling, ask students to alphabetize the names of the students in the class (first or last names) and to spell them. Adjust these activities for different age groups.

■ ■ Activity

Develop a first-week idea notebook to include:

1. First-day activities explained in detail.
2. Three bulletin board ideas for the classroom.
3. Three getting-to-know-you activities.

Make sure that you provide suggestions for both elementary and secondary students with special needs. ■ ■

Orientation Activities

The first week of school is the ideal time to orient students to the operating procedures of the classroom, including its organization and management. The time is also appropriate to introduce students to transition activities. The following activities may be used in both special and regular classrooms.

Management Activities

Develop a class calendar to include activities and events that are important to the students and that will help them manage and remember special occasions and deadlines. Record special

school events, student birthdays, field trips, important dates (e.g., report cards, parent-teacher conferences) on the calendar. Encourage the students to suggest calendar entries. Reproduce individual copies of the calendar and distribute them. To add a multicultural element to this activity, you may recognize Martin Luther King, Jr.'s, birthday in January, Black History Month in February, the Chinese New Year in February, Constitution Day in Puerto Rico in July, American Indian Week in November, and others (Mack, 1988).

Elementary classrooms frequently select a very important person (VIP), student of the week, or student assistant to the teacher. You may involve students in establishing the procedures for this selection (e.g., names in a hat or alphabetical order). In addition, during the first week of school, you may discuss the need to share the classroom responsibilities (passing out and collecting work, emptying the trash, being the line leader, etc.). You may assign responsibilities from the first day of school and develop a bulletin board displaying the assignments.

It is important to establish rules at the beginning of the school year. Some teachers have them posted when students enter the classroom for the first time. Other teachers enlist student assistance in developing rules for the classroom.

Transition Activities

Transition activities are short, motivating, and interesting activities used in both special and regular education settings during 10 to 15 minute time slots just before lunch, between classes or other assignments, or just before dismissal. They may include a variety of impromptu activities, such as the following:

1. Play a game by asking students questions about the subject matter that they have just completed. A variation of this is to have the students make up the questions.
2. Conduct activities with students following directions by writing or doing.

☐ Important Points

1. Effective methods for getting to know your students at the beginning of the year include autobiographical and biographical activities, and games.
2. Autobiographical and biographical activities include completing autobiographical report forms, interviewing other students, constructing time lines, and making scrapbooks.
3. Games include identifying from clues which student is being described and using students' names in reading, writing, and spelling activities.
4. Management activities help students manage their responsibilities.
5. Transition activities are impromptu, 10 to 15 minute activities used before lunch, between classes, and at the end of the day.

3. Make up the first line of a story and let each student add another.
4. Have students make an entry in their journals.

It may be helpful to use the following list to monitor the completion of first-week activities. Place a check mark or date next to an item as you complete it.

1. Set up the physical environment. Show the students where everything is located and how to use the different areas of the classroom.
2. Develop a class schedule and individual student schedules. Show the students where their individual schedules will be and explain how to use the schedules.
3. Select and develop instructional materials and orient the students to their location and use. Demonstrate new materials.
4. Establish feedback systems and demonstrate for students the monitoring, grading, and record-keeping procedures.
5. Demonstrate the use of equipment by walking students through the operating procedures for every piece of audiovisual equipment in the classroom.
6. Establish systems for leaving the room (with a pass), having free time, going to time-out, using learning centers, asking for help, turning in work, using materials, etc. Clearly communicate these procedures to students.
7. Clearly and systematically communicate classroom rules.
8. Explain the behavior management system (points, tokens, contracting, awards, graphs, charts, etc.).
9. Explain mainstreaming procedures, such as the amount of time students are to spend in mainstream classes, the roles of the special education and regular education teachers, and the ways in which grades will be awarded.
10. Explain consultative responsibilities. Tell the students that you may be working with them, with other students, or with their teachers in their regular classrooms.
11. Develop a set of transitional activities for the few minutes before lunch, at the end of the class period when everyone has finished early, and just before dismissal at the end of the day.

■ ■ Activity
Develop four 10 to 15 minute transition activities to use with students, two for elementary, and two for secondary. ■ ■

Summary

In this chapter, we focused on what teachers may do to ensure a smooth start to the school year. We gave special attention to the days preceding the arrival of students and to the first week of school. Systematic planning and preparation at these key times facilitate a smooth transition back to school and set the tone for the coming year.

In setting up the classroom at the beginning of the year, it is important to plan ways for providing feedback to students, identify grading systems, and develop record-keeping procedures. Factors to be considered in setting up the physical arrangement of the classroom include physical (size of room), student (age and grade levels), and environmental (instructional materials) variables. We also discussed instructional grouping arrangements. Instruction may be provided through large groups, small groups, individual arrangements, peer tutoring, and independent learning. Factors influencing the decisions about ways to provide instruction include the needs of students, the learning planned, and the activity.

We also discussed planning and scheduling. Planning requires the identification of long-term goals, short-term objectives, instructional strategies, materials, and evaluation. Sources for planning include curriculum guides, textbooks, and IEPS. The seven components of the IEP are (a) the student's present level of educational performance, (b) annual goals, (c) short-term objectives, (d) special and regular education services, (e) the amount of time in regular education, (f) the dates of initiation and duration of services, and (g) evaluation procedures.

Scheduling provides structure and organization. Scheduling is done for regular classrooms (consultative services), resource rooms, and self-contained settings. In scheduling, it is important to (a) alternate highly preferred and less preferred activities; (b) provide time cues; (c) require completion of one task before starting another; (d) group students by level, interests, and needs; (e) provide active involvement; (f) stress goals and objectives; (g) emphasize the connection between regular and special education, and (h) allot time for consultative work. Classroom time may be used more efficiently by considering housekeeping, transition, and allocated time in the class schedule.

We concluded the chapter by examining ways to get to know your students at the beginning of the year. We recommended using autobiographical and biographical activities, and games. We also suggested that you develop a series of management and transition activities to facilitate a successful start to the school year.

3

Informal Assessment for
Initial Planning

Key Topics

Planning begins with identifying the annual goals and short-term objectives on students' individualized education programs. Informal assessment procedures are frequently used to arrive at the short-term objectives of an IEP. According to Salvia and Ysseldyke (1988), informal assessment is "any assessment that involves collection of data by anything other than a standardized test" (p. 26). Informal assessment usually samples skills relevant to the curriculum. Because of this close alignment with the curriculum, informal assessment procedures are often recommended for all students with special needs, including those from various cultural and linguistic backgrounds (Duffey, Salvia, Tucker, & Ysseldyke, 1981; Fradd & Hallman, 1983; Hoffer, 1983; Sugai & Maheady, 1988).

In this chapter, we discuss the informal assessment techniques of error analysis, criterion-referenced tests, precision teaching assessment, curriculum-based measurement, and kidwatching (a term popularized by Yetta Goodman [Goodman, Goodman, & Hood, 1985]). We begin the chapter with a discussion of the influence of ethnic language patterns on student performance.

Ethnic Language Patterns

Before referring a student from a culturally diverse background for possible special education services, you should assess the student's competency with Standard English (Ortiz & Garcia, 1989; Ortiz & Yates, 1989). Although such assessment is usually completed by other professionals, you should still consider language differences when you are using informal measures to ascertain a student's performance, particularly in the areas of reading, written expression, spelling, and language arts.

Many experts argue that language differences, especially those dealing with phonemes, or sounds, should be of concern only if they impair meaning (Ortiz & Polyzoi, 1989; Saville-Troike, 1976). We agree that errors should be considered in terms of meaning and language differences. For example, if a Hispanic student reads *easy* as "iysi" or an African-American student reads *they* as "dey" and each understands the content of the message, you should note these substitutions as language differences and not reading errors. Thus, it is important for you to understand ethnic language patterns.

Table 3.1 lists some of the common language differences. Note that there are also variant dialects within other languages, just as there are differences in the English spoken in Boston and that spoken in Mississippi. Hispanics from a Cuban heritage do not necessarily speak the same dialect as those from a Mexican heritage. Therefore, there are always exceptions in classifications of individuals using group characteristics.

Table 3.1
Language Differences

Black English (Fasold & Wolfram, 1975; Gollnick & Chinn, 1990; Olson, 1987; Tiedt & Tiedt, 1986; Washington & Miller-Jones, 1989)

1. The suffix *s* is often deleted, such as:
   - In third person singular ("The girl play" for "The girl plays").
   - In plurals ("I have two penny" for "I have two pennies").
   - In possessives ("Jim father" for "Jim's father").
2. The verb *be* is often used as the main verb in place of *is, has, have,* and so on ("He be busy" for "He is busy").
3. The ending *ed* is often deleted ("He tie" for "He tied").
4. Forms of *have* are often deleted ("I five dollars" for "I have five dollars").
5. Contracted forms of *will* are often deleted ("He marry her" for "He'll marry her").
6. Contracted forms of *is* and *are* are often deleted, such as:
   - *Is* ("He here" for "He's here").
   - *Are* ("They here" for "They're here").
7. More than a single negative form is used ("I don't like candy no more" for "I don't like candy any more").
8. Stress often occurs in the first rather than the second syllable (*po'lice* for *po-lice'*). Alternately, the first syllable is absent when not stressed (*'cept* for *except*).
9. The vowel glides of *ay* and *oy* are often distorted (*boah* for *boy*).
10. The pronunciation of *th* is often distorted:
    - In the beginning of a word, *th* equals *d* (*dey* for *they*).
    - In the middle of a word, *th* equals *f* or *v* (*aufuh* for *author*, *muver* for *mother*).
    - At the end of a word, *th* equals *f* (*souf* for *south*).
11. The *r* and *l* are pronounced as *uh* (*sistuh* for *sister*, *steuh* for *steal*), omitted (*ca'ol* for *carol*, *fo'ow* for *follow*), or distorted when following *o* or *u* (*doe* for *door*, *tole* for *toll*).
12. The articles *a, an,* and *the* are often omitted ("I have book" for "I have a book").

Error Analysis

To establish the focus of instruction, you should examine errors. For example, if you target math facts for initial instruction, you should conduct an error analysis to determine which facts in particular are difficult for the student. If you find that Paul correctly calculates all facts except those involving the basic addition facts of 9 (e.g., 9 + 1 through 9 + 9), you know to teach just these addition facts.

Common Error Patterns

Successful error analysis requires both knowledge and recognition of common error patterns. Before you can systematically assess error patterns, you must be aware of different types of errors.

Reading

In the *Qualitative Reading Inventory*, Leslie and Caldwell (1990) discuss the following decoding errors: (a) omissions—the student omits words when reading, (b) substitutions—the student substitutes a similar word that often makes sense in the sentence, (c) insertions—the student adds words, and (d) reversals—the student reverses letters or phrases. Leslie and Caldwell do not count repetitions (repeating a word or phrase when reading), hesitations (pausing longer at some words when reading), or omissions of punctuation (e.g., not pausing at the end of a sentence) as errors because scoring is unreliable

Table 3.1
Continued

Spanish (Lado, 1964; Olson, 1987; Ortiz & Yates, 1989)

1. Possession is expressed by word order ("book of girl" for "girl's book").
2. There is no difference in pronunciation following certain sounds: *sh* and *ch, s* and *z, n* and *ng, b* and *v, d* and *th, y* and *j, t* and unvoiced *th,* unvoiced *th* and *s.*
3. The *r* is trilled, or rolled, when two *r*'s are together (*sorrrel* for *sorrel*).
4. Consonant clusters at the beginnings of words are often problems (*espeak* for *speak*).
5. *Ed, er,* and *est* are not used for endings, but *mas,* meaning more, is used for comparison.
6. The article *a* is often omitted ("I need drink" for "I need a drink").
7. Negation is expressed by *no* before the verb ("Juan no esta aqui" for "Juan is not here").
8. Tenses may not be expressed ("I play now" for "I am playing now").
9. The *s* suffix is dropped ("four bell" for "four bells").
10. One word is used for "there are" and "there is"—*hay* ("Hay muchos" for "There are many," "Hay un" for "There is one").
11. Adjectives follow nouns ("I have shoes white" for "I have white shoes").
12. Spanish usually operates on a three-tone system, while English operates on a four-tone system.

Native American (Gollnick & Chinn, 1990; Walker, 1987)

1. Final consonants are rare in Indian language.
2. Proper verb tenses are often problems (*winned* for *won*).
3. The articles *a, an,* and *the* are omitted.
4. Prepositions are often problems ("get on car" for "get in car").
5. Word order is subject, direct object, and verb ("boy ball hit" for "The boy hit the ball").
6. Suffixes are omitted (*boy* for *boys*).

Asian-American (D. Chan, 1987; Chinn & Plata, 1987)

1. There are no verb tenses, subject–verb agreement, number agreement, or verb conjugation in Chinese.
2. There are no prepositions in Chinese.
3. There are no designations of singular and plural nouns and masculine and feminine genders in Chinese.
4. There are no consonant clusters in Cantonese.
5. The sounds *sh, ch, r, x, l,* and *j* are difficult to pronounce.
6. Chinese has four to nine tones, while English has four. A change in the tone can alter the meaning.

---

for such factors and repetitions and hesitations do not alter the text's meaning. In another common error, called a none response, students do not attempt to pronounce the word and the teacher must supply it (Mercer & Mercer, 1989). In Table 3.2, we demonstrate examples of the errors in the reading of the sentence "The boy lives in the brick house." We again recommend that you consider any errors in terms of their effect on meaning, especially for students from diverse cultural backgrounds.

Most of the preceding reading errors are found when a student is attempting to decode words, but students also make errors when attempting to comprehend reading passages. Such errors frequently include mistakes in text-explicit, text-implicit, and script-implicit comprehension (Pearson & Johnson, 1978). Table 3.3 contains examples that measure each of these areas of comprehension.

Text-explicit comprehension, also termed literal comprehension, requires the reader to recall information specifically found in a selection. When you ask students to identify the main characters or actions of the main characters or to sequence events or recall significant details, you

Table 3.2
Categories of Reading Errors

- The boy lives in the brick house.
- The boy lives in the brick house. (omitted the word *brick*)
- The boy lives in the brick house. (substituted *block* for *brick*)
- The boy lives in the brick house. (inserted *large*)
- The boy lives in the brick house. (said "brick the house" instead of "the brick house")
- The boy lives in the ＿＿ house. (none response)

Table 3.3
Sample Comprehension Errors

A student read the following paragraph:

> There were 25 seconds left in the championship basketball game. The winner of the game would be high school state champion. The score was tied 98 to 98, but no one could believe that the Tigers were in contention. After all, the tallest player of the team was only 6′5″, the height of the shortest player of the opposition team, the Braves. But the Tigers had been deadly on the 3-point plays and had not missed a free throw.

After reading the paragraph, the student responded to the following sample questions:

1. How much time was left in the game?
   Answer: Twenty-five minutes. (text-explicit error)
2. What was the main idea of the paragraph?
   Answer: There was only a little time left in the game. (text-implicit error)
3. Why is height such an advantage when playing basketball?
   Answer: I don't know. (script-implicit error)

are checking text-explicit comprehension. Question 1 in Table 3.3 is an example, because students should find the answer directly in the first sentence of the paragraph.

Text-implicit comprehension, also referred to as inferential comprehension (Tindal & Marston, 1990), requires the reader to interact with information that is implied. It is not found directly from any one source in the passage. Forming opinions, predicting the next event in a story, and identifying the influence of the setting on the actions of the main character in a story are examples of text-implicit comprehension. Question 2 in Table 3.3 checks this type of comprehension because the reader must assimilate the information from more than one sentence.

In script-implicit comprehension questions, the reader must use the information from the text and provide additional personal information (Tindal & Marston, 1990). Undoubtedly, a person who is not familiar with the sport of basketball will not answer question 3 correctly. This type of comprehension question is generally difficult for students with special needs who are from diverse cultural backgrounds, because they often do not have the necessary background experiences.

Math
Engelhardt (1977) identified the following math error categories: (a) incorrect operations—the student selects one operation when another operation should have been selected, (b) basic fact errors—the student makes a mistake in basic number facts, (c) defective algorithms—the student employs the correct operation and knows the basic number fact but does not use the correct process or procedure, (d) grouping errors—the student does not attend to the place value of the number, (e) incomplete algorithms—the student performs the basic steps correctly but leaves out a step, (f) identity errors—the student confuses operation identities of 0s and 1s, (g) zero errors—the student has difficulty with the concept of 0, and (h) inappropriate inversions—the student reverses some critical

dimension of the operational procedures. Most of the errors fall in the areas of basic fact errors (38%), defective algorithms (18%), grouping errors (22%), and inappropriate inversions (21%). Engelhardt (1977) notes that the defective algorithm is the error that most frequently distinguishes competent math students from less competent ones. We present examples of math errors in Table 3.4.

Spelling

Common spelling errors include omission of silent letters and sounded letters, phonetic substi-

tutions, letter reversals, addition of letters, words with apostrophes (e.g., possessives and contractions), and rule overgeneralizations (Evans, Evans, & Mercer, 1986; Salvia & Hughes, 1990). Examples of these errors are presented in Table 3.5.

Handwriting

Errors in handwriting generally fall into three categories: physical difficulties, letter formation, and spatial orientation (Lewis & Lewis, 1965; Newland, 1932). Physical difficulties include improper pencil grip and poor writing posture.

Table 3.4
Common Math Errors

Incorrect Operations

$$\begin{array}{r} 25 \\ + 11 \\ \hline 14 \end{array}$$ (the student subtracted instead of added)

Basic Fact Errors

Errors made in any of the following:
- 1 + 0 through 9 + 9 (1 + 0 = 3; 9 + 8 = 16, etc.)

- 1 − 0 through 18 − 9 (1 − 1 = 4; 14 − 7 = 8, etc.)

- 1 × 0 through 9 × 9 (2 × 5 = 11; 9 × 6 = 53, etc.)

- 1 ÷ 0 through 81 ÷ 9 (7 ÷ 1 = 1; 21 ÷ 7 = 2, etc.)

Defective Algorithms

$$\begin{array}{r} 112 \\ \times 43 \\ \hline 146 \end{array}$$ (correct procedure not used)

Grouping Errors

$$\begin{array}{r} 35 \\ \times 6 \\ \hline 1830 \end{array}$$ (the student forgot to carry the 3 tens)

Incomplete Algorithms

$$3 \overline{\smash{)}125} \quad \begin{array}{l} 41 \end{array}$$ (the student forgot to subtract and failed to complete process)
$$\begin{array}{r} 12 \\ \hline 5 \\ \hline 3 \end{array}$$

Identity Errors

$$\begin{array}{r} 3 \\ \times 0 \\ \hline 3 \end{array}$$ (0 is treated as a 1)

Zero Errors

$$3 \overline{\smash{)}504} \quad 18$$
$$\begin{array}{r} 3 \\ \hline 24 \\ \hline 24 \end{array}$$ (0 is ignored)

Inappropriate Inversions

$$\begin{array}{r} {}^{5}45 \\ \times 7 \\ \hline 333 \end{array}$$ (the student reversed 35)

Table 3.5
Sample Spelling Errors

Word	Spelling	Error
climb	clim	(omission of silent letter)
	cimb	(omission of sounded letter)
	clime	(phonetic substitution)
	clibm	(letter reversal)
	climbe	(addition of letter)
haven't	havn't	(contraction error)
girls'	girl's	(possessive error)
deer	deers	(overgeneralization of a rule; add an *s* for plural)

Letter formation problems involve failure to close letters (*a* looks like *u*), closed top loops (*e* looks like *i*), use of straight up strokes instead of rounded strokes (*i* looks like *e*), not crossing letters (*t* looks like *l*), and letter reversals (*b* looks like *d*). Spatial orientation errors include inability to place the words correctly on the paper (such as not allowing enough space between words and letters), writing in the margins, failure to write letters on the line, inconsistent letter size, and improper slant of letters. Burns and Broman (1983) also identify spatial errors with the Arabic numerals of 0, 2, 5, 6, 7, and 9. We present examples of spatial orientation errors in Table 3.6. Another error, which is especially prevalent in older students, is slow writing speed.

Procedures

We recommend the following steps for analyzing errors: (a) list the student errors (e.g., on the addition fact worksheet, Jan is missing 9 + 8 , 7 + 8, 6 + 8); (b) make a hypothesis as to the error pattern (computational error, basic addition using the 8 facts); (c) test the hypothesis by examining the correct problems to see if any have the same pattern (Jan calculated 6 + 4, 5 + 6, and 9 + 2 correctly, so none of the correct ones involved the 8 facts); (d) if not correct, redo the hypothesis (steps a–c again); and (e) teach correction of the error (Jan needs to be retaught basic addition facts using 8).

In the preceding example, finding the error pattern was relatively easy. The following example is not so easy:

$$
\begin{array}{cccccc}
305 & 230 & 40 & 401 & 57 & 435 \\
-187 & -125 & -21 & -56 & -8 & -96 \\
\hline
288 & 105 & 19 & 255 & 49 & 339
\end{array}
$$

Jeff missed 305 − 187 and 401 − 56 (step a). It appears that Jeff has trouble regrouping, particularly with zero (step b). Calculating with zero is one of the common math errors identified in Table 3.4. However, a check of the hypothesis this time shows that Jeff was able to subtract 230 − 125 and 40 − 21 correctly, both of which involve the subtraction of zeros; thus, the error pattern is insufficiently identified (step c). A further comparison of the correct and incorrect problems with zeros indicates that zero is a problem in subtraction only when the zero is in the tens place of a three-digit minuend (step d). Thus, this example requires more careful analysis.

The process of identifying the general pattern of errors and then pinpointing the exact error may also be applied to the assessment of reading errors. For example, in identifying the general pattern of substitutions, you observe that the student reads many words incorrectly. However, pinpointing that the student makes these errors when reading words that contain the long *a* sound when it is spelled *ai* or *ay* makes instructional planning easier and more efficient. Sometimes, error analysis is made easier by asking the student to think out loud.

■ ■ Activity

Identify the following error patterns.

+ = correct
− = incorrect (The incorrect student response is in parentheses).

Reading Words

1. for	− (far)		4. man	+	
2. was	− (w)		5. fit	+	
3. of	− (off)		6. top	+	

Table 3.6
Common Handwriting Errors

Handwriting	Error
Spot	Not enough space between letters.
Space between	Not enough space between words.
within the margins	Writing in the margins.
line	Inability to write on the line.
Size	Inconsistent letter size.
slant	Improper slant.

Math Problems

36	29	47	55	26	26	45
+19	+68	+16	+79	+87	+13	+65
55	97	63	(34)	(73)	39	(20)

Spelling Words

1. might   − (mit)   4. flop   + _____
2. rain   + _____   5. mine   − (min)
3. run   + _____   6. sky   − (ski)

(Answers for this and other activities are found in the Instructor's Manual.) ■ ■

Criterion-Referenced Tests

Criterion-referenced tests (CRTs) measure the extent to which a student has mastered a skill or task based on an established criterion (Mercer, 1987). Unlike formal tests, which compare a student's performance to that of other students, a criterion-referenced test compares the student's performance to some expected level.

You may either design a criterion-referenced test or select one from the many commercial ones. Commercially produced CRTs assess either many subject areas or a single one. For

☐ Important Points

1. Informal assessment is any assessment that involves collection of data by anything other than a standardized test.
2. Informal assessments are frequently used to arrive at the short-term objectives on an IEP.
3. Language differences should be considered as errors only if they impair meaning.
4. In reading, there are decoding errors (e.g., omissions, substitutions, insertions, reversals, and none response).
5. Comprehension errors include problems with text-explicit, text-implicit, and script-implicit comprehension.
6. Math errors include incorrect operations, basic fact errors, defective algorithms, grouping errors, incomplete algorithms, identity errors, zero errors, and inappropriate inversions.
7. Common spelling errors include omission of silent letters and sounded letters, phonetic substitutions, letter reversals, addition of letters, words with apostrophes, and rule overgeneralizations.
8. Physical difficulties, letter formation, and spatial orientation are categories of handwriting errors.
9. The following steps are recommended for analyzing errors: (a) list the student errors; (b) make a hypothesis as to error pattern; (c) test the hypothesis by examining the correct problems to see if any of these have the same pattern; (d) if not correct, redo the hypothesis; and (e) teach correction of the error.

example, the *Brigance* diagnostic inventories (Brigance, 1977, 1981, 1983) are multiskill batteries that contain subtests measuring skills in such subject areas as reading, math, and spelling. Single-subject criterion-referenced tests available commercially include the *Standardized Reading Inventory (SRI)* (Newcomer, 1986), which measures only reading skills, and the *Basic Arithmetic Skill Evaluation (BASE)* (May & Hood, 1973), which measures only math skills. Commercially produced CRTs are available for preschool through secondary populations of students with special needs in academic and vocational areas.

Authors of CRTs typically consult curriculum scope and sequence lists for the selection of the items. For example, Brigance (1983) states that his test items are the direct result of checking the scope and sequence of the most recently published texts of several widely used basal series. In the *BASE,* May and Hood (1973) identify twenty key skills in each grade level from first through sixth based on an examination of the scope and sequence of math texts published by Addison-Wesley, Ginn, Laidlaw, and others. The scope identifies the breadth of the subject matter and the sequence identifies the sequential arrangement of the subject matter.

For example, the scope of the math curriculum for kindergarten through eighth grade, no matter the particular math series, usually includes math readiness (e.g., recognizing numerals), number facts (e.g., reciting basic facts, such as $4 + 6$), whole numbers (e.g., adding two-digit numbers with regrouping), fractions and mixed numbers (e.g., adding fractions), decimals (e.g., reading decimals), percents (e.g., converting percents to decimals), measurement (e.g., telling time to the hour, recognizing different coins), metrics (e.g., reading Celsius temperature), and geometry (e.g., recognizing squares) (Brigance, 1977, 1981, 1983).

In the sequence, math readiness skills such as rote counting are taught before basic facts, which are taught before fractions. There is also a sequence of skills within each area. For example, subtraction problems that do not require regrouping (e.g., 87 − 14) are taught before those that require regrouping (e.g., 87 − 19).

Using Criterion-Referenced Tests

Although teachers may design criterion-referenced tests, it is much easier for a beginning teacher to select commercial ones. Therefore, we concentrate on the use of commercial CRTs here. To use a commercial CRT for initial planning, we recommend the following steps: (a) select the test, (b) administer the test, (c) select the expected level of mastery, and (d) identify objectives.

Selecting the Test

There are two valuable sources of information to help you select CRTs. One is the curriculum scope and sequence of the subject area and grade level, and the other is the regular education teacher. A basic knowledge of the curriculum scope and sequence for various grade levels can help you. For example, if you are selecting reading tests to assess a first grader's reading performance, you are not likely to select a reading test that measures comprehension of colloquial and figurative expressions, because this skill is usually introduced much later. Instead, tests that measure basic sight vocabulary, initial consonant sounds, and short vowels are more appropriate, because these skills are introduced in the primary reading curriculum.

Most texts or text series have a scope and sequence that you can check for the various grade levels. For example, in Table 3.7, we present a partial scope and sequence found in the series *Mathematics in Action* (Hoffer, Johnson, Leinwald, Lodholz, Musser, & Thoburn, 1991). A glance at the sample scope and sequence finds that three- and four-digit subtraction is introduced in third grade and is a part of the math scope and sequence through eighth grade.

In addition to consulting a curriculum scope and sequence, it is a good idea to discuss a student's problem with the regular education teacher. For example, if Mr. Gonzalez, Jim's regular second grade teacher, tells you that Jim has problems telling time, as a first step, you should select a criterion-referenced test that measures math skills, not one that measures reading skills. You should select either a multiskill battery like the *Brigance,* which has various math tests, or a single-skill test like the *Basic Arithmetic Skill Evaluation (BASE)* (May & Hood, 1973).

Say that you select the *BASE*. Then, you should select items from the *BASE* that measure telling time. One such item is "Given pictures of clock faces the pupil can tell time to the hour and the half hour" (student answer sheet, item 215).

■ ■ Activity

Susan is a sixth grader. The regular education teacher and you have decided to test her math skills because she is failing in the basic math class. The regular education teacher reports that Susan seems to miss problems dealing with the calculation of fractions. Examine the scope and sequence of a sixth grade math text and identify some skills that you might select for testing. ■ ■

Administering the Test

You do not have to follow the directions for administration of a criterion-referenced test exactly. However, many of the commercially prepared instruments provide guidelines for where to start and stop testing and general directions and procedures for easy and quick administration. For example, the *Standardized Reading Inventory* (Newcomer, 1986) recommends that the student begin reading the passages of the test, starting with the passage that corresponds to the highest grade level scored by the student on the word list part of the test. Testing should always begin at the highest level at which you expect a student to be successful. That way the student is not discouraged by the items that are too diffi-

Table 3.7
Sample Series Scope and Sequence

	K	1	2	3	4	5	6	7	8
Subtracting Whole Numbers									
Understand subtraction concepts using models	•	•	•	•	•	•			
Understand subtraction concepts							•	•	•
Basic facts and fact families	•	•	•	•	•	•			
Problem solving	•	•	•	•	•	•	•	•	•
Subtraction with and without regrouping using models		•	•	•	•	•			
Subtraction with and without regrouping							•	•	•
Estimate differences			•		•	•	•	•	•
2- and 3-digit subtraction		•	•	•	•	•	•	•	•
3- and 4-digit subtraction				•	•	•	•	•	•
Subtract larger numbers					•	•	•	•	•
Multiplying Whole Numbers									
Understand multiplication concepts using models		•	•	•	•	•			
Understand multiplication concepts							•	•	•
Basic facts and fact families			•	•	•	•			
Problem solving				•	•	•	•	•	•
Estimate products				•	•	•	•	•	•
2- and 3-digit multiplication				•	•	•	•	•	•
3- and 4-digit multiplication					•	•	•	•	•
Multiply larger numbers					•	•	•	•	•
Dividing Whole Numbers									
Understand division concepts using models		•	•	•	•	•			
Understand division concepts							•	•	•
Basic facts and fact families				•	•	•	•		
Problem solving				•	•	•	•	•	•
1-digit divisors				•	•	•	•	•	•
Estimate quotients				•	•	•	•	•	•
With remainders				•	•	•	•	•	•
Interpret remainders				•	•	•	•	•	•
2-digit divisors					•	•	•	•	•
Zeroes in the quotient				•	•	•	•	•	•
3-digit divisors							•	•	•
Fraction Concepts									
Understand fractions	•	•	•	•	•	•	•	•	•
Explore fractions of regions and sets using models	•	•	•	•	•	•			
Explore fractions of regions and sets							•	•	•
Relate fractions and math language	•	•	•	•	•	•	•	•	•
Read and write fractions		•	•	•	•	•	•	•	•

Note. From *Teacher's Edition: Mathematics in Action* (p. 38) by A. R. Hoffer, M. R. Johnson, S. J. Leinwald, R. D. Lodholz, G. R. Musser, and T. Thoburn, 1991, New York: Macmillan/McGraw-Hill School Pub. Co. Reprinted by permission.

cult, nor is valuable time wasted by items that are too easy.

You may make adaptations during the testing process. For example, if Jason has a short attention span, you may decide to administer sections of the test for short time periods and then schedule a break. If you wish to hear Latasha's thoughts as she solves the math problems, you may ask her to think aloud as she writes the answers.

Selecting the Expected Level of Mastery

There are no absolutes as far as selection of mastery. Mastery, or acceptable performance, is most commonly determined by guessing, and 80% accuracy is usually the guess (Howell & Kaplan, 1980). However, Howell and Kaplan suggest using peer assessment as the criterion for acceptable performance (CAP). They recommend the following steps to establish the CAP.

1. Select a test.
   Example: Select the dictionary test of reference skills from the *Brigance Inventory of Essential Skills* (Brigance, 1981) for Carlos, a seventh grader.
2. Select the top 50% of successful grade-level peers by either teacher judgment or by standardized testing results. (There must be a minimum of ten students.)
   Example: Select 50% of the students from the seventh grade basic English classes.
3. Administer the test just as you plan to administer it to the specific student.
   Example: Administer the test following the directions in the examiner's booklet.
4. Rank order the scores and find the median.
   Example: The scores were 100%, 95%, 90%, 90%, 87%, 85%, 80%, 80%, 80%, 75%, 70%. To calculate the median score when there is an uneven number, count the total number of scores (11 in this example) and then divide by 2 to reach the midpoint, where the scores are divided into equal halves. In this case, 85% is the median, as 5 scores are larger than 85% and 5 scores are smaller.

When there is an even number of scores, the median is the number halfway between the two middle scores (Huck, Cormier, & Bounds, 1974). Thus, if 70% were eliminated and there were only 10 scores, the median would be 86%, because it lies between 85% and 87%.

5. Calculate a confidence band by multiplying and dividing the median score by 1.5 to make certain that it is representative of the performance of the students in that group.
   Example: $85 \times 1.5 = 127.5$ and $85 \div 1.5 = 56.6$. The confidence band is 56.6%–127.5%.
6. If most of the students' scores fall within the $\times 1.5$ or $\div 1.5$ confidence band, accept the median score as the CAP.
   Example: All of the scores fall between 56.6% and 127.5%; therefore, the mastery level of 85% is appropriate for Carlos on this skill.
7. If a large percentage of the scores fall outside the confidence band, double the sample size and repeat steps 2 through 6.

Many of the commercial CRTs recommend criteria for acceptable performance. However, as Howell and Morehead (1987) caution, any CRT that has a criterion statement included in the objectives should have a technical manual explaining the origin and validity of the criterion.

Identifying the Objectives

Once you have selected and administered the tests, identify the objectives for instruction. The objectives will consist of skills in which the student did not meet the mastery criterion. For example, if you expected Sharon to score 80% based on CAP procedures on a reading comprehension test but she scored only 60%, you should target reading comprehension as an area for remediation. Furthermore, you should examine the specific questions that Sharon missed. Did she miss text-explicit questions that required her to order and sequence events or did she miss questions that required her to remember significant details? Then, from this analysis, you should write a short-term objective, such as "When presented with numerous 200-word passages and four questions requiring recall of significant details, Sharon will answer 3 out of 4 questions correctly for at least three passages."

Some commercial CRTs even provide a suggested list of materials for teaching the skills. *The Brigance Diagnostic Inventory of Essential Skills* (Brigance, 1981) is correlated with instructional materials from the Janus Company (Taylor, 1984). The *BASE* skills are correlated with pages of the most commonly used math texts and multimedia and manipulative materials.

Planning Initial Instruction

So far, we have presented the steps separately for using a CRT, but to help you better understand the process, we relate Consuela's experience to each of the steps.

1. *Discuss the student's problem with the regular education teacher.* In a conference, Consuela's fifth grade teacher indicates that Consuela has problems reading words with silent letters and two or more syllables.

2. *Check the curriculum scope and sequence of the subject area and grade level.* A check of the reading scope and sequence from Consuela's classroom text shows that silent letters, prefixes, suffixes, and syllablication are some of the word analysis skills that students should master by fifth grade.

3. *Select a CRT.* Select a CRT that measures the skills identified by the teacher and the curriculum scope and sequence. In this instance, *The Brigance Diagnostic Inventory of Basic Skills* (Brigance, 1977) is appropriate for first through sixth grades, because it measures all of these skills.

4. *Administer the CRT.* Administer the following tests from the *Brigance:* phonetic irregularities to check silent letters, suffixes, prefixes, number of syllables auditorily, and syllabication concepts.

5. *Decide on a criterion of acceptable performance (CAP).* Then, administer these same tests to Consuela's peers. Their median score is 90%.

6. *Compare the student's performance to the peer criterion level.* Consuela reached the established criterion on phonetic irregularities only. She did not reach mastery on the tests dealing with reading suffixes, prefixes, and three-syllable words, nor was she able to apply the rules for syllabication.

7. *Identify short-term objectives for initial instruction:* (a) Presented with a list of fifty words, Consuela will read words containing the suffixes of *-ward, -ment, -ies,* and *-ness* and the prefixes of *inter-, ir-, anti-,* and *semi-* with 90% accuracy and (b) presented with a list of two-syllable words, Consuela will apply the syllablication rules dealing with two consonants–two vowels (*bot | tom*) and one consonant between two vowels (*a | bout*) to divide the words with 90% accuracy.

■ ■ Activity

Write a short-term objective in reading based on the following performance on a test of phonograms. The criterion for acceptable performance is 90%. Correct = +. Error = −.

The student reads the following words with common phonograms:

1.	*ail*	+	9.	*ell*	+
2.	*ble*	−	10.	*est*	−
3.	*ing*	+	11.	*all*	−
4.	*tion*	−	12.	*ack*	−
5.	*ter*	−	13.	*op*	−
6.	*ick*	+	14.	*ock*	−
7.	*et*	+	15.	*ill*	−
8.	*ide*	+			■ ■

⬜ Important Points

1. Criterion-referenced tests (CRTs) measure the extent to which a student has mastered a skill or task based on an established criterion.
2. The items on a CRT are often based on the curriculum scope (the skills or content taught at various grade levels) and sequence (the order in which the skills are taught).
3. In selecting a CRT, special education teachers often consult the regular education teacher and a curriculum scope and sequence.
4. A criterion for acceptable performance (CAP) is established by administering the test to at least ten students in the class, finding the median score, and calculating the confidence band to ascertain that the score is representative of successful performance in the mainstream class.
5. CRT assessments are usually used to identify the specific objectives for instruction.

Precision Teaching

Another informal assessment technique is precision teaching (PT). Precision teaching involves no specific teaching strategies. Instead, precision teaching is a precise and systematic way to measure student performance. Using precision teaching, you can decide on initial instructional strategies and evaluate their effectiveness. Precision teaching is one of the five practices recommended for students from various cultural backgrounds who are at risk for special education referral (Maheady, Towne, Algozzine, Mercer, & Ysseldyke, 1983).

Using rate of response, precision teaching emphasizes direct and continuous measurement of behavior (West, Young, & Spooner, 1990). Rate is the number of behavior movements divided by the number of minutes observed. In precision teaching, the average number of correct and incorrect responses per minute is calculated. The underlying principle is that a skill is mastered only if it can be performed both accurately and quickly. A student who is able to take notes at thirty words a minute will be more successful in the mainstream than one who is just as accurate in writing words but can transcribe only ten words a minute. A time limit of 1 minute is specified for measuring most academic skills, although the time limit may vary according to the amount of curriculum measured and student characteristics. For example, 3 minutes may be used when addition, subtraction, multiplication, and division facts (extensive curriculum) are measured at once, compared with 1 minute when measuring addition facts only. Fifteen seconds may be used for students who are highly distractible and cannot focus on a task for 1 minute (Binder, Haughton, & Eyk, 1990).

■ ■ Activity

Try an experiment. Time yourself for 15 seconds and with your usual writing hand, write the numbers from 1 through 9, starting with 1 again when you reach 9. How did you do? Can the numbers be read? Count how many numbers you wrote by counting each digit. You probably found this skill to be both accurate and fluent. Now, reverse hands and do the same task for 15 seconds. How are your numbers this time? They can probably be read, but how many digits did you write in the 15 seconds? Unless you are ambidextrous, you probably wrote more digits the first time. If a professor told you that you could take notes with your nonwriting hand only, your accuracy would be somewhat affected, but your proficiency would be more affected, and you would miss many notes. ■ ■

Using Precision Teaching

To use precision teaching for initial planning, follow these steps: (a) pinpoint the behavior to be taught, (b) design or select a probe, (c) select an aim, (d) take a baseline, (e) decide whether the skill is appropriate, (f) write an objective, and (g) decide on an intervention.

Pinpointing the Behavior

Pinpointing is choosing a behavior to change. In precision teaching, each behavior is counted, so the behavior must be repeatable and observable, and it must have a beginning and end (White & Haring, 1980) for it to be appropriately assessed with PT procedures. The skill of reading initial consonant clusters is appropriate to pinpoint. It is repeatable, as words requiring initial consonant clusters may be read again and again. It is observable, as you may listen while the student reads. Finally, each initial consonant cluster has a beginning and end. Other appropriate pinpointed behaviors are spelling words, writing letters, and saying letter sounds.

"Betty is intelligent" is not an appropriate behavior for pinpointing, as it does not meet the three requirements. How is intelligence repeated? How do you observe intelligence? Where does it begin and end?

■ ■ Activity

Mark *No* by all of the following descriptors that cannot be measured using precision teaching. Then, change them so that precision teaching can be used.

1. Counting money.
2. Answering questions at the end of a chapter.
3. Distractibility. ■ ■

Designing a Probe

Once the skill is pinpointed, you can either design a test, called a probe, or use a commercial one. Commercial probes may be secured from the following sources:

- Clearinghouse/Information Center
  Bureau of Education for Exceptional Students
  Division of Public Schools
  Florida Department of Education
  622 Florida Education Center
  Tallahassee, FL 32399-0400
- Precision Teaching Project
  Skyline Center
  3300 Third Street, Northeast
  Great Falls, MT 59404
- Regional Resource Center Diagnostic Inventories
  Clinical Services Building
  University of Oregon
  Eugene, OR 97403

If you plan to design a probe, you should follow certain guidelines. First, allow a standardized count in order to accurately assess the skill. To ensure a standardized count, the student must have freedom and opportunity to move (White & Haring, 1980). To allow the student freedom to move, design the probe so that you do not place physical constraints on the student. For example, if you use flash cards to test basic sight words, you are probably interfering with how fast the student can read the words, because the student's performance depends in part on how quickly you manipulate the cards. Changes in performance during assessment may be due to your dexterity in presenting the flash cards and not to the performance of the student. You are less likely to interfere with a student's freedom to move if you use a typed list instead of flash cards. In fact, most commercially designed probes measure math and reading skills with paper-and-pencil tests.

Opportunity to move requires that students never run out of problems to complete. White and Haring (1980) recommend that the probe contain more items than any student can possibly finish within the alloted time. (Remember, a 1-minute time limit is usually imposed.) They argue that an overabundance of items allows for a more accurate picture of the student's performance because it avoids ceiling effects. This is particularly important when you use precision teaching to evaluate the effectiveness of instructional planning. For example, if there were twelve problems on the probe on Monday and Sam answered all twelve correctly and then there were twenty problems on the probe on Tuesday and Sam answered all twenty correctly, you might conclude that Sam made progress when comparing his raw scores of 12 and 20. However, in reality, Sam's performance on Monday was limited by the number of opportunities he had to show his knowledge. In addition, inclusion of more items than a student can possibly finish within the particular time prevents rote memorization of the answers (Howell & Morehead, 1987).

Having more items on a probe than students can possibly finish does not mean including 140 different words or math facts. Ten words or 10 facts may be repeated 14 times to reach 140, or 2 words or facts may be repeated 70 times. See Table 3.8 for an example of a sight word probe. Notice that even though there are 100 total words on the sample probe, there are only 20 different words, and each word is repeated 5 times. Thus, a student is actually being assessed on 20 words, not 100. The amount of curriculum selected often depends on the student and the curriculum scope and sequence.

Once you have decided the content of the probe, you should identify the channels for measurement; that is, you should select the input and output channels (Hefferan & Diviaio, 1989). Input channels are the ways in which a student receives the information. In a school setting, input channels are usually visual or auditory. The student either sees the information when reading a text or hears the information when listening to the teacher read the text. Output channels are the ways in which a student expresses information. In a school setting, this is often with an oral (say) or written (write) response; for example, the student either says the answer to a math question or writes the answer.

The input and output measures may vary for any task; for example, you may test a student's addition skills by presenting him or her with a worksheet of addition problems. This is a visual (see) input, if the student looks at the problems on the worksheet. However, you can change this input to an auditory (hear) one simply by reading the problems from the worksheet instead of giving the paper to the student. In the same way, the output measure can be either a say response, if the student responds by orally telling you the answer, or a write response, if the student responds by writing the answer.

When designing a probe, you should select the channels that are used most often to perform

Table 3.8
Sight Word Probe

about	after	be	five	its	must	seven	there	(8)
well	sleep	call	from	him	let	old	around	(16)
upon	after	ask	cold	why	five	must	there	(24)
around	from	let	sleep	cold	why	about	its	(32)
seven	well	be	him	call	old	upon	ask	(40)
after	about	its	five	be	around	well	there	(48)
seven	must	old	let	him	from	call	sleep	(54)
call	about	must	upon	from	seven	after	why	(62)
him	upon	why	ask	cold	be	there	let	(70)
sleep	ask	let	well	five	around	cold	its	(78)
old	about	seven	him	ask	must	from	why	(86)
call	sleep	upon	let	after	be	around	there	(94)
well	old	five	its	about	seven			(100)

the skill in the classroom. For instance, in regular elementary classrooms, reading instruction usually involves students taking turns reading selections orally during reading groups, so the channels of see and say are appropriate for measuring reading skills at this level. However, the channels of see and write are probably more appropriate at the secondary level, where reading instruction often consists of students reading silently and answering questions. In both elementary and secondary regular classes, math instruction typically involves paper-and-pencil performance, so see and write are appropriate channels for measuring math skills.

The identification of the input and output channels leads to decisions concerning how to teach. For example, if Juan answered more math facts correctly when you read the problems than when he reads them, you may decide to use a language master to present the facts both auditorily and visually for him. If Sunfa performs better on a hear/say spelling probe than on a hear/write one, you may share that information with the regular education teacher so that Friday's spelling test is given orally to Sunfa. The last information to record on the probe is the cumulative score for each row of problems (see Table 3.8).

Selecting an Aim

You must specify a mastery level to show that the student has learned the skill for automatic application to different situations. In precision teaching, the mastery levels, or aims, are stated in terms of so many count correct (cc) responses and count error (ce) responses per minute, with an overlearning component (Alberto & Troutman, 1990). The overlearning component of an objective is the number of sessions that the student must remain on or above the aim. A sample precision teaching aim is 80 count correct responses and 2 count error (80 cc/2 ce) responses per minute for three sessions.

To determine if a student has mastered the content, you may use the performance standards suggested by the Precision Teaching Project in the Great Falls Public Schools (1981) (see Table

3.9). These standards are based on the performance of students who have demonstrated mastery of the skill. Performance standards are reported as the number correct within 1 minute. To use the performance standards, simply match the skill measured on the probe with the pinpoint that is most like it from the list. For example, if your probe consists of addition problems like 15 + 4 and 61 + 22, the matching pinpoint is "See/Write Math Facts," and the suggested standard is 70–90 correct digits per minute.

It may seem that 70–90 digits per minute is an impossible standard for mastery of basic facts. However, this standard considers each digit, not each problem. For example 35 + 42 = 77 is not counted as one problem correct, but as two correct digits:

$$
\begin{array}{ll}
(7 & 7). \\
+1 & +1
\end{array}
$$

An answer of 67 to the same problem is scored as one digit correct and one error:

$$
\begin{array}{ll}
(6 & 7). \\
-1 & +1
\end{array}
$$

In spelling, mastery aims are presented for letters and in reading, they are presented for sounds, letters, and words. Often, two or less is the count error aim (Koorland, Keel, & Ueberhorst, 1990). Errors are counted only as far as the student is able to progress on the probe. Thus, a student who finishes only ten of fifty problems on a probe is not penalized for failing to complete all fifty problems. Only the ten completed problems are scored.

If the performance standard appears too difficult for students to reach, you may use peer assessment or the adult-to-child proportional formula to determine mastery aims (Koorland, Keel, & Ueberhorst, 1990). Peer assessment uses a standard of peer performance similar to the criterion for acceptable performance. To establish a standard of peer performance, administer the probe to three peers from the student's regular (mainstream) classroom and then average the scores. The selected peers should be able

Table 3.9
Suggested Performance Standards

Pinpoint	Standard
Reading	
See/Say Isolated Sounds	60–80 sounds/min.
See/Say Phonetic Words	60–80 words/min.
Think/Say Alphabet (forward or backward)	400+ letters/min.
See/Say Letter Names	80–100 letters/min.
See/Say Sight Words	80–100 words/min.
See/Say Words in Context (oral reading)	200+ words/min.
See/Say Words in Context (silent reading)	400+ words/min.
Think/Say Ideas or Facts	15–30 ideas/min.
Handwriting	
Emphasizing Speed	
See/Write Slashes	200–400 slashes/min.
See/Write Circles	100–150 circles/min.
Think/Write Alphabet	80–100 letters/min.
Emphasizing Accuracy	
See/Write Letters (count of 3 for each letter: slant, form and ending)	75 correct/min.
See/Write—Cursive Letters Connected (count of 3 per letter)	125 correct/min.
Spelling	
Hear/Write Dictated Words	80–100 letters/min.
Hear/Write Dictated Words	15–25 words/min.
Math	
See/Write Numbers Random	100–120 digits/min.
Think/Write Numbers (0–9 serial)	120–160 digits/min.
See/Say Numbers	80–100/min.
Think/Say Numbers in Sequence (count by's)	150–200+/min.
See/Write Math Facts	70–90 digits/min.

Note. Reprinted from the *Great Falls Precision Teaching Project Training Manual* (p. 43), Great Falls Public Schools, Great Falls, Montana.

to perform the skill adequately. If the scores of the three peers for the skill of see/say multiplication facts 0 through 9 are respectively 95 cc, 85 cc, and 85 cc, the student's aim will be 88 cc (95 + 85 + 85 = 265 ÷ 3 = 88). Thus, it is likely that success in that classroom on that particular skill requires a mastery level of 88 cc with only 2 ce in 1 minute.

Another alternative for aim selection is based on an adult-to-child proportional formula (Eaton, 1978; Haring & Gentry, 1976; Koorland, Keel, & Ueberhorst, 1990). To use this alternative, calculate adult and student tool skill rates and adult performance rates. Then, plug these various rates into the following formula:

$$\frac{\text{Student aim (to be solved)}}{\text{Student tool skill rate}} = \frac{\text{Adult task performance rate}}{\text{Adult tool skill rate}}$$

To arrive at tool skill rates, you must first select the tool skill. Tool skills are the easiest skills in a subject area. For example, tool skills in math include writing digits and counting. In reading, tool skills include saying the alphabet and saying phonetic sounds. In writing, tool skills include writing the alphabet while looking at a visual model and writing the alphabet without a model (Hefferan & Diviaio, 1989).

Once you select the tool skill, the next step is for the student and you to take the tool skill probe. Administer the probe for 15 seconds and multiply the score by 4 to arrive at the minute performance. Now, enter the adult tool skill rate and the student tool skill rate scores in the formula. Then, take another probe to obtain the performance rate on the higher-level task and enter the result into the adult-to-child proportional formula.

For example, to establish a mastery aim for the pinpoint of see/write two-digit plus two-digit addition problems with regrouping (a higher-level skill), you must first identify the tool skill. A likely tool skill is writing numbers. Then, the student and you write numbers for 15 seconds, and you convert both scores to rates. Next, you take the probe on the higher-level task of adding two-digit plus two-digit numbers with regrouping and calculate your score. Say that you scored 180 digits a minute on the tool skill and 90 digits on the higher-level skill while the student scored 70 digits on the tool skill probe. Substitute these scores into the adult-to-child proportional formula:

$$\frac{x}{70} = \frac{90}{180} = (70 \times 90 = 6300 \div 180 = 35).$$

The aim is 35 correct digits a minute for the student.

Remember, the idea of an aim is to set a mastery level that the student will be able to apply at various times and in various settings. You are hoping that when the student reaches the aim of 35 correct digits a minute, he or she will be able to solve two-digit plus two-digit addition problems with regrouping on Friday, in a mainstreamed setting, or at home. If you find that a student reaches the mastery level but then forgets the information 2 days later, you probably did not set the appropriate mastery level.

■ ■ Activity

Practice setting aims for Damion, a seventh grader, for the pinpointed behavior of see/read science vocabulary words.

1. Use the performance standards found in Table 3.9.

2. Use a peer performance standard:

   - Jason 16 science vocabulary words a minute
   - Sally 15 science vocabulary words a minute
   - Jenni 20 science vocabulary words a minute

3. Use the adult-to-child proportional formula: The student said 20 alphabet letters in 15 seconds. The adult said 80 alphabet letters in 15 seconds and read 120 science vocabulary words. ■ ■

Taking a Baseline

A baseline is a repeated measurement of a sample behavior without any instruction. Put simply, you administer the same probe for at least three sessions without teaching. For most academic skills, this administration takes a minute. It is a good idea to tell the student that it is impossible to finish all of the problems but to do them as quickly as possible. If the student hesitates for more than 2 seconds on any item, tell the student to proceed to the next item. It is also important to stress to the student to be as accurate as possible. Leung (1987) notes that many Asian students, in particular, sacrifice accuracy for speed, because speed is reinforced in most Asian cultures.

Administer the probe for at least three sessions to determine if the student really needs remediation in the area. Since the probe always contains more problems than a student can complete within the time frame, it is permissible to change the starting point during each session. For example, if Latoya finishes the last problem in the second row during the first baseline session, have her begin the second baseline session with the first problem in the third row. By doing this, you may expose her to all of the problems during the baseline, and you may use the same sheet. Alternately, you may wish to staple a transparency to the probe sheet and instruct students to write with nonpermanent pens. That way, you may use the same sheet repeatedly. A squirt bottle filled with water and a cloth make the transparency easy to clean.

For accurate assessment, use some sort of timing device to time the probe. You may use a stopwatch or cassette tape that has recorded time signals (Hefferan & Diviaio, 1989). For example, a bell sound on the tape may signal the start of the timing, followed by a minute of soft music, followed by a bell sound to stop the timing. Follow this sequence with a 15-second interval of silence and then repeat the sequence (bell, soft music, bell, silence, bell, soft music, etc.). This way, you may place a total of 5 to 10 minutes of 1-minute timings on one tape.

If the probe does not require a written student response, as in the area of reading, mark the student's errors on a follow-along sheet, which is just a copy of the student's probe. Again, to conserve paper, laminate the follow-along sheet or staple a transparency to it.

Determining the Appropriateness of the Skill

As a general rule, a student must have at least 5 correct responses (cc) and not reach the mastery aim for two of the three sessions of baseline (White & Haring, 1976). If the student reaches the mastery level, the skill is too easy. If the student makes fewer than five correct responses, the skill is probably too difficult.

When the student makes fewer than five correct responses, you may either slice back or step down on the curriculum scope and sequence (White & Haring, 1980). To slice back, simply cut the curriculum into smaller pieces; that is, for example, use a probe of 0 through 4 multiplication facts to replace the probe of 0 through 9 facts. To step down, select an easier skill in the curriculum scope and sequence. For example, the student does not know addition facts yet, so multiplication is much too hard. You should take another baseline if you alter the skill.

The rule of five correct responses for selection of an appropriate skill is not absolute. White (1980) reports that some students with even no correct responses during the baseline still learn the skill once instruction begins. Teachers of students with speech and language problems have told us that their students are able to progress much faster and maintain interest when they score at least fifteen or more correct responses during the baseline.

If you don't seem to be able to apply the rule of five correct responses to the performance of a particular student, begin teaching and monitoring the student's progress. If the student who scored fewer than five correct responses makes little progress, the skill is probably too difficult and you should slice back or step down.

Identifying the Objective

With precision teaching, the input and output channels, the pinpointed behavior, and the aim are parts of the objective. For example, Consuela will see/say (input/output) initial consonant clusters in words (pinpointed behavior) at 70 cc and 2 ce per minute (aim) for 3 consecutive days. Notice that the overlearning component of 3 consecutive days has been added to the objective. This is an attempt to ensure that the student will obtain mastery.

Deciding on an Intervention

Although precision teaching may be used with any strategy, guidelines for the selection of a strategy are linked to the learning stages of acquisition, fluency, and maintenance or proficiency. Usually, anyone who learns a new skill, whether driving a car or recalling multiplication facts, proceeds through these three stages. In the first stage, acquisition, the driver attempts to keep the car in the correct lane between the middle line and the shoulder, while the math student tries to accurately answer problems such as 4 + 5. Acquisition involves performing the skill accurately and requires direct teaching. During acquisition, you should model, give immediate feedback, ask questions, and actively present the lesson content (Haring & Eaton, 1978). A student who scores 5–19 correct responses in a minute for 2 out of the 3 days of baseline is in the acquisition stage (Heffren & Diviaio, 1989).

The next stage in the learning hierarchy is fluency. The fluency stage occurs when the student is making few errors and is concentrating on pace or speed instead. At this stage, the driver is no longer worried about keeping the car on the road in the proper lane (accuracy) but is attempting to drive over 10 miles an hour (fluency) while remaining in the proper lane. The math student is trying to answer 4 + 5 before a second passes. In this stage, flash cards, drill activities, and reinforcements to increase motivation are recommended (Haring & Eaton, 1978). A student who scores at least 20 correct responses (cc) and 10 or fewer incorrect responses (ce) for 2 of the 3 baseline days is in the fluency stage (White & Haring, 1976).

The next stage, maintenance or proficiency, is reached when both count correct and count error aims have been obtained. The teaching strategy is to move to another skill when the student has mastered the content. The driver drives on the freeway at the speed limit. The math student adds accurately and quickly.

Planning Initial Instruction

Now that we have discussed all of the steps to precision assessment separately, we bring the steps together to write an instructional program for Rosa, a ninth grader.

1. *Pinpoint a behavior.* After a discussion with the regular classroom teacher, you determine that Rosa is having problems simplifying fractions to lowest terms.

2. *Select a probe, input and output channels, a time, and scoring procedures.* Your probe includes forty different problems like $4/12$ and $8/20$. Each of the problems is repeated once for a total of eighty problems. You decide to administer the probe to Rosa for 1 minute using the see/write channels, because Rosa is expected to perform the skill in the mainstream setting as a paper-and-pencil task. You score each digit of the answer (e.g., $1/4$ counts as two digits) only to where Rosa stops, but you count skipped problems as errors.

3. *Select a mastery aim.* You expect Rosa to be able to perform this skill at the performance standard of 70 cc and 2 ce per minute and feel that this aim will allow Rosa to apply this skill in other situations. You reach this aim by checking the pinpoint on the performance standard chart (Table 3.9) that is most like this skill. In this case, the pinpoint of simplifying fractions to lowest terms is most like "See/Write Math Facts" with an aim of 70–90 digits per minute.

4. *Take a baseline and determine the appropriateness of the pinpoint.* Administer the probe to Rosa three times without any teaching. She scores 10 cc (count correct) and 5 ce (count error) responses on day 1, 10 cc and 10 ce on day 2, and 15 cc and 9 ce on day 3. You conclude that this skill is appropriate for Rosa because she has at least five correct responses and has not reached her count correct or count error aim.

5. *Write a short-term objective.* The objective is "Presented with an eighty-item probe, Rosa will see/write fractions to lowest terms at 80 cc and 2 ce per minute for 3 consecutive days."

6. *Select the intervention.* Since Rosa is in the acquisition stage (she scored within 5–19 correct responses), you plan to use modeling of the simplification procedures as a teaching intervention. From your assessment, you have arrived at both a short-term objective and a teaching strategy for the initial instructional program.

■ ■ Activity

Look at the results of Jan's baseline performance in each of the following skill areas. Then, determine the skills to select for instruction, the learning stage, short-term objective, and an intervention for each. The first one is done for you.

See/Say Consonant Sounds
Session 1:   60 cc, 2 ce
Session 2:   65 cc, 3 ce
Session 3:   70 cc, 1 ce

(This skill is too easy; Jan reached the mastery level of 60–80 sounds per minute as suggested on the performance standards of "See/Say Isolated Sounds." Thus, the skill is not appropriate for instruction, so no short-term objective should be identified. The learning stage is maintenance, so move the student to the next skill.)

⬜ Important Points

1. Precision teaching is a precise and systematic way to measure student performance.
2. In precision teaching, behaviors that are repeatable and observable and that have a beginning and end are pinpointed.
3. Probes designed by teachers should not interfere with a student's opportunity or freedom to respond.
4. Aims may be based on performance standards, peer assessment, and the adult-to-child proportional formula.
5. A probe is administered for 3 days without any intervention to collect baseline data.
6. From the baseline data, appropriateness of the skill (at least five correct responses (cc) and aim not met), learning stage (acquisition, fluency, or maintenance), and instructional strategies are decided.
7. Precision teaching provides information from which to develop short-term objectives and instructional strategies.

See/Say Short Vowels

Session 1: 20 cc, 10 ce
Session 2: 24 cc, 7 ce
Session 3: 20 cc, 12 ce

See/Say Long Vowels

Session 1: 4 cc, 10 ce
Session 2: 7 cc, 12 ce
Session 3: 8 cc, 14 ce ■ ■

Curriculum-Based Measurement

Curriculum-based measurement (CBM) is a measurement and evaluation system developed over a period of 6 years, from 1977 to 1983, at the University of Minnesota's Institute for Research on Learning Disabilities by Deno, Fuchs, and their colleagues (Deno, 1985). Curriculum-based measurement is "one particular variant of curriculum-based assessment" (Fuchs, Fuchs, & Hamlett, 1989, p. 430). Material for curriculum-based measurement is selected from texts used in the classroom. Thus, if the school district has adopted the *Ginn Reading Series,* material for assessment is selected from the Ginn texts. This ensures that children are assessed on skills that have been or will be taught. The matching of

assessment and instructional materials is also recommended for students with cultural and linguistic differences. Such students often perform better when they are tested on material that is also presented in the classroom (Duffey, Salvia, Tucker, & Ysseldyke, 1981; Fradd & Hallman, 1983; Hoffer, 1983).

To date, curriculum-based measurement has been designed for reading, math, spelling, and writing curriculum at the elementary level and for vocational education at the secondary level. Deno, Mirkin, and Chiang (1982) demonstrated that a simple curriculum-based measurement, such as a 1-minute sampling of words read correctly from a basal reader, correlates highly with performance on standardized tests. They found a positive correlation between scores on this oral reading measure and scores on the *Stanford Diagnostic Reading Test* (Karlsen, Madden, & Gardner, 1977), the *Woodcock Reading Mastery Tests* (Woodcock, 1981), and the *Peabody Individual Achievement Test* (Dunn & Markwardt, 1970). Marston and Magnusson (1985) found a positive correlation of this measure of reading performance with the reading portion of the *SRA Achievement Series* (Naslund, Thorpe, & Lefever, 1978) and the Ginn 720 Reading Series (Clymer & Fenn, 1979).

Using Curriculum-Based Measurement

As in precision teaching, frequent, direct measurement is used in curriculum-based measurement, and student performance is measured according to rate. However, unlike precision teaching and most criterion-referenced measures, curriculum-based measurement may also be used for deciding a student's eligibility for special education placement. For more information concerning the use of these procedures for eligibility decisions, see Marston and Magnusson (1985).

Reading

Of the reading measures created by Deno and colleagues, the most efficacious, easiest, and best researched is the oral reading fluency measure (Deno, Marston, Mirkin, Lowry, & Sindelar, & Jenkins, 1982; Deno, Mirkin, & Chiang, 1982; Deno, Mirkin, & Wesson, 1984; Fuchs & Deno, 1981). In the assessment of reading performance, the oral reading fluency measure compares favorably with comprehension measures, although there is not a perfect relationship (Tindal & Marston, 1990).

To measure a student's oral reading fluency, ask the student to read three passages, each for 1 minute, from various reading texts. These passages should be approximately 100 words in length for young students and 300 words in length for older students. Select one passage from the beginning, one from the middle, and one from the end of various grade-level texts. Be careful to select prose paragraphs without much dialogue or many proper nouns or unusual words (Deno, Mirkin, & Wesson, 1984).

To begin the assessment process, instruct the student to read the passage as quickly as possible. If the student hesitates on a word for more than 2 seconds, say the word and tell the student to go on. Time the selection for only 1 minute (Salvia & Hughes, 1990). While the student is reading each passage, mark the student responses on a follow-along sheet. To make a follow-along sheet you may copy the pages from the text. (Be certain to check copyright laws concerning reproducing pages.) As suggested in precision teaching assessment, covering the text pages with a transparency while marking makes the material reusable. Count the words read correctly and incorrectly by the student for each passage and rank the numbers to find the median scores. Words misread (e.g., *house* for *horse*), words omitted (e.g., leaving out *horse*), words reversed (e.g., *was* for *saw*) and phrases reversed (e.g., "the beautiful, wild horse" for "the wild, beautiful horse") are counted as errors. Misread proper nouns, self-corrections, and insertions are not counted as errors (Tindal & Marston, 1990). Remember to check the information in Table 3.1 to consider language differences.

Continue testing with passages from different grade-level texts to determine the student's instructional reading level (the grade level at which to instruct a student). Find the student's instructional reading level by matching the student's median reading score on these three passages to an instructional standard. The instructional standard identifies the level at which the student should be taught and whether the area of reading should be targeted for remediation.

Various instructional standards have been developed for reading. Marston and Magnusson (1985) identify the following instructional standards based on the number of words per minute (wpm) read: 11–20 wpm for grades 1 and 2, and 41–50 wpm for grades 3 through 6. Deno, Mirkin, and Wesson (1984) suggest a range of 55–75 wpm correct with no more than seven errors for determining instructional reading level. These different ranges may create a problem during initial assessment, so you may want to select the instructional standard from a range of 11–55 wpm correct with no more than seven errors, using the lower score for young students.

For example, Mr. Smith used curriculum-based measurement to test Manu, a third grader.

After reading the referral problem, Mr. Smith decided to test Manu's reading performance using three passages from the Ginn third grade text (this is the series used in Manu's mainstream class). Manu read 15 wpm correctly, and 25 wpm incorrectly on the first passage of the third grade text, 8 wpm correctly and 22 wpm incorrectly on the second passage of the third grade text, and 10 wpm correctly and 20 wpm incorrectly on the third passage of the text. A ranking of the number of words per minute correct (8, 10, 15) and number of words per minute incorrect (20, 22, 25) resulted in a median score of 10 wpm correct and 22 wpm incorrect. This median performance is below the instructional standard of 11–55 wpm correct with fewer than seven errors. Thus, Manu's instructional level is not third grade, so Mr. Smith asked him to read three passages from the second grade reading text.

Manu's median scores for the second grade passages were 10 wpm correct and 14 wpm incorrect, still below the instructional standard. Finally, Manu scored a median of 40 wpm correct and 5 wpm incorrect on the first grade level passages. Thus, Manu's instructional reading level was first grade. The median score of 40 wpm correct and 5 wpm incorrect falls within the instructional standard of 11–55 wpm correct with no more than seven errors. Mr. Smith selected materials from the first grade level to begin reading instruction with Manu.

■ ■ Activity

Determine the appropriate instructional level based on the following reading scores of a sixth grade middle school student.

Third Grade Text

Selection 1:	90 wpm correct, 2 wpm incorrect
Selection 2:	105 wpm correct, 1 wpm incorrect
Selection 3:	100 wpm correct, 3 wpm incorrect

Fourth Grade Text

Selection 1:	40 wpm correct, 7 wpm incorrect
Selection 2:	45 wpm correct, 8 wpm incorrect
Selection 3:	42 wpm correct, 6 wpm incorrect

Fifth Grade Text

Selection 1:	10 wpm correct, 12 wpm incorrect
Selection 2:	21 wpm correct, 8 wpm incorrect
Selection 3:	25 wpm correct, 12 wpm incorrect

■ ■

Spelling

Curriculum-based assessment of spelling is also connected directly to the curriculum. Spelling measures typically include twenty words randomly selected from either the spelling series used in the district or from the basal reader (Deno, Mirkin, & Wesson, 1984; Marston & Magnusson, 1985). Begin by dictating words for 2 minutes, directing the student to write as many letters of each word as he or she can.

Score the test by counting the number of correct letter sequences. Counting correctly spelled words by letter sequences usually results in one more count than the number of letters; for example, the word *agent* consists of six possible correct letter sequences: one before *a*, because the student knew where to start (beginning to $a = +1$); one from *a* to *g* $(+2)$; one from *g* to *e* $(+3)$; one from *e* to *n* $(+4)$; one from *n* to *t* $(+5)$; and one after *t*, because the student knew where to end (t to end $= +6$) (White & Haring, 1976). *Agent* is marked in the following manner:

$$^{+1}a^{+2}g^{+3}e^{+4}n^{+5}t^{+6}.$$

A student who spelled *agent* as *agant* would score four correct letter sequences with two incorrect letter sequences. The student knew beginning to *a* $(+1)$, knew *a* to *g* $(+2)$, missed *g* to *a* (-1), missed *a* to *n* (-2), knew *n* to *t* $(+3)$ and knew *t* to end $(+4)$:

$$^{+1}a^{+2}g_{-1}a_{-2}n^{+3}t^{+4}.$$

A student who spelled *agent* as *egen* would score two correct letter sequences and four incorrect letter sequences. The student missed beginning to *e* (-1), missed *e* to *g* (-2), knew *g* to *e*, $(+1)$, knew *e* to *n* $(+2)$, missed *n* to *t* (omitted letter) (-3) and *t* (omitted letter) to end (-4):

$$_{-1}e_{-2}g^{+1}e^{+2}n_{-3}t_{-4}.$$

A student who spelled *agent* as *agente*, adding an extra letter, would score five correct letter sequences and two incorrect letter sequences. The student knew beginning to a ($+1$), knew a to g ($+2$), knew g to e ($+3$), knew e to n ($+4$), knew n to t ($+5$), missed t to e (added letter) (-1), and missed e (added letter) to end (-2):

$$^{+1}a^{+2}g^{+3}e^{+4}n^{+5}t_{-1}e_{-2}.$$

As with reading assessment, continue testing the student with different graded spelling lists until the following instructional standard is reached: 20–30 correct letter sequences (for students in grades 1 and 2) or 40–50 correct letter sequences (for grades 3 through 6) (Marston & Magnusson, 1985). For example, the instructional spelling level for Sharon, a fifth grader, is third grade. Sharon scored 20 correct letter sequences on a fifth grade spelling list, 30 on a fourth grade list, and 45 on a third grade list. A check of the instructional standards shows that a fifth grader is expected to write 40–50 correct letter sequences, and Sharon was able to perform at that level on a third grade spelling list only.

■ ■ Activity

Score the following spelling errors. Remember to count each letter sequence.

Spelling Word	Student Response
1. fast	fust
2. raise	ras
3. soon	sune
4. chicken	clickone

Hint: In each example, first mark the letter sequences in the correct word:

$$^{+1}f^{+2}a^{+3}s^{+4}t^{+5}.$$

Then, mark the errors:

$$^{+1}f_{-1}u_{-2}s^{+2}t^{+3}. \quad ■ ■$$

Math

Math measures have not been researched as thoroughly as language arts measures have. A curriculum-based measurement for math consists of a sampling of basic facts for 2 minutes (Shinn & Marston, 1985). Grades 1, 2, and 3 include addition and subtraction facts; grade 4 includes multiplication facts; and grades 5 and 6 include multiplication and division facts. Simply tell the student to proceed as quickly as possible. As in precision teaching, score the sample by counting each digit only to where the student finished the test. Thus, in the problem 6 + 7, an answer of 13 equals a score of 2 correct digits and 0 incorrect digit; an answer of 14 to the same problem results in a score of 1 correct digit and 1 incorrect digit.

Here again, administer tests until the student's score matches the instructional standard. Wilson (1987) suggests an instructional standard (placement score) of 20–39 correct digits per minute and 3–7 incorrect digits per minute. Thus, if Sharon scores 30 correct digits with only 5 incorrect digits on multiplication facts, you would target multiplication facts for the instructional level, because Sharon's score in this area approximated the instructional standard.

Written Expression

Curriculum-based measures for written expression consist of three story starters written or selected by the teacher, such as "The score was tied as the soccer ball rolled in front of my feet, I . . ." (Deno, Marston, & Mirkin, 1982). You may either read or write the story starter for the students. Administer all three story starters at one sitting or at three sittings. Give the student 3 minutes to complete the stories. Then, count the number of words in each story.

What constitutes a word is a teacher decision. Salvia and Hughes (1990) suggest considering grade level and linguistic backgrounds in scoring words. They recommend counting misspelled words as words for older students (e.g., *summer* spelled *sumar*) and counting any letter sequence that can be identified as a word for younger students (e.g., *summer* spelled as *sum*). For children whose first language is not English, they suggest counting word sequences that are acceptable translations of the native language.

Counting the number of words written demonstrates sensitivity to student growth in written expression (Marston, Fuchs, & Deno, 1985). The measure also effectively differentiates regular education students from special education students (Shinn & Marston, 1985) and is highly correlated with teacher judgments of quality of written expression at the elementary grade levels (Deno, Marston, & Mirkin, 1982).

There is no instructional standard for written expression, so the instructional level is the student's median score. Thus, if Jennifer writes 19 words on the first story starter, 13 words on the second, and 16 words on the third, her instructional level is 16 words in 3 minutes. In Table 3.10, we present a summary of the procedures for using curriculum-based measurement for determining instructional levels in reading, math, spelling, and written expression.

Planning Initial Instruction

As noted, curriculum-based measurement results in initial instructional decisions concerning behaviors targeted for remediation and materials targeted for intervention. Deno, Mirkin, and Wesson (1984) recommend using the results of curriculum-based measurement for writing annual goals and short-term objectives for individualized education programs (IEPs). They suggest writing annual goals by comparing a student's instructional level with mastery standards. The mastery standards they recommend for the language arts area include:

- *Reading.* 90–150 wpm correct and 7 wpm incorrect.
- *Spelling.* 60–80 correct letter sequences in 2 minutes for first and second graders and 80–140 correct letter sequences for third and fourth graders.
- *Written Expression.* 14.7 words in 3 minutes for first graders, 27.8 words for second

Table 3.10
Summary of Procedures for CBM Assessment to Identify Instructional Levels

1. Select classroom materials for assessment devices.
   - *Reading*—three passages from each grade level text.
   - *Spelling*—graded spelling lists.
   - *Math*—basic operations samples.
   - *Written expression*—three story starters.
2. Administer the test within a specified time frame.
   - *Reading*— 1 minute.
   - *Spelling*— 2 minutes.
   - *Math*— 2 minutes.
   - *Written expression*— 3 minutes.
3. Tabulate student scores.
   - *Reading*—words, correct and error responses.
   - *Spelling*—letter sequences, count correct responses.
   - *Math*—digits, correct and error responses.
   - *Written expression*—student's median score.
4. Compare these scores to the instructional standard.
   - *Reading*— 11–50 cc and 7 ce.
   - *Spelling*—20–39 cc (for grades 1 and 2). 40–50 (for grades 3 through 6).
   - *Math*— 20–39 cc and 3 through 7 ce.
   - *Written expression*—Student's median score. No instructional standard.
5. Continue testing until you reach the instructional level.
6. Select materials based on this instructional level and decide if the behavior is appropriate for an IEP goal.

graders, 36.6 words for third graders, 40.9 for fourth graders, 49.1 words for fifth graders, and 53.3 words for sixth graders.

Wilson (1987) recommends a mastery level for the math area of 40–100 correct digits and 2 incorrect digits per minute. Write annual goals and short-term objectives using the instructional level, the mastery standard, and the expected time (Deno, Mirkin, & Wesson, 1984). The steps are:

1. *Find the student's instructional level score.* Manu's instructional level score based on the *Ginn Reading Series* (Clymer & Fenn, 1979) was 40 wpm correct and 5 wpm incorrect on the first grade passage.
2. *Find the expected mastery standard for the content area and grade.* For reading, the mastery level is 90–150 wpm correct and 7 wpm incorrect. Since Manu is reading in the first grade book, you should select the lower mastery level of 90 wpm correct and 7 wpm incorrect.
3. *Write the annual goal.* The goal may be "When placed in Reader 1 of the *Ginn Reading Series,* Manu will increase his reading from an instructional level of 40 wpm correct to a mastery level of 90 wpm correct with no more than seven errors by the next IEP review."
4. *Subtract the instructional level from the mastery standard.* In Manu's case, this is 90 wpm correct − 40 wpm correct = 50 wpm correct.
5. *Check to see when the IEP is to be reviewed.* Manu's IEP is scheduled for review in 10 weeks.
6. *Divide the difference between the instructional level and mastery standard by the weeks before the next IEP review.* For Manu, the difference of 50 wpm divided by 10 weeks equals a gain of 5 wpm a week.
7. *Write the short-term objectives identifying the weeks that you plan to check the objectives.* The short-term objective may be "Every week, when presented with a random selection from the first grade Ginn reader, Manu will read aloud at an average increase of 5 wpm correct with not more than seven errors."

Since there are no instructional standards for written expression, you simply begin with a student's current score at step 1. Thus, if Manu's current median score is 15 words in 3 minutes, 15 is also his instructional level score.

■ ■ Activity

You have tested Latoya, a sixth grader, with reading passages selected from the *Macmillan Reading Series* used in her class. You found her instructional level was second grade because she scored the following on the sec-

Important Points

1. Curriculum-based measurement uses classroom materials for assessment, measures performance using rate, and compares a student's score with specified instructional and mastery standards.
2. Scores on curriculum-based reading samples correlate positively with standardized reading test scores.
3. Curriculum-based measures may be used to determine eligibility for special services when local norms are established and for determining annual goals and short-term objectives on an IEP for first through sixth graders.
4. The oral reading fluency measure requires a student to read passages for 1 minute from various reading texts to determine the instructional reading level (the grade level for instruction).
5. The spelling measure requires students to write as many spelling words as they can in 2 minutes and is scored by counting letter sequences.
6. In math assessment, addition, subtraction, multiplication, and division operations are tested, and instructional levels are indicated by the number of digits correct and the number of digits incorrect per minute.
7. In written expression assessment, students are given three story starters and instructed to write a story for each within 3 minutes.

ond grade passages: 30 wpm correct and 10 wpm incorrect, 20 wpm correct and 7 wpm incorrect, and 40 wpm correct and 5 wpm incorrect. Her IEP will be reviewed in 12 weeks. Now, write an annual goal and a short-term objective. ■ ■

Kidwatching Procedures

Kidwatching, a term used in the whole language literature, does not prescribe any specific techniques for collecting student information. Instead, teachers are encouraged to adapt and develop their own techniques for data collection from the many teacher-friendly ones proposed in the kidwatching procedures. As Baskwill and Whitman (1988) comment to teachers in their discussion of whole language alternatives to end-of-the-book tests and standardized testing procedures, "Evaluation and curriculum planning don't belong in anyone else's hands. They rightfully belong in yours" (p. 41). Thus, no matter the setting or service delivery options, teachers should rely on their own informal methods for collecting student data. Like the whole language approach, kidwatching is centered in the holistic approach to education. It emphasizes meaning and integrated learning. It sees learning as a whole, not as acquisition of separate skills.

In kidwatching, the observer analyzes both the content and thought processes used by a child or adolescent while providing a safe, natural, and nonthreatening environment. This combination of qualities is particularly important for students from diverse cultural backgrounds, because such students are often intimidated by a formalized testing process. For example, Leung (1987) cautions that when assessing Asian students, evaluators should be aware that they are often tense and stressed due to their high achievement motivation and their cultural background. In many Asian countries, assessment is used to keep students from pursu-

ing more advanced education programs instead of helping them.

Baskwill and Whitman (1988) describe the following scenario, which is typical of the kidwatching approach that has replaced their school district's administration of readiness tests to incoming kindergarten students. While a teacher meets with the parents briefly to discuss the required forms for enrollment, the child is allowed to look around the room and get acquainted with books and other items there. Once the interview with the parents is concluded, the teacher asks the child to select a book for them to read together. As the teacher reads aloud, the child is invited to discuss the pictures and to read along. Then, the child is asked to draw a picture and talk about it as he or she is drawing. Last, the child is asked to write something and then to read it. A child who says, "I can't write," can usually be persuaded to try with the directive to write the teacher a message. From this interaction, which is videotaped, information is gathered about such items as the child's language development, understanding of stories, understanding of print, and enjoyment of stories.

Kidwatching assessments frequently involve miscue analysis (Goodman & Burke, 1972), story frames (Au, Scheu, Kawakami, & Herman, 1990), interviews (Baskwill & Whitman, 1988), and checklists (Sharp, 1989). Suggestions for use of these typical kidwatching procedures follow. Note, however, that there is a limited research basis for most of these techniques.

Miscue Analysis

Miscue analysis helps you understand the strategies students are using when reading. It is a way to look at meaning as the focus of language learning. According to Goodman and Burke (1972), children develop as readers with the acquisition of semantic, syntactic, or graphophonic strategies. Semantic strategies involve understanding the meaning of words. Syntactic strategies involve understanding the grammatic function of words in a sentence. Graphophonic strategies involve the recognition of letter-to-sound correspondence. In graphophonic miscues, the reader misreads words where the letters are similar at the beginning, middle, or end (Leslie & Caldwell, 1990). For example, take the sentence "The brick house is located next to the supermarket." If Jane substitutes the word *home* for *house,* her miscue is a semantic one. If she substitutes *locate* for *located* in the sentence, she is making a syntactic miscue. If Jane reads the word *horse* for *house,* her miscue is a graphophonic one, because the first and last letters of the words are similar.

We suggest that you list the number of miscues and then only consider miscues that change the meaning of the text. In the example just discussed, the substitution of *home* for *house* and *locate* for *located* are not considered incorrect because they do not change the meaning of the sentence. However, the substitution of *horse* for *house* is considered incorrect because the meaning is changed.

Story Frames

Teachers use story frames to assess knowledge of a story and reactions to the story elements (Au, Scheu, Kawakami, & Herman, 1990). Students first read a literature selection silently and then write a summary to fit the story frame. We suggest having young students as well as secondary students who have problems with written expression complete story frames orally. After the student has completed the story frame, check the responses to determine whether or not the student included the following: the character or characters, setting, problem, events, solution, theme, application, and personal response.

In the example in Table 3.11, the student read *The Legend of the Bluebonnet: An Old Tale of Texas* (de Paola, 1983) and retold the story to the teacher, who recorded it. The student was able to identify and tell about the character, setting, problem, events and solution but had difficulty recognizing the abstract message of the story and applying the information (see Table

3.12). The student also did not give a personal response. From this brief sample, it appears that the student is able to retell the facts of the story and the main idea but is not able to communicate ideas that are not specifically found in the story. The skills of understanding the underlying message, applying information, and expressing a like or dislike for a story may comprise objectives for program planning.

Interviews

In the interviewing technique, students are asked to share their thought processes. Because of this, it is important to establish rapport and provide a safe, secure environment, where students can risk being wrong without penalty. Mercer and Mercer (1989) recommend focusing on one particular skill, such as two-digit subtraction with one regrouping in a math diagnostic interview. An interview may proceed in the following manner. First, you instruct the student, Kari, "Please complete these problems (e.g., 85 + 19, 67 + 18, 34 + 17) out loud so I can hear how you figure them out." As Kari is calculating the problems, she replies, "Well, 85 plus 19 means to add. Five plus 9 is 14, and 8 plus 1 is 9. So the answer is 9-1-4 [nine, one, four]." She proceeds with similar explanations and mistakes in the other two problems.

In analyzing Kari's thought processes and her answers, you find that she knows that plus means to add. She also knows to begin in the ones column, but she does not know place value and the regrouping process, nor does she monitor her computation by checking if the answer of 914 makes sense.

Sometimes, interviews are accompanied with recommended questions for the teacher to ask the student, as in the following spelling interview procedure (Baskwill & Whitman, 1988). To measure spelling using this procedure, select a list of twenty words from either the spelling or reading text that the student is using in the mainstream setting. To introduce the task in a nonthreatening manner, tell the student that you are really looking for a better way to teach spell-

Table 3.11
A Story Frame Form and Responses

*The problem in the story is

The Indians in Texas were suffering from no rain and many had died because they was drought. The holy man talked to the Great Spirits and asks what to do. The Gods say that the people are selfish and they must make a sacrifice.

The problem is solved

The girl takes her favorite doll that was made by her mother and father. Both of them died in the drought. And burns it and offers it to the Gods.

At the end of the story

The ashes from the doll turns into blue flowers and the rains come.

The author's message is

✓ I don't know

The message makes me think

✓ I don't know

Did you like the story? Tell why or why not

*The teacher recorded this verbatim as told by the student.

Note. This story frame form is based on the story frame in "Assessment and Accountability in a Whole Literacy Curriculum" by K. H. Au, J. A. Scheu, A. J. Kawakami, and P. A. Herman, 1990, *The Reading Teacher, 43*(8), p. 576.

ing and that it doesn't matter how many mistakes the student makes. Next, give the words in isolation. Then, give the same words in context. Add definitions if the student requests them.

Sit down with the student and go over the list together, asking such questions of the student as, Which words do you think you spelled correctly? Which ones aren't you sure about? Why did you decide on this particular spelling? How else could you have tried to spell this word? If this word is incorrect, how could you find the correct spelling? (Baskwill & Whitman, 1988). Remember that with the interviewing tech-

nique, you should assess both error patterns and strategies.

Checklists

Checklists are used in assessment to make teachers aware of what to look for and to communicate the proper vocabulary for observations. They also serve as devices for recording information (Sharp, 1989). Checklists may provide insight into the ways in which students approach tasks and the types of errors they make. You may use checklists to gain information concerning

Table 3.12
Scoring of the Story Frame Responses in Table 3.11

Characters	X
Setting	X
Problem	X
Events	X
Solution	X
Theme	—
Application	—
Personal Response	—

Note. Based on the checklist for the response to literature task in "Assessment and Accountability in a Whole Literacy Curriculum" by K. H. Au, J. A. Scheu, A. J. Kawakami, and P. A. Herman, 1990, *The Reading Teacher,* 43(8), p. 576.

any subject area or to find out about interests. Checklist items are frequently phrased positively to assess what a student can do instead of emphasizing the problems.

You should complete checklists using work samples (see Figure 3.1) or during observations. You may use the checklist found in Figure 3.2 to evaluate creative writing as this teacher did in evaluating the work sample in Figure 3.1. Questions for the checklist were compiled from the list of performance objectives of the ninth grade curriculum and suggestions from Tindal and Marston (1990), Rhodes and Dudley-Marling (1988), and Schumaker and Sheldon (1985).

Students may also complete checklists and be a part of their own assessment. Involving students in the assessment process can increase their motivation and interest.

Planning Initial Instruction

The information from various kidwatching procedures should lead to the planning of instruction and identification of short-term objectives, which usually involve identification of content to cover and strategies to use. Returning to Kari's math performance, with the interview technique, you assessed that Kari does not understand place value or regrouping and she fails to monitor her performance. Therefore, you target the following short-term objectives: (a) given two-digit plus two-digit addition problems with one regrouping, Kari will regroup in the ones column to 90% mastery for three assignments and (b) given two-digit plus two-digit addition problems with one regrouping, Kari will monitor her calculations by asking herself whether she remembered to trade her ones for tens on every problem for three assignments.

■ ■ Activity

Administer one of the kidwatching procedures to a secondary student and an elementary student with special needs. Write both skill and strategy objectives for each student. ■ ■

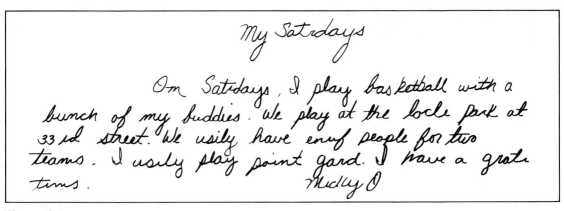

Figure 3.1
A Student's Work Sample

1. Is the student able to write a topic sentence?

yes

2. Is the student able to write supporting sentences?

yes - rest of sentences relate to topic

3. Does the student use descriptive words?

No, limited adjectives - "point, great"

4. Is the student able to use a variety of sentences (simple, compound, complex)?

No, all simple

5. Does the student use dialogue?

none used

6. Are there many mistakes in grammar?

none

7. Is the story organized?

yes, begins with a topic sentence, details and a closing

8. Are there many spelling errors?

yes, 10 out of 40 words

Figure 3.2
Scoring of a Student's Work Sample in Figure 3.1.

Important Points

1. In kidwatching, teachers are encouraged to design their own informal assessment devices.
2. Kidwatching procedures often assess both basic skills and strategies.
3. Miscue analysis assesses whether a student's semantic, syntactic, or graphophonic decoding strategies interfere with meaning.
4. Story frames assess a student's knowledge of story elements and personal reactions.
5. In interview assessment, students are asked to share their thought processes.
6. Teachers use checklists to gain information concerning subject areas and students' interests.

Summary

Informal assessment plays an important role in the instruction of students with special needs. It is particularly recommended for students from diverse cultural and linguistic backgrounds. In this chapter, we introduced you to criterion-referenced tests, precision teaching, curriculum-based measurement, and kidwatching. We feel that these techniques give you valuable information to use in planning instruction. In Table 3.13, we present a comparison of the informal measures discussed in this chapter.

Criterion-referenced assessment requires teachers to select or develop the tests for administration. The skills measured by criterion-referenced tests should correspond to the scope and sequence of the student's curriculum. Criterion-referenced assessment also allows teachers to administer tests with adaptations, if necessary, to identify objectives for planning.

Precision teaching procedures require pinpointing behavior, designing a probe, selecting a mastery aim, taking a baseline to determine whether the behavior is appropriate for instruc-

tion, and determining which instructional strategy is relevant. For a skill to be appropriate, the student must make at least five correct responses but not reach the aim. Direct instruction is recommended for the acquisition stage. Motivational strategies are necessary for the fluency stage.

Curriculum-based measurement uses the curriculum of the classroom for assessment materials: basal texts for reading and spelling, sentence starters for written expression, and basic math operations for math. Procedures are identified for teacher-constructed tests in each of these content areas and instructional and mastery level scores are suggested. Annual goals and short-term objectives are written based on the difference between the instructional level and mastery level scores.

Kidwatching is less formalized. It uses such techniques as miscue analysis, story frames, interviews, and checklists. Whether a student reads for meaning or simply to decode words is assessed in miscue analysis. Story frames assess a student's knowledge of story elements and personal reactions to a story. Interviews require a student to complete a task and to describe orally

Table 3.13
Comparison of Informal Measures

	CRT	PT	CBM	KW
Administration	Individual/Group	Individual/Group	Individual/Group	Individual
Content	Curriculum Scope & Sequence	Curriculum Scope & Sequence	Classroom texts	Classroom texts/Work samples
Mastery Measure	Percent	Rate	Rate	None
Identification	Objectives	Objectives/ Instructional strategies	Annual goals/ Objectives/ Instructional materials	Objectives
Assessment	Skills	Skills/Learning stage	Skills/Eligibility	Skills/Strategies/ Interests

the thought processes used. Checklists may be designed to measure interests, skills, and strategies.

No matter which informal assessment techniques you select, make certain that they assess the curriculum you plan to teach and that they provide useful information about students. Nothing is worse than spending the time to assess and then filing the results away instead of using them to plan instruction.

4

Informal Assessment for Monitoring Student Progress and Intervention Effectiveness

Key Topics

Performance Monitoring
  Precision Teaching Procedures
  Curriculum-Based Measurement Procedures

Mastery Monitoring
  Attainment of Objectives
  Lessons Completed
  Systematic Written Observations
  Portfolio Assessments

Data Collection
  Involving Students
  Software Packages

Organizing Materials
Establishing Routines

Task Analysis
  Analyzing the Task
  Altering the Task

Monitoring Progress in the Mainstream
  Teacher Monitoring
  Student Monitoring

Summary

The short-term objectives and annual goals written on a student's individualized education program (IEP) should be the focus of monitoring. After all, the objectives and goals are based on assessments by a team of professionals, and as such, they serve as blueprints for special educators.

According to PL 94–142, special educators must review the short-term objectives and annual goals on an IEP at least annually (*Federal Register,* August 23, 1977). Monitoring student progress and the effectiveness of interventions is important. Monitoring is a basis for making teaching decisions. With monitoring, progress is documented, and both students and teachers are reinforced. However, there is no consensus as to the best way to measure behavioral changes. There is even disagreement as to how frequently progress should be measured.

In the field of special education, there are essentially two types of assessment for the purpose of monitoring student academic performance. These types differ in the techniques and frequency for measuring changes. Adapting terminology from Tindal (1987), we refer to these two types of monitoring as performance monitoring and mastery monitoring. In performance monitoring, the same items are measured frequently. Precision teaching and curriculum-based measurement typify this monitoring be-

cause they depict growth by "an increasing score on a standard or constant task" (Deno, 1987, p. 41). In mastery monitoring, the items change each time a student masters a unit of curriculum (Tindal, 1987) and measurement is not so frequent as it is in performance monitoring. Many of the kidwatching procedures use the mastery approach.

Performance Monitoring

We suggest certain steps to follow when using performance monitoring procedures. These steps are (a) take a baseline, (b) teach and test, (c) graph scores, and (d) evaluate performance.

Precision Teaching Procedures
In performance monitoring with precision teaching, you should measure progress with the same probe until the student reaches a mastery level. Recall that a probe is an informal worksheet or test that is administered within a specified time frame.

Taking a Baseline
In using precision teaching, you administer the probe for at least three sessions without instruc-

tion. This repeated administration lets you know if the student needs instruction on that skill and provides a starting point for comparison once an intervention begins.

Teaching and Testing

Based on the learning stage during the baseline, you select a teaching strategy (see Chapter Three). Each day, after instruction is completed, administer the same probe to monitor the effectiveness of the intervention. For example, if Conseula's short-term objective is to increase her mastery of multiplication facts to 80 correct responses (cc) and 2 incorrect responses (ce) per minute, instruct her on multiplication facts, administer the probe, and then record the correct and incorrect scores. Some teachers become concerned that using the same probe to measure a student's progress allows the student to memorize the answers, but this is easily avoided by requiring the student to start with different problems on the probe.

Graphing the Scores

In math assessments, digits are usually counted; in reading and written expression, words are counted; and in spelling, letter sequences are counted. Once you record a raw score, you must convert it into a count per minute for display on a semilogarithmic chart or graph. In a semilogarithmic graph, the distances between the lines are adjusted proportionally. Proponents of this type of graph argue that a change of 10 to 20 is the same proportionally as a change from 20 to 40, as both are a doubling.

Many teachers graph data on a standard celeration chart (SCC) (Lindsley, 1990) (see Figure 4.1). Other teachers use adaptations of the SCC, such as the ABC-5 chart, which is an enlargement of a part of the SCC graph. (The SCC chart is enlarged from the 0.1 to 500 section.) We explain how to chart data using the ABC-5 graph. The vertical lines on the ABC-5 graph are called day lines (see Figure 4.2) (Hefferan & Diviaio, 1989). You can chart behaviors from Sunday through Saturday for 11 weeks, or 77 days. The short, dark marks at the top of the chart are

Sunday lines, an easy way to locate the beginning of the week. The horizontal lines are often referred to as number lines (Hefferan & Diviaio, 1989).

On the ABC-5 graph, we are able to count from 0.1 to 500 counts per minute. The graph is rarely marked above 300, because few behaviors may be accomplished at more than 300 counts a minute. Notice that there is a one-to-one correspondence between the numbers of 0.1 through 10. However, from 10 to 100, the numbers proceed 10, 15, 20 and then skip in increments of 10 until 100. Then, the count continues 100, 150, 300, 400, and 500. Therefore, to chart counts between 10 and 500, you must frequently estimate.

If you are monitoring your comprehension, you are probably wondering why it is necessary to have a count of 0.1 or 0.2 on the graph. Remember, however, that only count per minute is recorded on the graph, so to record a score of two items missed during a 10-minute probe, you must divide the 2 by the 10, which results in 0.2 incorrect responses per minute.

Steps for charting include (a) complete the student information, (b) mark the record floor, (c) mark the aims, (d) record the raw data, (e) convert the raw data to counts per minute, (f) chart correct and incorrect responses per minute, (g) identify ignored and no-chance days, and (h) connect data points.

1. *Complete the student information.* Identify the name and age of the student, the pinpointed behavior, and the aims at the bottom of the graph. Write the aims as cc (count correct) and ce (count error) per minute.

2. *Mark the record floor.* The record floor identifies the amount of time that you administer a probe. Record floor figures are found on the right side of the graph. Notice with the ABC-5 graph that you can administer a probe from 10 minutes to 0.2 minutes, or 12 seconds. Mark the record floor by drawing a horizontal line through each week at the appropriate minutes.

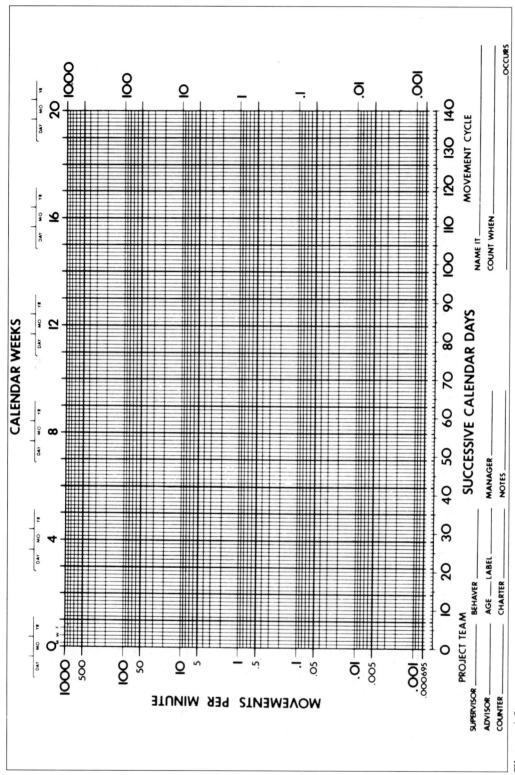

Figure 4.1

A Semilogarithmic Graph

Note. From Behavior Research Company. Reprinted by permission.

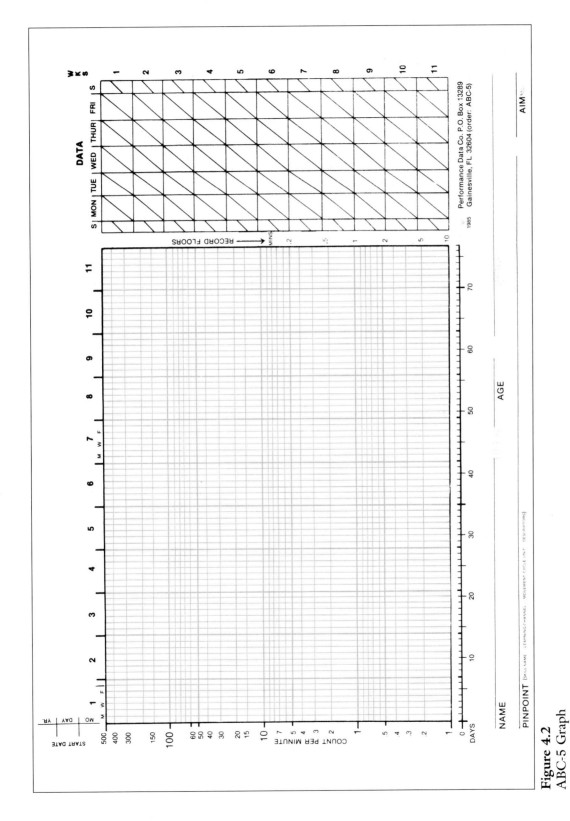

Figure 4.2
ABC-5 Graph

Note. The ABC-5 chart is a product of Performance Data Co. Reprinted by permission.

3. *Mark the aims.* Mark aims on the graph by finding the acceptable performance criteria of correct and incorrect responses per minute on the count lines. The count correct aim is frequently marked with a horizontal line and arrows pointing upward. The count error aim is frequently marked with a horizontal line and arrows pointing downward.

4. *Record the raw data.* Enter the raw scores in the data boxes at the right of the ABC-5 graph. Enter the count correct raw data at the top and the count error raw data at the bottom for each day that assessment occurred.

5. *Convert the raw data to counts per minute.* Before you record data on the graph, you must convert each raw score to a count per minute, dividing the score by the number of minutes. Thus, to record a student's score of 3 incorrect responses in 5 minutes, you would first divide 3 by 5 and then locate 0.6 on the chart. To show a 0 count, tradition states marking a data point just below the record floor.

6. *Chart correct and incorrect responses per minute.* Use a dot (.) to mark the correct responses per minute and an *x* to mark the incorrect responses per minute. To mark the correct responses on the chart, locate the first day you administered the probe on the day lines. Then, locate the count on the number lines. Follow the lines until they intersect, and place a dot at the intersection. Follow the same procedures to chart incorrect responses, only place an *x* at the intersection.

7. *Identify ignored and no-chance days.* Before you connect any of the data points, consider no-chance days and ignored days. No-chance days are days when you do not have an opportunity to assess the student, such as over the weekend or during an absence. Ignored days are days when you have an opportunity to assess the student but decide not to. Code IG for ignored

and NC for no-chance in the raw data boxes. Do not connect data across no-chance days, but do connect across ignored days. For example, if the student were absent on Tuesday, the picture would look like this:

If the student were present on Tuesday, but you decided to ignore data collection and did not administer a probe, the picture would look like this:

If there are many no-chance days, the student may not be progressing due to frequent absences. If there are many ignored days, the student may not be progressing due to the infrequency of data collection.

8. *Connect data points.* Connect count correct data points together and count error data points together. Do not connect data across no-chance days or phase change lines. Phase change lines (vertical lines) denote whenever something is changed; for example, a change in intervention, pinpointed behavior, or mastery aim. Always draw a phase change line between the last session of a baseline and the first day of intervention to note that teaching has started.

When the data are connected, you have a learning picture. Table 4.1 presents a pictorial summary of all the charting procedures.

■ ■ Activity
Chart the following data from a precision teaching assessment on a semilogarithmic graph.

- *Behavior:* See/write addition facts with sums 0–18.

Table 4.1
Summary of Steps for Charting with the ABC-5 Chart

Step 4: Record the raw data (Sara scores 30 correct responses and 10 incorrect responses on the first Monday.)

DATA

S	MON	TUE	WED	THUR	FRI	S	W K S
	30	25	30	35	40		1
	10	5	10	5	3		
	45	45	58	I	62		2
	2	2	2	9	0		
							3

Step 5: Convert the raw data to count per minute by dividing the number of correct and then the number of incorrect responses by the time. (Since the teacher administers the probe for only 1 minute, no division is necessary.)

Performance Data Co. P.O. Box 13289
Gainesville, FL 32604 (order: ABC-5)
1985

Step 1: Complete the student information at the bottom of the chart.

Step 3: Mark the aims. (Sara's aim is 120cc and 2ce per minute.)

Count Correct Aim

Step 6: Chart correct reponses per minute with dots and incorrect with x's.

Steps 7 and 8: Connect the dots and the x's, remembering phase change lines and other charting procedures. (Bravo, Sara has a learning picture.)

Count Error Aim

Step 2: Mark the record floor (Sara takes the probe for 1 minute.)

Record Floor

RECORD FLOORS

COUNT PER MINUTE

DAYS

NAME _Sara_

PINPOINT (SKILL NAME) _See / Say words in context_ (LEARNING CHANNEL) (MOVEMENT CYCLE) (UNIT) (DESCRIPTORS)

AGE _10_

AIM _120cc / 2cc per min 3 days_

93

- *Aim:* 80 cc, 5 ce.
- *Observation time:* 1 minute.
- *Baseline:*

    Monday— 10 cc, 10 ce.
    Tuesday— 15 cc, 10 ce.
    Wednesday— 5 cc, 15 ce.

- *Intervention:*

    Thursday— 20 cc, 10 ce.
    Friday— 20 cc, 8 ce.
    Monday— 24 cc, 8 ce.
    Tuesday—Ignored.
    Wednesday— 30 cc, 0 ce.

(Answers for this and other activities are found in the Instructor's Manual.) ■ ■

Evaluating Performance

Now that you have charted the data, it is time to decide whether the intervention plan is effective and whether the student is making progress. You can do this subjectively, just by eyeballing the data, or do it objectively, by comparing the data to an expected level of progress (White & Haring, 1976) or to an actual level (Fuchs, Fuchs, & Hamlett, 1989).

Subjective Evaluation. Subjective evaluation requires an examination of the direction of the count correct data points (correct responses) and count error data points (incorrect responses) and a comparison of the student's performance during the baseline and intervention. Effective learning pictures have in common that the count correct data points are moving up toward the count correct aim, the count error data points are moving down toward the count error aim, and both are improvements on the baseline. In Figure 4.3, we show effective learning pictures.

In each of these examples, after the baseline, the count correct data points are moving up toward the count correct aim and the count error data points are moving down toward the error aim. Student C displays a common pattern. There is a quick gain once instruction begins. This gain is apparent when you compare the last

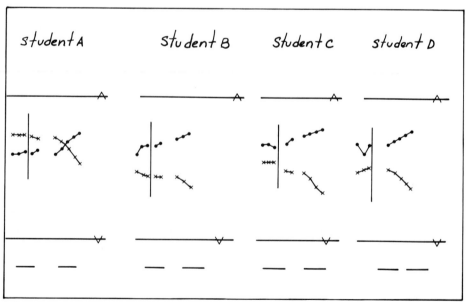

Figure 4.3
Effective Learning Pictures

data point of the baseline with the first one of intervention. Student A displays the best learning picture. This student had more incorrect responses than correct during the baseline and more correct responses than incorrect during the intervention. Thus, the intervention was very effective and resulted in a picture totally different from the baseline. When you see such pictures, you should continue with the intervention, because it is working and the student is progressing (Hefferan & Diviaio, 1989).

In ineffective learning pictures, the count correct data points and count error data points are moving away from the aims or are stagnant (Hefferan & Diviaio, 1989). Often, a comparison with the baseline shows that there is not much difference in progress. Figure 4.4 displays some ineffective learning pictures. Student A is not progressing, because the count correct data points have flattened out. Usually, when you see three consecutive sessions of flat data, you should make a change (Great Falls Public Schools, PT

Training Manual, 1981). Student B is not progressing either, because the correct responses are decreasing and the incorrect responses are increasing. Note, too, that for student B, the incorrect responses remain higher than the correct responses during the intervention. If you consider the intervention data only, you may think that student C's picture is effective, because the count correct data points are ascending and the count error data points are descending; however, when you compare the intervention data with the baseline data, the count correct data points are lower and the count error data points are higher. In Student D's picture the count error data points are decreasing, but so are the count correct data points. When you see pictures like these, you should change your intervention or make other program changes, because the student is not making adequate progress. Sometimes, data does not present a clear picture of progress, especially when there is much fluctuation. In these cases, an objective evaluation is much more effective.

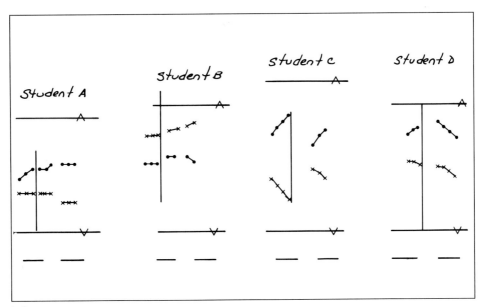

Figure 4.4
Ineffective Learning Pictures

■ ■ Activity

Examine the two students' charts below and tell whether you would plan to make changes based on the learning pictures. Why?

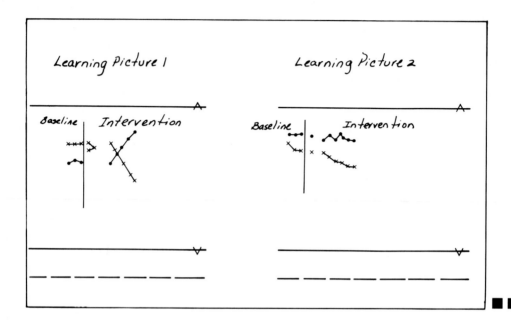

Objective Evaluation. In objective evaluation of a student's progress, you should analyze data trends and make changes based on certain decision rules. These decision rules differ, depending on whether you specify an expected rate of student change or you examine the actual rate of student change.

When you use a decision rule based on an expected rate of student change, you need both an aim and a date for achieving the aim. For example, you state that Otis should learn his basic multiplication facts at the rate of 80 cc (correct responses) and 2 ce (incorrect responses) a minute and that he should accomplish this by the end of the first 9 weeks (the grading period). To tell if Otis is progressing fast enough to meet your expectations, draw a trend, or celeration, line using aimline procedures, (see Table 4.2).

A decision rule states that you should change the intervention or make other changes when a

student scores three consecutive data points below the celeration line (White & Haring, 1980; White & Liberty, 1976). The reason for a change is that the student is not progressing as fast as you expected and will not meet the aim within the time available. For example, Otis is not learning the basic multiplication facts rapidly enough to be able to reach your expected aim of 80 cc and 2 ce per minute within 9 weeks, so it is necessary to change the intervention or make other changes.

Some students progress more rapidly than expected. What if Otis learned the basic multiplication facts at 80 cc and 2 ce within 3 weeks instead of 9 weeks. Your expectations of his rate of change were inaccurate. You should measure his actual rate of change so you don't lose valuable teaching time. When you measure actual rate of student change, you do not have a preconceived date in mind; instead, you rely on student behavior (the number of correct responses per minute during intervention) to evaluate performance. To measure student change based on a student's actual rate, use the quarter-intersect method to draw the celeration line (Haring, Lovitt, Eaton, & Hansen, 1978; White & Haring, 1980). White and Haring (1980) recommend that teachers draw celeration lines using the quarter-intersect method every 7 days to evaluate progress and change their instruction if the new celeration line based on student correct responses is flat or decreasing. Wesson (1987) recommends evaluating progress using the quarter-intersect method every 2 weeks. In Table 4.3, we present steps for drawing a celeration line using the quarter-intersect method and 7 days of intervention data.

Curriculum-Based Measurement Procedures

In curriculum-based measurement procedures for monitoring student progress and intervention effectiveness, the same steps of taking baseline, teaching and testing, graphing data, and evaluating performance are followed. In the initial assessment of reading, math, spelling, and written expression, collect behavioral samples more than one time to arrive at the instructional level. Use these scores for the baseline. During teaching and monitoring, assess the student at least twice a week (Fuchs, Fuchs, & Hamlett, 1989). Do not use the same material or allow the student to practice the material before assessment. For example, to monitor Luwanda's progress through Level 17 of the Ginn reader, select passages from the text that she has not read and assess her with these passages twice in one week.

You typically graph her scores on an equal interval graph (see Figure 4.5). An equal interval graph is a linear graph in which the distance between lines occupies equal space; that is, the distance between 5 and 10 is the same as the distance between 10 and 15 and 15 and 20. In charting on an equal interval graph, you should use some of the same charting procedures that you use on a semilogarithmic graph. For example, you should draw a phase change line to separate the baseline from the intervention or to signify changes. However, you do not follow the charting conventions of record floors, ignored and no-chance days, charting incorrect responses, and of converting a raw score to count per minute. To chart 20 words in 3 minutes, 40 words in 3 minutes, and 30 words in 3 minutes on an equal interval graph, simply locate the session (session 1), the score (20 words), and their intersection, and place a dot. The incorrect words are frequently not charted.

Fuchs, Fuchs, and Hamlett (1989) recommend that teachers consider both the expected and actual rate of student change when making decisions concerning intervention effectiveness and student progress. They draw a celeration, or trend, line based on expected rate using aimline procedures (aimline) and a celeration line based on actual rate using the quarter-intersect method (regression line). Then, they compare the aimline to the regression line. Their decision rules include (a) change a program if the regression line is less steep than the aimline (example A in Table 4.4), (b) raise the goal if the regression line is steeper than the aimline (example B), or (c) continue the intervention and draw another regression line, making a decision 7 or 10 days later if the regression line is close to the aimline (example C).

Fuchs, Fuchs, and Hamlett (1989) found that teachers who used the decision rules based on the level of actual student performance produced more achievement gains than did a control group of teachers who monitored progress with end-of-unit math tests, unsystematic observations, and workbook and worksheet performances. However, teachers who used decision rules based on expected student performance did not produce more achievement gains than did the control group.

Table 4.2
Steps for Drawing a Celeration Line Using Aimline Procedures

1. Select an aim rate for the student to master the aim, and mark it on the graph.

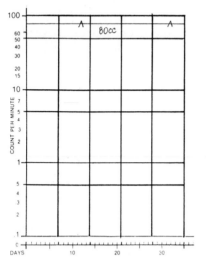

2. Select a date for the student to master the aim, and draw a line through the aim rate. Circle where they intersect; this is the end mark.

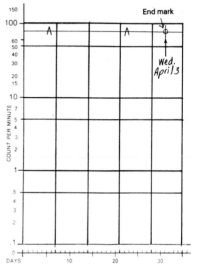

3. Record the baseline data on the graph.

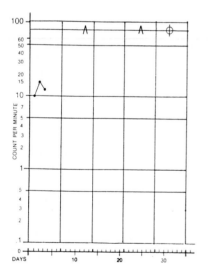

4. Find the mid-day during the baseline (the mid-day comes in the middle of the three baseline sessions), and draw a vertical line through it.

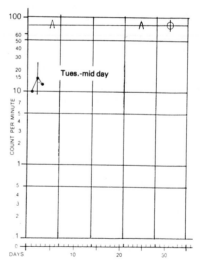

5. Find the mid-rate during the baseline (the middle count) by ranking the data points in order. If two data points are the same, select that number. Draw a horizontal line through it.

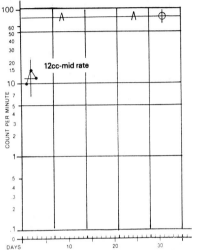

6. Put a circle where the lines intersect. This is the start mark, where the celeration line begins.

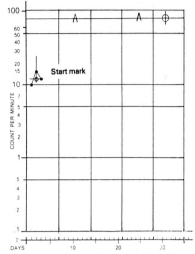

7. Connect the start mark with the end mark. The celeration line connects the two points.

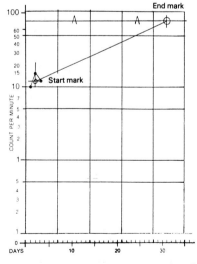

8. Chart the counts per minute during the intervention.

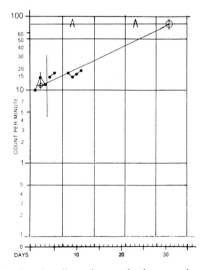

Decision Rule: If there are three consecutive data points below the celeration line, change the intervention or make other changes.

Table 4.3
Steps for Drawing a Celeration Line Using the Quarter-Intersect Method

1. Take intervention data for 7 days.

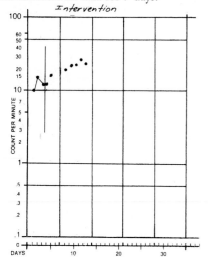

2. Divide the seven data points evenly.

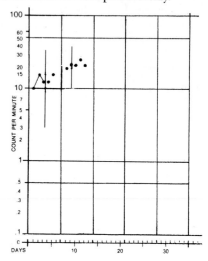

3. Mark the first three points as side A and the last three as side B.

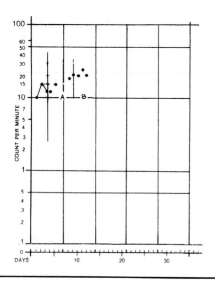

4. Find the mid-rate and the mid-day of side A.

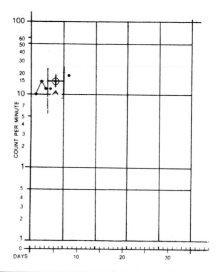

5. Find the mid-rate and the mid-day of side B.

6. Connect the two sides with a celeration line.

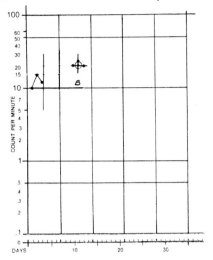

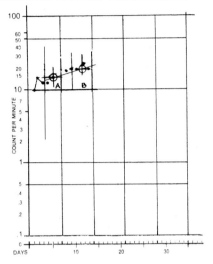

Decision Rules

(a) Continue the intervention with an increasing celeration line.

(b) Change the intervention with a flat celeration line.

(c) Change the intervention with a decreasing celeration line.

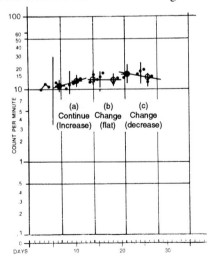

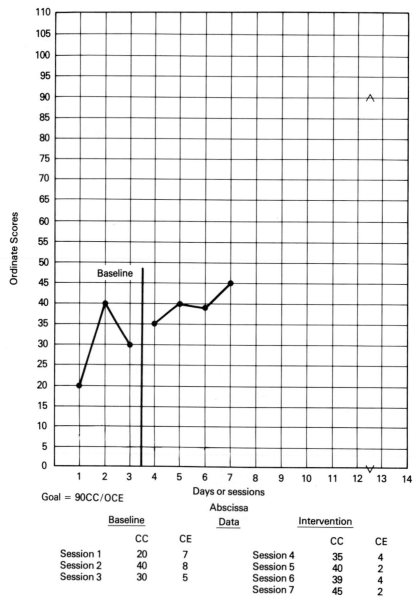

Figure 4.5
Equal Interval Graph

Goal = 90CC/OCE

	Baseline			Data		Intervention	
	CC	CE				CC	CE
Session 1	20	7		Session 4		35	4
Session 2	40	8		Session 5		40	2
Session 3	30	5		Session 6		39	4
				Session 7		45	2

Table 4.4
Steps for Comparing an Aimline and a Regression Line

1. Draw the celeration line using the aimline procedures (aimline).

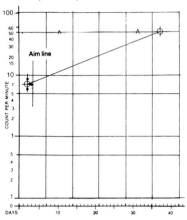

2. Draw the celeration line using the quarter-intersect method (regression).

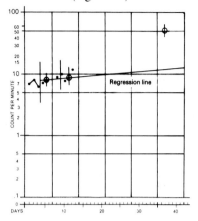

Decision Rules

(a) Change the intervention if the regression line is lower than the aimline.

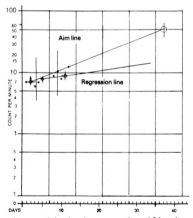

(b) Raise the aim if the regression line is steeper than the aimline.

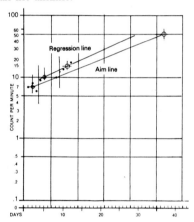

(c) Continue with the intervention if both celeration lines are the same.

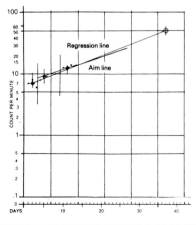

☐ Important Points

1. Performance monitoring procedures are integral parts of precision teaching and curriculum-based measurement.
2. The procedures for performance monitoring include taking baseline, teaching and testing, graphing data, and evaluating performance.
3. In subjective evaluation, a learning picture is effective when the count correct data points are moving up to the count correct aim, the count error data points are moving down to the count error aim, and both are improvements on the baseline.
4. Objective evaluation requires the drawing of celeration lines based on either the expected rate of student change or the actual rate of student change.
5. To determine the expected rate of student change, teachers identify both an aim and a date for reaching the aim and draw a celeration line using aimline procedures.
6. A decision rule states that teachers should change their intervention when a student scores three consecutive data points below the celeration line for the expected rate of change.
7. To determine actual rate of student change, teachers draw a cleration line every few days using the quarter-intersect method.
8. Decision rules state that teachers should change their intervention when a celeration line for the actual rate of change is flat or decreasing.
9. In curriculum-based measurement, teachers draw a celeration line based on the expected rate of student change (an aimline) and the actual rate of change (a regression line).
10. Decision rules state that teachers should change their intervention when a regression line is lower than the aimline or when a regression line is steeper than the aimline.

■ ■ Activity

Using the objective evaluation guidelines, decide whether the following student is progressing at an acceptable rate. First, draw a celeration line using the aimline procedures and then draw one using the quarter-intersect method. Apply one of the decision rules.

- *Aim Date:* Tues. of the third week.
- *Aim:* 70 cc, 4 ce.
- *Time of testing:* 1 minute.
- *Baseline:*

    Wednesday— 25 cc, 10 ce.
    Thursday— 30 cc, 7 ce.
    Friday— 20 cc, 18 ce.

- *Intervention:*

    Monday— 20 cc, 9 ce.
    Tuesday— 30 cc, 1 ce.

Wednesday— 35 cc, 9 ce.
Thursday— 45 cc, 5 ce.
Friday— 40 cc, 5 ce.
Monday— 45 cc, 4 ce.
Tuesday— 50 cc, 3 ce. ■ ■

Mastery Monitoring

Mastery monitoring is evaluation of student progress that occurs after teaching and learning have taken place. To assess progress using this type of monitoring, observe the product of your instruction. Remember, in mastery monitoring, the pool of items changes each time a student masters a unit of curriculum (Tindal, 1987). Measurement is not so frequent as in performance monitoring, nor is rate of behavioral change measured and evaluated. Instead, accuracy is the focus of measurement.

Many times, mastery monitoring is an integral component of popular curriculum programs. Many of these packaged programs, such as the learning strategies curriculum from the University of Kansas model, have built-in monitoring devices. For example, the *Sentence Writing Strategy* (Schumaker & Sheldon, 1985) from the Kansas model provides individual progress charts for depicting student progress in terms of "percentage of complete sentences, complicated sentences, and complicated sentences punctuated correctly" (Schumaker & Sheldon, 1985, p. 167). Mastery levels are identified and charts are provided for student performance on the pretest, written quizzes, controlled practice activities, and posttest. It is recommended that students use these charts to record their own progress. The authors also include a management chart, which records the date for individual student mastery of the various stages of the strategy. It is recommended that this chart be posted on a bulletin board in the class (see Chapter 9 for a more detailed description of the learning strategies curriculum).

In mastery monitoring, teachers can monitor attainment of objectives specified in a particular text or program or monitor completion of a certain number of lessons or amount of curriculum material. They may use systematic written assessments or portfolios for monitoring.

Attainment of Objectives

To measure the attainment of objectives, you must first identify the IEP objectives that you are monitoring and ways to evaluate whether the student has reached the objectives. Many times, these objectives may be correlated with text material. For example, Ms. Herbst, a teacher in a setting for students with special needs, prepared the monitoring device in Figure 4.6 from the objectives identified in a chapter from a math text that correlated with the students' IEP objectives. A score of 85% was required for mastery on all but the skip counting objectives,

which required 100%. Attainment of objectives was checked using worksheets, written tests, and oral tests.

Examine the chart. The first objective is "Reads and writes three-digit numbers." The teacher measured attainment of this objective with a test and the objective of "Recognizes even numbers" with worksheets. The columns indicate that Monica and Lashonda have mastered all the objectives in the chapter, while Manu, Raymond, and Sam have not.

Lessons Completed

A mastery device based on the evaluation of a student's progress using successful completion of lessons is found in the record-keeping system of Ms. Hernandez, a resource room teacher. She uses Reading Mastery materials, paragraph probes, Dolch sight words, the Troll Listening Lab, Distar Language, and the Sound Foundations Program for spelling, and she records the progress in each of these programs for each student on a checklist. See Figure 4.7 for the progress that Rashona has made in the various curriculum materials through the month of September. During the week of September 5 through 8, she completed lessons 41 through 43 of *Reading Mastery II-A*. She completed two checkouts on the lessons and received an A on the seatwork. She read an average of 50 words per minute with 2 errors on paragraph probe 1. She was working on the Dolch sight words in Unit 32. In the Sound Foundations Program 11, she received an A on Lessons 6 through 8. She was not given Troll listening or Distar language activities during the first week of September.

In Figure 4.8, we present an example of a mastery monitoring device based on a combination of assessment of objectives met and lessons completed designed by Ms. Vincur, a secondary teacher of students with special needs. The abbreviation of PS followed by a number indicates the performance standard expected of secondary students with mild disabilities. For example, PS 6.1 states that the student can calculate sales tax

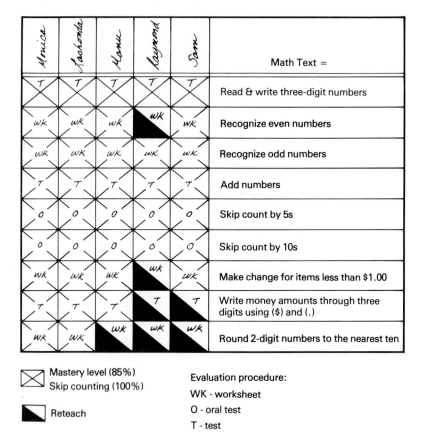

Monica	Lashonda	Manu	Raymond	Sam	Math Text =
T	T	T	T	T	Read & write three-digit numbers
WK	WK	WK	WK	WK	Recognize even numbers
WK	WK	WK	WK	WK	Recognize odd numbers
T	T	T	T	T	Add numbers
O	O	O	O	O	Skip count by 5s
O	O	O	O	O	Skip count by 10s
WK	WK	WK	WK	WK	Make change for items less than $1.00
T	T	T	T	T	Write money amounts through three digits using ($) and (.)
WK	WK	WK	WK	WK	Round 2-digit numbers to the nearest ten

Mastery level (85%)
Skip counting (100%)

Reteach

Evaluation procedure:
WK - worksheet
O - oral test
T - test

Figure 4.6
Objective Monitoring from Math Chapter.
Adapted from a monitoring device designed by Darci Herbst. Used with permission.

and figure out total price. The assignment pages for the objective are listed next. Any assignment is redone until a score of 80% is reached. Ms. Vincur records the date and scores only when the student meets the criterion of 80% or higher on an assignment.

Systematic Written Observations

Systematic written observation during lesson presentation is another monitoring technique. Identifying behaviors and preparing a recording sheet are essential for making observations systematic. For example, Ms. Pierce was teaching middle school students to make change in amounts less than a $1.00. Before her lesson, she identified the ten problems she was planning to ask the students to do during independent practice. Then, instead of trying to remember how the students did, she completed a chart as they were working the problems (Figure 4.9). She also recorded the number of trials and whether or not help was required. The chart shows that Rosa needed two trials to make change of $.60 and $.29. Maria needed assistance on every task.

Portfolio Assessments

Portfolio assessment is "the collection of periodic measures of oral reading, comprehension

Name: Rashona   **Subject:** Reading & Language Arts

Grade: Third

Materials

Date	Reading Mastery II-A — Lesson	Seatwork	Check out	Written tests	Precision Teaching — Paragraph Probes	Dolch Sight Words — Units	Identifying main idea	Recalling details	Recognizing sequence before + after	Finding cause & effect	Comparing & contrasting	Using context clues	Identifying facts + opinions	Distinguishing between fact & fantasy	Following directions	Discovering similes + metaphors	Spelling from Sound Foundations Program II — Lesson	Know a sentence	Cap./punct.	Naming - action	Compound words	Form plurals	Pronouns	Proper nouns	Verbs
Sept. 5-8	41-43	A	☆	☆	Probe 1 50/2	Unit 32											II 6-8 A								
Sept. 11-15	44-48	A		100	Probe 1 180/5	33											II 9-10 B	A	C						
Sept. 18-22	49-53	A			Probe 1 200/2	34											III 11-12B	A	B						
Sept. 25-29	54-56	A	☆	☆	Probe 2 60/3	34/35											III 13-15A	C	A						

Figure 4.7

Lesson Completion Monitoring

Adapted from a monitoring device designed by Ida Mazar. Used with permission.

checks, teachers' observational notes, creative writing samples, and a host of other work samples or more formal tests that are the physical ongoing evidence of a reader's progress" (Pikulski, 1989, p. 81). The portfolios are patterned after the portfolios prepared by professionals, such as artists, to show to their prospective employers. The following steps have been identified in creating a student portfolio: (a) plan the focus (Valencia, 1990), (b) select the content (Valencia, 1990), (c) select the times for adding materials (Jongsma, 1989), and (d) arrange periodic conferences (Farr, 1989; Valencia, 1990).

Planning the Focus

To prevent the portfolio from becoming a hodgepodge of papers, Valencia (1990) suggests that you provide a focus. A portfolio should consist of general reading and writing goals,

such as writing more creative stories or showing progress in summarizing a story theme. We suggest that the students or you select papers that focus on the goals or short-term objectives on each student's IEP for inclusion in the portfolio.

Selecting the Content

Portfolios may contain reading and writing samples of students' work selected by the teacher and student (Flood & Lapp, 1989; Valencia, 1990), teachers' observation notes (Flood & Lapp, 1989), student's periodic self-evaluations (Flood & Lapp, 1989; Valencia, 1990), progress notes written by the student and teacher (Valencia, 1990), a student-generated list of books and genre read each month (Flood & Lapp, 1989), and sample materials used in the school (Flood & Lapp, 1989). The key is selecting a variety of materials to depict a student's progress (Jongsma,

Name: Samantha
Units 4-6 *Consumer Mathematics*

	Date	Score
1. Objective: PS 6.1		
Sales Tax (p. 62, ex. 1–12)	10/16	10/12 83%
Total Price, (p. 64, ex. 1–10)	10/16	9/10 90%
Workbook, (pp. 23-24), if needed	10/17	10/10 100%
2. Objective: PS 1.1		
Unit Price & Best Buys		21/24 88%
(pp. 67-69, ex. 1-14, 16-23)	10/17	
3. Objective: PS 1.2		
Discount (p. 70, ex. 1-8)	10/18	8/8 100%
(pp. 72-73, ex. 20-27)	10/18	27/27 100%
(pp. 74-75, ex. 1.13)	10/19	11/13 85%
4. Unit Test (Object. PS 6.1, 1.1, & 1.2)		
(p. 78)	10/20	90%
5. Objective: PS 3.1		
Deposits (p. 84, ex. 1-14)	10/23	13/14 93%
Writing Checks (workbook, p. 29,		9/10 90%
ex. 1-10)	10/24	
Check Register (workbook, p. 30,		4/4 100%
ex. 1-4)	10/24	
6. Objective: PS 3.2		
Bank Statements (p. 91, ex. 1-8)	10/25	8/8 100%
(p. 93, ex. 1-7)	10/26	11/11 100%
7. Unit Test (Object. PS 3.1 & 3.2)		
(p. 98)	10/27	100%

Figure 4.8
Combined Objective And Material Monitoring
Adapted from a monitoring device designed by Lois Vincur. Used with permission.

1989). You may wish to include either the original copies or summaries of the materials. For example, the student-generated monthly list of books could be summarized into one list.

Selecting Times for Adding Materials

Materials may be added to a portfolio weekly or monthly (Jongsma, 1989). Wolf (1989) schedules periodic student checks for his eighth grade students. At this time, the students remove papers and keep those that best exemplify their progress.

Arranging Periodic Conferences

Regular sessions for portfolio discussions between teachers and students should be scheduled

throughout the year (Farr, 1989; Valencia, 1990). During a conference, you should discuss a student's progress (Valencia, 1990), plans for inclusion of other pieces for the portfolio (Valencia, 1990), and the student's thoughts about the portfolio. Ask such questions as, What is your favorite thing? Why did you organize the portfolio the way you did? Are you trying a new writing style? (Farr, 1989).

■ ■ Activity

You are co-teaching with Mr. Bangor during his sixth grade language arts class. During this 9-week period, Mr. Bangor and you are teaching the students to make their writing more in-

Date: 3/12/90

Activity: Makes change in amounts less than $1.00

0 = can't
✓ = can

	.14	.36	.92	.87	.55	.60	.85	.29	.43	.81
Rosa	✓	✓	✓	✓	✓	o✓	✓	o✓	✓	✓
Maria	✓ w/Help	✓	✓	✓	✓	✓	✓	✓	✓	✓
Michael	o✓	✓	✓	o✓	✓	✓	✓	o✓	✓	o✓
Latoya	✓	✓	✓	✓	✓	✓	✓	✓	✓	✓
Adam	✓	✓	ooo✓	oo✓	o✓	✓	✓	oo✓	✓	ooo✓
Manu	✓	✓	✓	✓	✓	✓	✓	✓	✓	✓

Figure 4.9
A Systematic Written Observation
Adapted from a monitoring device designed by Christi Pierce. Used with permission.

teresting with the use of descriptive words and more complicated sentence structures, such as compound and complex sentences. Design a system to monitor writing progress. ■ ■

Data Collection

Involving students, using computer software packages, organizing materials, and incorporating data collection as a part of the daily instructional routine help make frequent monitoring easy and practical for special education teachers.

Student involvement increases motivation and makes students feel more responsibility for their learning, plus it saves time for teachers. Software packages are valuable assets as more and more teachers have access to microcomputers. Organization and daily routines are crucial for data collection. Without them, the system tends to dominate the teacher.

Data collection still takes firm commitment. At the beginning, it may seem too time-consuming to keep track of your students, but the rewards far outweigh the time needed to develop a system. Baskwill and Whitman (1988)

☐ Important Points

1. In mastery monitoring, teachers can monitor attainment of objectives specified in a particular text or program or monitor completion of a certain number of lessons.
2. IEP objectives and techniques for evaluation are necessary to identify the attainment of objectives.
3. For lessons completed, the teacher tracks the units or materials completed to a specified criterion.
4. In systematic observations the behavior is identified and techniques for recording are specified.
5. Portfolio assessment is the collection of samples of the physical ongoing evidence of a student's progress in the areas of reading and writing.
6. Teachers must make decisions concerning the focus, the content, the times for adding materials, and when to hold periodic conferences.

---

offer these words of encouragement: "Continuous evaluation is a habit you won't want to break! . . . You'll recognize its impact on your effectiveness as a teacher and its positive influence on your interaction with the children. Getting in touch with your children is a truly rewarding and beneficial learning experience for both you and the children. No numbers, no letter grades have ever given you that before" (p. 34).

Involving Students

If you decide to incorporate performance monitoring procedures, teach students to grade their own probes and to chart the results in order to promote active student participation in the learning process. Wesson (1987) suggests setting up a measurement station in the class to involve the students in performance monitoring procedures. Place all materials, such as pencils or pens, a stopwatch with an audible beep, a tape recorder, probes, answer sheets, and graphs, at the center. It is best to file the answer sheets, graphs, and probes in a box for easy access. In fact, you may arrange the probes according to subject areas. Schedule the students at the measurement station and select the probes based on the IEP objectives, but then make the students responsible for the remaining activities. If a probe is a paper-and-pencil worksheet, have the

student proceed to the center, select the required probe as identified on his or her schedule, take the test, chart the information, and return all materials to their proper places.

Bott (1990) suggests placing a set of instructions at each measurement station. A sample set of instructions for collecting oral reading data is:

1. Put the timing tape in the Walkman and put the earphones on.
2. Find the assigned passage in your reading book and mark it with a bookmark.
3. Find the cassette tape labeled with your name, rewind it to the beginning, and press the record and play buttons down at the same time.
4. Allow the tape to run for 10 seconds, and then say your name, the date, the title of the book, and the page number.
5. Open your book, start the timing tape on the Walkman, and when you hear a tone, begin reading out loud. Read as fast and as accurately as you can. Skip any words you cannot figure out.
6. Stop reading when you hear a second tone.

7. Rewind the tape in the recorder and rewind the tape in the Walkman.
8. Put the tape with your name on it in the "in box for tapes." Put away all other materials. (Bott, 1990, p. 287).

Of course, you should model the use of a measurement system when you set up the measurement station.

You may increase student involvement by asking students to set weekly goals and to help evaluate their progress toward the goals. When asked by a teacher how to improve a student's performance, Dr. Lindsley (1990), a researcher and pioneer in the field of precision teaching, told the teacher to go back and ask the student, not him. Dr. Lindsley said, "After all, the child knows best" (p. 12). We agree with this analysis—a student often knows or can give clues to the best way of teaching.

Mr. Ramirez, a teacher of middle school students with special needs, shares this belief. He schedules individual conferences with his students every 2 weeks. In the Conferences, he discusses the charts and asks the students to estimate how much progress they will make before the next conference. The students also suggest interventions and materials to help them reach their goals. Once a goal is reached, a certificate of recognition is given to the student. Charts may also be displayed on a bulletin board.

You may ask students to complete checklists about their feelings concerning their writing and reading performances (Sharp, 1989). Items such as "I know I write better every time" and "Sometimes, I can sound out new words" may be on the checklist (Sharp, 1989). Ask the students to reevaluate their feelings at various intervals during the school term. Sharp contends that this type of monitoring introduces students to the idea that they "can be part of their own assessment as writers and readers . . . and empowers them to set their own expectations" (p. 26).

Diaries and logs are other ways for students to participate in their evaluation (Baskwill & Whitman, 1988). Students may identify a list of writing skills they have mastered under "Things I Can Do in Writing" in their writing diaries (Calkins, 1986; Graves & Stuart, 1985). These lists are updated monthly. In learning logs, students enter what they have learned in any subject area. The students date and compile the logs in a notebook. Logs indicate whether students can describe what they have learned, relate isolated ideas, and recognize relevant information (Baskwill & Whitman, 1988). For example, at the end of each day, Ms. Anderson has her students write one thing they learned and how they felt about the day in their logs.

Sometimes, students become discouraged with their perceptions of lack of progress. If you have kept records, such as charts, logs, and even samples of work completed at different periods during the school year, you can counteract this perception by presenting concrete evidence that the students have indeed progressed.

■ ■ Activity
Identify three ways to involve students with special needs at either the elementary or secondary level in data collection. ■ ■

Software Packages
Several microcomputer software packages generate displays of student data correlated with performance monitoring procedures. AC-CEL Computer Program (West, Young, West, Johnson, & Freston, 1985), Checkup (Fuchs, Hamlett, & Fuchs, 1988), and AIMSTAR (Hasselbring & Hamlett, 1983) are a few. The AC-CEL Computer Program analyzes student scores and recommends strategies for students to employ during peer tutoring sessions (West, Young, & Spooner, 1990). The Checkup program contains graded reading passages, spelling lists, and arithmetic probes that use curriculum-based measurement procedures. Students enter responses on the computer, which graphs the data and draws celeration lines. The program also communicates the appropriate decision: "Uh-oh! Make a teaching change", "Ok! Collect more data", "Ok! Raise the goal", "Move to a

higher grade level for measurement", or "Insufficient data for analysis."

AIMSTAR (Hasselbring & Hamlett, 1983) is available for Apple II. The teacher enters the data, the expected mastery level, and the expected date of mastery. The program keeps a record of progress for an unlimited number of objectives and students and calculates aimlines and regression lines.

Organizing Materials

Being organized helps you manage the monitoring system. Preparing materials ahead saves time later. Wesson (1987) has several practical suggestions for teachers who plan to use passage reading for the measurement of reading progress and story starters for the measurement of written expression as suggested with curriculum-based measurement. She suggests that teachers select ten pages from the beginning, middle, and end of each assigned text for measuring reading progress. The text and thirty slips of paper with a page number written on each slip are then placed in a container. Old ice cream tubs such as you see at Baskin-Robbins are ideal for storing the materials. A student randomly selects a slip of paper from the assigned text, turns to the page number, reads the passage, and initials the back. Once a student has read and initialed the slip three times, he or she can no longer use that page as a measure of reading progress.

She further recommends that teachers prepare thirty story starters at the beginning of the year to monitor written expression. These story starters are then placed on 3-by 5-inch cards. A student selects a card and initials the card on the back so that each story starter is not used more than once.

You should set aside places for students to keep their recording sheets. Graphs, assignment sheets, and checklists, may be three-hole punched and kept at the front of the notebooks of secondary students. Elementary students may use folders. For example, Ms. Anderson uses file folders for portfolio monitoring in her class. She lets the students select samples of items to keep

in the files, including work completed in the mainstream setting. The students date their samples using a date stamp. Her only requirement is that they select only one paper a month from each subject area.

Establishing Routines

Data collection is easier when it is part of the instructional routine. Routine procedures also make it easier for teaching assistants or others to collect data. We present examples from an elementary and a secondary setting that you may wish to adapt for your own data-collection routine. In each of these examples, the routine cycle consists of teach, assess, score, chart, evaluate, and check.

Mr. Chang organizes his elementary class into pairs to practice math facts. One student presents flash cards to the other student. The second student, in turn, writes any fact missed three times. Then, the roles reverse. During this time, Mr. Chang either monitors the tutoring procedure or works with individual students who need more direct instruction.

Following this 10-minute teaching session, Mr. Chang administers the probe. Different students have different probes based on their IEP objectives. Bill is working on addition facts and Yolanda is working on subtraction. Once the timing is up, the students check their problems from previously prepared correction sheets and chart their scores. Every once in a while, Mr. Chang grades the students' probes to check the accuracy of their scoring. After charting, the students complete the rest of the problems on the sheet untimed. This simple procedure of peer tutoring, probing, scoring, charting, and completing the problems takes between 25 and 30 minutes a day.

Every seventh day, the students and Mr. Chang evaluate their learning pictures and decide if any changes are necessary. At the beginning of class, the students spend 15 minutes examining their graphs and completing a monitoring evaluation sheet (see Figure 4.10). Mr. Chang schedules games and other independent activities on that day while he meets with

Date:_____

Name:_____

My learning picture looks _____ Terrific
_____ OK
_____ In Need of Repair

I think I'll try _____ The Same
_____ A New Method
_____ Other Problems
_____ Raise My Goal
_____ Other _____

I, Mr. Chang, agree with this evaluation. _____

I think _____ should try _____ .
    (student's name)
We agree to try _____
_____

Figure 4.10
Monitoring Conference Evaluation Form

each student individually for a 5-minute conference. Then, during the conference, Mr. Chang discusses and signs the evaluation sheet.

Mr. Otto, a history teacher, and Mr. Sims, the special education teacher, devised the following routine for their tenth grade cooperative history class. Every day, during the last 5 minutes of the period, Mr. Otto instructs the students to write the major points of the lecture or discussion and to turn them in before they leave class. Both teachers then divide the grading of the papers and score a point for each correct idea. The next day, Mr. Sims begins the lesson with a summary of the previous day's lecture, which he presents on an overhead projector. Then, he passes out the graded summaries and guides the students in charting the number of points earned for each correct idea.

Eventually, the students grade their own papers while Mr. Sims discusses each major point as he displays it on the overhead projector. Mr. Otto monitors the scoring at this time. The stu-

dents then chart their data. With this routine, the teachers save time grading papers and monitor student improvement in the identification of major points of lectures or discussions. In addition, the procedures identify the students who need prompting. The teachers do random checks so that each student's scoring of the summary is checked at least twice a month.

In Mrs. Ruble's class, a student orally reads a passage from the reading probe as the teaching assistant notes and corrects any errors. After the student has finished reading the passage, the teaching assistant goes over the student's errors by reading the words in context. Then, the student repeats the words missed and rereads the entire phrase or sentence (Peterson, Scott, & Sroka, 1990). The assistant administers the probe. With the student, the assistant counts words correct and words missed and charts the data. The session concludes with the student's reading the remainder of the passage untimed. The routine requires minimal time per student.

▢ Important Points

1. Student involvement, software packages, organization of materials and establishment of routines make data collection easier.
2. Actively involving students in data collection helps them learn and saves time for teachers.
3. Students may be involved in collecting, scoring, and charting probes; in completing self-evaluation checklists; and in compiling diaries and logs.
4. Preparing materials ahead of time and designing a place for students to store records are organizational strategies for efficient data collection.
5. Data collection should become a part of the daily routine and schedule.

Scheduling time for daily observations and for students to evaluate their progress as part of the daily routine demonstrates to the students the importance you place on monitoring their progress. Baskwill and Whitman (1988) suggest that teachers conduct observations during independent practice time. They also recommend that teachers carry around a spiral notebook for writing positive comments about the interactions of the children and the things that the children can do. Then, at the end of the week, the teachers should read the dated entries and highlight significant bits of information.

At the beginning of the observation procedure, we suggest that you identify the student for observation. Then identify the behavior you are attempting to observe. For example, "I plan to watch the strategies Thang uses to select his topic for the written assignment." If you teach students at the secondary level, you may select different days to monitor the progress in various classes; for example, Monday for first period, and Tuesday, for second.

■ ■ Activity
Describe how you might schedule data collection as part of your everyday routine. ■ ■

Task Analysis

When a student is making adequate progress, no change is necessary, for he or she will soon master the objective and progress to a new one. However, if the data show the student is not progressing, it is time for a closer assessment of possible problem areas and for some sort of an instructional change. An instructional program may not be working, because the student is not presented with the appropriate instructional techniques or materials or because the student has not mastered the prerequisite skills or component skills of the task.

To discover if a student is failing because of lack of prerequisite and component skills, you may wish to complete a task analysis. Task analysis involves breaking down a task or objective being taught into simpler components. To perform a task analysis, identify "the terminal behavior, list the necessary prerequisite skills and list the component skills in sequence" (Alberto & Troutman, 1990, p. 324.).

Analyzing the Task
Prerequisite skills are skills that students must master *before* they can be taught a terminal behavior. For example, if the terminal behavior is calculating the perimeter of an object, a student who cannot add does not have the prerequisite skill necessary to master the terminal behavior. Prerequisite skills are important to identify, because students often do not have the entry skills necessary for success. This is particularly true for students with linguistic and cultural differences.

Component skills must be mastered *on the way* to mastering a terminal behavior. For example, a

student must be taught the definition of perimeter on the way to being taught how to calculate perimeter. According to Desberg and Taylor (1986), both of whom have done extensive
work in the area of task analysis, component
skills may either be sequential or parallel. Skills
are sequential if their order is invariant; that is,
each component skill cannot be mastered unless
the previous one has been mastered. Parallel
component skills have no sequential order; that
is, it doesn't matter which component skill you
teach first. For example, if the terminal behavior
is to discriminate between mass and weight, it
doesn't matter whether you teach students to
define mass or to define weight first (parallel
component skills). However, you must teach
students the definition of mass and weight,
before you can teach them to discriminate between the concepts (sequential component
skills).

To complete a task analysis of the terminal
objective (presented with twenty problems requiring multiplication with percents such as
25% × 33, Heather will accurately calculate 18
of 20 problems on three different math assignments), you first identify the prerequisite skills.
These prerequisite skills include (a) solving multiplication facts correctly, (b) solving addition
facts correctly, and (c) multiplying two-digit
times two-digit problems with and without regrouping. To teach this objective, you should
make a quick check of students' entry-level skills
by including some two-digit times two-digit
multiplication problems. By including such
problems, you automatically check whether the
students know multiplication and addition facts,
the other specified prerequisite skills, and thus,
you know whether the student has the necessary
entry skills for success.

The component skills for the targeted behavior of multiplying percents are (a) converting
percents to decimals (25% = 0.25) and
(b) placing the decimal point in the proper place
in the product (8.25). These are sequential component skills, so you would first teach students
to change percents to decimals and then to place
decimals in the product.

It is no easy matter to identify the prerequisite
and component skills of a task, even for experienced teachers. Proceeding in a backward manner through a task analysis is one way to identify
the prerequisite and component skills of a task
(Moyer & Dardig, 1978). Begin with the terminal objective and then work back to the previous
objective. Once that is identified, use that objective to identify the preceding one. For example,
if the terminal behavior is "to count coins," the
behavior before may be to identify which coins
to count.

A second way to complete a task analysis is to
actually perform the task and record the component skills for completion (Moyer & Dardig,
1978). This is often effective for analyzing a motor skill such as tying a shoe. Moyer and Dardig
recommend using props, verbally stating the
steps as you perform them, and writing the steps
down. Finally, they recommend checking the accuracy of the task analysis by performing the task
a second time, and following the steps outlined,
or reading the steps to another person and asking that person to perform the task.

■ ■ Activity
Design a task analysis for sharpening a pencil. Identify the terminal objective, the prerequisite skills, and the component skills. Moyer
and Dardig (1978) identified six component
skills. Now, ask a friend to perform each step.
Did your friend end up with a sharpened
pencil? ■ ■

This use of task analysis is particularly important in coteaching, because special education
teachers often analyze the assignments to identify the necessary skills for successful completion. A task analysis of the worksheet in Table 4.5 shows that students must know the
following capitalization rules for successful completion.

1. Capitalize the beginning of a sentence
   (items 2 and 6).
2. Capitalize the pronoun *I* (item 3).

Table 4.5
Capitalization Worksheet

Directions: Circle the capitalization errors below in the nine sentences.

1. Look at the old Car with the shiny hubcaps.
2. they did a fun activity in class.
3. Yesterday i went to see dr. jones.
4. Did you like the movie, <u>gremlins?</u>
5. Chicago is a City in Illinois.
6. monkeys are funny to watch at the zoo.
7. We went to see mother.
8. Do you know dr. smith, the dentist?
9. I really enjoyed reading <u>a wrinkle in time.</u>

---

3. Capitalize the names and titles of persons and things (items 3, 4, 8, & 9).
4. Capitalize the word *mother* when it is used as a substitute for a name (item 7).
5. Do not capitalize common nouns (items 1 & 5).

After you analyze the task requirements of the assignment, you know which capitalization rules you need to teach or reteach for successful completion of the worksheet.

■ ■ Activity
Using task analysis, identify the capitalization rules that are involved in the following sentences. Circle the capitalization errors in each sentence.

1. we have left our airline Tickets at home.
2. Sunfa did not like the movie, *roger rabbit.*

■ ■

Altering the Task
A task may be altered in terms of color, size, number, or amount of stimulus material (Moyer & Dardig, 1978). For example, if Manu cannot discriminate between the letters of *b* and *d,* you may alter the task by making the *d* a darker color. This should help Manu make the discrimination. If Jon cannot cut a 1-inch line, then you may

have to change the size of the line to 3 inches for him to be successful. If Ramona cannot identify the main idea of a story, you may have to examine the story to determine that the story presents too much material for her to synthesize and memorize. Therefore, you may alter the task so she has to read only a paragraph. If this terminal behavior is still too difficult, you may alter it to just a sentence and ask Ramona to identify the main idea of a sentence.

Often, you may have to alter test items for students with special needs who are in a co-teaching situation. If Jason, a secondary student, cannot select the correct answer from three choices, his multiple choice test foils may be limited to two choices, an alteration of the number of stimulus materials. Of course, with task analysis you are making changes in the task with the idea that this is a first step in teaching the student to master the original objective. Eventually, Manu should learn to discriminate between *b* and *d* without the darker color, Jon should learn to cut a 1-inch line, Ramona should identify the main idea in a story, and Jason should answer multiple-choice questions with three foils.

■ ■ Activity
Alter the tasks below for success:

1. Towanda cannot remember three-step directions.
2. Kari cannot write a paragraph with a topic sentence, three detail sentences, and a closing sentence.
3. Jim cannot tell time to the minutes.

Monitoring Progress in the Mainstream

If you are directly involved with co-teaching or collaborative consultation with regular education teachers, communication and monitoring of student progress in the mainstream is continually occurring. If you find yourself in a different delivery model, monitoring mainstream progress is still essential, for the purpose of many special education pull-out programs is to return students to the mainstream once they can function there. Monitoring progress in the mainstream is essential for the success of mainstream programs (Jones, Gottlieb, Guskin, & Yoshida, 1978; Salend, 1984). Regular and special education teachers can work cooperatively to monitor a student's progress in the mainstream or they can teach children and adolescents to monitor their own progress.

Teacher Monitoring

Monitoring student progress in the mainstream goes hand in hand with communication with classroom teachers. In addition to frequent meetings with regular education teachers when students are first mainstreamed, written communication devices such as checklists are also effective. To use a checklist, ask the regular education teacher to monitor specific behaviors during the class and have the students return the checklist to you. Behavior and academic achievement items are often included on checklists. Some checklists even have a place for the students or teachers to write in homework assignments (see Figure

4.11). Many special education teachers include return of checklists among their classroom rules and provide consequences for nonreturn of checklists. Sometimes, too, special education teachers provide contracts regarding specific behaviors, such as tardiness and complying with classroom rules, for the regular education teacher to sign (Adamson, Matthews, & Schuller, 1990). However you decide to communicate with regular education teachers in monitoring a student's progress in the mainstream, it is best to remember that both of you are experts and that each of you has a contribution to make in educating students with special needs. We present other ideas for teacher communication in a co-teach setting in Chapter Six.

Student Monitoring

Students may be taught to monitor their progress in the mainstreamed setting through self-monitoring skills. Self-monitoring helps students transfer learning from the special education setting to the regular class (Anderson-Inman, 1986), makes students more acutely aware of their behaviors, and frees teachers for other tasks (Frith & Armstrong, 1986).

To teach students with special needs to monitor their own progress, use the following steps

	First		Second		Third		Fourth		Fifth		Sixth	
	Y	N	Y	N	Y	N	Y	N	Y	N	Y	N
Came on time	✓			✓								
Brought supplies	✓			✓								
Followed directions	✓		✓									
Completed work	✓		✓									
Grade on assignment	B		C *(late work)*									
Teacher initials	gEO		JMP									
Homework assigned	None		Page 91, 1–22									

Figure 4.11
Teacher Monitoring

compiled from those suggested by many practitioners (Anderson-Inman, 1986; Frith & Armstrong, 1986; Hughes, Ruhl & Peterson, 1988; Olson, 1982; Osborne, Kosiewicz, Crumley, & Lee, 1987).

1. *Define the behavior for monitoring.* Behaviors selected for self-monitoring should be easily identified as having occurred or not occurred. Try to select skills or behaviors that result in a permanent product, so that students have something visual to refer to. Behaviors such as turning in homework assignments, writing headings on papers, and bringing paper and pencil to class are appropriate for self-monitoring.

2. *Teach students to discriminate the behavior.* Model examples and nonexamples of the behaviors and then ask students to discriminate between the examples. For example, if you want the students to discriminate between appropriate and inappropriate comments during discussion in history class, model appropriate and inappropriate comments and ask the students to discriminate between the behaviors. Students cannot discriminate inappropriate comments

if they don't know what you mean by inappropriate comments.

3. *Design the form for data collection.* On the form, be sure to include the behaviors, dates, and key for coding. See Figure 4.12 for an example of a form. This form was used with secondary students to count the turning in of reading assignments on time.

4. *Demonstrate how to record using the form.* Model how to record on the form and explain the scoring code.

5. *Use a time routine.* Scheduling a specific time for students to complete the forms increases the chances that students will remember to monitor the behaviors when you are not around. Schedule the time for monitoring as close to the completion of the task as possible.

6. *Use teacher reliability checks.* A reliability check is easier if the student is monitoring a paper-and-pencil type of task, which leaves a permanent record. For example, a quick check of the regular teacher's grade book will let you know whether the student is correctly monitoring the turning in of reading assignments on time. Many times, teachers reward students when their counts match. Actually, however, more im-

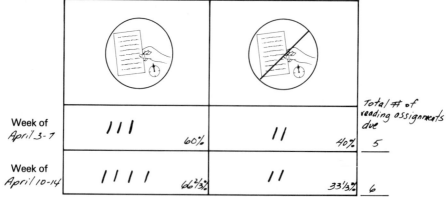

Figure 4.12
Student Monitoring

Important Points

1. Analysis of data lets teachers know if they should change the objectives, techniques, or materials in their instructional plan.
2. Task analysis requires the identification of prerequisite skills, component skills, and terminal behaviors or objectives.
3. Students may not be progressing because they do not have the prerequisite skills or component skills necessary to reach the terminal objective.
4. Prerequisite skills are skills that students must master before they can master the terminal objective.
5. Component skills are skills that must be mastered on the way to mastering a terminal objective.
6. Task analysis may be used to assess what skills should be taught or retaught for a student to successfully complete assignments.
7. Teaching prerequisite skills or altering the task may lead to improvement.
8. A task may be altered in terms of color, size, number, or amount of stimulus material.
9. Monitoring the progress of a student in the mainstream is essential for success.
10. Teacher monitoring and student monitoring are two monitoring procedures.
11. Checklists and contracts are ways to involve regular education teachers in monitoring student progress.
12. To initiate student monitoring, teachers should define the behavior, design the form for data collection, demonstrate how to use the form, use a time routine, use reliability checks, and introduce the monitoring gradually.

portant than checking accuracy is the use of the form. After all, the objective is for students to monitor their own progress in the mainstream.

7. *Introduce self-monitoring in one mainstream setting first, and add others gradually.* Anderson-Inman (1986) reports that allowing students to decide when and where to use the self-monitoring form makes them feel more committed to using it. Perhaps next a secondary student may want to monitor the turning in of math assignments on time.

Summary

In this chapter, we discussed performance and mastery monitoring procedures. Performance monitoring procedures measure and evaluate the rate of student progress, while mastery monitoring procedures evaluate the products of instruction. With performance monitoring procedures, a baseline is collected, teaching is begun, testing is done, data are charted, and student performance is evaluated. Student progress is monitored by either a subjective evaluation, where learning pictures are examined, or an objective evaluation, where celeration lines are drawn. With mastery monitoring procedures, progress is monitored as students complete materials or reach objectives. Systematic written observations or portfolio assessments may be used for collecting information.

Data collection may also involve students and teaching assistants. We presented ideas for setting up measurement stations, for systematically organizing data collection, and for establishing routines to make data collection easier and more efficient. Then, we examined task analysis procedures. In task analysis, you must identify the prerequisite skills and the component skills necessary for the successful completion of a terminal objective.

Special educators are responsible for monitoring the progress of their students in the special education and mainstream settings. Teacher monitoring for assessing the progress of students in the mainstream includes checklists and contracts. We also described steps for involving students in the monitoring of their progress in the mainstream.

5

Instructional Materials

Key Topics

Materials are the nuts and bolts of an instructional program, the vehicles through which instruction is delivered. If your students are to achieve success in the classroom, the materials they use must produce the learning outcomes you desire, motivate the students, and hold their interest. Teachers play a key role in instructional decision making (Gollnick, Sadker, & Sadker, 1982). In school districts where state-adopted textbooks and materials are used, teachers should be adept at modifying and adapting materials. In districts where teachers are given choices in the selection process, teachers should be skilled in selection, analysis, and development of materials. In this chapter, we focus on the use of commercial and teacher-made materials and present ways to select, analyze, adapt, and develop instructional materials.

Uses of Materials

Use and selection of instructional materials are part of the process of individualizing instruction for students (Walker, 1981). When choosing materials, teachers should be aware of a student's individual needs, strengths, weaknesses, characteristics, and levels of functioning. For example, Mico has difficulty understanding and remembering what he reads. Mico's teacher can, therefore, select or adapt texts and materials to include stop points where Mico can paraphrase what he has just read. Selection and modification of materials with attention to student needs help individualize instructional programs.

Motivation is an important factor to consider when you select materials for your students. Materials that are age appropriate, interesting, appealing, and related to real life are likely to be used by your students, particularly when you have given consideration to cultural backgrounds and interests. For example, some students benefit from using high-interest, low-vocabulary materials that are age and interest appropriate.

Teachers can use instructional materials, both commercial and teacher-made, to foster social interactions through peer tutoring, learning center activities, role playing, group projects, and cooperative learning activities. Interpersonal skills are important for school and community adjustment (Lovitt & Harris, 1987; Schloss & Schloss, 1987; Schloss, Schloss, & Harris, 1984; Schloss & Sedlak, 1986). For example, Joe and Mike, high school juniors, have been working with instructional materials that emphasize job-seeking skills. In addition to providing them with skills in finding and securing employment, the materials have given them valuable socialization experiences through role playing the employability activities.

Instructional materials may be used to help students recognize and celebrate the diversity and variety that exists among individuals and to share information about people from different cultural backgrounds. As you select materials, make sure that all groups are represented. Underrepresentation in instructional materials appears to occur most often for minority groups, women, people with disabilities, and older individuals (Gollnick & Chinn, 1990). Studies reveal that some books contain few female and minority illustrations, biographies, and characters and emphasize the majority male (Weitzman & Rizzo, 1974; Women on Words and Images, 1975).

In Mr. Rizzati's English class, students read and discuss books that incorporate different ages, both males and females, a variety of cultural groups, and people with disabilities. For example, the class examined the problems of the elderly in *Grandpa and Me* (Tolan, 1978), a story about a family that has to decide what to do about the aging grandfather who has always lived with them. The story highlights the special friendship between the grandfather and granddaughter. A particular favorite of the class was *Summer of the Swans* (Byars, 1974), a story told from the perspective of the sister of a boy with a mental disability. The story tells how the girl comes to know and understand herself better because of her brother.

Water Sky (George, 1987) is a story about a young man living with an Eskimo family in Alaska. There, he learns the importance of whaling to the Eskimo culture. *The Black Snowman* (Mendez, 1989) describes a young African-American boy who discovers the beauty of his heritage and self-worth. For a list of books about a variety of cultural groups, see Table 5.1.

You may use a variety of instructional materials to meet the needs of your students at each of the stages of learning. At the acquisition level, materials should provide opportunities for extensive teacher participation. For example, to teach writing skills to your students, you may use materials that explain how to write a variety of sentence types and then require you to model what to do when writing sentences.

After your students have acquired skills, they need to practice them to gain fluency. Students should practice first in a controlled or guided situation, under close supervision, and then in independent situations. Therefore, you should select and develop a wide variety of materials and provide opportunities for extensive student involvement. Practice materials should foster participation on the part of students. You may use workbooks, magazines, practice exercises, audiotapes, computer software, and games to develop fluency in writing skills. In addition, you may use charts and graphs to monitor each student's progress.

After students have demonstrated fluency, you should provide instructional materials that allow them to maintain the skills. At this stage, you should provide materials that will encourage frequent use of the skills. Students with special needs can practice writing a variety of things to maintain their writing skills (e.g., a monthly book report). In addition, maintenance is frequently enhanced by learning centers, where students work independently (e.g., writing different sentence types and writing reports).

The final stage of learning involves the generalization of skills across situations and settings. For example, you should help students identify the opportunities for using writing in real-life materials. Thus, you should select materials that require students to apply their writing skills to the types of writing they do in content area classes (e.g., English), on the job (e.g., taking orders), and personally (e.g., writing letters). A high school student confided to her teacher that her letters to her boyfriend were easier to write after she improved her writing skills.

Selecting and Analyzing Commercial Materials

Many commercially produced instructional materials for teaching specific academic skills and content area subjects are available for use with

Table 5.1
Multicultural Literature

African-Americans

Bryan, A. (1989). *Turtle knows your name*. New York: Atheneum.
Flournoy, V. (1985). *The patchwork quilt*. New York: Dial.
Greenfield, E. (1989). *Nathaniel talking*. New York: Writers & Readers.
Grifalconi, A. (1986). *The village of round and square houses*. Boston: Little, Brown.
Lester, J. (1989). *How many spots does a leopard have? and other tales*. New York: Scholastic.
Meltzer, M. (1984). *The Black Americans: A history of their own words*. New York: Crowell.
Mendez, P. (1989). *The black snowman*. New York: Scholastic.
Miller, D. (1988). *Frederick Douglass and the fight for freedom*. New York: Crowell.
Patterson, L. (1989). *Martin Luther King, Jr., and the freedom movement*. New York: Facts on File.
San Souci, R. (1989). *The talking eggs: A folktale from the American South*. New York: Dial.

Asian-Americans

Clark, A. N. (1979). *In the land of small dragon: A Vietnam folk tale*. New York: Viking.
Demi (1990). *The empty pot*. New York: Henry Holt & Company.
Goldman, P., & Fuller, T. (1983). *What happened to us in Vietnam?* New York: Morrow.
Huynh Quang Nhoung (1982). *The land I lost: Adventures of a boy in Vietnam*. New York: Harper.
Ike, J. H. (1982). *A Japanese fairy tale*. New York: Warne.
Luenn, N. (1982). *The dragon kite*. San Diego, CA: Harcourt Brace Jovanovich.
Newton, P. C. (1982). *The five sparrows*. New York: Atheneum.
Nguyen Ngoc Bich (1975). *A thousand years of Vietnamese poetry*. Translated by B. Raffel & W. S. Merwin. New York: Knopf.
Seros, K. (1982). *Sun and moon: Fairy tales from Korea*. Winslow, WA: Holly.
Vuong, L. D. (1982). *The brocaded slipper and other Vietnamese tales*. Reading, MA: Addison-Wesley.

Hispanics

Aardema, V. (1979). *The riddle of the drum: A tale from Tizapan, Mexico*. New York: Four Winds.
Belpre, P. (1978). *The rainbow-colored horse*. New York: Warne.
Bierhorst, J. (1986). *The monkey's haircut and other stories told by the Maya*. New York: Morrow.
Bierhorst, J. (1987). *Doctor Coyote: A Native American Aesop's fables*. New York: Morrow.
Griego y Maestras, J., & Anaya, R. A. (1980). *Cuentos: Tales from the Hispanic Southwest*. Santa Fe, NM: Museum of New Mexico.
Jagendorf, M. A., & Boggs, R. W. (1960). *The king of the mountains: A treasury of Latin American folk stories*. New York: Vanguard.
Lattimore, D. (1987). *The flame of peace: A tale of the Aztecs*. New York: Harper & Row.
Marrin, A. (1986). *Aztecs and Spaniards: Cortez and the conquest of Mexico*. New York: Atheneum.
Prago, A. (1973). *Strangers in their own land: A history of Mexican-Americans*. New York: Four Winds.
White, C. (1973). *Cesar Chavez, man of courage*. Champaign, IL: Gerrard.

Native Americans

Cleaver, E. (1985). *The enchanted caribou*. New York: Atheneum.
Esbensen, B. (1988). *The star maiden*. Boston: Little, Brown.
Freedman, R. (1988). *Buffalo hunt*. New York: Holiday.
George, J. (1987). *Water sky*. New York: Harper & Row.
Hamilton, V. (1988). *In the beginning: Creation stories from around the world*. San Diego, CA: Harcourt Brace Jovanovich.
Highwater, J. (1984). *Legend days*. New York: Harper & Row.
Highwater, J. (1985). *The ceremony of innocence*. New York: Harper & Row.
Highwater, J. (1986). *I wear the morning star*. New York: Harper & Row.
Hudson, J. (1989). *Sweetgrass*. New York: Philomel.
Monroe, J., & Williamson, R. (1987). *They dance in the sky: Native American star myths*. Boston: Houghton Mifflin.

students who have special needs. In choosing materials, you should consider the fact that you will work with students who have a wide variety of abilities and individual differences. A survey of over 30,000 teachers underscored the need for materials that address learner characteristics by calling for instructional materials that:

- Are adaptable to a variety of disabilities.
- Include supplements like manipulatives, games, visuals, etc.
- Have varied entry levels.
- Allow for monitoring of student progress.

Working in a regular elementary setting with students who have special needs as well as with other students, Ms. Gonzalez uses commercial materials called predictable books (see Table 5.2). According to Rhodes and Dudley-Marling (1988), "Books are predictable when they en-

able students to quickly and easily predict what the author's going to say and how the author's going to say it based upon their knowledge of the world" (p. 88). Ms. Gonzalez bases her decision to use these books with her students upon her knowledge of the characteristics of her students as well as upon some of the characteristics of predictable books that Rhodes (1981) has identified: (a) a match between the content and the reader's experiences; (b) rhythmical, repetitive patterns; and (c) familiar, well-known stories. Ms. Gonzalez selects books with characters, cultural backgrounds, and themes her students can easily relate to. She chooses books with repetitive patterns, such as *Alexander and the Terrible, Horrible, No Good, Very Bad Day* (Viorst, 1972) and books with which most of her students are familiar, such as tall tales or folktales. She includes many of the typical American folk

Table 5.2
Predictable Books

Aardema, V. (1981). *Bringing the rain to Kapiti Plain*. New York: Dial.
Ahlberg, J., & Ahlberg, A. (1978). *Each peach pear plum*. New York: Scholastic.
Barrett, J. (1980). *Animals should definitely not act like people*. New York: Atheneum.
Bishop, C., & Wiese, K. (1938). *The five Chinese brothers*. New York: Coward, McCann & Geoghegan.
Brand, O. (1970). *When I first came to this land*. New York: Putnam's Sons.
Burke, C. L., & Harste, J. C. (1983). *All kinds of cats*. Worthington, OH: School Book Fairs.
Carle, E. (1969). *The very hungry caterpillar*. Cleveland: Collins World.
Christian, M. B. (1973). *Nothing much happened today*. Reading, MA: Addison-Wesley.
de Paola, T. (1981). *Now one foot, now the other*. New York: Putnam's Sons.
Dodd, L. (1985). *Hairy Maclary*. Milwaukee, WI: Gareth Stevens.
Durrell, J. (1985). *Mouse tails*. New York: Crown.
Galdone, P. (1985). *Cat goes fiddle-i-fee*. New York: Clarion.
Hines, A. (1984). *Come to the meadow*. New York: Clarion.
Hoguet, S. R. (1983). *I unpacked my grandmother's trunk*. New York: Dutton.
Kalan, R. (1981). *Jump, frog, jump!* New York: Greenwillow.
Leydenfrost, R. (1970). *The snake that sneezed!* New York: Putnam's Sons.
Lobel, A. (1984). *The rose in my garden*. New York: Greenwillow.
O'Neill, M. (1961). *Hailstones and halibut bones*. Garden City, NY: Doubleday.
Petrie, D. (1982). *Joshua James likes trucks*. Chicago: Children's Press.
Plume, I. (1980). *The Bremen town musicians*. Garden City, NY: Doubleday.
Satchwell, J. (1984). *Odd one out*. New York: Random House.
Singer, M. (1981). *Will you take me to town on strawberry day?* New York: Harper & Row.
Thomas, P. (1971). *"Stand back" said the elephant, "I'm going to sneeze!"* New York: Lothrop, Lee & Shepard.
Viorst, J. (1972). *Alexander and the terrible, horrible, no good, very bad day*. New York: Atheneum.
Williams, B. (1974). *Albert's toothache*. New York: Dutton.

☐ Important Points

1. When choosing instructional materials, teachers should be aware of students' individual needs, strengths, weaknesses, characteristics, and levels of functioning.
2. Instructional materials should be motivating, age appropriate, interesting, and appealing.
3. Instructional materials may be used to foster social interactions and improve interpersonal skills.
4. Instructional materials may be used to help students recognize and share information about people from different cultural backgrounds.
5. Underrepresentation in instructional materials seems to occur most often for minority groups, women, people with disabilities, and older individuals.
6. Instructional materials may be used to address the needs of students at each of the stages of learning (acquisition, fluency, maintenance, and generalization).
7. When selecting commercially produced instructional materials, teachers should carefully consider the characteristics of the learners and the materials.

---

heroes, such as *Paul Bunyan, A Tall Tale* (Kellogg, 1984), and tales from other countries, such as the Asian legend *A Song of Stars* (Birdseye, 1990) and the Chinese tale *The Empty Pot* (Demi, 1990).

You should exercise care in your selection of commercial materials. Attention to individual learner characteristics and needs increases the probability of success with commercially produced instructional materials.

■ ■ Activity

Examine a commercially produced instructional material for reading, literature, history, or social studies. Count the number of times that different groups are represented as main characters and in illustrations. Do this for cultural groups (Hispanics, African-Americans, Asians, etc.) and for genders (males and females). Is the material equitable in its representation of cultural groups? Is it equitable in its representation of gender? Explain. (Answers for this activity and others are found in the Instructor's Manual.) ■ ■

Many commercial products are not appropriate because they possess characteristics that make

their use extremely difficult for students with special needs. The discrepancy between what is commercially available and what students actually need leaves you with two options. You may adapt commercial materials or develop your own instructional materials.

From 1981 to 1985, the Office of Special Education Programs in the United States Department of Education sponsored several materials adaptation projects to modify commercial materials to make them more appropriate for students with mild handicaps (Burnette, 1987). During the time these projects were being conducted, teachers reported that they were modifying approximately 40% of their instructional materials.

There are many reasons for the ineffectiveness of commercial materials, curricula, programs, and textbooks:

1. *The readability of text may be too difficult.* Many materials are written on a reading level that is higher than the publisher has indicated it to be. Sentences may be too long and complex, and vocabulary may be unnecessarily difficult, as in "The man, addressing the audience before him, told them that he had repented for all of his

past offenses" instead of "The man told the people he was sorry for what he did."

2. *The vocabulary is often highly sophisticated.* Complex words may be used when easier synonyms would be just as effective (see preceding example). Unfortunately, when technical terms are introduced in some content materials, definitions are omitted or not clearly stated. Wiig and Semel (1984) suggest the use of only five unfamiliar vocabulary words per lesson for students who are language or learning disabled.

3. *Too many concepts may be presented at one time.* Students with special needs benefit when concepts are introduced one at a time. Unfortunately, math materials sometimes present more than one type of problem on a page. For example, in one text we examined, the division problems ($24 \div 8 = $ _____ , $38 \div 5 = $ _____ , and $215 \div 3 = $ _____) required three different skills and levels of competence but were presented on the same page. Notice that the first problem can be divided evenly, the second has a remainder, and the third involves a two-digit quotient with a remainder. Each should be mastered before the next is introduced.

4. *The sequencing of the skills may be inappropriate.* Students with special needs may experience problems when skills are taught out of sequence. For instance, students should be taught initial consonant sounds before they are introduced to the concept of consonant blends (Spache & Spache, 1977).

5. *Directions are not always clear.* Some materials use different words for the same direction, as in the case of "Circle the best answer," and "Put a line around the best answer." It is less confusing for students if directions are handled consistently.

6. *Insufficient practice may be provided.* Many workbooks, textbooks, and other printed products jump from one skill to the next without giving students adequate prac-

tice (see the division examples in number 3 above). Students with special needs require practice to become fluent and to maintain a skill.

7. *There may be insufficient repetition, review, and application of previously learned tasks.* Many commercial materials do not revisit previously learned skills in practical, relevant situations. For example, once students in an employability skills class have learned the steps for job interviewing, they need to apply those skills through role playing, discussion, and videotaping.

8. *Key points and terms may not be given adequate emphasis.* Printed products do not always highlight, print in bold type, print in italics, or define the most important terms and ideas. This may cause difficulty for students who do not easily identify key points and terms.

9. *Organization, format, and layout are sometimes confusing.* Printed materials do not always begin with an advance organizer or introduction of what is to come (e.g., list of objectives, key vocabulary list, outline), nor do they conclude with a post organizer (e.g., summary, list of important points, questions). In addition, when tables, graphs, and illustrations are placed far away from the text that describes them, they may either confuse students or be ignored because the students do not see the connection between the text and the graphic aid. Imagine trying to follow an explanation of how to record checks in a check register when the instructions are on one page and a diagram of the check register is on another.

10. *The pace of the program may be too rapid.* Many commercial materials move too quickly, failing to provide sufficient practice, review, and application. For example, students should spend sufficient time learning how to subtract two-digit numbers from two-digit numbers without regrouping before attempting similar problems with regrouping.

11. *Materials may be unmotivating and uninteresting.* Some commercially produced materials simply are not attractive and interesting, because of format, level of difficulty, lack of color and illustrations, subject matter, age level targeted, or typeface. Thus, they may not hold the learner's attention.

12. *Pages may be cluttered with too much information.* Crowded formats can confuse students and discourage them from even beginning a task. Students may be unable to pinpoint relevant information and screen out nonessential information when a page is overcrowded.

13. *Materials and text are sometimes too abstract.* Some written materials contain long passages of text with no clues to the definitions of abstract vocabulary and concepts. For example, a social studies chapter on justice, democracy, and freedom, may not make these concepts concrete. Another example is math material that contains the term *congruent* with no examples, definitions, or illustrations of the term.

14. *Students may be limited in their response modes.* Unfortunately, some materials require only one type of response from students. For example, a science text that provides only a set of questions limits response. In contrast, a science text that provides suggestions for experiments, topics for discussion, suggestions for group activities, suggestions for field trips, and a set of questions provides a variety of response modes.

15. *A variety of ethnic and cultural groups may not be represented.* Some instructional materials do not include exposure to a variety of ethnic and cultural groups, thereby limiting their appeal. This omission may communicate to students that some ethnic and cultural groups are less important than others (Gollnick & Chinn, 1990).

16. *Some materials include descriptions of people and activities that stereotype individuals in terms of culture, ethnic group, religion, gender, or age.* Biases may exist within both the printed and graphic sections of materials (Baca & Cervantes, 1989).

Numerous forms and checklists are available for teachers to use when judging the suitability of instructional materials for students. You may use the Materials Analysis Form (MAF) in Table 5.3 to help you decide whether to use a given material as it is or to use it with modifications. Completion of the Materials Analysis Form provides you with the purpose and uses of the material, its distinguishing features, and a physical description. To analyze a material, write a few words or place a check mark by each of the categories that apply.

Forms and checklists may help you choose the most effective materials and individualize instruction. For example, the Department of Education Projects of 1981–1985 (Burnette, 1987), which focused on instructional materials for students with mild handicaps, identified features that are typically examined in a textbook analysis. Table 5.4 focuses on the identified features of vocabulary, reading level, and concept development. Knowing the reading levels of your students and of a text helps you judge the suitability of the text. The form also addresses the amount of repetition, review, and material presented. You should be sure that your students can handle the concept load and that the text provides ample opportunities for your students to check their understanding. Supplementary materials may include study aids, activity sheets, and overviews.

Finally, you should make sure that the format (layout, print, graphics) is compatible with the needs of your students. Table 5.4 provides a structured and systematic way for you to pinpoint the strong and weak features of a textbook. By analyzing elementary and secondary textbooks for content, organization, supplementary materials, and format, you can identify elements that cause problems for students and adapt the textbooks accordingly.

Table 5.3
Materials Analysis Form

Part I

Directions: Fill in the following information.

1. Title _____

2. Author(s) _____

3. Publisher _____

4. Instructional area(s) ___(e.g., Math)___
   a. Specific instructional skill(s) (e.g., addition facts)

   _____

   b. Suggested instructional level(s) (e.g., elementary)

   _____

5. Contents (e.g., teacher's guide, kit, worksheets, games)

   _____

Part II

Directions: Place a check mark in the column that best describes this material.

	Acceptable	Unacceptable
1. Readability level	_____	_____
2. Sentence length	_____	_____
3. Vocabulary control	_____	_____
4. Print	_____	_____
5. Color	_____	_____
6. Illustrations	_____	_____
7. Concept load	_____	_____
8. Sequencing of skills	_____	_____
9. Directions	_____	_____
10. Opportunities for practice	_____	_____
11. Repetition and review	_____	_____
12. Organization	_____	_____
13. Format and layout	_____	_____
14. Interest and motivation	_____	_____
15. Key points and terms	_____	_____
16. Pace	_____	_____

■ ■ Activity

Part 1. Select a classroom material (kit, program, game, workbook) and analyze it using the Materials Analysis Form (Table 5.3). Present the material and your findings to the class. *Part 2.* Select a content area textbook at the elementary or secondary level and use the textbook analysis form (Table 5.4) to judge its suitability for students with special needs. Report the results of this analysis to the class. ■ ■

Table 5.3
Continued

Part III

Directions: Respond to the following aspects of the material.

1. Mode of response
   a. Manipulation _____
   b. Copying tasks _____
   c. Written response _____
   d. Oral response _____
   e. Reading _____
   f. Mark a response _____
   g. Repeat information _____
   h. Role play _____
   i. Problem solving _____
   j. Other _____

2. Monitoring progress and providing feedback
   a. Immediate feedback process of some type _____
   b. Teacher checks student's work _____
   c. Student self-checks _____

3. Evaluation and record-keeping procedures
   a. How is the starting point of instruction established?
   b. How is the mastery of content demonstrated and recorded?

4. Teacher involvement
   a. Teacher preparation
      _____ Extensive
      _____ Minimal
      _____ Reasonable
   b. Teacher participation during time in use
      _____ Constant interaction
      _____ Teacher introduces and student completes
      _____ Virtually none or none at all
      _____ Supportive help or monitoring role

5. Affective Considerations   **Yes or No**
   a. Multicultural emphasis _____
   b. Age appropriate _____
   c. Interest appropriate _____
   d. Free of biases (cultural, ethnic, gender, handicap, minority, age, religious) _____

Adapting Materials

Once you have analyzed materials and identified any shortcomings, you may need to adapt the materials for use with students who have special needs. Materials should be usable under differ- ent instructional conditions with students who have varying abilities. As a consultant to regular classroom teachers, you often adapt instructional materials to better meet student needs.

Table 5.4
Textbook Analysis Form

Directions: Use this form to determine the suitability of a textbook for your students. For each item, place a check mark under *acceptable* or *unacceptable*.

	Acceptable	Unacceptable
Content		
• Vocabulary	_____	_____
• Readability	_____	_____
• Concept load	_____	_____
• Skill development	_____	_____
Organization		
• Sequencing of text	_____	_____
• Clarity of directions	_____	_____
• Amount of repetition/review	_____	_____
• Method(s) of checking for understanding	_____	_____
Supplementary Materials		
• Student study guides, outlines, or activity sheets	_____	_____
• Student glossaries, objectives, key concepts, games, software, etc.	_____	_____
Format		
• Layout, print, organization of topics	_____	_____
• Ease in using table of contents, index, etc.	_____	_____
• Inclusion of graphics, photographs, and illustrations	_____	_____
• Interest and age-appropriate	_____	_____
Comments:		

For example, Mrs. Perez asked the fifth grade teachers in her school to identify problems that students in their classrooms were experiencing with their social studies textbooks. The teachers reported that their students with special needs had difficulty comprehending the material, learning new terms and their definitions, and answering questions in class. Utilizing the feedback, Mrs. Perez developed study guides, glossaries, and questions to accompany the text.

These adaptations benefitted not only the students with special needs but also other fifth grade students in better understanding the text. The purpose of adapting instructional materials is to meet the academic, emotional, and physical needs of students (Lambie, 1980).

Printed Products

Printed products include textbooks, workbooks, worksheets, transparencies, kits with cards or written information, tests and quizzes, and flash cards; in short, anything that contains written text. Following are areas to modify and techniques that you may utilize for students with special needs.

Readability

To modify the readability level:

1. Shorten sentences.
2. Simplify vocabulary.
3. Provide outlines or study guides to accompany the text.
4. Highlight essential information.
5. Limit the amount of information on a page.
6. Make the topic sentence of a paragraph the initial sentence (Wood & Wooley, 1986).

Vocabulary

To modify vocabulary:

1. Use the marginal gloss technique. Write terms and their definitions in the margins of a textbook page (see Figure 5.1).
2. Underline or highlight key terms.
3. Locate all boldface, italicized, or new concept words from the text and list them with the corresponding page number (Wood & Wooley, 1986).
4. Record essential words, definitions, and sentences on language master cards or on audiotapes.
5. Provide vocabulary lists or glossaries with simplified definitions and use the words in sentences.

Presentation of Concepts

To modify the presentation of concepts:

1. Supplement print material with concept teaching procedures.
2. Present concepts one at a time.
3. Provide visual supplements, such as transparencies, illustrations, and diagrams.
4. Use modeling and demonstration to clarify concepts.
5. Use games, manipulatives, and hands-on activities to reinforce concepts.
6. Draw upon the different cultural backgrounds and experiences of your students to make concepts meaningful.

General Comprehension

To increase understanding of materials:

1. Include prereading organizers and end-of-text summaries.
2. Provide study guides or outlines.
3. Insert stop points in text and have students summarize what they have read.
4. Include periodic reviews in the form of statements or questions.
5. Have students generate their own questions about printed materials.
6. Highlight main ideas in one color and supporting details in another. Post a key to the coding system in the classroom.
7. Give short, frequent quizzes instead of one long test.
8. Provide summaries on tapes.
9. Use graphic organizers and semantic maps.
10. Conduct brainstorming sessions.

Directions

To clarify written directions:

1. Simplify the directions.
2. Shorten the directions.
3. Use concise, boldface directions.
4. Put the words typically used in directions on language master cards.
5. Highlight the key words in a set of directions (e.g., Write a *t* in the blank if the

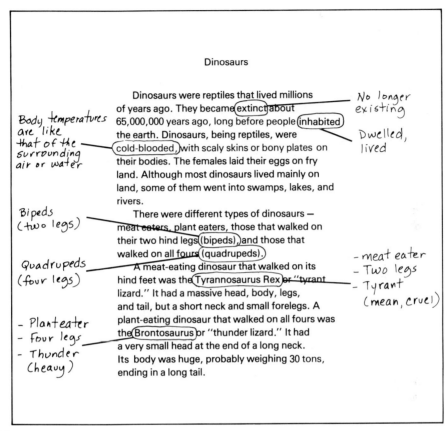

Dinosaurs

Dinosaurs were reptiles that lived millions of years ago. They became extinct about 65,000,000 years ago, long before people inhabited the earth. Dinosaurs, being reptiles, were cold-blooded, with scaly skins or bony plates on their bodies. The females laid their eggs on fry land. Although most dinosaurs lived mainly on land, some of them went into swamps, lakes, and rivers.

There were different types of dinosaurs — meat eaters, plant eaters, those that walked on their two hind legs (bipeds), and those that walked on all fours (quadrupeds).

A meat-eating dinosaur that walked on its hind feet was the Tyrannosaurus Rex or "tyrant lizard." It had a massive head, body, legs, and tail, but a short neck and small forelegs. A plant-eating dinosaur that walked on all fours was the Brontosaurus or "thunder lizard." It had a very small head at the end of a long neck. Its body was huge, probably weighing 30 tons, ending in a long tail.

Body temperatures are like that of the surrounding air or water

No longer existing

Dwelled, lived

Bipeds (two legs)

Quadrupeds (four legs)

*- meat eater
- Two legs
- Tyrant (mean, cruel)*

*- Plant eater
- Four legs
- Thunder (heavy)*

Figure 5.1
Marginal Gloss Technique

answer is true and an *f* if the answer is false).

6. Have the students underline what they are supposed to do (e.g., Write your answer in the blank provided for you).

7. In a set of multiple directions, use colored dots or numbers to differentiate the separate directions (Lambie, 1980).

8. Tape record directions on audiocassettes.

Practice

To provide sufficient practice:

1. Have students move laterally before they move vertically to a new skill (e.g., have students practice multiplying one-digit numbers by one-digit numbers for some time before you teach them to multiply one-digit numbers by two-digit numbers.

2. Supplement practice in printed products with games, tapes, and manipulatives.

3. Provide repetition, review, and application of skills.

Manageability of Materials

To adapt printed materials to increase manageability:

1. Shorten assignments by cutting worksheets in half or circling even-numbered questions for students to complete in a session.

2. Clip a piece of construction paper to half of a page and have the student complete the other half.
3. Draw a frame or border around the questions that the student should answer (see Table 5.5).
4. Use markers to help students locate words and keep their place.
5. Underline or highlight specific information that is being introduced or emphasized.
6. Mask out certain areas of print material to emphasize specific concepts, eliminate unnecessary visual stimuli, and encourage task performance.
7. Color code newly introduced material, major concepts, or material to be memorized.
8. During presentations with transparencies, star the important points and underline the details (Lambie, 1980).
9. Cover each transparency with a piece of paper and move the paper downward one line at a time (Lambie, 1980).
10. For students who have difficulty reading lengthy chapters, tape record every other page. Have the student read one page and listen to the next (Lambie, 1980).

Organization

To organize printed materials in a clear, consistent manner:

1. Use advance and post organizers for each activity (e.g., give students an outline or a set of questions at the beginning of a lesson and print a summary or list important points on a transparency to use for review at the end of a lesson).
2. Provide objectives, practice activities, and means of evaluation.
3. Use simple, easy-to-follow layouts and formats.
4. Provide graphics that are clear and understandable. Be sure that graphics clarify and support the printed text (e.g., give students a photocopy of a check that has been filled out so that as they read the text they

Table 5.5
Shortening an Assignment

Name _____ Date _____

Directions: Write your answers to the subtraction problems in the space provided.

Do the problems that are inside the frame

1. $5.10 − 2.51	2. $6.28 − 2.99	3. $4.43 − 1.76	4. $8.11 − 5.86
5. $7.56 − 6.78	6. $4.41 − 3.85	7. $9.05 − 2.79	8. $6.43 − 4.78
9. $3.10 − 2.98	10. $8.83 − 5.99	11. $6.76 − 3.97	12. $5.20 − 4.91
13. $5.84 − 1.96	14. $4.12 − 3.87	15. $8.03 − 5.75	16. $7.07 − 2.49

can see where the date, amount, signature, etc., belong).

Response Modes

To increase the options for student responses:

1. Allow students to tape their responses on audiocassettes.
2. Provide opportunities for students to work in groups with games, flash cards, and hands-on activities in response to printed assignments.
3. Allow students to take tests orally.
4. Let students dictate stories, themes, and book reports.
5. Provide role playing and discussions.

Motivation

To increase motivation and interest in printed materials:

1. Use concrete examples and demonstrations to supplement printed materials.
2. Draw upon prior knowledge to make material more interesting to students.
3. Supplement text materials with nontraditional printed materials, such as newspapers, magazines, comic books, and baseball cards. In Table 5.6, the teacher has used a story dictated by a student about a baseball player to develop a reading activity for the student.
4. Allow students to use self-correcting materials.
5. Use materials that interest students while simplifying vocabulary.
6. Let students use materials independently, in small groups, and in large groups.
7. Use audiovisual aids, such as filmstrips, videotapes, language master cards, computer software, and audiotapes to increase interest in printed materials.

Content Delivery

Use audiotapes to present printed materials (Deshler & Graham, 1979). When you prepare tapes:

Table 5.6
Teaching Reading with Baseball Cards

Vocabulary

1. always	6. farther
2. percentage	7. leagues
3. series	8. strikes
4. plays	9. high
5. join	10. right

Darryl Strawberry

Darryl Strawberry used to play for the New York Mets. The Mets always did well when Strawberry played for them. When Strawberry played, they were always one of the top teams in baseball. In 1986, the Mets won the World Series.

Now Strawberry plays for the Los Angeles Dodgers. He wanted to join the Dodgers so he could play in his hometown.

Strawberry plays right field. He has a high slugging percentage. He hits the ball farther than any other left-handed hitter in the major leagues. He strikes out a lot, but he hits lots of home runs.

What Is Your Batting Average?

1. For what team does Darryl Strawberry play?
2. Why did he change teams?
3. How did he help the team he used to play for?
4. What position does he play?
5. What is another way of saying *slugging percentage*?
6. If Strawberry strikes out a lot, how can he be a good player?
7. Find a sentence in the story that tells about something that happened in the past.
8. Find a word in the story that means "at a great distance."
9. Find a word in the story that means the opposite of *lost*.
10. The word *right* is used in the story. What does it mean? Now, think of another meaning of the word *right*.

1. Highlight important points.
2. Include questions to facilitate recall and critical analysis.
3. Repeat key concepts.
4. Provide feedback.

5. Differentiate between main ideas and supporting details.
6. Explain how to use graphics.
7. Explain how to use chapter titles, boldface subheadings, section summaries, and questions to gain information.

Show students how to use a marking system (see Figure 5.2) in connection with an audiotape (Deshler & Graham, 1979). Use a solid line to indicate that the material will be read verbatim on the audiotape. Use a dotted line to indicate that the material will be omitted from the audiotape. Use a wavy line to mean that the material will be paraphrased. Use a star to mean that students must stop the audiotape to complete an activity. Such a marking system helps students coordinate audiotaped material with printed material.

Abstractness
To make materials more concrete:

1. Provide demonstrations.
2. Use concrete examples.
3. Present or construct models.
4. Use role plays.
5. Associate concepts with music or art.

The Civil War was fought between the North and the South. Differences and major disagreements had developed between these two regions of our country. People on both sides tried to figure out ways to solve problems and work out differences. Although some of the suggestions were promising, nothing seemed to last. The two sides seemed doomed to disagree.

One of the reasons the North and the South differed to such a degree was that the two regions were developing so differently. The North was developing into a major manufacturing center with its textile mills and its emphasis on trade with other countries. Factories were plentiful and were run by thousands of immigrants arriving daily from across the sea.

On the other hand, the South was developing into a major agricultural area with cotton as its major crop. The Southern plantation thrived on its cotton crop and exported it to other countries.

These differences between an agrarian society (the South) and one that focused on manufacturing and trade (the North) further divided the two regions. The North wanted to pass laws that would help its interests such as a tax on imported goods. This tax would make goods produced in the North look very attractive.

A tax on imported goods would not help the South. The Southerners wanted to pay the lowest price they could for manufactured goods. They opposed the idea of a tax on imported goods.

★ **The Growth of Slavery in the South**

Southerners used slaves to work their plantations and produce a bountiful cotton crop. Therefore, the increased emphasis on cotton as the South's major crop lead to the growth of slavery.

Figure 5.2
Marking System

6. Relate materials to students' cultural backgrounds and experiences.

Chapter Questions
To modify end-of-chapter questions:

1. Ask fewer questions.
2. Reword the questions in simpler terms.
3. Increase responding time.
4. Write out the answers and the page numbers on which the answers are found. Then, have the students match the answers to the questions (see Table 5.7).
5. Write the page number where the response can be found next to each question at the end of a chapter. Or, next to the response in the chapter, write the number of the question. Highlight the response (Wood & Wooley, 1986).

Computer Software
Commercially produced computer software programs may not accommodate students with special needs. Furthermore, many commercial software programs are protected by programming codes that make them impossible to modify. An alternative to modifying commercial software programs is using public domain software, which is free to be copied and revised (Chiang, 1986). Because public domain software programs contain various types of problems for students who are mildly disabled, Chiang suggests a number of modifications:

Table 5.7
Chapter Questions

Bacteria are among the smallest and simplest of living things. Because they are so small, they are called micro-organisms. . . .

Page 16

Bacteria live in dirt, soil, and water. Bacteria live in milk and in most foods. Some live in the mouths, noses, and intestines of animals. They are everywhere! . . .

Page 18

Bacteria help decay dead plants and animals. Bacteria are used to combat pollution from oil spills. Bacteria are useful in sewage disposal plants because they break down impurities. . . .

Page 22

Chapter Questions
1. What are bacteria?
2. What shape are bacteria?
3. Where do bacteria live?
4. How are bacteria harmful to us?
5. How are bacteria useful to us?

---

1. *Add a word file editor.* A word file editor allows you to make a Dolch word list accessible to programs like Hangman and Spell-n-Time.
2. *Provide a performance summary upon quitting a program.* Performance summaries give students their scores in terms of number correct and rate before they abandon a program.
3. *Include clear, concise directions.* Make sure that students can review the directions at any time in case they have forgotten or are confused about them.
4. *Provide opportunities for self-correction.* Self-correction encourages self-monitoring of performance and allows for error analysis.
5. *Provide prompts about the location of entry.* Use a flashing cursor or question mark to show students where to enter the next response.
6. *Control the duration of the screen display.* Lengthening the display may also prove advantageous to students.

For a more extensive discussion of computer software, see Chapter 12 and consult Appendix B.

Selecting, Analyzing, and Adapting Materials for Students from Culturally and Linguistically Diverse Populations

Baca and Cervantes (1989) suggest ten guidelines to follow in making decisions about materials. Some of their suggestions overlap suggestions in the previous discussion and therefore are not repeated; however, others have not been mentioned and are important to consider. Baca and Cervantes recommend that teachers include appropriate cultural experiences in the materials they adapt or develop. For example, when Ms. Higgins developed a unit called "Holidays Around the World" for her primary students, she taught the students to sing a song in five different languages. For her discussion of customs, she presented a different holiday custom from each country and encouraged the students to share a holiday custom that their families practiced.

Baca and Cervantes suggest that teachers continue to try out different materials and adaptations until they achieve an appropriate education for all students who are culturally and linguistically diverse. For example, in her history class, Mrs. O'Mara had to significantly adapt and supplement the history textbook to include the perspective of Native Americans in the study of Western expansion. The textbook presented only the United States government's perspective. She felt that the Native American students in her class and students of other cultures should read more than one perspective.

Teachers should be knowledgeable about particular cultures and heritages and the compatibility of the cultures and heritages with selected materials. For example, a text that is limited to the contributions of the European settlers in the United States does not present a balanced perspective (Gollnick & Chinn, 1990). Many students would fail to learn about the contributions of their own cultural groups in the development of their country. Such a text would have to be significantly modified or supplemented.

Ortiz (1989) recommends that teachers consider specific factors when adapting materials for students who have limited English proficiency (LEP). He suggests that teachers analyze vocabulary and syntax for verbal load and regional forms and rewrite the text if necessary. He feels that teachers should support texts with pictures, media, and action to make the content understandable. For example, Mr. Bonavidez uses videotapes to supplement his discussion of famous inventors. His students are able to see different parts of the United States and the world. Each videotape traces the origins and background of one inventor. Mr. Bonavidez also provides glossaries that contain terms, definitions, and pictures to help students who are not proficient in English.

▢ Important Points

1. Materials and texts that are not appropriate may be adapted.
2. Strategies for adapting printed products and computer software include highlighting, color coding, and simplifying, among others.
3. To facilitate the effective and appropriate use of instructional materials with students who are culturally and linguistically diverse, strategies include modification of vocabulary; use of media, pictures, and glossaries; and incorporation of supplementary materials that emphasize different languages and cultures.

■ ■ Activity

Locate the instructional material that you analyzed in the last activity and think about the limitations you identified. Now, use some of the strategies presented and modify the material to make it more appropriate for students with special needs. Remember to include multicultural and gender considerations. ■ ■

Developing Materials

Some instructional materials cannot be adapted or modified to a level that is acceptable for use with students who have special needs. For example, we have worked with some math and spelling materials that required an almost complete reconstruction because of inappropriate sequencing of skills, problems with format, and print quality. Other materials have been inappropriate because of cultural or gender bias. Another material introduced too much new vocabulary within a story.

Because of such problems and others, you may choose to develop your own materials. When developing instructional materials, avoid the problems that are characteristic of ineffective commercial products. For example, design materials that provide sufficient practice, repetition, and review, and consider factors that will affect the performance of your students. For example, consider how the learner is going to interact with the material. The input may be auditory, with directions given on an audiotape, and the output may be written, with the student required to write something. You may want to vary the input (auditory, visual) and output (written, verbal), depending upon the activity and the characteristics of your students.

You should also attend to the complexity of the material and match it to the level of your students. For example, some teachers develop manipulative materials to help their students better grasp abstract concepts. The complexity of the material can also be related to the stages of learning. For example, when Mrs. Roberts initially taught place value to her students, she gave them Popsicle sticks to help them understand the concept (acquisition stage).

As you develop materials, consider how your students will receive feedback. Some of your materials should be self-correcting, so that your students can monitor their own performance. Computers can provide automatic feedback. With other materials, *you* should provide positive and corrective feedback to your students.

In materials development, you should give careful consideration to the concept load of the material. This includes the number of new concepts you present at one time, the amount of practice you provide, and the rate of presentation. For example, Mr. Saunders spent a class period with his high school students going over a diagram that he developed after examining several textbooks. He had consolidated into one diagram nearly everything he could find on the topic of prejudice. Concentrating on the one concept, the class defined prejudice, identified characteristics of it, and gave examples.

In materials development, you should also consider your level of involvement with the materials, whether it is extensive (teacher-directed) or minimal (student-directed, individual, or group). Rewriting materials and then presenting them to your students (teacher-directed) will require quite an investment of your time. If you give your students a problem to solve through group discussion, your involvement will be much less. Finally, you should consider the affective aspects of materials, such as cultural emphasis, age bias, and gender bias.

Teacher-made materials may include worksheets, books, learning and tutoring packets or folders, games, and self-correcting materials. These materials may increase the effectiveness of the overall instructional program because they ensure individualization and because they are designed to reinforce, motivate, and enhance pupil participation. For example, Marco, a third grader, had trouble learning vocabulary in its written form in his reading workbook. Miss Micelli, his special education teacher, made him a word bank that contained the reading vocabulary on language master cards. Marco practiced his words on the language master, which presented the words to him both visually and auditorily. Marco said each word aloud as he practiced and again, later, as Miss Micelli checked him. Miss Micelli noted Marco's progress on a chart that listed each of the words. Marco learned the words quickly because he received positive and corrective feedback and found the approach interesting and motivating.

Laurie, a seventh grade student, had just been taught a technique to improve her comprehension of reading material. Because she works successfully in groups and learns well from others, her teacher, Mr. Nohmura, grouped her with two other students to practice, repeat, and review the steps of the comprehension monitoring technique. Mr. Nohmura developed worksheets for the students to use for written prac-

tice, let them verbally rehearse the steps with one another, and then, using a teacher-made checklist, evaluated each student for mastery of the steps. Use of the teacher-made materials, attention to affective concerns, learner interactions with the materials, and feedback and evaluation increased Laurie's opportunities for success.

Worksheets

In developing worksheets for students, you should make directions clear and concise and be careful not to put too much on a page. Worksheets should focus on one concept at a time and provide adequate practice. You may make worksheets self-correcting by printing the answers on the back, on the bottom (upside down), or along the right margin, which can be folded over to conceal them. You may also provide access to a key for self-checking or be available to provide oral and written feedback. Whenever you utilize worksheets, be certain that they serve a valid purpose and are not used merely to fill time.

Teacher-Made Books

Commercially produced reading materials do not always move at a pace that is acceptable for students with special needs, nor do they consistently provide sufficient repetition and practice of vocabulary. Cox and Platt (1985) developed a set of paperback, consumable books at the pre-primer, primer, first, second, and third grade levels. As soon as their students master a Dolch word list (consisting of twenty-five to thirty words), they are able to read a new book. *No words other than the words on that Dolch word list are included* (see Figure 5.3). The books have been prepared in coloring-book format, enabling students to personalize their books with crayons and markers. After they have shown that they can read their books in school, students are encouraged to take their books home to read to their parents. You can develop similar materials by selecting a word list and then developing a story around the words in the list. Students find

Figure 5.3
Dolch Word Book

Note. From *Dolch Word Books* by V. F. Cox and J. M. Platt, 1985, unpublished educational materials. Reprinted by permission of the authors.

it enjoyable when you incorporate their names and experiences.

Cox and Platt (1986) also developed Read-with-Expression books out of a need to improve the reading fluency of their students. These books are consumable, short, humorous stories written at a second grade reading level and prepared in coloring-book format. The intent is to encourage fluent reading by providing humor-ous high-interest, low-vocabulary content and by showing students how to use punctuation marks to help them read with expression. Both the Dolch books and the Read-with-Expression books were created out of a need to teach the skills that commercial products were neglecting. Remember, you can create stories like these by incorporating your students' background expe-riences into topics of interest to them.

Packets and Folders

In meeting the needs of exceptional students, it may be helpful to prepare learning packets. Learning packets contain materials that students are to use in the classroom. Because packets are usually student directed, they should contain clear, concise directions. Packets may include some means of self-monitoring, such as access to an answer key. You may develop tutoring packets for teaching assistants or volunteers to use. Such packets may list activities to complete with the student. A packet may consist of a practice activity that the teaching assistant or volunteer supervises, drill or practice using a game or flash cards, and a brief review. Learning packets require knowledge of the sequential development of skills.

File folders meet the needs of students by providing opportunities for practice and reinforcement of a wide range of skills. File folders are convenient to use and store. Teachers who float from classroom to classroom can easily transport them. Folders may be constructed to include activities that are multilevel. For example, in preparation of a math unit, Mrs. Barkwell sets up a folder to include a restaurant menu. In the first activity, students are asked to locate the cost of various items, such as hamburgers, soft drinks, french fries, and milkshakes. In the second activity, students must order several items and compute the total cost. In the third activity, students are required to figure the total cost plus tax. In the fourth activity, students determine the total cost, the tax, and then figure out how much change they will receive from $10.00 and $20.00. The activities may be set up to be self-correcting, with an answer key provided or the answers written on the reverse side (e.g., a card with a picture of a hamburger on one side and the price on the back). As you can see, file folders may be used effectively with students who have a wide range of abilities.

Games

Educational games do not take the place of instruction, but they do provide motivating ways to help reinforce skills (Heit, 1980). By creating your own games, you help your students attain skills and solve problems that are important to their success both in and out of school. A teacher-made game must provide (a) a clearly stated purpose or rationale and outcome, (b) complete yet uncomplicated directions and rules, (c) reinforcement and practice of skills already acquired, and (d) a method of monitoring and evaluating progress.

You may construct your own game board, as in Figure 5.4, or use a commercial board. Little Kenny Publications has wipe-off game boards, cards, spinners, and game pieces available for purchase. With the needs of your students in mind, you can use this generic equipment to create your own instructional games to support the sequential development of academic skills. The game boards can be adapted to any academic skill and content that you want to reinforce, including math facts, science vocabulary, and long vowels. You may also construct a spinner for a game by attaching a paper fastener to the center of a transparency. By drawing a circle on the transparency, dividing it into eighths, and writing numbers 1 to 8 in each section, you can make a generic spinner that is appropriate for use with any game and is usable with the entire class or a group.

Self-Correcting Materials

You may develop self-correcting materials that are easy to make and fun for students to use. The following ideas are based on suggestions by Mercer, Mercer, and Bott (1984). For more information about their textbook on self-correcting materials, consult the reference section.

You may write a problem on one side of a card and put the answer on the back. You may use such cards for math facts and their answers and for terms and their definitions. Alternately, you may write terms or math facts and their answers on the same side of the card. Then, cut each card in half in a different zigzag pattern, so that the question is on one half of the card and the an-

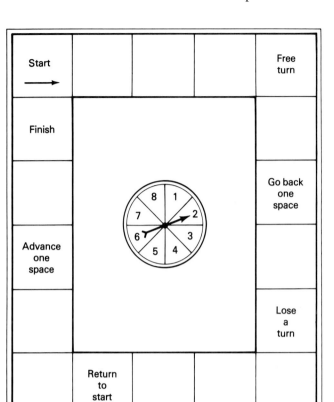

Figure 5.4
Game Board

swer is on the other half. That way, the two parts fit together each time your students respond correctly. You may also use this technique for the states and their capitals.

You may use an audiocassette to record a problem, question, or direction and then pause before dictating the answer. This self-correcting technique is also effective with spelling words, science vocabulary, and word problems.

For practicing a word and its abbreviation, a math problem and its answer, or a date in history and the event that took place on that date, you may prepare sets of cards with a problem or question on one card and the answer on another card. Be sure the back of each pair of cards contains some type of picture completion. After students respond to the problems, they should turn

the cards over. If the answer is correct, the pictures should either match or fit together to complete an object or design.

These are just a few of the examples of self-correcting materials that you can develop. Such materials offer students with special needs a variety of ways to respond as they complete learning activities.

■ ■ Activity
Part 1. Develop a math worksheet on telling time for a third-grade student. Make sure the directions are clear and the worksheet is self-correcting.
Part 2. Develop a self-correcting activity appropriate for an elementary student (such as

states and their capitals) and one for a secondary student (such as subject-verb agreement). ■ ■

Multilevel Learning Centers

An effective way to individualize instruction is to use learning centers. A learning center is an area within the classroom that contains a collection of activities and materials to reinforce initial teaching, clarify concepts, provide drill and practice, enrich, and motivate (Cooper, 1981; Kaplan, Kaplan, Madsen, & Taylor, 1973).

Learning centers do not replace the teacher, nor are they responsible for initial teaching. Instead, they provide opportunities for students to work independently with materials on their own level and with activities that are interesting and motivating. Learning centers may help your

students become more self-directed, independent, and task-oriented. Items you should consider in developing learning centers include (a) goals and functions, (b) key components, (c) organization, (d) development, (e) scheduling, (f) teacher and student roles, (g) record keeping, and (h) evaluation.

Goals and Functions

Kaplan et al. suggest using learning centers as vehicles for independent study, as follow-ups for teacher-taught lessons, as enrichment or extension activities, and as substitutes for regular assignments. You may use learning centers for either individual or group activities. Learning centers perform varied functions, including assessing, monitoring, and evaluating; reviewing, drilling, and practicing; reteaching; reinforcing; contracting; and increasing interest and motiva-

A learning center should contain a collection of activities and materials that reinforces teaching.

tion. You may develop and organize learning centers by specific topic, content area, or skill, as illustrated by the following themes: creative writing center, listening center, following directions center, map skills center, computer center, fractions center, writing center, and famous people center. Figure 5.5 illustrates a learning center in which students are required to read and write about Alaska. Materials and activities revolve around the theme of the center. Student-developed materials, such as the scrapbook and summaries of articles or news broadcasts, could also be included as part of the center display.

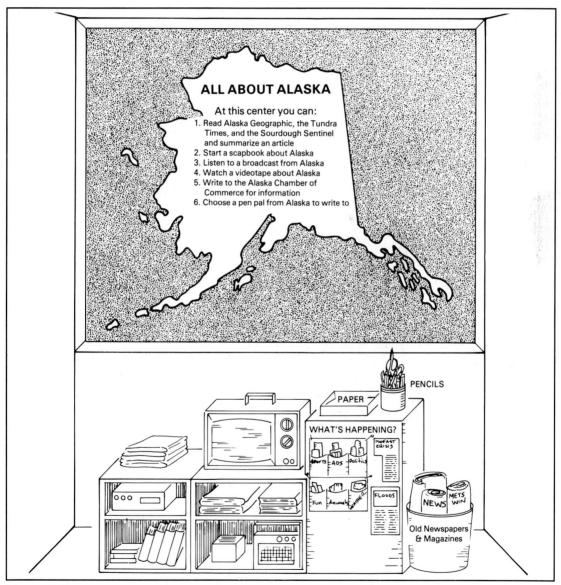

Figure 5.5
Learning Center

Key Components

A learning center should possess multilevel capabilities; that is, it should include a variety of activities at various levels so that each of your students has work on his or her level. The materials and activities must not only cover a range of abilities from simple to complex but also include tasks that are concrete and abstract. A learning center should be geared to the interests, abilities, and needs of the students in that classroom (Kaplan et al., 1973). The basic components of a learning center are:

1. A name or theme.
   Examples: Alphabetizing, tall tales, or mollusks.
2. A wide variety of materials to support the theme, concept, or skill.
   Examples: Filmstrips, games, tapes, worksheets, charts, books, manipulatives.
3. Clear, complete directions about who can work at the center, how to complete the activities, how to correct work and record performance, when students are scheduled at the center, how many students can work at the center at one time, and which materials each student should use.
   Example: "Please consult the learning center schedule to find out what center to report to (see Figure 5.6). Centers will be open from 9:00 to 10:30 for all groups on Friday morning. Check the folder in your center for directions."

Organization

As you develop learning centers, consider how to organize the centers within the physical environment. Special education teachers in pull-out models are frequently given small classrooms and therefore must make optimal use of the space they have while providing a variety of resources for their students. Other special education teachers must be able to set up learning centers in regular classrooms, work with existing centers in those classrooms, or transport their learning centers on a cart.

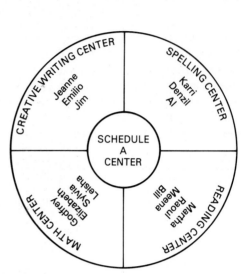

Figure 5.6
Learning Center Schedule

Development

Construction of a learning center should be systematic and careful. You may use the following ten steps as a guide:

1. Identify an area of need.
   Example: Reading comprehension.
2. Determine the objectives.
   Examples: Identifying main idea, identifying supporting details, answering questions and retrieving information from text, paraphrasing, summarizing, sequencing, and selecting a title.
3. Develop the area of skill or concept into a learning activity.
   Example: Students learn about reading comprehension by matching main idea and detail statements to the correct category.
4. Design the area of skill or concept into an application activity.
   Example: Students apply a reading comprehension skill to a game in which they read a short story and then select the best name or title for the story.
5. Incorporate the area of skill or concept into an extending activity.

Example: Students extend their reading comprehension skills by constructing their own questions about a reading passage, giving them to another student, and correcting the responses.

6. Prepare clear, concise directions for each activity in the learning center.
7. Select, develop, and collect the materials and equipment to be used in the learning center.
8. Construct the learning center (drawing a sketch or floor plan may be helpful).
9. Develop a time schedule for learning center use.
   Example: The center may be open for 2 hours in the morning and 1 hour in the afternoon with specific students assigned to use it at different times.
10. Develop a record-keeping system and a method of providing feedback and monitoring student progress.
    Example: After students complete an activity, such as sequencing the events in a story, they check the answer key for the accuracy of their responses. They enter the name of the activity and their scores before and after corrections on the learning center log or checklist.

Scheduling

The type of scheduling you use in a classroom depends upon how you use learning centers in that setting. You must decide whether you want your students to have a voice in the scheduling or whether the scheduling will be teacher-directed. The times when students are assigned to learning centers may be incorporated into their daily assignment sheets or be indicated on a separate schedule for learning centers.

Once you have determined your needs and those of your students, select the scheduling technique that best suits your situation. You may utilize a variety of techniques to schedule students into learning centers, including (a) rotational scheduling, (b) use of contracts, and (c) assignment to centers based on diagnosed

needs, interests, and daily work. Rotational scheduling involves having students rotate from one center to another at times that you specify. In contracting (Blackburn & Powell, 1976), teachers and students develop a contract, set goals, and decide what the student will accomplish in each learning center (see Figure 5.7). In scheduling after you have assessed each student's skills and interests, you assign students to centers or let them choose from specified centers. For example, after instructing students in small groups, Ms. Peterson assigned them learning center activities for practice.

Teacher and Student Roles

Teachers and students have different roles and expectations in relation to the development, use, maintenance, and evaluation of learning centers. You should develop learning centers in relation to the needs and interests of your students. Then, you should identify the objectives that will meet these needs and incorporate them into the learning centers. You are responsible for setting up meaningful activities, clear directions, and effective methods of evaluation.

You should introduce one learning center at a time. Remember to change learning centers frequently to maintain student interest, motivation, and participation. Finally, prepare your students by providing a thorough orientation, including modeling and role playing, to include the use and maintenance of centers as well as student behavior standards. During the orientation, thoroughly explain the roles of students in relation to learning centers. You should expect your students to follow directions, keep accurate and thorough records, exercise care when using materials and equipment, adhere to the prearranged schedule, and clean up and put away activities when finished. Also, you may ask students to evaluate the effectiveness of learning centers.

Record Keeping

Record keeping is extremely important in planning for and evaluating student learning. It makes your students more aware of their

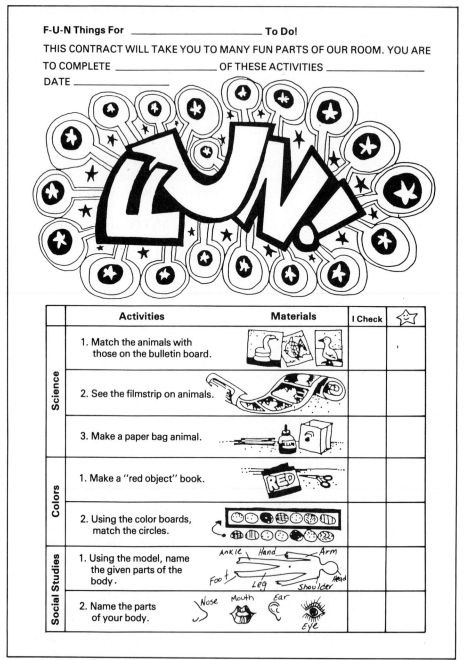

Figure 5.7
Learning Center Contract

Note. From *One at a Time All at Once: The Creative Teacher's Guide to Individualized Instruction Without Anarchy* (p. 130) by J. E. Blackburn and W. C. Powell. A Good-Year book. Copyright © 1976 by Scott, Foresman and Company. Reprinted by permission.

☐ Important Points

1. In developing instructional materials, it is important to provide sufficient practice, repetition, and review.
2. Key variables during materials development include the learner's interactions with the materials, the concept load, the extent of teacher involvement, and affective aspects.
3. Teacher-made materials may include worksheets, books, learning and tutoring packets, folders, games, self-correcting materials, and learning centers.
4. Learning centers should possess multilevel capabilities and be geared to the interests, abilities, and needs of students.
5. Teachers may use learning centers as vehicles for independent study, follow-ups to lessons, enrichment activities, and substitutes for regular assignments.
6. Teachers may use learning centers for either individual or group activities.
7. The basic components of a learning center include a name or theme, a variety of materials, and clear directions.
8. The steps involved in developing a learning center include (a) identify an area of need; (b) determine the objectives; (c) develop the skill or concept into learning, application, and extending activities; (d) prepare directions for the activities; (e) collect the materials; (f) construct the center; (g) develop a time schedule; and (h) develop a record-keeping system.
9. Teachers and students have different roles in the development, use, maintenance, and evaluation of learning centers.
10. Teachers should evaluate each learning center before they present it to students.

progress and increases their responsibility for their learning. It assists you in making data-based decisions about your students' performance. You can show records to parents to report participation in specific activities and to demonstrate overall progress. You can share records with mainstream teachers and use them to make decisions about participation in regular classroom activities. Because record keeping is so valuable, it is important to include it in learning center activities.

Records should be kept to evaluate progress. Both you and your students may evaluate progress in learning center activities. You may perform spot checks; evaluate folders, products, and completed work on a daily basis; review contracts; and schedule individual conferences with students. Your students may set goals and evaluate their progress toward those goals, utilize self-checking procedures, monitor their progress toward meeting the terms of their contracts, chart and graph their performance, and request conferences with you. Table 5.8 shows an example of record keeping used to monitor a student's progress. Notice how the teacher, Mrs. Tinsdal, has provided feedback and how Mandy has set her own goals to work on. Records should be simple and uncomplicated and should communicate at a glance what the student has accomplished and how well he or she has done.

Evaluation

Of equal importance to the development of a learning center is evaluation. Before presenting a learning center to your students, you should ask yourself the following questions:

1. Does it possess multilevel capabilities?
2. Is it interesting and age appropriate?
3. Does it have clear, concise directions?
4. Are a wide variety of activities and materials included?

Table 5.8
Record Keeping

Learning Center Check Sheet

Name _____Mandy Markowicz_____

Directions: Put a check mark next to the center you worked in each day. For example, if you worked on Creative Writing on Monday, put a check mark next to Creative Writing and under Monday.

	Days				
Centers	**Mon.**	**Tues.**	**Wed.**	**Thur.**	**Fri.**
Measurement	✓		✓		
Creative Writing		✓		✓	
Social Studies		✓		✓	
Reading	✓		✓		✓

Feedback from teacher:

Measurement _____Excellent progress — all work correct._____

Creative writing _____Loved your story about "trip around the world."_____

Social Studies _____You need to redo your map — I'll get you started._____

Reading _____Good score on vocabulary. Comprehension is improving._____

Goals for next Check Sheet:

_____I need to concentrate on my map in social studies and do activity #3 in reading_____

Teacher _____Mrs Tinsdal_____ Date ___11/19___

Student _____Mandy Markowicz_____ Date ___11/19___

5. Will students have opportunities to use different response modes?
6. Does the center have a clear purpose along with objectives that relate to student needs?
7. Does the center have eye appeal?
8. Is the schedule workable?
9. Are record-keeping procedures included?
10. Is there a plan to orient students to the center?

If you respond positively to these questions, then you are ready to introduce learning centers into your instructional program.

■ ■ Activity

In a group of four to five members, assume the role of a teacher of students with special needs (choose an age group). Identify the needs of your students, develop objectives, and select a theme for a learning center. Then, simulate the steps and procedures you would follow in developing the learning center, dividing the responsibilities for this task among the group members. Be sure to include a list of materials, a sketch, directions, a time schedule, and methods for record keeping and monitoring progress. Present your learning center to the class. Ask another group to consider the ten evaluation points provided in the chapter and evaluate your center. ■ ■

Summary

Instructional materials are essential parts of instruction. In this chapter, we examined several aspects of instructional materials, beginning with uses for them, including motivation, socialization, recognition of the diversity of cultures, and meeting students' needs in conjunction with the stages of learning. We described how to select, analyze, adapt, and develop instructional materials.

When selecting materials, it is important to consider the characteristics and needs of students. In addition, instructional materials should be motivating, age appropriate, interesting, and appealing. They should relate to real life and to the cultural backgrounds and interests of students.

Commercial materials are not always appropriate for students with special needs because of problems with readability levels; vocabulary; concept load; sequencing; directions; opportunities for practice; repetition, review, and application; format; pace; and representation of cultural, gender, and age groups. Materials analysis forms and textbook analysis forms are useful for judging the suitability of materials and textbooks.

We discussed two options for teachers who find that materials are inappropriate for their students: adapting existing materials and developing materials. We described strategies for modifying printed materials, computer software, and materials for culturally and linguistically diverse populations. Those strategies include highlighting, color coding, simplifying, providing graphics, tape recording, supplementing, using advance organizers and postorganizers, using marginal gloss, providing outlines and study guides, using visuals, and providing glossaries.

Finally, we described ways to develop instructional materials such as worksheets, books, learning and tutoring packets, folders, games, self-correcting materials, and multilevel learning centers.

6

Communication and
Collaborative
Consultation

Key Topics

The field of special education is undergoing many changes. Attention has focused on redefining or restructuring the relationship between general and special education (Stainback & Stainback, 1985; Will, 1986). Increasing numbers of students with special needs are receiving services in regular classrooms. Therefore, communication and collaboration are becoming necessary tools (Idol, Paolucci-Whitcomb, & Nevin, 1986). Teachers of students with special needs are working less in isolation and more as members of the educational team. Your ability to communicate and collaborate with other members of the team (regular classroom teachers, administrators, paraprofessionals, other direct- and related-service providers, and parents) may have a significant impact on the quality of services you provide for your students.

Consultation-Based Programming

Teachers are exploring alternatives to traditional practices for providing educational services to students with special needs in the least restrictive environment. Many regular and special education professionals have indicated a need for alternative service delivery options for students with mild handicaps and for other students with special needs (Boyer, 1987; Friend, 1988). Clearly, alternatives must be explored in light of the students that teachers are being asked to serve. The Regular Education Initiative, a merger between regular and special education, has been suggested as a way to meet these needs. This merger "would create a shared responsibility for educational programming for all students, regardless of specific individual student characteristics" (Bauwens, Hourcade, & Friend, 1989, p. 17).

The movement toward the use of indirect services has potential for reducing many of the problems that exist in current practices (Graden, Casey, & Christenson, 1985). Indirect services, or consultative services, are services provided by special education teachers working with regular education teachers to meet the needs of exceptional students (Ysseldyke & Algozzine, 1990). Consultation-based programming is receiving support as an alternative service delivery option (Phillips & McCullough, 1990). Studies have shown that the use of consultation may contribute significantly to reducing the number of students referred for special education and may facilitate the sharing of the expertise of regular and special education professionals (Gable, Young, & Hendrickson, 1987). However, even with the current trend toward sharing responsibility, collaboration and consultation exist sporadically or not at all in most schools (Phillips & McCullough, 1990).

Evidence suggests that few special education teachers receive formal training in consultation (Idol-Maestas & Ritter, 1985; Lilly & Givens-Ogle, 1981). In fact, in a national survey of special education undergraduate and graduate programs, Gable, Young, and Hendrickson (1987) found that little emphasis was given to indirect teaching skills, namely consultation and collaboration. To participate fully as a special education professional and a member of an educational team, you should possess skills in collaborative consultation. We agree with West and Cannon's (1988) statement regarding collaborative consultation: "Preservice preparation of both regular and special education teacher trainees will provide for better transition to actual school situations in which the classroom and special education teachers share instructional responsibility for mainstreamed exceptional students" (p. 63).

School Consultation

Reviews of research in school settings have yielded positive effects on attitudes of consultants, consultees, and recipients, or clients (Sibley, 1986). Following are theoretical perspectives and models available for you to use.

Theoretical Perspectives

Conoley and Conoley (1988) discuss three theoretical perspectives that have influenced the development of school consultation models. These models are mental health consultation, behavioral consultation, and process consultation.

Mental Health Consultation. In the mental health orientation, consultants act as facilitators by guiding consultees in problem clarification. The focus is on establishing and maintaining a positive relationship between the consultant and consultee in order to change attitudes and improve learning or behavior. Caplan (1970), a psychiatrist, practiced what he called "one downsmanship," by seeking input from consultees, avoiding taking credit for ideas, and emphasizing equal status of consultees (Conoley & Conoley, 1988). Bear Bryant,

former football coach for Alabama, put it another way when he said:

> If anything goes wrong, I did it.
> If anything goes semi-good, then we did it.
> If anything goes real good, then you did it.
> That's all it takes to get people to win football games for you. (Bryant, 1984, p. 5)

As you work with classroom teachers, you may borrow some of the principles from mental health consultation by guiding teachers in the solving of their own problems. Consider this example. When Ms. Briggs (special education teacher) was approached by Mrs. D'Angelo (fifth grade teacher) with several concerns about Carlos, one of her students, Ms. Briggs listened. She soon led Mrs. D'Angelo to state that Carlos really had only *one* problem, not several. He never finished his work (problem clarification). Soon, Mrs. D'Angelo was offering several reasons for Carlos's problem with assignment completion and even mentioned a couple of things that she had done to aggravate the problem. After an exchange of ideas, Mrs. D'Angelo decided to use time cues and an assignment completion contract, to make a point of monitoring Carlos's progress, and to offer frequent praise and encouragement. Two weeks later, during the next fifth grade team meeting, Ms. Briggs enthusiastically told the group about Mrs. D'Angelo's efforts in bringing about a significant improvement in Carlos's performance.

Behavioral Consultation. The behavioral consultation orientation also employs a problem-solving approach (Bergan, 1977). The tasks are to define the problem, identify the environmental variables contributing to the problem, design strategies to solve the problem, implement these strategies, and evaluate the results. The behavioral consultation orientation emphasizes mutual problem solving by a consultant and consultee (Babcock & Pryzwansky, 1983). In school settings, behavioral consultants work with teachers to change their interactions with their students, with the ultimate goal of changing the behavior of the students.

You may incorporate behavioral consultation principles into your work with classroom teachers by keeping in mind that the key is mutual problem solving. For example, Jeff was a sixth grade student who attended a pull-out program for assistance in math. He was typically late arriving at the resource room and again late returning to his sixth grade class after math. Mrs. Pancheski, the resource teacher, and Mr. Franklin, the sixth grade teacher, decided that Jeff's tardiness was affecting his progress in both settings (defining the problem). They noted that Jeff had to walk from his sixth grade class on the second floor of the school building outside to the resource room, which was housed in a portable classroom (identifying environmental variables contributing to problem). Therefore, they decided to give Jeff the opportunity to earn points for promptness in reporting to both classes. The teachers made it part of his participation grade, along with coming prepared and actively participating. They also made sure that they let Jeff leave with adequate time to reach the other class (designing strategies to solve problem). After explaining the plan to Jeff, they tried it for 2 weeks (implementing the strategies). Jeff was on time for class 9 out of 10 days. Therefore, the two teachers agreed to continue using their plan and monitoring its effectiveness (evaluating the results).

Process Consultation. The process consultation orientation focuses on increasing the awareness of individuals about the dynamics in their environments and how those dynamics affect their work (Schein, 1969). This orientation helps teachers lead groups, give feedback, solve problems, make decisions, and communicate with other teachers and parents. According to Conoley and Conoley (1988), process consultants focus on improving the productivity and interactions of groups (e.g., teachers, students, multidisciplinary team members).

You will be able to use process consultation techniques when you participate in peer coaching. As a peer coach, you will learn effective ways to give feedback to colleagues, such as by saying, "I thought your questioning skills were super. You showed a good balance of low-level and high-level questions. How do *you* think your lesson went?"

As a member of a support team, you will learn how to act as a facilitator by saying things such as, "This looks like a great agenda for our next meeting. We have divided the time evenly between discussing successes and concerns. Hey, Barb, you haven't given me anything to include yet. What'll it be? . . . (pause) . . . That's a great suggestion. I know we all want to discuss that."

Consultation Models

There are two basic consultation models: expert and collaborative.

Expert Model. In the expert model, the relationship between the consultant and consultee is hierarchical, with the consultant in the role of the expert and the consultee in the role of the recipient of advice (Pryzwansky, 1974). We are reminded of a scene from "Marcus Welby, M.D.," in which Dr. Welby gives advice to one of his patients, Mrs. Gonzalez, about her son's behavior. In turn, she thanks him, pays her fee, and leaves. In expert model consultation, there is no attempt at generating solutions through mutually defined problems.

Collaborative Model. Collaborative consultation originates from a triadic model (Tharp, 1975; Tharp & Wetzel, 1969). The triadic model consists of three components: (a) the target (T), or student with a problem; (b) the mediator (M), or someone who has the ability to influence the student; and (c) the consultant (C), or someone with the knowledge and skills to work with the mediator. Idol, Paolucci-Whitcomb, and Nevin (1986) indicate that consultants and mediators may be regular education teachers, special education teachers, speech pathologists, paraprofessionals, principals, parents, or other members of the educational community. Correct use of the model results in collaborative solutions to carefully specified problems. Special education professionals refer to this as collaborative consultation. According to Idol, Paolucci-Whitcomb, and Nevin (1986):

> Collaborative consultation is an interactive process that enables people with diverse expertise to generate creative solutions to mutually defined problems. The outcome is enhanced, altered, and produces solutions that are different from those that the individual team members would produce independently. The major outcome of collaborative consultation is to provide comprehensive and effective programs for students with special needs within the most appropriate context, thereby enabling them to achieve maximum constructive interaction with their non-handicapped peers. (p. 1).

The purpose of collaborative consultation in special education is to facilitate the cooperative efforts of regular and special educators in developing specific interventions for students with learning and behavior problems (Pugach & Johnson, 1988). Consultation may be the only service provided by a special education professional or it may be one of many services (Idol, 1988). For example, Ms. Jones provides only indirect services at Charles Elementary School. Her entire day is spent working with regular classroom teachers who have students with special needs enrolled in their classes. At a middle school across town, Mr. Petrovski teaches students with special needs for four class periods and provides consultative assistance to teachers for two class periods.

Which model do you think teachers prefer—collaborative or expert? Right, teachers prefer

Important Points

1. Indirect services are provided by special education teachers working with regular education teachers and others to meet the needs of exceptional students.
2. Consultation-based programming is an indirect service that can be used as an alternative service delivery option for students with special needs and for other low-achieving students.
3. Consultation can contribute to reducing the number of students referred for special education and enhance the cooperative efforts of regular and special education teachers.
4. Three theoretical perspectives that have influenced the development of school consultation models are mental health consultation, behavioral consultation, and process consultation.
5. In mental health consultation, the consultant acts as a facilitator, guiding the consultee in problem clarification.
6. In behavioral consultation, the consultant and consultee define the problem, identify the environmental variables contributing to the problem, design strategies to solve the problem, implement the strategies, and evaluate the results.
7. Process consultation focuses on improving the productivity and interactions of groups by helping teachers lead groups, give feedback, solve problems, make decisions, and communicate with other teachers and with parents.
8. The two consultation models are expert, in which the relationship between consultant and consultee is hierarchical, and collaborative, in which the relationship is collegial.
9. Collaborative consultation is an interactive process in which people with diverse expertise work together to exchange ideas and generate solutions to mutually defined problems.

the collaborative model over the expert system (Pryzwansky & White, 1983), and studies indicate that a continuous, dynamic exchange of information is vital to effective consultation (Heron & Kimball, 1988).

■ ■ Activity

Ms. Sullivan discovers that several sixth graders who are mainstreamed in her class for English have poor or minimal skills using a dictionary. They need this skill for the work she is having them do in class. The rest of her students appear to have good dictionary skills. She has come to you (their resource teacher) for assistance. Ms. Sullivan says, "Most of my students are fine—no problem. I end up spending most of my time with the six who are having trouble. It's not fair to the others, but if I don't help those six, they'll never get anywhere. They may even start disrupting the class. What should I do?"

Look back at the discussion of behavioral consultation. Describe how you would work with this teacher. (*Hint:* You may want to work with a partner for this activity. Sometimes, it is helpful if you each role-play one of the parts. Remember to include the steps of behavioral consultation: define problem, identify the environmental variables contributing to problem, design strategies to solve problem, implement the strategies, and evaluate the results). (Answers for this and other activities are found in the Instructor's Manual.) ■ ■

Implementation of Collaborative Consultation

Consultation-based programming has been called the foundation on which alternative services are built (Curtis & Meyers, 1988). Collaborative consultation, a type of consultation-based programming, focuses on working together, exchanging ideas, and generating solutions to mutually defined problems. The intent is to facilitate the efforts of regular and special education teachers as they plan instruction for students with special needs. According to Bauwens,

Hourcade, and Friend (1989), "This approach holds great potential for enhanced educational integration of students of widely differing academic abilities, including those students eligible for special educational services" (p. 17).

Following are options for implementing collaborative consultation: teacher assistance teams, prereferral intervention, consulting teacher, and co-teacher (Chalfant, Pysh, & Moultrie, 1979; Graden, Casey, & Christenson, 1985; Haight, 1985; Hawisher & Calhoun, 1978; Idol-Maestas, 1983; Jenkins & Mayhall, 1976; Lilly & Givens-Ogle, 1981). To varying degrees, these options represent consultative assistance to regular classroom teachers who are responsible for students with special needs in the mainstream (Idol & West, 1987).

Teacher Assistance Teams

Teacher assistance teams (TATs) are support systems for teachers (Chalfant, Pysh, & Moultrie,1979). Such teams provide opportunities to brainstorm solutions to problems and exchange ideas, methods, and techniques for developing instructional alternatives to help students referred to the team (Hayek, 1987). The philosophy behind teacher assistance teams is that classroom teachers have the skills to teach students with learning and behavior problems by working together in a problem-solving, collaborative manner. Teacher assistance teams are composed of regular classroom teachers, and function to help these teachers resolve problems. See Figure 6.1 for TAT operating procedures.

Teacher Referrals. A teacher who is having difficulty with a student submits a referral to the team. The referring teacher describes the student's performance, strengths, and weaknesses; the interventions already attempted; and other pertinent information, such as health history or assessment results.

Reviews of Referrals. The team coordinator reviews the referral and asks the team members to read the referral prior to a team meeting so that the team members may devote the meeting time to actual problem solving (Chalfant & Pysh, 1981).

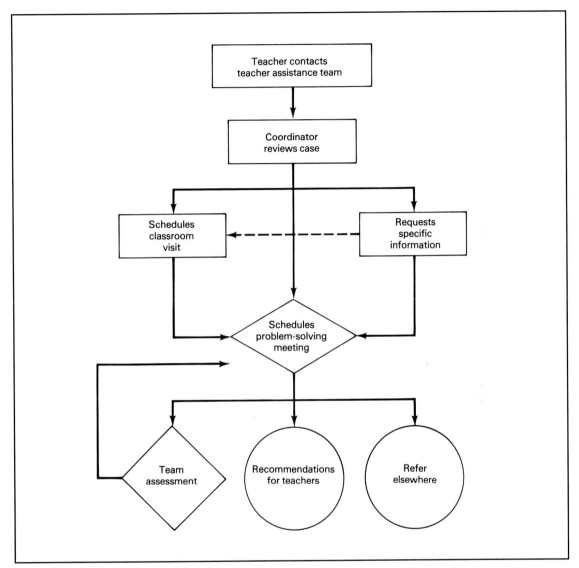

Figure 6.1
Teacher Assistance Teams

Note. From "Teacher Assistance Teams: A model for Within-Building Problem Solving" by J. C. Chalfant, M. U. Pysh, and R. Moultrie, 1979, *Learning Disability Quarterly, 2,* p. 91. Reprinted by permission.

Requests for Specific Information. The team coordinator may need to contact the referring teacher for clarification of information submitted or for additional information.

Classroom Visits. It may be helpful if one of the team members observes the student in the classroom. This team member may be able to collect additional, pertinent information through observation of the student and the environment.

Problem-Solving Meetings. The teacher assistance team meeting lasts for 30 minutes and includes the following steps recommended by Chalfant and Pysh (1981):

1. Reach a consensus about the nature of the problem.
2. Negotiate one or two objectives with the referring teacher. Be sure that the objectives are in terms of the behaviors the student should achieve.
3. Brainstorm alternatives.
4. Select the methods the referring teacher would like to try and define the methods.
5. Assign responsibility for carrying out the recommendations (who, what, when, where, why, how).
6. Establish a follow-up plan for continued support and evaluation.

Chalfant and Pysh indicate that training may be necessary for teachers to complete these steps in 30 minutes. With emphasis on communication and group dynamics, the process consultation orientation has merit for this situation.

Recommendations. The meeting should result in recommendations for the referring teacher to implement, recommendations for informal assessment for the teacher or a team member to complete, or referral for special help.

Prereferral Intervention

The prereferral intervention model is an indirect model of service delivery that focuses on providing intervention assistance at the point of initial referral (Graden, Casey, & Christenson, 1985). The aims are preventing inappropriate placements in special education and helping regular classroom teachers interact effectively with students who have special needs. It is an indirect service model because the students are helped through assistance provided to classroom teachers. Prereferral consultation does not employ the expert system. Rather, it provides assistance in a highly collaborative manner (Welch, Judge, Anderson, Bray, Child, & Franke, 1990). The emphases are instructional and behavioral interventions as opposed to testing and placement. The model was developed through the collabo-rative efforts of a school district and the Minnesota Institute for Research in Learning Disabilities. The prereferral system is composed of six stages, four in the prereferral process and two in the referral, assessment of eligibility process (Graden, Casey, & Christenson, 1985):

Stage 1: Referral for Consultation. The classroom teacher requests assistance from a consultant (e.g., school psychologist, social worker, special education teacher, counselor) or seeks assistance from a school-based problem-solving and screening team (e.g., school psychologist, other classroom teachers, special education teacher, principal, social worker, counselor).

Stage 2: Consultation. Similar to Bergan's (1977) behavioral consultation orientation, the consultant or team collaborates with the teacher to define the problem, explore intervention strategies, try them, and evaluate the outcomes. If the intervention attempts are successful, the process ends. If they are not, the process moves to a third stage.

Stage 3: Observation. During the observation stage, additional information is collected through observation of the student and the environment. Then, alternate intervention plans are implemented and evaluated. At this stage and the previous one, the participants must specify the roles and responsibilities of those implementing the plan. For example, the school psychologist may be responsible for observing the student, the classroom teacher may be responsible for collecting work samples and performing an error analysis, and the special education teacher may be responsible for adapting instructional materials.

Stage 4: Conference. At this stage, a conference is held with a child review team to communicate the results of interventions and make decisions. This team is composed of some of the school resource people mentioned in Stage 1 (school psychologist, regular classroom teachers, special education teachers, etc.). All information is reviewed and the team makes recommendations to continue the interventions, try alternative interventions, or refer the student for consideration for special education placement.

Stage 5: Formal Referral. At this stage, the student may be referred for a psychoeducational assessment. Information previously gathered and interventions tried during the previous stages can be vitally important. The team members may want to ask themselves what additional data are necessary to make a decision. They may want to reexamine student work samples, records of assignment completion, observations of classroom behavior and participation, screenings of academic skills, and modifications made in the classroom. Further assessment could include curriculum-based assessment, criterion-referenced testing, and additional observation measures.

Stage 6: Formal Program Meeting. A formal meeting of the child study team is held to review information from the first five stages. The team discusses alternative placements and services (direct or indirect), and writes IEP goals if appropriate.

The teacher assistance team and the prereferral model are two examples of problem solving through a team approach. The members of the teacher assistance team are regular classroom teachers, while the prereferral team members may be special education teachers, counselors, social workers, and other members of the school community. In both cases, the intent is to work collaboratively through formal, structured stages to solve problems and make decisions about students. These approaches tend to reduce the number of inappropriate referrals, provide support to students, and expand the instructional alternatives that teachers have at their disposal.

Cultural and Linguistic Diversity as Factors in the Prereferral Process

Ortiz and Garcia (1989) report that regular education teachers have difficulty distinguishing between Hispanic students whose learning problems can be addressed by modifying the regular program and those who may need to be referred for comprehensive evaluation. One reason is that the language and cultural characteristics may be interpreted as disabilities instead of differences. Heller, Holtzman, and Messick (1982) state, "The major issues related to the disproportionate placement of minority children in special education are the quality of instruction provided in the mainstream and the validity of referral and assessment processes" (p. 6). The prereferral process should, therefore, include considerations related to the education of multicultural populations. Ortiz and Garcia (1989) suggest a prereferral process (see Figure 6.2) that addresses the following questions during prereferral:

1. *Is the student experiencing academic difficulty?* It is hoped that the sources of problems will be identified through prereferral interventions and that attempts will be made to improve performance in the mainstream.

2. *Is the curriculum known to be effective for Hispanics?* Members of the prereferral team should investigate the success that other Hispanic students have experienced with the curriculum. If the fault is with the curriculum and not the student, then changes should be made in the instructional program.

3. *Is there evidence that the child did not learn what was taught?* Student performance should be assessed by observing the student in various settings, comparing the student's work to that of others, checking with other teachers and the parents, and collecting work samples. Work samples may be more representative of student performance than standardized tests, which may not be culturally or linguistically fair (Ortiz & Garcia, 1989).

4. *Is there evidence of systematic efforts to identify the source of difficulty and take corrective action?* At this stage, attention is directed to the teacher, student, curriculum, and factors related to instruction. In other words, teachers may have to change something they are doing, the student may lack background experiences (which would have to

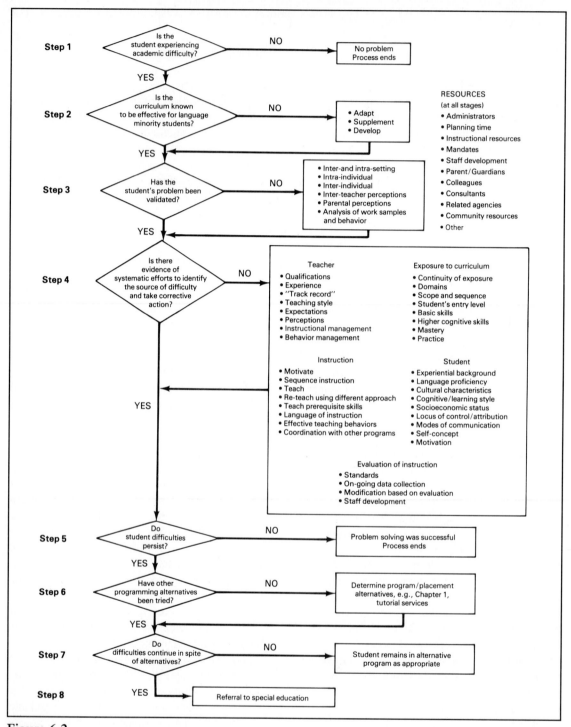

Figure 6.2
Prereferral System for Hispanic Students

Note. From "A Prereferral Process for Preventing Inappropriate Referrals of Hispanic Students to Special Education" by A. A. Ortiz and S. B. Garcia. In *Schools and the Culturally Diverse Exceptional Student: Promising Practices and Future Directions* (p. 9) edited by A. A. Ortiz and B. A. Ramirez, 1989, Reston, VA: Council for Exceptional Children. Reprinted by permission.

be taught), the curriculum scope and sequence may have to be modified, or specific teaching strategies may be required.

5. *Do the difficulties persist?* If the problems continue after interventions have been tried, then additional strategies should be investigated.
6. *Have other programming alternatives been tried?* Alternative programs such as bilingual education or migrant education should be tried before referral to special education (Garcia, 1984).
7. *Do difficulties continue in spite of the programming alternatives?* If all of the other possibilities have been exhausted and procedures have been systematically followed, then a referral to special education may be appropriate.

Although Ortiz and Garcia provide this pre-referral model to use with Hispanic students, it may be used effectively with members of other multicultural populations. We include it because a disproportionate number of racial and language minority students are assigned to special education classes, possibly due to problems with screening, referral, and assessment procedures (Benavides, 1989). Studies suggest that teachers may judge students on the basis of race, sex, socioeconomic characteristics, or linguistic differences as opposed to their abilities (Jackson & Cosca, 1974; Ysseldyke, Algozzine, Richey, & Graden, 1982). Therefore, it is important that you recognize and accommodate the cultural and linguistic characteristics of students during the prereferral process.

Consulting Teacher
Consulting teaching is "a process for providing special education services to students with special needs in which special education teachers, general education teachers, other school professionals, or parents collaborate to plan, implement, and evaluate instruction conducted in general classrooms for the purpose of preventing or ameliorating students' academic or social be-

havior problems" (Idol, 1986, p. 2). As a service delivery system, the pure consulting teacher model is one of indirect service to students (Idol, 1986; Lilly & Givens-Ogle, 1981). It is meant to be highly collaborative, with regular and special education teachers working as partners in planning instruction. Bergan (1977) suggests following four steps in consultation: problem identification, problem analysis, plan implementation, and plan evaluation. Following this sequence of steps allows special education and regular education teachers to utilize systematic procedures in working collaboratively, thus providing an excellent vehicle for consultation. Figure 6.3 contains an example of the type of form that may be used during consultation. Notice that the form is completed cooperatively by the special education and regular classroom teacher.

Although consulting teachers occasionally model a teaching technique with a class or small group, or team teach with the classroom teacher, the intent of the consulting teacher model is to provide regular classroom teachers with the skills necessary to instruct students who have special needs. In other words, the goal is not to relieve regular classroom teachers of the responsibility for instructing students who are mildly handicapped and other low-achieving students (Huefner, 1988). Idol (1988) feels that consultation should support, not supplant, regular education programs.

Consulting teachers must possess excellent listening, interpersonal, communication (verbal and nonverbal), problem-solving, and teaming skills. This role requires knowledge of large- and small-group instruction, familiarity with the regular curriculum, ability to adapt and modify materials and instruction, and expertise in helping others. For example, a high school teacher was concerned that the readability level of her history textbook was too high for many of her students and that by failing to represent the contributions of different cultural groups to the development of the United States, it did not present a balanced perspective. She got together with the consulting teacher and they secured and devel

Cooperative Planning Guide

Student's Name: Marcus Wyler
Date: 11/10

1. Define the problem:

Marcus doesn't pay attention in science class and this affects his performance on tests and projects.

2. Analyze the problem:

   a. List the factors in the environment which may be contributing to the problem

   • The pace is fast
   • The class is large
   • The class is primarily lecture

   b. List the behaviors of the student which may be contributing to the problem

   • He doesn't come to class prepared with pencil and paper
   • He doesn't watch when information is put on the board
   • He doesn't write anything down, so he probably doesn't study

   c. Discuss the student's strengths

   • He likes working with peers
   • He has excellent attendance
   • He learns well from visuals

3. Implement a plan:

   a. List and prioritize five recommendations

   • Award points for coming prepared (1)
   • Teach him to take notes (2)
   • Cue him when to write something down (3)
   • Present material on transparencies when possible (4)
   • At the end of class, review the key points of the presentation and let him compare his notes to a peer's (5)

   b. Go back and write the initials of the person responsible for implementing each recommendation next to that recommendation

Figure 6.3
Cooperative Planning Guide

4. Evaluate the plan:

For each recommendation
listed in 3(a), specify how it will
be monitored and evaluated

- Science teacher will keep a record of points earned (1)
- Special education teacher will check notes for technique and science teacher for content (2)
- Science teacher will keep track of the effectiveness of cueing (3)
- Science teacher and special education teacher will check notes for evidence of material presented on transparencies (4)
- Science teacher and special education teacher will check notes for key points (5)

Special education teacher: Judy Hernandez
Content teacher: Don Whitley

Comments:

Figure 6.3
Continued

oped materials to supplement the text. They used videotapes, books, and reference materials from the media center. Consulting teachers may also design curriculum units, participate in pre-referral systems, and co-teach with regular classroom teachers.

Co-Teacher
According to Bauwens, Hourcade, and Friend (1989), "Cooperative teaching (or co-teaching) refers to an educational approach in which general and special educators work in a coactive and coordinated fashion to jointly teach academically

and behaviorally heterogeneous groups of students in educationally integrated settings (i.e., general classrooms)" (p. 18). Co-teaching is a collaborative effort that takes place in the regular classroom. In co-teaching, cooperative planning and instructing are emphasized. Both the regular and special education teachers are present in the classroom and assume responsibility for instruction. Roles and responsibilities are determined on the basis of the strengths and skills of the teachers. Most regular education teachers are skilled in content and curriculum and in providing instruction to large groups, while most special education teachers are adept at analyzing and adapting materials and are knowledgeable in special teaching methodologies. By combining the skills of these two professionals in a cooperative arrangement, it may be possible to achieve successful reintegration of students with special needs into regular classrooms.

In our world of specialists, the contributions of regular education teachers may be overlooked. Pugach and Johnson (1989) relate how during an informal discussion presented by a collaborative team of two regular education teachers and one special education teacher, participants in the audience commented on what a wonderful opportunity the model gave the regular education teachers to learn from the special education teacher. At that point, the special education teacher asked, "Why doesn't anyone ask about all the things I have learned from them?" We hope that you will think about this as you work collaboratively with classroom teachers.

Figure 6.4 lists some of the tasks that special education teachers may perform as co-teachers to help students with special needs succeed in regular classrooms. Of course, both teachers should provide input into the appropriateness of these tasks for a given situation.

Cooperative teaching may be implemented through complementary instruction, team teaching, and supportive learning activities. At times, one or more of these approaches may occur simultaneously.

Lectures and Presentations

1. Provide visuals.
2. Prepare study guides and chapter outlines.
3. Use modeling and demonstration.
4. Prepare glossaries.
5. Teach note taking.

Textbooks and Other Printed Materials

1. Physically alter printed material.
   a. Insert stop points in text.
   b. Use marginal gloss.
   c. Highlight.
   d. Underline.
2. Tape-record printed material.
3. Have the students develop their own end-of-chapter questions.
4. Teach the use of mnemonic devices.
5. Show the students how to preview a textbook and chapter.

Interest and Motivation

1. Use story starters.
2. Alternate listening and doing activities.
3. Allow students to demonstrate knowledge in a variety of ways (e.g., writing, telling, making, working with a partner or group).
4. Provide written feedback.
5. Use calculators, games, word searches, puzzles, audiovisuals (videotapes, language master cards, slides, and filmstrips).
6. Develop learning centers.
7. Develop self-correcting materials.

Teacher Assistance

1. Cooperatively plan lessons and activities.
2. Help teachers locate and adapt materials.
3. Monitor student progress (academic and social).
4. Help grade assignments.

Figure 6.4
Possible Tasks of the Special Education Teacher in Cooperative Teaching

Complementary Instruction. Students in intermediate grades, middle school, and high school may have difficulty with some of the skills necessary for school success, such as organization, studying, test taking, report writing, use of reference materials, and note taking. In the complementary instruction approach to cooperative teaching, regular education teachers assume the responsibility for presenting specific content (e.g., science) while special education teachers instruct students in how to access that content by teaching strategies in listening, note taking, and test taking.

For example, Mrs. Latoya (a special education teacher) spent the first 12 minutes of science class instructing students in note taking. She had the students divide their papers into two columns. Next, she showed them how to write the science teacher's key words and points on the right side of the page during the teacher's presentation. Then, she showed them how to summarize the teacher's notes and jot down questions on the left side of the page after the presentation. While Mr. Peterson (a regular classroom teacher) presented some information on ecosystems, Mrs. Latoya took notes so that she would have a model to show the students later. Mr. Peterson stopped about 10 minutes before the end of class so that he and Mrs. Latoya could circulate and give feedback to the students about their note-taking content and technique. Then, Mrs. Latoya showed her notes to the class on the overhead projector. With this type of cooperative teaching, generalization may be facilitated, because students are presented with strategies to access content directly.

Team Teaching. In the team teaching approach, regular and special educators jointly plan and present content to all of the students. At times, one teacher takes the lead for some aspect of instruction, such as teaching the steps for a bill to become a law. At other times, the other teacher takes the responsibility for part of a lesson, such as instructing students in how to interpret the graphics in their social studies texts.

For example, Mr. Webster's sixth grade class was involved in writing as part of a schoolwide project during American Education Week. The intent was for all students to write something (e.g., short stories, magazine articles, newspaper

articles, fiction, and nonfiction). Several of the students in Mr. Webster's class had reading, writing, and spelling problems; therefore, he and the special education teacher, Mr. Milaki, had been co-teaching during language arts activities.

For the writing activity, Mr. Milaki and Mr. Webster planned collaboratively about how to work with these students. The two teachers decided that many students in the class would need support, encouragement, and assistance during the activity. They decided to set up assistance stations in Mr. Webster's classroom. One station contained pictures, cartoons, magazines, books, and articles designed to motivate students and give them ideas about what to write. Another station contained paper, pens, pencils, sketch pads, markers, dictionaries, thesauruses, English books, and posters with samples of stories from famous, well-known writers. A third station was set up like a book-binding center with paper, a paper cutter, scissors, rulers, and wallpaper samples to use as covers (from floral pastel prints to sports scenes to pictures of wildlife). There were two computers with software that the students could use to create graphics, borders, designs, and various prints. Finally, there was a station designed to be used to proof the final product and put it together. Mr. Webster and Mr. Milaki worked collaboratively during class time, each teacher taking charge of two of the stations. Each was responsible for directly teaching the skills needed at his particular stations. These teachers were truly co-teaching. They determined in advance who would be responsible for what, and they followed through.

Supportive Learning Activities. In this approach to cooperative teaching, both regular and special education teachers plan and present content. Regular education teachers present the essential content, while special education teachers are responsible for designing and implementing supplementary and supportive learning activities. Both teachers are present during instruction to monitor student performance.

For example, Ms. Parrish (regular classroom teacher at the high school level) presented a lesson on the different forms of government. She described the forms of government, provided examples, and discussed characteristics. She asked the students several questions to check their understanding of the material. After she finished her presentation, Ms. Ramirez (the special education teacher) organized the students into cooperative learning groups and asked them to describe how their history class would be run under a democracy, dictatorship, parliamentary government, etc. She also planned a trip to the media center later in the week to examine some supplementary materials on the topic. Through cooperative teaching, these teachers provided their students with the essential content as well as supplementary and supportive activities to reinforce, enrich, and supplement the content.

■ ■ Activity

Read the following two scenarios. Decide which one represents the collaborative consultation system and which one describes the expert system. Work with a partner to complete the collaborative consultation model scenario using the cooperative planning guide in Figure 6.3.

Scenario 1

Teacher: Say, I'm glad I caught you, Gina. I have five LD kids in my class, and they can't pass my tests in science.

Consultant: It's probably because they're having trouble reading the book or taking notes during class.

Teacher: Yeah, probably.

Consultant: I can tutor them just before the tests or help them with their notes when they come to my class. Or if you'd rather, you can give them an outline of your notes before you lecture. That's called an advance organizer.

Teacher: O.K. Thanks, I knew you'd know what to do.

Consultant: . . .

Scenario 2

Teacher: Bertha, thanks for stopping in. I have a problem I need help with.

Consultant: What seems to be the problem?

Teacher: The LD kids in my third period class can't seem to write a theme. Every time I assign one, they fail.

Consultant: What is it about the assignment that's giving them trouble?

Teacher: Well, they can't seem to write enough. Actually, they can't even write a variety of sentences. In fact, they don't always write complete sentences.

Consultant: I can see this is a real problem for you. Let me see if I understand the situation. They are having trouble writing themes because they don't know how to write a variety of sentences and sometimes their sentences aren't correct.

Teacher: Right. I thought maybe you could help me.

Consultant: . . .

Note: Remember to complete only the scenario that represents the collaborative consultation model. ■ ■

Comparison of Consultation-Based Programming Alternatives

Let's look even more closely at the four options for implementing collaborative consultation: teacher assistance teams, prereferral intervention, consulting teacher, and co-teacher. These four options may be examined by using the categories of (a) knowledge base, (b) goals, (c) stages or steps, and (d) responsibilities (Idol & West, 1987). Under the category of knowledge base, Idol and West specify two areas: (a) teaching/content skills and (b) communicative/interactive skills. All four options focus on teaching such skills as individualizing instruction, adapting material, and on managing behavior. Although communicative and interactive skills are evident in all four options, these different options for implementing collaborative consultation emphasize different skills. Problem solving is emphasized in prereferral intervention; adapting to change is stressed in prereferral, consulting teacher, and co-teaching; and negotiating and questioning are emphasized in teacher assistance teams, prereferral, and consulting teacher options. All four options appear to emphasize teaching/content skills over communicative/interactive skills.

Idol and West categorize goal responses of the service options into teacher change, student change, and system change. The goal of the consulting teacher and teacher assistance team is indirect service to classroom teachers (teacher change). The co-teacher alternative provides direct services to students and indirect services to teachers (teacher and student change). The prereferral option emphasizes teacher change, student change, and system change.

The teacher assistance team and prereferral options employ stages or steps, and the consulting and co-teacher service options identify roles and responsibilities. Finally, the responsibilities of the participants in these approaches include sharing decision making, exchanging ideas, planning and implementing instruction, and solving problems collaboratively.

Barriers to and Ingredients of Effective Consultation

Although consultation has many benefits as a service option, a number of barriers may interfere with its effectiveness (Haight, 1984; Idol, 1988). In this section, we discuss some of the barriers to consultation and provide suggestions for overcoming them.

1. *Problem:* Insufficient time and overwhelming caseloads (Evans, 1980; Idol-Maestas & Ritter, 1985). This problem is frequently cited by special education teachers who provide both direct and indirect services. Because of the demands of multiple roles and responsibilities, some of them state that consultation is just one more thing to do.

Solutions: In situations where cooperative teaching has been implemented, time has not been found to be a problem, perhaps because with more efficient communication, duplication of instruction to students with mild handicaps is minimized (Bauwens, Hourcade, & Friend, 1989). Furthermore, as teachers gain more experience with the roles of consulting teacher and co-teacher, responsibilities may become more evenly distributed. In addition, teachers who participate as members of collaborative consultation teams such as prereferral and teacher assistance teams may initially find the procedures time-consuming; however, with increased use, these structured procedures may expedite decisions about students. Finally, it appears that school administrators play an important part in easing the time and scheduling problems of teachers. Administrators may help alleviate the time problem by providing adequate planning and scheduling time for teachers and by assigning the same preparation periods to those who need them.

2. *Problem:* Lack of administrative support. This was found to be the major barrier to developing and implementing consultation efforts between regular classroom and special education teachers (Nelson & Stevens, 1981).

Solutions: School administrators have opportunities to create a climate in which collaborative consultation is valued. Their involvement in promoting consultation, controlling caseloads, providing adequate time for consultation, financing programs, facilitating teachers' efforts, breaking down barriers, and addressing implementation issues is crucial to the success of consultation-based programming.

Active involvement of teachers in planning and decision making helps increase collaboration (Rozenholtz, Basler, & Hoover-Dempsey, 1985) and ensures ownership (Duke, Showers, & Imber, 1980) and implementation (Fullan & Pomfret, 1977). Administrators may want to secure the participation of teachers from the initial planning stage through implementation and evaluation.

3. *Problem:* Poor teacher attitudes and resistance to consultation. Idol-Maestas and Ritter (1985) found negative attitudes toward mainstreaming exceptional children. Phillips and McCullough (1990) cited a lack of understanding between regular and special educators in regard to the other's role. In fact, regular and special education teachers may have very different priorities. According to Glatthorn (1990), "the special education teacher is more often concerned with one student and how learning might be individualized; the classroom teacher worries about the entire class and how overall achievement might be advanced. The special education teacher tends to be concerned with developing a wide range of learning and coping skills; the classroom teacher focuses on academic skills and content" (p. 307).

   Solutions: The options for implementing collaborative consultation, such as the consulting teacher and the co-teacher, may reverse negative attitudes, misunderstandings, and resistance. The combining of a professional who possesses knowledge in curriculum, content, and large-group instruction with a professional who is skilled in adapting instructional materials and implementing effective teaching strategies may enhance the progress of all students.

4. *Problem:* Lack of training. Few preservice special educators receive training in consultation (Idol-Maestas & Ritter, 1985; Lilly & Givens-Ogle, 1981) and similarly few preservice general educators are given formal preparation in school consultation (Pugach & Johnson, 1988).

   Solutions: Comprehensive training programs should be developed for preservice special education teachers, in-service spe-

cial education teachers, regular education teachers, and school administrators. For teachers, the training should include but not be limited to clarification of roles, consultation skills, and techniques for adapting to change (Idol, 1988). For administrators, training should include but not be limited to role and responsibility clarification, techniques for implementing change, awareness of barriers to implementation, and strategies for promoting and implementing school consultation (Idol, 1988).

   Studies involving adapting to change indicate that people move through specific stages. Hall and Hord (1984) report seven stages: (a) awareness ("I'm really not involved that much"), (b) informational ("Tell me more"), (c) personal ("What is my role going to be?"), (d) management ("How will I implement this?"), (e) consequence ("Let's see how this is going to impact . . ."), (f) collaboration ("By cooperating on this we can . . ."), and (g) refocusing ("This has worked well, but I have a suggestion for making it even better"). Teachers and administrators need training in consultation-based programming in adapting to change.

   Once consultation-based programming has been established, ongoing training and support to maintain it are essential. Effective support strategies include observation, practice, experimentation, feedback, formation of support teams, and peer coaching (Joyce & Showers, 1983).

5. *Problem:* Special education teachers may use a communication code not easily understood by regular classroom teachers (Stamm, 1980). Teachers of students with special needs may use acronyms such as LRE, IEP, FAPE, WRAT, ITP, CRT, and CBM, unaware that classroom teachers may not understand them. This may pose a major barrier to effective communication.

   Solution: Little (1982) suggests that teachers use a shared language to communicate

☐ Important Points

1. The following are options for implementing collaborative consultation: teacher assistance teams, prereferral intervention, consulting teacher, and co-teacher.
2. The Teacher Assistance Team is a support system for teachers that provides opportunities for brainstorming solutions to problems in order to develop alternatives for students referred to the team.
3. In prereferral intervention, a consultant or team collaborates with a teacher to define a problem, explore intervention strategies, try them out, and evaluate the outcomes.
4. The prereferral process should include considerations related to the education of multicultural populations.
5. Consulting teaching is conducted in regular classrooms and involves providing sup-

port services to teachers and students in order to prevent or ameliorate students' academic or social behavior problems.
6. Barriers to effective consultation include insufficient time and overwhelming caseloads, lack of administrative support, teacher attitudes and resistance to consultation, lack of training, and communication problems.
7. Ingredients of effective consultation include administrative support, teacher involvement in decision making, training in collaborative consultation, support teams, peer coaching, and use of a shared language with regular education teachers.

about students and school-related activities. This may help strengthen the bond that should exist among professionals who share responsibility for the same students.

■ ■ Activity

Examine the following statements made by regular education teachers about consultation and work in a group to brainstorm ways of responding to these concerns:

1. "I don't have time for all those meetings. I have too much to do."
2. "When will I plan with the special education teacher? She has planning during sixth period and I have it during fourth."
3. "I don't understand all those terms they use in special education."
4. "There's too much paperwork. How will I keep up?"
5. "How will these consultation procedures help my students?" ■ ■

Paraprofessionals in Special Education

Over the last few years, a substantial growth in the use of paraprofessionals in special education has had a positive impact on the delivery of services to students with handicaps (Harrington & Mitchelson, 1987; Pickett, 1988). Frith and Lindsey (1982) report a 42% increase in the use of special education paraprofessionals, or teaching assistants, since 1976. This phenomenal growth rate has been attributed to (a) the high marks that paraprofessionals have received in serving exceptional students (Frith, Lindsey, & Edwards, 1981; Guess, Smith, & Ensminger, 1977; Palmer, 1975), (b) the ability of paraprofessionals to work with a variety of exceptionalities in a variety of settings (Bayes & Neill, 1978; Frith & Lindsey, 1980), (c) the cost effectiveness of utilizing paraprofessionals (Frith & Lindsey, 1982), and (d) a change from the emphasis on performing clerical tasks to that of providing instructional support (Boomer, 1982; Evans & Evans, 1986).

Unfortunately, although paraprofessionals have a great deal to offer, their skills are not always accurately identified or utilized to enable them to contribute in a meaningful way (McKenzie & Houk, 1986). Training and supervision have been informal, haphazard, or nonexistent (Frith & Lindsey, 1982), and placement decisions have not always been made systematically. Therefore, it is necessary to examine ways to improve current practices and maximize the positive effects that these important members of the educational team can have on students.

Planning Paraprofessional Programs

There are several aspects to consider in order to best maximize the skills and talents of paraprofessionals in meeting the needs of teachers and students. We believe it is important to match the skills of paraprofessionals with the needs of teachers, to examine ways to utilize the skills of paraprofessionals in working with culturally and linguistically diverse populations, and to clearly define the role expectations and responsibilities of paraprofessionals.

Matching Skills with Needs

From time to time, you may overhear special education teachers discussing their needs, such as "I could really use some help making flash cards, self-correcting materials, and games for my students" or "I am trying to get my class checked out on their job application and job interview competencies, but it's impossible to do by myself." A paraprofessional should be placed with a teacher whose needs and expectations match the skills of the paraprofessional (Frank, Keith, & Steil, 1988; McKenzie & Houk, 1986).

McKenzie and Houk suggest the use of an inventory (see Figure 6.5) that is filled out by both the special education teacher and the paraprofessional. Teachers can use the inventory to identify the types of support they need, while

paraprofessionals can use it to indicate their skills and interests. In this way, a paraprofessional who is skilled at materials development may be assigned to a teacher who needs self-correcting materials and games, while someone with effective instructional skills and good rapport with students may be assigned to a teacher who needs someone to go over vocabulary with the students, monitor progress during practice activities, or help students review for tests. Special education teachers who are co-teaching with regular classroom teachers may want to enlist the assistance of a paraprofessional in preparing study guides, making transparencies, tape-recording portions of textbooks, and making supplementary activities, such as games, word searches, and crossword puzzles.

Utilizing Paraprofessionals with Culturally and Linguistically Diverse Populations

Teachers are expected to possess the knowledge, skills, and experience to be effective with an increasing number of students from diverse cultural, linguistic, and socioeconomic backgrounds (Ortiz & Garcia, 1989). It may be helpful to have a teaching assistant who can work effectively with culturally and linguistically diverse groups and can speak other languages in addition to English.

Paraprofessionals can and have assisted non-English-speaking students and students from culturally diverse backgrounds. One of the authors of this text set up a volunteer program that utilized volunteers to work individually and in small groups with students to teach them to speak English. Through one of the volunteers, the students were able to share some of their culture, language, and customs with their peers. What an asset to the classroom to have an assistant who could explain in two languages something about the diversity within cultures and who could create learning activities compatible with student characteristics!

Another way to involve assistants in ensuring that students from culturally and linguistically diverse backgrounds succeed is to have them de-

Name _____ Date _____

Directions: Listed below are a number of tasks which a paraprofessional may perform. If you are a paraprofessional, mark with a "P" those activities/duties which you feel you could conduct. If you are a teacher, mark with a "T" those areas in which you intend to use a paraprofessional.

Instructional Support

1. _____ Reinforce concepts already presented by the teacher, by assisting students in reading, math, spelling, articulation, vocabulary development, signing, mobility, and/or self-care.
2. _____ Listen to students read.
3. _____ Read to students.
4. _____ Supervise independent or small group work.
5. _____ Modify written materials, e.g., tape record stories, rewrite to lower level.
6. _____ Help students work on projects or assignments.
7. _____ Help students select library books.
8. _____ Assist physically disabled students, e.g., feeding, positioning.
9. _____ Help students explore careers and special interests.
10. _____ Practice vocabulary with non-English speaking students.
_____ Other. Please describe.

Behavior Management Support

11. _____ Provide and/or supervise earned reinforcement.
12. _____ Supervise time out.
13. _____ Be a resource for students who are experiencing stress.
14. _____ Monitor progress on contracts.
15. _____ Enhance students' self-concept by providing positive feedback.
_____ Other. Please describe.

Diagnostic Support

16. _____ Correct and grade assigned activities.
17. _____ Observe and record academic behavior and progress, e.g., math facts learned, vocabulary growth, reading rate.
18. _____ Observe and record social behavior(s).
19. _____ Administer informal assessments, e.g., unit tests and criterion-referenced measures.
_____ Other. Please describe.

Classroom Organization

20. _____ Make instructional games.
21. _____ Develop and manage learning centers.
22. _____ Prepare displays.
23. _____ Locate instructional materials.
24. _____ Assist in daily planning.
25. _____ Make bulletin boards.
_____ Other. Please describe.

Clerical Support

26. _____ Type.
27. _____ Duplicate materials.
28. _____ Take attendance.
29. _____ Record grades.
_____ Other. Please describe.

Figure 6.5

Inventory of Paraprofessional Skills and Teacher Needs

Note. From "Paraprofessionals in Special Education" (p. 249) by R. G. McKenzie and C. S. Houk, 1986, *Teaching Exceptional Children, 19* (4). Reprinted by permission.

velop multisensory teaching aids, such as language master cards, games, audiovisual aids, and learning centers in which material can be learned in a variety of ways. Assistants may also help you monitor diversified grouping patterns, such as cooperative learning and peer tutoring. These instructional arrangements allow more students to participate, regardless of their cultural and linguistic backgrounds.

Defining Role Expectations and Responsibilities

The lack of a clear job description appears to be one of the problems most commonly experienced by paraprofessionals. According to Frith and Mims (1985), "Paraprofessionals who possess a realistic perception of what is expected of them are more likely to perform admirably and to be more satisfied with their work" (p. 226). Teachers should clearly specify what the teaching assistant is expected to do within the areas of instructional support, behavior management support, diagnostic support, classroom organization, and clerical support. As you can see from Figure 6.5, a paraprofessional can accomplish many tasks in the special education setting and in the regular classroom. The key is careful communication of the tasks, roles, expectations, and responsibilities.

Carefully specifying role expectations and responsibilities may also help prevent the awkward situation of what to do if your teaching assistant tries to assume a supervisory role. Regularly scheduled conferences in which you and your assistant talk about student progress, clerical activities, development or modification of materials, and scheduling are ideal for reviewing and clarifying the assistant's assignments and responsibilities. Some teachers prepare a written schedule each day for their assistants in order to clarify roles and responsibilities. Praising and reinforcing your assistant for performing agreed-upon assignments is an effective way to ensure that these and not other assignments are carried out.

Does this sound like good communication? That is exactly what it is. We believe that the key

to working with paraprofessionals and other members of the educational team is good communication.

According to Frank, Keith, and Steil (1988), the specific competencies that your teaching assistant requires may differ from those of another teacher's assistant. With the increased emphasis on educating students with special needs in regular classrooms, special education teachers need to explore ways to involve paraprofessionals.

Implementing Paraprofessional Programs

Planning is the first step in organizing a paraprofessional program. In order to effectively implement the program, you should include orientation and training, scheduling, communication and feedback, and evaluation.

Orientation and Training

Lindsey (1983) suggests that paraprofessionals attend an initial meeting with other members of the school faculty and staff. Such a meeting should include the following activities: (a) introductions, (b) definition of the paraprofessional's role, (c) distribution of information about diagnostic and instructional techniques, (d) audiovisual presentations, (e) simulations, (f) and a question and answer session. An initial session may include discussions about confidentiality, rules, and school procedures. Then, a general orientation from a building-level administrator may occur, followed by specific training on the part of the teacher. The training session provides an excellent opportunity for the teacher to clarify roles and responsibilities. Training may involve anything from how to operate the copying machine to how to develop study guides for students in mainstream settings.

Training is necessary at the outset and then on an ongoing basis. Training may be provided by the teacher and in separate training workshops as needed. Separate training sessions may involve topics such as how to work with culturally diverse populations; how to implement the whole language approach, learning strategies, and cooperative learning; how to use effective questioning; or how to work effectively in mainstream settings. Lindsey suggests providing ongoing in-service activities to maintain the diagnostic, instructional, and interpersonal relationship competencies of the paraprofessional and recommends monthly staff meetings to provide support.

Once a teacher and paraprofessional clarify role expectations, they should decide on (a) the specific tasks the paraprofessional will complete (e.g., collecting data on students' knowledge of multiplication facts), (b) the skills necessary to accomplish the tasks (e.g., charting and graphing), and (c) any training or modeling of strategies that would help the paraprofessional complete the tasks (e.g., strategies for monitoring students' performance). For example, if a paraprofessional were going to help a teacher make data-based decisions about a student's learning by using precision teaching to monitor progress, he or she would need specific training or instruction in how to use it. McKenzie and Houk (1986) suggest developing a plan that specifies the skills a paraprofessional must have in order to accomplish the tasks assigned. The plan should indicate exactly how the paraprofessional will acquire the skills, such as through on-the-job training, through in-service workshops, or by reading information on the topic.

Scheduling

The tasks, or job descriptions, once identified, may be written up on a task sheet (Salvia & Hughes, 1990) or schedule (see Figure 6.6). Daily and weekly schedules are helpful in clarifying assignments and structuring the activities of an assistant. This is an important point. What is written down is more likely to be accomplished than what is just mentioned. You may have encountered this when you made a "to do" list in the morning compared with when you had some ideas in your mind of things you wanted to do that day. On which day did you accomplish more?

The responsibilities of a teaching assistant should change as the classroom needs change. For example, during the month of September, Ms. Hernando's students were preparing for a young author's conference to be held in October. Ms. Hernando's teaching assistant, Mrs. Talbot, helped students write stories, complete illustrations, type them in final form, and bind them in covers. During late October, Mrs. Talbot helped students prepare for their end-of-the-quarter exams. Her responsibilities changed because the needs of the students and classroom changed.

Communication and Feedback

Kahan (1981) suggests including time each day for you and your teaching assistant to meet. You may use this time to review the day, plan the next one, make modifications and adjustments, revise job responsibilities, and most importantly keep communicating. You should make a point of providing both positive and corrective feedback to your assistants.

For example, Mrs. Brizo provided positive feedback to her teaching assistant, Mrs. Grant, by praising her for the many multicultural activities she had developed to go with her learning center on famous American poets. She also reported this to her principal. You can imagine Mrs. Grant's surprise when the principal came into the classroom to congratulate her and to look at the learning center. On another occasion, when they were having a weekly planning session, Mrs. Brizo noticed that Mrs. Grant had left out some information on a chapter outline that she had been developing for some of the mainstreamed sixth graders. Mrs. Brizo showed Mrs. Grant a new technique to use in pulling the essential information out of a chapter. Mrs. Grant used the technique to rework the outline, and Mrs. Brizo praised her for her efforts.

Evaluation

Some teachers plan a brief conference in the morning before school begins and another brief meeting at the end of the day. Others plan a

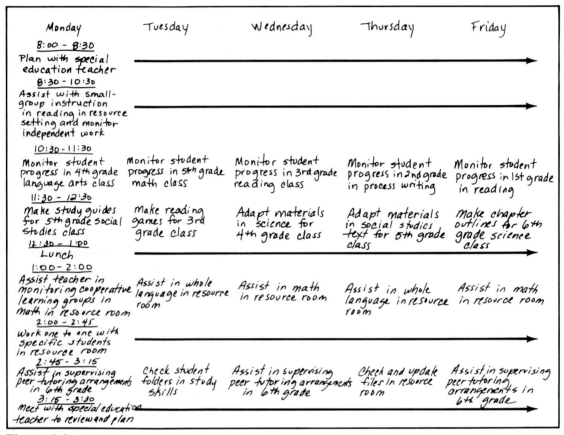

	Monday	Tuesday	Wednesday	Thursday	Friday
8:00 - 8:30	Plan with special education teacher	→			
8:30 - 10:30	Assist with small-group instruction in reading in resource setting and monitor independent work	→			
10:30 - 11:30	Monitor student progress in 4th grade language arts class	Monitor student progress in 5th grade math class	Monitor student progress in 3rd grade reading class	Monitor student progress in 2nd grade in process writing	Monitor student progress in 1st grade in reading
11:30 - 12:30	Make study guides for 5th grade social studies class	Make reading games for 3rd grade class	Adapt materials in science for 4th grade class	Adapt materials in social studies text for 5th grade class	Make chapter outlines for 6th grade science class
12:30 - 1:00	Lunch	→			
1:00 - 2:00	Assist teacher in monitoring cooperative learning groups in math in resource room	Assist in whole language in resource room	Assist in math in resource room	Assist in whole language in resource room	Assist in math in resource room
2:00 - 2:45	Work one to one with specific students in resource room	→			
2:45 - 3:15	Assist in supervising peer tutoring arrangements in 6th grade	Check student folders in study skills	Assist in supervising peer tutoring arrangements in 6th grade	Check and update files in resource room	Assist in supervising peer tutoring arrangements in 6th grade
3:15 - 3:30	Meet with special education teacher to review and plan	→			

Figure 6.6
Paraprofessional's Schedule

conference once each day in the morning to plan the day and then meet again the next morning to review the previous day and make adjustments, if necessary, as they devise a schedule for that day. Still others prefer to meet at the end of the day for planning and scheduling.

Evaluation is greatly facilitated when teachers and assistants schedule daily conferences. First, a teacher and assistant may evaluate the responsibilities of the paraprofessional to make sure that they are still an important use of the assistant's time. Second, a teacher may use the time to provide positive or corrective feedback to the assistant. The greater the specificity of the assistant's duties and the greater the structure in identify-

ing the tasks in writing, the easier it is to evaluate performance. If paraprofessionals are to provide services to students with special needs, then special education teachers must provide adequate training, schedule their time effectively, and give them ample feedback and recognition.

■ ■ Activity

Part 1. Suppose you are an elementary school teacher of students with special needs. Several of your students are mainstreamed for math and reading. Make a list of the ways you would utilize a paraprofessional to help these students in the mainstream setting. In addition,

Important Points

1. There has been substantial growth in the use of paraprofessionals in special education, and this growth has positively affected the delivery of services to students with special needs.
2. In planning paraprofessional programs, it is important to(a) match the skills of the paraprofessional with the needs of the teacher, (b) examine ways to utilize the

skills of paraprofessionals in working with culturally and linguistically diverse populations, and (c) clearly define role expectations and responsibilities.
3. Implementation of paraprofessional programs should include (a) orientation and training, (b) scheduling, (c) communication and feedback, and (d) evaluation.

---

list the ways you would utilize your assistant in a resource room with you.

Part 2. Suppose you are a teacher of secondary students with special needs. You work with your students in school in the morning and in the community by supervising them on the job in the afternoon. In what ways could you utilize a paraprofessional in these situations? ■ ■

Parents in Special Education

Public Law 94–142 (1975) mandated parent involvement in decision making and program implementation for children with disabilities. This role was not always the role that parents in special education played. Historically, parents were often totally excluded from participation in the education of their children. School districts assessed and placed children in special education settings without parental input or notification (Turnbull & Turnbull, 1986).

The roles of parents are also changing in society at large. Ever-increasing numbers of women are entering the work force. Single-parent families are prevalent due to such factors as escalating divorce rates, desertion, and the growing acceptance of single parents (Ascher, 1987; Peterson, 1987; Turnbull & Turnbull, 1986). Nearly half of African-American families are headed by females, while Hispanic and An-

glo households headed by women are rising (Ascher, 1987). Because of these life-style changes, parents are relying more and more on alternative caregivers, such as day care centers. Moreover, children and adolescents are being reared by foster parents, extended family members, or persons other than a biological parent (Peterson, 1987). With all of these factors affecting families, it is not an easy task for special educators to meet child, parent, family, and program needs. Flexible, individual, and alternative options are necessary.

Models of Parent Involvement

Beale and Beers (1982) propose three approaches to soliciting parent involvement in special education: parent education, parent volunteering, and parent communication. In the parent education approach, parents are directly taught specific skills or techniques effective for working with the child. The most common parent education programs teach parents ways to manage their children's behaviors and ways to teach their children academic skills. In the parent volunteer approach, parents, most noticeably mothers, provide direct services to the school by volunteering to be room mothers, to chaperone school dances, to supervise field trips, or to help in fund-raising. Many school districts organize parent volunteer groups to assist in the classroom. In the communication approach, parents are involved with their children's education informally and from a distance. Contact involves parent-teacher conferences, phone conversations, or communication via written notes. Of the three approaches, surveys show that parents of children with special needs prefer the communication approach whether they have preschoolers (Winton & Turnbull, 1981), young children (McKinney & Hocutt, 1982; Turnbull, Winton, Blacher, & Salkind, 1983), or adolescents (McCarney, 1986).

■ ■ Activity
Interview some parents and ask them to share their preferences for involvement with their child's special education program. Be certain to select a parent with a child in an elementary special education program and one with a child in a secondary program. Then, match their answers to those reported in the previously discussed studies. ■ ■

Communicating with Parents
To communicate effectively, you must be aware of some of the barriers to effective communication, the content of both nonverbal and verbal messages, and ways to communicate during a crisis confrontation.

Communication Barriers
Sonnenschein (1981) identified attitudes of professionals that interfere with communication. These include the beliefs that parents are helpless, that parents and professionals should not become overly friendly, that parents are responsible for the child's conditions, that parents' opinions are not worthwhile, and that parents are pushy or adversarial. Sonnenschein further asserts that these attitudes hinder the development of productive and rewarding communication.

A first step in communicating with parents is viewing parents as partners, showing trust and respect and having empathy for their problems. An attitude of respect and trust is particularly important when working with parents from various cultural groups (S. Chan, 1987; Johnson, 1987; Olion, 1989). Lack of respect from teachers and other school personnel is often mentioned by African-American parents as one of the reasons for their choice of infrequent involvement with their child's educational program (Marion, 1981).

Imagine what it would be like to have a child with you all day who is in constant motion, or one who has frequent temper tantrums, or to constantly worry how that child will function as a productive adult. The old Indian saying of "Oh, Great Spirit, grant that I may not criticize my neighbor until I have walked a mile in his moccasins" (author unknown) reminds us to consider the perspectives and experiences that parents bring to the communication process.

Nonverbal Skills
Eighty-five percent of communication is a type of primal, nonverbal communication (Crisis Prevention Institute, 1983). Nonverbal communication is essentially all communication other than the spoken or written word. It is an important component of communication, because when there is a discrepancy between a person's verbal and nonverbal message, people more often attend to the nonverbal message (Argyle, 1975; Mehrabian, 1969). If your friend says everything is fine, but has a scowl on his face, do you really want to ask if you can borrow his car? Nonverbal communication consists of proxemics, kinesics, and paraverbal components.

Proxemics. Proxemics refers to personal space, or the amount of distance you need in order to feel comfortable in your interactions with others. It is an imaginary circle that surrounds your body and is your comfort zone. When others cross it, you become uncomfortable. If you have ever worked with students who have behavior problems, you know that many problems develop because these students frequently do not respect the personal space of others. In fact, some teachers even take masking tape and tape personal spaces around each student's desk with the stipulation that other students can cross only with permission.

Culture influences a person's comfort zone. Many Asian-Americans require more personal space and are uncomfortable with physical closeness of a teacher, whereas people from the Hispanic culture frequently need less personal space (Briganti, 1989). Most Arabs and southern Europeans stand closer when they talk than do Indians, Pakistanis, northern Europeans, and African-Americans (Baxter, 1970; Watson, 1970).

The personal space you are comfortable with is also often influenced by the sex, age, race, and size of the other person. Do you stand closer to an unfamiliar female or male? Anxiety also plays a part in personal space. A person who is anxious usually requires more personal space. When communicating with parents during a conference, you may want to place the chairs so that there is room for the parents to move and adjust their comfort zone.

■ ■ Activity

Try a little experiment. Stand directly across from a friend. Looking at the friend, have her or him walk silently toward you. Hold your hand out and say, "Stop," when you begin to feel uncomfortable. Now reverse roles. Was your friend's personal space different from your own? Try the same experiment without the stop cue when you are out shopping or with people you do not know as well. Did your comfort boundary change or did it differ from theirs? ■ ■

Kinesics. Body language, such as postures and gestures, also conveys a message. Again, cultural effects are evident in this nonverbal communication. For some cultures, looking down, not at the teacher, is a sign of respect. Many Native Americans avoid eye contact (Simpson, 1982), as do many Asian-Americans, who are taught that avoiding direct eye contact conveys respect (S. Chan, 1987). Individuals from the Hispanic (Briganti, 1989) and the African-American cultures (Grossman, 1990) teach children to lower their heads and not maintain eye contact when they are being reprimanded. In fact, eye contact with authority figures is frequently a sign of disrespect in the African-American culture (Gilliam & Van Den Berg, 1980; Johnson, 1971). If you have ever read *The Naked Ape,* (Morris, 1967), you are aware that there is a body posture that might keep you from getting a speeding ticket.

It is a good idea when communicating with parents to maintain a supportive stance, which considers body positioning. A supportive stance requires physical positioning so you are not sitting or standing directly in front of a parent, but off to the side. Too many people connect a straightforward position with an authoritarian figure, which may decrease verbal communication (Crisis Prevention Institute, 1983). Instead of sitting or standing in front of parents, try sitting or standing to the side.

Paraverbal Communication. The tone, volume, and cadence of your voice are involved in paraverbal communication. Paraverbal communication is what your dog understands when it hops around when you say "Let's go for a walk," or hides when you say, "It's bath time." It's the type of communication that interfered with the first speech you ever had to give in front of a large unfamiliar audience—remember, the sweaty palms and the quaking voice. Suggestions for desirable nonverbal language communications with parents are found in Table 6.1.

Verbal Skills

The verbal skills of active listening, rephrasing, open-ended questioning, and summarizing are powerful during communication (FDLRS East, 1982; Roberds-Baxter, 1984; Turnbull & Turnbull, 1986). Coupled with nonverbal skills, they can lead to productive communication sessions.

Active Listening. Many teachers use active listening. In active listening, you communicate to parents that you are interested in what they have to say, will work to understand what they mean, and are comfortable with the feelings underlying

Table 6.1
Nonverbal Communication Skills

Desirable	Undesirable
Facial Expressions	
• Direct eye contact (except when culturally proscribed)	• Avoidance of eye contact
• Warmth and concern reflected in facial expression	• Eye level higher or lower than client's
• Eyes at same level as client's	• Staring or fixating on person or object
• Appropriately varied and animated facial expressions	• Lifting eyebrow critically
• Mouth relaxed; occasional smiles	• Nodding head excessively
	• Yawning
	• Frozen or rigid facial expressions
	• Inappropriate slight smile
	• Pursing or biting lips
Posture	
• Arms and hands moderately expressive; appropriate gestures	• Rigid body position; arms tightly folded
• Body leaning slightly forward; attentive but relaxed	• Body turned at an angle to client
	• Fidgeting with hands (including clipping nails or cleaning pipe)
	• Squirming or rocking in chair
	• Slouching or placing feet on desk
	• Hand or fingers over mouth
	• Pointing finger for emphasis
Voice	
• Clearly audible but not loud	• Mumbling or speaking inaudibly
• Warmth in tone of voice	• Monotonic voice
• Voice modulated to reflect nuances of feeling and emotional tone of client messages	• Halting speech
• Moderate speech tempo	• Frequent grammatical errors
	• Prolonged silences
	• Excessively animated speech
	• Slow, rapid, or staccato speech
	• Nervous laughter
	• Consistent clearing of throat
	• Speaking loudly
Physical Proximity	
• Three to five feet between chairs	• Excessive closeness or distance
	• Talking across desk or other barrier

Note. From *Direct Social Work Practice: Theory and Skills*, Third Edition by Dean H. Hepworth and Jo Ann Larsen. © 1990 by Wadsworth, Inc. Reprinted by permission of the publisher.

their message. You echo what parents say, including their emotions, and they can either confirm or correct your understanding. An example of active listening is:

Parent Message:	I just can't understand why Janet is the way she is!
Active Listening:	You sound very sad about Janet's disability.

Parent Response 1: No, I can handle her slowness. It's the distance she puts between us that hurts me.

Parent Response 2: Yeah, I really am down. I'm so tired of coping. (Roberds-Baxter, 1984, p. 58)

In parent response 1, the parent is correcting your perception that she or he cannot handle Janet's disability, while in parent response 2, the parent is agreeing with your interpretation. Active listening allows parents the freedom to express their feelings, to feel accepted, and to accept themselves (FDLRS, 1982).

Rephrasing. When you reframe, or rephrase, what a parent is saying, you are attempting to use your own words to restate the parent's message (FDLRS, 1982). Unlike active listening, in which you concentrate on both the affective and cognitive parts of the message, in rephrasing you concentrate on the meaning, or cognitive part. For example, look again at the parent's message of "I just can't understand why Janet is the way she is." The active listening response was "You sound very sad about Janet's disability." A possible rephrasing response is "You seem confused about Janet's disability." With this response, you are not attempting to describe the feeling (e.g., sadness), but the cognitive part of the message. Reframing changes the words to help parents hear what they are saying and perhaps approach their problems from a different perspective.

Open-Ended Questioning. Open-ended questions encourage parents to share information and participate more. The questions may be unstructured (e.g., "What do you think about Hector's program?") or structured, which limits the responses (e.g., "What have you found that works with Susan when she begins to cry?") (Turnbull & Turnbull, 1986). Furthermore, according to Hepworth and Larsen (1982), open-ended questions may take the form of a polite command (e.g., "Would you please tell me how

the notes are working with Jock?"), or an embedded question (e.g., "I'd like to know how the notes are working with Jock."). This doesn't mean that you should never ask a closed-ended question, such as "Do you feel Lashonda is making progress?" or "Does Lashonda frequently appear tired?" Such questions are useful for finding out factual information, but a preponderance of these questions limits discussion.

Summarizing. It is always best to summarize the communication interaction at the end of a conference or periodically. To summarize, simply restate what the parents said, highlighting the major points. Summarization helps to acknowledge that a topic has been exhausted and that the major points are understood.

■ ■ **Activity**

A parent has said that she is upset that you are allowing the other children to pick on her daughter. Write down two active listening statements and an open-ended question in response to this comment. ■ ■

Crisis Confrontations

Handling an upset parent is never easy, even for veteran teachers. If you know that communication with a particular parent has the opportunity of becoming quarrelsome, you may wish to practice what you plan to say with other people first and ask them for feedback (Roberds-Baxter, 1984). However, many times, this type of situation occurs without prior knowledge. How do you handle communication when you are surprised by an irate parent? The Crisis Intervention Institute (1983) for handling verbal aggressive behavior recommends the following procedures.

1. *Stay calm.* Trying to remain calm when a parent is shouting at you or maligning various parts of your anatomy is easier said than done. Normal reactions are usually twofold: to shout back or to escape.

Breathe deeply or think a pleasant thought before you engage in conversation.

2. *Isolate the parent.* Remove the parent from the public area. There is no need for others to be involved, and it is often difficult to change an attitude when others are observing. For example, you might say, "Ms. Herman, I'm sorry you're upset about Joe's quiz score. Let's go to my classroom, so I can find a copy of his paper and we can sit down and talk about the problem." Don't forget the nonverbal behaviors of a calm, steady, low voice and the supportive stance.

3. *Listen and be aware of nonverbal cues.* Remember the nonverbal postures specified in Table 6.1. Try to pick up on any nonverbal cues, such as relaxation of the shoulders to show that the parent is moving from an anxious stage and is ready to listen and discuss the problem rationally.

4. *After listening to the complaint, attempt to restate the parent's comment.* Restating what the parent said gives you time to think and possibly break the parent's pattern of irate communication. For example, "I can see that you are upset with Joe's grade because you feel the test was unfair and I'm picking on him." You may even agree with part of the criticism (e.g., "I know this was a difficult quiz").

5. *Question for specifics.* When you question for specifics, try to promote a rational reaction to the problem and show that you are willing to look at the problem from the parent's viewpoint. Open-ended, structured questions are often the best (e.g., "I have the test. Let's see what questions you feel were unfair."). Try never to be judgmental with comments like, "Oh, Ms. Herman, you are so wrong."

6. *Keep communication simple.* Refrain from long explanations until the parent has calmed down. An anxious person is usually not ready or willing to listen to others. Spend more time listening than talking.

⬜ Important Points

1. The three common approaches of involving parents in the home and school partnership are parent education, parent volunteering, and communication.

2. Thinking of parents with respect and having empathy for their problems removes some of the communication barriers.

3. Eighty-five percent of communication is nonverbal.

4. Nonverbal communication includes proxemics (personal space), kinesics (postures and gestures), and paraverbal components (tone, volume, and cadence).

5. Nonverbal behaviors such as proxemics are influenced by a person's culture (e.g., Hispanics require less personal space than Asian-Americans and African-Americans).

6. Effective verbal communication skills include active listening, rephrasing, open-ended questioning, and summarizing.

7. Active listening involves echoing the cognitive and affective components of a verbal message.

8. Rephrasing involves restating the cognitive component of a verbal message.

9. Open-ended questioning such as "How is sending the note home working with Jock?" tends to foster active interchanges.

10. Summarizing requires highlighting the major points of an interaction.

11. During a crisis confrontation, teachers should stay calm, isolate, listen, restate, question, keep the communication simple, view it as not personal, and be assertive.

7. *Try not to take the action personally.* Do not automatically assume that the parent dislikes you. People lose control for many reasons besides personal animosity, including displaced anger, loss of personal power, confusion, fear of the unknown, attention getting, or psychological or physical disorders (Crisis Prevention Institute, 1983). Think of the reasons people lose control and try not to take the comments personally.

8. *Be assertive.* This is a step we have added in training our students to deal with verbal aggression. If Ms. Herman continues to scream, attempt to reschedule the conference with an assertive comment, "Ms. Herman, I appreciate your concern and I would like to resolve the problem with you, but it is difficult to do when you are very upset. Let's reschedule for tomorrow morning" or "Ms. Herman, we don't seem to be able to resolve this. Sometimes, it helps to talk to another person. Would you like to come in tomorrow and we'll talk with the principal, Ms. Martinez, and maybe she can help us with our discussion."

Parent–Teacher Conferences

Effective communication skills should be practiced during parent conferences. Parent–teacher conferences generally involve the three steps of (a) planning for a conference, (b) conducting the conference, and (c) following through on the conference. We present a checklist identifying procedures for these three steps in Table 6.2.

Conference Planning

Since many parents feel that a parent–teacher conference signifies some sort of problem (Flake-Hobson & Swick, 1984), be specific about the purpose of the meeting in addition to specifying the date and time. You may notify parents of the parent–conference meeting by a note or by phone. A phone call provides an opportunity for the parents to ask questions and for you to check their understanding of the purpose of the meeting. You should try to schedule conferences when both parents can meet, such as on Saturdays or after 5:00 P.M. (Young, 1983).

Before the conference, review the student's folders, gather examples of work, and prepare materials, including a skeleton script of what you are planning to say. Scripting the content allows you to check your communication to determine whether or not it is free of educational jargon, to organize your thoughts, and in many cases, to listen carefully to the parents (because you have planned the important points you want to mention). A script also allows you to check with other teachers to obtain their input. In a co-teaching situation, it is essential that you meet with the regular education teacher ahead of time for his or her input. In fact, you may want to sit down together and complete the script.

Professional educational jargon often interferes with communication. If you must use educational jargon, define or give examples of the terms. For instance, if you use the term *short-term objective,* add a definition, "the small steps students must master to reach a goal," or an example, "Jason must be able to master the short-term objective of changing percents, such as 70%, to decimal numbers, such as 0.70, before he can figure out sales tax."

When scripting the content, include student strengths, your concerns, and possible solutions. Remember cultural implications of solutions. For example, in many cultures, such as the Asian-American (Chinn & Plata, 1987), Hispanic (Briganti, 1989), and Native American (J. L. Walker, 1988), child raising is shared by grandparents or others who live in the home. Therefore, consistency in helping youngsters with disabilities can be achieved only if whole families agree to participate in the intervention. Also, African-Americans often have kin networks in which a child with special needs may be given emotional support. Therefore, you would not recommend a formal community support system, but instead training for the extended family members to learn how to care for the child (Turnbull & Turnbull, 1986).

Table 6.2
Conference Checklist

Planning the Conference

_____ 1. Notify
- Purpose, place, time, length of time allotted

_____ 2. Prepare
- Review student's folder
- Gather examples of work
- Prepare materials

_____ 3. Secure co-teacher's input, if appropriate

_____ 4. Script important points you wish to make

_____ 5. Arrange environment
- Select site
- Choose comfortable seating
- Eliminate distractions

Conducting the Conference

_____ 1. Build rapport
- Welcome
- Introduce yourself and others
- Introduce role of all individuals at conference

_____ 2. Preview meeting
- Purpose
- Time limitations
- Note taking
- Emphasize importance of parents' input

_____ 3. Share information
- Use open-ended questions
- Use active listening/rephrasing
- Discuss strengths, concerns, and solutions
- Pause once in a while
- Look for nonverbal cues

_____ 4. Complete parent-conference form

_____ 5. Summarize information
- Review high points
- Schedule other meetings or follow-ups
- Thank them for taking the time to come and for their contributions

Following Up on the Conference

_____ 1. Review conference with student, if appropriate

_____ 2. Share information with other school personnel, if needed

_____ 3. Mark calendar for planned follow up

_____ 4. File parent–teacher form

Note. Adapted from the University of New Mexico/Albuquerque Public Schools Center for Parent Involvement, Albuquerque, 1979.

Another consideration in offering solutions is to recognize that some resources may not be available to the parents. For example, Johnson (1987) cautions that it is not appropriate to suggest that a child play with water at home, if water must be hauled to the home. For these reasons, it is important to secure parent input concerning solutions; the ones you write during the planning should never be etched in stone. A sample script appears in Table 6.3.

A final item in the planning step is selection of the environment for the conference. Try to use the classroom. You have immediate access to the files, plus the setting serves as a reminder of things the student said or did and that the purpose of the meeting is to discuss educational goals (Stephens, Blackhurst, & Magliocca, 1988).

Some schools encourage conducting parent–teacher conferences in the child's home. Home visits are frequently recommended when dealing with parents from diverse cultural backgrounds (Chinn & Plata, 1987; Johnson, 1987; Olion, 1989; J. Walker, 1988). Check district guidelines concerning home visits. You should probably have another professional, such as a social worker, accompany you. Also, remember that the parents may speak a language other than English. Olion (1989) suggests that schools contact local ministers to help transport African-American parents to schools. Frequently, transportation is listed as a major deterrent to the involvement of African-American parents in the education of their children with special needs (Patton & Braithwaite, 1984).

Table 6.3
Sample Script

Student's Name <u>Bill</u>
Grade <u>Ninth</u>

1. *Strengths* (Check vocabulary.)
   - Participates in discussions.
   - Makes insightful comments that often describe the point the author is trying to make.
   - Is a leader during cooperative learning groups. (Cooperative learning groups involve students of different ability working together on a project.) For example, Bill helps organize the other students by suggesting how they might all work together, asking such questions as, Who wants to draw the graph? and, Who wants to look up the information in the encyclopedia?
2. *Concerns* (Check jargon and specific examples.)
   - Bill is constantly late for his first period history class, which is resulting in a failing grade.
   - His regular class teacher and I kept a record of the number of times late the past 3 weeks—late 11 of 15 days an average of 20 minutes each day. On time about 1 day a week.
   - Bill says he oversleeps or he rides with a friend who oversleeps.
   (Ask parents if they have any idea why he is late?)
3. *Possible Solutions* (Initiate by asking parents if they have any solutions? If none, ask them to look at each of the following and see if they think any one would work.)
   - Bill rides the bus instead of riding with a friend.
   - Set up a home reinforcer system. At the end of the week the teacher will call the parent. If Bill is on time 3 out of 5 days, he can go to the football game or dance or out on Friday night. If not, he stays at home.
   - Bill and both teachers write out a contract. If Bill is on time 3 out of 5 days, he earns the negotiated reinforcer at school, such as leading a small-group discussion with materials provided by the teacher.

Spend time prior to the meeting relaxing. Roberds-Baxter (1984) recommends that you visualize yourself before the conference as being nondefensive, assertive, listening, and showing confidence.

■ ■ Activity

Examine the case study below and script the information using the script in Table 6.3 as an example. Include strengths, concerns, and possible solutions.

Rosa is having problems turning in homework. She keeps telling the regular teacher and you that her younger brother rips it or that she forgets it, but it is finished. At this time, her grade is a D due to her incompleted homework assignments. She is able to score Bs and Cs on the weekly quizzes. ■ ■

Conducting Conferences

Establishing rapport, previewing the conference, sharing information, and summarizing the information are ingredients for successful completion of a conference. We also recommend the completion of a conference form during the conference to serve as a written verification of the content. A completed form dealing with the problem of Bill's lateness is found in Table 6.4. The information beginning with solutions was completed with parent input during the conference.

Establishing Rapport. Begin the conference by introducing yourself and any other individuals and indicating their responsibilities. Be certain to address the parents respectfully. The names of Hispanic children often incorporate both father and mother's surname. In the name, Juan Perez Diaz, Perez is the father's name and Diaz is the mother's. Be certain you call the parents Mr. and Mrs. Perez, as the use of Diaz implies the child is illegitimate (Briganti, 1989). It is also disrespectful to address an Asian by the last name. For example, in the name, Hoang Hy

Vinh, Hoang is the surname, Hy is the middle name, and Vinh is the first name. Thus, this person should be addressed as Mr. Vinh (Banks, 1987).

If you are part of a co-teaching situation and the regular education teacher and you are both present, the person who contacted the parents first should take charge. If you are in charge, remember to ask opinions of your co-teachers as well as of the parents as you conduct the conference.

Previewing the Conference. At this time, state the purpose of the meeting, the time limitations, and emphasize to the parents their importance in providing input and solutions. If you plan to take notes, inform the parents and ask them if they would like a copy. Take the notes openly, so that they can see what you are writing (Turnbull & Turnbull, 1986). If you are going to complete a conference form similar to that in Table 6.4, show and explain the form at this time.

Sharing Information. In sharing information, remember to use open-ended questions, active listening, and rephrasing. Make every attempt to actively involve the parents. In many cultures, parents are passive receivers of information in school matters. For example, in the Asian culture, schooling is viewed as the unilateral responsibility of the school (Chinn & Plata, 1987). In the Hispanic culture, parental involvement in school matters is not expected or encouraged (Echevarria-Ratleff & Graf, 1988). The inclination to be a passive receiver of information is also often found in the Native American parent, whose culture promotes a reluctance to share information with authorities (Johnson, 1987).

Always start on a positive note, mentioning the strengths of the student. Next, move to concerns, using specific examples or work samples. You may want to ask parents if they see some of this similar behavior at home. Once your concerns are thoroughly discussed, move to possible solutions, asking for parent input. Throughout the conference, remember to listen

Table 6.4
Conference Form

Parent-Teacher Conference Form

Student's Name __Bill__   Grade __9th__

Date __Sept. 12, 1991__

Place __Milton High School__

Purpose: To discuss Bill's lateness to his first period history class, which is resulting in a failing grade. Tardy-11 out of 15 days the past 3 weeks. On time-4 out of 15 days, about once a week.

Possible Solutions:

Solutions	Evaluation
1. Parents talk with Bill	?
2. If late for more than 3 days during the week, he must ride the bus the entire week.	Negative, too long of a punishment.
3. If on time for 3 days a week father will take Bill out to drive the car on Saturday.	Positive, must do every week.
4. If on time for 3 days a week for 5 or 6 weeks, Bills father will take him to a professional football game.	Positive, 6 weeks time.

Solution Selected:
#4 because father feels Bill will work for football & wants him to take driving lessons at school. Teachers will make up chart for Bill to view progress.

Follow-Up Procedures:
Call parents weekly to tell of Bill's progress.

Signatures __L. J. Jacobs__ (parent/s)

__Ms. J. Gonzalas__ (teacher)

to the parents, refrain from interruptions, and give the parents many opportunities for input. Wait for the parents to respond before adding another point, because in some cultures, it is impolite to interrupt others. For example, in some Native American tribes, it is an unwritten rule that an individual waits for the speaker to finish talking before saying anything (Johnson, 1987).

Summarizing the Information. Before concluding the conference, review the high points, including the concerns and the solution agreed upon. Schedule any future meetings, phone calls, or follow-through plans. Be certain to thank the parents for their ideas and contributions, and offer to send them a copy of your notes or the conference form.

Follow-Through

If you are planning to review the conference with the student, you should mention this at the end of the parent conference and ask the parents for their permission or summarize what you plan to say. If you need to share the information with other professionals, remember that any written information that is shared with other school personnel must be revealed to parents upon request (Morgan & Jensen, 1988). Finally, be certain to file the conference form.

School–Home Communication Techniques

Since parents and families need individual interventions, educators need a variety of ways to communicate with parents besides conferencing. You may survey your parents to secure their input on the types of information they are interested in and ways they would like you to communicate information.

Software Programs

Minner, Prater, and Beane (1989) describe a software program to use with Apple computers. Titled *Parent Reporting,* the program generates brief statements to parents. Teachers may also generate their own statements about a specific student. For more information, contact Sam Minner, Ph.D.; Center for Excellence in Education, Northern Arizona University; Flagstaff, AZ 86011.

Notes and Newsletters

Notes and newsletters are common communication systems. You may send notes home on a regular basis, so that parents may continually monitor their child's progress, or for special occasions, to inform parents of an outstanding accomplishment or a problem. The notes may require the parents to sign and return them. (We present a sample home note for middle school in Figure 6.7.) No matter which type of note you select, remember to check the vocabulary and to determine if you need to write the note in a language other than English.

If you plan to use notes, you must schedule time to write them. In a transitional classroom, where the children were mainstreamed for 1 or 2 hours a day, Ms. Kaumeheluva organized the last 30 minutes of the day for student activities while she wrote notes. For the first 15 minutes, the students listened to a story that she had tape-recorded. For the last 15 minutes, they participated in free time. After finishing writing each note, she stapled it to the student's graded papers as part of the take-home packet that parents expected to see. Another teacher in a resource room incorporated notes into the language arts program every Friday. The children reviewed the week's activities as the teacher wrote the information on the board. Then, the students copied the information to take home to their parents. D'Alonzo (1983) suggests letting secondary students see any notes before you send the notes home to parents.

Kerr and Nelson (1989) indicate that parents are more willing to attend to notes if you let them know what to expect, when to expect it, and how to respond. For example, if you are planning to send notes home once a week, alert the parents so that they will watch for the notes. In addition, to make the system more motiva-

Date _____   Student _____
Teacher _____

(S = Satisfactory, U = Unsatisfactory)

Academic Behaviors

S	U	Completed all assignments in:
		Math
		English
		Learning Strategies
		Science
		Social Studies
		Was prepared for classes (pencil,paper, etc.)
		Completed homework

Social Behaviors

S	U	
		Followed directions
		Participated in class discussions
		Cooperated with peers
		Cooperated with teachers
		Followed school rules

Parent: I have read this note.   Yes   No
I would like a conference.   Yes   No
Comments _____
Signature _____

Figure 6.7
Home Note

tional for the students, you may recommend that the parents respond by praising or rewarding a child for a certain number of positive teacher statements.

Students may also participate in the written communication process between school and home. In co-teaching an eighth grade English class, a special education teacher and regular education teacher organized a newsletter writing activity to motivate the students. At the same time, the newsletter communicated with the par-ents. At the beginning of each month, the teachers assigned the students to cooperative groups to work on the various topics of the monthly newsletter. The topics usually included information about the objectives and activities completed in the English class, interviews about students' reactions to the activities, biographies of several students, horoscopes, quotations, and television reviews. The teachers also had their own article for any separate information that they wished to share.

Every Friday during English class, the students met in each group and worked on the newspaper assignment they had selected for that month. For example, the group assigned to write about the objectives and activities of the class summarized the week's events, while the group working on television reviews voted on the best and worst shows of the past week and wrote commentaries. During the last week of the month, two class periods were devoted to editing and publishing the newsletter. Both teachers were involved with either typing the information on the computer or facilitating the group interactions.

Home-Based Reinforcers

Another means of maintaining communication with parents is the use of home-based reinforcers (deBettencourt, 1987; Jensen, Sloane, & Young, 1988; Kerr & Nelson, 1989). Often, in home-based reinforcement systems, students earn points for specific behaviors at school and the parents supply the reinforcers. The reinforcers should be something other than the usual treats (see Table 6.5). Jensen, Sloane, and Young (1988) suggest that at the first parent–teacher conference or during open house, teachers ask parents to list two or three reinforcers, such as a trip to the ice cream parlor, that they are willing to do for or with their child.

One of the most unusual experiences we have heard of concerning a home-based reinforcement system was related by Dr. John Trifiletti during a personal conversation. He described how one of his students earned a bicycle piece by piece. The parents had bought the boy a bicycle for his forthcoming birthday when they and Dr. Trifiletti agreed instead to offer the bike as a reinforcer for the boy. Dr. Trifiletti prepared a poster that showed the parts of the bicycle, such as handlebars and tires, and how much each part was worth. The child then earned points for following the classroom rules and traded these points weekly for various bicycle parts. What was even more reinforcing to the child was that he and his father began to put the pieces together as he earned each piece.

Table 6.5
Possible Home Reinforcers

Preschool Children
Tangibles: Any food the child likes which is limited because of concern about nutrition or dental health
Small toys
Activity or coloring books
Activities: Television time
Playing music
Trips—to library, museum, zoo, toy store
Helping parents with housework
Games

Elementary School-Age Children
Tangibles: Food otherwise unavailable
Records, tapes
Toys
Comic books, magazines
Money
Activities: Television time
Late bedtime
Reading in bed
Renting a video tape
Playing Nintendo
Sleeping on the floor with a sleeping bag
Having a friend sleep over
Cooking

Adolescents
Tangibles: Money
Clothing
Records, tapes
Something expensive and possibly unattractive (to parents) done to hair, face, or body (e.g., frizzy perm)
Activities: Access to car keys
Late curfew
Getting a part-time job
Going to a rock concert
Staying at a friend's house
Hanging out at the mall
Going to a school dance or football/basketball game

Note. From *Applied Behavior Analysis for Teachers* (3rd ed.) (p. 432) by P. A. Alberto and A. C. Troutman, 1990, Columbus, OH: Merrill. Adapted by permission.

In addition to point systems, contracts may also be used in home-based reinforcement systems. A contract is a written statement of the agreement among the child, parent, and teacher. The student's, teacher's and parent's responsibilities are identified in the contract (see Figure 6.8). Here again, the child is responsible for displaying appropriate behavior and the parents for furnishing the reinforcer.

Telephone Answering Machines

Telephone answering machines provide time-efficient, systematic contacts for both parents and teachers. Bittle (1975) tried the following technique for a second grade class. The parents called a special number and listened to a recorded message played by an automatic answering device. The message from Bittle's study included a list of spelling words for practice and a request for nonacademic materials. The results were that the children's spelling performances improved and more parents complied with the teacher's request for various materials.

Chapman and Heward (1982) replicated Bittle's procedures with students in a learning disabilities setting and reported the same results.

Parents could call anytime from 5:00 P.M. until 7:00 A.M. Sunday through Thursday and hear messages similar to the following one:

> Good evening. The children worked very hard today. We are discussing transportation. They enjoyed talking about the airport and all the different kinds of airplanes. The spelling words for tomorrow are: *train, t-r-a-i-n; plane, p-l-a-n-e; truck, t-r-u-c-k; automobile, a-u-t-o-m-o-b-i-l-e;* and *ship, s-h-i-p.* Thank you for calling. (p. 80)

Minner, Beane, and Prater (1986) recommend that teachers record brief reports about the academic and social behaviors of individual students by assigning each student a code number. For example, "Student 1 completed all assignments during the school day. Student 2 spent too much time talking to other students." One teacher just decided to make only positive comments about each student. Olion (1989) recommends this type of system to increase involvement of African-American parents because such recorded messages are nonthreatening.

Date of Initiation of Contract _____
Date of Conclusion of Contract _____
I _____ (student) promise to arrive on time for history class 3 out of 5 days. On time means in my seat with paper and pencil ready as soon as the first bell rings.
I _____ (teacher) promise to remind Bill the first time he is late. I also promise to repeat the contract specifications at that time.
I or We _____ (parents) promise to take Bill to a football game if he arrives on time 3 out of 5 days for 1 month. Whenever this goal is met, tickets will be purchased for the next game.

Signed _____

_____

_____

Figure 6.8
Home Contract

Important Points

1. During a parent–teacher conference, a teacher should establish rapport; preview the meeting; share strengths, concerns, and possible solutions; and summarize the conference content.
2. Software programs, notes and newsletters, home-based reinforcers, and telephone answering machines are school–home communication techniques.
3. Teachers may use notes to help parents monitor the progress of their child and to inform them of special accomplishments.
4. Scheduling time to write notes and including notes as part of language arts activities are two ways to handle note writing.
5. In home-based reinforcement, the parents are responsible for providing reinforcers for the child's classroom behavior.
6. Telephone answering machines provide time-efficient contacts for both teachers and parents.

■ ■ Activity

Describe or design two school–home communication techniques, one appropriate for elementary students and the other for secondary students. Share the ideas with a neighbor.
■ ■

Summary

In this chapter, we discussed the changing expectations of special education professionals and the importance of communication and collaboration with other members of the educational team. We focused on indirect services, those provided by special education teachers working with regular education teachers and others to help them meet the needs of exceptional students. We described consultation-based programming as a service delivery option for students with special needs.

Three theoretical perspectives have influenced the development of school consultation models: (a) mental health consultation, in which the consultant guides the consultee in problem solving; (b) behavioral consultation, in which the problem is solved collaboratively; and (c) process consultation, in which the consultant focuses on improving group interactions. There are two consultation models: expert and collaborative. In the expert model, the relationship between consultant and consultee is hierarchical, while in the collaborative model, the relationship is collegial. Collaborative consultation is a process in which people with diverse expertise work together to exchange ideas and generate solutions to mutually defined problems.

Options for implementing collaborative consultation include teacher assistance teams, prereferral intervention, consulting teacher, and co-teacher. Teacher assistance teams provide opportunities for brainstorming solutions to problems. Prereferral intervention is a system in which a consultant or team collaborates with a teacher to define a problem, explore intervention alternatives, try them out, and evaluate the outcomes. The prereferral process should include considerations related to the education of multicultural populations. Consulting teaching is conducted in regular classrooms and involves providing support services to teachers and students to prevent or ameliorate academic or social behavior problems of students. Co-teaching involves regular and special education teachers working together to teach students in the regular classroom.

We described barriers to effective consultation, such as insufficient time and overwhelming caseloads, lack of administrative support, poor teacher attitudes and resistance to consultation, lack of training, and communication problems. We also described ingredients of effective consultation, such as administrative support, teacher involvement in decision making, comprehensive training in collaborative consultation and techniques for implementing change, formation of support teams, participation in peer coaching, and use of a shared language with regular education teachers.

Paraprofessionals and parents are important members of educational teams. We described matching the skills of paraprofessionals with the needs of teachers, utilizing paraprofessionals and volunteers in working with culturally and linguistically diverse populations, and defining role expectations and responsibilities. In addition, we discussed the implementation of paraprofessional programs through orientation and training, scheduling, communication and feedback, and evaluation.

Three ways of involving parents in the school–home partnership are parent education, parent volunteering, and communication. Parental involvement is beneficial, and parents prefer informal contacts with teachers.

An important aspect involved in working with parents is communication. Eighty-five percent of communication is nonverbal, including proxemics (personal space), kinesics (postures and gestures), and paraverbal components (tone, volume, and cadence). Nonverbal behaviors, such as proxemics, are influenced by a person's culture. Effective verbal communication skills include active listening, rephrasing, open-ended questioning, and summarizing. We also described the steps to follow in the event of a crisis confrontation with a parent: stay calm, isolate, listen, restate, question, keep the communication simple, view it as not personal, and be assertive.

Part II

Instructional Techniques

7

General Instructional Techniques

Key Topics

In Chapter 1, we referred to a general frame-work for making decisions about the teaching of students with special needs. Teachers make decisions everyday about techniques for presenting information, activities to use for practice, and types of feedback. Researchers have identified the variables of presentation, guided practice, feedback, and independent practice as necessary whether you are teaching explicit skills (Berliner, 1984; Brophy, 1979; Rosenshine, 1980; Rosenshine & Stevens, 1986) or implicit skills (Rosenshine, 1990). Remember, explicit skills are basic, well-structured skills that can be taught in a step-by-step manner, while implicit skills are higher order skills that do not follow step-by-step procedures (Rosenshine & Stevens, 1986). An example of an explicit skill is regrouping in addition. An example of an implicit skill is solving word problems. Teachers also make everyday decisions about instructional language, learning time, student downtime, motivation, and subject content.

Instructional Language

Providing clear, explicit instructions is a strategy related to positive academic achievement (Coker, Medley, & Soar, 1980; Fisher, Berliner, Filby, Marliave, Cahen, & Dishaw, 1980;

Rosenshine, 1983). Yet, many teachers have problems communicating with students who have special needs, especially with students from diverse language backgrounds (Wohlge, 1983). To give directions, you must gain the attention of the students, examine the syntax and semantic content of the message, give visual cues, rephrase instructions, use comprehension checks, and select appropriate vocabulary.

■ ■ Activity

This is a quick check of your instructional language. First, find a cooperative friend and sit your friend with his or her back to you. Now, describe the following figures to your friend and have him or her draw them:

To make the task even more realistic, do not allow your friend to ask questions (students with special needs tend not to ask questions to clarify misunderstanding) (Bryan, Donahue, & Pearl, 1981). How did you and your friend do? The chances are that you did not achieve 100% communication. ■ ■

A first step in giving directions or beginning instruction is to make certain that everyone is listening, but this is easier said than done. Sometimes, teachers are in such a hurry to teach a concept that they forget that John isn't going to learn it if he is asleep or is talking to Susie. A verbal cue such as "Listen" or "Look at me" followed by silence and then praise for the students who are attending can ensure that all are listening. "May I please have everyone's attention" followed by "Thank you" is appropriate for secondary students. This cue is particularly effective when stated while standing close to a nonattending student. Other effective cues are silently standing in front of the room until all are quiet at the secondary level and gesturing with one finger in front of the lips for silence at the elementary level.

Syntax and semantics are also considerations for instructional language. An active sentence, such as "The boy hit the ball" is easier to understand than a passive sentence, such as "The ball was hit by the boy" (Wiig & Semel, 1984). Passive sentences require more processing by children of all ages (Bryan, Donahue, & Pearl, 1981). Watson, Northcutt, and Rydele (1989) suggest avoiding idiomatic expressions, such as "busy as a bee," when instructing bilingual students. Simple sentences to control for semantic complexity are recommended for multicultural students, whose ability to understand instructional language lags behind their understanding of social language (Wohlge, 1983). Wiig and Semel (1984) suggest a sentence length of not more than eight to ten words.

Visual cues also help students understand instructional language. Simply writing the number 74 on the board clarifies the direction "Turn to page 74 in your math book." Writing the major points of a lecture on a transparency makes the lecture easier for secondary students to follow. Likewise, repeating a concept or direction in a different way often helps students comprehend instructional language. For example, it is much better to rephrase the direction "Locate all the adjectives and underline them in the ten sentences" to "Find the descriptive word, or adjective, in each of the sentences and then underline it" than to repeat either direction verbatim.

Comprehension checks are a necessity when working with students who have special needs. Specific questions are more effective than are general questions (Rosenshine & Stevens, 1986). "Are there any questions?" often results in silence, even though the students do not understand the task, whereas the question "Robert, what are you to do first?" clarifies whether Robert understands the task and lets you know whether or not you should repeat it. In addition, specific questions give students opportunities to listen to information again.

Vocabulary selection is another important consideration for instructional language. Wiig and Semel (1984) suggest the use of only five unfamiliar vocabulary words a lesson for language learning disabled. Marker words such as "remember," or "the first step is," or "this is important," and voice emphasis assist poor listeners (Alley & Deshler, 1979; Burns, 1980). Vague vocabulary not only prevents understanding of instructional language but also correlates negatively with achievement (Hiller, Fisher, & Kaess, 1969; Smith & Cotten, 1980; Smith & Land, 1980). Some of the most frequently used vague terms in secondary social studies classes and middle school math classes are, "some, many, of course, things, a little, might, few, actually, and much" (Florida Performance Measurement System, 1984, p. 151).

■■ Activity
Borrow your friend again and notice the improvement in your instructional language and your friend's performance as you describe these four figures:

■■

Learning Time

Academic learning time is the amount of time that students spend engaged in successful completion of relevant learning activities (Wilson,

1987). It is closely linked to achievement in elementary students (Fredrick & Walberg, 1980) and students with disabilities (Rieth & Frick, 1982; Sindelar, Smith, Harriman, Hale, & Wilson, 1986), including those from culturally diverse backgrounds (Gettinger & Fayne, 1982).

A stronger correlation of achievement than academic learning time (Greenwood, Delquadri, & Hall, 1984), academic responding time is the time that students spend making active, overt responses. Answering teacher questions and modeling the steps of a problem are active, overt responses, while listening and attending are not. Later in the chapter, we present ideas on ensuring active student responding during lesson presentation.

Students must be on task and achieving at a high accuracy level during academic learning time. Time on task varies, depending on the special education setting and the instructional techniques. Rich and Ross (1989) report that elementary students in resource room settings have higher levels of on-task behavior than do those in special classes and special schools. They also observed that students spent about 90% of the time on task during teacher instruction and only 60% during seatwork activities. Englert and Thomas (1982) found that presenting shorter and more frequent lessons per hour, using appropriate positioning and eye scanning to monitor the class, and reinforcing appropriate behavior facilitated student task involvement.

Another variable that affects time on task is off-task talk. Sometimes in answer to a question, students talk about a personal experience that is totally unrelated to the task. To redirect the student to the task at hand and to maintain the momentum or pace of the lesson, you may state that what the student has said does not have anything to do with the topic ("This doesn't relate to our topic. Remember, we are talking about electricity") or suggest that the topic should be talked about at a later time ("I know that's important, but let's talk about it later")—of course, you must remember to discuss the topic later.

For academic progress to occur, a student must not only attend to the task but also achieve an accuracy level of approximately 80% when answering questions or participating in teacher-led practice connected with presentation of new material (Christenson, Thurlow, & Ysseldyke, 1987; Englert, 1984; Wilson, 1987). Moreover, during independent practice and review, Christenson, Thurlow, and Ysseldyke (1987) recommend a success rate between 90% and 100%. Alternatives for what to do when waiting for assistance from the teacher or waiting for others to finish their work decrease the amount of time students spend engaged in nonacademic activities.

Student Downtime

Student downtime in class typically occurs as students wait for teacher assistance or for other students to finish assignments. Rich and Ross (1989) found that student downtime comprised a large part of the noninstructional time for students with special needs in all types of delivery systems. Frequently, a great deal of downtime can lead to inappropriate behavior, especially if students are sitting with nothing to do. Thus, you should provide alternative activities.

Sometimes, students just sit and wait for help because they do not know any alternatives. Listing alternatives, such as "go on to the next problem" and "ask for help from your assigned partner," helps students alleviate downtime (Olson, 1989). Other times, students may wait because they cannot continue to work and raise their hands at the same time. If this is the case, you may design a help sign for students to place on their desks so they can continue working. Alternately, you may have the students write their names on the board when they need help. For older students, you may use a deli format, having the students take a number for help. The students continue working and you write the number being served on the board (Olson, 1989).

When this student finishes his assignments early, he enjoys reading to the class rabbit.

Motivation

As a teacher, you will be faced with the challenge of motivating your students. Offering structured choices relative to curriculum content and procedures can be motivational (Adelman & Taylor, 1983). Even simple choices of whether to do the odd- or even-numbered problems and times to do various worksheets may motivate reluctant adolescents. You may schedule a variety of activities for student selection during independent practice. Moreover, you may offer a variety of ways for students to demonstrate their knowledge. One of the most popular responses in education is a paper-and-pencil response that requires students to answer questions on dittos, workbook pages, or at the end of a chapter (Rieth, Polsgrove, Okolo, Bahr, & Eckert, 1987). However, students can present their knowledge in other ways. In Table 7.1, we present a sample choice sheet designed for secondary students. The sheet lists different ways to exhibit content knowledge. A student or you may select the total number of tasks for completion. In Figure 7.1, a secondary student with learning disabilities demonstrates her knowledge of a chapter on the Civil War by developing a filmstrip (choice 2 on the sample choice sheet).

Motivation is further enhanced when learning is personally relevant (Good & Brophy, 1984). Explaining why the material is necessary to learn and applying objectives to real-life experiences are adaptations that teachers can easily make to motivate students (Adelman & Taylor, 1983). "We are studying about business letters because next week we will be writing to the embassies of various countries to ask for information" is an

In addition, you should plan activities to accommodate the work completion rates of your students. For students who finish assignments early during class, set up a free area or learning center with games or listening activities. Collect magazines such as *National Geographic, People, Seventeen,* and *Hot Rod* for students to read at their desks. Arrange an area in the room for quiet talk (especially appropriate for secondary students who enjoy peer interaction). Create a worksheet area where students can select papers to complete for extra credit. On 3-inch by 5-inch index cards, create enjoyable tasks, such as reading to the rabbit or calculating the area of the teacher's desk (Olson, 1989). Such activities are motivating and appropriate for students who finish tasks quickly and accurately.

Table 7.1
Sample Choice Sheet for Secondary Students

Name _____

Date _____

I will do _____ of these to show I understand the material found in Chapter _____ of _____ .

_____ 1. Take a test.

_____ 2. Design a filmstrip of the major points.

_____ 3. Write a summary and answer the questions at the end of the chapter.

_____ 4. Tape a summary and the answers to the questions at the end of the chapter.

_____ 5. Complete _____ worksheets.

_____ 6. Discuss the major points with two peers over a tape recorder.

_____ 7. Complete a notebook of major facts.

_____ 8. Your option as approved by the teacher _____ .

(The following numbers are required by all _____ .)

example of giving relevance to the study of business letters.

Making a commitment to learning and setting goals gives students a sense of participation in the learning process. One of the techniques used in the learning strategies curriculum model from the University of Kansas (Deshler & Schumaker, 1986) is to ask adolescents to make a commitment to learning a new strategy before you introduce it. Some teachers even write individual student contracts. Often, in these contracts, students set their own goals (Sprick, 1985). However, we have found that students frequently set unrealistic goals, such as "completing 100 prob-

lems in a minute" or "scoring 100% on all spelling tests," compared with performance standards. Therefore, it is helpful to share with the students the common performance standards (see Chapter 3) in order to instill realistic expectations of success. In Table 7.2, we present a sample contract for a secondary student.

Setting goals and making commitments actively involve students. Mercer and Mercer (1989) note in a discussion of motivation that one of the recurring themes that "permeates the literature on managing and motivating adolescent low achievers is involve the student" (p. 492). For example, while teaching a secondary basic science class, Ms. Moore motivated students with special needs by asking for student volunteers to lead the class in a discussion of science questions. Before the science discussion, she had written the questions on transparencies and the answers on a piece of notebook paper. Each volunteer took turns sitting on the teacher's high stool at the front of the class and acting as the teacher. The acting teacher read a question and called on a student to read the section of the textbook that contained the answer. The acting teacher then showed the transparency with the question printed on it, called on a different student for the answer, and wrote the answer on the transparency using the teacher's model. Some of the students led lively discussions and wrote their own answers, while others just followed the procedures.

Task-attraction and task-challenge behaviors motivate students to become involved in lesson presentations (Florida Performance Measurement System, 1984). Task attraction is teacher behavior that "expresses or shows genuine zest for a task" (p. 157). Challenges are statements that indicate "to the students that an exercise or activity will be hard to do" (p. 157). Enthusiastic statements like "This next activity is going to be fun" (task attraction) and "This is a very difficult concept" or "You'll need your thinking cap on for this one. Hope I don't fool you" (task challenge) are easy to incorporate into a lesson.

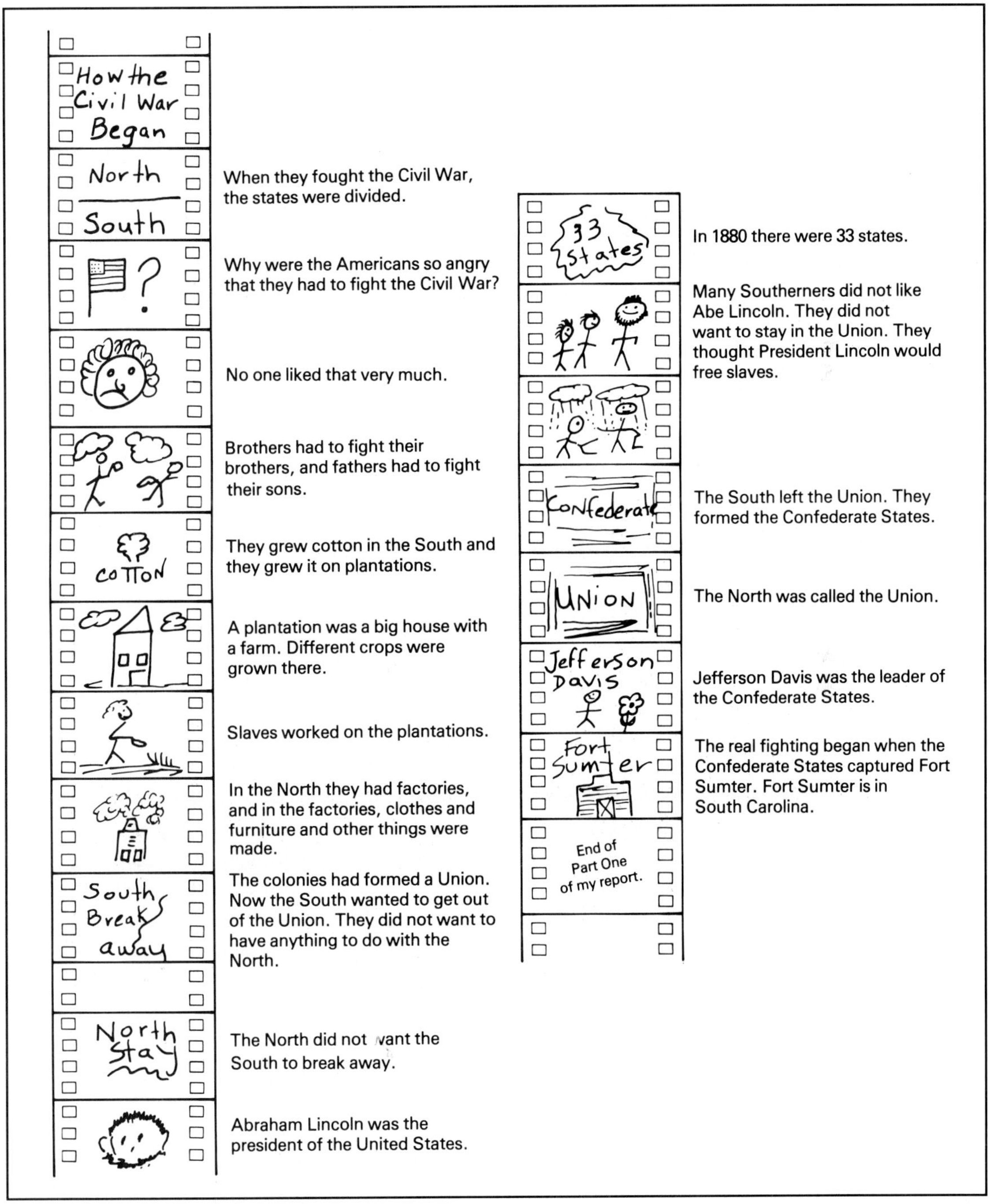
How the Civil War Began
North
South
When they fought the Civil War, the states were divided.
Why were the Americans so angry that they had to fight the Civil War?
No one liked that very much.
Brothers had to fight their brothers, and fathers had to fight their sons.
cotton
They grew cotton in the South and they grew it on plantations.
A plantation was a big house with a farm. Different crops were grown there.
Slaves worked on the plantations.
In the North they had factories, and in the factories, clothes and furniture and other things were made.
South Break away
The colonies had formed a Union. Now the South wanted to get out of the Union. They did not want to have anything to do with the North.
North Stay
The North did not want the South to break away.
Abraham Lincoln was the president of the United States.
33 States
In 1880 there were 33 states.
Many Southerners did not like Abe Lincoln. They did not want to stay in the Union. They thought President Lincoln would free slaves.
Confederate
The South left the Union. They formed the Confederate States.
Union
The North was called the Union.
Jefferson Davis
Jefferson Davis was the leader of the Confederate States.
Fort Sumter
The real fighting began when the Confederate States captured Fort Sumter. Fort Sumter is in South Carolina.
End of Part One of my report.

Figure 7.1
Student Choice Example

Table 7.2
Academic Contract

Math Contract

Objective I Will Be Working On:

> *I will learn to add, subtract, multiply, and divide like fractions and reduce the answers to the lowest terms.*

Materials & Techniques:

> *Participation in teacher-directed lessons during the weeks of November 1-29. Completion of all worksheets and assigned activities.*

Goal:

> *90% on at least ½ of the worksheets and activities.*
> *80%-90% on the exit exam.*

I have selected the goal and feel it is one I can achieve.

Signed ___*Jose H.*___
(Student)

The fooler game is a task-attraction activity to motivate elementary students to pay attention during lesson presentations. Demonstrated by Engelmann during a Distar reading program workshop (personal observation, Chicago, 1978), it involves a game playing the teacher against the class. First, write sounds, facts, words, or whatever on the board. Then, explain to the children that they will play a fooler game to practice a particular skill. Continue with, "In this game, I'm going to try to fool you. If I fool you, I get a point, but if I don't, the class gets a point. I'm going to write some letters on the board and tell you the sound. You have to tell me whether I'm right or wrong. Remember, I'm going to try to fool you, so I won't always say the correct sound. Let's see if I can fool you." Then, point to the letter *ii* and say, "This is *aa*. Right?" If children say no, reply, "What sound? Yes, a point for you." If the children answer incorrectly, reply, "No, it's *ii*. What sound?" and then, following

student repetition of the correct sound, say, "A point for me." Engelmann adapted components of this game into his Direct Instruction reading program.

Ms. Gaines plays a similar game during controlled practice of writing skills with her primary class of students with special needs. After teaching the correct printing of a letter, she writes the letter on the board, sometimes correctly and other times incorrectly, and asks each student to tell her whether the letter is correctly printed. If the student is correct, the class gets a point; if not, the teacher does.

A classroom reinforcement system may motivate students to reduce disruptive behaviors and increase academic efforts (Sprick, 1985). We discuss more about disruptive behaviors in Chapter 14; however, now, we want to share with you a lottery reinforcement system that is an adaptation of one recommended by Canter and Associates (1986) in a videotape presentation of various reinforcers appropriate for use with

Important Points

1. Teachers enhance instruction when they gain the attention of the students, examine the syntax and semantic content of the message, give visual cues, rephrase instructions, use comprehension checks, and select appropriate vocabulary.
2. Short, active sentences that do not contain idiomatic expressions are easier for students to understand.
3. Comprehension checks involve the asking of specific questions instead of general ones and require students to repeat the information.
4. Marker words and voice emphasis to stress important points help students comprehend instruction.
5. Academic learning time is the amount of time students spend engaged in successful completion of relevant learning activities.
6. Active academic responding time is the amount of time students spend making active, overt responses.
7. Time on task is influenced by setting (e.g., students in resource rooms spend more time on task than do those in special classes or schools), instructional strategies (e.g., students spend more time on task during teacher-directed presenta-

tions and less time during seatwork activities), and off-task talk.
8. For profitable academic learning time, students should maintain an accuracy level of 80% during lesson presentation and between 90% and 100% during independent practice.
9. Alternatives for what to do when waiting for assistance from the teacher or waiting for others to finish their work decrease the amount of time that students spend not engaged in academic activities.
10. Offering choices, making learning personally relevant, asking students to make commitments and to set goals, actively involving students, making task challenges and task-attraction comments, and implementing a reinforcement system motivate students to achieve academically and to display appropriate behaviors.
11. Task-attraction statements are statements that indicate teacher interest or zest for the task, such as "This next activity is going to be fun."
12. Task challenges are statements that indicate that a task may be hard to complete or understand, such as "This is a very difficult concept."

assertive discipline. Our student interns have used the adaptation effectively with both middle school and secondary students. In the lottery system, identify the behaviors that you wish to reinforce. Then, instead of giving points, give the students slips of paper when they display appropriate behaviors. Have the students write their names on the slips of paper and place them in a container. At the end of the week, draw two names. Have the two winners then draw cards to determine what they have won. Each card should have a number from 1 to 7, representing the number of the reinforcers

except for one card, which says the student wins all seven prizes.

In Table 7.3, we show a lottery system designed to increase the academic performance of a class of secondary students. The teacher uses both tangible reinforcers, such as NFL pencils, and privileges, such as homework passes.

Subject Content

Teacher effectiveness research has identified some common categories of subject matter and

Table 7.3
Lottery Motivation Example

You will earn chances for the room lottery held every Friday by:

- Returning homework on time.
- Bringing in paper and pencil.
- Participating in class.
- Scoring 80% or above on assignments.
- Turning in assignments.

The homework and paper-and-pencil tickets will be given out at the beginning of class. All other tickets will be given out at the end of class. Write your name on the tickets and drop them into the lottery container.

On Friday, two winners will be drawn. Being a winner entitles you to draw a card to determine which prize you have won. Each card has a number from 1 to 7, representing the numbers of the prizes. However, one card allows you to win all seven prizes.

concomitant teaching strategies. The academic subject matter found in classrooms typically falls into the categories of concepts, rules, laws, law-like principles, and value judgments (Florida Performance Measurement System, 1984). An example of a concept is "a verb is a word that indicates action or state of being." Concepts are found in all subjects and are best taught through the inclusion of a definition, examples, and non-examples (Engelmann & Carnine, 1982; Florida Performance Measurement System, 1984). You may include characteristics of the concept and comparisons with related concepts.

For example, to teach the concept of a verb, identify the definition (a verb is a word that in-dicates action or state of being) and some exam-ples (*run, jump, is, are*) and nonexamples (*girl, man, to, and*). You may also want to add char-acteristics, such as verbs often follow subjects in the English language. Then, proceed to contrast verbs with other parts of speech (a verb doesn't name a person, place, or thing, like a noun does). The sophistication of the examples and

nonexamples and the contrasts depend on the age and knowledge of the students.

Some basic concepts cannot be clarified through definitions but are usually described with examples, such as *red, under, back, smooth, over*, and *happy*. With these basic concepts, def-initions are impossible, so it is best to include concrete examples and nonexamples (Engle-mann & Carnine, 1982).

A rule is a prescribed guide for action. Rules often serve as the basis of content of language arts and mathematics. There are spelling, gram-mar, phonics, and math rules. Effective teachers identify the rules to teach and examples for stu-dent application (Florida Performance Measure-ment System, 1984). To teach a rule, first iden-tify it (e.g., Begin a sentence with a capital letter). Give examples (*the boy is my friend*) and nonexamples (*off the chair*) for student applica-tion. Englert (1984) found that effective student teachers of students with mild disabilities also required students to justify whether or not the rule applied.

Laws are principles that describe and explain the physical environment. "Electricity can pass through a closed circuit only" is a law that is often taught in a discussion of electricity. Laws form the content of the natural sciences. To teach a law, identify the law, explain the cause and the effect, and select experiments or prob-lems where students can apply the principle. Words such as *if* and *then, because, thus, therefore,* and *consequently* and phrases such as *in order to* relate the cause to the effect and increase under-standing (Florida Performance Measurement System, 1984).

For example, to teach the preceding law of circuitry, select linking words when describing the principle (If the circuit is closed, then elec-tricity can pass through) and outline the impor-tant points to discuss concerning the cause (closed circuitry) and the important points to discuss concerning the effect (the passage of electricity). Then, select a way for students to apply the law (an experiment—use wires and a battery cell to turn on a light bulb).

Lawlike principles are similar to laws, although they are usually used to explain human or animal behavior. They usually form the content of social studies, and in special education, social skills. Lawlike principles include the following: "If people have no support groups, then they often feel alienated." When teaching lawlike principles, be sure to identify the principle, the cause and the effect, and to use linking words.

Value judgments consist of statements about worth. Social skills and self-help skills are often based on value judgments. Value judgments require the development of criteria and then evaluation of whether or not the facts meet the criteria. For example, the statement "Pam's behavior was appropriate" is a value judgment. To determine whether or not Pam's behavior was appropriate, develop criteria: "Did Pam voice her request in a polite, calm voice? Did she remember to say 'please' "? Then, gather facts to answer the questions, such as "Pam smiled and said 'please' when she asked to borrow the pencil." Ask the students to decide whether or not the facts meet the criteria. In this case, smiling and saying "please" are appropriate behaviors based on the previously posed criteria.

In teaching your students to analyze social situations using value judgments, you may also design role-playing situations in which the students compare various behaviors to the specified acceptable criteria.

Structuring and Sequencing of Subject Content

Once you have identified the content for instruction, you must structure and sequence it. From a review of the effective teaching research, Berliner (1982) reports that presenting concepts in small steps is particularly successful when teaching young students, slow students, and students of all ages and abilities during the acquisition stage of learning. Englert (1984) found that effective special education teachers present a small

number of sequenced concepts in one lesson. In teaching the explicit skills of long division, effective teachers of low-achieving students in math taught the students the estimation step and had the students practice that step. Then, the teachers described the next step and followed it with practice. They taught the entire procedure one step at a time (Evertson, 1982).

To structure subject content in teaching implicit skills, begin with simple materials or tasks and then increase the complexity (Rosenshine, 1990). In the learning strategies curriculum, the students first practice the strategy with easier tasks or materials, and then they apply the strategy to grade-appropriate tasks or materials (Deshler & Schumaker, 1986).

In teaching implicit skills, effective teachers also use procedural facilitators and anticipation of students' errors in order to decrease material complexity (Rosenshine, 1990). Procedural facilitators are prompts to help students successfully complete a task (Scardamalia & Bereiter, 1985). For example, Short and Ryan (1984) improved fourth graders' note taking with narrative stories by teaching them to underline using the following questions as procedural facilitators: "Who is the main character? When and where does the story take place? What does the main character do? How does the story end? How does the main character feel?" Then, the students used the underlined material to help them write their notes.

In anticipating student errors, effective teachers attempt to decrease the material complexity. For example, in planning to teach reading comprehension, you should select the vocabulary that you feel may give the students problems and then discuss the words to prevent possible misunderstandings (Palincsar & Brown, 1989). At first, it may be difficult to anticipate mistakes, but with experience, you will begin to recognize which content in a lesson will prove particularly troublesome for students.

Teacher's manuals often assist in the selection, structuring, and sequencing of subject matter. Definitions, characteristics, examples, an instructional sequence, and objectives are frequently found in manuals. For example, the following teacher information is presented in the *Guide to Basic English Grammar* (B. Walker, 1988), the manual accompanying a text used to teach English to middle school students with special needs: "Remind students that the subject of a sentence is the person, place, or thing that is being talked about" (p. 37). This statement furnishes the definition of subject as used in the text. There is also a suggested sequence for instruction: "Discuss the meaning, pronunciation, and spelling of each vocabulary word. Remind students that the subject of a sentence is the person, place, or thing that is being talked about. Discuss the information and examples on pages 101 and 102. Have students complete the three Warm-Up exercises" (p. 20).

In some popular commercial curriculum programs used in the teaching of students with special needs, such as *Reading Mastery 1* (Engelmann & Bruner, 1988) and the learning strategies curriculum (Deshler & Schumaker, 1986), the subject matter is clearly specified and the lessons are scripted. In addition to teachers' manuals, students are also valuable sources of information. They bring in ideas and background information concerning the lesson.

■ ■ Activity

Part 1. Label each of the following statements as a concept, rule, law, lawlike principle, or value judgment:

1. A triangle is a figure with three sides and three angles.
2. Flossing your teeth is a good health habit.
3. When you round off a number, you should compare it to 5.
4. If water reaches 212 degrees Fahrenheit, then it will boil.

Now, select a concept, rule, law, lawlike principle, or value judgment and tell the type of information you plan to teach. For example, if you select a concept, identify the definition that you plan to teach the students and name some

---

☐ Important Points

1. Teachers must be able to identify the important content of a lesson when teaching concepts, rules, laws, lawlike principles, and value judgments.
2. Definitions, examples, and nonexamples are usually presented when teaching concepts.
3. Examples, nonexamples, and defense of whether or not a rule applies are necessary in teaching rules.
4. When teaching laws and lawlike principles, effective teachers state and discuss cause and effect and lead students in applications.
5. Criteria are necessary in the teaching of value judgments.

6. In teaching implicit skills, teachers should decrease the complexity of the materials by using procedural facilitators and anticipating possible student errors.
7. Procedural facilitators are prompts that help students when they begin to learn a skill.
8. Effective teachers anticipate the errors that the students will make on a task and then try to avoid the errors.
9. When students are first learning an explicit skill, effective teachers present a number of small, sequenced steps.
10. To structure content in teaching implicit skills, effective teachers begin with simple materials or tasks.

of the characteristics, examples, and nonexamples.

Part 2. Examine a lesson that teaches implicit skills, such as some of the learning strategies curriculum, and identify the procedural facilitators. For example, a procedural facilitator in the sentence writing strategy (Schumaker & Sheldon, 1985) is "SV" (subject, single verb or verb phrase), which cues students into one of the patterns of simple sentences. ■ ■

Lesson Presentation

Presentation is one of the essential variables described in research for teaching both explicit skills (Englert, 1983; Rosenshine & Stevens, 1986; Thurlow, Christenson, & Ysseldyke, 1987) and implicit skills (Palincsar & Brown, 1987, 1989; Rosenshine, 1990). Archer and Isaacson (1990) divide strategy lessons into three parts: opening, body, and closing. We borrow this terminology for our discussion.

Opening

To teach students, you must gain their attention. Sometimes, this is done by verbally cueing the students with "Look at me" for young students or "I need everyone's attention" for older ones. Sometimes, nonverbal cues, like silently waiting in front of the room or flicking the light switch, are used. Once you have everyone's attention, Rosenshine and Stevens (1986), in their summary of the teacher effectiveness research, suggest beginning a lesson with a short review of prerequisite skills or relevant prior information when teaching explicit skills.

Remember that prerequisite skills are the skills that students must bring with them to successfully complete a task. For example, a student must know how to regroup in addition (e.g., $150 + 75 = 225$, not 900) in order to successfully learn multiplication problems with multidigit factors (e.g., 75×12). Reviewing relevant information may include relating the lesson to existing knowledge, previewing the lesson, and providing an organizer or outline for the lesson (Rosenshine & Stevens, 1986). Relating the current lesson to previous lessons is also recommended when introducing a new skill to exceptional students (Cohen, 1986; Englert, 1984; L. Goodman, 1985). For example, a review of the definition of a paragraph from the previous lesson should precede a new lesson dealing with various kinds of paragraphs.

Following these guidelines, Ms. Holmes, a resource room teacher of students with special needs, spends the first 5 minutes of every math lesson reviewing information from the previous lesson. If calculating the perimeter of an object was discussed one day, she prepares a worksheet, a timing drill, or a group game reviewing the calculation of perimeter for the first 5 minutes of class the next day. A junior high teacher of students with special needs uses rapid-fire drills for review. The teacher says "rapid-fire drill" and asks the students to respond to a review question such as "Rapid-fire drill. Jim, what are the three branches of government?" "Rapid-fire drill. Sam, one half equals what percent?"

An overview or outline emphasizing the key points is an effective opening for the teaching of content lessons on the secondary level (Darch & Gersten, 1986). For example, as an overview of a chapter on France after World War I, Mr. Durkin listed such points as (a) the land was ruined because many battles were fought there and (b) as the victor, France claimed the coal of the Saar Valley.

An introduction that is especially effective for students with problem behaviors is sharing your expectations concerning the behavior rules of the lesson (Borg & Ascione, 1982; Emmer, Evertson, & Anderson, 1980; Englert, 1984; Evertson & Emmer, 1982; Rosenberg, 1986b). You should inform students if you expect them to raise their hands to answer a question and tell them about any other class rules that apply to a particular situation. This is particularly important at the beginning of the year and when new students enter a program. In addition, review reminds both the students and the teacher of the appropriate behaviors.

Some of these same strategies are frequently employed in the teaching of implicit skills. For example, Schumaker (1989) recommends that students be told the expectations regarding their involvement in a learning strategies lesson: "(a) watch the demonstration, (b) pay particular attention to what the teacher says and does, and (c) imitate what has been demonstrated" (p. 1). However, other suggestions for opening a lesson apply mostly to the teaching of implicit skills. These include sharing rationales (Archer & Isaacson, 1990; Palincsar & Brown, 1989; Schumaker & Sheldon, 1985), discussing situations where the skill may be used (Palincsar & Brown, 1989; Schumaker & Sheldon, 1985), noting results that students may expect (Schumaker & Sheldon, 1985), and activating background knowledge (Palincsar & Brown, 1989).

Sharing the objective of a lesson and trying to relate its importance to real life motivates readers who are reading 1 or more years below grade level (Duffy, Roehler, & Rackliff, 1986). Rationales such as "This lesson should help you read the back of a cereal box" influence the amount of information that low achievers remember from the lesson. Rationales that describe the benefits of using different learning strategies in school, for employment, and in general also motivate secondary students with mild disabilities (Lenz, Alley, & Schumaker, 1987).

Prediction activates background knowledge and purpose setting (Langer, 1984; Ogle, 1986). Prediction requires students to ask essentially two questions: (a) What do I need to know? and (b) How well do I already know it? (Orange County Curriculum Guide, 1986). In Figure 7.2, we present a form for using prediction as an introductory activity. Notice that in the first column, guided by the teacher, the students discuss what they already know after reading the title and looking at the pictures and captions. For example, in preparation for reading an article about Christa McAuliffe, the first teacher scheduled to make a shuttle flight, Ted said, after looking at the title "I know she was a teacher." The next column, "Think You Know," relates the students' perceptions to the topic. For example, Ted said "She likes children" as his perception is that teachers like children.

What Do You . . .			
Know You Know?	**Think You Know?**	**Think You'll Learn?**	**Know You Learned?**

Figure 7.2
Prediction Form

Note. From *Orange County Curriculum Guide* (p. 38), 1986, Orlando, FL: Orange County Public Schools. Reprinted by permission.

In the "Think You'll Learn" column, the students predict the author's purpose and orientation. In the preceding example, Ted might question whether the author plans to include information about Christa McAuliffe's early life or limit the discussion to the time just before the shuttle disaster. The last column, "Know You Learned," completed at the end of reading the content, requires students to compare their predictions to the events described. This type of activity is particularly effective for students from different cultural backgrounds. Research shows that activating background knowledge pertinent to the text helps learners with limited English proficiency (Hudson, 1982).

Ruiz (1989) describes a variation on the preceding prediction technique. For students from different cultural backgrounds, Ruiz suggests that the teacher identify the major idea of the text, ask the students to relate any of their similar experiences, and then ask the students to predict what will happen in the story for successful previewing.

■ ■ Activity

Part 1. For a group of elementary students with special needs, decide how you would open a lesson with the following objective: When presented with two-digit numbers and asked to round them off to the nearest 10, students will round off the numbers at a rate of at least 20 digits correct and no more than 2 digits incorrect per minute for three sessions.

Part 2. For a group of secondary students with special needs, decide how you would open a lesson with the following objective: When presented with a paragraph from the reading text, students will paraphrase the content with 100% accuracy. ■ ■

Body

Demonstrations, prompts, practice, and questioning to check for comprehension are recommended for teaching explicit skills (Christenson, Ysseldyke, & Thurlow, 1989; Good & Grouws, 1979; Rosenshine & Stevens, 1986). Modeling, prompting, checking for comprehension (Archer & Isaacson, 1990; Deshler & Schumaker, 1986: Palincsar & Brown, 1989), and anticipating student difficulties (Rosenshine, 1990) are frequently used in teaching implicit skills. Both areas employ questioning and student participation.

Modeling

Modeling, or demonstration, as part of teacher presentation is defined as a "teacher's active performance of a skill" (Haring & Eaton, 1978, p. 25). Teacher modeling is recommended when students are just acquiring a skill, during the acquisition stage. For explicit skills, teachers usually model the steps to a problem, while for implicit skills, they add think alouds. In think alouds, teachers model their thought processes (Rosenshine, 1990). Modeling is used in explicit and implicit skill teaching, but think alouds are particularly important in implicit teaching. Modeling is effective for all levels and ethnic groups of exceptional students (Cohen, 1986; Englert, 1984; Graham, 1985; Haring & Eaton, 1978; Leinhardt, Zigmond, & Cooley, 1981; Rivera & Smith, 1988).

An example of modeling correlated to the teaching of explicit skills is found in Mr. Clarke's oral introduction to long division: "The first step to work the problem 365 divided by 5 is to ask if 3 can be divided by 5. It cannot be, so 36 will have to be divided by 5. Thirty-six divided by 5 is about 7 because 7 times 5 is 35. The next step is to subtract 35 from 36, which is 1. One cannot be divided by 5, so bring down the 5, which makes the number 15. Fifteen divided by 5 is 3. The answer is 73." Of course, Mr. Clarke is drawing a visual model of each step of the problem on the board as he completes each step verbally.

In an examination of teacher communication with low-achieving readers, Duffy, Roehler, and Rackliff (1986) described a think aloud. We have modeled the following think aloud after theirs.

Mr. Clarke begins: "Today, I'd like to share with you a strategy I use when I come to a word that I don't know when I'm reading. I'll talk out loud so you can hear my thoughts." Mr. Clarke reads the first sentence: " 'The weatherman said there will be snow flurries.' I know I've heard the word *flurries* before, but I don't know what it means. The word before *flurries* is *snow,* so it has something to do with snow. Hmmm. It may mean it's going to snow a lot or it may mean it isn't going to snow much. How can I find out? I'll read on. The next sentence says, 'When the little boy heard the weather report, he became angry, because he wanted to build a snowman.' I think that can help me, because I know that you have to have a lot of snow to build a snowman. My brother and I used to make snowmen all the time. Now, I may know what the word means. I'll bet it means light snow. Let me go back and check, 'The weatherman said there will be snow flurries. When the little boy heard the weather report, he became angry, because he wanted to build a snowman.' Yep, I'm right."

In some implicit skills teaching, the steps to the procedures are also added to the think aloud in order to prompt the strategy use (Albion, 1980; Rosenshine, 1990). For example, returning to the preceding example, you would add the procedural facilitators of (a) read the unknown word in the sentence, (b) see if any other words in the sentence can help you figure out the unknown word, (c) use any background information you have to help you, (d) read more of the sentences, (e) repeat steps b and c, (f) substitute the new meaning, and (g) reread the sentences.

Now, Mr. Clarke incorporates these steps into the modeling: "I'd like to share with you a strategy that I use when I come to an unknown word when I'm reading. I'll think out loud so you can hear my thoughts. First, I read the unknown word in the sentence: 'The weatherman said

▢ Important Points

1. Research has identified the following for opening activities in lesson presentation when teaching explicit skills: gaining the learner's attention, reviewing prerequisite skills, reviewing prior relevant information, sharing expectations, and sharing goals and objectives.

2. Activities for reviewing prior relevant information include relating the lesson to what students have already learned, previewing the lesson, and providing organizers and outlines for the lesson.

3. An overview or outline emphasizing the key points is an effective opening in the teaching of content lessons on the secondary level.

4. An introduction that is especially effective for students with problem behaviors is sharing your expectations concerning behaviors.

5. Research has identified the following for opening activities in lesson presentation when teaching implicit skills: cuing attention, sharing expectations, sharing rationales, discussing where to use skills, noting results that students may expect, and activating background knowledge.

6. Introducing a lesson with prediction activates background knowledge and purpose setting.

7. In the teaching of implicit skills, teacher modeling involves think alouds, in which the teacher shares his or her thought processes and steps that help the students use the strategy.

8. In the teaching of explicit skills, teacher modeling usually involves orally presenting the steps to a problem.

there will be snow *flurries.*' I know I've heard the word *flurries* before, but I don't know what it means. Let's see, my next step is to look at the other words and see if they can help me. The word before *flurries* is *snow,* so it has something to do with snow. Hmmm. It may mean it's going to snow a lot or it may mean it isn't going to snow much." Mr. Clarke continues, incorporating the remaining supports into his think alouds. In an examination of teacher communication with low-achieving readers, Duffy, Roehler, and Rackliff (1986) report that the most effective teachers not only talk about their thoughts but also tell how to use context clues.

■ ■ **Activity**
Add the rest of the think aloud script to Mr. Clarke's think aloud concerning context clues.
■ ■

Questioning

Teachers use questioning during lesson presentation to elicit student involvement (Engelmann & Carnine, 1982), to foster cognitive learning (Florida Performance Measurement System, 1984), to reinforce concepts, to prompt (Alberto & Troutman, 1990), and to monitor and adjust instruction (Christenson, Ysseldyke, & Thurlow, 1989) when teaching either explicit or implicit skills. Other considerations in teacher questioning are nonacademic questions and wait time.

Involving Students. Even though teacher questioning can effectively involve all students, minority and low-achieving students are not given as many opportunities to respond in class as are other students (Reid, 1986; Stanley & Greenwood, 1983). Teachers advance the following reasons for not calling on low achievers: to protect the student from embarrassment, to prevent a slowdown of the lesson, and to assure that everyone will hear a good answer (Christenson, Thurlow, & Ysseldyke, 1987). To ensure that every student is given an opportunity to respond to questions, you should elicit unison

responses, call on students in a fixed order, or put each student's name on an index card, which you flip once the student is called on.

Fostering Cognitive Learning. A number of studies (Englert, 1984; Gall, Ward, Berliner, Chaen, Winne, Elashoff, & Stanton, 1978; Goodman, 1985) show that when teaching basic, or explicit, skills, it is best to use low-level, fast-paced questions that produce many correct responses and elicit much involvement of special students. High-level, slower-paced questions are generally required in the teaching of implicit skills.

Even if you are teaching a curriculum that emphasizes explicit skills, you should try to ask questions that demand high-level thought processes. For example, instead of giving directions such as "Put the materials in the box. It's time to clean up the room," to make the students think, you ask a question, such as "What do you have to do to make the room the way it was before we started?" (Bailis & Hunter, 1985).

Reinforcing and Repeating Information. Questioning may also be used to reinforce and repeat information (Engelmann & Carnine, 1982). You may ask any number of questions to reinforce the fact that three fourths of the earth is covered with water, such as, "How much of the earth is covered with water? Three fourths of the earth is covered with what?" Thus, with these questions, students have an opportunity to hear the fact two more times in varied formats.

Prompting. Questions also serve as prompts to help students arrive at the correct answer. In prompting, teachers sometimes increase assistance until the student is able to respond correctly (Alberto & Troutman, 1990). For example, if you receive no response or an incorrect one after asking the question, "How do we change *lady* to *ladies?*" you should proceed with a more intrusive verbal prompt: "What is the rule?" (to remind the student that there is a rule). If necessary, you should continue with, "What do we do when a word ends in *y* to make it plural?" (to give the student a part of the rule). A fault of many teachers during this process is impatience as they give more clues (Alberto & Troutman, 1990).

Monitoring and Adjusting Instruction. Specific questions, such as, "What is the next step in the operation, Bob?" or, "What kind of punctuation marks do you use at the end of a sentence?" serve as checks of comprehension and enable you to monitor and adjust instruction. The answers to specific questions will inform you if you should reteach concepts or skills or if you should change the content of the lesson. If the students cannot answer the questions, you should reteach the concept instead of continuing with a new one. Rosenshine and Stevens (1986) identify three frequent errors teachers make in monitoring for understanding: (a) asking a general question (e.g., Do you understand?) and then assuming that everyone understands if there are no questions; (b) calling only on a volunteer, who usually knows the answers, and then assuming that other students know from hearing the volunteer's answer; and (c) asking only a few questions.

Nonacademic Questioning. Nonacademic questions frequently disrupt the flow of a lesson (Florida Performance Measurement System, 1984) and may lead to noncompliant behavior. Remember, an academic focus increases academic learning time, which results in higher achievement for students with special needs. For example, during her experience in a primary setting with students with special needs, a student teacher asked a 7-year-old student, "Joey, will you read the next two paragraphs?" To which he replied, "No, let Jamey do it." Now, the student teacher was faced with another problem. This type of response to a nonacademic question is not unusual for noncompliant students. A nicely stated command, "Please read the next two paragraphs, Joey" is a better way to proceed.

Wait Time. There are two types of wait time connected with questioning. One involves the amount of time a teacher waits for a student's response after asking a question. The other concerns the amount of time a teacher waits after a student's response to ask another question.

Rowe (1974) investigated both types of wait time in elementary science classes and found that teachers waited an average of 1 second for a student's response after asking a question and 0.9 seconds after a student's response. When teachers increased the amount of wait time, students responded with longer answers, volunteered answers more frequently, and even initiated more questions. In a review of wait time research, Tobin (1987) stated that a 3- to 5-second wait time enhanced achievement in all content areas with all levels of students, kindergarten through twelfth grade. Wait time is also important for bilingual students, who have language processing difficulties (Watson, Northcutt, & Rydele, 1989).

This discussion of wait time may seem contradictory to the instructional procedure of asking many questions that require quick, short student responses when teaching explicit skills. It certainly is not appropriate for a teacher to wait 5 seconds when asking a child what sound a short *a* makes. Tobin (1987) suggests that the amount of wait time is a function of the type of question. He contends that low-level cognitive questions require less wait time and high-level questions require more. This is a logical explanation of the difference between the results of the wait-time research, which shows achievement enhanced by a 3- to 5-second pause after questioning, and the teacher effectiveness research, which shows that a brisk pace of teacher questioning and a high frequency of accurate student responses for teaching explicit skills is effective.

■ ■ Activity

Part 1. Change the following ineffective questioning techniques to effective ones:

1. A secondary teacher asked, "Sarah, why is this an example of a narrative paragraph? What is the relevant cue?"
2. A secondary teacher asked, "Why do we hear a long sound in that word?" (No response.) The teacher continued, "Because it has a silent *e* at the end."

Part 2. Identify some questions to initiate thinking for the following situations:

1. One student is distracting another.
2. One student is whining.
3. Peg says she can't work the problem.

■ ■

Participation

Active student involvement is essential in teaching both explicit skills (Christenson, Ysseldyke, & Thurlow, 1989) and implicit skills (Schumaker, Nolan, & Deshler, 1985). Actively involving low achievers not only increased academic gains but also reduced absenteeism and discipline referrals in the teacher expectations and student achievement (TESA) project (Kerman, 1982). Remember, active academic responding time, with students making many active, overt responses, relates positively to student achievement. The three-statement rule (The teacher will make no more than three statements without having a student make a response) (Schumaker, Nolan, & Deshler, 1985) typifies the importance of student participation.

Active student involvement is not difficult to initiate. Instead of having students sit and watch while one student is calculating a problem on the board, the other students could be completing the problem at their desks. A regular education secondary teacher in a co-teaching situation uses peer discussion throughout the lecture to actively involve students, including students with special needs. She lectures for 15 minutes and has the students repeat the important points in small peer groups for about 5 minutes while she and the special education teacher monitor the comments of the various groups. Both teachers then list the major points on an overhead projector, ask questions of the groups to summarize the relevant features of the lecture, and clarify misunderstandings they heard while monitoring the group discussions.

Learning is also enhanced when students are taught to display overt, rapid, and accurate responses to teacher questions in explicit skills (Englert, 1983; Hall, Delquadri, Greenwood, & Thurston, 1982; Stevens & Rosenshine, 1981). In addition to low-level, fast-paced questions, unison responding is a way to elicit overt, rapid, and accurate responses.

Verbal Unison Responding. Unison, or choral, responding is cued group responding to either a teacher question or a request following a signal. For example, after telling students that an adjective tells which, what kind of, and how many, the teacher would signal and ask, "Everyone, what does an adjective tell?" Then, all students would respond. Notice, in the preceding example, a cue word *everyone* was used to elicit the group response. If a cue word is not used, the fastest and brightest students often blurt out the answers, defeating the purpose of the unison response.

It is easy to incorporate choral responding during a reading group. For example, one student may read one paragraph aloud while the whole class or subgroups of the class (e.g., all the children with blue eyes, all the children with freckles) read the next.

Nonverbal Unison Responding. Nonverbal responding may be used with older students who consider it babyish to read together or to answer after a signal. With older students, practice is frequently less overt (Rosenshine, 1983). Moreover, nonverbal unison practice may be effective for students from linguistically different backgrounds who feel uncomfortable or have difficulty communicating verbally. For example, a special education teacher required a unison response when teaching place value to her middle school students. The students answered questions like, "What number is in the tens place?" by putting the correct number of fingers under their chins.

You may also use index cards to elicit unison response. First, give yourself and each student a set of labeled 3-inch by 5-inch cards. Then, ask a question that can be answered by one of the cards. Finally, have each student hold up the card with the selected answer so you can check the correctness of the response. This practice activity has been used successfully with students of all ages and with all content areas.

For example, to practice the identification of parts of speech, such as adverbs and adjectives, pass out two cards to each student. The word *adjective* is written on one card and the word *adverb* on another. Then, write or say a sentence, followed by a question and a cue word such as "The dilapidated window shutter was flapping wildly in the breeze. What part of speech is *dilapidated*? (pause) Now." *Now* cues the students to hold up one of the cards. At the same time, flash the correct answer from your set of cards, so that you give the students immediate feedback. With this feedback, it is not so embarrassing for students to have the incorrect answer because they usually correct it before their peers notice. You also receive immediate feedback as to who is having problems with the concept. A quick glance can tell you which students look at the cards of others for the answer or which are holding up the incorrect card. To cue a faster response, you may eventually shorten the question, "What part of speech is *dilapidated?*" to only the key word, *dilapidated*. Such a format for eliciting active participation is effective when teaching bilingual students (Watson, Northcutt, & Rydele, 1989).

In the teaching of implicit skills, teachers prompt student involvement in their modeling and asking of questions until the students become proficient enough to use the skill independently. For example, students eventually model the think alouds and other teacher behaviors. This increased student participation and decreased teacher support is called scaffolding (Palincsar & Brown, 1986, 1988). At the beginning of the scaffolding process, the teacher demonstrates the think alouds and supports the students with prompts, suggestions, procedural facilitators, and other hints. Eventually, the teacher fades the support and the students provide the support for each other until they become independent.

■ ■ Activity

Use what you've read about active involvement to correct the following mistakes made by two student teachers.

1. This student teacher was teaching a reading lesson to primary students with special needs by calling on one student to sound out ten words and then calling on another student to sound out ten words.
2. This student teacher was teaching a math lesson to a group of five middle school students. He spent the first 20 minutes lecturing to the students. ■ ■

Closing

When teaching explicit skills, at the close of the lesson you may summarize or review for the students or elicit their participation in arriving at the major points of the lesson (Rosenshine & Stevens, 1986). You should also summarize how the students met your expectations, especially if you shared your expectations at the beginning of the lesson. Then, you should introduce independent work.

Frequently, in implicit skill teaching, the lesson ends with (a) a review of the information presented (Archer & Isaacson, 1990; Schumaker, 1989), (b) a preview of the future use for the information (Archer & Isaacson, 1990, Schumaker, 1989), (c) a statement of expectations (Archer & Isaacson, 1990; Schumaker, 1989), (d) a cue to chart progress (Palincsar, 1986; Schumaker, 1989), and (e) an introduction of the independent work (Archer & Isaacson, 1990). Following is an example of each feature. The first three examples are taken from the teacher script in *The Error Monitoring Strategy* (Schumaker, Nolan, & Deshler, 1985).

- *Review.* "Today we've begun to learn about the Error Monitoring Strategy. It consists of six steps that we can remember using the word *WRITER*. In the *I* step, we interrogate ourselves about four types of errors

Important Points

1. Questioning is used to elicit active student involvement, to foster cognitive learning, to reinforce concepts, to prompt, to monitor, and to adjust instruction when teaching either explicit or implicit skills.

2. It is best to use low-level, fast-paced questions that produce many correct responses and elicit much involvement when teaching basic, or explicit, skills.

3. High-level, slow-paced questions are generally required in the teaching of implicit skills.

4. In prompting, teachers often increase assistance until the students are able to respond correctly.

5. Specific questions, such as "What is the next step in the operation, Bob?" serve as checks of comprehension and enable teachers to monitor and adjust instruction.

6. Nonacademic questions frequently disrupt the flow of a lesson and may lead to noncompliant student behavior.

7. Wait time involves the amount of time a teacher waits for a student's response after asking a question and the amount of time a teacher waits after a student's response to ask another question.

8. Active student involvement is essential in teaching both explicit and implicit skills.

9. Verbal unison responding is effective for involving young students, while nonverbal unison responding is effective for older students.

10. In teaching implicit skills, teachers should prompt student involvement in their modeling and asking of questions until the students become proficient enough to use the skill independently.

11. Increased student participation and decreased teacher support is called scaffolding.

12. Reviews, summaries of important points, summaries of how students met expectations, and introductions of independent work are effective closing activities for teaching explicit skills.

13. Frequently, in implicit skill teaching, the lesson ends with a review of the information presented, a preview of the future use for the information, a statement of expectations, a cue to chart progress, and an introduction of the independent work.

which we can remember using the word *COPS*" (p. 33).

- *Preview.* "From now on, you will be applying the *WRITER* step each time you write a paper" (p. 33).
- *Expectations.* "You can expect the number of errors you commonly make in your written products to decrease drastically and, as a result, you can expect your grades on written products to improve" (p. 33).
- *Charting.* "Turn to progress charts . . ."
- *Independent work.* Give a specific assignment that relates to the content taught.

Guided Practice

Guided practice is teacher-led practice of concepts, rules, and other information presented in a lesson. If you are teaching the rule to begin a sentence with a capital letter, you may model use of the rule first and then provide examples and nonexamples for rule application as guided practice until students perform with minimum errors. Often, guided practice is alternated with teacher demonstration so that the two variables appear as one (Rosenshine & Stevens, 1986). Generally, low-achieving students need more guided practice than do high-achieving students to reach the overlearning stage (Rosenshine, 1986). Guided practice activities should always relate to the objective of the lesson and actively involve the students.

During guided practice of explicit skills, effective teachers provide prompts, check for understanding, repeat and rephrase lesson content, provide examples and nonexamples, and give feedback (Gettinger & Fayne, 1982; Good & Grouws, 1979; Rosenshine & Stevens, 1986). Often, in such teaching, a mastery level, such as 80%, is identified (Brophy, 1980). Some guided practice activities used in special education include repeated reading and repetitive activities.

In repeated reading, the teacher first reads the selection. Then, the students read it in unison. Then, the teacher and students reread together before the students read it alone. This activity is easily adapted to independent practice by having students practice reading over a tape recorder after listening to a teacher or peer read the selection (O'Shea & O'Shea, 1988). In a comparison with worksheets, repeated readings result in improved reading rate and comprehension for students with special needs (Henk, Helfeldt, & Platt, 1986; O'Shea & O'Shea, 1988; O'Shea, Sindelar, & O'Shea, 1985). Other suggestions for repetitive guided practice for both elementary and middle school students with special needs include telling students, "Repeat the rule with your eyes closed," "Whisper the rule to a neighbor," and "Say it with your right hand raised."

Teachers also guide students in practice of implicit skills by giving hints, reminders of procedural facilitators, suggestions for improvement, corrections, and feedback (Palincsar & Brown, 1989; Rosenshine, 1990). Cue cards (Rosenshine, 1990), half-done examples (Rosenshine, 1990), and verbal rehearsals (Schumaker & Sheldon, 1985) are also frequently used. Mastery levels are specified for some skills (Palincsar & Brown, 1986; Schumaker, Nolan, & Deshler, 1985), such as "The student must make fewer than 0.05 errors per word in the final draft" (Schumaker, Nolan, & Deshler, 1985, p. 53).

Cue cards are visual prompts of procedural facilitators. Remember, procedural facilitators are clues, or supports, that help students when they begin to learn an implicit skill. Cue cards are often made to prompt students to practice the steps of a strategy. For example, cue cards containing the important components of the Sentence Writing Strategy (Schumaker & Sheldon, 1985) are provided for the students in Cue Card #6, which states:

Steps for Sentence Writing
    Step 1: Pick a Formula
    Step 2: Explore Words to Fit the Formula
    Step 3: Note the Words
    Step 4: Subject-Verb Identification (Search and Check)
        • Look for the action or state-of-being word(s) to find the verb.
        • Ask the "Who or What Question" to find the subject. (p. 150)

The Learning Strategies Curriculum also uses first-letter mnemonics to cue students into strategies or components of a strategy, such as PENS, for prompting students in the Sentence Writing Strategy (Schumaker, 1989).

Half-done examples provide questions or statement starters, such as "That doesn't sound right because *cold* means _____," for students to complete (Rosenshine, 1990). In verbal rehearsals, the students imitate the modeling procedures of the teacher during practice until they can repeat the modeling independently.

Feedback

Feedback involves responding to students' answers and correcting students' errors. It is an essential part of the teacher-student interactions during teaching of both explicit and implicit skills. Rieth and Frick (1983) report that only

8% to 9% of academic learning time is given to feedback, even though research shows that 12% to 14% increases the likelihood of student engagement and achievement gains. Teachers can give feedback by acknowledging, amplifying, rephrasing, and correcting (Anderson, Evertson, & Brophy, 1979; Florida Performance Measurement System, 1984).

Acknowledgement
Acknowledgement involves telling a student that an answer is correct or wrong, such as "Yes, that is correct" or "No, that is not correct." Acknowledgement also involves the use of specific praise. Specific praise requires specification of the appropriate behavior. It is not merely, "Good," but "Good reading" or "Good remembering." Stating the specific behavior (reading, remembering) helps students recognize why they are receiving positive statements from you. They know the exact behavior that earned your approval. In response to a general statement like "Good boy," a student may think, "Oh, yes, I read well," or the student may think, "Oh, the teacher must be in a good mood today." Many students with special needs have problems connecting a behavior with the praise when the behavior is not specified. Soldier (1989) recommends praising a Native American's efforts rather than the product.

Positive verbal reinforcement is related to increased student attention and achievement gains in both elementary and secondary populations (George, 1986; Reid, 1986; Stallings, Needels, & Staybrook, 1979). Positive comments may also be made in feedback of written products. Marking the correct items in color with a pen or writing positive comments on the paper ("Excellent printing," "Great idea") takes a little more time, but it helps students view school more positively.

Amplification and Rephrasing
Amplification is expansion of a student's response by either the teacher or another student, such as "Yes, Jim, you are correct. We do multiply to solve that problem and the reason we do

that is . . ." and "Yes, Sue, that is a good start. Now, Pat, would you explain it further?" Amplification is used during the teaching of learning strategies to help students discriminate between good and poor student modeling of the think alouds of the teacher (Schumaker, 1989).

Rephrasing is often used to emphasize facts that make an answer correct or to emphasize the steps or methods used to arrive at a correct answer (Anderson, Evertson, & Brophy, 1979). It is also used to repeat the relevant points of a lesson, such as "Yes, that's correct, the rule is *i* before *e* except after *c*" and "Yes, Jimmy, you first divide and then multiply. Exactly correct."

Correction
Correcting a wrong response usually takes two formats and adaptations to them. With the supply format, which is used mostly in explicit skill teaching, you or a student supply the correct answer. With the prompt format, which is used in teaching both explicit and implicit skills, you prompt or in some way lead the student to the correct answer. However, with both, the process should end with the student's responding with the correct answer. Using the supply format, you model the correct answer or call on another student to model it (model), lead the student (lead), and then have the student repeat the correct answer (test), as in "No, the word is *some* (model). Let's say it together (lead). Now, say it alone (test)" or just model and test as in "No, the word is *some* (model). What word? (test)" (Engelmann & Carnine, 1982; Meyer, 1986).

Although used in teaching explicit skills, the prompt format is particularly useful in teaching implicit skills (Palincsar & Brown, 1989; Schumaker, 1989). You may prompt the correct answer or suggest a strategy or information that the student can use to deduce the correct answer ("Not quite. Remember, the first step is the *D* step" or "Why don't you try sounding out the words?") (Collins, Carnine, & Gersten, 1987).

Rosenshine and Stevens (1986) believe that appropriate feedback depends on a student's response. If a student answers correctly in a quick and firm manner, they suggest a quick acknowledgement of "Right" followed by another question. If a student answers correctly but is hesitant, they recommend specific praise, repeating the part that is correct, or explaining why it is correct. An incorrect but careless response requires a quick correction, while an incorrect response due to a lack of knowledge of facts or process requires elaborated feedback with reteaching if the student cannot correct in a short time. Whichever technique you use, note that feedback is more effective than ignoring errors altogether (Sindelar, 1987).

■ ■ Activity

Student teacher 1 asked a third grade student to make up a sentence with the word *me*. The student said, "*Me* am happy," to which the teacher replied, "me and my shadow" and then asked the student to write the word *fan*. How could the student teacher have given the student more appropriate feedback?

Student teacher 2 responded, "That's correct," when a student answered the question of why the astronauts are weightless in space by saying that there is no gravity. Provide a rephrasing type of feedback to emphasize the effect of gravity. Provide a specific praise acknowledgement. ■ ■

Independent Practice

Added to guided practice, independent practice should result in fluency and maintenance of skills. It is recommended that students move to independent practice activities when they are making few errors during guided practice (Rosenshine & Stevens, 1986). Most of what is said in this section concerning independent practice applies in the teaching of both explicit and implicit skills. Perhaps, the major difference between the two is that individual seatwork is the most common context for independent work in the teaching of explicit skills (Rosenshine &

Stevens, 1986), while a variety of instructional contexts are used in the teaching of implicit skills (Rosenshine, 1990). In many cases, individual seatwork is replaced with work in groups or pairs to promote generalization of the skills. This doesn't mean that these techniques cannot be used in the teaching of explicit skills. In fact, research (Delquadri, Greenwood, Whorton, Carta, & Hall, 1986; Johnson & Johnson, 1986; Slavin, 1988a) shows that peers helping each other promotes positive achievement of both explicit and implicit skills.

Independent practice is not to be confused with a student's interacting with a worksheet. Ineffective teachers often expect students to learn too much from worksheets (Medley, 1979; Rieth, Polsgrove, Okolo, Bahr, & Eckert, 1987; Rosenshine & Stevens, 1986; Squires, Huitt, & Segars, 1983). It is appropriate to use worksheets or dittos during independent practice, but only to reinforce a concept that has already been taught. Thus, independent practice should relate to guided practice activities even though new examples are provided. If the objective of the lesson is to identify possessive nouns, then students should practice the identification of possessive nouns during independent activities.

A success rate of 90% to 100% is suggested for independent practice of basic, or explicit, skills for effective learning (Christenson, Thurlow, & Ysseldyke, 1987). Instructing middle school students with learning disabilities, Rivera and Smith (1988) did not assign independent worksheets of long division problems until the students were able to compute a sample long division problem with 100% accuracy during guided practice.

To ensure a 90% success rate, you should give instructions telling what you expect during the independent activity, and if necessary, adapt the activities. Wong, Wong, and LaMare (1982) caution against the use of general instructions like "Read the assignment carefully." Instead, to promote optimal learning and on-task behavior, they suggest that teachers inform students of the specific objectives of the assignment. Teachers

Important Points

1. Guided practice is teacher-led practice of concepts, rules, and other information presented in a lesson.
2. During guided practice of explicit skills, effective teachers provide prompts, check for understanding, repeat and rephrase lesson content, provide examples and nonexamples, and give feedback.
3. Effective teachers guide students in practice of implicit skills by giving hints, reminders of procedural facilitators, suggestions for improvement, corrections, and feedback.
4. Cue cards are visual prompts of procedural facilitators.
5. Half-done examples provide questions or statement starters to complete.
6. Verbal rehearsals provide students with practice as they imitate the modeling procedures of the teacher with prompting until they can repeat the modeling independently.
7. Feedback involves responding to students' answers and correcting students' errors.
8. Acknowledgement involves telling a student that an answer is correct or wrong.
9. Specific praise requires specification of an appropriate behavior.
10. Amplification is expansion of a student's response by either the teacher or another student.
11. Rephrasing is often used to emphasize facts that make an answer correct or to emphasize the steps or methods used to arrive at a correct answer.
12. Correction procedures often consist of either a supply format or a prompt format.
13. Individual seatwork is the most common context for independent work in the teaching of explicit skills, while a variety of contexts are used in the teaching of implicit skills, including work in groups or pairs to promote generalization of the skills.
14. Independent practice activities should relate to guided practice activities and reinforce previously taught information even though new examples are provided.
15. Instead of sitting at their desks, effective teachers give extra help and individual feedback during independent practice.

may adapt the directions or content of worksheets for independent practice. (Refer to Chapter 5 for an extensive discussion of ways to adapt materials.)

Instead of sitting at their desks, effective teachers give extra help and individual feedback during independent practice (Brophy & Evertson, 1977). However, if you spend more than a few minutes explaining a problem to a student, you should probably reteach that lesson. Beginning teachers often run into management problems during independent practice because they spend too much time with one student or they position themselves with their backs to the other students, making it impossible to monitor behaviors.

Summary

In this chapter, we related the teacher effectiveness research to the presenting of lessons for the teaching of both explicit and implicit skills to elementary and secondary students with special needs. We discussed instructional language, academic learning time, active academic responding time, motivation, subject content, and structuring and sequencing of subject content. Then, we discussed the variables of lesson presentation, guided practice, feedback, and independent practice.

Active simple sentences, visual cues, marker words, and voice emphasis make instructional language easier to understand. Students must be successfully involved in academic activities and in active responding to increase achievement. Active student involvement, student choices, task attractiveness, and task challenge are just a few ways to motivate students.

In subject content, we discussed concepts, rules, laws, lawlike principles, and value judgments. Presenting material in small steps is effective for teaching explicit skills. Using simple materials to introduce a task, providing procedural facilitators, and anticipating student errors are effective for teaching implicit skills. Lesson presentation should include activities to open the lesson, activities for the body of the lesson, and activities to close the lesson. Modeling, teacher questioning, and student participation are just a few of the instructional methods to present new content. Guided and independent practice activities are vital parts of lesson presentation. They should relate to the objectives and each other. Regardless of the type of feedback, some feedback should always be given.

8

Teacher-Directed Content Instruction

Key Topics

In this chapter, we concentrate on some of the more teacher-directed instruction approaches in such areas as reading, math, social studies, and science. The teacher-directed approaches in this chapter include Direct Instruction and unit teaching. Direct Instruction focuses on the teaching of explicit skills, while unit teaching is frequently used in teaching content information. The Direct Instruction model and the various commercial materials connected with the *Distar Reading, Distar Arithmetic, Corrective Mathematics, Corrective Reading, and Reading Mastery 1* (e.g., Engelmann and colleagues) has been used in special education for many years.

As you read the discussion of the Direct Instruction model in this chapter, you will notice some of the same features that were found in the teacher effectiveness research as effective strategies for teaching explicit skills. These include well-structured sequences of subject matter, student participation, immediate feedback, and fast-paced questions with many correct responses. Other predominate features are the teaching techniques of modeling, prompting, testing or checking for comprehension, and cuing unison responses.

Unit teaching has also been used extensively, especially in classes for students with mental handicaps (Meyen, 1981). In this chapter, we expand the concept of unit teaching to consider the needs of students from diverse cultural backgrounds and to its use in a collaborative setting.

Direct Instruction

Direct Instruction (DI) is used in this chapter to refer to the structured, teacher-directed curriculum program first designed by Becker and Engelmann as a model for Project Head Start, a federally funded preschool intervention program for disadvantaged children from low-income homes. In 1967, when Head Start was extended to Project Follow-Through, with a focus on intervention through the primary grades, Direct Instruction with the Distar language, math, and reading programs was retained as one of the twenty-two experimental models selected for evaluation (Peterson, 1987). The Direct Instruction approach consists of well-sequenced, unambiguous tasks presented to small groups of students at a rapid, repetitive pace, requiring the students to participate individually and in unison.

Following is a typical Direct Instruction presentation that was adapted from *Reading Mastery 1* materials (Engelmann & Bruner, 1988). A small group of students is sitting in a semicircle in front of the teacher as the teacher models, saying, "This sound is *aa*," and pointing to the letter *a*. The teacher asks the students to respond in unison, saying, "Everyone, what sound?" and dropping the other hand. The teacher continues to test the students: "Again. Get ready." (Hand drop.) "Again. Get ready." (Hand drop.) Then, the teacher presents positive examples, asking, "Is this *aa*?" pointing to *a* and dropping the other hand. The teacher presents a negative example, asking, "Is this *aa?*" pointing to a picture of a tree and dropping the other hand. The students answer the questions in unison and the teacher gives feedback, saying, "Yes, this is *a,*" or "No, this is a tree." The lesson closes with individual tests and the teacher asking, "Brendan, is this *aa?*" and pointing to *a.*

Research conducted by an independent agency, ABT Associates, documented the effectiveness of Direct Instruction in increasing academic performance of low-income, disadvantaged children in the 3-year Follow-Through program (Stebbins, St. Pierre, Proper, Anderson, & Cerba, 1977). In a longitudinal study, Meyer (1984) followed graduates of Direct Instruction programs and a matched inner-city control group through high school graduation. The 85% black and 11% Puerto Rican students had participated in the Direct Instruction model for 3 or 4 years and completed three levels in reading, language, and math programs. Compared with the control group, more of the students from the Direct Instruction program graduated from high school, completed school without retention, and applied to college (Meyer, 1984). In addition, the graduates posted higher ninth grade reading and math scores. Furthermore, the Direct Instruction model was the only one of seven Follow-Through models located in New York City schools to succeed (Meyer, Gersten, & Gutken, 1983).

The Direct Instruction model began to be used with special education elementary students in the late 1960s with similar success, especially in the teaching of basic skills (Gersten, 1985; Gersten, Woodward, & Darch, 1986; Lloyd, Cullinan, Heins, & Epstein, 1980; Stein & Goldman, 1980). Direct Instruction has also increased the academic performance of adolescents with mild disabilities (Polloway, Epstein, Polloway, Patton, & Ball, 1986), senior high school readers with reading problems (Gregory, Hackney, & Gregory, 1982), and preadolescents and adolescents with mild mental retardation (Ger-

sten & Maggs, 1982). The program has been identified as one of the five alternative instructional practices effective for working with students from diverse cultural backgrounds who are at risk for special education referral (Maheady, Towne, Algozzine, Mercer, & Ysseldyke, 1983).

Rationale

The Direct Instruction model is based on behavioral principles. The fundamental premise is that students must master basic academic skills before they can master higher-level cognitive skills. According to Tarver (1986), "Instruction begins with specific decoding skills and strategies and progresses in a highly structured, spiraling fashion to higher level comprehension skills and strategies" (p. 370).

The premise of Direct Instruction is that the best way to teach both basic and higher-level skills is to present carefully sequenced content using task analysis and mastery learning principles. In discussing the basis of *Distar Arithmetic* (Engelmann & Carnine, 1972, 1975, 1976), Gersten and Carnine (1984) posit that "all children can learn mathematics if the lesson is designed so students can understand what is being presented, if they are given adequate practice with corrective feedback and their progress through the curriculum is assessed regularly" (p. 396).

Description

The Direct Instruction model features a well-designed curriculum and detailed instructional procedures. As described by Tarver, "The curriculum design components constitute the cognitive elements of DI and the presentation components constitute the behavioral elements" (p. 369). The curriculum features include sequential order, examples, well-constructed formats, prompts, independent practice activities, and mastery learning.

Curriculum Features

In Direct Instruction, skills and concepts are presented in sequential order and in logical steps within well-constructed, repetitive formats. All skills are taught directly, without any reliance on incidental learning. Each lesson includes teacher-scripted presentations, individual tests, and independent practice activities. In addition, mastery tests are interspersed throughout the curriculum.

Sequential Order. In all of the content areas, skills and concepts are analyzed thoroughly to make certain that preskills necessary for success are taught, easy skills are taught before more difficult ones, similar skills are taught nonconsecutively, and high-utility skills are taught before less-used ones. *Preskills are skills that must be taught before a task is introduced* (Silbert, Carnine, & Stein, 1990). Examine the following script from a Direct Instruction program designed for teaching math created by Silbert, Carnine, and Stein (1990). This example shows the beginning of a lesson on teaching students to add the fast way:

Write on board: $5 + 3 = \square$

1. "I'LL TOUCH AND YOU READ."
2. "WE'RE GOING TO WORK THIS PROBLEM A FAST WAY. WE DRAW LINES UNDER THE NUMBER AFTER THE PLUS" Point to + 3. "WHAT DOES THIS SAY?" "SO HOW MANY LINES ARE WE GOING TO DRAW?" "I'LL MAKE THE LINES." Draw three lines under the 3.
3. "WATCH ME COUNT THE FAST WAY." Touch 5 and then each line. "FIIIIVVVE, SIX, SEVEN, EIGHT." (p. 147)

In previous lessons, the students were taught the preskills of (a) drawing lines to correspond to a numeral (making 3 lines to represent 3), (b) rote counting from a number other than 1 (beginning with 5), (c) rational counting (to touch lines as they counted), and (d) reading equations

$(5 + 3 = \underline{\hspace{1cm}})$. Thus, the objective of teaching students to add the fast way was made easier by ensuring that each preskill was taught and mastered before this lesson.

Skills are also sequenced according to difficulty levels. In symbol identification, the teen numerals of 14, 16, 17, 18, and 19 are taught before 11, 12, 13, and 15 due to the regularity in reading the numerals (Silbert, Carnine, & Stein, 1990). The first numerals are read beginning with the numeral in the ones, such as 14 (four-teen) and 16 (six-teen), while the last set are not read beginning with the numeral in the ones; that is, 11 is not read "one-teen, nor is 12 read "two-teen." Sounding out words that begin with continuous sounds is taught before sounding out words that begin with stop sounds (Carnine, Silbert, & Kameenui, 1990) because it is much easier to sound out words beginning with sounds that can be held, such as *a* in *an* and *m* in *mat*, than with sounds that cannot be held, such as *p* in *pan* and *t* in *tot*.

Similar information or strategies that are likely to be confused are not introduced together. For example the sound of *d* is introduced in Lesson 27, Presentation Book A, and the sound of *b* is introduced in Lesson 121, Presentation Book C. The letters are not introduced close together because students frequently have difficulty discriminating the letters visually. The skip counting series for 4 and 6 are not introduced together, since they both contain many similar numbers (e.g., 4, 8, *12*, 16, 20, *24* and 6, *12*, 18, *24*) (Silbert, Carnine, & Stein, 1990).

High-utility skills are taught before less-used ones. Irregular words such as *was, said,* and *have* are taught before the less-used ones of *tomb, heir,* and *neon* (Carnine, Silbert, & Kameenui, 1990). Letter sounds are taught before letter names, as letter sounds are used more than letter names in beginning reading.

Examples. According to Engelmann and Carnine (1982), inclusion of a wide range of positive examples, negative examples, and test examples assists in unambiguous communication and in teaching generalizations. The range of positive examples must demonstrate "only one identifiable sameness in quality" (Engelmann & Carnine, 1982, p. 5). For example, when teaching the concept red, the example of red should not always be accompanied with round objects, because students might incorrectly conclude that red is round. The only sameness of the objects should be red. Thus, red apples, red wagons, red squares, and other objects that are red are used. If teaching fraction to decimal conversions, you should include examples that show variations, such as $8/100 = 0.08$, $80/100 = 0.80$, and $800/100 = 8.00$, not just variations of the first example, $x/100 = 0.0x$.

In turn, a negative example must be minimally different from a positive one to prevent students from overgeneralizing and to help the students make discriminations. For example, returning to the teaching of red, negative examples should differ only in the color attribute. A red ball should be compared with a yellow ball (difference only in color attribute) instead of a red square with a yellow ball (difference in color plus shape attributes). In the latter example, students may use the shape and interpret red as something that has corners, instead of using the color as the discriminating factor. In teaching the adjective *rough,* positive examples may include a piece of sandpaper and a rough book cover, contrasted with the negative examples of a piece of paper and a smooth book cover (Carnine, Silbert, & Kameenui, 1990). In the test examples, you should present new positive and negative examples that require students to apply their knowledge. For instance, in a test example of red, present a red scarf if it was not one of the objects used as an example during the lesson.

One last guideline in example selection is to include examples that are consistent with the strategy before exceptions (Carnine, Silbert, & Kameenui, 1990). If the rule that the letters *ea* in the middle of a word often say the long *e* sound, then examples such as *thread* and *breath,* which are exceptions to the rule, should not be selected until students become proficient with the rule.

■ ■ **Activity**

Part 1. In teaching elementary students, identify some positive, negative, and test examples you might use to teach the following concept: "A sum is the answer you get when you add." A positive example may be $3 + 8 = \underline{\hspace{1cm}}$.

Part 2. In teaching middle school students, identify some positive, negative, and test examples you might use to teach the following rule: "We change a decimal to a percent by adding a percent sign after the number and moving the decimal point two places toward the percent sign" (Silbert, Carnine, & Stein, 1990, p. 414). (Answers for this and other activities are found in the Instructor's Manual.)

■ ■

Formats and Procedures. Well-constructed, fast-paced, repetitive formats are designed to teach skills, basic concepts, related concepts, rules, and cognitive operations (Tarver, 1986). There is a different format for each of the parts of a lesson. For example, there are five formats for classification of story problems (Silbert, Carnine, & Stein, 1990): formats for "language training problems, structured worksheet problems, less-structured worksheet problems, supervised practice problems, and independent worksheet problems" (p. 276). In each format, the wording is consistent and specific to make the information easier for the students to acquire and for the teacher to present (Engelmann, Osborn, & Hanner, 1978). Formats contain the specific wording for the teaching procedures, feedback, and independent practice activities.

Silbert, Carnine, and Stein (1990) describe three basic teaching procedures found in Direct Instruction formats for teaching mathematics. The procedures involved essentially modeling and testing. They differ depending on whether the task is a motor, labeling, or strategy one. A motor task involves counting, saying a rule, or executing a precise movement, like writing numerals. A labeling task requires a student to label items, such as saying "square" when seeing a figure with four equal sides. A strategy task involves the integration of a series of steps to solve a problem. Although Silbert, Carnine, and Stein correlate the teaching procedures to the motor, labeling, and strategy tasks involved in mathematics instruction, these tasks, and thus the teaching procedures, apply to other academic areas, too. For example, teachers ask students to say and spell words in spelling, to label in writing, and to follow steps to reach a solution in reading.

To teach the motor task of counting, saying a rule, or making a precise movement, the teaching procedures of model, lead, test, and delayed test are used (Silbert, Carnine, & Stein, 1990). For example, in the format for introducing numbers, the teacher models by saying, "Listen, 12345678910 11 12 13. Listen to the new part: 11 12 13"; then leads with "Say the new part with me"; then tests, telling the students to "Say the new part all by yourselves" (p. 67). As a delayed test, the teacher presents the counting task again later in the lesson. This same procedure applies in the rhyming format in *Reading Mastery 1*: the teacher models ("My turn. First I'll say the sound. Then I'll say (pause) *an*"), leads ("Do it with me . . ."), and tests the students (calls on different children) (Engelmann & Bruner, 1988, Presentation Book A, Lesson 28, p. 172).

In a labeling task, the teaching procedures of *modeling, alternating test,* and *delayed tests* are used in the format (Silbert, Carnine, and Stein, 1990). The teacher points to a symbol, such as 5, tells the students what it is called, and asks the students to repeat the label. The teacher then presents the alternating test, using the new example 5 and previous examples (other numerals). Later in the lesson, the teacher asks the students to identify the new example. This same procedure is used in teaching letter sounds. For example, in teaching the new sound of *s*, the teacher points to it ("Here's a new sound"), says the sound ("My turn to say it. Get ready. *Sss*"), and asks the students to say it ("Your turn. Get ready. Yes, *sss*") (Engelmann & Bruner, 1988, Lesson 16, p. 102). The teacher then presents the alternating test and asks the students to discriminate between the *s* sound and the letter

sounds of *m* and *a*, which were taught in previous lessons. The teacher also presents the *s* sound again later in the lesson.

A *model, guided practice,* and *testing* procedure is basically used on strategy tasks that require the integration of sequential steps (Silbert, Carnine, & Stein, 1990). The teacher first models and asks questions that prompt the students to apply the skills to solve the problem, then fades some of the modeling during guided practice, and lastly tests the students. For example, in teaching the strategy for subtraction with renaming, the teacher models and says, "The ones column tells us to start with 3 and take away 6," and then asks, "What does the ones column tell us to do?" (Silbert, Carnine, & Stein, 1990, p. 176). Eventually, the modeling is faded, until the students complete the task independently many lessons later, the test step.

The same procedure may be used in teaching spelling rules. For example, the teacher says, "Here's a rule about spelling words that end with an *e*. An *e* at the end tells us to say the name of this letter," and the teacher points to the *a* in *game*. The teacher then guides the students in applying the rule by asking, "Is there any *e* at the end of this word?" (Carnine, et al., 1990, p. 201).

■ ■ Activity
Describe the teaching procedure used in the following format. Choose from (a) model, lead, and test; (b) model, alternate test, delayed test; and (c) model, guided practice, test.

Teacher: Everyone, all eyes up here. You are going to sound out these words. What are you going to do? (Signal.)
Student: *Sound out these words.*
Teacher: Right. My turn first. *Sh-u-t, shut.* The first word is *shut.* Say it with me. (Signal.)
Student: *Shut.*
Teacher: Your turn. Sound it out alone. Get ready! (Signal.)
Student: *Shut.*
Teacher: Good sounding out the word *shut.*
■ ■

Prompts. A prompt is a visual detail that is added to an example to highlight a relevant feature (Engelmann & Carnine, 1982). Eventually, the prompts are faded. Some of the frequently used visual cues in the beginning reading program are exemplified in the following word:

līke

A macron (-) marks the long *i* vowel sound, the silent letter *e* is reduced to smaller print to prompt students that "when a word has a little sound, you don't say that sound" (Engelmann & Bruner, 1988, Presentation Book A, p. 221), and an arrow underlines the word to prompt students to proceed from left to right when reading. Dots, or balls, under a word tell students that they must make that sound. A larger dot prompts students where to begin, for example:

man

In beginning math, one 10 is written as 1°, so 16 is $1^\circ 6$ and 106 is $1^{\circ\circ}6$.

Independent Practice. With independent practice activities, students complete exercises in their workbooks. Such written activities reinforce the content taught during the oral presentation. The activities include a mixture of examples where the new skill or rule is applied and some where previously taught skills are applied. For example, after Mr. Phillips introduces subtracting with regrouping, he gives the students independent assignments containing problems that require regrouping (application of the new skill), such as $35 + 27$, and problems that do not require regrouping (application of a previously taught skill), such as $35 + 12$ (Silbert, Carnine, & Stein, 1990). In *Reading Mastery 1* (Engelmann & Bruner, 1988), the independent practice activity for Lesson 16, which introduces the *s* sound, involves activities dealing with not only the *s* sound but also the *a* and *m* sounds, which were taught in earlier lessons.

Mastery Learning. Mastery learning, which requires students to reach a certain criterion, is built into the Direct Instruction model during the lesson presentation. According to the authors, students do not practice material alone

until the group response is firm. For example, in choral reading of a story, the students must read to a certain point with a limited number of errors. If they make more errors, they must reread the section as a group until the error goal is reached, and then they read individually.

In addition to group tests, individual tests are interspersed throughout the oral presentation to check individual mastery. The individual tests evaluate a single student's performance and let the teacher know which students are having problems, which skills to reteach, and which lessons to reteach. In addition, the teacher continually monitors student progress with mastery tests interspersed throughout the curriculum. For example, the first mastery test in *Reading Mastery 1* (Engelmann & Bruner, 1988) appears after Lesson 8. Placement tests are also available for the initial placement of students in the program.

Presentation Components

As is evident from the various well-constructed formats used in Direct Instruction, teachers model, question, and test. Other presentation components include cuing attention and providing overviews to begin the lesson; eliciting student participation, providing immediate feedback, and guiding practice activities during the body of the lesson; and introducing independent practice activities to close the lesson.

Opening. Often, lessons begin with cues to students to attend. For example, some lessons begin with "Everyone, look at me." Attention getters such as "Listen" and "Your turn" are also frequently interspersed throughout the lesson. Each section of the lesson usually begins with an overview, such as, "First, you're going to say the word slowly without stopping between the sounds. Then, you're going to say the word fast" (Engelmann & Bruner, 1988, Presentation Book A, p. 190).

Body. Unison responding ensures that students are attending to the lesson and participating (Silbert, Carnine, & Stein, 1990). Unison responding requires all students to respond at the same time and is frequently prompted with a question followed by a signal. This signal is to prevent some students from shouting out the answer before others get a chance. The sequence usually proceeds from giving directions, to providing a thinking pause, to cuing the response (Silbert, Carnine, & Stein, 1990). For example to teach the word *of* in Lesson 108 of *Reading Mastery 1,* the teacher says, "Everybody, you're going to read this word the fast way" (overview); pauses 3 seconds (thinking pause); and says, "Get ready" (verbal signal) while moving one finger quickly along the arrow (visual signal) (Presentation Book C, Lesson 108, p. 3). Likewise, the signal may be a "hand drop, clap, or simply a change in voice inflection" (Carnine, Silbert, & Kameenui, 1990, p. 18). After leading the group in practice, the teacher asks individual students to respond. Continuing the previous example, the teacher would call on individual students to read the word the fast way.

Throughout lesson presentation, the teacher gives structured, immediate feedback for both incorrect and correct answers. The correction procedure is specified and frequently consists of a variation of a model, lead, test, and retest format (Engelmann & Carnine, 1982). For example, to use the procedure when a student does not say the short *a* sound correctly, first model the correct answer (*aaa*), repeat the correction with the student ("Say it with me. Get ready"), test the student ("Your turn. Get ready"), and retest ("Again. Get ready") (Engelmann & Bruner, 1988, Presentation Book A, Lesson 2, p. 9). Sometimes, the teacher asks

---

▢ Important Points

1. The Direct Instruction model as demonstrated commercially in such programs as *Distar Arithmetic, Corrective Reading,* and *Reading Mastery 1* materials is effective in teaching basic skills to students from ethnically diverse cultural backgrounds and students with special needs.

2. Curriculum features of Direct Instruction include the components of sequential order, examples, well-constructed formats, prompts, independent practice activities, and mastery learning.

3. The guidelines for sequential order are (a) teach preskills, (b) teach easy skills before more difficult, (c) teach similar skills nonconsecutively, and (d) teach high-quality skills before less-used ones.

4. Negative, positive, and test examples should be selected.

5. Examples should consistently follow the rule, with exceptions introduced later.

6. A model, lead, test, and delayed test teaching procedure is recommended for teaching motor tasks; a model, alternate test, and delayed test procedure is recommended for teaching labeling tasks; and a model, guided practice, and test format is recommended for strategy tasks.

7. Prompts are visual details that are added to an example to highlight the relevant features.

8. Independent activities in the workbook are presented after the lesson.

9. Mastery learning activities are presented in the lessons and mastery tests are interspersed throughout the Direct Instruction program.

10. Cuing attention and providing overviews to begin the lesson; eliciting student participation, providing immediate feedback, and guiding practice activities during the body of the lesson; and introducing independent practice activities to close the lesson are presentation components often used.

students to model the correct answer during the modeling step.

Often specific praise statements for academic behaviors are written into the program, such as "Good, now you said it fast." The *Corrective Reading Program* even includes a sample point sheet (Engelmann, Becker, Hanner, & Johnson, 1980).

Closing. Most lessons close with introduction of practice activities in the workbook. Often, the teacher will complete the first few problems with students.

■ ■ Activity

Identify the correction procedure you might use when a student mispronounces the word *over.* ■ ■

In Table 8.1, we identify format and presentation procedures of Direct Instruction. We use the same sample that we used in a previous activity. You should have already identified the format as model, lead, and delayed test.

Lesson Plan

Many school districts have adopted commercial programs for Direct Instruction in the areas of reading, spelling, math, and language. Thus, you may find a kit with a teacher's manual, student workbooks, and other materials in the classroom. Although you should try to follow the scripted teacher presentation, Gersten, Carnine and Woodward (1987) discovered that immediate correction of student errors and the number of correct student responses were linked more to student success than was following the script word for word.

Even if Direct Instruction commercial programs are not available, it is possible to incorporate the curriculum design features and presentation components into a lesson. Here again, teaching involves making decisions and monitoring their effectiveness. If students are not mastering the information or progressing at an acceptable rate, one of your choices is to reexamine how you incorporated the curriculum design features and presentation components into your lesson. In the following sections, we use the curriculum design features and presentation

Table 8.1
Identification of Format and Presentation Components of a Direct Instruction Lesson

	Script	Format	Presentation Component
Teacher:	Everyone, all eyes up here.		Attention
	You are going to sound out these words.		Overview
	What are you going to do? (Signal.)		Cuing for unison response
Students:	*Sound out these words.*		
Teacher:	Right.		Feedback
	My turn first. *Sh-u-t, shut.*	Model	
	The first word is *shut.*		
	Say it with me.	Lead	
	(Signal.)		Cuing for unison response
Students:	*Shut.*		
Teacher:	Your turn.	Test	Attention
	Sound it out alone.		
	Get ready! (Signal.)		Cuing for unison response
Students:	*Shut.*		
Teacher:	Good sounding out the word *shut.*		Feedback
	Your turn, Jim. Sound out the word.	Individual test	

components of Direct Instruction to design a lesson for the rule "When a word has a short vowel sound followed by one consonant, double the consonant before adding *ing*," adapted from a fourth grade spelling book (Silver Burdett, 1986).

Adapting Curriculum Features

Plan your lesson around the curriculum features of sequential order, examples, well-constructed formats, prompts, independent practice activities, and mastery. Then, consider the presentation components.

Identifying the Sequence. Identify the preskills that should have been taught and mastered by students. These preskills include recognizing short vowel sounds, identifying consonant sounds, doubling letters, and spelling *ing*. If students do not know these preskills, teach them. If they know the preskills, proceed with teaching when to apply the rule (e.g., "Do you double the consonant *t* and add *ing* to the word *bat*?") and then how to apply the rule (e.g., "Double the *t* and add *ing* to spell *batting*").

Selecting Examples. In selecting examples, remember to present a range of positive examples, negative examples that are minimally different, and test examples that require students to apply the rule. Use the two positive examples of *bat* and *slip* when teaching the lesson. These examples represent different vowel sounds (short *a* and *i*) and different beginning consonants (a single consonant, *b*, and a blend, *sl*). Use the negative examples of *jump* and *rain*. *Jump* differs in the number of consonants and *rain* in the vowel sound. Test examples include positive ones like *skip*, *hem*, and *hop* and negative ones like *batch*, *bow*, and *meet*.

Adapting Procedures. Adapt the basic teaching procedure of model, guided practice, and test to teach students when to apply the rule. Model with questions, present examples, fade the prompts during guided practice, and then test. A scripted format appears later in the chapter. The feedback procedure includes specific praise with rule repetition for correct answers and a model and test procedure for incorrect answers.

The outline for the lesson format is:

1. Model the rule, question, and give feedback.
2. Model one positive example, question, give feedback, test individuals, and give individual feedback.
3. Model two negative examples, question, give feedback, test individuals, and give individual feedback.
4. Model another positive example, question, and give feedback.
5. Present six test examples, give feedback, test individuals, and give individual feedback.

Selecting Prompts. Visual cues should prompt students to apply the rule. You should want the students to be aware of the vowel sound and the one consonant in this rule, so at the beginning of the lesson color or darken the vowels and circle the consonants following the vowels to cue the students into these relevant features.

Designing Independent Practice Activities. Give the students ten items that require rule application to complete on their own after the lesson. Use the visual prompts that were used in the lesson on the worksheet and then eventually fade them out. In the following example, the vowels are darkened in the first three words and the consonants following the vowels are circled.

Directions: Decide if you can use the rule for adding *ing* to these words. If you can use the rule, mark *yes*. If you cannot use the rule, mark *no*. The first two are completed for you.

Word	Yes	No
1. game		X
2. fan	X	
3. sit		
4. slop		
5. rob		
6. drink		
etc. (10 examples total)		

Including Mastery Checks. Be sure to include both group and individual comprehension checks during the lesson presentation. Also, make sure that every student is able to answer whether or not the rule can be applied before you ask the students to complete the worksheet independently.

Adapting Presentation Components

Instead of discussing each of the instructional procedures separately, we present them in a scripted format to show how the lesson might actually be taught. We have attempted to include the two critical factors in writing the script: (a) uniform and unambiguous wording and (b) many opportunities for overt student responses. By including many opportunities for overt responses, you can tell which steps to reteach and which students are having problems. A hand drop is the signal for unison responding.

Modeling the Rule, Questioning, and Giving Feedback.

1. *Model the rule.* Say, "Listen. I'm going to present a new spelling rule and teach you when to use it. Here's the new spelling rule: 'When a word has a short vowel sound followed by one consonant, double the consonant before adding *ing*.' "
2. *Question.* Say, "What do you do when a word has a short vowel sound followed by one consonant?" (Signal.) Ask, "When do you double the consonant?" (Signal.)
3. *Give feedback.* If the students are correct, say, "Yes," and repeat the rule. If the students are incorrect, say, "No, listen, the rule is 'when a word has a short vowel sound followed by one consonant, double the consonant before adding *ing*' " (modeling). Continue, "Say it with me" (leading) and "Say it alone" (testing). Practice the rule until firm.

Modeling One Positive Example, Questioning, Giving Feedback, Testing Individuals, and Giving Individual Feedback.

4. *Model a positive example.* Write *bat* on the board with colored chalk and circle the *t*. Say, "Look at this word, *bat*. My turn. Does *bat* have a short vowel sound? Yes. Does one consonant follow the vowel? Yes. Do I double the consonant? Yes. How do I know? Because the word has a short vowel sound followed by one consonant."
5. *Question.* Say, "Your turn. Does *bat* have a short vowel sound?" (Signal.) "Does one consonant follow the vowel?" (Signal.) "Do you double the consonant?" (Signal.) "How do you know?" (Signal.)
6. *Give feedback.* If the students are correct, say, "Good knowing to double the consonant." If they are incorrect, say, "No, listen," and repeat steps 4, 5, and 6.
7. *Test individuals and give feedback.* Repeat steps 5 and 6 with individual students.

Modeling Two Negative Examples, Questioning, Giving Feedback, Testing Individuals, and Giving Individual Feedback.

8. *Model a negative example.* Write *jump* with colored chalk on the board and circle the consonants following the vowel. Say, "Look at this word, *jump*. My turn. Does *jump* have a short vowel sound? Yes. Does one consonant follow the vowel? No. Do I double the consonant? No. How do I know? Because one consonant doesn't follow the vowel."
9. *Question.* Say, "Your turn. Does *jump* have a short vowel sound?" (Signal.) "Does one consonant follow the vowel?" (Signal.) "Do you double the consonant?" (Signal.) "How do you know?" (Signal.)
10. *Give feedback.* If the students are correct, say, "Good knowing not to double the consonant." If they are incorrect, correct them, repeating steps 8, 9 and 10.
11. *Test individuals and give feedback.* Repeat steps 9 and 10 with individuals as needed.
12. *Present another negative example.* Say, "Look at this word, *rain*. My turn. Does *rain* have a short vowel sound? No. Does one consonant follow the vowel? Yes. Do

I double the consonant? No. How do I know? Because it doesn't have a short vowel sound."

13. *Question.* Say, "Your turn. Does *rain* have a short vowel sound?" (Signal.) "Does one consonant follow the vowel?" (Signal.) "Do we double the consonant?" (Signal.) "How do you know?" (Signal.)

14. *Give feedback.* If the students are correct, say, "Good knowing not to double the consonant." If they are incorrect, correct them, repeating steps 12, 13, and 14.

Modeling Another Positive Example, Questioning, and Giving Feedback.

15. *Model another positive example.* Write *slip* with colored chalk on the board and circle the consonant. Say, "Look at this word, *slip.* My turn. Does *slip* have a short vowel sound? Yes. Does one consonant follow the vowel? Yes. Do I double the consonant? Yes. How do I know? Because the word has a short vowel sound followed by one consonant."

16. *Question.* Say, "Your turn. Does slip have a short vowel sound?" (Signal.) "Does one consonant follow the vowel?" (Signal.) "Do you double the consonant?" (Signal.) "How do you know?" (Signal.)

17. *Give feedback.* If the students are correct, say, "Good knowing to double the consonant." If they are incorrect, say, "No, listen," and repeat steps 15, 16, and 17.

Presenting Six Test Examples, Giving Feedback, Testing Individuals, and Giving Individual Feedback.

18. *Present a test example.* Write the words *hop, hem, bow, skip,* and *rate* on the board without the prompts. Say, "Look at this word, *hop.*" (Point to hop.) "Do we double the consonant before we add *ing?*" (Signal.)

19. *Give feedback.* If the students are correct, say, "Good knowing that we double the consonant before adding *ing.* If they are

incorrect, model the correct rule and question again. Follow steps 18 and 19 with the rest of the words.

20. *Test individuals.* Call on each individual to do one of the samples with the wording in step 18. Give feedback.

21. Proceed to the independent practice activity.

■ ■ **Activity**

Continue writing the script for the lesson. Teach the students how to apply the rule of "when a word has a short vowel sound followed by one consonant, double the consonant before adding *ing.*" You may use the same positive and negative examples in your lesson that we used in ours. Use the following outline:

1. Model spelling positive and negative examples, question, test students, and give feedback.
2. Question, test individuals, and give feedback. ■ ■

The Unit Method

In some special education settings at both the elementary and secondary levels, teachers are expected to teach science, social studies, health, and other content areas. A frequent technique used in teaching these content subjects is to have students either read orally or silently from the text and then answer the questions at the end of the chapter. Use of this technique often leads to an uninspiring, boring lesson. An alternative to the textbook approach is unit teaching.

Unit teaching relates instruction to a topic, problem, theme, or an area of interest (Hittleman, 1983). Unit teaching is designed around a unit comprised of "smaller bits and pieces of information that are grouped together into a larger, meaningful mass of subject matter" (McPhie, 1983, p. 52). For example, instead of gaining information about a topic such as electricity by reading from page to page in the science text, you would teach about electricity through interrelated activities that connect the study of electricity to other academic areas. With the unit method, students might be calculating the average cost of the school's electric bill for the past 6 months, setting up an experiment demonstrating the idea of a circuit, or reading about Thomas Edison and his experiments with electricity.

Most of the support for the unit method of teaching comes from expert testimonials. Meyen (1981) commented that unit teaching is effective for students with handicaps and students from diverse cultural backgrounds. In an analysis of the various types of units, Kelly (1979) suggested that integrated units connecting language arts, math, science, and other content areas are best for special education teachers. Units are also recommended for integrating multicultural content into the curriculum (Baker, 1983; Banks, 1987; Grant & Sleeter, 1989; Tiedt & Tiedt, 1986). For example, if you are teaching a unit dealing with different shelters, it is easy to include such diverse cultural elements as shelter on a reservation and shelter in a ghetto. A unit on nutrition may easily include foods native to various cultures in a discussion of the four basic food groups. A unit on folktales may include a selection of tales of African origin, such as *Mufaro's Beautiful Daughters* by John Steptoe (1987); tales of Native American origin, such as de Paola's (1983) *The Legend of the Bluebonnet;* and tales of Hispanic origin, such as Belpre's (1973) *Once in Puerto Rico.*

There is some empirical support for unit teaching with students who have special needs. Roser, Hoffman, and Farest (1990) found that literature units contributed to increased performance in language arts and reading test scores on the California Test of Basic Skills for second graders at risk, many of them from the Hispanic culture. In addition, Singer, McNeil, and Furse (1984) report a positive influence on reading and writing development.

Rationale

The unit method of teaching is based on the premise that students learn and assimilate information by actively participating in a variety of activities. As such, the philosophy of unit teaching is "learning by doing," which was articulated by John Dewey (Berry, 1983; Mickelson, 1983). Inclusion of a variety of activities also fosters individualization of instruction, an important component of special education instruction (Meyen, 1981). Integration of information promotes real purposes and audiences for language, factors important in learning (Rhodes & Dudley-Marling, 1988). A further premise is that units are motivational because they often take advantage of a students' special interests, natural curiosity, experiences, and cultural backgrounds.

Description

Units may be subject centered or interdisciplinary (integrated). Subject-centered units concentrate on one major content area, while integrated units incorporate the areas of math, language arts, and other content into the topic. A thematic unit is an integrated unit that focuses on reading and writing needs (Rhodes & Dudley-Marling, 1988).

It is possible to create either a subject-centered unit or an integrated unit for almost any topic. If a unit on Mexico includes only social studies objectives, it is a subject-centered unit. However, if a unit on Mexico includes objectives from other areas, such as math (requiring students to chart and compare the temperatures of different regions), reading (requiring students to read about Benito Juarez), and writing (requiring students to write reports about Mexican festivals, it is an integrated unit).

Units may also differ in the amount of student input (Baker, 1983). In a teacher-prepared unit, the teacher decides the topics and information to be presented. In a teacher-student prepared unit, the teacher generally selects the topic but guides the students in their selection of the content and ways to learn the information. In a student-prepared unit, the students totally decide the topic, the approaches, and the length of time. In a comparison of all three types, Baker (1983) recommends teacher-prepared units as the easiest for the integration of multicultural content. No matter the type, all units usually contain subtopics, general goals, specific objectives, activities to correspond with the objectives, ways to evaluate the objectives, and a list of resources.

Planning

The suggestions for planning a unit are a compilation of ideas from Baker (1983), Kelly (1979), Meyen (1981), Muessig (1983), Rhodes and Dudley-Marling (1988), and our own experiences. At the beginning, the unit method of teaching is time-consuming, but once the units are in place, they may be used again and again, often with only slight modifications. We suggest the following steps for creating a unit: (a) select the unit topic, (b) select the subtopics, (c) identify the general goals, (d) identify the specific objectives, (e) develop activities to meet the objectives, (f) evaluate the objectives, and (g) compile a list of resources. The steps are not always sequential, as sometimes it is easier to identify the general goal before the subtopics or sometimes the activities before the objectives.

Selecting the Unit Topic

The selection of the unit topic is often dictated by district curriculum guides, which list the required topics and objectives in social studies, language arts, science, history, health, and other subject areas for various grade levels. However, if curriculum guides are unavailable, you may examine the content of classroom textbooks for ideas. Roser, Hoffman, and Farest (1990) used children's literature to select unit topics. They selected and grouped ten children's books that focused on character traits and the ways in which these traits made the characters special into the unit topic of "Being Different Is Being Special" (p. 556). Rhodes and Dudley-Marling (1988) suggest, "The topic can be selected because the

teacher knows that it will inspire students' interests and meet some of their needs, or because the students themselves have suggested the topic or revealed a great interest in it during another instructional experience" (p. 93).

Muessig (1983) recommends using a single textbook as a basis for selecting topics for unit teaching at the secondary level. He recommends that you first write all of the chapter titles found in the class text on separate 3-inch by 5-inch cards. Then, separate the cards into essential, helpful, and possible topics. From the essential and helpful piles, select about six to eight overall topics for unit construction. For example, the following chapters of "Indian Life in America," "France in the New World," "Spain in the New World," and "England in the New World," found in the text *American History* (Abramowitz, 1979), may be grouped under the overall topic of the first settlers in America. Muessig further recommends that each unit contain three to six chapters.

Selecting Subtopics

Subtopics comprise the major areas that the unit topic may be divided into. If you are using Muessig's one-textbook approach, the subtopics of Indian, French, Spanish, and English settlers in America have already been indicated. In other cases, before identifying subtopics, you should become familiar with the unit topic. A quick and easy way to gain information on any subject in a short amount of time is to consult encyclopedias and easy-to-read library books. In addition, students may help choose subtopics.

To identify subtopics, you may use a type of clustering, or webbing, activity to assess students' knowledge or attitudes (Tiedt & Tiedt, 1986). Clustering is a brainstorming technique. In clustering, you write the unit topic, circle it, and space the subtopics around it. In Figure 8.1, we present a clustering activity that identifies subtopics for a subject-centered unit dealing with famous African-Americans. Notice that the major unit topic, famous African-Americans, led to the subtopics of various occupations, such as

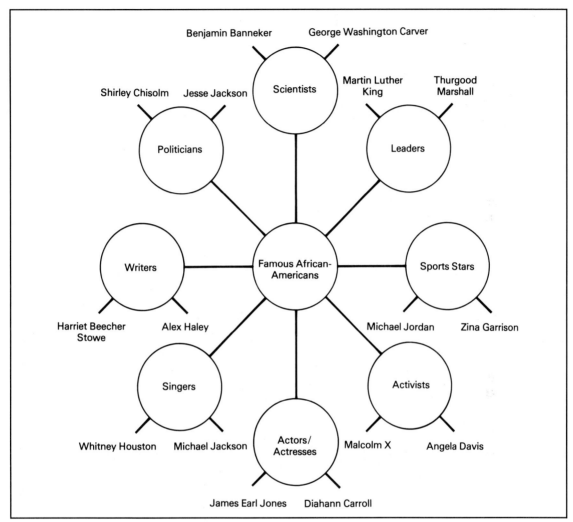

Figure 8.1
Clustering Approach to Subtopic Selections

scientists, activists, and singers. After spending time in the library and from past knowledge, the students identified particular scientists, activists, singers, etc., whose lives they wanted to study.

Rhodes and Dudley-Marling (1988) say that subtopics may serve as a basis for dividing students into interest groups. Thus, Hector, Sarah, and Michael may select to study the lives of famous African-American scientists such as Ben-

jamin Banneker and George Washington Carver and their contributions, while Jenni, Omar, and, Jason may select to study the lives of famous African-American politicians.

■ ■ Activity
Create subtopics for the general topic of Hispanic immigration to the United States. Use the information in Appendix A to help you. For

example, one of the subtopics may be the differences and similarities of family life of the various Hispanic groups. ■ ■

Identifying General Goals

In unit planning, general goals are "statements of broad, general outcomes of instruction and they do not state or convey meaning in a behavioral sense" (Burns, 1972, p. 3). General goals may include such words and phrases as "to have a greater appreciation, to better understand, to be able to enjoy, to develop respect for" (Baker, 1983, p. 108). A general goal found in a multicultural unit is "to help students understand the role and contributions of different ethnic groups in the development of the District of Columbia" (Baker, 1983, p. 109). General goals serve as bases for identifying objectives for individual lessons (Meyen, 1981).

To arrive at general goals using a text, Muessig (1983) suggests reading the content of the chapters selected under a particular theme, listing the basic facts in each chapter on 3-inch by 5-inch fact cards, and then combining related facts into a general goal. For example, continuing with the unit theme of the first settlers of America, Mr. Smith grouped related facts concerning the reason for the immigration to America from his chapter readings on Indian, English, Spanish, and French settlers into the following general goal: To help students understand the various reasons that the first settlers came to America and the effects the reasons had on the establishment of colonies.

Identifying Objectives

Behavioral objectives specify the learner, condition, criterion, and target behavior. They describe outcomes that can be measured. In the unit method of teaching, they are written to correlate with the subtopics and the major goals of the unit. For example, an objective for the general goal just discussed may be, After a discussion of English exploration of the New World, the students will list three reasons for English

settlements at 100% accuracy. Kelly (1979) recommends identification of enough objectives to cover a period of 3 to 6 weeks, as this is the usual time suggested for each unit.

Developing Activities and Learning Experiences

Ideas for activities may come from suggested experiments, enrichment activities found in teacher's manuals, or your own creativity and experiences. The activities depend on whether the unit is an integrated unit or a subject unit. In an integrated unit, the activities relate to other content areas. Meyen (1981) suggests encompassing the core areas of math, social competency, communication skills, safety, health, and vocation. For example, in teaching an integrated unit on time, Meyen (1981) suggests the following activities: "(a) make a calendar for this month as a group or individual project for *math*, (b) list some problems that result from being late for school for *social competency*, (c) obtain timetables from bus depots to read for *communication skills*, (d) role-play possible accidents that might occur because you are late for a meeting for *safety*, (e) read to determine the amount of sleep needed a night for *health*, and (f) investigate the number of hours various community workers spend on the job for the *vocational* core." If you plan to use integrated units based on core activities, you may wish to create a chart similar to the one found in Table 8.2.

■ ■ Activity

Look at the core activities in Table 8.2. Add a second activity to each of the core subject areas to meet the identified goal. ■ ■

In a subject-centered unit, many activities may be related to each objective. Such activities as (a) whole-class viewing of films on African-American scientists, (b) preparing a small-group chart of the list of contributions made by African-American scientists, (c) preparing individual dioramas of scenes from the lives of fa-

Table 8.2
Identification of Core Activities

Goal	Math	Social Competence	Communication	Health	Vocation
To develop an awareness of likenesses and differences among people.	Measure height and weight of students in class.	In small groups, develop a checklist to evaluate behaviors and appearances of people.	Read stories about famous people who are disabled and note their likenesses and differences in overcoming their disabilities.	Use a microscope to look at similarities and differences in peer's strands of hair and other objects.	Study want ads to determine how differences are related to job qualifications.

Note. These activities were adapted from *Developing Instructional Units for the Regular and Special Teacher* (3rd ed.) (pp. 102–105) by E. L. Meyen, 1981, Dubuque, IA: Wm. C. Brown Co.

mous scientists, and (d) illustrating inventions or discoveries of the scientists on a class mural correlate with the objective of describing contributions of African-American scientists. As you can see from the sample activities, different instructional arrangements—individuals (preparing dioramas), small groups (preparing a chart), and large groups (viewing films)—may be assigned.

Many times, teachers plan a culminating activity to tie together the information and understandings the students have developed. For example, in one cooperative teaching model, the fourth grade regular education teacher allowed the students to sign up for subtopics that interested them in the unit on Mexico. In the subtopic groups of three or four students, some members read and compiled the information; some wrote reports or stories about the information; and others drew the charts, graphs, murals, and diagrams. The children chose their major roles, but at the same time, they participated in all of the activities. Half of the groups reported and worked with the regular education teacher and half with the special education teacher.

As a culminating activity, the teachers and students held a fair and invited parents and members from other classes to visit the various booths designed by each subtopic group. Visitors were treated to sample foods, dramatizations, oral reports, and visual displays concerning Mexico. During the fair, the following booths were presented: food, folklore, city life, village life, history, religion, and government. In the government booth, a student who was essentially a nonreader volunteered to read the group prepared report. He was so motivated by his selection that he memorized the report but pretended to read from the typed project.

Evaluating the Objectives
Evaluation may be in the form of paper-and-pencil tests, experience stories, group reports, or individual reports. Muessig (1983) suggests that secondary teachers use paper-and-pencil tests at first and then develop checklists, inventories, observations, and open-ended evaluation procedures. Meyen (1981) suggests that elementary teachers use experience stories with each lesson.

Compiling a List of Resources
Since no one text is used in unit teaching and since you want to include many activities when presenting the information, you must compile a list of resources. The resources may include library books, vocabulary word lists, workbook

pages, worksheet pages, speakers, films, film-strips, field trips, and experiments (Meyen, 1981). (In Figure 8.2 we provide ideas for other

Free Stuff for Kids
Meadowbrook Publishers
1230 Avenue of the Americas
New York, NY 10020

Free Publications from U.S. Government Agencies
Library Unlimited
P.O. Box 3988
Englewood, CO 80155-3988
(*Phone:* 800–237–6124)

Kid's America
by Steven Caney
Whitman Publishing Co.
708 Broadway
New York, NY 10003

Educator's Guide to Free Health, Physical Education, and Recreation Materials and *Educator's Guide to Free Social Studies Materials*
Educator's Progress Service, Inc.
214 Center Street
Randolph, WI 53956
(*Phone:* 414–326–3126)

How to Get Free Software
St. Martin's Press, Inc.
Subsidiary of Macmillan Publishing Co.
175 5th Avenue
New York, NY 10010
(*Phone:* 800–221-7945)

Fress Resource Builder for Librarians and Teachers
McFarland and Company Inc. Publishers
Box 611
Jefferson, NC 28640
(*Phone:* 919-246-4460)

Figure 8.2
Sources of Free Materials

resources and free materials.) Sometimes, students may secure supplemental materials. One teacher who organized the social studies curriculum into subject area units with various countries as topics had the students write to the embassies located in Washington, DC, for information about each country. Frequently, embassies send not only free brochures and pamphlets but also addresses of other places for free materials. At the beginning of the school year, this same teacher had parents identify any special skills or topics they or their friends might share from a list of planned unit topics for the coming school year. Crocker (1983) recommends having students file information and materials that they collect in large vertical files for use by other students in the future.

In Table 8.3, we present a summary of the steps of unit preparation with examples. Notice that the unit is integrated to incorporate math and other subject areas.

Instead of following the preceding steps to design your own units, you may wish to adapt some units prepared by others. In *Planning and Organizing for Multicultural Instruction* (Baker, 1983) and in *Multicultural Teaching: A Handbook of Activities, Information, and Resources* (Tiedt & Tiedt, 1986), the authors suggest ideas for various multicultural units. Other sources for prepared units include *Developing Instructional Units for the Regular and Special Teacher* (Meyen, 1981), with such elementary-level topics as time, health habits, and community helpers, and *The 4MAT System* (McCarthy, 1987), with such elementary-level topics as living and nonliving things, middle school-level topics as probability and energy, and secondary-level topics as due process and respiration/breathing.

Lesson Plan

Once the planning steps are completed, a final step is to develop individual lesson plans. Meyen (1981) suggests writing the first ten to fifteen lessons in detail and merely outlining the remaining lessons. As suggested by Baker (1983),

Table 8.3
Preparation of Unit with Examples

Step 1. Select a topic or theme from texts or curriculum guides.
Example: Mexico (selected from a history text).
Step 2. Select subtopics of the unit theme.
Example: People, climate, animals, shelters, customs, government, history, and natural resources.
Step 3. Identify the general goals.
Example: Students will develop an understanding of the various people who comprise the population of Mexico.
Step 4. Identify specific objectives for each general goal.
Examples: (a) given a chart, student will identify five differences between the life-styles of city dwellers and village dwellers in Mexico with 100% accuracy; (b) given 40 minutes, students will write about life in a city, making at least five comparisons with life in a village; (c) given milk cartons, paints, and other materials, students will build a replica of a typical Mexican village as evaluated by the teacher; and (d) given specific vocabulary items, students will use them accurately in their written reports.
Step 5. Develop activities and learning experiences.
Examples: For math, compare the number of people who live in the city with the number who live in villages. For language arts, read library books and write both individual and group stories or reports concerning what it feels like to live in Guadalajara. For art, build a replica of a Mexican village.
Step 6. Evaluate the objectives.
Example: Complete the following chart in small groups:

	City Dwellers	**Village Dwellers**
Occupation	_____	_____
Population	_____	_____
Shelters	_____	_____
Clothing	_____	_____
Life of children	_____	_____

Step 7. Compile a list of materials and resources.
Examples: Survey parents of Mexican-American students as possible resources. Check film catalogs. Check the library for student books, vertical picture files, and teacher reference books. Check *National Geographic* and other magazines. Have students write to the Mexican embassy. Prepare a vocabulary list with housing words like *adobe, patio, petates* (straw mats), and *plaza* and clothing words like *bolero, sombrero, huaraches* (sandals), and *rebozos* (shawls).

we recommend the use of a grid with objectives, activities, and evaluation identified within a time framework. In Table 8.4, we present lesson plans for one of the general goals and three objectives of the unit specified in Table 8.3. The following week, students will be presented with some different objectives within the same general goal and subtopic.

■ ■ **Activity**
Select a subtopic, such as customs or animals, and identify the general goal and objectives to continue a unit about Mexico. Then, list activities to correlate with the objectives, including evaluation activities. Write a 5-day plan. You may wish to consult an encyclopedia or easy-to-read children's books. ■ ■

Table 8.4
Sample Weekly Unit Plan

Goal: Students will develop an understanding of the various people who comprise the population of Mexico

STO: (1) Given a chart, students will identify five differences between the life styles of city and village dwellers in Mexico with 100% accuracy. (2) Given 40 minutes, students will write about life in a Mexican village and in a city. (3) Given specific vocabulary terms, students will use these terms in their writings accurately.

Eval: (1) In small groups, students complete the categories of occupation, population, clothing, shelters and life of children sections on chart (check of objective 1) with 100% accuracy. (2) In individual writing activity, students include three facts and at least five new words (check of objectives 2 and 3)

Monday	Tuesday	Wednesday	Thursday	Friday
Working on Obj 1+2+3	Working on Obj 1	Working on Obj 1+3	Evaluate Obj 1	Evaluate Obj 2+3
View film on life in Mexican village. Present new vocabulary terms. Discuss and list major points as a class. Individuals write a story about living in a Mexican village (tell at least 3 things) (Include 2 vocab terms).	Divide students into small groups to read and draw charts and bar graphs of population and of various occupations in city and village.	Guest speaker - Ms Gonzalez talks about and shows slides of city life in Guadalajara and villages around the city. Read and discuss story section about city life and discuss new vocab. terms. List 3 things on board and 3 vocab terms in group language experience story.	Students complete sections on chart and present and discuss their charts with other students.	Students individually write about city and village life. Have those who finish early plan the building of a replica of a typical Mexican village and city. Discuss plans as a group.

Summary

In this chapter we included information concerning Direct Instruction and unit teaching. Empirical evidence shows that the Direct Instruction model is effective for teaching explicit skills to students with special needs. The curriculum features of Direct Instruction include the components of sequential order, examples, well-constructed formats, prompts, independent practice activities, and mastery learning. Cuing student attention and providing overviews to begin the lesson; eliciting student participation, providing immediate feedback, and guiding practice activities during the body of the lesson; and introducing independent practice activities to close the lesson are presentation components often used in presenting a lesson.

Unit teaching is a technique used for teaching in content area subjects. It involves integrating instruction in a variety of academic areas to a topic, a problem, a theme, or an area of interest. Expert opinion often endorses the effectiveness of unit teaching. In planning a unit, (a) select the unit topic, (b) select the subtopics, (c) identify the general goals, (d) identify the specific objectives, (e) develop activities to meet the objectives, (f) evaluate the objectives, and (g) compile a list of resources. Planning a new unit requires much time; however, once a unit is complete, it may be used again and again.

Important Points

1. Unit teaching is a method of teaching that relates instruction in a variety of academic areas to a topic, a problem, a theme, or an area of interest.

2. There is some empirical evidence as to the effectiveness of unit teaching, but unit teaching is mostly supported by expert opinion, which extols student involvement, individualization, motivation, and multicultural concerns.

3. A subject-centered unit draws objectives from one major subject area.

4. An integrated unit incorporates objectives from various subject areas.

5. In planning a unit, (a) select the unit topic, (b) select subtopics, (c) identify the general goals, (d) identify the specific objectives, (e) develop activities to meet the objectives, (f) evaluate the objectives, and (g) compile a list of resources.

6. Unit topics may be selected from curriculum guides, classroom texts, children's literature, and students' interests.

7. Clustering is a way to enlist student input that identifies subtopics for a general topic.

8. General goals are the general outcomes of a unit.

9. General goals form the bases for identifying the objectives for individual lessons.

10. Objectives identify specific behaviors and correlate with the subtopics and major goals of the unit.

11. Activities and learning experiences should relate to the unit objectives, require student participation, and provide for various grouping arrangements.

12. A culminating activity is often used to tie together the information and understandings students have developed.

13. Evaluations of the objectives may be in the form of paper-and-pencil tests, experience stories, and reports.

9

Teacher-Directed
Strategy Instruction

Key Topics

"Give me a fish and I eat for a day. Teach me to fish and I eat for a lifetime" is an old adage that typifies the current emphasis in special education on teaching students *how* to learn. If you teach students *how* to learn, then you do not have to help them prepare for every test, assist them with each report, or help them answer the questions at the end of every chapter they are assigned. In other words, you provide them with the strategies that will enable them to master implicit skills. These skills may include finding the main idea in a paragraph, summarizing a passage, accessing information on their own, and writing a research paper (Rosenshine, 1990).

In this chapter, we present techniques for teaching implicit skills. We specifically focus on metacognition, reciprocal teaching, and task-specific strategy instruction. Metacognition is the knowledge and control that individuals have over their learning. Reciprocal teaching involves gaining meaning from text. Task-specific strategies are approaches that facilitate the completion of tasks. Although we introduce you to metacognition separately, you will notice that the features of metacognitive instruction are present in reciprocal teaching and task-specific strategy instruction. Those features include "(a) careful analysis of the task at hand, (b) the identification of strategies which will promote successful task completion, (c) the explicit instruction of these strategies accompanied by metacognitive information regarding their application, (d) the provision of feedback regarding the usefulness of the strategies and the success with which they are being acquired, and (e) instruction regarding the generalized use of the strategies" (Palincsar & Brown, 1987, p. 73). In implementing these procedures, teachers initially assume the major role and responsibility for teaching. Gradually, through scaffolding, the responsibility shifts to the students.

Metacognition

The general knowledge (awareness) and the control (monitoring) that an individual has over his or her thinking and learning is known as metacognition (Flavell, 1976; Paris, Lipson, Jacobs, Oka, Debritto, & Cross, 1982). Awareness, the first component of metacognition, involves a person's knowledge about his or her cognitive resources and the relationship between those capabilities and the demands of the task. For example, if you notice that you can study better with the television off, you are demonstrating an understanding of how you best function in a specific situation. If you are aware of what you need to do to perform effectively, then you may be able to regulate and control your activities to solve a problem or complete a task. For example, when Chris observes that he does better in afternoon and evening classes because he performs better later in the day, he is demonstrating metacognitive awareness.

The second component of metacognition involves self-regulatory mechanisms that enable a person to monitor, adjust, correct, and control his or her cognitive activities and task performance. For example, when you estimate the length of time it will take to complete an activity and then adjust your pace to allow yourself sufficient time to finish, you are exercising control and regulating your actions. You are actively participating in and assuming control over the learning situation. Active monitoring of cognitive activities is necessary for efficient learning (Baker & Brown, 1980). For example, Ranjit, a high school student, has learned self-regulation by adjusting his rate when he reads different materials. He reads quickly through *Auto Trader* magazine and the daily comics but reads his history and science textbooks more slowly and methodically, looking back frequently to check his comprehension. Notice how he first demonstrates an *awareness* of the need to read materials at different rates (metacognitive awareness) and then exercises *control* over the situation by actually adjusting his reading rate with different materials (metacognitive monitoring).

■ ■ Activity

Part 1. Read the following passage. As you read it, try to observe what you do as you read by asking yourself these questions, which are based on Robinson (1975):

1. Do I look back at the words I have just read?
2. Do I look at each word?
3. Do I think of other things when I read?
4. Do I read and think about the meaning of every word, or do I put words together into groups?
5. Do I really know what I am reading?

When you finish reading, write out all of the things you did while you were reading (activity adapted from Platt, 1987; Platt & Williams, 1988).

Passage

Beneath their feet the diesel engine thudded slowly, sending a thrust of power trembling through the deck. Across Tauranga Harbor, against the wharf at Mount Maunganui, a Japanese timber ship lifted her long black hull fretfully on the tide, dragging at the hawser with a dark, clumsy impatience. Farrer looked away, out to the harbor mouth, mentally checking off Matakana Island, impatient to be past it, as though the approaching bird sanctuary barred their passage to the open sea and the thing he knew awaited him there. The sun, still rising, spread hot, multi-fingered hands across the water. (Burns & Roe, 1985)

Part 2. Now that you have completed a metacognitive awareness activity, try a metacognitive monitoring activity. If you were to read this passage again, what would you do to improve your reading of it? Write down any strategies you would use or adjustments you would make. For example, did you look back or adjust your pace? (The answers for these and other activities are found in the Instructor's Manual.) ■ ■

Cognitive psychology is an important source of information for teachers working with students who have mild disabilities. Using the contributions of cognitive psychology, special educators can design interventions that emphasize maintenance and generalization of skills and strategies (Wong, 1986). For example, a self-questioning procedure taught to students with learning disabilities resulted in systematic self-monitoring and enhanced reading comprehension (Wong & Jones, 1982). Other investigations have studied the effects of metacognitive instruction on memory skills (Paris, Newman, & McVey, 1982) and written expression (Harris & Graham, 1985) of students with academic problems. Researchers in the fields of cognitive developmental psychology and instructional psychology have developed systematic procedures for teaching metacognitive strategies (Collins & Smith, 1980; Garner & Kraus, 1982; Palincsar, 1982; Taylor & Beach, 1984; Wong & Jones, 1982), and teachers may use these procedures with students who have special needs.

These procedures may be used to teach a variety of metacognitive strategies to students with special needs. We could compare a student's having a variety of metacognitive strategies to a good rock group that has a repertoire of hits that it can perform at a concert. So too, do students with special needs require a number of strategies at their disposal to respond to the academic demands of the classroom. Besides knowing a variety of strategies, students need to know which ones to use and when to use them. The members of the rock group will consider their audience and the acoustics in the facility in which they are playing (setting demands), the lighting, equipment, their voices, instruments (strengths and weaknesses), and what they are trying to accomplish at each concert they hold, such as fund-raising or plugging a new album (personal goal or objective). Students need to consider the demands and problems they encounter in the classroom, what strengths they bring to a learning activity, what typically gives them problems, and what they are trying to do, such as understand a reading passage, remember a list of words, or write a theme. Successful musicians monitor throughout the concert how they are going over with the crowd. They may decide to rearrange the sequence of numbers they are performing based upon the reaction of the audience, or they may resurrect some of their old hits if they get lots of requests for them or if the new ones are not getting a good reaction. You may have been to a concert that started out in a sequenced and organized manner and then noticed signals being passed among the group members to change the original plan and try something else.

Just as the rock group members monitored and made adjustments in their performance at the concert, students who are metacognitively aware and know how to regulate their learning make adjustments as they proceed through a task.

Karim could not remember what he had read when he got to the bottom of the page in his history book (awareness), so he reread the page, this time pausing after each paragraph to paraphrase what he had just read (monitoring). Angel was having difficulty studying for tests at the end of a unit because she could not understand her own notes or remember what the teacher had said (awareness). She began to rewrite her notes after each class, thereby engaging in a cumulative review (monitoring). These two students were demonstrating metacognitive knowledge. When students possess good metacognitive skills, they are able to interact effectively with learning situations and perform independently.

■ ■ Activity
Give an example of a metacognitive awareness activity and a metacognitive monitoring activity. ■ ■

Rationale
The reason we teach metacognitive strategies to students is to influence how students interact with a learning task (Palincsar, 1986a). Metacognitive instruction is designed to empower students to assume control over their own learning and problem solving. It allows students to be more independent, to understand the purpose behind their academic assignments, and to realize the results of their actions. Metacognitive instruction is designed to promote generalization and transfer of skills across content areas and settings and is effective in teaching implicit skills, such as summarizing, paragraph writing, and self-questioning.

Description

Wong (1986) and other advocates of metacognition believe that students should be made aware of the purpose of metacognitive training and the relationship between the learned strategy and improved performance in the areas targeted for use—Why am I learning this and how will it help me? The procedures typically used for training metacognitive skills include informed training and self-control training (Brown & Palincsar, 1982).

Informed Training

With informed training, students are told the rationale underlying each of the activities they are asked to do. Informed training helps students understand the significance of the strategy as well as the potential benefits. Paris, Newman, and McVey (1982) trained two groups of children in mnemonic activities. One group (informed training group) was given the rationale for each of the training activities and feedback regarding their performance of the activities while the other group (blind training group) was not. The group receiving informed training (elaboration) experienced greater gains than did the group receiving blind training (no elaboration). It appears that when students are given information about the purpose of a skill or strategy, where and when it will be useful, and how to monitor their use of it, they acquire it more readily and later spontaneously apply it in other contexts (Palincsar, 1986b).

Self-Control Training

Self-control training includes the training of general executive skills, or self-regulation, such as planning, self-monitoring, self-questioning, self-testing, and self-evaluation (Brown & Palincsar, 1982). For students with special needs, instruction in self-control is extremely important if transfer and generalization are to occur. For example, Day (1980) instructed junior college students in comprehension strategies. Students who did not have learning problems performed well with informed training only. However, students with demonstrated learning problems required self-control training (instruction involving rules and how to monitor the application of those rules) before showing significant improvement.

Implementation

Teachers initially assume the responsibility for helping students identify tasks with which they need metacognitive training (awareness). They begin metacognitive training by modeling self-regulation activities. Then, gradually, through scaffolding, they shift the responsibility to the students, who participate in applying metacognitive skills. Metacognitive strategies become student-directed when students show independent application of them, or generalization.

A review of the literature in metacognition suggests the existence of specific elements to include in metacognitive instruction. We present the following critical steps adapted from the work of Palincsar and Brown (1987) and Pressley, Borkowski, and O'Sullivan (1984), in combination with our own thoughts.

1. Identify the task.
   Example: Remembering what you read.
2. Choose a strategy to facilitate completion of the task.
   Example: Inserting stop points in text at which you must put into your own words what you just read.
3. Explicitly teach the strategy.
   Example: Modeling for students what they should do when they come to a stop point.
4. Explain the benefits to be expected.
   Example: Describing that grades will improve, frustration will decrease, and reading will be easier and more fun.
5. Provide guided practice.
   Example: Working through an activity with students, having them apply the strategy.
6. Provide feedback.
   Example: Giving positive and corrective feedback regarding consistent and appropriate use of the strategy.

7. Teach students how to generalize use of the strategy.
   Example: Showing students how to use this technique with reading materials in school (content area subjects) and out of school (magazines, mail, assembly directions).

Let's take a look at a metacognitive intervention for increasing class participation (Ellis, 1989). It consists of four parts (PREP, SLANT, RELATE, and WISE) that teach students thinking ahead, thinking during class discussions, and thinking after class discussions. PREP (prepare materials, review what you know, establish a positive mind set, and pinpoint goals) activates students to prepare themselves for class discussions. During actual class discussions, SLANT (sit up, lean forward, act like you're interested, nod, and track the teacher) cues students to demonstrate appropriate nonverbal behaviors. RELATE (reveal reasons, echo examples, lasso comparisons, ask questions, tell main idea, and examine importance) directs students to the verbal behaviors essential for class participation.

WISE (were goals met, itemize important information, see how information can be remembered, and explain what was learned) requires students to think back and evaluate their participation after class is over. Figure 9.1 shows the WISE strategy for thinking after a lesson, and Figure 9.2 shows the PREP/WISE Score Sheet.

Ellis's (1989) class participation intervention (CPI) for students with mild handicaps addresses metacognitive awareness ("Am I prepared for class?") and monitoring ("Does that make sense? No, I had better ask a question"). Ellis recommends teaching PREP and WISE together, and after they are mastered, he recommends teaching SLANT and RELATE together. Ellis specifies that the CPI strategies should be taught by (a) motivating students to learn them, (b) describing and modeling the strategies, (c) requiring verbal elaboration and then rote memorization of the strategies, (d) providing group and individual practice, and (e) periodically checking for maintenance of the strategies. He reports that students who master the CPI strategies come to class better prepared and increase academic responding during class.

Important Points

1. Metacognition is the general knowledge (awareness) and control (monitoring) that an individual has over his or her thinking and learning.
2. Metacognitive awareness involves a person's knowledge about his or her own cognitive resources and the relationship between those capabilities and the demands of the task.
3. Metacognitive monitoring involves self-regulatory mechanisms that enable a person to monitor, adjust, correct, and control his or her cognitive activities.
4. Metacognitive instruction is designed to improve student problem solving and in-

crease student independence, generalization of the skills, and mastery of implicit skills, such as self-questioning.
5. The teaching of metacognitive skills involves informed training, which explains the rationale and benefits, and self-control training, which teaches executive skills such as planning, self-monitoring, self-testing, and self-evaluation.
6. Metacognitive teaching procedures include the following: (a) identify the task, (b) choose a strategy, (c) teach the strategy, (d) explain the benefits, (e) provide guided practice, (f) provide feedback, and (g) teach generalization.

```
┌─────────────────────────────────────────────┐
│          Think Back with WISE                │
│  Were goals met?                             │
│                                              │
│  • Did you learn what you wanted to learn?   │
│  • Did you meet your participation goals?    │
│                                              │
│  Itemize important information               │
│                                              │
│  • Review study guide, notes, or textbook    │
│  • Mark key information                      │
│                                              │
│  See how information can be remembered       │
│                                              │
│  • Draw graphic displays                     │
│  • Create mnemonic devices                   │
│  • Create study cards                        │
│                                              │
│  Explain what was learned to somebody        │
│                                              │
│  • Use your notes to teach somebody about    │
│    the topic                                 │
│                                              │
└─────────────────────────────────────────────┘
```

Figure 9.1
The Metacognitive Strategy for
Thinking After a Lesson
Note. From "A Metacognitive Intervention for Increasing
Participation" by E. S. Ellis, 1989, *Learning Disabilities Focus*, 5(1), p. 37. Reprinted by permission.

Reciprocal Teaching

Like the other approaches in this chapter, reciprocal teaching concentrates on teaching students how to learn, specifically how to gain meaning from reading text. Essentially, "reciprocal teaching is a dialogue between teachers and students for the purpose of jointly constructing the meaning of the text" (Palincsar, 1986a, p. 119). The approach helps students understand how to study and learn from a text and promotes metacognitive monitoring of comprehension (Palincsar & Brown, 1986, 1987). The instruction is teacher-directed at first, but then a student assumes the teacher's role as other students comment upon the student's questions, elaborate upon the student's summary, and assist in constructing meaning. To move from teacher-

directed to student-directed instruction, the teacher uses a scaffolding procedure, decreasing the intensity and frequency of the prompts and supports (Palincsar & Brown, 1984).

The technique is usually taught to students individually or in groups of four to seven, and the lessons last for approximately 30 minutes for 20 days (Palincsar & Brown, 1986, 1988). Since reciprocal teaching involves teaching implicit skills, many of the techniques identified by research as effective for teaching implicit skills (see Chapter 7) are the same as those effective in reciprocal teaching. We point out the similarities in our discussion of reciprocal teaching.

Much of the research on the effectiveness of reciprocal teaching was conducted by the creators of the model with junior high students in remedial reading classes as the subjects and expository or informational text as the reading material. The students were identified as "adequate decoders but poor comprehenders" (Palincsar & Brown, 1986, p. 775). In the studies (Brown & Palincsar, 1982; Palincsar & Brown, 1984), students improved in comprehension, measured by daily curriculum-based tests of 450-word passages and ten comprehension questions. They also improved in comprehension of material presented in their regular classes, demonstrating that reciprocal teaching produced generalization. Recently, the research program has been extended to investigate the effectiveness of reciprocal teaching with first and second graders determined to be at risk for academic failures (Palincsar & Brown, 1989). In these studies, teachers, instead of the students, read the text. It was found that 75% of the first grade children achieved criterion performance. In addition, the first grade children attempted to apply the procedure to spontaneous discussions and were able to maintain the procedures in a follow-up study conducted when the students entered second grade.

Rationale

The idea behind reciprocal teaching is that the teacher is teaching the students a strategy that will enable the students to learn how to gain

```
                         PREP/WISE score sheet

        PREP                                                        WISE
                          Student name: _____

Prepare materials for class                                  Were goals met?
                          ┌──────────────────────────────┐
yes no N/A                │   PREP/WISE Process          │   yes no N/A    Noted whether topic question
 □  □  □   Textbook       │  # of "yes" boxes            │    □  □  □      had been answered during the
 □  □  □   Notebook       │   □              Score       │                 lesson/what answer was
 □  □  □   Pen/pencil     │                  _____    │   Itemize important information
 □  □  □   Homework       │   □              Process Score│   yes no N/A    Marked on notes/book
 □  □  □   Study guide    │  # categories evaluated      │    □  □  □      perceptions of most important
 □  □  □   Other _____ └──────────────────────────────┘                 information from lesson
yes no N/A
 □  □  □   Difficult areas marked on notes/book              See how information can be remembered
                                                             yes no N/A
                                                              □  □  □      Remembering devices created

Review what you know                                         Explain what was learned to somebody
                                                             yes no N/A
(at least 3 items    What I already know:                     □  □  □      Explained what was learned to
known about topic                                                           someone else
listed)              1. _____

                     2. _____
yes no N/A
 □  □  □             3. _____

Establish positive mind set

yes no
 □  □               Positive statement about myself: _____
Pinpoint goals      _____

Question about the topic
has been noted       I want to find out _____   I found out        I still don't know
yes no N/A                                                   □                  □
 □  □  □             _____

yes no N/A           My participation goal is to _____
 □  □  □                                                     □                  □
                     _____
Participation goals noted                                 I met my goal     I didn't meet my goal
```

Figure 9.2
PREP/WISE Evaluation Sheet

Note. From "A Metacognitive Intervention for Increasing Participation" by E. S. Ellis, 1989, *Learning Disabilities Focus, 5*(1), p. 39. Reprinted by permission.

information from the printed page. Once the students learn the strategy, they can apply it to different situations without the presence of the teacher. The strategy improves self-concept, because students learn to attribute success to their ability to use the strategy and not to luck (Palincsar, 1986a). The emphasis on ensuring that the students are well-informed about the procedures, purposes, and applications finds its basis in metacognition and the premise that students with learning problems acquire information

more readily when they are well-informed. (Duffy, Roehler, Meloth, Putnam, & Wesselman, 1986). The interactive nature of the approach, which requires a joint construction of meaning, is based on the belief that students can learn from each other. (Palincsar & Brown, 1988).

Description

The essential components of reciprocal teaching are strategies that teach students how to gain information from text, guided interactive instruction, and informed learners. The teacher instructs the students in the strategies of summarizing, questioning, clarifying, and predicting. In guided interactive instruction, control of the lesson moves from the teacher to the students. Students are informed about the procedures, purposes, and applications.

Strategies

The teacher teaches the four strategies of summarizing, questioning, clarifying, and predicting. For the first 4 days of the procedures, the teacher teaches the students each of the strategies and then on the fifth day, the teacher begins modeling the strategies in constructing a dialogue. For example, Palincsar and Brown (1986a) suggest that you teach students to generate information-seeking questions by first asking them to generate questions concerning everyday events, such as, "If you are interested in knowing what time the afternoon movie begins, you call the theatre and ask: _____" (p. 773). The teacher spends only about a day introducing each strategy, because the emphasis is on teaching the strategies through the interaction between teacher and students in a dialogue (Palincsar & Brown, 1986a).

Summarizing. Summarizing involves identification and paraphrasing of the main ideas. Students are taught first to summarize the content in a paragraph or section and then to integrate the content across paragraphs.

Questioning. Questioning requires students to question themselves about the content. Students become more involved when they must generate questions than when they must respond to teacher questions (Palincsar & Brown, 1986). At the beginning, students often generate questions that cannot be answered using the information presented in the text, which is a clue that they are not focusing on the text information (Palincsar & Brown, 1988).

Clarifying. Clarifying is discerning when there is a breakdown in comprehension and identifying appropriate strategies to restore

meaning. To do this, students must know that they are not comprehending the information (metacognitive awareness). Readers who have comprehension problems often cannot discriminate when they do not understand materials, as they are more interested in decoding words than in making sense of the words (Palincsar & Brown, 1986a). At first, students attribute lack of vocabulary knowledge as the cause for not understanding the meaning of a passage, so they focus on the unknown words in a selection for clarification. Eventually, however, they realize that unfamiliar ideas or difficult content may block understanding of the text, so they attempt to clarify these concepts (Palincsar & Brown, 1988).

Predicting. Predicting is hypothesizing the next event in the text. Students often use pictures and text structures such as headings and italicized words to aid them in making predictions. Predicting requires students to activate background information concerning the passage and to link that information to the author's intent. Often, however, students who come from different cultural backgrounds find that their background information does not relate to the classroom materials that they are using, and they have difficulty comprehending the author's message (Ruiz, 1989). For example, if you are reading a selection about plants of the desert, you probably will predict that sometime in the text the author will mention cactus. Think of the advantage of the student who has read about or visited a desert compared with one who has never encountered the desert environment before.

Predictions can also let teachers and students know when there is a breakdown in comprehension and a student's background knowledge is incorrect. Palincsar and Brown (1988) relate the following incident of an example when students did not use the facts of a selection to check an incorrect prediction. In reading the title and looking at the picture in the selection "Ships of the Desert," some students predicted that the author would talk about camels storing water in their humps. When asked to summarize, these same students said the author told how camels stored water in their humps, when in fact the author had stated that camels store fat in their humps. The students did not correct their prediction and, thus, didn't glean the correct meaning from the selection. They failed to use metacognitive monitoring to check their incorrect prediction.

Guided Interactive Instruction

During guided instruction, model the use of the preceding four strategies. Remember, you have already spent 4 days teaching the strategies. During the initial modeling, attempt to involve the students by having them answer questions, elaborate upon your summary, and add predictions and clarifications (Herrmann, 1988). Gradually, transfer responsibility for these activities to the students, until eventually, you just provide feedback and coach the students through the dialogue as they interact with each other.

This procedure is a form of scaffolding (Palincsar & Brown, 1984). During the scaffolding process, teachers provide supports by prompting students and changing the demands of the task (Palincsar & Brown, 1989) or by modeling the task or giving feedback (Bos & Vaughn, 1988). For example, if the student discussion leader cannot generate a question, you may prompt by suggesting that the student begin the question with *when*. If that doesn't work then you may modify the task by asking the student to identify a fact, instead of a question. If that doesn't work, then you may model the task: "I might ask the question . . . ." You may also give corrective feedback using the prompt format (i.e., "I think you forgot an important point in your summary. Remember . . .") and praise for correct answers: "Good summary."

High-risk students frequently have difficulty constructing summarizing statements and generating appropriate questions, so during the beginning stages, you should construct paraphrases and questions for the students to mimic (Brown & Palincsar, 1982). Eventually, however, high-risk students are able to use the strategies on their own. In a comparison of student performance on the beginning dialogue sessions (when the teacher assumed most of the responsibility) and the end sessions (when the students assumed most of the responsibility), Brown and Palincsar (1982) report that nonquestions were reduced from 19% to 0% and student responses needing clarification were reduced from 36% to 4%. At the same time, in the beginning sessions, only 11% of the students' summary statements described main ideas, while 60% of the statements did at the end.

Informed Learners

At the beginning of every reciprocal teaching session, inform learners about the strategies they will be using, the importance of using the strategies, and ways to generalize them. In addition, inform learners of the consequences of learning the strategies. Specifying consequences of what happens when a strategy is employed leads to a better understanding of the relationship between the strategic learning and successful performance (Paris & Oka, 1986). Students must feel that the effort of learning the strategies produces success with a task (Paris & Oka, 1986). Direct and frequent measurements are suggested as means to convince students of the worth of reciprocal teaching (Palincsar, 1986b). Frequent graphing of the results of comprehension testing and taping of the reciprocal sessions help prove to students that the use of reciprocal teaching leads to positive consequences (Palincsar & Brown, 1984).

Implementation

Implementation of reciprocal teaching requires careful planning and incorporation of the activities of summarizing, questioning, clarifying, and predicting into the lesson presentation. The steps are adapted from the works of Palincsar and Brown (1986, 1988, 1989) and Herrmann (1988). These steps are not rigid, nor is the exact wording given for the modeling, the prompting, or the feedback. Unlike Direct Instruction, with the emphasis on teacher control and scripted lessons, much of the learning interaction in reciprocal teaching is controlled by the students, so teacher responses cannot be specifically worded. In addition, reciprocal teaching is used to teach an implicit, higher-order skill or a body of knowledge that does not lend itself to step-by-step procedures.

Planning

To prepare for a reciprocal teaching session, first select text segments. Criteria for text selection are that the students can decode the material with at least 80 words-per-minute (wpm) accuracy with no more than 2 errors and that the text is representative of the materials that students read and study in the regular class (Palincsar, 1986b). Remember, also, that most of the research was completed with expository or informational materials.

The other planning activities include (a) generate possible predictions, (b) identify questions ahead; (c) summarize each section, (d) circle difficult vocabulary or concepts, and (e) identify supports that students will need to help them learn the information (Herrmann, 1988). We present each of these activities with an example in Table 9.1.

Presentation

We suggest the following steps for presentation in a reciprocal teaching lesson during the initial stages of teacher modeling and after the students have been taught the four strategy skills. We follow each step with an example of its implementation in teaching a group of middle school students with special needs. Since this is an initial lesson, the teacher is more in charge and the students are participating more by answering questions generated by the teacher, elaborating on the summary, and adding predictions and clarifications. The teacher explains, instructs, models, guides the students, and praises (Palincsar & Brown, 1986). We use the plan in Table 9.1 to assist in generating the dialogue.

1. Begin with a review of the four strategies, their importance, and the context in which the strategies are useful (informed learners).
2. Read the title and ask the students to predict what they will learn. An example is:

> T: The title of the passage is *Langston Hughes: He Believed Humor Would Help Defeat Bigotry and Fear.* In your own words and looking at the pictures, what do you think this story will be about?
> S1: A man.
> T: Correct. Any other predictions?
> S2: A black man.
> S3: He thinks humor is powerful and can beat fear.
> S4: I bet he's a comedian.
> S5: No, look at the picture. He's signing autographs. I bet he's a writer.
> T: Those are excellent predictions. Let's begin.

3. Read a small portion of the text orally or have the students read it silently, depending on the group.
4. Ask a question about the content. In the beginning ask students to answer the question. Also ask if students have any additional questions to ask. An example is:

> T: After reading the first three paragraphs my question is, Why did Langston's father leave home?
> S1: To go to Mexico.
> T: To do what?
> S1: To become a lawyer.
> T: Why did he go to Mexico?
> S1: Because he was black.
> T: And . . .
> S1: Oh, yeah, he couldn't practice law in this country.
> T: That's correct. Does anyone else have a question to ask?

5. Summarize the section and invite elaboration from the group members. Herrmann

Table 9.1

Planning Steps with Examples for Reciprocal Teaching

---

1. *Select the text segment for the first modeling.*

   Langston Hughes: He Believed Humor Would Help Defeat Bigotry and Fear by L. Morgan (Ed.). (Seattle, Washington: Turman Publishing Company, 1988)

   "I've known rivers," wrote Langston Hughes in *The Negro Speaks of Rivers,* one of his best-known poems. "I've known rivers ancient as the world and older than the flow of human blood in human veins. My soul has grown deep like the rivers."

   Langston, one of America's greatest writers, was a powerful artist. He was able to capture in his writing both the humor and sadness of life.

   Langston had a very difficult childhood. Not long after he was born in Missouri on February 1, 1902, Langston's father James left home. James had studied law for years and learned he could not become a lawyer because he was black. Angry and bitter, James moved to Mexico to become a lawyer there. (p. 9)

2. *Generate possible predictions.*
   He was an author.

3. *Identify questions ahead.*
   - How do you think Langston's father's leaving affected his writing?
   - Why did Langston's father leave home?
   - Why did his father have to leave for Mexico?
   - Did Langston think life was only funny?
   - What did he compare his soul to?
   - Who is Langston Hughes?

4. *Summarize each section.*
   Include who he was and why he had a difficult childhood.

5. *Circle difficult vocabulary or concepts.*
   Bigotry. "My soul has grown deep like the rivers." Effect that a difficult childhood may have on writing.

6. *Identify supports.*
   - Kendra will need help on questions.
   - Ali will need a prompt for prediction.

7. *Generate possible predictions for the next section.*
   It will tell more about Langston's childhood.

(1988) recommends that you explain how you arrived at the summary also.

T: My summary begins with the statement that Langston Hughes was a famous black writer who wrote about the humor and sadness in life. He had a difficult childhood. His father left to become a lawyer in Mexico, because he wasn't allowed to practice law in this country. This is a summary, because I have included only information that we have already read.

6. Discuss any clarification that needs to be made concerning ideas or words.

T: Let me ask you something. Do you know what *bigotry* in the title means?

S1: No.

T: Let's see if we can find the meaning somewhere in the text. I see an example in the story. Langston's father had to move to Mexico to practice law because he was black. This is an example of bigotry. Does anyone know what it means now?

☐ Important Points

1. The essential components of the reciprocal teaching model are strategies that teach students how to gain information from text, guided interactive instruction, and informed learners.
2. The comprehension and monitoring strategies of summarizing, questioning, clarifying, and predicting are taught to structure the dialogue of reciprocal teaching.
3. Teachers employ a scaffolding procedure, decreasing and adjusting support as they model the techniques, assist the students in the transfer of the technique, and move into a coaching and feedback role.

4. Careful planning includes identification of the text segment, possible predictions, questions, a summary, difficult words or concepts, and supports that students may need.
5. The steps of presentation include (a) share a brief review of the strategies, (b) read the title for student predictions, (c) read a small portion of the text, (d) ask questions, (e) summarize and encourage the students to elaborate upon the summary, and (f) add clarifications.

S4: Oh, it's when people do not like you because your skin is black.

T: Any other ideas?

S2: Yes, *bigotry* means having bad feelings about someone.

T: I guess you could say that it is having bad feelings without a good reason.

7. Predict the next section of the text.

T: I think the next part of the story may be about some more unhappy childhood experiences. Anyone have another prediction?"

■ ■ Activity

Prepare a reciprocal teaching lesson identifying possible predictions, questions, a summary, and difficult words or concepts from the following continued selection from *Langston Hughes.* Check the plans in Table 9.1.

Carrie Hughes, Langston's mother, moved to Topeka, Kansas. She worked in a law office. Carrie wanted Langston to go to a public school that did not allow black children. She went

to the school board and won her fight to place Langston in the school.

Even though his mother won that fight, Langston had to struggle every day to fit in at the school. Many of the children, and one teacher especially, were mean to Langston and made fun of him. Langston later wrote about his school years in *The Big Sea,* a book about his life. (Morgan, *Langston Hughes* [Seattle: Turman Publishing Company, 1988], p.9) ■ ■

Task-Specific Strategy Instruction

Students with special needs frequently experience difficulty with academic and social demands (Deshler & Schumaker, 1988). Research indicates that low-achieving students and students with learning disabilities arrive in the secondary school without the skills to effectively meet the curricular demands (Sinclair & Ghory, 1987). Attempts to teach the skills in which students are deficient have been ineffective because mastery is not required and generalization of skills to mainstream classes is not promoted (Deshler & Schumaker, 1986). Students with learning problems appear to lack certain strategies, fail to use them, or choose them inappropriately (Swanson, 1989).

Certain strategic procedures facilitate the performance of educational tasks (Pressley, Symons, Snyder, & Cariglia-Bull, 1989). Teachers of students who do not spontaneously or appropriately use strategic procedures should teach such skills as summarizing and paraphrasing just as they teach addition facts, the digestive system, and subject-verb agreement. A strategy is an individual's approach to a task, or how a student thinks and acts when planning, executing, and evaluating a task (Lenz, Clark, Deshler, & Schumaker, 1988).

In learning to use a strategy, students eventually progress from following the teacher's directions, cues, and prompts to incorporating and applying the strategy in a self-directed plan (Paris & Cross, 1983). For example, initially, students may be specifically taught how to memorize facts or items for later retrieval, perhaps by clustering. Gradually, through scaffolding, they assume more responsibility for accomplishing each task (e.g., using rehearsal to remember a phone number or mnemonics to remember lists). Students may learn how to plan to complete a task, to monitor their progress, and to modify or adjust their plan according to incoming information (Gelzheiser, Shepherd, & Wozniak, 1986).

Rationale

There are four reasons for including task-specific strategy instruction in the curriculum for students with special needs. First, as students progress through the grades, the gap widens between what they can do and what they are expected to do. By the time such students reach secondary school, the demands in listening and writing have increased more than their skills in these areas (Moran, 1980). Research conducted at the University of Kansas Institute for Research in Learning Disabilities (KU−IRLD) indicates that low-achieving students just after tenth grade appear to plateau at about a fourth to fifth grade level in reading and writing, and at a sixth grade level in math (Deshler, Schumaker, Alley, Warner, & Clark, 1982). It seems appropriate to change the curricular approach to one that teaches students how to learn, solve problems, monitor performance, and take control of their cognitive processing.

Second, research conducted at the University of Kansas Institute for Research in Learning Disabilities indicates that low-achieving students do not use effective or efficient study techniques, have difficulty completing assignments, do not organize information well, and have problems distinguishing important information from unimportant information (Alley, Deshler, Clark, Schumaker, & Warner, 1983). These problems may be adequately addressed with task-specific strategy instruction to help students select appropriate strategies, monitor execution of the strategies, and generalize the strategies across situations (content) and settings (school, home, and work).

Third, students with special needs may not be actively involved nor assume responsibility for learning and applying specific strategies to help themselves acquire the skills needed to meet the demands of the curriculum (Torgesen, 1982). Investigations involving academic tasks have shown that students with learning disabilities do not typically apply techniques to facilitate their comprehension of reading materials (Wong & Jones, 1982). However, students have shown significant improvement in performance when taught appropriate task strategies (Torgesen, 1977). Through strategy instruction, a teacher actively involves students in learning, and gives them opportunities to set their own goals.

Fourth, students may have been taught with an approach that did not require mastery and generalization of skills to the mainstream environment or to novel situations. Strategy instruction emphasizes mastery and includes specific procedures to promote generalization.

Description and Implementation

In recent years, a variety of approaches to task-specific strategy instruction have been recognized. Most approaches involve the teaching of self-monitoring, planful action, systematic application of carefully sequenced steps, and the importance of strategy use. Additionally, most approaches incorporate the use of strategies within the existing curriculum content (solving word problems in math, paraphrasing a reading passage, taking notes in science, and memorizing information in history).

Although many task-specific strategy instruction approaches exist, it is not our intention in this chapter to describe all of them, for it would take an entire textbook to do so. If you would like more in-depth information, consult the references at the end of the textbook. In this section, we describe two approaches, the *Strategies Intervention Model* (Deshler & Schumaker, 1988) and *Skills for School Success* (Archer & Gleason, 1989). The *Strategies Intervention Model* targets the adolescent population, while the *Skills for School Success* program focuses on elementary-aged and middle grade students.

The Strategies Intervention Model

The purpose of the Strategies Intervention Model (SIM) is to teach students how to learn and perform academic, social, and job-related tasks so that they can cope with immediate setting demands and generalize these skills across situations and settings throughout their lives (Deshler & Schumaker, 1988). The Strategies Intervention Model consists of three components: (a) a strategic curriculum (what strategies are taught), (b) strategic instruction (how strategies are taught), and (c) a strategic environment (how the environment is arranged to enhance strategic performance). (See Table 9.2.)

Strategic Curriculum. The strategic curriculum component consists of four types of strategies: (a) learning strategies (memorizing information, paraphrasing, test taking), (b) social skill strategies (getting along, conversational skills, problem solving), (c) motivation strategies (goal setting), and (d) executive strategies (selecting and designing appropriate strategies). We discuss learning strategies in this chapter in detail because such strategies deal specifically with academic learning. The curriculum compo-

Table 9.2
Strategies Intervention Model

Strategic Curriculum	Strategic Instruction	Strategic Environment
● Learning strategies	● Acquisition procedures	○ Teaming techniques
● Social skill strategies	● Generalization procedures	○ Management techniques
● Motivation strategies	○ Strategic teaching behaviors	○ Evaluation techniques
○ Executive strategies	○ Content enhancement procedures	○ Development techniques

● Available Commercially

Note. From "Learning Strategies: An Instructional Alternative for Low-Achieving Adolescents" by D. D. Deshler and J. B. Schumaker, 1986, *Exceptional Children, 52*(6), pp. 483–590. Reprinted by permission.

nent has been the focus of much of the work at the KU-IRLD, with a great deal of attention given to learning strategies. The Learning Strategies Curriculum is divided into three strands: (a) the acquisition strand helps students acquire information from printed materials, (b) the storage strand helps students store important information, and (c) the expression and demonstration of competence strand helps students with writing, proofreading, and organization. The Learning Strategies Curriculum is organized in the form of a series of instructor's manuals with accompanying student activities, lesson plans for teachers, and teaching materials.

Strategic Instruction. The strategic instruction component consists of four parts that are critical to the success of the model: (a) stages of acquisition, (b) stages of generalization, (c) strategic teaching behaviors, and (d) content enhancement procedures. Within these four areas are such elements as communicating expectations and rationales, using think alouds, providing feedback, and using procedural facilitators.

Stages of Acquisition. Utilizing the following stages of acquisition, teachers can teach students such strategies as Error Monitoring, Paraphrasing, Sentence Writing, and Word Identification published by the University of Kansas Institute for Research in Learning Disabilities. The following systematic application of these stages is vital to the success of the model:

1. *Pretest and make commitments.* Establish the student's current level of performance and secure his or her written agreement to learn a strategy. For example, after Rudy takes his pretest, he and his teacher, Ms. Olan, review the results and determine that his written work is messy and filled with errors. Ms. Olan makes a commitment to help him improve and motivates Rudy to make a commitment to learn how to proofread his work.

2. *Describe the strategy.* Discuss the rationales and benefits for learning the strategy. Then, carefully describe the steps of the strategy. You may notice that this step was also included in reciprocal teaching and metacognitive instruction. For example, Ms. Olan shows Rudy how the Error Monitoring strategy will help him improve his grades in school, his chances for employment, and his ability to write error-free letters to his girlfriend. Then, she describes and gives examples of each step of the error monitoring strategy.

3. *Model the strategy.* The modeling stage is based upon the premise that students learn a skill better if they see it performed rather than just hear it described. Therefore, Ms. Olan models the steps of the strategy by thinking aloud and using self-instruction, self-regulation, and self-monitoring. For example, she says, "Let's see. I will look at this sentence to see if there are any capitalization errors. Hmmm, I have capitalized the first word and the proper nouns. Oh, I forgot to capitalize *I*. Good, now, I don't have any capitalization errors." After Ms. Olan models the cognitive processes by thinking aloud as she examines a written passage for errors, she enlists Rudy's participation in finding errors in the passage.

4. *Verbal practice.* Review and rehearse the steps of the strategy until the student knows them at an automatic level. For example, Rudy and Ms. Olan practice the steps to error monitoring until he has committed them to memory.

5. *Provide controlled practice and feedback.* Provide ample guided practice in easy materials (controlled) until mastery is reached. Give individual feedback to reinforce efforts and prevent practice of incorrect responses. For example, Ms. Olan gives Rudy practice exercises and then provides verbal and written feedback regarding his performance in detecting and correcting errors in passages.

6. *Provide advanced practice and feedback.* Provide advanced practice in grade-level materials found in the mainstream setting while providing positive and corrective feedback. For example, Ms. Olan checks

some of Rudy's work from selected mainstream classes and gives him feedback regarding his ability to detect and correct errors in these more difficult materials.

7. *Posttest and make commitments.* Give a posttest to determine progress and provide feedback. Ask the student to agree to generalize use of the strategy to other settings.

■ ■ Activity
Use the describe stage of the stages of acquisition to teach someone to parallel park a car. Remember to include the rationale and benefits of the strategy and to carefully describe the steps. ■ ■

Stages of Generalization. The following stages of generalization provide students with the steps necessary to ensure successful transfer of skills across situations and settings: For strategy instruction to be effective, students must generalize the use of strategies. The stages . . .

1. *Orientation.* Make the student aware of the need to apply the strategy. For example, Ms. Olan and Rudy discuss where Rudy could use the strategy and how he will remember to use it.
2. *Activation.* Prompt the student to use the strategy, and monitor his use of it. For example, Ms. Olan checks with mainstream teachers to see if Rudy is using the strategy and helps Rudy set goals.
3. *Adaptation.* Prompt the student to examine the strategy for the cognitive behaviors he or she is using (e.g., self-questioning) and to modify the strategy to the demands of new situations. For example, Rudy and Ms. Olan work together to figure out how Rudy can use the error monitoring strategy as he takes tests.
4. *Maintenance.* Promote long-term use of the strategy across situations and settings. For example, Ms. Olan conducts periodic checks to see that Rudy is still using the error monitoring strategy effectively in a

variety of situations (home, school, and on the job).

Strategic Teaching Behaviors. Strategic teaching behaviors are the effective teaching routines that you should utilize throughout all phases of strategy instruction. Strategy instruction is more effective when you use advance organizers and postorganizers, monitor student performance, clarify expectations, actively involve students, and make instruction motivating and interesting. For example, Ms. Olan actively involves Rudy as he practices the steps of the strategy and she monitors his performance, both verbal and written.

Content Enhancement Procedures. Content enhancement procedures are the procedures teachers utilize to make content material more meaningful and more easily remembered. You may remember the day your third grade teacher leaped up on his desk, claimed to be the sun, assigned nine students in your class to be the nine planets, and had them walk around his desk in their orbits, each at a prescribed distance from him. What a meaningful and vivid procedure to explain the solar system! For those of you less theatrically inclined, you may want to present some material and then help students develop a mnemonic (a memory technique) to remember it, construct a bulletin board with key information, or prepare an outline with important points and essential vocabulary. In Rudy's situation, Ms. Olan uses the WRITER mnemonic.

Strategic Environment. The Strategies Intervention Model consists of four types of techniques designed to promote a learning environment that is strategic: (a) teaming techniques, (b) management techniques, (c) evaluation techniques, and (d) development techniques. Teaming techniques relate to preparing the members of the educational community (mainstream teachers, parents, psychologists, vocational rehabilitation counselors, etc.) to work together cooperatively. Management techniques are related to managing people, time, and materials in order to facilitate student learning and performance. For example, each day that Rudy comes to class, he looks in a designated place in the classroom for his folder. Ms. Olan puts his assignments there along with a progress chart, cue cards with the steps of the strategy, and completed work with written feedback. Evaluation techniques emphasize the provision of feedback to teachers and students. Finally, development techniques refer to the continued development of strategies to meet student needs.

The Strategies Intervention Model stresses collaboration among support agents: mainstream teachers, special education teachers, students, parents, and administrators. It employs techniques that encourage students to think and act strategically (e.g., know what information to memorize for a test, know when an outline will be helpful) in their problem solving. For additional information or training in the Strategies Intervention Model, contact Dr. Donald D. Deshler or Dr. Jean B. Schumaker, Institute for Research in Learning Disabilities, 3061 Dole Center for Human Development, University of Kansas, Lawrence, KS 66045.

■ ■ Activity

Part 1. Choose a partner to work with. You are a special education teacher in a secondary setting (choose middle school or high school). You want to use the Strategies Intervention Model in your class. Ask your partner to assume the role of your principal. Convince your principal that this model should be implemented in your school. (*Hint:* Look back at the preceding rationale section.)

Part 2. Play the part of a high school student. Ask your partner to assume the role of your special education teacher. You have always had difficulty preparing for and taking tests. Have your partner convince you to make the commitment to follow the procedures of the Strategies Intervention Model and learn a strategy to help you improve your studying and test-taking skills (*Hint:* Look at the describe stage under "Stages of Acquisition.") ■ ■

Skills for School Success

Skills for School Success is a four-level, teacher-directed program designed by Archer and Gleason (1989). This program teaches organization and study strategies. It includes skills required for success in school, such as appropriate school behaviors, organization, learning strategies, textbook reference skills, graphics skills, and use of reference materials. The program is appropriate for students in both regular and special education settings, is designed for students in elementary (intermediate grades) and middle school, and may be used across grade levels.

The Skills for School Success program employs a spiral curriculum, meaning that skills introduced at one level are reviewed at subsequent levels with more advanced applications. In addition, new skills are introduced at each level. For example, there are four books in the program (Books 3, 4, 5, and 6). Book 6 contains skills that are not present in Book 3, such as taking notes on lectures, using reference lists, and interpreting and comparing information from different types of graphs.

Components. The strategies taught in the program are organized into strands and are arranged in a suggested scope and sequence. The authors recommend levels at which to introduce, extend, and review each skill.

1. *School behaviors and organization strategies.* Students are taught important school behaviors, such as (a) organizing and maintaining notebooks, desks, and assignments; (b) keeping an assignment calendar; (c) managing homework; and (d) using effective before-, during-, and after-class behaviors. Figure 9.3 illustrates HOW your paper should look (H— heading, O—organized, and W—written neatly). For example, Felipe used this strategy to prepare his papers in a neat and organized manner. His efforts resulted in a better grade in English because his English teacher awards points for organization and appearance.

2. *Learning strategies.* Students are taught specific strategies to increase their indepen-

---

Name _____

Teacher _____ Date _____

HOW Should Your Papers Look?

H = Heading

1. First and last name	1. yes	no	yes	no
2. Date	2. yes	no	yes	no
3. Subject	3. yes	no	yes	no
4. Page number if needed	4. yes	no	yes	no

O = Organized

1. On the front side of the paper	1. yes	no	yes	no
2. Left margin	2. yes	no	yes	no
3. Right margin	3. yes	no	yes	no
4. At least one blank line at the top	4. yes	no	yes	no
5. At least one blank line at the bottom	5. yes	no	yes	no
6. Good spacing	6. yes	no	yes	no

W = Written neatly

1. Words and numbers on the lines	1. yes	no	yes	no
2. Words and numbers written neatly	2. yes	no	yes	no
3. Neat erasing or crossing out	3. yes	no	yes	no

Comments: _____

_____

_____

_____

_____

Figure 9.3
HOW Organization Strategy
Note. From Archer, A., & Gleason, M.—*Skills for School Success* © 1989—Curriculum Associates, Inc., N. Billerica, MA. Reproduced by permission of the publisher.

dence in completing tasks. They include strategies in (a) assignment completion, (b) memorizing information, (c) previewing chapters, (d) taking notes, (e) answering questions, and (f) proofreading. For example, when students need to study and remember information, they may use the RCRC strategy (read, cover, recite, check) by reading the material, covering it, telling themselves what they just read, and uncovering it to check for accuracy.

3. *Test-taking strategies.* Strategies are presented to help students prepare for and take tests. Students are shown strategies for taking multiple-choice, true–false, and short-answer tests. The strategies provide systematic procedures to follow in test taking. At the end of each strand, students may practice using their test-taking strategies by taking a multiple-choice, short-answer, or true–false test.

4. *Textbook reference strategies.* This strand teaches students to access information from their textbooks, a skill they need during the school years and may need later, on the job. Students are taught how to use the

☐ Important Points

1. Many students with special needs fail to use strategies or they use them inappropriately.

2. Task-specific strategy instruction facilitates the performance of academic tasks.

3. The Strategies Intervention Model is a teacher-directed model that includes a strategic curriculum component, a strategic instruction component, and a strategic environment component.

4. The strategic curriculum component addresses what to teach, the strategic instruction component includes how to teach, and the strategic environment component incorporates how the environment is arranged to enhance performance.

5. The Strategies Intervention Model focuses on teaching strategies directly to students,

having the students practice the strategies in controlled materials, and then having the students apply the strategies in regular classroom materials and generalize their use.

6. Skills for School Success is a teacher-directed program that teaches organization and study strategies to elementary and middle school students.

7. Skills for School Success includes skills necessary for success in school, such as appropriate school behaviors, organization, learning strategies, textbook reference skills, graphics skills, and use of reference materials.

---

parts of a textbook, such as the table of contents, glossary, and index. For example, Barbara was able to find information for a report she was preparing just by scanning the table of contents in several books. This helped her locate the material she needed.

4. *Strategies for interpreting graphics.* Students are taught how to read and interpret graphs. For example, Bev admitted that she used to avoid the graphs, charts, and diagrams in her textbooks, but after her teacher taught her how to access the information in graphics, she began to learn from them.

5. *Strategies for using reference materials.* In this strand, students learn how to use dictionaries and encyclopedias. They also learn how to locate words and how to select the best definition (decision making). For example, Niki was glad that she had learned reference skills, because they helped her with her papers, reports, and other assignments in English and social studies.

■ ■ Activity

Look back at the description of the RCRC (read, cover, recite, check) strategy for memorizing and studying. Now, turn to another section of this textbook. Use the RCRC strategy to study what is on that page. Did it help? In what situations would you use it with elementary or middle school students? ■ ■

Content and Procedures. Skills for School Success is a teacher-directed program, not an independent practice program (Archer & Gleason, 1989). The lessons contain objectives, rationales, lists of materials needed, outlines of the general teaching procedures, scripted teaching procedures, and maintenance and application activities. Teachers are expected to teach these strategies to a high level of mastery, ensure active student involvement, review the strategies, prompt application of the strategies, and provide feedback on their use and application. Materials are provided for teachers to use in meeting these expectations. Skill maintenance and application activities appear throughout the program along with review games for reinforcement. Posters containing the steps of the strategies are available to support instruction. Awards and record-keeping sheets may be reproduced for students. Checklists are available for students to use in monitoring their progress and for teachers to use in giving feedback to students regarding their before-, during-, and after-class behavior. For example, the "during-class checklist" states that students should follow the rules, listen, work during class, and ask for help when needed. Finally, the program contains an assignment calendar to help students assume responsibility for their assignments. For more information contact Dr. Anita Archer, 5300 Campanile Drive, San Diego, CA 92182.

Summary

In this chapter, we focused on instructional techniques that are appropriate for teaching implicit skills: metacognition, reciprocal teaching, and task-specific strategy instruction. Metacognition is the knowledge (awareness) and control (monitoring) that individuals have over their learning. Metacognitive instruction is designed to increase students' independence, problem-solving abilities, generalization and transfer of skills, and mastery of implicit skills such as self-questioning. The teaching of metacognitive skills utilizes informed training (which explains the rationale and benefits) and self-control training (which teaches executive skills such as self-monitoring). Metacognitive teaching procedures include identifying a task, choosing a strategy, modeling the strategy, explaining the

benefits that may be expected, providing guided practice, providing feedback, and teaching generalization.

We also discussed reciprocal teaching, which is defined as a dialogue between teachers and students for the purpose of helping the students gain meaning from text. Reciprocal teaching incorporates the use of guided interactive instruction and emphasizes the importance of informed learners. As with metacognitive instruction, a scaffolding procedure is used to transfer control from the teacher to the student (in reciprocal teaching, through the use of a dialogue). Teaching procedures include generating predictions, asking questions of students, summarizing, encouraging students to elaborate, and adding clarifications.

In the next section, we discussed task-specific strategy instruction. Strategic procedures help students complete academic tasks. We described two approaches to the teaching of task-specific strategies: the Strategies Intervention Model and the Skills for School Success program. The Strategies Intervention model is a teacher-directed model that includes a strategic curriculum component (what to teach), a strategic instruction component (how to teach), and a strategic environment component (how to facilitate access to information). Students (usually secondary) are taught strategies that they practice with controlled materials, apply in regular classroom materials, and generalize to new situations. Skills for School Success is a teacher-directed program that teaches organization and study strategies to elementary and middle school students. It includes appropriate school behaviors, organization, learning strategies, textbook reference skills, graphics skills, and use of reference materials.

10

Teacher-Directed Study Skills Instruction

Key Topics

Students with special needs who exhibit an inability to achieve may be doing so because of poor organizational and information-processing skills. Study skills and strategies can help your students acquire, organize, and express information and facilitate their performance of academic skills. Study skills and strategies may be thought of as alternative ways of approaching learning situations: techniques, tools, or steps to systematically complete tasks or solve problems. For example, students may be taught how to take notes, organize information to be memorized and studied, prepare for tests, and write reports, all of which are implicit skills (see Chapter 7).

Students do not often receive training and practice in study strategies (McKeachie, 1974). Teachers typically grade learning activities for accuracy rather than for the study skills used to complete them. By teaching study skills, you may show your students the relationship between their approach to a learning task and the result of that approach (e.g., using a mnemonic device to memorize a list of words may facilitate memorization of that list better than simply repeating the words in the list). Students improve their metacognitive skills as they become aware of situations in which to use study skills and then apply them and monitor their performance. The application of study strategies may, therefore, increase the independent functioning of learners. The purpose of this chapter is to present study skills and strategies that will help students with

special needs acquire information, organize it, and express it.

Rationale

The use of study strategies usually results in improved achievement (Kulik, Kulik, & Schwalb, 1983; Weinstein, Goetz, & Alexander, 1988). Incorporation of study skills instruction into the curriculum may help students attribute their learning successes to the systematic selection and application of strategies instead of luck or the assistance of others. It is possible to teach students to develop effective repertoires of study skills. Studies utilizing different task strategies have shown significant improvement in student performance following instruction in the strategies (Torgesen, 1977; Wong & Jones, 1982). Utilization of study skills may lead students with special needs to exhibit more active learning styles and to demonstrate proactive approaches to academic tasks, behaviors connected to academic achievement.

Components

In order for study skill training to be effective, teachers must be aware of the components that contribute to its success. The following five criteria derived from Paris (1988) should be included in study skill training. These are similar to the critical features of strategy instruction and the teaching of implicit skills.

1. *Strategies should be functional and meaningful.* Identify your students' needs and determine the study skills that would be most effective in meeting those needs. For example, if Jesse is required to memorize lists of terms for his biology class, you may want to teach him a mnemonic strategy to help him memorize material and prepare for the tests. Suppose Jesse has to memorize the parts of the digestive system. He may make a list with all the parts and then look at the first letter of each of the words. Perhaps, they spell a word, or maybe he can make a sentence out of them.

2. *Students should believe that strategies are useful and necessary.* Your students must be convinced that study strategies are important, necessary for success, worth using, and effective in solving problems; therefore, demonstrate to your students that their current methods are not effective and explain the rationale for each specific strategy (Alley & Deshler, 1979). For example, Mr. Waldo asked his students to take notes on one of his presentations in science. When he evaluated their notes with them, he pointed out the shortcomings and ineffective practices. He elicited from the students the rationale for taking effective notes and had them suggest situations in which they might need to use this skill. One student mentioned she could use it in her history class, while another said that it would help him as a reporter for the school newspaper. Then, Mr. Waldo presented some effective note-taking techniques to the class. By first demonstrating how note-taking techniques are useful and necessary, he was able to motivate and interest the students in note taking.

3. *Instruction should be direct, informed, and explanatory.* According to Rosenshine (1983), direct instruction should include (a) presenting material in small steps, (b) focusing on one aspect at a time, (c) organizing the material sequentially for mastery, (d) modeling the skill, (e) presenting many examples, (f) providing detailed explanations for difficult points, and (g) monitoring student progress. For example, in her instruction of report writing, Ms. Tartaglia took her class to the media center and modeled the steps that she wanted the students to follow as they used reference materials. She provided several different topics and modeled the steps sequentially for each one. She spent time teaching the students how to use the card catalog before she assigned them topics to look up. Then, as the students worked through the steps she had modeled, Ms. Tartaglia carefully monitored their progress.

4. *Instruction should demonstrate what strategies can be used, how they can be applied, and when and why they are helpful.* For example, Mr. Johansen, working with his high school students on test taking, taught the students two strategies to apply when taking tests. Next, he elicited from the students when and why the strategies would be helpful (mainstream classes, job seeking, and taking the driver's test or the test for the military). Finally, he showed the students how to apply the strategies to each of the situations they had identified.

5. *Instructional materials must be lucid and enjoyable.* The materials you use as a part of study skills instruction must be motivating, meaningful, relevant, and easy to understand. For example, working with a group of fourth graders in a regular classroom, Mrs. Barnhart incorporated information about the students into a lesson that showed them how to use the graphic aids in textbooks. She taught her students to read graphs by graphing the students' ages, birthdays, interests, and favorite music groups. These activities were instru-

mental in holding student interest and attention.

Because we believe the preceding components of effective study skill instruction should be included in the teaching of all of the study skills and strategies presented in this chapter, we do not mention them each time a new strategy is introduced.

Acquisition of Information

As mentioned in Chapter One, students with special needs often have difficulty with reading, mathematics, oral and written language, attending, and organizing. Therefore, they must be taught techniques to help them acquire the skills and content expected of them. In this section, we present strategies for listening, taking notes, and comprehending.

Listening

Students with mild disabilities should be made aware of the fact that listening is more than hearing words and it may require practice and training (Masters & Mori, 1986). The following strategies are provided for students who have difficulty listening effectively, have developed poor listening habits, do not attend to relevant stimuli, or are inattentive.

Prelistening Strategies

In adaptations of the work of Nichols and Stevens (1957), Barker (1971) and Taylor (1964), Alley and Deshler (1979) present the following prelistening strategies:

Mental Preparation. Before your students attend a class lecture or presentation, they should prepare for listening by practicing the three *R*'s of listening preparation: review, read, and relate, using procedural facilitators or cues. They can do this by reviewing previous notes, reading about the topic that is going to be covered, and relating the topic to what they already know and to what they have learned in class. You may model this for them by thinking aloud what

you want your students to say and do. For example, you may say, "Let's see, I need to look back at Monday's notes. Oh, I remember. We were talking about clouds, and today, we are going to talk about two types: cumulus and cirrus. I know how clouds are formed, because I put hot water in a jar and held ice over the jar. I watched a cloud form in the jar. O.K., I'm ready to learn more about clouds. I'm ready for today's class."

Physical Preparation. Your students should select seats that will increase their opportunities for attending to and concentrating on what is presented. They should come to class with the necessary materials, such as textbook, notebook, pens, pencils, tape recorder, and/or highlighter.

Vocabulary Preparation. If the class topic is known in advance, students may be able to ask for a list of the vocabulary that will be included. Teachers of students with special needs sometimes tape-record words and their definitions or prepare glossaries for students to use in the mainstream. Students may be taught to prepare their own note cards with the word, a brief definition, or a picture that relates to the word.

Listening Strategies

Alley and Deshler (1979) suggest the following strategies to improve listening skills.

Organizing Cues. Students may attend to cues that indicate how the teacher is organizing content or information. Some teachers use verbal cues to emphasize the most important points of a presentation. Teach your students to listen for statements like "The main reasons Cuban Americans immigrated to the United States are . . . " or "The most important thing to remember about crop rotation is . . . " Also, teach students to look for written cues to spoken content. Some teachers identify the main points of their presentation by writing them on the chalkboard or an overhead projector. Students may take this as a cue to copy the information.

Verbal and Nonverbal Cues. Show students how to identify important points by attending to speaking pace, volume, pauses, and stress on words and phrases. Also, alert students to the nonverbal behaviors that teachers use to make important points while speaking. These include eye contact, hand signals, facial expressions, and posture. You may model these verbal and non-verbal cues by videotaping class lectures and then pointing out cues as they occur. For example, Ms. Jackson videotaped herself teaching a history class. She played the videotape for her students and pointed out the fact that each time she mentioned a new term, she wrote it on the board and underlined it. She also alerted her students to other cues, such as holding her hand up, increasing her volume, and slowing her speaking rate each time she emphasized an important point.

Main and Supporting Ideas. Specific activities may help students distinguish main ideas from supporting material during a lecture or presentation. For example, Mr. Wong presented the following three statements and asked the students to identify which was the main idea and which were supporting statements:

- The air is becoming polluted.
- The environment is undergoing significant changes.
- Our water supply is insufficient in some areas.

Then, Mr. Wong showed his students how the first and last sentences were actually examples, or supporting details, of the second sentence.

Another activity involves having the students listen to a class presentation and then identify the main ideas. At first, give your students a worksheet from which to choose the main ideas. After they select the main ideas, the students should explain why the other choices are not main ideas. Such activities prepare students to separate essential information from extraneous, irrelevant material—a skill that is essential to listening comprehension.

Questioning. One way to determine if your students have listened effectively is to have them ask questions about what they have heard. For example, after a presentation about dolphins to a

third grade class, the teacher was convinced that her students had listened when they asked these questions: Where did the word dolphin come from? What is the difference between a dolphin and a porpoise? Is the dolphin a fish or a mammal? What do dolphins eat? How do dolphins breathe?

Students may practice asking questions in a role-playing situation with you or with taped materials. This technique may be used effectively in mainstream classes with feedback given by the mainstream class teacher.

Additional listening activities for students with special needs at both the elementary and secondary level are:

1. Alert your students before they listen to a class presentation that there will be at least one factual error in the presentation. Ask the students to write down the error(s) after the information has been presented (Wallace & Kauffman, 1986). For example, during a presentation on the size, population, major cities, and important industries of New Jersey, Mr. Feldman erroneously identified the capital as Newark.

2. Prior to a lecture or presentation, list on the chalkboard, an overhead projector, or a handout the five most important points of the talk. Then, ask your students to listen for those five points and arrange them in the correct sequence before the conclusion of the presentation (Devine, 1981).

3. Show a videotape containing subject matter that is interesting and age-appropriate. Ask the students to listen for specific information, such as the speaker's intent, definitions of certain words and how context affects them, factual information, or the general theme. You may stop the videotape at any time to ask questions about the content or ask for predictions of what will happen next. For example, Mr. Suwana showed a series of videotapes to his students about the lives of four African-Americans who made great contributions

to our country: (a) Paul Lawrence Dunbar, (b) Booker T. Washington, (c) Dr. Martin Luther King, Jr., and (d) Dr. George Washington Carver. He periodically stopped the videotape to ask questions and to give his students a specific fact to listen for.

4. Ask your students to listen to television or radio advertisements and explain how the advertisers are trying to influence listeners to buy their products. For example, some advertisers ask celebrities to advertise and endorse their products, others use catchy tunes, and some tell about the money you will save. This listening activity may be done in the classroom or as a homework assignment (Lerner, 1985).

■ ■ Activity

Part 1. In order to appreciate the necessity and importance of listening in your daily life, record the amount of time in a single day that you spend listening. This could include listening to the weather report in the morning, listening to the news, listening in classes (e.g., discussions, instructions for assignments, questions), listening to friends and family members, and listening on the telephone. Now, calculate the total percentage of time that you devote on a daily basis to this vital communication skill.

Part 2. During your next class lecture, note all of the verbal and nonverbal cues that the instructor utilizes. Compare these to what other class members identify. (Answers for this and other activities are found in the Instructor's Manual.) ■ ■

Note Taking

Note taking is difficult and tedious for many students with learning and behavior problems. Therefore, many of them do not take notes in class. You may need to convince your students of the importance of taking notes. One effective way is to make them aware of what they currently do during a lecture or class presentation.

For example, Ms. Malone presented information on the recycling of products as a way to protect the environment. She asked her students to take notes during her presentation, using the activity as a pretest to show the students that improvement may be needed. After instruction in note-taking techniques, she used the activity as a post test to show the students their improvement in note taking. Pauk (1984) found that non-notetakers forget 80% of a lecture within 2 weeks. Therefore, it is important for you to directly teach note taking and to reinforce its use.

Many strategies are available to improve note taking. You may want to show your students a variety of ways to take notes so that they can find one or more that are effective for them.

The Five-Step Method for Taking Lecture Notes

The five-step method for taking lecture notes (Bragstad & Stumpf, 1987) includes the following:

1. *Surveying.* Many teachers give an advance organizer or preview of what they are going to cover. Students can take notes on these points, thereby alerting themselves to what is coming and to what to expect during the lecture.
2. *Questioning.* Encourage your students to have a questioning attitude to help them focus on what is happening in the presentation. They may ask themselves, What is the main idea of this presentation? What am I supposed to know when the speaker is finished? What is being said about the topic? Effective ways to teach students to have a questioning attitude during a lecture presentation include (a) modeling question asking for them and (b) setting up role plays so that they can practice with each other.
3. *Listening.* Encourage students to employ listening strategies to help them listen carefully for content, cues, organization, main points, and supporting statements.

4. *Organizing.* Have your students determine how you are organizing the information being presented. Perhaps, you use the chalkboard, an overhead projector, or handouts to organize content. If you do not provide these clues, then your students may listen for verbal cues to organization, such as "The most important point to remember is . . . " or "Note this . . . " You may also repeat important points or say them slowly with emphasis and then a pause.

5. *Reviewing and revising.* As soon after the lecture or presentation as possible, your students should review their notes. In this way, they can add, change, or delete material while the information is still fresh in their minds. Encourage your students to conduct frequent cumulative reviews of their notes. By going back over that day's notes along with all previous notes after each class session, your students will be commiting the material to memory.

Outlining and Highlighting

Wallace and Kauffman (1986) recommend showing students how to follow an outline when taking notes. An outline helps students look for a main idea followed by supporting statements and perhaps clarifying details or examples. Wallace and Kauffman further suggest teaching students to use abbreviations (e.g., + for *and*, % for *percent*, # for *number*) to make note taking faster and easier. They also recommend encouraging students to use highlighters to emphasize main ideas or key points.

The Two-Column Method

The two-column method (Aaronson, 1975; Bragstad & Stumpf, 1987) may be varied and modified for individual purposes. With this system, students divide their papers into two sections by drawing a line from top to bottom, thus forming two columns. The wider column is used to record the teacher's ideas as presented in class. The narrower column is used after the lecture to write questions or to summarize the major

---

☐ Important Points

1. To listen effectively, students should physically and mentally prepare to listen; identify organizational, verbal, and nonverbal cues; learn how to identify main and supporting ideas; and practice self-questioning.

2. Three other ways to give students purposes for listening are (a) alerting them to listen for factual errors in a presentation, (b) listing the five most important points of the lesson and directing the students to listen for those points, and (c) asking students to listen for certain information as they view a videotape.

3. A five-step method of taking notes includes (a) surveying, (b) questioning, (c) listening, (d) organizing, and (e) reviewing and revising.

4. Following an outline, using highlighters, and using abbreviations are effective techniques in note taking.

5. Teachers can model note taking by playing a videotape of a lecture and then taking notes on an overhead projector as the class watches.

6. Students can practice taking notes as they watch how-to-do-it presentations, (e.g., how to change a tire).

7. For additional practice, teachers can give students notes with errors to correct.

8. Teachers can reinforce the importance of taking notes with a note-taking contest in which students produce notes for points.

points and ideas. Some students prefer to have a third, narrow column to define key terms or to paraphrase material from the class presentation.

In teaching note taking to students, you should model effective note taking. Bragstad and Stumpf (1987) suggest playing a tape of a lecture, and while the class is watching, taking notes on an overhead projector so that the students see what you write. At the conclusion of the demonstration, you and your students can discuss the note-taking techniques that you utilized.

You should provide your students with ample practice in note taking before asking them to take notes in mainstream classes. Devine (1981) recommends using how-to-do-it presentations, such as how to change a tire, how to use a card catalog, or how to make a peanut butter sandwich. Have your students take notes as you present one of these topics.

Bragstad and Stumpf (1987) suggest giving students a set of notes that contain errors. Then, have the students work in groups to correct the errors and to improve the notes. To reinforce the importance of taking notes, Devine (1981) recommends having a note-taking contest in which main ideas and supporting details are each worth a specified number of points. Then, have the students calculate the scores of the different sets of notes. You may also specify other aspects to look for in a set of notes, such as underlining of key points or defining of technical vocabulary in the margins, and then ask the students to judge which notes contain all of the important elements.

Comprehension

In order to succeed in content classes, students with special needs are expected to acquire information from textbooks and from material presented orally in lectures, class discussions, demonstrations, and student presentations (Herr, 1988). Because your students may lack a systematic approach to comprehending content material, you must provide specific strategies to help them structure their efforts. In this section we present suggestions in the use of advance orga-

nizers, paraphrasing, mapping, concept teaching, study methods, and textbook usage.

Advance Organizers

An advance organizer is material that is presented "in advance of and at a higher level of generality, inclusiveness, and abstraction than the learning task itself" (Ausubel & Robinson, 1969, p. 606). Advance organizers may be verbal or written (Gleason, 1988). Advance organizers set the stage for and contribute to comprehension.

Teachers may use bulletin boards as advance organizers, as did Mrs. Gonzalez, who wanted to introduce a unit about people who immigrated to the United States from other countries. Her students placed family names on the appropriate country on a map of the world. Mr. Row used a handout (written advance organizer) to introduce a lesson on the parts of a story. The handout listed the six parts and then identified them in an actual story. While co-teaching with a regular classroom teacher, Mr. Johnson used a verbal advance organizer to introduce a lesson on rocks. He began by saying, "Today we are going to learn about three types of rocks: igneous, sedimentary, and metamorphic." In all three of these classrooms, the teachers used advance organizers to provide clues to important information that they wanted their students to acquire.

Paraphrasing

Paraphrasing requires students to rephrase, or to put material into their own words. You may stop in your lecture or presentation and ask your students to paraphrase by writing or verbalizing in their own words what you just presented. You may also teach your students to periodically stop at designated points in their textbooks and paraphrase what they have just read. This forces students to concentrate on the meaning of the material. You may mark textbooks and other printed material ahead of time with stop signs for young children and lines, dots, or dashes for older students. Eventually, you may phase out these symbols and let the students assume the responsibility for paraphrasing.

Mapping

Mapping is making a word picture of ideas. Students can use maps to organize their ideas, stories, reports, notes, and textbook chapters. There are five steps in designing a map (Bragstad & Stumpf, 1987). (Figure 10.1 provides an illustration of these steps.)

1. Find the topic (usually in the title).
   Example: Picnic.
2. Hypothesize what the major concepts may be before actually looking. These become the questions you want to address.
   Examples: Food, drinks, games, insects.
3. Read for answers to these questions.
   Example: Find out what the characters in the story took to their picnic and did on it.
4. Read the story while thinking about the major concepts and recite from memory the supporting details.
5. Review the map frequently to retain the information.

Mapping is an excellent method for acquiring information from printed materials. It enhances comprehension, allows students to think about the relationships among concepts and ideas, and facilitates the condensing of material to be studied.

Concept Teaching

Concept teaching possesses many of the same characteristics as mapping. Concept teaching routines, which utilize concept diagrams (Bulgren, Schumaker, & Deshler, 1986), are effective for helping students acquire information. Such routines are particularly useful in facilitating the comprehension of content material (e.g., science, social studies, history). Bulgren, Schumaker, and Deshler successfully taught regular classroom teachers to use concept diagrams with students who had learning disabilities as well as with their own students by using the following procedures:

1. Select a concept (a word or phrase that represents a category or idea).
   Example: Colonization.

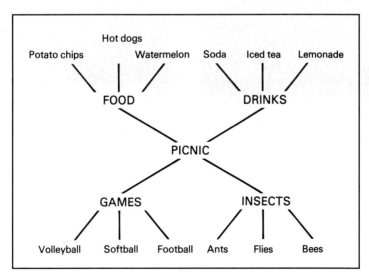

Figure 10.1
Sample Map

2. Construct key words or phrases that are related to the concept.
   Example: Settlers, religious freedom.
3. For each word or phrase, decide if it is an example or a nonexample and whether it is a characteristic that is always present, sometimes present, or never present in the concept.
   Example: In colonization settlers are always present. An example of a colony is St. Augustine. A nonexample is Cortez in Mexico.
4. Plot this information on a concept diagram.
   Examples: See Figure 10.2.
5. Based on the information printed in the diagram, define the concept.
   Example: Colonization is a group of people settling an undeveloped country but remaining under the rule of the country from which they came.

Like mapping, concept teaching routines help students comprehend content material. Concept diagrams condense material into manageable chunks of information and facilitate the acquisition of information.

Study Methods

Several study methods help students comprehend what they read in textbooks and other printed materials. These methods structure the attempts of students to deal with key points and vocabulary, paraphrase reading passages, and identify the overall theme. You may teach the following study methods to students with special needs to facilitate comprehension.

SQ3R Method. This approach, developed by Robinson (1961), utilizes a five-step procedure. It is extremely effective for content area subjects.

1. *Survey.* Students scan the reading passage for general ideas. This includes headings, subheadings, bold print, summaries, and illustrations. For example, in a passage from a social studies text, students may find headings and illustrations that tell them the passage is about Montezuma, ruler of the Aztecs.
2. *Question.* The students restate headings as questions. Encourage who, what, why, when, where, and how questions. For example, students may turn headings into the following questions: Who was Montezuma? When and where did he live? What did he do?
3. *Read.* At this stage, students read to find the answers to the questions they have posed. This should be meaningful, since they are addressing their own questions.
4. *Recite.* The students attempt to answer their own questions *without* looking at the reading passage.
5. *Review.* For this step, the students review the material in order to assure that they have retained it. They may restate key points and check their answers to their questions.

EVOKER Method. This study method, developed by Pauk (1984), utilizes the following six-step procedure. It is effective with content material and poetry.

1. *Explore.* Students read the entire passage silently to determine the overall theme. For example, Ms. Barro's social studies class read about people who have worked for the rights of American Indians.
2. *Vocabulary.* Students look up any unfamiliar words, terms, or events. For example, as Ms. Barro's students read about the Spanish priest Bartolome de Las Casas, they decided to check on the correct pronunciation of his name. What a wonderful opportunity for the Spanish-speaking students in the class to help the students who did not speak Spanish with some of the names and terms!
3. *Oral reading.* Students read the passage aloud.
4. *Key ideas.* Students determine the overall theme and major points. For example,

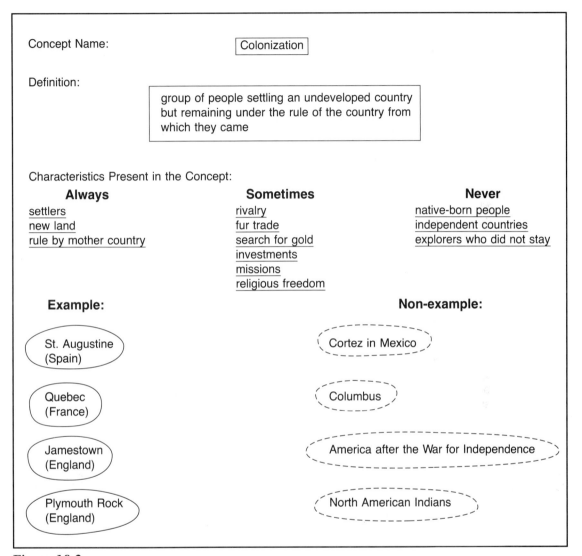

Concept Name: | Colonization |

Definition:

group of people settling an undeveloped country but remaining under the rule of the country from which they came

Characteristics Present in the Concept:

Always
settlers
new land
rule by mother country

Sometimes
rivalry
fur trade
search for gold
investments
missions
religious freedom

Never
native-born people
independent countries
explorers who did not stay

Example:

St. Augustine (Spain)

Quebec (France)

Jamestown (England)

Plymouth Rock (England)

Non-example:

Cortez in Mexico

Columbus

America after the War for Independence

North American Indians

Figure 10.2
Concept Diagram

Note. From J. Bulgren (1986). *Concept Diagrams,* Research Report. Lawrence: University of Kansas Institute for Research in Learning Disabilities.

reading about the Spanish priest, Ms. Barro's students discovered that in 1516, he worked for laws to give American Indians rights and freedom and brought peace to the Indians of the West Indies.

5. *Evaluation.* Students identify the key words, terms, and sentences to ensure un-

derstanding of the major ideas. For example, Ms. Barro's students identified terms and sentences to support the ideas they found in their reading about Bartolome de Las Casas.

6. *Recapitulation.* Students reread the entire selection.

☐ Important Points

1. Oral and written advance organizers for increasing comprehension are used before a lesson or unit and may include bulletin boards and handouts.

2. Paraphrasing requires students to restate in their own words what they have just heard or read.

3. Mapping is making a word picture of ideas.

4. Mapping includes the steps of finding the topic, hypothesizing what the major concepts may be, reading to answer questions, reciting supporting details, and reviewing the map.

5. Concept teaching consists of selecting a concept; constructing key words or phrases; identifying examples, nonexamples, and characteristics; plotting this information on a concept diagram; and utilizing this information to define the concept.

6. The SQ3R approach includes survey, question, read, recite, and review.

7. The EVOKER method includes a six-step procedure: explore, vocabulary, oral reading, key ideas, evaluation, and recapitulation.

■ ■ Activity

Select one of the following concepts and develop a concept diagram: conservation, democracy, pollution. ■ ■

Textbook Usage

Students with special needs frequently encounter problems when trying to read, use information, or locate it in textbooks. Study skills and strategies in textbook usage provide valuable assistance, particularly to students who are expected to use textbooks independently in mainstream classes. We present suggestions in previewing and surveying textbooks and textbook chapters and in chapter mapping.

Textbook Previewing. Davis and Clark (1981) indicate that by focusing on ten specific aspects of a textbook, students concentrate on the fewest number of words that contain the greatest amount of information. After previewing these ten parts, your students will know a great deal about the textbook. Following are the ten keys to textbook previewing (Davis & Clark, 1981):

1. Title.
2. Introduction.
3. Summary.
4. Pictures and maps.
5. Chapter questions.
6. Subtopic titles.
7. First paragraphs following subtopics.
8. First sentences of paragraphs.
9. Special print (italics).
10. Bold print.

Textbook and Chapter Surveying. Prior to beginning to use a new textbook, a valuable activity for your students to perform is surveying that textbook. This allows the students to become familiar with the parts of a textbook: table of contents, preface, glossary, appendix, bibliography, and index. This activity may be performed in small groups or individually.

After a textbook is surveyed and students become familiar with its contents, an additional activity may be performed; that of surveying a chapter. This allows students to predict from the title what the chapter is about, to turn headings into questions, to identify study aids (e.g., bold print, italics, graphs, and charts), and to divide the chapter into manageable sections. Imagine the excitement that could be generated in a social studies or history class when students from culturally diverse backgrounds find a chapter that describes their native country, customs, and language! Class discussions, cooperative learning activities, or class presentations may facilitate the sharing of information about the chapter before the students read and study it. Table 10.1 illustrates textbook and chapter surveying.

If students know how to use a textbook and are aware of how to read and study individual chapters, they are more apt to interact with content material presented. This interaction may promote more independent functioning in both special and regular classes.

Chapter Mapping. Another technique that helps students acquire information from textbooks is that of chapter mapping, a student-

prepared outline using only the titles, subtitles, and minor topic headings provided by the textbook author (Davis & Clark, 1981). This technique utilizes print in different sizes to illustrate the importance of the topic and helps students compress lengthy chapters to one page. The benefits of this procedure are that the students have a one-page list of the topics discussed in the chapter and a visual overview of the scope and sequence of the chapter (Davis and Clark, 1981).

Graphic Aids. Many students with learning problems do not automatically activate and utilize strategies to help them acquire information from text (Torgesen, 1982). This problem is intensified in the content areas because of the prev-

Table 10.1
Surveying a Textbook and Chapter

Surveying Your Textbook

1. Name of textbook _____
2. Author(s) _____
3. List two things you can tell about the book by its title. _____
_____
4. List three points that the author makes in the introduction. _____
_____
5. Look at the table of contents. List three things you know about the textbook by reading the chapter titles. _____
6. Does the textbook contain an index, glossary, and appendix? If so, how will you use each of them? _____

Surveying a Textbook Chapter

1. Title of chapter _____
2. List two things that the chapter title suggests. _____
_____
3. Read the first and last paragraphs and the boldface headings in the chapter. What do you think the author wants you to learn? _____
_____
4. What graphic aids does the chapter contain?
   _____ maps   _____ italics
   _____ graphs   _____ questions
   _____ charts   _____ definitions
   _____ illustrations _____ bold print
   _____ diagrams   _____ other
5. What other clues does the chapter have that might help you understand it? _____
_____

alence of inconsiderate text—lack of structure, unity, coherence, and audience appropriateness (Armbruster & Anderson, 1981). Graphic aids may alleviate the problems inherent in content area textbooks. Graphic aids may take the form of a table of contents; chapter headings; maps, graphs, and other illustrations; tables; a glossary; an appendix; a bibliography; and an index. These graphic aids help students gather clues about the content of the text and organize facts so that they are easy to understand.

You may want to specifically teach the use of each of the graphic aids rather than assume that your students know *how and when* to use them to acquire information. For example, Mr. Alonzo taught beginning map skills to his primary students by drawing a map of the neighborhood around the school. He showed the students how to use the compass rose (the symbol that has lines or arrows that point in the four main directions on the map). He gave them many opportunities to practice by asking them questions such as, If you wanted to walk from Anderson Street in front of the school to Third Street behind the school, in which direction would you walk? Next, he showed them how to use the distance scale on the map to determine how far apart streets, stores, and houses were. On his map, the scale stated that 1 inch is equal to 3 miles. After modeling how to figure distance with the distance scale and a ruler, he asked them questions such as, If I live on Bellvedere Street and I want to walk to school, how far will I have to walk?

Another effective graphic aid is the graphic organizer, a tree diagram that contains vocabulary related to a specific concept (Barron, 1969). Alvermann (1983) suggests using a modified graphic organizer. It contains empty spaces that represent missing information for students to fill in while reading their textbooks. It focuses their attention on what is important in the textbook and secures their involvement by requiring them to search for the missing information.

Once you have taught the use of graphic aids, provide opportunities for practice. For example, for practice in using maps with intermediate and middle school students, Ekwall (1985) recommends setting up a travel bureau in the classroom. Students (customers) may visit the travel bureau to plan family vacations, identify the best mode and route of travel, and locate landmarks and historical sites. After students have practiced using graphic organizers, they may try constructing graphic organizers, individually or in groups.

■ ■ Activity

Part 1. Utilize the form in Table 10.1 and survey this textbook and one of its chapters.

Part 2. Select a content area textbook (intermediate, middle school, or high school) and choose one of its chapters. Make a list of all of the graphic aids that you can find. Based on the graphic aids you identify, write down five things you already know about the chapter. ■ ■

▭ Important Points

1. A textbook may be previewed by attending to the title, introduction, summary, pictures and maps, chapter questions, subtopic titles, first paragraphs following subtopics, first sentences of paragraphs, italics, and bold print.
2. A chapter map is a student-prepared outline that uses only the titles, subtitles, and minor topic headings provided by the textbook author.
3. Graphic aids, the parts of a textbook that provide clues to content and organize facts, include the table of contents; chapter headings; maps, graphs, and other illustrations; tables; glossary; appendix; bibliography; and index.

Organization and Memorization of Information

In this section of the chapter, we present strategies that relate to how students organize and remember information. We describe mnemonic and general memory strategies, underlining and highlighting, and study guides and outlines.

Memory Strategies

Memory plays an important part in the academic success of students. Memory skills affect the organization and storage of information for later retrieval. However, memory skills are among the most commonly reported areas of weakness among students in special education and remedial classes (Scruggs & Mastropieri, 1984). Therefore, you should specifically teach strategies that will enhance memory skills.

Mnemonic Strategies

Mnemonic strategies are systematic strategies to facilitate the organization, storage, and retrieval of information (Bellezza, 1983; Levin, 1985; Masters & Mori, 1986). The term *mnemonics* comes from Greek and refers to the art of improving memory by using formulae or other aids (Bragstad & Stumpf, 1987). The following mnemonic strategies may be helpful to students who have difficulty with remembering.

Keyword Method. The keyword mnemonic method has been used successfully for learning and recalling information (Mastropieri, Scruggs, & Levin, 1986b; Mastropieri, Scruggs, Levin, Gaffney, & McLoone, 1985). Atkinson (1975) used the keyword method in foreign language vocabulary tasks. More recently, the keyword method has been used in the teaching of content area subjects such as history and science to students with learning disabilities (Scruggs, Mastropieri, Levin, & Gaffney, 1985; Veit, Scruggs, & Mastropieri, 1986).

The keyword method is a mnemonic strategy that assists in the retention of facts by using auditory and visual cues as well as visual imagery

(Mastropieri, 1988). It employs the steps of recoding, relating, and retrieving. In recoding, an unfamiliar word is associated with a familiar, acoustically similar keyword. The relating element allows the learner to link the keyword to the actual word through a picture or image. Finally, the retrieving component enables the learner to systematically call to mind the original word (Mastropieri, Scruggs, & Levin, 1986a). For example, Mastropieri (1988) suggests that to learn the word *apex,* you recode it to a word that sounds similar, like *ape.* This is a good keyword for students who are familiar with the concept of ape. Next, relate the keyword, *ape,* by creating an image of the keyword and the definition of the word *apex.* Since *apex* means highest point, you would picture an ape at a highest point. A good interactive image may be an ape (possibly King Kong) sitting on the highest point of something, for example, the Empire State Building. To retrieve the word *apex* and its definition, you would tell the student to think of the keyword, think back to the picture, and state the definition. It is important to consider students' experiential and cultural backgrounds when choosing keywords. You want to be sure to include concepts with which they are familiar.

Pegword Method. A method for learning and remembering a list of items is the number rhyme, or pegword, method. A pegword is a rhyming word for the numbers from 1 to 10:

1.	Bun.	6.	Sticks.
2.	Shoe.	7.	Heaven.
3.	Tree.	8.	Gate.
4.	Door.	9.	Vine.
5.	Hive.	10.	Hen.

To learn a list of words, you create an image that associates the number 1, the word *bun,* and the first word on the list of items to be learned. For example, if you wanted to remember the five senses (sight, hearing, smell, taste, and touch), you would picture (1) a large bun wearing glasses, (2) a shoe with big ears, (3) a tree with an oversized nose sniffing its blossoms, (4) a door with an open mouth licking its lips, and

(5) a beehive with long arms extending from its sides that were getting stung by bees because they kept touching the hive. This technique utilizes the visualizing and associative potential of the learner to help aid memory.

Other Mnemonic Aids
Although mnemonic aids are not to be used as a substitute for studying and understanding, they may provide useful cues for students who are required to memorize lists, items, causes, laws, or equations. Some commonly used mnemonics are suggested:

1. Directions (north, east, south, west)—Never eat soggy waffles.
2. Continents (North America, South America, Europe, Asia, Australia, Africa, Antarctica)—Never say elephants are angry at aardvarks.
3. Parts of the atom (proton, electron, neutron, shell)—PENS.
4. Planets (Mercury, Venus, Earth, Mars, Jupiter, Saturn, Uranus, Neptune, Pluto)—My very energetic mother just served us nine pizzas.
5. Simple machines (lever, pulley, wheel, axle, inclined plane, screw, wedge)—Lisa pushed Wendy Adams in pretty Susan's way.
6. Parts of the solar system (comets, sun, asteroids, planets, meteors)—Come see Angie's pretty marbles.
7. Spelling *dessert*—Two s's because so sweet.
8. Colors of the spectrum (red, orange, yellow, green, blue, indigo, violet)—Roy G. Biv.
9. Great Lakes (Huron, Ontario, Michigan, Erie, Superior)—HOMES.
10. Time changes—spring forward, fall back.
11. Coordinating conjunctions (for, and, nor, but, or, yet, so)—fan boys.
12. Days of the week (Sunday, Monday, Tuesday, Wednesday, Thursday, Friday, Saturday)—Silly Mother told William to find Snoopy.
13. Operations (multiplication, division, addition, subtraction)—My Dear Aunt Sally.
14. *b* and *d* reversals—thumbs-up sign to represent the headboard and foot of a bed.
15. Spatial-relations in handwriting:
    - *Grass letters*—grow only to middle line (a, s, c).
    - *Sky letters*—reach to the top line (b, f, l).
    - *Root letters*—grow as high as grass letters and then dig down (g, j, p).

■ ■ Activity
Part 1. Develop a mnemonic strategy for each of the following situations:

a. Teach a sixth grader to memorize the following parts of speech: noun, verb, adverb, adjective, preposition, conjunction.
b. Show a ninth grader an effective way to memorize the following types of trees: spruce, oak, willow, sycamore, elm, palm, maple.

Part 2. Ask a friend to time you while you look at the following list of words for 60 seconds. Now cover the list and write as many of the items as you can remember:

flamingo	bicycle
wagon	van
tangerine	banana
pear	sparrow
pelican	orange
motorcycle	plum
truck	vulture
robin	

How many items did you remember? What memory strategies did you use? What other suggestions could you give to elementary and secondary students? ■ ■

Underlining and Highlighting
Some study strategies help students organize information by physically altering the text or material. Underlining is one of the most popular and frequently used study strategies (Ander-

son & Armbruster, 1984; Annis & Davis, 1978; Glynn, 1978). It is accomplished by drawing a line under the important text. Highlighting is accomplished by going over the text with a transparent marker. Underlining and highlighting are particularly useful with consumable materials. Underlining and highlighting may facilitate studying by isolating the information to be recalled (Blanchard, 1985). Effective underlining identifies the main ideas and supporting statements in a passage and conveys the same meaning as the entire passage (Raygor, 1970). For example, consider the following passage that Mrs. Rodriguez used with her students:

> Every now and then, a <u>moving light</u> may appear in the <u>night sky.</u> That light may be a <u>comet.</u> A comet has a <u>head</u> and a <u>tail.</u> The <u>head</u> of the comet is <u>made up of</u> a large cloud of <u>gases called</u> the <u>coma.</u> The <u>tail</u> actually <u>forms when</u> the cloud of <u>gases</u> is <u>blown back by</u> the <u>wind.</u>

Notice that the same meaning is conveyed when you read the entire passage and when you read only the underlined portions.

The results of many of the studies conducted in the area of underlining (Anderson & Armbruster, 1980; Cashen & Leicht, 1970; Fowler & Barker, 1974; Idstein & Jenkins, 1972; Johnson & Wen, 1976; Rickards & August, 1975) suggest that teachers should do the following:

1. Give preunderlined material whenever possible.
2. Provide training in effective underlining.
3. Encourage students to underline important general ideas.
4. Remind students that with underlining, less is more.
5. Encourage students to use the time saved by underlining to study the material.

For example, Mrs. Rodriguez frequently gives handouts to her students to accompany their fifth grade science textbook chapters. Her handouts contain sections that she has underlined prior to assigning the chapter. This has helped her students focus on important concepts, key terms and their definitions, study questions, and other elements that she wants them to study in preparation for a quiz or test. Sometimes, she passes out handouts that have not been underlined and models for her students what they should underline. She uses cognitive modeling techniques to demonstrate by saying, "I am going to underline *moving light* and *night sky* because it is important to know that comets move and that we can see them against the dark sky at night. I will underline *comet, head,* and *tail* because I need to remember that a comet has a head and tail. I am going to underline *head made up of gases called coma* so that I will remember what the head is composed of. That sounds as if it might be a test question."

After modeling for her students, she gives them another handout and asks them to practice underlining the way she has shown them. When Mrs. Rodriguez began this procedure, her students tended to underline almost everything on a page, but after repeated practice, the amount of underlining decreased and was limited to the most essential information, and her students have learned to focus on the underlined information to prepare for tests.

Study Guides and Outlines

Study strategies that help students organize information, both visual (e.g., textbook, overhead transparency, chalkboard) and auditory (e.g., lecture, audiotape, and videotape) may take the form of study guides or outlines. Because many students with special needs have difficulty organizing information, they benefit from a guide or outline presenting information in a well-sequenced, structured format. Study guides and outlines may help students with poor reading skills gain information from texts that have heavy concept loads and high readability levels (Olson, 1980). By directing attention to specific points, study guides and outlines provide organized ways to view a videotape or listen to an audiotape.

Study guides and outlines may be used with elementary and secondary students. For example, a child in the elementary grades would benefit from a guide illustrating the four steps in long division or an outline with the names of the five parts of a friendly letter and an example of each. Mario, a second grade student, was given a study guide with the five short vowels (*a, e, i, o, u*) on it. Next to each vowel, was a picture that represented the sound that the vowel made (apple, elephant, igloo, octopus, umbrella).

Bonita, a fifth grade student, received the following guide prepared by her teacher:

Topic: Writing four types of sentences.
Terms: Declarative, interrogative, exclamatory, and imperative.
Definitions:
- *Declarative*—a sentence that states or declares something.
- *Interrogative*—a sentence that asks a question.
- *Exclamatory*—a sentence that expresses emotion or surprise.
- *Imperative*—a sentence that gives a command or order.

Examples:
- Don ran all the way home from Bob's house. (declarative)
- Do you think I could have left my notebook in school? (interrogative)
- I'll never do that again as long as I live! (exclamatory)
- Close the door. (imperative)

Students at the secondary level may profit from a listing of (a) title or subject, (b) purpose, (c) key vocabulary and definitions, (d) a brief outline of subject matter, (f) questions, and (g) text references with pages. For example, Leroy needed to prepare for a test on Japan. Utilizing the six elements just listed, his teacher, Miss Delgado, developed a study guide to help structure his studying and organize the information.

1. *Title/Subject:* The island of Japan.
2. *Purpose:* To describe the environment of Japan and the way of life of its people.
3. *Key vocabulary and definitions:*

- *bonsai*—potted plants and trees kept small through specific cultivation techniques.
- *monsoon*—a periodical wind that reverses direction seasonally.
- *archipelago*—a body of salt water interspersed with numerous islands.
- *typhoon*—a tropical cyclone that occurs in the western Pacific.
- *tsunami*—a huge wave caused by an underwater disturbance.
4. *A brief outline:*
   A. Climate
   B. Population distribution
   C. Landforms
      1. Mountains
      2. Plateaus
      3. Plains
   D. Natural resources
   E. Life in Japan
      1. Urban
      2. Rural
5. Questions:
   - What are the advantages and disadvantages of Japan's geography?
   - What are Japan's greatest natural resources?
   - Describe urban and rural life in Japan.
6. *Text references:*
   - *World Cultures,* pages 56–67.
   - *Japan Today,* page 34 and pages 117–129.

Next month, after Leroy has become used to the format of the study guide, Miss Delgado may leave some blanks in his study guide and require him to fill in these sections, increasing his involvement with the material. Perhaps, he will have to supply some of the definitions, generate some questions about the topic, or fill in parts of the subject matter outline.

Study guides and outlines may take many different forms, depending on the age of the student, the purpose of the guide, the subject matter, and the needs of the students. They provide still another way to facilitate the organization of information for students with special needs.

▢ Important Points

1. To organize information effectively, students may use memory strategies, underlining or highlighting techniques, and study guides or outlines.
2. Mnemonic strategies are strategies that facilitate the organization, storage, and retrieval of information.
3. The keyword method uses auditory and visual cues as well as visual imagery to enhance memorization.
4. The pegword method utilizes a number rhyme technique to remember a list of items.
5. Underlining and highlighting help students organize information to be studied by physically altering the material.

6. Effective underlining identifies the main ideas and supporting statements and conveys the same meaning as the entire passage.
7. Study guides and outlines help students organize information presented visually, in texts or on the board, and auditorily, through lectures and audiotapes or videotapes.
8. Study guides may include items such as the title or subject, purpose, key vocabulary, definitions, an outline of subject matter, questions, and text references.

■ ■ Activity

Part 1. Examine a set of directions. Underline or highlight the information that you think is important for your students to know. Compare what you underlined or highlighted with what someone else in the class underlined or highlighted. How similar were your sections? Justify your choices.

Part 2. Select a chapter from this textbook, and develop a study guide. Switch with someone else. Would their guide help you prepare for a test on the chapter? Critique their guide using some or all of the suggestions given in the chapter. Now, have them do the same for yours. ■ ■

Expression of Information

In this section, we present study skills and strategies that relate to how students express information. Students are expected to possess skills that will enable them to demonstrate their knowledge and mastery of competencies in school. Therefore, in this section, we provide

techniques to improve two skill areas important for success in school and later at work and in life: (a) test taking and (b) report writing and presentation.

Test Taking

Most students are required to take tests before they enter elementary school, during the elementary and secondary years in school, and before they leave high school. Even though students spend their school years taking quizzes, unit tests, and minimum competency tests, they are not necessarily proficient at doing so. Students with special needs encounter special problems taking tests because of difficulties with organization, comprehension, memory, task completion within time limits, studying, self-confidence, and test-wiseness.

Just as you prepare your students in computation, hand-writing, and theme writing, you may also prepare them to take tests. After all, your students are tested in every aspect of the curriculum from reading to vocational skills. We provide the following suggestions for you to teach your students before they take a test, during the completion of a test, and after a test is returned (Bos & Vaughn, 1988; Bragstad & Stumpf, 1987; Mercer & Mercer, 1989).

Before the Test

Following are some of the specific procedures you can suggest to your students as they prepare for a test.

1. *Keep reviewing.* You may suggest that your students keep a study log to help keep up with information. They should review after each class, week, or section. A spaced review is more effective than a massed review of the information just before a test. The study log may contain things to do, such as review prior work, rewrite notes, or highlight important information and things to remember (e.g., key words, dates, and formulas).

2. *Determine the specifics about the test.* Suggest the following ideas to your students to find out from the teacher: date of test, sources to be studied (text, notes, presentations), types of questions (objective, essay), and time allowed.

3. *Guesstimate about the test.* Prompt your students to use past tests and quizzes, clues from their teachers, and brainstorming with other students to predict questions on the test. This will help them more efficiently allocate study time.

4. *Think positive thoughts.* Encourage your students to tell themselves that they will do well because they have studied the right sources of information, prepared for specific types of questions, and thought about how to allot their time.

During the Test

Following are some specific techniques you can suggest your students use as they actually take a test:

1. *Situate yourself where you can concentrate.* If seats are not assigned, remind the students to choose one that will allow them to concentrate. For some, it will be in the back,

and for others in the front, away from friends, noise, or other distractions.

2. *Survey the test.* Suggest that the students take a few deep breaths before starting. They should then put their names on their tests and look over the entire test before beginning. This will help them decide how much time to spend on each section and how the points are allocated. If this is not clear to them, they should ask the teacher.

3. *Complete the test.* Alert the students to read the directions carefully and to respond as directed, since failure to do so may result in a loss of points. They should answer the easy questions first (to earn points quickly and gain confidence) and place a mark by each question that they are unsure of. Then, they can go back to the questions they left unanswered. Unless there is a penalty for guessing, they should answer all of the questions even if they must guess.

4. *Review the test.* Remind the students that after they have completed the test, they should look it over again. They should make sure they have followed the directions, answered all of the questions, and put their name on the test. They should check to see if their writing is legible and their words are spelled correctly. Caution the students to change an answer only if they are absolutely certain it is incorrect.

After the Test

Following are some of the suggestions you can give to your students after they turn in their tests. Have the students systematically analyze their test-taking strengths and weaknesses.

Directions: This is an analysis of your test-taking performance. Please mark *Yes* or *No* for each of the following statements.

	Yes	No
1. Studied for test	____	____
2. Put name on paper	____	____
3. Surveyed test	____	____

	Yes	No
4. Decided order to do test	___	___
5. Read and followed directions	___	___
6. Answered easy questions first	___	___
7. Marked/left difficult questions	___	___
8. Went back to unanswered questions	___	___
9. Answered all questions	___	___
10. Proofread test	___	___

Report Writing and Presentation

Students are frequently required to express information through the writing and presentation of reports. This begins in the elementary schools with young children using show-and-tell activities, language experience stories, and process writing, and with older students creating paragraphs, short stories, book reports, and themes. Students at the secondary level express themselves in writing through paragraph and theme writing, preparation of written reports, and research papers requiring extensive use of references and orally through presentations of themes and reports.

It is helpful for students to have a time line to follow in the development of a paper or report. Some teachers ask for a topic, outline, and first draft by specific dates. These deadlines may be planned cooperatively with students, thus involving them in setting their own goals. You may want to instruct your students in how to do the following:

1. *Choose a topic.* When possible, topic choices should reflect student interests. For example, Mr. Bruno wanted his elementary students to write a report in his science class. He gave his students several choices of topics (e.g. the greenhouse effect, environmental pollution, depletion of resources, waste disposal) to motivate them to do the research and prepare the report. With choices, students had more involvement in the assignment from the start.

2. *Use reference materials in the media center (e.g., Reader's Guide, encyclopedia, fiction and nonfiction, audiovisual aids).* It may be necessary to demonstrate for students how to locate reference materials and use them effectively. Some teachers take their classes to the media center during class time to give them guided practice in using reference materials. For example, Miss Taylor took her tenth grade students to the media center and showed them how to make a card for each reference they used. This helped them later as they put together their bibliographies.

3. *Prepare an outline (for organization and prioritization) and submit it for approval.* Many teachers require their students to submit outlines of their reports prior to the preparation of the actual report. This is an excellent way to monitor the progress of your students and to guide them in organizing and expressing themselves. For example, Mr. Tseng helped two of his students sequence the events of the Civil War by changing the order of the items on their outlines.

4. *Write and submit a thesis statement.* Your students should begin with a thesis statement and make sure that all of their information contributes to and supports that thesis. Show your students how to write a sample thesis statement such as "Insects have an effect upon people and the environment." Then, list several facts about insects and ask your students to decide which statements contribute to the thesis.
   - Insects have three body regions: the head, thorax, and abdomen.
   - Insects are the largest class of organisms, comprising three fourths to five sixths of all known types of animals.
   - Some insects transmit diseases to man, his plants, or animals.

- Some insects feed on crops and stored products.
- The expense in combating insects and the cost in loss or damages is at least $4 billion.
- Insects play an important role in soil improvement.

This step helps your students organize their writing so that what they write relates to and supports the topic.

5. *Prepare a rough draft of the report.* Many teachers require a rough draft of a report as a monitoring device. They assign points or credit to emphasize its importance in the preparation of a report. Suggestions, adjustments, and corrections can result in an improved final product. For example, out of a possible 300 points, Jeremy received 30 points for his outline, 90 points for his rough draft, 15 points for his bibliography, and 110 points for his final report.

6. *Prepare a bibliography.* Your students should include a list of the references they used in completing their reports. This task is made easier when they make a card for each of their references as they find them.

7. *Develop a final copy of the report.* By incorporating any changes suggested during the rough draft stage of the report preparation, students have the opportunity to earn the maximum points possible. If students voice reluctance with "doing the report twice," remind them that their work will be more complete and polished, and likely to earn them a better grade when they complete the final copy.

8. *Proofread all work.* Some teachers award extra points when students turn in perfect papers because this indicates that they have proofread their work.

9. *Submit the paper or give the report orally.* Whether your students are presenting the information orally or in writing, they should follow the preceding steps.

You may want to give your students the nine points listed above in the form of a checklist. Have them mark a section or insert a date each time they complete an item on the checklist. Let this form serve as a monitoring tool for your students as they complete each stage of the presentation or the report.

■ ■ Activity

Part 1. Evaluate your test-taking skills. Think of the last test that you took. How many of the suggestions for what to do before, during, and after taking a test did you follow? What are your favorite types of test items to answer?

☐ Important Points

1. Students express information through (a) tests and (b) oral and written reports.
2. Techniques to use before taking a test are to review using a study log, determine specifics about the test, guesstimate about the test, and think positive thoughts.
3. Techniques to use during a test are to sit where it is possible to concentrate, survey the test, complete the test, and review the test.

4. A suggestion to use after taking a test is to analyze test-taking performance, including strengths and weaknesses.
5. The steps for developing an oral or written report are to choose a topic, use reference materials, prepare an outline, write a thesis statement, prepare a rough draft, prepare a bibliography, develop a final copy, proofread all work, and submit or give the report.

What are your least favorite? How many of the tips for answering specific question types did you follow? What aspects of your test-taking performance do you think you should change? Be specific.

Part 2. Work with a partner for this activity. Practice writing a thesis statement. List several facts about the topic, including both extraneous and relevant issues. Justify which ones relate to the thesis statement and which ones do not. Now switch roles. ■ ■

Summary

Study skills and strategies are techniques, tools, or steps to use in completing tasks. In this chapter, we presented strategies to help students acquire, organize, and express information.

The strategies we presented that relate to how students acquire information are listening, note taking, and comprehension. To listen effectively, students should physically and mentally prepare to listen; identify organizational, verbal, and nonverbal cues; learn to identify main and supporting ideas; and practice self-questioning.

Although there are a variety of ways to take notes, students should survey the topic being presented, approach the task with a questioning attitude, utilize listening strategies, organize the information and listen for cues, and review and revise after the presentation. Advance organizers for increasing comprehension include a statement of objectives and the use of bulletin boards, maps, and handouts. Paraphrasing is used to increase comprehension during a presentation or during the reading of printed materials

by requiring students to stop and state the material in their own words. Mapping is making a word picture of ideas. It includes finding the topic, hypothesizing about the major concepts, reading to answer questions, reciting supporting details, and reviewing the map. Concept teaching consists of selecting a concept; constructing key words or phrases; identifying examples, nonexamples, and characteristics; plotting this information on a concept diagram; and utilizing this information to define the concept.

Strategies that relate to the organization of information are memory strategies, underlining and highlighting, and the use of study guides and outlines. Mnemonic strategies facilitate the organization, storage, and retrieval of information. Underlining and highlighting help students organize by physically altering the material. Study guides improve organization and include title or subject, purpose, key vocabulary words, definitions, an outline of the subject matter, questions, and text references.

Finally, we suggested strategies in test taking and oral and written report preparation for students to use in their expression of information. Techniques to use before taking a test include reviewing, determining specifics about the test, guesstimating about the test, and thinking positive thoughts. Techniques to use during the test include surveying, completing, and reviewing the test. A suggestion for after the test is for students to analyze test-taking performance. The steps in developing a report include choosing a topic, using reference materials, preparing an outline, writing a thesis statement, preparing a rough draft, preparing a bibliography, developing a final copy, proofreading all work, and submitting or giving the report.

11

Student-Directed
Instruction

Key Topics

In the early days of American education, when one-room schoolhouses were prevalent, older students instructing younger students was often a necessity, because the teacher usually taught four to eight grades (Allen, 1976). Recently, the technique of peers working with and instructing each other is enjoying resurgence in American education. Now, cooperative goal structure is being added to the competitive and individualistic goal structures found in the schools (Johnson & Johnson, 1986). As described by Johnson and Johnson, in the cooperative goal structure, students work together to accomplish goals, while in the competitive structure, students work against each other to achieve a goal only some can attain, and in the individualistic structure, students work by themselves to achieve a goal unrelated to the goals of other students.

Recently, empirical data show substantial benefits both academically and socially in the use of the cooperative goal structure (e.g., Delquadri, Greenwood, Whorton, Carta, & Hall, 1986; Johnson & Johnson, 1986; Slavin et al., 1981, 1984, 1985, 1988). As Algozzine and Maheady (1986) comment in a special issue of *Exceptional Children* focusing on effective instructional strategies for students with special needs:

> It is also evident in effective instructional approaches that the teacher alone cannot, and perhaps should not, be viewed as the primary determiner of academic and/or social success in the classroom. On the contrary, there is ample evidence that substantial benefits accrue for the use of peers as instructional agents. These benefits are not limited to acquisition of basic academic skills; rather, improvements in important social behaviors . . . also are products in peer-mediated instructional strategies. (p. 488)

In this chapter, we examine some student-directed strategies that focus on students helping others and themselves to learn. These strategies include peer tutoring, cooperative learning, and whole language. In peer tutoring and cooperative learning, students assume the role of the teacher, or they assist their peers. Whole language techniques are included as the approach and activities are mostly student-directed from students making decisions about the curriculum to the forming of cooperative groups for the purpose of discussing the content of a story.

Peer Tutoring

Defined by Cohen, Kirk, and Dickson (1972) as a "situation in which a person provides instructional assistance and guidance to another person" (p. 1), peer tutoring originated in the early nineteenth century. Peer tutoring consists of one student acting as a tutor, or the person who transmits the information, and one student acting as the tutee, or the person who receives the information. A tutor may be either the same age as the tutee (same-age tutoring) or a different age (cross-age tutoring).

Research studies show that peer tutoring is effective for teaching students with special needs in elementary and secondary grades whether the students are tutors or tutees (Eiserman, 1988; Maheady, Sacca, & Harper, 1987; Maher, 1984; Scruggs & Richter, 1986). Peer tutoring increases academic performance in the areas of reading (Chiang, Thorpe, & Darch, 1980; Eiserman, 1988); spelling (Maheady & Harper, 1987; Mandoli, Mandoli, & McLaughlin, 1982); math (Greenwood, Dinwiddie, Terry, Wade, Stanley, Thibadeau, & Delquadri, 1984; Maheady, Sacca, & Harper, 1987); social studies when facts are presented (Maheady, Sacca, & Harper, 1988); and language arts when punctuation and capitalization are emphasized (Maher, 1984). Peer tutoring not only increases academic performance but also improves social attitudes and attitudes about school learning (Eiserman, 1988); social acceptance of and attitudes toward students with special needs (Johnson & Johnson, 1980; Schuler, Ogulthorpe, & Eiserman, 1987); and positive interactions and attitudes toward tutor, tutee, and content (Scruggs, Mastropieri, & Richter, 1985; Scruggs, Mastropieri, Veit, & Ogulthorpe, 1986). Peer tutoring programs have also decreased absenteeism (Lazerson, Foster, Brow, & Hummel, 1988; Maher, 1982), tardiness (Lazerson, Foster, Brow, & Hummel, 1988), and number of disciplinary referrals (Maher, 1982, 1984).

Classwide peer tutoring is one of the five alternative instructional practices recommended for students with special needs from different cultural backgrounds who are at risk for special education referral (Maheady, Towne, Algozzine, Mercer, & Ysseldyke, 1983). Remember, the culture of many of these groups promotes a cooperative learning structure (Briganti, 1989; Grossman, 1990).

Rationale

The rationale behind peer tutoring is that a peer who has similar experiences and is closer to the developmental age of the tutee can often interpret the teacher's ideas or content in the child's language. Both tutor and tutee benefit from the experience. By feeling useful and needed, tutors learn positive social behavior both in and out of school (Allen, 1976). Additionally, they are given the opportunity to practice an adult role of responsibility (Olson, 1982b). In turn, tutees learn as they are given more opportunity to respond (Greenwood, Delquadri, & Hall, 1984).

Furthermore, peer tutoring is another way to accomplish individualized instruction. The material to be learned can be matched closely to the learner's interest and ability, and immediate feedback is provided. Peer tutoring is also an effective way to reinforce concepts that have been previously taught by the teacher.

Description

Peer tutoring approaches may be either informal or structured, depending on the subject area and purpose. If the purpose is for students to share an enjoyment of literature, an informal peer tutoring approach is often employed. For example, in one fifth grade class, students participated in shared reading with primary students by first reading a short book to the students, talking about the story and pictures, asking the first graders to read with them during the second reading, and, finally, asking the first graders questions (Mossip, 1985).

In contrast, when the purpose was teaching word-recognition skills, Chiang, Thorpe, and Darch (1980) trained their tutors to follow a structured presentation. The tutors first modeled the correct pronunciation of each word with the tutee. Then, the tutor asked the tutee to say each word. The tutor praised each correct response and corrected any errors. The tutor repeated the first two steps with any misread words until the 20-minute tutoring session was over or the tutee read all words correctly.

The classwide peer tutoring system, a combined peer-team approach found to be effective with students who have learning disabilities and students from various cultural backgrounds, is another peer tutoring alternative (Maheady, Sacca, & Harper, 1988). In the combined peer-team approach, students with special needs are paired with regular students. The pair is assigned to one of two teams by randomly drawing colored squares. The students then contribute points to each team as the teams compete with each other. The team membership stays the same for 2 weeks.

Maheady, Sacca, and Harper (1988) instituted the following classwide peer tutoring system in a regular secondary social studies class using study guides developed by the regular and special education teachers. On Monday and Tuesday, the regular teacher presented the material; on Wednesday and Thursday, the peer tutoring occurred; on Friday, the students took a quiz during class time.

As in the cross-age tutoring example of Chiang, Thorpe, and Darch, the presentation format was structured. During the peer tutoring sessions, the tutor dictated the study guide questions to the tutee, who wrote and said the correct answer. The tutors gave feedback: either "that's right" and 3 points for each correct answer or "wrong" and the correct answer. The tutor then instructed the tutee to write the correct answer three times and awarded the student 2 points instead of 3.

The teacher's role was also well structured. The teacher moved around the classroom and awarded bonus points up to 10 to tutors for following the presentation format. The individual scores of tutor and tutee were totaled for the daily team scores and posted on a chart in front of the class. On Friday, an individual quiz was given over the material and each student earned 5 team points for each correct answer. The winning team was announced following the weekly quiz.

Maheady, Sacca, and Harper (1987) identify structured presentation format, contingent point earning, systematic error correction strategies, and public posting of student performance as essential components of this classwide peer tutoring system. They also suggest the scheduling of surprise check days to monitor the accuracy of students' point counts and an awarding of points for each accurate total. Similar classwide peer tutoring techniques were effective in a mainstream secondary math classroom. The major difference in the techniques in the math study was that the tutor and tutee interchanged roles so that students with special needs served as both tutors and tutees.

■ ■ Activity
Look at the example of the classwide peer tutoring system. Notice that it is specific as to how tutees earn points for the team, yet does not describe specific ways that tutors may earn points other than for following the presentation format. In some classes, it is also necessary to identify specific tutor behaviors that earn points. Specify which tutor behaviors earn points and the number. For example, a tutor may earn 3 points for the team if he or she dictates the study guide questions correctly. (Answers for this and other activities are found in the Instructor's Manual.) ■ ■

Implementation
Teachers must carefully plan the use of peer tutoring. In a description of a tutorial community project begun in the Pacoima, California, school system, Melaragno (1976) reported that unplanned efforts at tutoring resulted in dissatisfaction on the part of tutees, tutors, and participating teachers. Steps necessary for a successful peer tutoring program include selecting objectives, selecting and matching students, preparing materials, selecting sites and determining schedules, planning the presentation format, training

tutors, monitoring progress, evaluating the tutoring session, and informing significant others.

Selecting Objectives

Your first step in deciding to institute peer tutoring is to formulate the objectives of the peer tutoring program. Is the major concern academic skills or social skills? Usually, basic academic skills are taught directly, and the concomitant purpose of promoting positive social interaction skills is achieved indirectly. However, Eiserman (1988) organized a peer tutoring activity where elementary students with learning disabilities tutored regular students in sign language for the primary purpose of promoting improved attitudes among the students. Delquadri, Greenwood, Whorton, Carta, and Hall (1986) designated the following target behaviors as appropriate for peer tutoring selection: "answering comprehension questions; practicing in reading workbooks; practicing spelling word lists; practicing math facts; and practicing vocabulary words, their meanings, and definitions" (p. 536).

Selecting and Matching Students

Once you decide the purpose for peer tutoring, you need to select and match the tutors and tutees. To select tutors (a) choose students who have demonstrated the initial acquisition of a skill but need more practice for mastery and application or (b) choose students who are eager to participate and capable of learning appropriate procedures (Chiang, Thorpe, & Darch, 1980; Olson, 1982b; Scruggs, Mastropieri, & Richter, 1985).

Of course, tutees should be selected from students who need to be taught the skill or information. Students with special needs have benefited from peer tutoring, both as tutors and tutees, although Eiserman (1988) recommends that students with learning disabilities be assigned a stable role.

Research provides no clear guidelines for the best matching procedures. Students with special needs have been matched to both same-age and

younger regular and disabled students with similar results (Eiserman, 1988; Webb, 1985). However, you must make certain that the tutor is more competent than the tutee in the subject being taught, as nothing is so embarrassing to an older student than to be constantly corrected by a younger one. Many times, selection between cross-age and same-age tutoring will depend on the objectives of the program. If an academic objective is selected, younger and older students are often matched.

Frequently, students show a preference for same-sex pairs (Devin-Sheehan & Allen, 1976) although Cosden, Pearl, and Bryan (1985) found that boys without learning disabilities often had to be given incentives and instructions before they were willing to work with boys with learning disabilities. In contrast, girls without learning disabilities were eager to work with girls who had learning disabilities. You must be careful not to pair argumentative students together. On the first day of class, Mr. Herman had his students list their strengths and interests to assist him in the selection of peer tutors (see Table 11.1).

Preparing Materials

Depending on the objective, either you or the student tutor may prepare the materials. If you target spelling words as the objective for peer tutoring, the tutor may just use the class text. If you select memorizing math facts, the tutor may write each fact on a 3-inch by 5-inch card. If the objective is studying for a test, you should prepare a study guide. For a shared reading objective, you may guide tutors in selecting a book for the session. Monitoring sheets may also be prepared by the tutors or you.

Determining Schedules and Selecting Sites

The popular length of a tutoring session is 30 minutes two or three times a week for 5 to 7 weeks with about 15 to 20 minutes for the actual student contact time, while the rest of the time is spent organizing materials. Devin-Sheehan and Allen (1976) recommended that tutors learn the

Table 11.1

Peer Tutor Application

Name _____ Grade Level _____
Date _____

I am good at:

_____ Listening to younger children read.
_____ Holding up flash cards for younger
            students.
_____ Reading to younger children.
_____ Remembering math facts.
_____ Drawing with younger children.
_____ Watching and talking about a
            filmstrip with younger children.
Other — _____
       _____

I like:

_____ Talking about sports.
_____ Talking about movies.
_____ Talking about stories I have read.
_____ Working with numbers.
_____ Talking to students who have had
            different experiences than I have had.
Other — _____
       _____
       _____

presentation format on Monday; tutor on Tuesday, Wednesday, and Thursday; and discuss the lesson with feedback from the teacher on Friday. In classwide peer tutoring, Maheady, Sacca, and Harper (1987) schedule teacher-directed instruction for 2 days, peer-tutoring of practice activities for 2 days, and a quiz on the fifth day. Delquadri and colleagues (1986) suggest a 30-minute block divided into 10 minutes for each student to serve as tutor and 5 to 10 minutes to add and post individual and team points.

The site should be a place where the tutors and tutees can work together undisturbed. It may be in the classroom with partitions separating the tutoring pairs to eliminate distractions. If peer tutoring is scheduled as part of the class routine, there is no problem with site selection; students may just be instructed to move their desks together. Two unsatisfactory areas are outside the school building and in the hallways, where distractions tend to be excessive.

Planning the Presentation Format

You may decide on the presentation format alone or with student input. You may wish to use a structured format similar to that used in classwide peer tutoring or in the teaching of word recognition skills or you may choose an informal format. We recommend that you begin peer tutoring using a structured format, as it is much easier to train tutors to follow a structured format. In a structured presentation format, you should identify how the tutor presents the information, gives feedback, and monitors the progress of the tutee.

We have found the following presentation format to be effective in the initial institution of a peer tutoring program:

1. The tutor shares the objective with the tutee.
   Example: The tutor says, "I'm going to work with you to teach you your multiplication facts so you won't have to use your fingers to multiply."
2. The tutor describes the steps in the lesson.
   Example: The tutor says, "First, I'll show you a fact on a flash card. Then, I'll ask you to tell me the answer. If you are correct, you get to keep the card. If you are wrong, I get to keep the card."
3. The tutor asks the tutee to repeat the directions.
   Example: The tutor says, "So, what are you going to do?"
4. The tutor presents the task.
   Example: The tutor holds up a flash card for a few seconds and asks for the answer.
5. The tutor gives feedback.
   Example: If the student is wrong, the tutor says, "No, the answer is 15." If the student is correct, the tutor says, "Good, you know these facts. Wow!"
6. On a recording form, the tutor monitors by marking each fact that the student knows with a plus and each fact that the student does not know with a minus.
7. The tutor goes over the errors by stating the correct answer and then having the tutee repeat the answer.

☐ Important Points

1. Peer tutoring consists of one student acting as a tutor, or the person who transmits the information, and one student acting as the tutee, or the person who receives the information.
2. A tutor may be either the same age as the tutee (same-age tutoring) or a different age (cross-age tutoring).
3. Depending on the objective, peer tutoring approaches may be informal or structured.
4. The steps for implementating peer tutoring procedures consist of (a) selecting objectives, (b) selecting and matching students, (c) preparing materials, (d) selecting sites and determining schedules, (e) planning the presentation format, (f) training tutors, (g) monitoring progress, (h) evaluating the tutoring sessions, and (i) informing significant others.
5. Tutors must be taught to follow a lesson presentation format, wait for a response, and avoid sarcasm and criticism.

Example: The tutor says, "Six times 7 is 42. Your turn. Say the whole thing."
8. The tutor retests the student by showing the tutee the missed facts again and giving the student the card if he or she is correct.
9. The tutor closes the session with a pleasant comment.
Example: The tutor says, "Thanks for working with me today. I hope you enjoyed our time together."

Training Tutors

Once you have decided on the presentation format, you must train your tutors to follow the format and to display appropriate teaching behaviors (Devin-Sheehan & Allen, 1976; Lippitt, 1976). These behaviors include waiting for the response instead of immediately telling the answer, avoiding sarcasm and criticism, and proceeding in a positive, friendly manner.

You should plan an orientation session where you share the purpose, expected outcome, and information about the tutees with the tutors (Devin-Sheehan & Allen, 1976; Maher, 1984). This is also a good time to teach the tutors how to set up and put away the tutoring materials (Schuler, Ogulthorpe, & Eiserman, 1987). For example, in Mossip's fifth grade tutoring program as a part of the orientation session, the

tutors visited the primary teacher, who explained the value of shared reading for her students, how to enter the classroom, and how to help the primary student rejoin the whole-class activity.

Following the orientation session, you should model the presentation format, guide the tutors in their imitation of the model, and point out the important behaviors. In a co-teaching situation, modeling is frequently presented with one teacher acting as the tutor and the other as the tutee.

Mossip (1985) videotapes his students during the role-playing sessions. The students then view the videotape and discuss what worked and what didn't. One teacher prepared a checklist for tutors as a reminder of the essential behaviors before each tutoring session. The items were (a) I have all the materials, (b) I have examined the materials, (c) I plan to _____ when my student says something wrong, (d) I know when to say, "Good answer," and other nice things, (e) I will remember to smile, (f) I will count to 5 to give my tutee a chance to answer after I ask a question.

Monitoring Progress

Charting of the tutee's progress should occur. For example, the tutor may count and chart the number of words the student read correctly each day or the number of addition facts the tutee answered correctly. Be sure to monitor and praise tutors for following the procedures.

Evaluating the Tutoring Session

Both tutors and tutees should evaluate the tutoring session. After each session, you should give tutees forms to mark whether they learned anything and how the session went. If students cannot read the form, you may read the form to them. See Figure 11.1 for a sample elementary evaluation form.

Maher (1984) suggests tutor support conferences where tutors as a group can discuss concerns and meet with the teacher individually if necessary. In Figure 11.2, we present feedback forms for tutors to complete.

Informing Significant Others

You should be certain to notify parents of peer tutoring programs. Parents need to understand when their children come home and talk about working with other students. Tell them why, when, and how tutoring will be used. It is important to include that teacher-directed instruction is still occurring.

■ ■ Activity

With a partner, design a peer tutoring system for elementary, middle school, or secondary students who have special needs. Identify the objective, plan the presentation format, and prepare a parent notification form. ■ ■

Figure 11.1
Elementary Evaluation Form

Tutor Form

Date: _____

Name: _____

My tutee learned: _____

_____

_____

He/She made ___ many ___ some ___ few mistakes

	Yes	No
He/She seemed to like the sessions.	___	___
I enjoyed the sessions.	___	___
I used praise.	___	___
I paused after I asked a question.	___	___

Next week I plan to: _____

_____

_____

Figure 11.2
Tutor Feedback Form

Cooperative Learning

Like peer tutoring, cooperative learning relies on peers working together to solve problems or share information. However, unlike peer tutoring, which consists of a tutor and tutee, cooperative learning groups consist of teams of three or four students working together to master academic tasks or content. The students help each other learn the information or complete the project. The students are usually of varying ability levels, races, and ethnic groups. Cooperative learning has been studied extensively by Slavin and his colleagues at the Center for Research on Elementary and Middle Schools at Johns Hopkins University and by Johnson and Johnson at the University of Minnesota.

In a meta-analysis of ninety-eight studies from 1944 to 1982 involving students with special needs at elementary and secondary levels, Johnson, Johnson, and Maruyama (1983) found that cooperative learning increased achievement and promoted positive attitudes toward the subject areas and other students. Cooperative learning increased academic achievement in reading comprehension (Slavin, Stevens, & Madden, 1988); math (Slavin, Leavey, & Madden, 1984); and science and social studies (Slavin, 1988b). In addition, cooperative learning positively affected social outcomes. The rejection of mainstream special education students is decreased in cooperative learning, although there is no growth in friendship outside the school (Madden & Slavin, 1983; Slavin, Leavey, & Madden, 1984). However, Johnson, Johnson, Warring, and Maruyama (1986) did find that pure cooperation generated more frequent interaction during unstructured class and school activities.

Race relations were improved in classes using the cooperative learning structure (Slavin, 1985; Slavin & Oickle, 1981). Furthermore, cooperative learning has been proposed "as a successful teaching strategy for bilingual and English as a Second Language (ESL) programs and as a way to improve relationships among students of different racial or ethnic backgrounds" (Slavin, 1988a, p. 31). The model capitalizes on the heritage of students with diverse cultural backgrounds, such as the Mexican-American, whose culture emphasizes a working together for the good of the group (Grossman, 1990) and other Hispanic cultures, which value friendship and cooperation (Briganti, 1989).

Rationale

Cooperative learning is proposed as a way to ensure successful mainstreaming of students with special needs (Johnson & Johnson, 1986; Slavin, 1988a) based on the premise that students who work together tend to come to like each other (Johnson & Johnson, 1980). A long tradition of research in social psychology "has shown that people working for a cooperative goal come to encourage one another to do their best, to help one another do well, and to like and respect one another" (Slavin, 1988b, p. 8).

Cooperative learning also relies on peer pressure, a powerful reinforcer for adolescents, in particular (Alberto & Troutman, 1990). Urging other students to complete a task for the good of the group frequently motivates reluctant adolescents.

Description

There are essentially four models of cooperative learning: (a) the jigsaw approach, (b) the group project, (c) the competitive team approach, and (d) Team-Accelerated Instruction, formerly titled Team-Assisted Individualization. Each has a different purpose and format. All models except for Team-Accelerated Instruction are generic. Team-Accelerated Instruction has specific materials that accompany the model and the procedures apply only to the math area (Barbara Luebbe, personal conversation, January 10, 1991).

The Jigsaw Approach

In the jigsaw format (Aronson, 1978), each member of the jigsaw group becomes an expert in some aspect of the task or material and teaches the others what he or she knows. For example, in preparing a report or answering a worksheet about the life of Martin Luther King, Jr., each student in the group may select to study, or you may assign each student to study, one aspect of Reverend King's life. Once each student has mastered the specific content, he or she shares the information with the rest of the group. Then, the group as a whole combines the individual information for the final project, whether it is a report or a worksheet about King's life.

The idiom of jigsaw is appropriate for this technique, for each student has a puzzle piece (e.g., Hector has information concerning Reverend King's childhood and Lashonda has information concerning King's educational background) that must be joined together with the puzzle pieces of the other students before it is possible to complete the entire puzzle (a report on the life of Martin Luther King, Jr.). In the jigsaw approach, student absenteeism can be a problem. If Hector is absent, then he cannot contribute the information concerning Reverend King's childhood. Slavin (1988b) suggests assigning two students from each group to the same subtopic (Hector and Kendra would both be assigned to gather information concerning Reverend King's childhood) or selecting an activity that may be completed during one class period if absenteeism is a problem.

An adaptation of the jigsaw technique is a "counterpart" group (Aronson, 1978). In this adaptation, all students who are assigned or who select a particular subtopic meet together. After sharing information on this subtopic, they rejoin their original group members and complete the report.

Group Projects

In this format, students pool their knowledge and skills to create a project or complete an assignment. Typical group assignments include

(a) making a tower with straws and masking tape (Anderson,1985), (b) completing a chart on objects that sink or float (ERIC, 1988), and (c) figuring out how to build a crystal rock garden (Ruiz, 1989). In using the cooperative learning model to teach the concept of area, Wells (1981) suggests that more complex tasks, such as measuring areas of the floor and other objects in the classroom, produce more cooperation than do simple ones, such as completing a worksheet of problems dealing with the calculation of area.

Competitive Teams

In the competitive teams approach, competition among different groups is emphasized. Slavin and his colleagues at Johns Hopkins University have created two different cooperative learning techniques that emphasize team competition. These two structured formats include Student Teams-Achievement Divisions (STAD) and Teams-Games-Tournaments (TGT).

Student Teams-Achievement Divisions (STAD). In Student Teams-Achievement Divisions, the students are divided into learning teams of three to five members. The teacher introduces new material in a lecture or discussion, usually on Mondays and Tuesdays. The team members study worksheets concerning the material on Wednesdays and Thursdays. Answer sheets are also provided to the team because the idea is to learn the concepts, not to simply complete the worksheets. Students may study in pairs, quiz each other, or choose whatever techniques they want to ensure that everyone on the team knows and understands the material.

On Fridays, the students, individually, take thirty-item quizzes over the material to demonstrate the knowledge that they gained from the class presentations and team practice. Then, the individual scores are added to total the team score. Slavin (1988b) suggests giving points based on the "amount the student's quiz score exceeds his or her past quiz average" (p. 26). The past average quiz score is called the base score. For example, if Keisha's base score was 20, then she has the possibility of contributing 10 points if she scores 100% on the thirty-item quiz. Since there is the possibility of a ceiling effect on improvement scores (i.e., a student who scores a base score of 30 can show no improvement score on a thirty-item quiz), Slavin (1988b) suggests setting base scores that are 5 points below the student's average past quiz scores. You also may want to administer the quiz on Monday before teaching a concept (pretest) and then administer the same quiz after team study on Friday (posttest) to arrive at improvement scores. You may adjust the base scores at any time.

Teams-Games-Tournaments (TGT). An adaptation of the STAD is TGT (Teams-Games-Tournaments) (Devries & Slavin, 1978). The procedures are the same as in STAD except the students participate in a tournament at the end of the week instead of taking a quiz. The teacher still presents the concepts and students still study in teams to master the information. However, students earn points for their teams by participating in the weekly tournament. Students performing on similar skill levels are assigned to each tournament table. For example, the top performers of each team based on past test performance or teacher judgment are assigned to the number 1 table to compete against each other; the middle ones to the number 2 table, and the poorest performers to the number 3 table.

The game materials are a quiz, an answer sheet, and cards. The number of items on the quiz and the number of cards vary depending on the size of the group. You should be able to divide the cards evenly among the group members (Slavin, 1988b). For example, if the team consists of either three or five members, you can maintain a thirty-item quiz and thirty cards, printing a single question or problem from the quiz on each card. However, if the team consists of four members, you may reduce the number of items on the quiz to twenty-eight, so each student will have seven chances to answer questions and earn team points.

To play the game, the students draw cards and the person who draws the card with the highest number begins the game. Play proceeds in a clockwise direction. The rules appear in Figure 11.3

Slavin (1988b) recommends a somewhat complicated scoring procedure, allowing 6 points for the person at each table with the highest number of cards, 4 points for the second, and 2 points for the third. However, we have found it just as equitable and much easier for the students to count the number of cards they earn, to add this number to the other team members' scores, and to divide by the total number of members on the team. For example, if Sunfa earned seven cards at table 1, Juan earned ten cards at table 2, and Jenni earned ten cards at table 3 for the Tigers team, then the total team score would be 9 points ($7 + 10 + 10 = 27 \div 3 = 9$).

The members at the tables change, depending on the scores. When the tournament is held again, the student who scored the highest at each table advances to the next higher table except the student who won at the first table remains there, as it is the highest table. The student with the middle score stays at the same table. The student with the lowest score moves to a lower table except the student who lost at the lowest table remains there, as it is the lowest table (Slavin, 1988b). For example, Brendan, Hector, and Tai were seated at table 2 for the first tournament. Hector scored 14 points, answering fourteen items correctly; Brendan scored 9 points; and Tai scored 7. For the next tournament, Hector would move up to table 1, Brendan would stay at table 2, and Tai would move down to table 3.

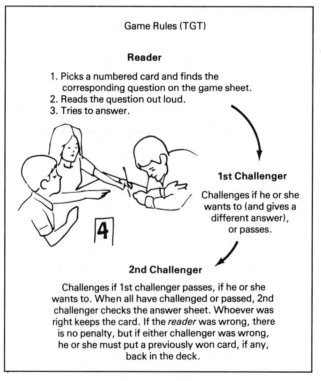

Figure 11.3
Teams-Games-Tournaments Rules

Note. From *Student Team Learning: An Overview and Practical Guide* (2nd ed.) (p. 34) by R. E. Slavin, 1988, Washington, DC: National Education Association. Reprinted by permission.

Team-Accelerated Instruction (TAI)

In Team-Accelerated Instruction, Slavin and colleagues (1984, 1988) combine individualized instruction and cooperative learning. Unlike the other cooperative learning techniques, in which all group members are working on the same objective, project, or set of materials, in TAI, students are first tested to determine their skill levels and then assigned to materials that pertain to these levels only. For example, in math, there may be a student working on addition, one working on fractions, one on decimals, and one on word problems in the same group (Slavin, 1984). The students are given individual math units that they bring to the group.

The units consist of (a) a guide sheet, (b) several skill pages of twenty problems each, (c) formative tests of two parallel sets of ten problems, (d) a unit test, and (e) answer sheets for the skill pages, the formative tests, and the unit test. The guide sheet explains the skill to be mastered and gives a step-by-step method to solve the problems. The skill pages contain problems for students to work. Skill pages consist of the subskills of the task identified by a task analysis. For example, if the final skill is to add with regrouping or renaming, the unit would consist of "a skill page on deciding whether or not renaming is necessary, a second skill page on adding the tens column, and a final skill page on adding the ones column, performing the renaming, and adding the tens column to get the final answer" (Slavin, 1988b, p. 48). Thus, on the first skill page, students would have to answer "yes" to problems such as 75 + 37 or "no" to problems such as 75 + 23; on the second page, they would have to complete the addition process by adding the regrouped 10 to the original tens; on the third page, they would complete the entire problem, such as 75 + 37 = 112.

The formative test contains ten problems at the same difficulty level and similar to those found on the final skill sheet. Most unit tests consist of fifteen problems, again at the same difficulty level and similar to those found on the formative test. Materials are available for the areas of addition, subtraction, division, multiplication, fractions, decimals, numeration, percentages, ratios, statistics, algebra, and word problems.

The procedures are somewhat complicated. Each student reads the guide sheet, asking the teacher or other students for help. The teacher also teaches groups of students who are on the same skill for 15 to 20 minutes a day. Then, the student proceeds to complete four problems on the first skill page. Using the answer sheet, another student in the group checks these problems. If the student completes all four problems correctly, the student moves to a new skill page. If the student completes fewer than four correct, the student asks a peer or the teacher for assistance and then continues with the next four problems on the skill page.

Once all of the skill pages are completed, the student moves to the first formative test sheet and answers ten problems. If the student scores 8 out of 10 correct, the student takes the unit test, which is given and checked by a monitor from another group. If the student does not score 8 correct on the first formative test, the teacher may decide to instruct the student or assign more problems from the skill pages. Then, the student must take the other formative test of ten parallel problems. At the end of the week, the teacher computes the team score.

Team members earn points for their teams. Completion of a unit is worth 10 points, each perfect unit test is worth 2 points, and each unit test with only one error is worth 1 point (Slavin, 1988b). For more detailed information concerning the program procedures and the commercial materials, contact Barbara Luebbe, Project Director, The Johns Hopkins University Team Learning Project, Center for Social Organization of Schools, Johns Hopkins University, 3505 North Charles Street, Baltimore, MD 21218. There is also a similar program for reading instruction, entitled Cooperative Integrated Reading and Comprehension (CIRC).

In 1,371 third, fourth, and fifth grade math classes with mainstreamed students who had special needs, TAI produced positive effects on the academic performance of all of the students and better acceptance of the students with special needs by teachers and pupils (Slavin, 1984). CIRC was also effective in improving reading comprehension in third, fourth, and fifth grade mainstream reading classes (Slavin, Stevens, & Madden, 1988). Salend and Washin (1988) report an increase in on-task and cooperative behaviors in adjudicated youth with TAI procedures. We present a summary of the cooperative models and their components in Table 11.2.

■ ■ Activity

Part 1. Describe an appropriate activity for use with the jigsaw approach to cooperative learning for elementary students with special needs. Describe one for secondary students.

Part 2. With a peer, discuss the role you might play in the STAD procedure in a co-teaching situation. ■ ■

Table 11.2
Comparison of Cooperative Models

Model	Teacher's Role	Student's Role	Outcome	Grade Level/ Subject Area
Jigsaw	Facilitator	Serves as expert.	Product or assignment completed.	Grades 3–12 in social studies, literature, science. Any material with no one right answer.
Group Project	Facilitator	Member of group	Product or assignment completed.	Grades 1–12 in any subject.
Teams				
• STAD	Instructs 2 days.	Members of team study information together.	Quiz passed. Earn points for team.	Grades 2–12 in mathematics, language arts, science, graph reading, geography. Any material with one right answer.
• TGT	Instructs 2 days.	Members of team study information together.	Weekly game. Earn points for team.	Grades 2–12 in mathematics, language arts, science, graph reading, geography. Any material with one right answer.
• TAI	Varies—direct teaching, monitoring.	Complete individual worksheets and certify group members.	Pass skill/sheets, checkout sheets, final test. Earn points for team.	Grades 2–8 in mathematics.

Note. Data in last column from *Student Team Learning: An Overview and Practical Guide* (2nd ed.) (p. 19) by R.E. Slavin, 1988, Washington, DC: National Education Association. Reprinted by permission.

Implementation

You should follow certain steps when implementing cooperative learning procedures. These steps apply no matter what the model is.

Specifying Objectives

You should be certain to specify both academic and collaborative objectives. You may emphasize collaborative objectives, such as all students need to know how to do the work and students need to help each other learn. Slavin (1988a) further insists that the group objective must be important to the group members and suggests that awarding certificates, free time, or bonus points for appropriate group participation may motivate each group member to cooperate.

Selecting the Model

Decide which of the previously discussed models to select. In addition to the following considerations, Table 11.2 should help in your decision. Remember, TAI follows explicit procedures and requires the purchasing of materials. The jigsaw approach and the group project models are more appropriate for the teaching of implicit skills, as there is not one correct answer. The other procedures are more appropriate for the teaching of explicit skills, as there is one correct answer and the steps are usually very specific.

TGT is competitive. Individuals compete face to face against each other, even though the individual scores contribute to the team score. Thus, TGT may not be appropriate for students who cannot handle losing in a game format or have problems in relating to others. Both STAD and TGT are more teacher-directed. Students work with each other completing worksheets or independent practice activities from information already presented by the teacher.

The jigsaw technique and the group project models may not be as motivating because team points are not earned. Plus, more safeguards must be designed to ensure participation by all students, so that the project is not completed by only one or two students instead of the group.

Assigning Students to Groups

Once you decide the model to use, assign the students to the various groups. It is recommended that you assign students of various ethnic backgrounds and ability levels to each group (Johnson & Johnson, 1986; Slavin, 1988a). In a co-teaching situation, make certain that students with special needs are evenly distributed among the different groups. In a review of best practices of cooperative learning, Webb (1985) recommends a range of only two ability levels for each group and the same number of boys and girls. Much of the research that shows positive effects for students with special needs has combined two students who are performing the skill or task at a low level and two who are performing the skill at a higher level in each group (Slavin, 1984; Slavin, Stevens, & Madden, 1988). The recommended size of a group is three to five members (Johnson & Johnson, 1986). To ensure the cohesiveness of the team, Slavin (1988b) stresses that you should make clear to the students that "putdowns, making fun of teammates or refusing to help them are ineffective ways for teams to be successful and not acceptable kinds of behavior" (p. 52).

Deciding Team Schedules

As with anything new, you should first try the cooperative learning approach with one class or in one area. Students may stay on one team anywhere from 4 to 10 weeks. However, if teams do not work out, reassign the students after 3 or 4 weeks (Slavin, 1988b). The idea is to give every student an opportunity to work with all students in the classroom.

Planning Room and Material Arrangements

Group members should be grouped close together, and groups should be far apart (Schniedewind & Salend, 1987). Johnson and Johnson (1986) recommend a circle arrangement to accommodate student communication. Such an arrangement allows students to share and discuss materials and maintain eye contact. The physical arrangement must allow clear access for the teacher. The group also needs an area to store materials or the group project. One teacher bought square laundry baskets that each group decorated and used for the storage of their materials. The decorations were removable to accommodate the frequent changes in group membership.

Guaranteeing Individual Accountability and Participation

Make certain that each member is participating in the group and that the project or activity is not being completed by only one or two students. This is not a problem with STAD or TGT, because individual accountability is ensured by the weekly quiz or tournament, nor is it a problem with TAI, as students are assigned different materials to complete. However, to ensure participation of all members when using the jigsaw and group project techniques, assign student roles. Johnson and Johnson (1986) recommend the assignment of the roles of checker, accuracy coach, summarizer, elaboration seeker, and reporter to specify a responsibility for each group member. The checker makes certain all students can understand the information. The accuracy coach corrects any mistakes in another member's explanation or summary. The summarizer restates major conclusions or answers of the group. The elaboration seeker asks members to relate material they previously learned. The reporter writes down the information or completes the worksheet. Assigning a specific role to students is particularly important for cooperative learning activities in a regular classroom with mainstreamed students. Often, mainstreamed students are left out if no particular role is assigned to them.

Another way to ensure individual accountability and participation is to select only one student's product to represent the group effort (Johnson & Johnson, 1986). Of course, this selection is kept secret until the end of the project. Salend and Allen (1985) ensure participation of all students by limiting the number of times each student may talk. Before the group activity, each member is given a certain number of tokens.

Each time a student addresses the group, he or she must surrender a token. Once all of the tokens are used, the student may no longer address the group. A final technique for ensuring group participation is to limit the amount of material given to the group (Slavin, 1988a). If only two worksheets are given to the group, then four members cannot complete the worksheet individually.

Role-Playing Cooperative Behaviors

For students with special needs, role-playing such cooperative behaviors as "use a quiet voice," "stay with your group," and "say one nice thing to everyone in your group" (Putnam, Rynders, Johnson, & Johnson, 1989) is necessary, because many of these students have an inability to relate in socially appropriate ways with others. You should model cooperative behavior first. Then, have students role-play appropriate and inappropriate ways to show cooperation and evaluate whether the demonstrated behavior is an example of cooperative or noncooperative behavior. For older students, a checklist of cooperative behaviors for students to self-monitor is often useful. Example items may include (a) I listened to others' opinions, (b) I complimented a person's idea in the group, (c) I spoke in a pleasant voice, (d) I didn't get angry if my ideas weren't used, and (e) I made constructive comments when I thought another's idea was outrageous or not appropriate.

As part of a collaborative effort with regular education teachers, Johnson and Johnson (1986) recommend that special education teachers complete the activity with the students ahead of time, before it is performed in the regular class. Thus, if the students are assigned to various groups in the regular science class to determine which objects sink and which float, you may set up the sink-float experiment before the students participate with their cooperative group in the regular setting.

Monitoring Cooperative Behaviors

Once you have taught the concept or given directions for the required activity or project and modeled cooperative behavior, your role becomes typically that of a monitor. Monitor each member's cooperative behavior; keep the group on task; and intervene, when necessary, to provide task assistance. For young students, praise the sharing or helping behaviors publicly (Putnam, Rynders, Johnson, & Johnson, 1989) with such comments as "Sunfa shared her article with Juan. She was being very cooperative."

Evaluating Both the Product and Process
You should evaluate both the product and process of the group. If you are using STAD, TAI, or TGT procedures, you already have evaluated the product, respectively, from the quiz grades, unit test grades, and the points earned during the tournament. You may elect to grade the group project or the individual student's project selected to represent the group work in the jigsaw or group project approaches. Some teachers, when they know what individual members have contributed, grade the students' individual contributions. Research has not demonstrated any

one particular evaluation as more effective than another (Webb, 1985).

However, according to Slavin (1988a), in the identification of best practices of cooperative learning teams, the group grade should be based on an average of the performances of all of the students. Johnson and Johnson (1986) suggest using different criteria to evaluate the project of a student with special needs, giving bonus points to the groups who have members with special needs.

Some teachers also give grades for the group process. Remember, Slavin (1988b) recommends giving points to the students for appropriate participation. Even if you don't grade the process, you and the students should evaluate how the group functioned. The students might answer such questions as, What was a helpful action? What was not a helpful action? What could be done differently next time? (Schniedewind & Salend, 1987). (See Table 11.3 for a sample evaluation form.) In fact, you may want to have students role-play problem areas

Table 11.3
Student Evaluation of Cooperative Session

What was learned in the group today? _____
_____

Describe an example of cooperative behavior.

• You did _____
_____

• Others did _____
_____

Describe an example of noncooperative behavior.

• You did _____
_____

• Others did _____
_____

Examine the example of noncooperative behaviors and change them to cooperative behaviors. _____
_____

The completion of this sheet is worth 10 points toward your grade.

☐ Important Points

1. Cooperative learning groups consist of teams of three or four students who work together to master academic tasks or content.

2. Research studies show that cooperative learning increases achievement and promotes positive attitudes toward subject areas and other students.

3. There are essentially four models of cooperative learning: (a) the jigsaw approach, (b) the group project, (c) the competitive team approach, and (d) Team-Accelerated Instruction.

4. In the jigsaw approach, each student has a piece of the puzzle that must be combined to facilitate a group report or project.

5. In the group project, students pool their knowledge and skills to create a project or complete an assignment, such as a chart on objects that sink or float.

6. In Student Team-Achievement Divisions (STAD), students are divided into learning teams of three to five members who work together to master content presented by the teacher.

7. The students in STAD earn points for the team, depending on their score on the weekly quiz.

8. In the Teams-Games-Tournaments (TGT) approach, the students also work together to learn the information; however, they earn points for their team by answering questions correctly during a weekly tournament.

9. In the TAI approach, students help each other work on individual objectives and sets of materials, earning points for the team by completing materials that pertain to their objectives only.

10. To implement cooperative learning, the following steps are recommended: (a) specifying objectives, (b) selecting the model, (c) assigning students to groups, (d) deciding team schedules, (e) planning room and material arrangements, (f) guaranteeing individual accountability and participation, (g) role-playing cooperative behaviors, (h) monitoring cooperative behaviors, (i) evaluating both the product and the process, and (j) recognizing the group effort.

and possible solutions for evaluation of the process.

Recognizing the Group Effort

In STAD and TGT, Slavin (1988b) recommends the use of newsletters or bulletin boards to recognize team accomplishments. If you select the group project model, invite your principal, secretary, or colleagues to judge the projects. Then, display the projects with pictures of the group members. In Table 11.4, we present a checklist of items for you to decide on before you use cooperative learning techniques. Remember, teachers make instructional decisions and monitor their effectiveness.

■ ■ Activity

With a group of three other students, solve the following problems that Mr. Hernandez identified when working with cooperative groups. First, identify the problem. Then, describe a solution.

1. Sam is frequently absent during the jigsaw procedure.

2. Manu contributes no points to the team, as he always scores 20 out of 20 on his papers.

3. Rupert monopolizes the group discussion.

4. Only two of the four members of the Tiger Team are completing the projects. ■ ■

Table 11.4
Teacher Checklist

1. Specify group objective.
   Academic:

   _____

   _____

   _____

   Motivated to attain by:
   _____ a. Points
   _____ b. Certificates
   _____ c. Free time
   _____ d. Praise
   _____ e. Homework pass
   _____ f. Other

2. Specify group objective.
   Collaborative:

   _____

   _____

   Motivated to attain by:
   _____ a. Points
   _____ b. Certificates
   _____ c. Free time
   _____ d. Praise
   _____ e. Homework pass
   _____ f. Other

3. Select model.
   _____ a. Jigsaw
   _____ b. Group project
   _____ c. STAD
   _____ d. TGT
   _____ e. TAI

4. Assign students.
   _____ a. Even number of girls/boys
   _____ b. Two high-level/two low-level
   _____ c. Special students divided
   _____ d. Students of various cultures/interests
              divided
   _____ e. Random

5. Decide team schedule.
   Time Frame:
   _____ a. No. of weeks
   _____ b. No. of days

6. Arrange room materials.
   _____ a. Clear access for teacher
   _____ b. Storage for materials

7. Guarantee individual accountability.
   _____ a. Grade individual quizzes or projects
   _____ b. Assign roles
   _____ c. Select one student's project
   _____ d. Tokens
   _____ e. Other

8. Have students evaluate their own cooperative
   behaviors.
   _____ a. Complete student evaluation form
   _____ b. Answer questions

9. Evaluate the students' work.
   Products:
   _____ a. Points
   _____ b. Grades
   _____ c. Other

   Process:
   _____ a. Points
   _____ b. Grades
   _____ c. Other

10. Recognize the group effort
    _____ a. Bulletin board
    _____ b. Newsletter
    _____ c. Other

The Whole Language Approach

The whole language approach is difficult to define and operationalize. Proponents advance that it is not a practice, but a set of beliefs (Altwerger, Edelsky, & Flores, 1987; Goodman & Goodman, 1979; Newman, 1985). As Judith Newman (1985) lamented in her book *Whole Language: Theory and Use* when a reviewer suggested she begin by defining *whole language,* there is "no simple definition of 'whole language.' . . . 'Whole language' is a shorthand way of referring to a set of beliefs about curriculum" (p. 1). Thus, it is difficult to separate the definition of *whole language* from its rationale. The whole language model stresses a student's own language production as a bridge from oral to written language. The meaningfulness of language is emphasized, so instruction proceeds within the context of a whole text instead of within nonmeaningful segmentation of language, such as individual sound–symbol relationships (Stahl & Miller, 1989). It is immersing students "in an environment in which language is being used in purposeful ways" (Newman, 1985, p. 58).

Empirical support of the whole language model with students who have special needs is difficult to find, probably due to the relative newness of the use of the model with this population and the insistence of many proponents of whole language that it is more a philosophy than a specific method. In a review of fifty-one studies from 1960 to the present, Stahl and Miller (1989) studied the effects of the whole language approach combined with the language experience approach, contending that both are part of a "continuous evolution" (p. 87). They concluded that overall, there are no differences between basal readers and the whole language/language experience approach in standardized and nonstandardized measures of reading performance. However, they did find different effects for grade levels, ethnic backgrounds, and reading skills. Whole language/language experience produced better results with kindergarten children than with first graders, with middle or upper class populations than with disadvantaged populations, and with word recognition skills than with reading comprehension.

There are basically three reasons for the inclusion of whole language approaches in this text: (a) the paucity of studies dealing specifically with students who have special needs, (b) the individualized nature of special education, and (c) the role of the special education teacher. Of the fifty-one studies reviewed by Stahl and Miller (1989), only one dealt with the disabled population, although the study reported no significant differences in subjects with mental retardation (Woodcock, 1967). In addition, Stahl and Miller found that there was "not enough research available to evaluate the effects of whole language programs in the later grades" (p. 110).

Moreover, it is important for teachers of students with special needs to be aware of different approaches. The whole language approach or certain components of it may be the best to use with some students. Remember, you will be monitoring progress, so you will know whether a particular technique is working with a student. In addition, the role of special education teachers in co-teaching or collaborative situations makes it necessary to know the curriculum being used in the regular class, and whole language is being used extensively in many regular education classrooms (Stahl & Miller, 1989).

Furthermore, recent research on effective teaching strategies for bilingual students with disabilities supports the adoption of interactive models of instruction (Swedo, 1987; Willig & Swedo, 1987). Whole language, of course, is an interactive model. The approach emphasizes social interaction among students and between the teacher and students (Strickland & Morrow, 1989).

Rationale

The whole language approach is based on the holistic theory of learning. Highlighted in a special issue of the *Learning Disability Quarterly* in the fall of 1984, holism is proposed as a movement whose time has arrived in special education (Poplin, 1984). A basic premise of holism is that all learning is meaningful and naturalistic and a product of the learner's discoveries (Tarver, 1986). Learning is presented as a whole, not divided into segments.

Another premise of whole language is that children learn written language the way they do oral language, through exposure to a literate environment (Goodman & Goodman, 1979). Language is acquired by using it as a whole, not by practicing the separate parts (Altwerger, Edelsky, & Flores, 1987). In the literate environment, speaking, listening, writing, and reading are interrelated and interdependent. They are not learned in a hierarchical order from listening, speaking, reading, and then writing. As Newman (1985) describes, "Whole language activities are those which support students in their use of all aspects of language; students learn about reading and writing while listening; they learn about writing from reading and gain insights about reading from writing" (p. 5). Goodman and Goodman (1983) concur with this analysis in their statement that "people not only learn to read by reading and write by writing, but they also learn to read by writing and write by reading" (p. 592).

In reply to the many myths concerning whole language, Newman and Church (1990) list the following assumptions of the whole language approach:

> Learning
>> is social;
>> requires risk-taking and experimentation;
>> involves constructing meaning and relating new information to prior knowledge;
> occurs when learners are actively involved,
>> when they have real purposes,
>> when they make choices and share in decision-making;

uses language, mathematics, art, music, drama, and other communication systems as vehicles for exploration. (p. 24)

Description

Although there is no consensus for the exact content and structure of a whole language model (Leigh, 1980), we have identified the following components from reading the literature and observing whole language teaching in special and regular settings. The components include the teacher's role as a facilitator (Fagan, 1989; Newman & Church (1990); Staab, 1990; Tunnell & Jacobs, 1989), the student's role as the initiator (Fagan, 1989; McWhirter, 1990; Newman, 1985), functional materials (Strickland & Morrow, 1988; Toliver, 1990; Tunnell & Jacobs, 1989), invented spellings (Newman, 1985), silent and shared sustained reading (Bode, 1989; Tunnell & Jacobs, 1989), journal and functional writing (Bromley, 1989; McWhirter, 1990), and integration of curriculum areas (Leigh, 1980; Newman & Church, 1990).

The Role of Teachers

The role of teachers is to provide a language-enriched environment (Newman, 1985). Teachers are facilitators who do not impose their interpretations of events on students, but help the students construct their own. Teachers also help students relate their prior knowledge to new information (Newman & Church, 1990). Newman (1985) relates the following instance. When children were preparing instant pudding in their group as part of a reading activity and they came across the direction "Add the ingredients in the box to the milk," they asked the teacher how to pronounce the word *ingredients* and what it meant. The teacher replied that they should try to read the rest of the recipe to look for clues and think about what other people did when they made pudding at home. Suddenly, one student replied, "Oh, yes, that means add all the stuff in the box to the milk." Even without pronouncing the word, the student was able to figure out the steps and bring meaning to reading. The teacher served as a facilitator to remind the students to use other information that they could read from the recipe and to think about their own experiences with mixing pudding.

Teachers also correct students with strategies that emphasize meaning and self-correction. Such strategies are based on observations of how good readers correct themselves when they cannot read words. Good readers usually reread, read further, skip words, or substitute words when they come to something they don't know, while poor readers often try to sound out the unfamiliar words (Newman, 1985). Good readers try to bring meaning to the passage, and poor readers try to bring grapheme–phoneme relationships. Thus, teachers in the whole language approach prompt students to reread something, read ahead, skip, or substitute a word when they encounter information they can't decode or don't understand.

Teachers also model a love and enthusiasm for reading and writing. Thus, during sustained silent reading, teachers read along with the students. During journal writing, teachers write in a journal and share the entries with the class. In process writing, teachers assume the same roles as students, that of helping, praising, and appreciating a piece of creative work (Zaragoza, 1987).

Staab (1990) describes another teacher behavior prevalent in the whole language approach. For your information (FYI) is information presented briefly when students need it. For example, Staab relates how a teacher emphasized that *ea* says the *e* sound during a 10-second segment and mentioned it again later in the day when the children were attempting to use another word with that sound. For incidental teaching, Staab recommends that new teachers examine the skills in the curriculum scope and sequence.

The Role of Students
In the whole language approach, students are active learners, often selecting the activity, books to read, or topics to write about. With these choices, students feel ownership, a necessary ingredient for valuing their ability to read and write (Fagan, 1989). McWhirter (1990) found that students with special needs in high school were motivated to read more when they were able to select their reading materials and their writing topics. Zaragoza (1987) notes that students with special needs who are given time and opportunity to write, choose and develop personal writing topics, feel control, and become less passive and more independent as they learn to make choices. Thus, student decision making is emphasized throughout the curriculum.

Students are also given the role of learning from each other (Balajthy, 1989; Newman, 1985). Whole language practices foster cooperative learning. As explained by Fagan in a discussion of the roles of teachers and students in whole language: "Teachers must try to control what appears to be a 'teacher instinct' of giving, telling, describing, explaining . . . , but quite often this same information can be provided by the students" (p. 577). Students can help each other learn. For example, during process writing, they critique their peers' stories and make constructive suggestions for improvement.

Functional Materials
The whole language classroom is filled with printed materials that are natural and relevant (McNutt, 1984). Often, the materials are placed in centers. Cereal boxes, environmental print found at places such as McDonald's or Burger King, road signs, menus, recipes, candy bar wrappers, and other natural instances of print are a part of the whole language environment. Objects in the room are even identified with printed labels. Print is also included in daily oral activities. McNutt (1984) suggests the use of printed sentence strips, such as "Today is Monday," while students talk about calendar events.

Stationery, envelopes, stamps, memo lists, and other functional writing materials are kept at a writing center. Often, a tape recorder is placed there for children to dictate their stories for other students or the teacher to transcribe. The library center frequently has a podium to hold oversized books and has comfortable sitting areas where the students either read books written by each other or library books. See Chapter Five for a discussion of learning centers.

Instead of basals and Direct Instruction materials, trade books and predictable materials are used. Unlike basals, with controlled vocabulary, these materials are rich in vocabulary and syntax. Trade books are children's literature books written by children's writers. Often, the illustrations provide support for the text, and the content deals with a topic relevant and familiar to the child or adolescent. Trade books may be either fiction or nonfiction.

Predictable materials include songs, nursery rhymes, poems, and classical and contemporary children's stories. They use repetitive language patterns and rhythms, which allow the children to predict the content and language as they listen or read. The illustrations in predictable books are bright and vivid, and they match the text. One predictable book is Bill Martin's book, *Brown Bear, Brown Bear* (1970), in which Martin repeats the phrases so that the pattern is evident. For example, the lines "Brown bear, brown bear what do you see? I see a blue bird looking at me" become "Blue bird, blue bird what do you see? I see a . . ."

Sometimes, predictable books are published commercially as big books. These oversized books, anywhere from 18 inches by 15-1/2 inches to 18 inches by 12 inches, allow all of the children to see the page as they read along with the teacher.

Wordless picture books are used to motivate writing. These books may be unfamiliar stories, such as *The Bear and the Fly* (Winters, 1976), or familiar stories, such as *Jack and the Beanstalk* (DeRegniers, 1985).

Language experience stories are other materials used in the whole language approach. Language experience stories are stories dictated by children to the teacher. The children relate some event or experience and the teacher writes their exact words on large chart paper (for young children) or notebook paper (for older students). No attempts are made to limit or control the vocabulary used (Newman, 1985).

■ ■ Activity
With two peers, brainstorm other printed environmental materials that may be brought into the class. For example, what about paper and plastic bags with different writing? ■ ■

Invented Spelling
Invented spelling is simply spelling as done by the students. In other words, the students are encouraged to generate their own spellings of words. Spelling usually develops in the following stages: prephonemic, phonemic, letter name, transition, and correct (Rhodes & Dudley-Marling, 1988). Prephonemic spellers use strings of letters, numbers, and other markings to represent words. They spell words with either markings of some kind, as ∿᷍᷍ for *baby*, or conventional letters, as *jym* for *baby*. Most words are represented by random strips of letters (e.g., *babadada*).

Phonemic spellers attempt to spell words using sounds, although not necessarily all of the sounds in the word. They have discovered phonetic principles of spelling. For example, *baby* may be spelled as *ba* (the first two sounds of the word) or *speck* as *pek*. Phonemic spellers become letter name spellers when they attempt to represent all of the sounds of words with letter names. For example, *baby* may be spelled *babe* or *open* as *opn*. Many students with special needs are letter name spellers (Rhodes & Dudley-Marling, 1988). Transitional spellers are becoming aware of differences between their own spellings and conventional spellings. They incorporate some of the visual features of the words into their own spellings, such as *babey* for *baby* or *lite* for *light*. In the final, correct stage, students begin to employ the visual features of Standard English spelling to spell words, and they regularly spell words correctly. Rhodes and Dudley-Marling (1988) caution that these stages are not necessarily discrete. Many students revert to earlier strategies when they attempt to spell difficult words.

In a whole language model, a formal spelling program is usually not taught, as spelling is not taught in isolation (Scibior, 1985). Instead, students are given opportunities to spell functionally. Students are immersed in writing activities that eventually lead to the adaptation of conventional spelling patterns. Spelling generalizations such as "the *oi* sound is spelled *oy* at the end of the word" are taught only if the children ask or if the teacher feels it is necessary (Gunderson & Shapiro, 1988).

Silent and Shared Sustained Reading

For students of all ages, sustained silent reading and shared reading are recommended. In sustained silent reading, time is set aside for everyone in the class, including the teacher, to read something, whether it is a magazine, a library book, or a peer-authored text. During shared reading times, the students read together. Older children may read to younger or younger children to older. Shared reading not only gives students opportunities to practice reading but also provides functional and social activities. Children who are just starting to read usually spend the time looking at pictures or reading along with a recorded book.

Journal and Functional Writing

Journal writing is recommended to help students continuously practice writing and view writing as a functional, meaningful skill. The premise is that writing is learned only by writing, reading, and perceiving oneself as a writer (Newman, 1985). Journal writing also serves as two-way communication between teacher and students. The teacher encourages the students to write what is of interest to them. There is no required length or duration, and the journals are never corrected or graded. At the same time that the students are writing in their journals, the teacher is also writing in a journal. Both teacher and students may share journals. It is also sug-

gested that once a week, the teacher write to each individual student in the journal (Bode, 1989; Unia, 1985). Bode (1989) suggests that you may want to write the first entry in a student's journal for young or reluctant writers.

When young students write in their journals, the teacher rotates around the room. For first graders on the first day of writing, Gunderson and Shapiro (1988) recommend that teachers write the words for the children who ask. If the children just scribble, which is appropriate for this stage of development, Gunderson and Shapiro further recommend that the teacher ask the students what the scribbles say and then write the words above the scribbles.

Other informal writing activities in a whole language setting give students a purpose for writing (Newman, 1985). One such activity is writing to pen pals at other schools, in different states or countries, or from different service organizations. One teacher of students with special needs shared pen pals with another teacher's class in a different state. The teachers had met at the International CEC Conference. Letters plus videos were shared between the classes. Another class adopted a group of sailors on a submarine for pen pals. A student teacher had her unmotivated middle school students with special needs write letters requesting free materials.

Another teacher of students with special needs created a bulletin board that correlated the social skill of giving compliments. In the center of the board was a pocket filled with sheets that had "Something to Brag About" written at the top. At any time, a student, the teacher, even a visitor could write complimentary items about anyone at the high school. All items dealing with the teacher or students were posted on the bulletin board, while the student or teacher delivered the other comments to the designated persons outside the classroom.

Integrated Curriculum

Thematic units that integrate different aspects of the curriculum are frequently used in the whole language approach (Balajthy, 1989; Strickland &

Morrow, 1990). We discussed units thoroughly in Chapter 8, so we do not discuss them again here. Newman and Church (1990) state that whole language doesn't promote integration of just reading, spelling, writing, and listening, but that the literacy curriculum should be planned around investigations in math, science, and social studies content, also.

Strickland and Morrow (1990) describe the following activities with animals as a theme. Books about animals appear in the library corner. The science table has pictures of the four different animals, and live animals, such as gerbils and hermit crabs, are in the class. The teacher discusses with the children their upcoming trip to a farm. As they sing, she points to the words of "Old MacDonald Had a Farm." The children build a pretend zoo and make animals from clay. In the writing area are animal pictures and word lists meant to encourage the children to write books about animals. During reading, the teacher selects books with repetitive patterns, such as "Not I, said the Little Red Hen." With these activities, emergent literacy skills and content areas are integrated into the curriculum.

Implementation

There are no formal steps in teaching whole language. However, for clarity of discussion and to help explain the whole language intervention, we discuss previewing the lesson, presenting it, and correlating activities to incorporate the whole language approach into the teaching of both elementary and secondary students with special needs in the reading and writing areas. The organization is not meant to imply that these components occur in sequential order or in isolation.

Previewing the Lesson

In previewing, supply the students with background knowledge pertinent to reading, social studies, science, and so on. The background knowledge that readers have about texts has a powerful effect on their comprehension (Anderson & Pearson, 1984; Pearson, 1982). We dis-

cussed the importance of background knowledge in Chapters 7 and 9, so previewing is not an activity connected with whole language only. However, as it is an integral part of the whole language approach, we present examples that are consistent with the whole language philosophy of making learning meaningful for students.

Reading. In "The Optimal Learning Environment (OLE) Curriculum Guide: A Resource for Teachers of Spanish-Speaking Children in Learning Handicapped Programs," Ruiz (1989) describes one activity that links the knowledge areas to text for language-minority children and adolescents with mild disabilities. In this activity, the teacher first identifies the central idea of a text. Then, the teacher asks the students about their experiences with the situation. The students' accounts are either recorded on the chalkboard or are discussed, followed by predictions of what will happen in the chapter. After the text is read, possible connections between these experiences and what occurred in the text are discussed.

Often, when using previewing with primary students, you should introduce a predictable book or big book to the children by reading the title and asking them to make predictions. For instance in the book *Fire! Fire! Said Ms. McGuire* (Martin, 1970), you ask the children what and who they think the book will be about. Remember, prediction is one of the strategies taught in reciprocal teaching (Chapter 9).

■ ■ Activity

Look at a predictable book. With a peer, list three questions you might ask students about the pictures for a preview activity. ■ ■

Writing. Previewing is also suggested for written activities, because often, students with special needs have difficulty selecting topics (Bos & Vaughn, 1988). Zaragoza (1987) suggests that students will be able to decide their own topics after they have listened to and discussed trade books, so you may want to begin by reading a book and discussing how the author decided on his topic, characters, and vocabulary before asking students to write. In designing whole language experiences for remedial readers, Wicklund (1989) suggests that teachers share their writings with the students and even share their metacognitive thoughts in story writing, such as "I included this part in my story because I wanted the audience to feel scared," as a prelude to student writing. Wicklund also recommends brainstorming activities and thorough discussion of the topic before assignment of a writing activity.

Bos and Vaughn (1988) suggest that you have students prepare lists of possible topics, following these directions:

> Give each student and yourself a piece of paper; say to them, you know lots of things about yourself, about your family, and about your friends. You have hobbies and activities that you like to do. You have stories about things that have happened to you and/or to others. I want you to make a list of things you would like to share with others through writing. Do not put them in any specific order—just write them as you think of them. You will not have to write on all of these topics. The purpose of this exercise is to think of as many topics as you can. I will give you about ten minutes. Begin. (p. 158)

As the students are writing, model the process of writing a list. When time is up, share your topics with the students and tell them to pick a partner to share their topics with. Now, the students have possible topics to refer back to when they can't think of one.

Presenting the Lesson

The lesson may proceed with your leading the students or with the students working together. Remember, there are no locked-in steps; however, some adaptations of the whole language approach are suggested for students with special needs.

Reading. Farris (1989) identifies seven steps in reading a big book to primary students: (a) the teacher briefly introduces the book; (b) the teacher asks students to make predictions concerning what they think this book is about; (c) the teacher reads the book to the class, pointing to the text; (d) the teacher has students make predictions throughout the book; (e) the teacher rereads the book, encouraging students to read along; (f) individual students or pairs of students volunteer to read along; and (g) the book is reread every day for 1 week. After reading, the teacher helps the children relate key concepts and recall important or favorite parts of the story.

For remedial and younger students, discussion usually occurs after repeated readings of the text (Wicklund, 1989). For remedial students, repeated reading continues until most of the children can read the book independently, although this may not occur during one lesson. As noted, predictable books lead to easy memory of the content. Children enjoy the rhythm and repetitive language patterns, as in *Horton Hatches the Egg* (Dr. Seuss, 1940): "I meant what I said and I said what I meant, an elephant's faithful, one-hundred percent" when Horton sits on "that good for nothing Lizzy's" egg (p. 3).

It is suggested that decoding skills also be taught formally to high-risk young children (Trachtenburg & Ferruggia, 1989), remedial readers (Wicklund, 1989), and children in the lowest reading groups (Bridge, Winograd, & Haley, 1983). In teaching first graders in the lowest reading group, Bridge, Winograd, and Haley (1983) describe the teacher first reading the book aloud to a group of eight children and then leading the children in choral reading of the text until they take individual turns reading the material. Then, the teacher copies the text on a chart without the illustrations and has the children read isolated single words and sentences by matching them to the sequenced text on the chart until they can read without matching.

Trachtenburg and Ferruggia (1989) recommend a structured activity that involves teaching high-risk students to use context clues and memory to decode individual words. In a page of text that has been read frequently by teacher and students in unison, the teacher covers all words except the word of interest. The teacher asks the student to read the word. If the student cannot, the teacher exposes more of the text until the student can decode the word through memory or other context clues. For example, to use the strategy to decode the word *blow* in the familiar line of "I'll huff and I'll puff and I'll blow your house down," said by the wolf in the *Three Little Pigs* (Galdone, 1970), cover all of the words except *blow*. Then, expose the word *I'll* (e.g., "I'll blow"), then *your* (e.g., "I'll blow your"), then *house* (e.g., "I'll blow your house") until the student is able to read the word *blow*.

Sometimes, the teacher points out common consonant clusters and other word patterns, for example, "Notice that if you can read the word *huff*, you can read the word *puff*, as only the first sound is different." Another adaptation for students with special needs is letting the students select a word for the day that they would like to learn and putting it in a word bank for practice. Thus, the students learn sight words and decoding skills in the context of whole words and with meaningful text.

Teachers often use cooperative learning activities in presenting lessons to adolescents. For example, Harste (1984) suggests assigning two students to work together during a reading activity. The students decide how they will read, whether they will read silently or orally, and how much they will read before they stop and talk. When they reach the stopping point, they talk and compare the information with their past knowledge, including the information discussed with the teacher during previewing. Then, at the end of the selection, they share their insights with other pairs of students and the teacher.

Ruiz (1989) suggests a literature study activity for language-minority students with mild disabilities. After the teacher previews the books, the students select the ones that they wish to read. Students who select the same book meet in groups to discuss their reading. Students also keep reading dialogue journals in which they write their thoughts, feelings, progress, and problems with the day's reading.

Writing. With young children, the writing lesson often involves using a predictable book pattern and writing language experience stories as a group or individually. After repeated readings of a book, the children either retell the story for the teacher to transcribe or write their own story.

For remedial readers and students with mild disabilities, more structure in the form of story starters is often provided in the writing activity. Rhodes and Shannon (1982) describe students in a resource room rewriting the pattern from Bill Martin's *Brown Bear, Brown Bear* (1970) to make it a Christmas story. As created by the children, the line, "Brown Bear, Brown Bear, what do you see?" became "Santa Claus, Santa Claus, what do you see? I see an elf looking at me. Elf, elf, what do you see?" (p. 5).

Wicklund (1989) suggests using patterns found in poetry to structure composition for remedial readers. In the poem "Oodles of Noodles" by Lucia and James L. Hymes (1972), a group of fourth grade students inserted their own ideas in the blanks:

> I love _____ . Give me _____ .
> Make a _____ (tell how much).
> _____ is my favorite _____ .
> I eat _____ (when) _____ .

The fourth graders completed the poem with:

> I love *macaroni*. Give me *macaroni*.
> Make a *pile up to the sky*.
> *Macaroni* is my favorite *snackaroni*.
> I eat *macaroni every night*." (p. 480)

■ ■ Activity

With two peers, select a predictable book and write a story starter for adolescents. ■ ■

In process writing, writing activities are less structured. Students are often just given class time for composing with no other assistance. Zaragoza (1987) recommends a 20- to 30-minute daily writing period for process writing. After the students have written the first draft of the composition, they revise, edit, and publish the creative piece.

In revising, students focus on mistakes made dealing with the ideas, while in editing, they concentrate on grammatical errors and other mechanical errors. During the revising and editing stages, the students may ask their peers or the teacher to critique their stories. Lamme (1989) recommends an author's chair for the revising stage. Students sign up for the chair to ask their peers for ideas and opinions concerning their writing. Zaragoza (1987) teaches her students to positively receive the work of other students by the acronym TAG: "(a) T—Tell what you like, (b) A—Ask questions, and (c) G—Give ideas" (p. 293). Instead of providing an author's chair, you may let older students work together to provide and receive feedback.

Revising and editing may also be done during a teacher–student conference. Bos and Vaughn (1988) recommend scheduling brief, frequent conferences, usually lasting only 2 to 3 minutes. In the revising conference, they suggest that you listen and ask questions to help the students correct their writings. Zaragoza (1987) suggests open-ended questions like, What are you trying to describe? or, Can you tell me more about . . .? Be certain that you do not rewrite a student's story or attempt to change the writing style (Newman, 1985).

In the editing stage, the student and you should focus on the mechanics of writing (Zaragoza, 1987) and spend time checking grammar and punctuation errors. To assist students during the editing stage, Bos and Vaughn (1988) suggest posting a list of editing skills the students already know.

The publishing phase of the writing process is often in the form of books that have cardboard bindings and laminated pages. Usually, there is a brief biography of the author and the date of publication. After publication, many teachers schedule sharing time for the students to read their published books to peers as they sit in the designated author's chair, ask questions about the story, and then answer any questions the peers have about the story. Of course, the reading is followed by applause. Sometimes, at the beginning of the writing process, teachers allow students with special needs to move to publication without revision (Bos & Vaughn, 1988).

Selecting Activities to Correlate with the Lesson

In a review of different basic elements of whole language programs, Tunnell and Jacobs (1989) found that most of the lessons ended in writing or other culminating activities. Such culminating activities usually occur in conjunction with predictable trade books. In other words, these activities usually occur after the class has spent much time discussing and working with a particular story.

The following culminating activities, which are representative of the many found in whole language classrooms, emphasize the social, functional, and meaningful parts of learning. The students or you may direct the activities. Some activities are completed individually; some, in small groups; and some, with the teacher. As Altwerger, Edelsky, and Flores (1987) describe, whole language is "very eclectic in having a large repertoire of materials, modes of interacting, and ways of organizing classrooms" (p. 43).

Big Books. Making a big book requires that children be quite familiar with a literary work, so the activity occurs only after much repetitive reading and discussion of a story or book. After the students are familiar with the story, ask them to retell it and transcribe this retelling on chart paper. Print one or two sentences at the top of each 12-inch by 18-inch piece of light cardboard until the children's version of the story is complete. Then, have the children, either individually or in small groups, draw illustrations that correspond to the text on each page. A cover page with the title and author along with a preface page that explains why the children selected the story to retell is also suggested (Herald-Taylor, 1987). The pages are then sequenced by the children and either stapled with a heavy-duty stapler or bookbinding tape. Before putting the book together, you may elect to display the separate pages around the class and use them for various activities, such as sequencing.

Serebrin (1985) suggests that students start out with familiar literature books, such as *Jack and the Beanstalk* (DeRegniers, 1985), and that teachers reproduce just the illustrations and let the students individually or as a group write their own stories. Whenever reproducing published materials, remember to check the copyright laws.

An adaptation of the big book activity for remedial students uses similar word patterns to

This big book was designed by primary-age students with special needs.

make big books, such as the *ing* big book and the *oy* big book (Wicklund, 1989). The activity may also be adapted for adolescents with special needs by dividing the students into groups to design big books for the media center or for use in a younger grade.

Another adaptation is to create ethnic feelings books to help students develop a more positive understanding of their cultural heritage. Ford and Jones (1990) had twelve students from 9 to 12 years of age with developmental disabilities collaborate on a book concerning the historical experiences of African-Americans.

Art and Drama. Literature lends itself easily to art and creative drama activities. After reading a story about a paper bag princess and conducting a class discussion of the favorite parts, Boyer (1985) had the 9- to 13-year-old high-risk students in a mainstream setting make masks that looked like helmets for fighting dragons.

When teaching twelve students with special needs during a summer program, one of the authors had the students read, reread, and finally retell the story of *The Three Billy Goats Gruff* (Galdone, 1973) by tape-recording different students rephrasing the dialog of the various characters. The teacher transcribed the script and gave each student a copy. As a culminating activity for the summer program, the students made puppets for each of the characters, constructed a puppet stage from a refrigerator box, and performed the show for different classes.

Literature stories may also lead to a class mural project. For example, Ms. Anderson and her

As the culminating activity of an animal unit, Ms. Anderson's class created a mural of the different kinds of animals aboard Noah's Ark.

primary children prepared a mural after reading *Noah's Ark* (Spier, 1977). A secondary teacher had her class make relief treasure maps after they had read *Treasure Island* (Stevenson, 1883). She used a soap-based clay. The project had an ancillary outcome, too. Her students had the cleanest hands in the school!

Games. Hornbeck created games from trade books for her elementary and middle school students with learning problems (Midgett, Olson,

& Hornbeck, 1985). First, she designed the game board with a path consisting of colored squares that lead to the goal, or end. Next, she created literal, interpretive, and critical questions plus vocabulary questions based on the story. Students moved closer to the goal by spinning a homemade spinner and moving the number of spaces indicated. A player landing on a blue square had to answer a literal question (a question of fact) about the story. A player landing on

Important Points

1. Whole language is a set of beliefs about curriculum based on the premise that learning is a meaningful activity.
2. Empirical data as to the effectiveness of the whole language approach with students who have special needs are inconclusive, although many educators recommend the approach for teaching students with special needs from diverse cultural backgrounds.
3. Following are components of whole language: the teacher as a facilitator, the student as an initiator, functional materials, invented spelling, silent and shared sustained reading, journal and functional writing, and integration of curriculum areas.
4. In the whole language approach, teachers provide a language enriched environment, help students connect their prior knowledge with new information, correct students with prompting and encouragement of self-correction, model an appreciation of books and writing activities, and teach information based on student need.
5. In the whole language approach, students make decisions concerning the topics for writing and books for reading, and they help others gain knowledge in a meaningful and functional manner.

6. Functional materials are printed materials that are natural and relevant, such as cereal boxes, environmental print found at places such as McDonald's or Burger King, road signs, menus, and other printed items that students see every day.
7. Invented spelling is spelling as done by students and not corrected by teachers.
8. In sustained silent reading, time is set aside for everyone in the class to read, including the teacher, whether it is a magazine, a library text, or a peer-authored text.
9. During shared reading times, the students read together.
10. Journal writing provides students with a purpose for writing and serves as a two-way communication between the teacher and each student.
11. In the whole language approach, curriculum is treated in an integrated manner, planned around investigations in math, science, reading, and other content.
12. Previewing the lesson, presenting it, and selecting activities are components of the whole language approach.
13. Structured activities such as decoding words and writing with story starters are often used with students who have special needs.

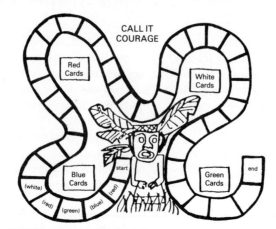

CALL IT
COURAGE

Red Cards

White Cards

Blue Cards

Green Cards

start

end

(white)

(red)

(green)

(blue)

(red)

LITERAL COMPREHENSION QUESTIONS (Blue)

1. What did Mafatu fear the most?
2. Why did Mafatu fear the sea so much?
3. Why didn't Mafatu go fishing with the other boys?
4. What was Mafatu's inseparable companion?
5. Why did Mafatu never let his fire go out?
6. What did Mafatu use to make his knife?
7. Why did Mafatu feel confident and have a new belief in himself after he built his lean-to?
8. How did Mafatu make his canoe?
9. What broke into Mafatu's trap and ate his fish?
10. What made Mafatu know that his homeland lay ahead?
11. How old was Mafatu when the story takes place?

VOCABULARY (Red)

1. The warriors of that island killed pigs with naught but a knife for a weapon, bracing themselves so that the animal impaled itself upon the blade.
2. He stood there taut with purpose, high above the demon sea.
3. The stems where the fruit had grown had been severed cleanly by a knife.
4. Some premonition of danger kept him poised, and wary.
5. The boy was filled with unaccountable dread.
6. Those eaters-of-men had wrought well.
7. Mafatu seized him by the scruff and dragged him up to safety.
8. But the boar toppled, gave a convulsive shudder, lay still.
9. Somewhere below in darkness, black hands drew forth from hollowed logs rhythm that was a summation of life, a testament of death.
10. The boy fell upon the thwart, shoved the craft into the water.
11. He put his little craft first on one tack, then on another.

CRITICAL LEVEL QUESTIONS (White)

1. If you had been Mafatu, would you be afraid of the sea?
2. Do you think Mafatu had good reason to be afraid of the sea? Why or why not?
3. How can you explain Mafatu's realization that the sea was only another element to conquer?
4. How did Mafatu win a victory for himself when he took the spearhead from the sacred place?
5. What kind of courage did it take to kill the wild pig?
6. Do you think it takes courage to face loneliness? Explain.
7. What courage did Mafatu show in saving his dog, Uri?
8. How would the story have been different if Mafatu had climbed to the lookout the last day?
9. How do you think Mafatu showed resourcefulness?
10. Do you feel Mafatu won by his own wits and skills? Why or why not?
11. Do you think it would be fun to be on an island all alone?
12. What would you do for survival if you were stranded on an island?
13. What could have happened to Mafatu if the men didn't turn back?
14. How do you think Mafatu felt when he realized he no longer feared the sea?

INTERPRETIVE LEVEL QUESTIONS (Green)

1. Why did Mafatu need to conquer his fear of the sea?
2. How did Kivi, the albatross, give Mafatu hope when he thought he was lost at sea?
3. Why did Mafatu feel Moana, the Sea God, had been cheated?
4. Why was Mafatu alarmed when he saw the fruit had been severed by a knife?
5. What kind of bones did Mafatu find on the platform of the idol?
6. What gave Mafatu the knowledge that he had found the sacred place where the eaters-of-men made sacrifices?
7. Why was it so important for Mafatu to finish making his canoe?
8. Why do you think Mafatu stabbed the octopus again after it was dead?
9. Why did Mafatu feel he had to climb the plateau to his lookout every day?

Figure 11.4
A Game Created from a Trade Book

Note. From "Comprehension Games! Yes! Yes!" by J. Midgett, J. Olson, and D. Hornbeck, 1985, *Florida Media Journal, 10* (2), p. 14. Reprinted by permission.

a green square had to answer an interpretive question, which required understanding of implied meanings. A player landing on a white square had to answer a critical question, which required judgment and evaluation. A player landing on a red square had to answer a vocabulary question. The other players evaluated the correctness of the answers by looking at the prepared answer sheets for the literal questions and vocabulary items or by a majority vote for the critical and interpretive questions. If the answer was incorrect, the player moved back a square.

Eventually, Ms. Hornbeck turned the designing of the game boards over to cooperative groups of students. The students turned their homemade games over to the library for other students and teachers to use. A sample of one of the games made after the class read *Call it Courage* (Sperry, 1940) appears in Figure 11.4.

■ ■ Activity

Select a trade book. With two peers, design three meaningful and integrated activities that correlate with the topic of the book. ■ ■

Summary

In this chapter, we discussed the more student-directed strategies of peer tutoring, cooperative learning, and whole language. In these approaches, students are actively engaged in learning and helping each other. In peer tutoring, one student tutors another student to provide extra practice and more opportunity for responding. In cooperative learning groups, students work together to either finish a joint project or to help each other learn and understand teacher-presented material. The whole language model often finds children working together to complete projects or to provide feedback.

We discussed each of these models extensively, and we gave you ideas that you can use in your particular setting, whether at the elementary level or the secondary level. The steps for implementing peer tutoring procedures are (a) select objectives, (b) select and match students, (c) prepare materials, (d) select sites and determine schedules, (e) plan the presentation format, (f) train tutors, (g) monitor the progress, (h) evaluate the tutoring session, and (i) inform significant others.

For cooperative learning, we discussed the various models of jigsaw, the group project, competitive teams, and Team-Accelerated Instruction. The following steps were recommended to implement cooperative learning: (a) specify objectives, (b) select the model, (c) assign students to groups, (d) decide team schedules, (e) plan room and material arrangements, (f) guarantee individual accountability and participation, (g) role-play cooperative behaviors, (h) monitor cooperative behaviors, (i) evaluate both the product and the process, and (j) recognize the group effort.

For the whole language procedures, we discussed techniques and activities that emphasize the use of meaningful and functional materials for teaching language arts. Previewing the lesson, presenting it, and selecting activities are components of the whole language approach. Whole language activities are usually more structured for students with special needs.

Part III

Factors Affecting Instruction

12

Computer Technology for Teaching and Learning

by Donna Baumbach

Key Topics

As little as a decade ago, computers were seldom in any school or classroom. Now, however, technological advances, increased sales, decreased costs, improved software, and interest from parents and teachers make it possible for you and almost every teacher to use technology to improve teaching and learning. The computer has become one of the most powerful tools in schools today. Effectively utilized, it enables teachers to change the ways they teach and the ways students learn.

Research indicates that microcomputers with appropriate software have the potential to raise the quality of instruction (Roblyer, Castine, & King, 1988). Students are excited about using computers, and their learning is enhanced by the wide variety of instructional software that is available. Teachers use computers to make planning, record keeping, materials preparation, and classroom management faster and easier. This gives them more time to spend with their students. Teachers can use technology to help individualize instruction as well as to foster cooperative learning. Computers can help teachers work with students whose native language is other than English. In short, computers can en-

Donna Baumbach is a professor of instructional technology at the University of Central Florida.

hance most classroom instruction and management.

Perhaps, just as importantly, students are growing up in a world of computers, information, robots, and automation. New models of instruction for students with special needs must prepare these students for life in a world of information and technology (Cain, 1984). According to Roblyer, Castine, and King (1988), "The children of our society will never again know schools without computers. While technology's rapid evolution makes it difficult to predict its exact role in our future, the Computer Age has already had an irrevocable impact on our educational system" (p. 11). The purpose of this chapter is to describe the role of the computer and related technology in the education of children with special needs at both the elementary level and the secondary level.

Advantages of Computer Technology

The impact of computers in education has been the subject of much research. Generally, studies reveal several advantages for using computers in instruction. Using computers can result in improved achievement, reduction in learning time, improved attitudes toward learning, and improved self-esteem.

Many studies show that the use of computers in instruction either improves learning or makes no difference when compared with traditional classroom instruction (Carnine, 1989; Chambers & Sprecher, 1983; Roblyer, 1988), but low achievers and students with special needs show substantially higher achievement when learning through computer-assisted instruction (Niemiec, Samson, Weinstein, Walberg, 1987). Carefully designed and implemented computer-assisted instruction can lead to improved learning in most content areas.

Computers are useful with students who have special needs because instructional techniques demonstrated to be effective for teaching such students can be easily incorporated into computer-assisted instruction (Budoff, Thormann, & Gras, 1984). Different learners have different abilities and different ways of processing information. Computers can be used to combine approaches and to tailor individual learning experiences. Good instructional software incorporates good teaching practices and produces success for students. According to Budoff, Thormann, and Gras (1984), the advantages of using computers with students who have special needs include the following:

1. *Individualization and self-pacing.* Students working at computers may set their own pace, and each student may work at a different pace. Students often control how long a paragraph or image is displayed. Computers wait patiently for students to respond. With some software programs, you or your students can regulate the presentation rate and the response time.

2. *Immediate feedback.* Instructional computer programs can provide immediate feedback to each student about his or her performance. For each response, the student may receive feedback of "good," "great," "super," or "try again." Depend-

ing on the program, specific feedback and even the student's name may be used. For example, "Good, Carolyn, you remembered the rule about *i* before *e.*"

3. *Consistent correction procedures.* Computer-assisted instruction programs can provide specific, concise correction. Students sometimes get confused with wordy or conflicting corrections. For example, you may correct a student's spelling one time by saying, "Did you remember to change the *e* to an *i* and add *ng?*" Another time you may say, "Did you remember to drop the *e* and add *ing?*" This may be confusing to a learner. Watch for consistent correction procedures in software.

4. *Repetition without pressure.* Computers are infinitely patient and never get frustrated with a student. Students can repeat a task or problem without embarrassment until they get it correct. They can try different solutions to solving a problem without penalty or fear of failure.

5. *Immediate knowledge of correct responses.* In traditional classroom instruction, students must often solve several problems and then wait to have them corrected. Computer programs can provide feedback after each problem, and many computer-assisted instruction programs offer hints to help students avoid making an error again. Spelling checkers and grammar checkers also give immediate feedback. In addition, feedback as a form of positive reinforcement for correct answers motivates students.

6. *Well-sequenced instruction.* Just as you break a task into small steps and allow students to master one step at a time, so does good software. For most students with special needs, well-designed, well-sequenced instruction is essential.

7. *High frequency of student response.* Good software is highly interactive, demanding student response. Students cannot remain passive in front of a computer, so students remain on task and get more

practice than they might get from large-group response techniques or even worksheets.

8. *Repeated demonstration of mastery of academic subject matter.* For students who have experienced failure, software programs may allow success by providing review and recall of previous learning. Many software programs are designed not only to increase the difficulty level of problems when a certain number of problems are answered correctly but also to drop back a level when several problems in a row are answered incorrectly. This helps students avoid frustration and feel successful, yet remain challenged.

9. *Peer response.* Many students with special needs have experienced failure and frustration and are viewed by their peers as incompetent. Success with a computer makes them more successful in the eyes of their peers.

10. *Motivation.* Most students like to work at a computer and are excited to have the opportunity. Highly motivated students have fewer behavior problems and more success at learning. Some teachers use computer time as a reward for other good behavior, but this is not generally recommended. Students should know that computers are an integral part of instruction, not an extra. It is also possible that students who never get computer time when it is offered only as a reward may be those who will benefit the most from its use. Allowing *additional* computer time or allowing the student time to work with a favorite program may be a more acceptable reward.

11. *Increased time on task.* Given a choice, students readily spend more time working with computers than they do with traditional seatwork. Several studies have shown significant correlations between time on task and achievement in settings with students who have special needs

(Roblyer, 1988; Thormann, Gersten, Moore, & Morvant, 1986).

12. *Minimizing disabilities.* Often, students with special needs understand a concept but are unable to write the correct answer due to poor memory, problems with visual perception, or other problems. With computers, students can manipulate letters and numbers without having to write. Using a computer as a word processor allows students to write without having to worry about correct letter formation. Students can edit their work without erasing or copying and recopying.

■ ■ Activity

Jorge has trouble writing and spelling, so he dislikes both. He seldom finishes his written work, and although he thinks clearly, his thoughts seldom find their way to paper. Jorge has become discouraged and frustrated with school. He frequently shows his frustration by misbehaving. His attention span is short. Discuss the advantages of using computer technology with this student. (Answers for this and other activities are found in the Instructor's Manual.) ■ ■

Uses of Computer Technology in Instruction

According to Stein (1984), "Computers will not and cannot replace teachers any more than did the advent of chalkboards, books, and audiovisual materials; some teacher roles and functions should be augmented by this new and powerful tool available for our use" (p. 41). Today's powerful microcomputers used in combination with appropriate software programs are highly versatile. During the few years, teachers have found many ways to use computers in instruction. The uses of computers in instruction generally fall into three main categories: (a) computer literacy, (b) computer-assisted instruction, and (c) computer-managed instruction.

Computer Literacy

All students in our schools need to be computer literate. Computer literacy exists along a continuum that has computer awareness at one end and programming at the other end (Heinich, Molenda, & Russell, 1989). This makes defining computer literacy difficult. To some people, it means being able to turn on the computer and turn it off. To others, it means knowing the history of computers. Most people now believe that computer literacy means being able to live and work in a computer-oriented world. We use this broad definition; for we are preparing our students to live and work in such a world.

Teaching about computers leads students to an understanding of what computers do, what computers cannot do, and how computers work. It also leads students to an awareness of the impact of computers on society and their daily lives. Computers have affected existing careers and have created new career opportunities. They have made information about each of us instantly accessible, so privacy and security issues must be addressed. Legal and ethical concerns are also a part of computer literacy.

Teaching and learning about computers does not always require a computer. Students see computers in offices and businesses every day. They hear their parents complain that "the computer made a mistake" in computing the electric bill or in addressing a magazine label. Television programs, magazine articles, and newspaper articles in which computers play a role can help you initiate discussion and activities about many of the areas of computer literacy.

Computer literacy does not have to be taught as a separate subject. In fact, many of the skills of computer literacy are best learned when computerized instruction is part of other instruction. While using computers for lessons in mathematics or language arts, for example, students can also learn how to care for disks, how to save and load data and programs, and how to use peripheral devices, such as printers. Students should be taught equipment operation and care when they first begin to use computers. Like other skills, computer skills must be reviewed, practiced, and reinforced.

Students using computers quickly learn that they must follow directions in order to interact with programs. For example, if the program tells them to press the return key after entering an answer, they learn that they must press the return key. If they forget, they are reminded with a prompt or by lack of computer activity. They also learn that directions can vary from program to program, and they learn to adjust to those variations.

Students who are computer literate can make computers do what they want them to do and

---

☐ Important Points

1. Use of computers in instruction can save time and improve learning.
2. Use of computers can improve students' attitudes and self-esteem.
3. Software for students with special needs incorporates many of the instructional strategies that have proven effective for them.
4. Computers are widely used in almost every job setting today, and students must be able to use computers to compete in the job market.
5. Computer literacy means being able to live and work in a computer-oriented world.
6. Computer literacy skills are best integrated into the curriculum; that is, they are taught as students learn to use computers for other tasks.
7. Students who are computer literate use computers and appropriate software to accomplish specific tasks.

use them as tools for learning and communicating. Students who are computer literate can identify software programs that will perform tasks they need to do. They can select word processing programs to write a report or paper, graphics programs to illustrate a point or to prepare a bulletin board display, game programs when they have time for recreation, and instructional programs when they are appropriate. Students with special needs are no exception. Like all of us, such students must recognize the important role that computers play in improving productivity and managing information.

■ ■ **Activity**

For 1 week, read, clip, and collect newspaper and magazine articles that discuss computers, computing, or software. Make a list of places you see computers and how they are used during the same week. Did you find more or fewer articles on computers than you thought you would? What was the most interesting thing you read about computers? Where was the most surprising place you found a computer? Think about your own computer skills? Are you computer literate? ■ ■

Computer-Assisted Instruction

Computers can be used to deliver instruction effectively and efficiently. In computer-assisted instruction, students interact with the content through instructional software, or lessons delivered by the computer. Computer-assisted instruction (CAI) programs are available for every grade level and every subject area.

Instructional software must be carefully designed, developed, and programmed in order to be effective. You must select the software for your students carefully, and you must plan for its utilization by students. Computer-assisted instruction software programs differ not only in content and suitability for different grade levels and abilities but also in the methods of instruction used. The methods include drill and practice,

tutorials, games, simulations, discovery learning, and problem solving. Just as teachers use several methods to deliver instruction, many programs combine two or more of these methods.

Drill and Practice Programs

About 85% of the computer-assisted instruction programs available are drill and practice programs. Drill and practice programs give students opportunities to practice concepts and skills. For example, *See the U.S.A.* (CompuTeach) provides varied practice for students in naming states and capitals. *Fraction Fuel-Up* (DLM) allows students to practice working with equivalent fractions. *The Human Pump* (Sunburst) allows students to practice identifying parts and functions of the heart. *Chariots, Cougars, and Kings* (Hartley) and *The Amazing Reading Machine* (MECC) provide practice in reading comprehension.

Drill and practice programs are similar to workbooks in purpose. However, drill and practice with computers offers distinct advantages over workbooks for students with special needs. Students are usually more excited when working at computers than when completing workbook pages. Students generally work longer at computers, and good drill and practice programs do not allow students to make the same mistakes over and over again because they offer corrections and hints for improvement.

Repetition in drill and practice programs provides increased dexterity and fluency in skills. Drill and practice programs generally provide a number of questions in a variety of interesting ways. Several levels of difficulty may appear in a program. Programs also provide immediate positive and negative feedback as well as rewards and reinforcement.

Drill and practice programs may be used just after a lesson, just before a test, or to recall prerequisite skills before beginning instruction at a higher level. Drill and practice programs help students gain and retain skills, making the students feel successful and competent.

Perhaps because so much of the software available is drill and practice software, surveys of teachers of students with special needs reveal that this is by far their most prevalent use of computer software (Thormann, 1982, 1985). Results of the surveys indicate that "as currently utilized, computers primarily serve a 'workbook' function" (Thormann, Gersten, Moore, & Morvant, 1986). Because of this, the use of computers is receiving much criticism in education, much as the use of the workbook pages and ditto sheets have in the past. Much power and potential remain untapped if computers are used for this purpose only. Drill and practice software is most effective when it is well designed, appropriate to the learner, and integrated into the overall curriculum through good instructional planning.

Tutorials

Tutorial programs are designed to teach new concepts and skills. In a tutorial program, instruction is presented much as it might be by a teacher. An example of a tutorial is *Poetry Express* (Mindscape), which teaches students how to write poetry like haiku, limericks, and cinquains. IBM's *Reading for Meaning Series* teaches students to understand and interpret charts and graphs while reading stories, to differentiate between fact and opinion, to use context to determine word meaning, to make inferences, and generally to improve comprehension. *Un Viaje En Tren* (D. C. Heath) provides practice with the Spanish language.

Tutorial programs offer four distinct advantages for children with special needs (Budoff, Thormann, & Gras, 1984). First, interactive tutorial programs may provide individualized instruction and repetition when you cannot, which may lead to enhanced student performance. To learn a task completely, much repetition is necessary for many students with special needs. Repetition can be both boring and frustrating for you, but computers don't get bored or frustrated. Second, tutorials provide the structure and consistency in instruction that is particularly important for teaching students with special needs, so students may learn specific skills

more rapidly. Third, tutorials provide sequence and structure important to the learning process. Students must go through a specified sequence to produce a specified outcome. Fourth, students must respond correctly to each step in the sequence. They receive immediate feedback for their responses as well as appropriate reinforcement.

Tutorial programs range from simple to extremely complex in design. Many are linear, with all students completing the same program, although the pace may be different for each student. Complex programs may offer multiple branching opportunities, with different responses taking students to different parts of the program for review, remediation, or advanced information. With extremely complex tutorial programs, it is possible for two students to go through the program on completely different paths as well as at different paces; however, learning outcomes for the program are the same.

Games

The use of game software in schools is controversial. Many educators dismiss games as inappropriate instructional methods. However, games can be useful in developing problem-solving skills and in increasing motivation. It is important to remember that not all games are educational; some are merely intended for recreation. Instructional games include *Alien Addition* (DLM), *Monster Math* (IBM), and *Word Munchers* (MECC). These may also be considered drill and practice programs with the added excitement and challenge of arcade games. Often, instructional games allow a student to compete against the computer or against another student. Sometimes, games allow a student to compete against his or her best time or score.

Students generally find educational games challenging but nonthreatening. Instructional games provide more focus and concentration than do other methods of instruction for limited periods of time. Games often improve response rate and accuracy. They foster cooperative learning and teamwork. Computer games also increase fine and gross motor skills and eye–hand coordination (Budoff, Thormann, & Gras, 1984). Instructional game programs should not be underestimated. They can help students gain skills as well as develop logic and strategy. In addition, games are usually described as "fun," so students like them and don't mind repeating them again and again.

As beneficial as games may be, however, games should not be the only type of software available for students. Competition can be frustrating, and the excitement that games provide can be overwhelming to some students. Like other computer-assisted instruction software, however, games must be carefully evaluated, selected, and integrated into instruction.

Simulations

Simulation programs offer students opportunities to see the consequences of their choices. Often, simulations present graphic demonstrations of abstract concepts. Simulations model reality but allow students to interact without the risks or expenses that might otherwise be involved. Students involved in simulations may be asked to use math skills, to develop problem-solving strategies, or to use observation and note-taking skills. Simulations usually involve reading skills, mathematics skills, and reasoning skills.

A variety of simulation programs are available for instruction, including programs that allow students to dissect a frog (*Operation Frog*, Scholastic), drive through a city (*Jenny's Journeys*, MECC), manage the environment (*Odell Lake*, MECC), travel across the United States (*Oregon Trail*, MECC), or relive events in history (*Revolution*, Britannica Software). Simulation programs may provide students who have special needs with extensive practice of vocational skills (Maddux, 1986). In *Math Shop* (Scholastic) and *Math Shop Junior* (Scholastic), for example, students simulate the role of a clerk in different types of stores and practice a wide variety of math skills. As they work, they are faced with long lines and impatient customers, pressures

and frustrations of a real job. Simulations generally are time-consuming methods of instruction, but retention and transfer to real-world experiences are high. Simulations are highly motivating, although some students with special needs become frustrated and bored if a program takes too long or seems too difficult.

Discovery Learning

Discovery software uses the inductive approach to learning. Students can manipulate variables and observe results, approximating a laboratory environment. Few directions are provided by the program or the teacher in most discovery learning. In *Incredible Laboratory* (Sunburst), students use trial and error to discover how fifteen chemicals combine to create different monsters. Each chemical determines a variation of one of the monster's body parts: the head, arms, body, legs, or feet. This program has accompanying lesson plans, transparency masters, and worksheets that allow you to guide students to discover what you want them to learn. Without these, students could use the program for hours without discovering anything. In fact, they might not even know that there was a problem to be solved.

Logo is a computer language that has been used by students with special needs in discovery learning. Papert's (1980) work with the Logo programming language and young children endorses this approach to learning. Using Logo, students enter a simple command in English to make a turtle move on the screen. For example, students can type "FORWARD 10" and see the turtle move ahead, drawing a line 10 units long. If they want the line longer, they experiment with the FORWARD command, substituting larger numbers until it draws a line the length that they want. Simple commands move the turtle, change the color of the line, and turn the turtle. Students experiment with commands, observe the movement of the turtle, and design more complex sets of commands that they assign names. The programming becomes more and more complex as students create problems and discover ways to solve them. For many students with special needs, a more structured application of Logo, such as *Logowriter* (LCSI), may be desirable (Budoff, Thormann, & Gras, 1984).

With discovery learning programs, you may need to ask carefully sequenced questions and give hints that lead students to discover what you want them to discover. Because discovery learning programs lack the structure, sequencing, and practice required by students with special needs, you should use discovery learning programs with discretion.

Problem Solving

Much is being written about the need for students to acquire problem-solving and higher-order thinking skills. You can use computers to teach such skills as well as to apply them. *The Factory* (Sunburst) is a graphic puzzle program that shows students a finished product. In this program, students must recreate the product by designing an assembly line to produce it. Students learn how to collect information, discover patterns, make generalizations, produce charts, apply strategies, and use inductive reasoning. They also learn the importance of sequencing, and they can use their creativity to develop and produce a product of their own.

Gnee or Not Gnee (Sunburst), *Perplexing Puzzles* (Hartley), *Bounce* (Sunburst), and the *Carmen SanDiego Series* (Broderbund) also provide excellent problem-solving and critical thinking opportunities for students. Problem-solving software generally gives practice in identifying the problem, finding alternative solutions, selecting appropriate strategies, and evaluating the results of decisions made. Problem-solving software provides excellent opportunities for cooperative learning when pairs or teams of students work together.

Like discovery learning software, however, problem-solving programs may not provide the repetition, feedback, and structure that students with special needs require. Because higher-order thinking skills are involved, it is important to be sure that students have mastered the basic skills

required. These may include reading; mathematics; note taking; inference making; map, chart, and table reading; and comparisons.

■ ■ Activity

Locate an educational software catalog. Find an instructional program that might help students learn each of the following: mathematics, reading, grammar, history, science, and geography. Read the description of each program. Determine the type or types of computer-assisted instruction used in each package — drill and practice, tutorial, game, simulation, discovery, or problem solving. Remember, a program may combine two or more different types. If possible, preview several programs and determine the type of CAI (computer-assisted instruction) used. ■ ■

Computer-Managed Instruction

While computer-assisted instruction (CAI) provides computer-based lessons for students, computer-managed instruction (CMI) uses computer systems to manage information about learner performance and learning resource options in order to prescribe and control individualized lessons (Heinich, Molenda, & Russell, 1989). Maddux (1986) describes this as computer-assisted educational planning (CAEP), insisting that only people can be managers. CMI programs are designed to administer diagnostic tests, score them, prescribe remediation, monitor progress, and keep records of student achievement. Many CAI programs have some elements of CMI built into them. For example, testing and reporting features may be available for a drill and practice program. Generally the term *CMI* is reserved for large systems of individualized instruction in one or more subject areas. These are generally offered through a network of computers connected to a central file server, which stores the instructional programs and keeps track of student progress.

Important Points

1. Most of the instructional software available provides for drill and practice of skills that have already been taught.
2. Tutorial programs present information and require learner response.
3. Games can provide enjoyable ways to learn and to practice what has been learned.
4. Simulation programs allow students to experience approximations of real-life events that may otherwise be too costly or too dangerous for use in the classroom.
5. Discovery software uses the inductive approach to learning, so it provides few directions.
6. Problem-solving software provides students with opportunities to apply higher-order thinking skills.
7. Computers can be used to help diagnose, teach, test, remediate, score, and report student progress.
8. The use of computer-managed instruction is relatively new and will be increasing as technology and demand develop.

Josten's Learning Systems, Wicat, Wasatch, and other large education companies are installing computer-based, computer-managed instructional systems in many schools. A CMI program can keep track of each student in the school, addressing him by name, diagnosing, teaching, remediating, and printing out progress reports for you, the student, and the parent. CMI programs will become more prevalent as technology advances and as teachers' demands for this type of management system increase.

Activity
Use an educational software catalog to locate two software programs that (according to the descriptions) manage student learning in some way (diagnose, prescribe, report progress, etc.).

The Computer as a Tool for Teachers

Many of the everyday tasks that teachers perform can be made easier and faster with com-

puters. Computer-enhanced instruction (CEI) refers to using computers to bring additional dimensions to traditional teaching methods, dimensions that may be otherwise impractical (Troutman & White, 1988). This includes using computers to create instructional materials, slide shows, videotapes, worksheets, tests, bulletin board materials, rewards, incentives, games, and displays. It also includes using computers to increase personal productivity through gradebook programs and word processing programs.

Teachers who use computers in these ways find that instruction is indeed enhanced. They are more productive, more organized because of the thought and planning required, and more efficient because of better record keeping. The learning environment is more appealing when materials are neatly and professionally generated. Finally, students generally have more positive impressions of teachers when they use the computer in the classroom.

Planning
Good planning is critical to successful instruction. Any good word processing program (*Appleworks*, Claris; *Microsoft Word*, Microsoft;

MacWrite, Claris; *Bank Street Writer III,* Scholastic; *Magic Slate,* Sunburst) allows you to enter, edit, format, and print text. A word processing program can be used to enter, store, revise, and print your lesson plans. Using a template in word processing is like using a blank form. The template provides the basic outline, and you fill in the details. Using a word processor for lesson planning allows you to organize the lesson and print out a neat, clean copy for your use during instruction. After the lesson, you can make changes in the lesson plan by editing, and you can use it again at a later date or with another group. Storing your lesson plans on disk also allows you to keep your plans together and to retrieve them quickly when needed.

One popular use of computers in classrooms with students who have special needs is producing individualized education programs (IEPs) (Krivacska, 1986; Maddux, 1986; Male, 1988). You can use a word processor to enter, store, retrieve, and modify the form of your school or district, or you can use an IEP generation program. At least twenty such programs are intended to automate paperwork from referral to IEP, including long-term and short-term educational objectives. Automated IEP software such as *IEPWorks* (K–12, Micromedia) (see Figure 12.1) also offers the ability to conduct evaluation across common goals and objectives because of the specificity, accuracy, and accessibility of information (Krivacska, 1986). The number of objectives included in such programs range from several hundred to several thousands. These objectives are selected by you or the team. Most IEP programs can be adapted to particular classrooms, objectives, goals, prescriptions, and diagnoses.

Computerized IEPs can save much time. One study found that such systems saved teachers from 1 to 28 minutes per student per meeting (Enell, 1984). Computerized IEPs are usually easier to read and more professional in appearance than those generated in other ways. Computerized IEPs offer the ability to enter data and edit without retyping. Large IEP-generating systems allow access to information about instructional materials that have been correlated to specific objectives, annual goals and objectives, and assessment data. They also allow the generation of a variety of reports (Male, 1988).

Some educators warn that computer-generated IEPs tend to reduce the individualization of the process because goals and objectives may be selected by a single person or may be selected too quickly (Krivacska, 1986; Maddux, 1986). It is important to remember that IEPs should be planned and written by *teams of people.* However, computers can facilitate the process, reduce the preparation time, and free personnel for direct-instruction activities.

Record Keeping and Classroom Management

Computers can be used for a variety of computational activities, such as managing gradebooks and scoring tests. They also, however, can handle text, graphics, and a variety of classroom management tasks. You can improve your record keeping and your accuracy in computing grades through the use of a computerized gradebook program such as *Gradebusters 1/2/3* (Gradebusters, Inc.) or *Grade Manager* (MECC). Many gradebook programs allow you to print out an individual student's scores as a report to the student or the parents. Many gradebook programs allow such options as dropping the highest and lowest grade, assigning weights to assignments, and customizing reports.

Many standardized tests offer computerized scoring, such as the *Woodcock Reading Mastery Test,* and *Wechsler Intelligence Scale for Children—Revised (WISC—R),* and the *Peabody Individual Achievement Test-R.* Using scoring programs, educators who work with students who have special needs can save themselves hours of time and be more accurate in their computation of scores. Programs are also available for testing readability and sampling language (Male, 1988).

Computers can also be used to record observations of students with special needs and to record notes about their progress. The notes can

```
HELP for IEPWorks
    (Options are also shown at the bottom of the screen)

    To START an IEP
        Press <SA> - <I> for a new IEP

            <I> to enter I.D. information
                Then
            Use the arrows to highlight the desired Goal, File, or Objective!!!
                <G> - to add an entire Goal/objectives group to the IEP
                <F> - to load a File of objectives
                    LIST:   O  - to select objectives from a slist on GOALSLIST
                        <T> - to type in search information to find Objective
            or
                FILE: <O> - to select Objectives from above File
                    <ESC> - to return to GOALSLIST from File
                <P> - TP ADD A COVER PAGE FROM THE PREVIOUS YEAR
                <E> - to end the IEP      <SA> - <H> - continue a stopped IEP
                <ESC> - to quit                   (use in GOALSLIST only)
```

LEARNING DISABILITIES

Directions and W questions	[O]bjectives fot this [F]ile below
Location and retrieval of information	[O]bjectives for this [F]ile below
Math skills improvement	(Select from File after [F]ile)
Money concept skills	[G]oal OR File after [F]ile
Reading Comprehension	[O]bjectives for this [F]ile below
Word Recognition Skills	[O]bjectives for this [F]ile below
Grammar skill Improvement	[F]ile

1.1.1	Adjectives	(Use [O] or [T] to add
1.1.2	Adverbs	these objectives to IEP.)
1.1.3	Conjunctions	
1.1.4	Contractions	
1.2.1	Sentences - terms/phrases	
1.2.2	Punctuation	

Written Communication Skills Improvement   [Upper elementary]
          (Multiple objective clusters for [G]oal)

MULTIPLE AREA GOALS: (no header)

Improve study skills.
Time usage habit improvement.
Test taking skills.

OTHER

HEADER   [An empty header for individualized goal]
Page 1   [An uncompleted IEP Page 1]

- -

[O]bjectives lists for [F]iles indicated above

Directions and W questions   [F]ile name

DW 1.1	Following directions - related parts
DW 1.2	Following directions - unrelated parts
DW 1.3	Giving directions
DW 1.4	Giving positive & negative directions
DW 1.5	Following 'before' & 'after' directions
DW 1.6	'Before' & 'after' in life situations
DW 2.1	Answer 'w' questions
DW 2.2	Ask 'w' questions
DW 2.3	Ask 'w' questions - present progressive verb
DW 2.4	Ask 'w' questions - past tense verb
DW 2.5	Ask 'w' questions - future tense verb

Figure 12.1
Part of file from *IEPWorks*

Note. From *IEPWorks* by K–12 Micromedia Publishing, Ramsey, NJ. Reprinted by permission.

be used to generate reports for the parents or for special referrals. *HyperCard for Educators* (Apple), a free program for educators, includes a special section designed for recording such comments (see Figure 12.2).

You may also use computers for storing and generating lists. Mailing lists, lists of students-with specific characteristics, inventories of classroom supplies, and records of frequently used instructional materials may be stored in the computer, edited, and printed in a variety of formats.

Preparation of Classroom Materials

Computers can enhance instruction by generating materials for your students and classroom. In most cases, using a computer to generate materials not only saves time but also makes your work appear more professional. Note that while this section concentrates on teachers' use of

computers, materials can also be generated by students.

Computers can generate worksheets. With computers, problems can be randomly generated so that each student receives a different worksheet. In fact, each student can receive a different worksheet every day of the year, a task that would be nearly impossible without a computer. Programs generate mazes, crossword puzzles, word find puzzles, and other drill and practice formats (*Multiple Choices*, Mindscape; *Crossword Magic*, Mindscape; *Designer Puzzles*, MECC; *Studymate*, CompuTeach). These programs print answer keys for each worksheet as well.

Computers can also be used to generate tests (*TestMaker*, Sage Productions; *TestWorks*, Microcomputers for Education). While a word processor can be used to construct and print a test, test generation programs allow you to enter ques-

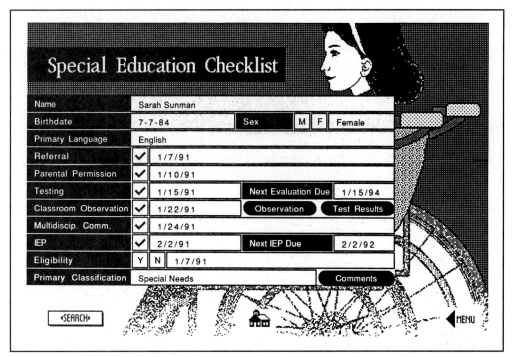

Figure 12.2
Computer-Generated Checklist
Note. From *HyperCard for Educators* by Apple, Cupertino, CA. Reprinted by permission.

tions and key them to specific objectives, customize tests for students, and randomly generate a variety of test forms. Some programs (*Study Guide*, MECC) even allow students to take the test on the computer, minimizing the use of pencil and paper and presenting the student with only one question at a time. Written tests with many questions on a single page may be obstacles to accurate measurement for students with special needs. Programs also score the tests and save and print the results.

Overhead transparencies can be generated by computer. Computer-generated transparencies are generally more legible, more organized, and more attention getting than are transparencies produced by mere drawing or writing on transparency film while in front of the class. Some programs are specifically designed for producing transparencies, but other programs can be adapted to this purpose. For example, *Power Point* (Microsoft) is designed to produce masters for overhead transparencies, or to print several small versions of the transparencies on a single page. You or your students can add notes to these mini-transparencies, and you can duplicate them and use them as handouts. Almost any graphics program that produces a "sign," such as *Print Shop* (Broderbund) or *PrintMaster Plus* (Unison World) can also be used. To make transparencies, print the sign on paper and then use a photocopy or thermal machine. Some transparency films can be used directly by dot matrix printers, and others can be used by laser printers.

Print Shop (Broderbund), *Create with Garfield* (DLM), *Clifford's Big Book Publisher* (Pelican), *SuperPrint* (Scholastic), and similar programs allow you to combine text and graphics to create cards, banners, signs, book pages, big books, posters, and bulletin board materials for your students and your classroom. These programs are limited only by your creativity in putting them to work for you.

Some programs produce certificates, awards, and badges (*Certificate Maker*, Springboard; *Award Maker Plus,* Baudville). Others print bookmarks that you can use as rewards. Several

programs print progress reports for parents, permission slips for field trips, tickets, name tags, visitor logs, and notepads for your use (*Library Magic, Holiday Magic,* and *School Magic,* McCarthy-McCormack; *Certificates and More,* Mindscape). These programs provide infinite variety to the materials available to you. Colored paper or colored ribbons in printers can enhance the use of these already popular programs.

Desktop publishing refers to the use of page-arrangement programs that allow users to combine text and graphics from other programs and that add columns, rules, boxes, shading, and more. Desktop publishing programs add professional polish to instructional materials and reports, especially when you print with a high-quality laser printer. Desktop publishing titles include *PageMaker* (Aldus) and *Publish It!* (Timeworks).

A relatively new use of computers is desktop presentation. This application uses the computer to produce a slide show or animation program on the computer screen. The presentations can be viewed by individual students or small groups, or they can be projected for large groups. Desktop presentations include text, graphics, color, transitions, and special effects. You can transfer them to videotape by use of a single cable from the computer to a videocassette recorder, and you can add sound to the videotape through the audio dubbing process. Two popular programs for desktop presentations are *Slide Shop* (Scholastic) and *VCR Companion* (Broderbund).

Authoring Programs and Languages

While an enormous number of software programs are available, you may have difficulty finding software tailored to the specific objectives or content for particular students. Sometimes, good instructional software can be identified, but often, it is unavailable in the school, funds are not available to purchase it, or you need it immediately. While few teachers have programming skills (or need to have them), most teachers say they need customized software. For example, you might combine a history unit on the Civil War with a geography lesson on the states and their capitals. It would be almost impossible to find one software program that provided practice on the facts and concepts in both areas.

Some commercially available programs have authoring capabilities built into them. Drill and practice programs and instructional games often allow teachers to input information about content being taught in a unit of instruction. If you cannot find software that fits the content and the needs of your students precisely, explore programs that allow some authoring, such as *The Game Show* (Advanced Ideas), *Garfield's Trivia Machine* (DLM), *All Star Drill* (Tom Snyder), and *Square Pairs* (Scholastic). These allow you to add your own content easily.

When you need tailor-made programs, you may use authoring programs and authoring languages. *SuperPILOT* (Apple), *E-Z PILOT* (Hartley), and *Authorware Professional* (Authorware) are common examples of these programs. Authoring programs allow you to input questions or information for use in the student lesson. You can specify correct answers and, in some cases, even provide some latitude for the answers. For example, you may specify that certain misspellings of an answer are acceptable. In some authoring programs, the program itself provides feedback for correct and incorrect responses. In more complex authoring programs, you may specify hints, remediation, and branching. Instructional software created with authoring programs can be as long or as short, as simple or as complex, as plain or as fancy as you wish within the constraints of the authoring program itself.

Hypermedia programs such as *Tutor-Tech* (TechWare), *HyperCard* (Apple), and *LinkWay* (IBM) are also authoring programs. Hypermedia programs allow you to create a stack of electronic pages or a deck of electronic cards that are linked together and cross-referenced by buttons, or hot spots on each card. Each card can also contain an unlimited amount of text, graphics, sound, animation, music, or other information.

With hypermedia programs, you do not have to access information in a linear fashion. While reading a paragraph, for example, you can choose (or not choose) to explore related images, sounds, or text. Hypermedia programs can access data and images on peripheral devices, such as CD-ROMs, videotapes, and videodiscs to supply information, graphics, and sound. You can easily add music, your own voice, and electronic photographs to your hypermedia program.

Many teachers are creating their own hypermedia programs, and hypermedia programs, called stacks or folders, are available through hypermedia clearinghouses or stack exchanges. You can submit your program to a clearinghouse and receive others developed by teachers in exchange. Hypermedia programs are also available commercially.

Authoring programs, including hypermedia programs, can be used by teachers with little or no knowledge of programming or computer languages, and they require considerably less time to produce a finished product than do programming languages such as BASIC, PASCAL, or C. However, a good knowledge of instructional design principles is very useful.

Telecommunications

Computers can be used to contact people and to locate resources outside the classroom and school. Peripheral devices called modems connect two or more computers together using existing telephone lines. Many schools are using telecommunications to help teachers—and students—communicate. The use of electronic mail, frequently called e-mail, and computerized bulletin boards has become increasingly popular with busy teachers, who retrieve messages others have left for them, leave messages for someone else, get information about meetings and deadlines in a timely manner, and provide or retrieve information of interest to others.

The use of modems can also provide access to large bibliographic databases such as *ERIC* (Educational Resources Information Center), *Excep-*

Important Points

1. Teachers who use computers as tools find that they are more productive, organized, and efficient.
2. Computers can improve management functions such as IEP generation and record keeping.
3. Computers can be used to generate instructional materials such as worksheets, transparencies, posters, and certificates.
4. Computers can be used to generate tests as well as to administer and score them.
5. Computers can be used to generate bulletin board materials, rewards, and progress reports.
6. Computers can be used for desktop publishing and desktop presentations.
7. Software can be created or customized through authoring programs and languages.

---

tional Child Education Resources, encyclopedias, and almanacs. Perhaps the catalog of your school library media center or your district's instructional materials catalog is available through telecommunications.

SpecialNet is a communications network designed to provide information, resources, and electronic mail services for those involved with programs for the disabled. While not all teachers have access to SpecialNet, district administrators may be able to print out information and pass it on to you.

■ ■ Activity
Using an educational software catalog, find some programs designed specifically to help you. Locate at least one title that will help you:

1. Write a lesson plan.
2. Generate an IEP.
3. Generate a puzzle, game, or worksheet.
4. Generate a test.
5. Generate a certificate, bookmark, or reward.
6. Store and calculate your grades.
7. Make materials for the bulletin board.
8. Generate an overhead transparency.
9. Author a program.
10. Contact an electronic bulletin board.

If possible, preview at least one of these programs. Do you think the program would be useful to you? How would it help to make you more productive? More professional? ■ ■

The Computer as a Tool for Students

Computers can be used as enabling tools for all students, and especially for students with special needs. Students who have difficulty with writing, spelling, mathematics, organization, and sequencing find that computers make these tasks easier. You can use applications such as word processing programs, database programs, spreadsheets, and graphics programs as instructional tools. Such applications may help students overcome problems that interfere with learning.

Word Processing
According to Male (1988), "Word Processing is a necessity, not an option" (p. 49) for most students with special needs. When students must write, a word processing program can make the task easier. Handwriting may be difficult for students with special needs, and word processing programs make it easier for such students to express themselves. Editing and rewriting are also

critical to improving writing skills, and they are parts of the writing process for all writers. These tasks are made easier by word processing programs. Students who use word processors are actively involved in their work. Maddux (1986) says, "The ease of revision encourages children to experiment with new ways of expressing themselves. Spelling and grammar checkers such as *Sensible Speller* and *Sensible Grammar* (Sensible Software) or *RightWriter* (RightSoft) enable them to produce polished final drafts without adult help and criticism" (p. 8).

Word processing programs for students range from very easy for elementary students (*Once Upon a Time,* CompuTeach; *Cotton Tales,* Mind-Play; *Magic Slate,* Sunburst) to extremely powerful for older students as well as for adults (*Appleworks,* Claris; *Microsoft Word,* Microsoft) and include public domain (free programs) such as *FrEdWriter* (CUE Softswap).

There are also several word processors that "speak"! *Talking Textwriter* (Scholastic), for example, reads what the student has typed in a human-like digital voice. It can read letter by letter, word by word, sentence by sentence, or complete paragraphs.

A number of programs allow students to combine graphics with their text (*Muppet Slate,* Sunburst; *StoryMaker,* Scholastic; *Cotton Tales,* MindPlay; *Clifford's Big Book Publisher,* Scholastic; *Transportation Transformation,* Pelican; *Appleworks GS,* Claris) to produce complete pages and books. *Once Upon a Time . . .,* (Compu-Teach) provides an additional dimension with digitized sound.

Students should learn to use all of the features and power of word processors. For example, students can use the search function of a word processor to improve their writing. If the adjective *nice* is frequently used, the student can search for the word *nice* and replace it with a different adjective each time it is found. This is an excellent function for using synonyms, building vocabulary, and bringing life to students' writing.

Word processors may be used in instruction with very little typing. Students can use the cut

and paste function of a word processor to rearrange sentences. Students can read paragraphs you have entered into the word processor, underlining topic sentences or answers to specific questions. They can erase any sentences that don't belong in a paragraph. These activities improve not only writing but also reading.

Spreadsheets
Spreadsheets help students with their mathematics in much the same way as word processing programs assist their writing. Spreadsheet programs organize numerical information into rows and columns and are useful in gathering, calculating, and analyzing numerical data. Spreadsheet programs such as *AppleWorks* (Claris), *MicroSoft Works* (MicroSoft), *MouseCalc* (International Solutions), and *MultiPlan* (Microsoft) perform all of the calculations. They allow students with special needs who have poor mathematics skills to learn from the manipulation and comparison of numbers. For students with special needs, "an electronic spreadsheet helps students organize their math problems and print them out so they can be read. Since computers do most of the calculations, students can only get the correct answer by understanding how to set up the problem, a key thinking and problem-solving skill" (Male, 1988, p. 68).

There are many opportunities to learn to work with spreadsheets in any classroom. Using a spreadsheet, a student can keep track of expenses for a field trip or project. The student can estimate expenses item by item, calculate the actual total, and compare the differences. Along the way, the student can use the spreadsheet to project "what if?" What if we have only $20 to spend? What if lunch costs twice as much as we expected? What if we get a 10% discount on our admission?

A unit on weather yields many statistics that can be stored, sorted, calculated, and analyzed. Hypotheses can be tested. Which month has the hottest average temperature in Florida? Is it the same month as it is in Alaska? Which day of the week had the most snow during an entire year? Are warm months more windy than cool months?

Students are often involved in fund-raising programs for the school or classroom. Spreadsheets are useful in keeping track of receipts and projecting results. Which student sold the most? How much would the school make if only a small, specified amount were sold? How much if everyone were able to sell twice as many as they did last week?

Many students who have poor math skills have excellent abilities to recall and interpret sports statistics. Spreadsheets can be used to record statistics from the daily paper, make comparisons, and predict outcomes. Who will have the best batting average? Which team had the most touchdowns at the end of the season? If Michael Jordan continues to score 2 points above average for the remainder of the season, how many points will he score by the end of the season? Students can also use spreadsheets to manage their allowances and prepare personal budgets or keep statistics during simulations.

Databases

Databases, too, are useful for students with special needs, who are frequently lacking in organizational skills. A database program such as *Friendly Filer* (Grolier), *Bank Street Filer* (Scholastic), *Stuff and Fetch* (MECC), *Appleworks* (Claris), or *MicroSoft Works* (MicroSoft) is a generic program that like a word processing program or a spreadsheet program can be used with a variety of subjects to create, sort, and retrieve files. Frequently, students can locate information, but they cannot break it down into useful parts or remember it. Database programs require students to break large amounts of material into small chunks and to compare data systematically. Information management is becoming an essential life skill, and databases are programs that allow people to manage information. Learning to use databases gives students more control over their learning and access to information.

Using databases, students can put things in alphabetical order or sequential order. Students can compare and contrast data, test hypotheses, or organize and share information. For example, students are frequently asked to gather information about the fifty states. Frequently, they forget to get the same information about each state, and they have trouble organizing their reports without all the information. You can create a database that lets students organize the important information into separate fields: state, nickname, population, state bird, state motto, date of admission into the union, and so on. When a field is blank, it is immediately visible on the report. The data can then be sorted, arranged, and compared in a variety of ways, and the printed reports are easily and neatly generated. Students can list the states alphabetically, in order by size of population, or by date of admission to the union. Each of these provides an important comparison for students. What is the largest state in population? How many states have the same state bird? Which states were admitted to the union in the same year?

A database on U.S. presidents may be sorted by the computer in a variety of ways: first to last, last to first, oldest to youngest, tallest to shortest, by political party, by size of family, or by length of time in office in days, months, or years. It allows a student to print out a list of presidents who were born after 1900 or before 1800, or to list the vice-presidents who later became presidents (see Figure 12.3).

Students can also create their own databases. Membership lists, address lists, and information about collections of cards, coins, or stamps can be organized into databases.

Graphics

Graphics programs allow students to illustrate their work, make the abstract concrete, and express themselves without words. Graphics programs can also encourage discovery learning and promote general problem-solving strategies. Students enjoy using programs such as *Print*

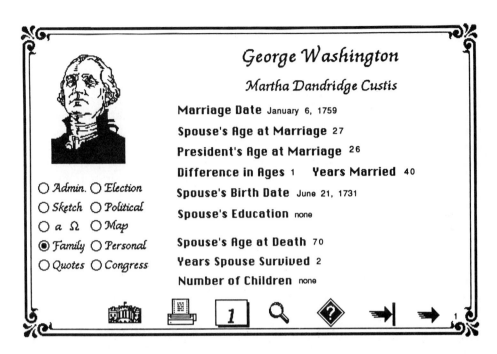

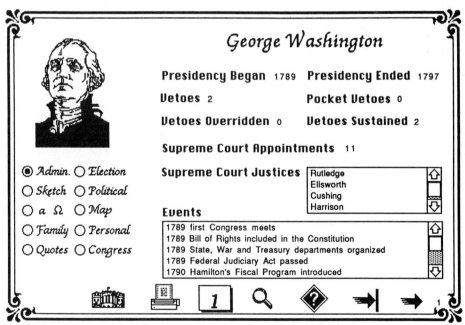

Figure 12.3

Screen Dump from *The Presidents* Hypercard Stack

Note. From *The Presidents* by ISTE, Eugene, OR. Reprinted by permission.

☐ Important Points

1. Students with special needs may use the computer as a tool to assist with writing, computation, data comparison, graphing, and visualization.
2. Students may improve their writing skills by using word processing programs.
3. Students who have difficulty with mathematics may manipulate numbers and per-

form complex calculations using spreadsheet programs.
4. Students may use database programs to organize, sort, compare, retrieve, and report information and to improve their organizational skills.
5. Students may use graphics programs to produce charts, illustrations, and graphs.

Shop (Broderbund), *Print Magic* (Epyx), and *SuperPrint* (Scholastic) to print illustrations in different sizes and styles. Graphing programs such as *MagnaCharta* (Third Wave Technologies), *Easy Graph* (Grolier), and *Cricket Graph* (Cricket Software) allow students to take data from their spreadsheets and databases to create pie graphs, bar graphs, pictographs, and even three-dimensional graphs for comparison. Creating graphs, charts, and tables can help students learn to interpret those they find in textbooks and reference materials.

■ ■ Activity

Name the type of application software that would be most appropriate for students to use in each of the following situations:

1. Writing a thank you note for a birthday gift.
2. Producing a pie chart showing the portion of time they spend on various activities during the day.
3. Comparing the size and population of each of the countries in South America.
4. Establishing a personal budget.
5. Producing a resume to accompany a job application.
6. Compiling an address list for friends and relatives that can be sorted by ZIP code, last name, or state.

7. Producing a "no smoking" sign for the school cafeteria.
8. Finding the title of a book about monkeys.
9. Calculating the average price of television sets advertised in the daily paper.
10. Creating a get well card for a hospitalized friend. ■ ■

Finding and Evaluating Software

Thousands of software programs are available, covering every grade level and almost every subject area. Many of these programs are, unfortunately, of poor quality. Many more programs simply do not meet an individual student's needs or yours. Finding and evaluating software are not easy tasks, but they are essential to the successful use of computers in instruction.

Finding Software

Education journals such as *Teacher, Social Studies Teacher,* and *Technology & Learning* frequently provide listings of software appropriate to a particular subject area or unit of instruction. The Technology and Media Division of the Council for Exceptional Children includes information about computer software in its newsletter. These and other sources frequently present ideas for integrating computers into the curriculum and for using application programs in the classroom.

Professional journals provide two other sources for finding software: software reviews and advertisements. Software reviews are reports of evaluations by experts and are intended to help educators with software selection. You should use reviews as initial screening devices. Reviews sort out good software from bad. However, even though a piece of software has received a good review, it may not be appropriate for a particular situation or student. You need to review software before your students use it. Software advertisements frequently make you aware of software that is available. However, believing all of the claims for the effectiveness or the content of software as described in advertisements may lead to disappointment. Remember, no producer is going to point out the poor qualities or features of the program in an advertisement.

Your school library media specialist is trained in the selection and evaluation of materials, including computer software. You should consult these professional colleagues to obtain not only catalogs and journals but also indexes, access to on-line databases, and printed directories, as well as reviews and evaluations.

Evaluating Software

Computer software must be evaluated from two different perspectives (Truett & Gillespie, 1984). First, you should evaluate the program on its own merits. How effective is it at producing specified outcomes? Secondly, you should evaluate it in light of specific learning objectives and students. What may be an outstanding program for some students may not be at all appropriate for your students. Evaluations by others may always be used as second opinions but should *never* replace preview, review, and evaluation by you. No one knows the students' learning styles and needs better than you.

Software producers have many different policies about previewing software. Many will loan a program to a school for a 30-day preview period. Others will not, providing preview copies to only an authorized preview center or the district office. Many districts and universities have established authorized preview centers so that you can come and spend uninterrupted time previewing and evaluating software. Most preview centers also keep catalogs, directories, and reviews on file.

When you evaluate text materials, you can easily scan them, flipping through the pages and spot-checking sections of particular interest. Slides and overhead transparencies can be held up to the light to determine quality and content. Evaluation of software, however, is not quite so easy and can be time consuming. You really must use a program several times in order to begin to judge its quality.

First, use the software as you believe an average student might, getting some questions right and some questions wrong in order to see how the computer handles correct and incorrect responses. This will also provide an overall picture of the program and its content. Next, work through the software as you believe a poor student might. What happens when wrong answers are given repeatedly? Is there remediation? How many tries does a student get? Are there prompts and hints? What happens if control keys are pushed? The escape key? How easy is it to crash the program? After using the software program several times, you may apply the criteria found in Table 12.1.

Software designed specifically for students with special needs is not easily found. Yet, you should evaluate software with the specific needs of your students in mind. Therefore, we present the following additional criteria to consider when selecting software for students with special needs (Budoff, Thormann, & Gras, 1984; Powers, 1986):

1. *Flexibility.* Can the software be used by many students? Can it be used by a single student many times? Does the software of-

Table 12.1
Software Evaluation Form

Title _____ Date _____

Publisher _____

Address _____

Subject area _____ Grade level _____ Price _____

Directions: Place a check mark under <u>Y</u> if yes and <u>N</u> if no, or <u>NA</u> if not applicable.

Appropriateness:	Y	N	NA
• Age	_____	_____	_____
• Interest	_____	_____	_____
• Level	_____	_____	_____
Hardware considerations:			
• Compatible with computer	_____	_____	_____
• Sufficient memory	_____	_____	_____
• Color monitor required	_____	_____	_____
• Peripherals required (printer, mouse, etc.)	_____	_____	_____
Documentation:			
• Manual provided	_____	_____	_____
• Additional materials included (worksheets)	_____	_____	_____
• Adaptations suggested	_____	_____	_____
Program:			
• Content interesting	_____	_____	_____
• Content accurate	_____	_____	_____
• Information up to date	_____	_____	_____
• Information free from stereotypes	_____	_____	_____
• Content well organized	_____	_____	_____
Interaction:			
• Active participation required of learner	_____	_____	_____
• Varying levels of difficulty available	_____	_____	_____
• Learner control of presentation rate	_____	_____	_____
• Learner control of exit function	_____	_____	_____
• Feedback provided	_____	_____	_____
• Concepts and skills reinforced	_____	_____	_____
Technical Considerations:			
• User friendly	_____	_____	_____
• Sound optional	_____	_____	_____
• High-quality graphics	_____	_____	_____
Record Keeping:			
• Reporting of scores option	_____	_____	_____
• Capable of printing out scores	_____	_____	_____

fer a large number and variety of presentations to facilitate the acquisition of new skills? Can you use an authoring mode to insert vocabulary and other content appropriate to the objectives? Can you select parts of the program for a specific student or group?

2. *Student or teacher control of the presentation of the materials.* Can students work at their own pace? Is the rate of movement through the program response-controlled rather than time-controlled? Can you control the response time in timed drill and practice programs? Can the response time be set at a very slow rate? Is the slowest rate slow enough for students with special needs? Can the rate be increased in small increments? Is the material presented and practiced in a variety of formats, contexts, and arrangements to facilitate transfer of skills? Are a variety of presentation techniques varied throughout the program to maintain the learners' attention?

3. *Number of problems or length of lesson.* Does the program maintain the students' attention? Can you control the number of problems presented so that students are challenged but attention is maintained? Are students able to stop a program and continue it later from the same point?

4. *Type of feedback.* Does feedback include an indication of correct responses, incorrect responses, and reasons why a response is incorrect? Does the feedback compare an incorrect response to the correct response in order to help the student judge his or her performance? Is feedback intermittent and varied? Does the program refrain from negative feedback? Does the program refrain from providing better rewards for incorrect answers than for correct answers?

5. *Program content.* Is the software built upon clearly specified learning objectives? Is the mode of instruction direct? Is the instruc-

tion focused on predetermined objectives? Does the program offer content flexibility and personalization? Are record-keeping mechanisms present and adequate? Is the reading level of information presented in the program carefully controlled and specified in the program manual? Do supplementary materials which provide extensive and varied practice accompany the software? Do the content and the presentation meet the needs of the students? Do they fit the curriculum?

6. *Instructional design.* Are directions simple and clear? Do they remain on the screen throughout the program? Are initial tasks required by the program designed in such a way as to assure a high probability of successful responses? Are prerequisite skills clearly specified in the program manual? Is the program design based on a task analysis? Is step size carefully controlled? Is progression from one skill level to the next carefully sequenced and controlled? Are multisensory experiences provided as often as possible? Is help available throughout the program?

7. *Screen design.* Is the screen display simple and uncluttered? Is color used to add interest and motivation? Does the use of color complement the content. Is the visual display free of unnecessary distractions? Are relevant stimuli clearly identified and emphasized through flashing, underlining, color, or contrast? Are graphics utilized to provide realistic and concrete illustrations of abstract concepts? For students with visual problems, is the lettering large and clear?

■ ■ Activity
Reexamine the preceding seven criteria to consider when selecting software for students with special needs and use these criteria to evaluate a piece of instructional software. ■ ■

Adapting and Using Software

As a teacher, you will regularly adapt materials in all formats to meet the special needs of your students. Computer software can be adapted as well. More and more software producers are providing flexibility in their programs, varying levels of difficulty, offering control of presentation and response rates, and providing adjustable feedback and reinforcement.

Software need not always be used as the documentation or teacher's manual prescribes. Most software, for example, relies to a great extent on the reading abilities of students. For poor readers, this can be a major barrier to learning from the program. You can adapt the program by having two students work together. The good reader reads the screens and the less able reader provides the decisions and input.

You may also find it necessary to introduce new vocabulary words before students use the program, much as you would introduce new words before beginning a new reading assignment in any content area. It may be necessary to record directions on a tape recorder for use with students who have poor reading skills.

Students with visual problems may benefit from the use of a large television monitor or a projection device. Students may also benefit from the use of bright stickers to code keys that are frequently used with a program. You might use *Print Shop* (Broderbund) to produce some special help cards for use near the computer. These can list frequently used commands or summarize directions in large, clear print with illustrations.

Printers and screen dump programs that allow you to print the image on the screen are critical for students with special needs. You can use the printout to produce flash cards, to review a program when the computer cannot be used, to prepare transparencies and task cards for a computer program, to display and file exemplary work, and to provide concrete products of the learning experience.

Many programs give you and your students the option of using a speech synthesizer. A speech synthesizer allows the computer to pronounce words on the screen. Some programs use the speech synthesizer to read directions and to give feedback. Others use it to pronounce what the student has entered.

Students usually respond to instructional software programs by typing on the computer keyboard. However, other popular input devices are the joystick and the mouse. A joystick is a small box with a stick and a handle, similar to a gearshift on a car. By moving the joystick, the student changes the location of the cursor on the screen. To select something on the screen, you press a button on the joystick box. The mouse has also become a very popular input device. Attached to the computer by a special cable, the mouse is a hand held device that you glide across the surface of the table or desk to move the cursor on the screen. Selections are made by pushing a button on the mouse. Although using a mouse or a joystick requires some eye–hand coordination, it may be easier than manipulating the many keys on the keyboard, and practice usually improves ability quickly.

A number of computers and programs also offer touch-sensitive screens and response pads that use a finger, stylus, or light pen for input. To make a selection, the student simply points at the computer screen with a finger or a special pen-like device. This often allows students who have fine-motor-skill problems, inaccurate keyboard skills, or problems with spelling to complete programs without frustration.

A graphics pad is also an input device on which students can draw or write. The image is displayed on the monitor. A graphics pad can be used for tracing, illustrating, producing shapes and colors, and other psychomotor skills.

Key guards reduce the possibility of hitting the wrong keys as students attempt to enter information. Key guards are most useful when only a few keys are needed and reduce the chance of making an error.

☐ Important Points

1. Software can be located through education journals, reviews, advertisements, and catalogs.
2. Software reviews provide expert evaluations of software packages and can be used to screen good software.
3. Advertisements should not be used to select software for purchase.
4. Teachers should always preview and review software themselves if possible.
5. Specific criteria to look for when evaluating any software include appropriateness, hardware considerations, documentation, program, user interaction, technical considerations, and record-keeping ability.
6. Good instructional strategies for students with special needs should be reflected in software selected for use with these students.
7. Software must be evaluated in light of learners' needs and ability of the software to meet those needs.
8. Very little software is written for students with special needs; however, much software can be easily adapted for such students.
9. As well as meeting other selection criteria, software that is flexible and adaptable is most useful to teachers of students with special needs.
10. Speech synthesizers allow students to hear parts of a computer program.
11. Consideration should be given to the use of alternative input devices, such as the mouse, joystick, and graphics pad for use with students who have special needs.

Voice entry systems allow students to enter information into the computer simply by speaking into a microphone attached to the computer. Voice entry systems are still in the early stages of development and are extremely expensive and inaccurate.

■ ■ Activity

List five characteristics of students with special needs. Then, describe how you might use or adapt software to meet those needs. ■ ■

Using Computers in the Classroom

Computer-assisted instruction is most effective when it is a carefully planned and integrated part of instruction. You have already learned to integrate worksheets, flash cards, and learning centers into the instructional program (see Chapter Five). This may be because such materials are familiar and readily available. When you were in school, you probably used these materials to learn, but you may not have been able to use computers. Integrating computers into instruction takes a bit more planning and, perhaps, a lot more skill.

You must be aware of when and how computers can enhance instruction. You must also be familiar with the students, the learning objectives, and the computer software. You must know which kinds of instructional activities can be enhanced by computer software and what kind of software can accomplish each activity. The question is not, How can I make use of the computer for this lesson? but rather, What is the best way to assist the learner in accomplishing an objective? When the answer is "through a software program," successful integration may take place.

A general model of instructional design can help you integrate computers into the instructional process. One such model is the ASSURE instructional design model. When the first letters of the steps are combined, the word *assure* is spelled, making the model easy to remember (Heinich, Molenda, & Russell, 1989):

1. *Analyze the students.* Determine if the students have the entry-level skills and competencies required. Assess their knowledge, attitudes, and skills. Determine their learning needs.
2. *State the objectives.* What should the students be able to do after the instruction has taken place? What should the students be able to do after using the software program?
3. *Select the media and materials.* Identify formats and materials appropriate to meet the objectives and the needs of the students. (This may or may not include computers and software, but for this discussion, we assume that it does.)
4. *Utilize the materials.* Allow for individual use of the computer or adapt the instruction to group presentation through use of a data display unit for the overhead projector or a splitter cable that allows display of the computer output on a large television monitor.
5. *Require student performance.* Allow interaction between the students and the computer to take place. Monitor the students' performance.
6. *Evaluate and revise.* Examine the reports generated by the scoring and record keeping of the software. Did the students master the skill or concept? Is additional review necessary? Would a repetition of the software program produce additional practice and knowledge? How did the students feel about the instruction? Did the students feel successful? Was the program too hard or too easy?

Table 12.2
Software Integration Checklist

√ Identify needs for computer applications in the curriculum.
√ Search for software to meet the needs.
√ Review and evaluate software using established criteria.
√ Plan for integration. Be sure to know:
  • At which points in the lessons computer activities will fit.
  • What skills will need to be taught with other resources both before and after the software is used.
  • What computer skills and directions students will need prior to using the computer.
√ Follow up on computer use.

Note. From *Making the Most of Microcomputers in the Classroom* by M. D. Roblyer, 1989, Tallahassee, FL: Florida Department of Education. Reprinted by permission.

Roblyer (1989) prefers a five-step integration checklist (see Table 12.2).

Integrating computers into existing classroom instruction can promote increased learning and more positive attitudes toward learning. It is no more appropriate to use a computer program totally unrelated to the curriculum than it is to provide worksheets merely to keep students busy.

Summary

Computers are part of the information age, the age in which we live. They should be integral to the experiences provided for students with special needs. Computers can provide tools for teacher productivity in planning, record keeping, classroom management, and the preparation of materials. They can be used for lesson plans and IEPs. Electronic gradebooks, test generation programs, test scoring, and instructional materials generation programs are available. Computers can be used to produce bulletin boards, rewards, and incentives for students. You

☐ Important Points

1. Instructional software is most effective when it is an integrated part of the instructional process.
2. Computers should be used only when the format and software are appropriate for the learners and the learning objectives.
3. While planning a lesson, it is important to plan the use of a computer program.
4. The ASSURE model is a systematically designed approach to including computer software.
5. The image from a computer screen may be enlarged with a data unit device for an overhead projector or a large television monitor.
6. Teachers should always follow up on the use of computers to determine whether or not the objectives were met and additional instruction is required.

---

can create customized software packages with authoring programs and languages. You can communicate with other people and places through telecommunications hardware and software.

Students can use application programs to enhance their learning. Word processing programs can make writing and editing easier. Spreadsheets can be used to perform calculations and make projections. Databases can assist in accessing and managing large amounts of information, in comparing and manipulating data, and in preparing reports. Graphics programs can show relationships and provide illustrations for papers and presentations.

Thousands of software programs are available commercially; however, not every one is appropriate for students with special needs. Good software must fit the learning needs of the students, must be appropriate to the content and

objective being taught, and must demonstrate sound instructional strategies. Reviews provide some information about software, but you must preview and evaluate software packages yourself to be sure they fit into the curriculum and your instructional plan. There are general criteria for evaluating software, and there are special considerations when evaluating programs that will be used with learners who have special needs.

While not much software is designed specifically for students with special needs, good software is available. Good software is flexible and adaptable. You can adapt software for use with your students in many ways. Students may choose from several input devices, such as the keyboard, mouse, joystick, graphics table, and touch screen. The ASSURE model of instructional design provides a framework for planning and integrating computers into the classroom.

13

Transition Skills: Career Education and Related Social Skills

by Warren J. White and Linda P. Thurston

Key Topics

In a report on the postschool adjustment of special education students, Edgar (1987) documented that only 18% of the students who had graduated from special education programs earned minimum wage or better. When individuals with learning disabilities and behavior disorders were removed from the sample, only 5% earned minimum wage or better. Minimum wage, based on a 40-hour workweek, currently equates to a monthly gross salary of $737, clearly inadequate for independent living.

Nationally, between 40% and 50% of students in special education drop out of school before they graduate (Edgar, 1987; Zigmond & Thorton, 1985). The dropout rate is particularly high for students with mild disabilities who are Hispanic (Ascher, 1987). Many Mexican-Americans do not go beyond sixth grade, while the average Puerto Rican usually completes 8.7 years of school (Briganti, 1989). It is probable that the standard of living of these individuals is less than that of individuals who graduate.

In a national study of more than 600 adults with learning disabilities, Chesler (1982) stated that the five most frequently mentioned areas in which the respondents reported that they needed help were developing social relationships and social skills, career counseling, developing self-esteem and confidence, overcoming dependence, and vocational training. The academic areas of reading and writing, typically the cause of their problems in school environments, barely made the top ten.

Warren J. White and Linda P. Thurston are associate professors of special education at Kansas State University.

White, Alley, Deshler, Schumaker, Warner, and Clark (1982) conducted a study comparing adults with and without learning disabilities. While approximately the same percent of learning disabled and nonlearning disabled adults were employed and the distributions of income for these groups were approximately the same (at least in the first few years after high school), the adults with learning disabilities were much less satisfied with their employment situation and their social lives. The respondents with learning disabilities were significantly less involved in community, civic, religious, and leisure activities than their non-learning disabled counterparts and had significantly lower aspirations for further education or training.

Like those with learning disabilities, individuals with mild mental retardation have also been reported to have difficulty adjusting to community and vocational settings upon leaving school. Fewer than 20% are employed full-time (Edgar, 1987), earnings are minimal (Hasazi, Gordon, & Roe, 1985), marriages tend to be unstable (Halpern, Close, & Nelson, 1986), and many require one or more nondisabled advocates to provide support in their lives (Mithaug, Horiuchi, & Fanning, 1985). What little is known about the adjustment of adults with behavior disorders appears to parallel that of adults with learning disabilities, at least in the area of occupation outcomes (Edgar, 1987).

The unsuccessful postschool adjustment of special education students lends credence to the belief that career education skills and competencies should play a role in the curriculum for all special education students, even for those who pursue postsecondary education or training. The purpose of this chapter is to discuss the importance of career education and related social skills in the preparation of students with special needs for all of life's roles.

Career Education

While a variety of definitions of career education are proposed, one of the more widely accepted ones in special education is:

> Career education is the process of systematically coordinating all school, family, and community components together to facilitate each individual's potential for economic, social, and personal fulfillment and participation in productive work activities that benefit the individual or others. (Kokaska & Brolin, 1985, p. 43)

This definition gives the work aspect (e.g., productive work activities), personal–social skills (e.g., social and personal fulfillment), and daily living skills (e.g., economic skills) equal emphasis. Many earlier definitions emphasized only the work aspect. In addition, this definition assumes that not only the school must be involved in the career education activities of an individual but also the family and community. Kokaska and Brolin (1985) identify twenty-two competencies within these three broad curriculum areas, which they call (a) daily living skills, (b) personal–social skills, and (c) occupational guidance and preparation (see Table 13.1)

Also included in the concept of career education is the idea that career education progresses through four basic stages (Kokaska & Brolin, 1985). Career awareness, the first stage, begins about kindergarten. During this stage, children develop an understanding of the roles that people assume in the world and fantasize about their place in the world. Career exploration, the second stage, begins about grade 6. During this stage, students begin to let go of their fantasies

Table 13.1
Life-Centered Career Education Curriculum Competencies

Daily Living Skills

1. Managing Family Finances
2. Selecting, Managing, and Maintaining a Home
3. Caring for Personal Needs
4. Raising Children—Family Living
5. Buying and Preparing Food
6. Buying and Caring for Clothes
7. Engaging in Civic Activities
8. Utilizing Recreation and Leisure Time
9. Getting Around the Community

Personal–Social Skills

10. Achieving Self-Awareness
11. Acquiring Self-Confidence
12. Developing Socially Responsible Behavior
13. Maintaining Adequate Interpersonal Skills
14. Achieving Independence
15. Achieving Problem-Solving Skills
16. Communicating Adequately with Others

Occupational Skills

17. Knowing and Exploring Occupational Possibilities
18. Selecting and Planning Occupational Choices
19. Exhibiting Appropriate Work Habits and Behavior
20. Seeking, Securing, and Maintaining Employment
21. Exhibiting Sufficient Physical–Manual Skills
22. Obtaining Specific Occupational Skills

Note. From *Career Education for Handicapped Individuals,* Second Edition, (pp. 71, 105, 147) by C. J. Kokaska and D. E. Brolin, 1985, New York: Macmillan.

and take a more realistic look at their abilities and interests. Career preparation, the third stage, begins at grade 8 or 9. The fourth stage, career placement, follow-up, and continuing education, begins about grade 10. In following these stages, students typically develop job and daily living skills, obtain employment, and move into the community.

Career education must be distinguished from vocational education, which is primarily concerned with skill training in one or more of the following areas: vocational agriculture and agribusiness, marketing and distribution occupations, health occupations, technical occupations, and trade and industrial occupations. While there are many excellent vocational education programs around the country, the majority of students with special needs have not been welcomed into vocational programs in most schools (Clark & Kolstoe, 1990), and even in settings where students are provided services from vocational education, special education programs may have to assume the responsibility for providing training in personal–social and daily living areas.

The Content of Career Education

Will (1984) calls transition a bridge between the security of the school environment and the complex experiences of the world of work and life in the communities. Effective career transition programming does not just happen with the inclusion of a few work-type skills, by having a few parents come to class to talk about their jobs, or by including a unit on interviewing and completing job applications. Teachers must include career skills and competencies in all curriculum areas and must explicitly show students how these skills and competencies relate to the world beyond the school walls. While this may sound overwhelming, it is not. In fact, generally, it motivates students.

The following strategies for the successful transition of students with special needs from school to the community were identified by the staff from the Secondary Transition Intervention Effectiveness Institute, University of Illinois at Urbana-Champaign, when they analyzed over two hundred program applications for federal funding to improve transition programming (Rusch & DeStefano, 1989).

1. *Begin planning for the transition from a school environment to the community well in advance of graduation.* Planning should begin as soon as a student has been placed in a special education setting, but no later than seventh grade. Early intervention can help ensure a long-term, coordinated plan for each student.

2. *Identify a team of school personnel, adult service providers, parents, and community representatives to help plan and develop transition services.* Parents may play a critical role by being vocal advocates of planning for the transition to community life and by informing the team of the anticipated needs of students who are exiting school. Community service agencies (e.g., vocational rehabilitation agencies, the Job Training Partnership Act, vocational and technical centers) can help identify community resources and provide employment training, placement, and support. Transition services should be tailored to individual needs and should be sensitive to cultural and linguistic differences.

3. *Develop an individualized transition plan (ITP).* Similar to an IEP, an ITP is a systematic, written, multiagency plan that outlines the critical areas of need in transitions from school to community. It is important to include annual goals and short-term objectives in such areas as employment, social skills, residential placement, income support, and transportation, as well as the person or agency responsible for each goal or objective (see Figure 13.1).

4. *Integrate students into as many environments as possible.* It is important to expose students to work and community environments and to individuals of different cultural backgrounds with whom they may eventually live and work. This is especially true early in the transition process. By definition, students with special needs do not easily learn nor readily generalize. High school is much too late to begin career education. Too often, elementary teachers, and sometimes even middle school teachers, do not understand the need to begin career education early in the school years,

Individualized Transition Plan

Student's Name _____ Age _____ Date _____

School _____ Date of Graduation _____

| Planning Areas | Status as of _____ | Responsibilities | | | | | | Completed |
| | | Student/Parent | | School | | Adult/Community Service Providers | | |
		Action	Time Line	Action	Time Line	Action	Time Line	
1. Life skills								
2. Living arrangements								
3. Medical needs								
4. Financial/ income								
5. Vocational training/ placement								
6. Leisure options								
7. Transportation								
8. Advocate/ guardianship								
9. Social/ behavior								

The undersigned agree to carry out the recommendations of the ITP for _____ .

Signature/Title/Date	Signature/Title/Date
_____	_____
_____	_____
_____	_____
_____	_____
_____	_____

Figure 13.1
An ITP

so that students have the time they need to learn and generalize to all of the environments they will encounter.

5. *Teach community-relevant living skills.* Research has shown that employment success and community adjustment are only moderately correlated (Benz & Halpern, 1987). A student may be successful in the workplace but unable to live independently in the community. Therefore, you need to include specific instruction in community-relevant living, such as transportation, healthy meals, and banking. Students should also become familiar with local social service agencies. Because communities are very different in the nature of the skills necessary and customs practiced, school personnel must assess local housing markets, transportation demands, and cultural influences to determine the skills needed in that location.

6. *Teach necessary living skills in natural settings.* Because many students in special education classes have difficulty generalizing from the classroom setting to other environments, you should teach skills in real employment, community, and residential settings. For example, students should learn to shop in actual supermarkets and department stores instead of responding only to worksheets about shopping.

7. *Include employers, employees, and families in searching for real jobs with advancement opportunities for students.* While the majority of special education graduates are employed, fewer than 20% earn enough to live independently (Edgar, 1987). One of the reasons is career stereotyping on the part of parents, teachers, and employers. Too often, students with special needs do not receive appropriate career or vocation information and experience because of perceptions that they can be successful only in low-level, menial jobs, which require little more than motor skills and strength (Cummings & Maddux, 1987). Despite empirical evidence demonstrating that the voca-

tional interests and personalities of individuals with special needs are just as diverse as those without special needs (Cummings & Maddux, 1987), individuals with disabilities are still overwhelmingly placed in low-paying jobs such as food service, auto mechanics, and domestic occupations (Cummings & Maddux, 1987). It is important to work with parents, local civic organizations, private industry councils, and state vocational rehabilitation agencies to identify employment opportunities that have the *potential* for allowing employees to live independently.

8. *Evaluate programs and outcomes in order to improve the transition process.* It is important that you monitor the progress of former students (both graduates and nongraduates) in order to evaluate and improve career education programs. Changing local economic conditions and community values are just two factors that necessitate the need for follow-up information. Information about types of jobs held, wages earned, benefits, hours worked, performance ratings, extent of community integration, living arrangements, and social–interpersonal status are some indicators of program effectiveness. One high school teacher kept yearly records on each of his students who had left his program, showing where they were working and what they were earning. You can do this by keeping in close contact with your former students and their employers.

In addition to the preceding eight strategies for successful transition of students with special needs from school to the community, we have found that successful programs are based upon assessments of the needs in the local community and school curricula. For example, several school districts have surveyed different types of businesses, and in larger population centers sometimes even different sizes of businesses, to determine the skills necessary for entry-level employment in that specific location. This is necessary because the current economic climate, types of businesses, and geographic constraints affect the skills needed in a particular area.

White (1983) found that when employers were asked about the importance of occupational skills in published career education curricula, the skills rated as important differed depending on the type, size, and location of the business. The format found in Table 13.2 has proven useful in local employer surveys.

Community surveys are not difficult to conduct, as you can usually complete one in 5 to 8 minutes over the telephone, and employers are typically enthusiastic about being asked what they think is important in their businesses. It gives them the feeling that someone out there cares what they think. Thus, you can obtain useful information for program development and promote good public relations for the program. After conducting the interviews, you may either average the responses from the different

Table 13.2
Local Employer Survey Example

Survey

Directions: Please rate each skill based on the types of entry-level jobs you supervise. If you supervise more than one type of job, use the one that represents the greatest number of workers you supervise. Please use a 1 to 5 rating scale, with 1 meaning this skill is very important to an entry-level person in your workplace and a 5 meaning this skill is not important to an entry-level person in your workplace.

Rating	**Skill**
_____	1. Count money in coin and bill denominations.
_____	2. Recognize potential methods for dealing with work-related problems.
_____	3. Know appropriate action to take in an emergency situation.
_____	4. Identify potential safety hazards on jobs.
_____	5. Recognize general job categories.
_____	6. Recognize education/training requirements of various common jobs.
_____	7. Know resources for obtaining occupational information.
_____	8. Recognize self as worker.
_____	9. Know meaning of leisure time.
_____	10. Recognize appropriate behavior in public/work settings.
_____	11. Know proper listening techniques.
_____	12. Recognize importance of goal setting.
_____	13. Recognize skills necessary for interpersonal relationships in work settings.
_____	14. Identify work roles that fit own characteristics.
_____	15. Demonstrate proper use of deodorant, hair care products.
_____	16. Identify steps in decision making.
_____	17. Know importance of quality standards on the job.
_____	18. Identify personal aptitudes.
_____	19. Recognize value of him/herself as a person.
_____	20. Demonstrate ability to use local transportation.
_____	21. Identify sources of assistance in calculating/filing common taxes.
_____	22. Identify basic steps in job finding.
_____	23. Identify their interests in education/occupations/leisure.
_____	24. Follow written/spoken directions.
_____	25. Know personal abilities/aptitudes/interests with regard to job choice.

Note. Adapted from "The Validity of Occupational Skills in Career Education: Fact or Fantasy?" by W. J. White, 1983, *Career Development for Exceptional Children, 6*, pp. 51–60. Adapted with permission.

Important Points

1. Research shows that students with special needs have difficulty adjusting to community and vocational settings upon leaving school.
2. Career education is the process of systematically coordinating all school, family, and community components to facilitate each individual's potential for economic, social, and personal fullfillment and participation in productive work activities that benefit the individual or others.
3. Career education should give the work aspect, personal–social skills, and daily living skills equal emphasis.
4. Career education progresses through the four stages: (a) awareness, (b) exploration,

(c) preparation, and (d) placement, follow-up, and continuing education.
5. Career education programs should contain the following eight components: (a) transition planning that begins early; (b) a team approach, including school personnel, parents, adult service providers, and community representatives; (c) ITPs for all students; (d) integration of students into many environments; (e) education in community-relevant living skills; (f) the teaching of skills in natural settings; (g) involvement of employers, employees, and families in finding opportunities for students; and (h) program evaluation.

types of businesses or compile the information so it can be compared with information from other sources (e.g., curriculum needs assessments).

You may compare the information from the community surveys with the school curriculum to determine which skills are already being adequately covered and which ones need to be added. This is a relatively simple but extremely important step in program development. The same skills found on the local employer survey (see Table 13.2) are measured, but they are rated differently. The result of this process will be lists of skills, ranging from those that are high priority but already in the curriculum, to low priority and in the curriculum, to high priority and not in the curriculum, and low priority and not in the curriculum. These lists will give you an overview of the strengths and weaknesses of the program and will provide a place to begin program development. You may use the same type of process with daily living skills or community living skills, utilizing either students or parents as sources of information.

■ ■ Activity
Using the survey items in Table 13.2 or from a competency list, survey three employers, including retail, manufacturing, and service businesses. After you collect and compile the information, summarize the differences and similarities of the needs of the businesses. (Answers for these and other activities are found in the Instructor's Manual.) ■ ■

Teaching Career Education Skills
A remark commonly made by special education teachers (particularly elementary teachers) is "OK, I understand the need for a community-referenced curriculum and I realize that most students with special needs don't do well after they leave school. However, I already have more to teach from the basic skill areas than I will ever be able to teach, and they need these basic skills. Remember, these kids don't learn as fast as some of the other kids. There is no way to juggle all of this and include career education skills." This comment is based on the mistaken notion that

career skills must be taught as a separate unit or class, thereby adding to an already crowded curriculum. While career skills may be taught separately, it is not always necessary or even desirable to do so. You may teach career skills by infusing them into the existing curriculum or by teaching them separately. For most teachers, the best approach is probably to combine infusion with separate programming to provide a balance. This way, both critical academic skills and critical career concepts and skills are taught (Clark, 1980).

The Infusion Approach

The definition given by Clark (1980) for the infusion approach is:

> Infusion is an approach that incorporates or integrates career education concepts and skills into other subject matter content, to make that content more motivating, more relevant, more clear, or more concrete. In this approach, the primary learning objectives are focused on the subject matter content. For example, when an instructional objective in a science class focuses on the concept of toxicity, instructional activities can include learning about poisons in the home. This presents a science concept in the context of a daily living skill. (p. 68)

The infusion approach tends to make abstract content more concrete and relevant and therefore easier to learn. It is also easier to expose students to a wide range of career concepts and skills within the context of what schools are already doing (Clark, 1980). Conversely, since the focus of the instruction is not the career concepts but the concepts and skills associated with other subject matter, career concepts and skills are frequently left to incidental learning, are more difficult to evaluate, and many times, do not lend themselves to the number of instructional repetitions necessary for students with special needs.

With a little imagination, career education may be infused into nearly any subject area. For example, if the students in an English class are working on communicating with others in writing, they may write directions for another student to walk to some other location in the school building and then see if the directions can be followed. Students may work together to make the directions as accurate as possible. Later, students may write letters of complaint or write letters of inquiry about jobs. In mathematics, when working on decimals, students may also learn about and use different tax rates (e.g., state income tax, city tax, sales tax). In this way, the students get the practice that they need using decimals while learning about the tax system. In social studies, students may discuss consumer rights and due process.

The Separate Programming Approach

In the separate approach, career education is taught as another subject area. According to Clark (1980):

> Separate programming is an approach that separates career education concepts and skills from other subject matter to the extent that the career education concepts and skills are, and remain, the primary objectives for learning. While basic skill subjects or other subject matter content may be used as activities or means to reach the career education concept or skill objectives, they remain secondary to the primary objectives directed toward student attainment of career education concepts and skills. (p. 68)

The separate programming approach is demonstrated by the teacher who elects to teach consumer rights as a separate unit, apart from any connection to social studies, or has a separate 9-week class on comparative shopping without a specific connection to math instruction. Separate programming assures concentrated attention on career concepts and skills and makes it easier for

☐ Important Points

1. In the infusion approach, career education is integrated into other subject matter content.
2. The infusion approach tends to make career concepts and skills more concrete and relevant, but it frequently leaves them to incidental learning and makes them difficult to evaluate.
3. In the separate programming approach, career education content is taught as a separate unit or course.
4. The separate programming approach makes it easier for teachers to control the scope and sequence of desired skills, but it adds to an already crowded curriculum.
5. Career education must be incorporated into IEPs for it to be a viable option for students.

---

teachers to control the scope and sequence of the desired skills. However, teachers today have many instructional responsibilities, and separate programming of career education adds to an already crowded curriculum.

■ ■ Activity

Outline how you might use both the infusion approach and separate programming approach to teach the daily living skill of demonstrating knowledge of traffic rules. Be sure to provide suggestions for both elementary and secondary students with special needs. ■ ■

Individualized Education Programs

The case for including career skills into all special education curricula is indisputable. Regardless of which approach you use, you must cover the concepts and skills. To return to an earlier question of why all special education teachers do not incorporate career education into their programs, we examine the IEP process. In writing an IEP, teachers tend to first concern themselves with curriculum areas, such as reading, math, and writing. These basic skill areas have a long history of experimentation with methodology and individualization and have strong advocates within the schools. Career education does not

have the same history of experimentation and has not developed the same type of advocacy base. Therefore, it is critical that at each IEP conference, you determine the appropriateness of the programming decisions being made. If you ask about the career education needs of the students, then other IEP conference participants will begin to keep the career education needs of each child or youth in mind (Meyen & White, 1980).

■ ■ Activity

Examine an IEP that has been developed for a student in the elementary grades and one for a student at the secondary level. List the goals and objectives that apply to career education. If you cannot find any, rework the IEP to include career competencies. Remember, career education provides instruction in critical life skills. ■ ■

Social Skills

In addition to academic, daily living, and occupational skills, social skills are an important part of total life skills. In fact, social skills (personal–social) are part of career education. Just as career skills are important in preparing students to survive successfully in the real world of their mainstream classrooms, homes, communities, and employment settings, so are social skills. A student's competence in social skills makes a difference in his or her success first as a student and later as an adult.

Teachers should be concerned about students' social skills for several reasons. Adolescents with special needs exhibit significant deficits in social skills when compared with their nondisabled peers. Empirical evidence suggests that the effectiveness with which adolescents and young adults who have special needs interact on a social basis is directly related to their success and adjustment (Hazel, Schumaker, Sherman, & Sheldon-Wildgen, 1983). Rose (1983) reports that socially isolated students have a greater incidence of school maladjustment and dropping out of school.

Chesler (1982) indicates that among the most problematic areas for adults with learning disabilities are social relationships and social skills. Goldstein (1972) found that employers tend to view vocational adjustment problems as more related to socialization deficits than to the actual job or task performance. We frequently hear comments from employers like, "He could do the work, he just couldn't get along with the other employees," or "Her job skills were fine, but her attitude was so negative." Evidently, social skills play a major part in a student's success in life, both personally and occupationally.

Defining Social Skills

In general, social skills are socially acceptable, learned behaviors that enable a person to interact with others in ways that elicit positive responses and avoid negative responses (Cartledge & Milburn, 1986). In connection with social skills, the social validity of behaviors (Wolf, 1978) is an important consideration in educational programs. Therefore, you should teach only behaviors that are likely to be reinforced in the real world, because only these behaviors will be functional for students. In the real world, asking

questions if you don't understand the job and talking with the boss when there is a problem are social skills that help produce job success.

As teachers, you deal with a wide variety of specific social skills. These skills may be grouped into the following categories:

1. *Working (employment or school) skills:* following the instructions of teachers or bosses, doing your best work, deciding what to do next.
2. *Basic interaction skills:* making eye contact, listening, asking questions.
3. *Getting-along skills:* using polite words, helping others.
4. *Making and keeping friends skills:* starting a conversation, giving a compliment, smiling.
5. *Coping skills:* staying out of fights, negotiating, resisting peer pressure.

■ ■ Activity

Think of three students you know, have observed, or have read about, one in elementary school, one in middle school, and one in high school. Give each a name and remember or imagine his or her strengths and deficits in social skills. List problems in social skills for each student. For example, Alecia is a fourth grade student who is shy and does not ask questions in the classroom. She doesn't do her homework, and you suspect this is because she doesn't understand the directions. Now, identify the category. For example, she needs to learn some listening and question-asking skills, which are in the category of basic interaction skills. ■ ■

Components of Social Skills Training

Social skills training is a generic term that includes any structured individual or group activity facilitating the acquisition or learning of expressive or interpersonal social behavior. In other words, it is the planned teaching of skills that include communication and interactions with others. Based upon the well-researched paradigm of social learning theory (Bandura, 1977), social skills training programs utilize a wide variety of procedures, such as instruction, modeling, behavioral rehearsal, role playing, reinforcement, coaching, shaping, and feedback (Rathjen, 1984). Other commonly used strategies are cognitive self-statements, homework assignments, problem-solving strategies, and systematic desensitization.

Social skills training programs are aimed at modifying students' interpersonal behaviors with peers and adults (Conger & Keane, 1981). Socially important and valued outcomes for students include acceptance in peer groups, acceptance by significant adults, school adjustment, mental health, and lack of contact with the juvenile court system (Gresham & Elliott, 1984).

There are commercial social skills training programs such as *Social Skills for Daily Living* (Shumaker, Hazel, & Pederson, 1988), but there can also be teacher-developed or -modified programs based on the specific needs of students. When selecting or developing social skills curricula for students with special needs, Schumaker, Pederson, Hazel, and Meyen (1983) suggest using the following five criteria for evaluation:

1. Does the curriculum promote social competence?
2. Does the curriculum accommodate the characteristics of students with special needs?
3. Does the curriculum target social skills deficits?
4. Does the curriculum provide training in situations as well as in skills?
5. Does the curriculum incorporate instructional methodologies found to be effective with students who have special needs?

Teachers who adhere to the preceding criteria may help their students become more socially competent because they address the characteristics, needs, and social skills deficits of their students. When you develop or select curricula to provide students with practice in a variety of situations and settings and then employ effective teaching strategies, you increase your students' abilities to respond appropriately in social situations. Most successful programs are based on assessing the students' social skills, organizing the classroom, teaching the skills, assessing attainment of the skills, and informing significant others about the social skills program.

Assessing Social Skills

It is necessary to assess the strengths and deficits students have before you start training. You should determine the current levels of performance and select skills to teach or strengthen. You will want to include skills that are important and appropriate, but you do not want to teach skills the students have already mastered.

Gresham and Elliot (1984) list six methods of assessing social skills: (a) sociometrics, (b) ratings by others, (c) naturalistic observation, (d) behavioral role plays, (e) behavioral interviews, and (f) self-report measures. Hops and Greenwood (1981) suggest that sociometrics, ratings, role plays, and self-reports are useful for diagnostic purposes. Naturalistic observation means you watch the student at school or on the job and take notes on social skills strengths and deficits. You may use a checklist for this purpose. Role plays are social situations that are conducted in a classroom or training setting. Students take various roles that require them to solve problems, make friends, resist peer pressure, and so on. You may judge competence in social skills by observing these situations. Self-reports and interviews allow students to talk about or rate themselves and their strengths and problems in social situations. In Table 13.3, we list various assessment instruments. You have the option of using commercial assessments or developing your own instruments. Whichever you select, be sure to choose the instrument that provides you with the most useful information about your students.

Commercial Assessments. Most of the published social skills programs have assessment

Table 13.3
Social Skills Assessment Instruments

Name	Type
Waksman Social Skills Rating Scale (Waksman, 1985)	Rating scale for parents, teachers, other adults.
Social Skills Rating System (Gresham & Elliot, 1990)	Rating scale for various adult raters.
Walker Social Skills Curriculum (Walker, McConnel, Holmes, Todis, Walker, & Golden, 1983)	Teacher rating scale.
Social Behavior Assessment (Stephens, 1980)	Rating scales.
ASSET (Hazel, Schumaker, Sherman, & Sheldon-Wildgen, 1981)	Rating by parents and teachers, role plays.
Guess Who (Gottlieb, Semmel, & Veldman, 1978)	Peer ratings.
MESSY (Matson, Rotatori, & Helsel, 1983)	Self-report rating scale.
Children's Assertive Behavior Scale (Michelson & Wood, 1980)	Self-report rating scale.
Teacher-designed instruments	Ratings, role plays, checklists, surveys, observational instruments.

methods and instruments as part of the package. Assessment methods that are frequently used include ratings by various significant persons in the student's life, role plays, naturalistic observations, and self-reports. One commercially available instrument is the *Waksman Social Skills Rating Scale* (Waksman, 1985), which has gender and age norms. The Waksman specifically measures social skills that involve assertive behaviors. The instrument is a rating scale to be completed by teachers, parents, and other adults in a student's environment. Another published assessment tool is the *Social Skills Rating System* (Gresham & Elliott, 1990), which offers norms for males and females, ages 3 through 18, and for disabled and nondisabled students. It too, uses a multirater approach to assessing social skills and problem behaviors.

The *Walker Social Skills Curriculum* (Walker, McConnel, Holmes, Todis, Walker, & Golden, 1983) includes a twenty-nine-item teacher rating scale. The *Social Behavior Assessment* (Stephens, 1980) contains 136 skills divided into the four categories of environmental, interpersonal, self-related, and task-related skills. Both of these scales have been empirically validated. The *ASSET* curriculum (Hazel, Schumaker, Sherman, and Sheldon-Wildgen, 1981)

includes rating scales for parents and teachers. The *Guess Who* scale (Gottlieb, Semmel, & Veldman, 1978) is rated by peers. Self-report measures include the *MESSY, Matson Evaluation of Social Skills with Youngsters* (Matson, Rotatori, and Helsel, 1983), and the *Children's Assertive Behavior* scale developed by Michelson and Wood (1980).

Teacher-Designed Assessments. If you plan to design your own instruments, you should decide on the skills for inclusion and the method of measurement. In the selection of skills, keep in mind the social behavior requirements of the situations in which students are and will be working. These are called setting demands (Shumaker & Deshler, 1984), because the settings in which students are working make special social demands on them. For example, one teacher's expectations of students may be different from those of another teacher, and Grandma's ideas of appropriate social behavior at dinner may be different from Dad's. The supervisor of a worker in a fast food restaurant probably has different demands for behavior than does the farmer who hires a student to help at the dairy in the summers. If you want to prepare students for these various settings, you must know what social behaviors are required or demanded. Sometimes,

---

☐ **Important Points**

1. Social skill competence in students relates to life adjustment as adults.
2. Social skills are socially acceptable learned behaviors that enable a person to interact in ways that elicit positive responses and avoid negative responses.
3. Social skills training is any structured individual or group activity facilitating the acquisition or learning of expressive or interpersonal social behavior.
4. Social skills programs should include assessing the students' social skills, organiz-

ing the classroom, teaching the skills, assessing student attainment of the skills, and informing significant others of the social skills program.

5. The first step in developing social skills programs is to assess the skill level of all students.
6. Skills may be assessed using commercial or teacher-made instruments.
7. In making their own assessment instruments, teachers should ask about important skills required in other settings.

---

teachers are tempted to teach only the skills they think are important. But many times, they must do some investigation to discover which behaviors are appropriate. In this way, teacher-developed assessment instruments meet the standard of social validity; that is, the behaviors they assess are relevant to the student's real world.

In addition to assessing the setting demands, you may wish to ask other teachers, administrators, and significant others their perceptions of the setting demands. If you plan to teach social skills to secondary students, you may want to ask supervisors in employment settings to identify the social behaviors they expect of their employees (Thurston & White, 1990).

Once you identify the skills, you must decide how to measure them. You may wish to design checklists, surveys, or observational instruments. Most often, a checklist identifies the skill and then asks the evaluator to check *yes* or *no*, whether the student does or does not perform the skill. Sometimes, the list is made into a rating scale that designates behaviors from 1 to 5, with 1 representing "not at all" and 5 representing "all the time." As with many of the commercial assessment devices, you may ask numerous people, such as teachers, parents, employers, and the students themselves, to complete the checklist.

Instead of a checklist, you may want to design an instrument to be used in directly observing

the behaviors of students as they take place. This method does not rely on the judgment of others, nor does it rely on ability to remember if the behavior took place frequently or seldom. Although this is often the most accurate method of assessing social skills, it is the most difficult for teachers to utilize because it requires an observer with the student in various settings to measure the behaviors.

■ ■ **Activity**

Part 1. List the setting demands of a university library. Design an assessment instrument (e.g., rating scale or checklist) that could be used to assess appropriate behavior in the library.
Part 2. List the setting demands of a Friday night party. Develop an instrument different from that designed in Part 1 to assess appropriate behavior in that setting. ■ ■

Organizing the Classroom

To organize the teaching of social skills, you must decide on instructional arrangements and scheduling. Students with similar skill deficits may be grouped for training into large groups or into small groups of two or three, or they may be taught individually. The small-group format of four to twelve students is considered optimal

(Rose, 1983). The group may consist of students in one special education classroom or may include students from several classes. Some teachers teach a social skills class to students from regular and special education together when the prerequisite for entering the class is having a skill deficit rather than a special education classification. Collaboration between regular and special educators is successful for many teachers who want to improve the social skills of their students. Working with small groups within a class or with the entire class on social skills relevant to the course, the special education teacher and the regular education teacher may co-teach.

Social skills classes may be held once a week, several times a week, or for a short time each day. Some teachers integrate social skills training into other classes, such as science, social studies, speech, drama, language arts, and home economics, and classes where cooperative learning is utilized. Social workers, guidance counselors, school psychologists, teaching assistants, or the teacher may work with students on developing social skills.

Teaching Social Skills

Most successful programs are based on the following steps:

1. Introducing and defining the skill.
2. Discussing the skill steps.
3. Modeling the steps of the skill in many situations.
4. Providing practice and feedback.
5. Generalizing the skill to other settings and situations.

The preceding steps ensure that students understand and practice the social skills being taught.

Introducing and Defining Social Skills. You may present a specific skill, such as resisting peer pressure or responding to criticism. Then, have your students tell their definition of the skill and rationales for its use. Next, lead the students in a discussion of the usefulness of the skill. They may say the skill is useful because it keeps them out of trouble with parents, helps them retain privileges at home, helps them get a promotion at work, or keeps them out of trouble with the law. It is important to have the students state their own examples and give their own rationales for the use of a skill. This aspect of the program helps students see the relationship of the skill to their own lives and helps you decide if the students understand the meaning and usefulness of the new skill. Students should do most of the talking. Effective teachers resist the temptation to lecture during social skills classes.

Discussing Skill Steps. At this time, list the specific nonverbal and verbal behaviors that make up the new skill. You can use task analysis or let students work together to develop the skill steps. Task analysis is discussed in Chapter 4.

The listing of specific skill steps helps students discriminate the behavior, remember the steps, and perform the skill. Goldstein, Sprafkin, Gershaw, and Klein (1980) recommend six steps for the skill of negotiating: (a) decide if you and someone else are having a difference of opinion, (b) tell the person what you think about the problem, (c) ask the other person what he or she thinks, (d) listen carefully, (e) think about what was said, and (f) suggest a compromise.

Modeling Skill Steps. In this phase of the program, students see someone else demonstrate the appropriate behavior. The model may be on a videotape, or it may be the teacher or a competent student. You may include models from different cultural backgrounds, such as models who are Asian, African-American, Hispanic, or Native American. You should use both male and female models. Students learn better when models are like themselves. Some commercial programs, like ASSET (Hazel, Schumaker, Sherman, & Sheldon-Wildgen, 1981), have accompanying videotapes. The model should demonstrate both the nonverbal and verbal steps of each social skill. For example, for the skill of negotiating, the model would first demonstrate nonverbal skills, such as (a) facing the person, (b) making eye contact, (c) using a serious voice, (d) having a serious facial expression, and (e) keeping a straight body posture (Schumaker, Hazel, & Pederson, 1988). Then, the model would proceed to the verbal steps of the skill. The modeling should be clear and detailed so that students can later imitate the behavior. After the demonstration, have the students discuss whether the model performed the behavior correctly, examine the relevance of the situation to their own lives, and raise questions. The model should be repeated often with different problem situations.

At this point, some programs include nonexamples of the appropriate social skill (Walker et al., 1983). For example, the model may demonstrate failure to use the skill or incorrect use of the skill. If students can discriminate whether the social skills are demonstrated correctly or incorrectly, they are better able to use the skills appropriately.

Providing Practice and Feedback. After the students see the behavior demonstrated, they should practice the behavior. Students may role-play situations in their own lives or common situations for students their age. Ask the students to take the role of another person during the practice. For example, if Jessie has a problem standing up for her rights in the science lab, she may take the role of her lab partner and the teacher or another student may take Jessie's role to demonstrate how to apply the skill of standing up for your rights in this setting. Then ask Jessie to practice as herself in the same situation.

As the students practice new skills, give them immediate feedback about their performance. Corrective feedback helps students improve their performance of the skill and positive reinforcement promotes learning. The feedback should be given by the other students and you. When students give feedback to their peers, they learn to discriminate successful performance of social skills, and they learn to give and receive feedback. If this is difficult for your students to do, you may want to begin the social skills program with teaching these skills.

The feedback given to students, whether it is positive or corrective, must be descriptive; that is, it must tell the students specifically what they are doing well and what specific aspects of the

behavior they need to improve. For example, saying "Jose, you need to practice that skill some more" is not as helpful as saying, "Jose, next time, remember to look your employee in the eye, speak politely, and stand up straight when you ask for time off during finals week."

It is important that the students get plenty of practice. Students with special needs may require more practice for every skill they learn, and social skills are no exception. In addition, unlike academic skills, these skills often need to be used in conflict or stressful situations, so overlearning is important in assuring success outside the classroom.

Generalizing Social Skills to Other Settings and Situations. All social skills programs must contain generalization objectives. It doesn't matter if students can perform the behaviors in the social skills class if they cannot perform the behaviors in other settings. Thus, generalization must be planned and must be a component of all career education activities.

There are many ways to promote generalization of social skills. (Table 13.4 lists several suggestions.) Homework is one way you may solve the transfer of social skills from an isolated setting. Homework in social skills means planning and executing the use of the new skill during appropriate situations outside the classroom. For example, Latoya is learning how to respond

Table 13.4
Generalization Strategies for Social Skills

1. Practicing the skills in other settings using planned homework.
2. Asking parents to practice and reinforce use of new social skills.
3. Involving job supervisors or other teachers in providing practice and reinforcement for new skills.
4. Teaching students to provide feedback to themselves.
5. Providing many examples of situations where skills can be used appropriately.
6. Reviewing skills learned previously.

to a complaint. She has told the group that her mother often complains about the way she cleans her room. For homework, Latoya plans how she will practice the new skill with her mother at home the next time her mother complains. Latoya tells the group what she will do, and the teacher has her actually demonstrate what she will do. The teacher or another student may play the role of the mother.

Students are often asked to use a homework form or checklist or to take notes immediately after their use of a skill. This helps the students provide feedback to themselves. Latoya may practice responding to a complaint at home and then keep a diary of what happened, what she did, and her thoughts about how she did. Because the teachers and other students are not there to provide support and positive reinforcement for using a new social skill, Latoya's diary must help her reinforce herself for a job well done. Young children who cannot write may draw happy faces on a chart or put stickers on a list of behaviors illustrated with stick figures to provide themselves with feedback for practicing the new skills in settings outside the classroom.

Involving mainstream teachers and parents is helpful in promoting generalization of social skills. These individuals may provide opportunities for students to practice their new skills and feedback about the performance of the skill to students and to the social skills teacher. Many parents and teachers are willing to cooperate in helping students learn appropriate social skills.

Teachers may use several other procedures to promote the transfer of training (Alberto & Troutman, 1990; Stokes & Baer, 1977). One procedure is to provide many examples of the new social skill. Have the students contribute examples of situations in which the skill was used, as they do when the skill is introduced. Also, describe many other situations in which the skill can be used by students. Utilize these procedures during the practice and role-playing step of the program.

Another means of promoting generalization is to bring in others to practice with the students, such as other teachers, potential employers, playground monitors, parents, vocational supervisors, and other students. When students practice a new social skill during the social skills class with a variety of people, generalization of new skills is promoted.

A final way to help students generalize their new skills is to provide review practice sessions of skills already learned. Students need review, and over time, they will have new and different situations that they need to practice. Many teachers report that students sometimes request review or practice of a specific skill because the students see the need for the skill and are unsure of how to perform it in the new problem situation.

Assessing the Attainment of Social Skills

Have the students learned and applied the social skills? This is a question you must ask, and to answer the question, you must conduct post-assessments. Usually, this means replicating the assessment procedure you used earlier. Using checklists, rating scales, or observation, you can determine if your students have learned the skill and are ready to progress to the next skill. Careful comparison of pretraining measures to post-training measures will tell you which skills have been learned, generalized, and used appropriately. At this point, you may need to reteach some skills or develop more generalization activities to promote transfer of training to other settings.

Informing Significant Others

When implementing a new program, you must communicate the nature and intent of the social skills program. Relationships, developed when communicating with parents, teachers, and employers about setting demands and skill priorities, enhance the programs that teachers develop.

Positive relationships lead to on-the-job training opportunities and career sampling programs for students, and they increase parent involvement and schoolwork support for programs in special education. A rural Kansas teacher de-

☐ Important Points

1. Students should define and give rationales for using a skill.
2. Listing skill steps helps students discriminate and perform the behaviors.
3. Modeling should be clear and detailed so that students can later imitate the behavior.
4. Practice activities should include role playing of situations common to the students' lives.
5. Feedback must tell the students specifically what they are doing well and what aspects of the behavior they need to improve.

6. Generalization of social skills is enhanced with homework assignments, the help of others such as mainstream teachers and parents, and review practice sessions that require students to practice the skills with many different examples and different individuals.
7. Assessment may be accomplished by replicating preassessment procedures.

---

scribed the usefulness of communicating with other school personnel and family and community members (Thurston & White, 1990). She asked employers the expectations they had for social skills of prospective employees. She found that these employers were pleased to be asked these questions and that they were willing to come into the class and talk with the students about career education skills. Some of the employers were even willing to actually practice skills with the students. Finally, these employers were also willing to provide feedback to the students and to the teachers about the students' performances when they were on the job. This participation by local employers was valuable to the teacher and the students. In addition, the Kansas teacher reported that her program gained credibility in the eyes of the students and the administration, because she could pinpoint specific career education skills, including social skills, that local employers require in prospective employees.

■ ■ Activity

Choose a social skill that you would like to improve yourself, such as handling embarrassing situations or responding to anger or criticism. Maybe you would like to be more assertive or give negative feedback easily. Analyze the behavior you chose and then make up several role-playing situations for practicing the skill. Develop three assessment procedures to determine whether or not you have mastered the skill. ■ ■

Summary

In this chapter, we discussed the importance of career education and related social skills in preparing for the successful transition and adjustment of students with special needs. According to Kokaska and Brolin (1985), "Career education is the process of systematically coordinating all school, family, and community components together to facilitate each individual's potential for economic, social, and personal fulfillment and participation in productive work activities that benefit the individual or others" (p. 43).

Career education is developmental. It should begin in the elementary years and proceed through adulthood. Career development progresses through four stages: (a) awareness, (b) exploration, (c) preparation, and (d) placement, follow-up, and continuing education. The eight components that all career education programs should possess include (a) early transition planning; (b) the team approach; (c) individualized transition plans for all students; (d) integration of students into many environments; (e) education in community-relevant living skills; (f) skills teaching in natural settings; (g) involvement of employers, employees, and families; and (h) program evaluation.

Career competencies may be taught through the infusion approach or the separate programming approach. In the infusion approach, career competencies are integrated into other subject matter content, while in the separate programming approach, competencies are taught as separate units.

We also discussed social skills. Just as career education skills are important in the transition to the real world of mainstream classes, homes, communities, and employment settings, so are social skills. Social skills are socially acceptable, learned behaviors that enable a person to interact with others in ways that elicit positive responses and avoid negative responses. The components of social skills training include (a) assessing social skills with commercial or teacher-designed assessments, (b) organizing the classroom for instruction, (c) teaching social skills, (d) assessing attainment of social skills, and (e) informing significant others about the program. Most successful social skills programs are based upon the following steps: (a) introducing and discussing social skills, (b) discussing the skill steps, (c) modeling the steps, (d) providing practice and feedback, and (e) generalizing the skills.

14

Identifying and Managing
Teacher Stress

Key Topics

Without doubt, teaching students with special needs is a stress-producing occupation. As a special educator, you are expected to design and implement individualized education programs, manage behavior, and document progress of students who are often disruptive and difficult to teach. In addition, you must communicate and collaborate with regular educators, parents, supervisors, administrators, and myriad other professionals and nonprofessionals.

According to Alschuler, Carl, Leslie, Schweiger, and Unistal (1984), "*Stress* could be a one-word definition of teaching" (p. 7). Sometimes, stress is facilitating (Farber, 1984). A student who is exhibiting problem behaviors often creates stress for the teacher, but this same stress often leads to a search for a solution and, if resolved, a reduction of the problem. However, many times, stress leads to teacher health problems, absenteeism, or attrition (Kyriacou & Sutcliffe, 1978; Litt & Turk, 1985).

The special education profession cannot afford to lose good teachers, who take 4 or 5 years to prepare for teaching and then leave after a 3- or 4-year period. Smith-Davis, Burke, and Noel (1984) found that 30% of the teachers who taught students with severe disabilities left their jobs within 4 years. Lawrenson and McKinnon (1982) reported a 48% loss over a 3-year period of teachers of the emotionally disturbed population. Platt and Olson (1990) found an average length of stay of 4 years for teachers of the emotionally disabled population, of 7 years for teachers involved with students who have specific learning disabilities, and 5 years for those involved with students who have mild mental retardation. In many states, the turnover rate of teachers is so high that all areas of special education have been identified as critical shortage areas. Likewise, the profession cannot afford the effects of stress on teachers remaining in the field, who tend to become less tolerant and less patient, interact less with students, and emphasize rote learning (Blase, 1986; Galbo, 1983).

It is impossible for you to avoid stress while teaching, but it is possible to keep it at a tolerable level and to be able to cope with and profit from it (Bradfield & Fones, 1985). The purpose of this chapter is to discuss the various causes and symptoms of stress and to present some suggestions to prevent its debilitating effects. The suggestions come from a literature review and our own personal experiences with handling stress during a combined 40 years as professionals in the field of special education.

Identifying Teacher Stress

You should be aware of the definition, symptoms, and causes of stress. Stress is present in all aspects of our personal and professional life. Nothing runs as smoothly as anyone would like. Being caught in a traffic jam on the way home or being evaluated by the principal can create stress. Stress can lead to burnout, a much more serious problem. Burnout is a distinctive kind of work-related stress (Jones, 1987). Burnout is defined as "progressive loss of idealism, energy, purpose, and concern as a result of conditions of work" (Edelwich & Brodsky, 1980, p. 5). It is "a syndrome of emotional exhaustion and cynicism that frequently occurs among individuals who do 'people work'—spend considerable time in close encounters with others under conditions of chronic tension and stress" (Maslach & Jackson, 1979, p. 1).

Symptoms

Three symptoms of burnout have been identified (Maslach & Jackson, 1979). One symptom is a feeling of boredom, overwork, emotional exhaustion, and fatigue. Often, teachers feel this way even though there are no physical reasons for the exhaustion or fatigue. Another symptom is the development of negative, cynical, or depersonalizing attitudes toward students. Teachers suffering from this symptom become increasingly rigid and inflexible and often withdraw from students, other people, or activities (e.g., eating lunch alone). Finally, there is the development of a lack of sense of accomplishment from the job. Teachers feel ineffective and receive no satisfaction from the job. These feelings can also affect physical health, creating depression, ulcers, migraine headaches, and so on (Fimian & Santoro, 1983; Greer & Wethered, 1984).

Causes

The causes of burnout in teachers of students with special needs have been studied extensively, most often by asking current teachers to complete surveys or inventories identifying stress factors. The *Maslach Burnout Inventory* (MBI) (Maslach & Jackson, 1986) has been used in many studies. The MBI correlates with the symptoms of burnout as teachers rank the frequency and intensity of items measuring exhaustion, depersonalization, and lack of personal accomplishment. A high score on exhaustion and depersonalization and a low score on personal accomplishment result in an assessment of burnout or severe stress.

Other surveys require teachers to rank or rate stress-producing factors such as low pay, and still others ask teachers to complete open-ended questions, such as "Do you feel your job is stressful?" In an analysis of the various burnout studies that have included special educators in the surveyed population, stress factors tend to fall into the general categories of time management, behavior problems, interpersonal relationships, and role expectations (Platt & Olson, 1990).

Managing Teacher Stress

We hope that the following stress management techniques will make you more capable of handling the demands of teaching and better able to appreciate the joys. We devote the rest of the chapter to providing you with techniques for managing time, student behavior, interpersonal relationships, unclear role expectations, and personal concerns.

Time Management

As a special education teacher, you face tremendous demands on your time. Your days and sometimes your evenings may be filled with a series of tasks that must be accomplished to satisfy some aspect of your many and varied professional responsibilities. These demands may involve completion of paperwork, scheduling of students, preparation for meetings, development of instructional materials, consultation with teachers, assessing student performance, and grading daily work.

Symptoms of Poor Time Management

Due to the extensive demands on their time, some teachers of students with special needs show signs of poor time management. Mathews (1984) describes these as (a) uncontrolled rushing, (b) chronic vacillation between unpleasant alternatives, (c) fatigue or listlessness with many slack hours of nonproductive activity, (d) constantly missed deadlines, (e) insufficient time for rest or personal relationships, and (f) the sense of being overwhelmed by demands and details. Teachers exhibiting these symptoms usually rush into classes or meetings late. They find themselves trying to decide whether to work on IEPs or fill out administrative forms for the office, perhaps eventually accomplishing neither. These individuals experience chronic fatigue and spend endless hours sitting around worrying about how much they have to do and what little time they have in which to do it. Individuals with these symptoms may not get adequate rest and may not know that there is "life after school."

Some teachers have difficulty coping with all of the details that are so much a part of the special education teacher's responsibilities, such as maintaining IEPs; keeping up with paperwork; scheduling meetings with parents and teachers; and administering, scoring and interpreting tests. Another sign of poor time management manifests itself in a lack of organization of time and materials. Some teachers feel that they are drowning in a sea of paper and cannot locate the specific form or memo they need at the moment. Teachers who are experiencing problems with time management may feel overwhelmed, helpless, and out of control. Sound and practical time management techniques may help alleviate these stressors.

Techniques for Improving Time Management

Time management encourages effective time use by eradicating time wasters in the day (Mathews, 1985). Sisley (1983) indicates that "the goal of time management is to maximize production capabilities and minimize the time you waste" (p. 75). Therefore, it is important for you to learn ways to effectively and systematically manage your time.

Self-Management. George (1983) suggests five steps in the effective self-management of time: (a) time analysis, (b) goal setting, (c) prioritization, (d) delegation, and (e) action. The purpose of time analysis is to make you aware of how you currently spend your time. Therefore, you should record what you do every day for a period of 2 weeks. At the end of this time period, see how you actually spend your time. Record activities both within and outside work hours, such as, paperwork, staffings, telephone calls, conferences, diagnostic workups, cooking, exercise, and television (See Figure 14.1).

■ ■ Activity

Evaluate your own time management skills by performing a time analysis. Record what you do each half hour of the day for the next week. (Answers for this and other activities are found in the Instructor's Manual.) ■ ■

Time	Activity
6:00–7:00	Eat breakfast and get ready for school
7:00–7:30	Drive to school
7:30–8:00	Consult with teachers or plan
8:00–9:30	Work with students
9:30–10:30	Testing or staffing activities
10:30–11:30	Work with students
11:30–12:00	Paperwork/Telephone calls
12:00–12:30	Lunch
12:30–1:00	Lunch or playground duty
1:00–3:00	Work in regular classrooms
3:00–3:30	Consult with teachers and/or bus duty
3:30–4:00	Paperwork or plan conferences
4:00–4:30	Drive home
4:30–5:00	Do errands
5:00–6:00	Fix and eat dinner
6:00–6:30	Do dishes and clean up
6:30–7:00	Relax
7:00–8:00	Help kids with homework
8:00–9:00	Grade papers
9:00–10:00	Watch television or read
10:00–10:30	Go to bed

Figure 14.1
Sample Time Analysis

You should use the information that you collect through time analysis to help you set goals. List all of the goals you would like to accomplish in the next year. These should be both long- and short-term goals and should be measurable and realistic. For example, if you find, as a result of your time analysis, that you are spending too much time on paperwork, you can set goals to improve the way you handle records, correspondence, and student papers.

Goals are effective when they are positive, have a deadline, and are specific (Potter, 1987). When you set a goal, you should state what you want to do or accomplish (positive), include a date or time by which you will accomplish it (deadline), and be specific about what you want to do. Following are some examples of poorly written goals and well-written goals.

- *Poor:* I will get my paperwork done. This goal is stated positively, but it does not have a deadline, nor is it specific. It does not specify what "paperwork" means.
- *Poor:* I will get my paperwork done by October 15. This goal is stated positively and contains a deadline; however, it still does not identify "paperwork."
- *Better:* By October 15, I will write five IEPs. This goal is stated positively, has a deadline, and is specific; therefore, you can observe or measure its completion.

Consider the teacher who wants to increase her interactions and consultations with regular classroom teachers.

- *Poor:* I will increase the number of collaborative contacts I have with the intermediate grade teachers. This goal is stated positively, but it is not specific enough, nor does it have a deadline.
- *Poor:* By March 6, I will increase the number of collaborative contacts I have with the intermediate grade teachers. This goal has a deadline and is positive, but it is still lacking specificity.

- *Better:* By March 6, I will meet with the intermediate grade teachers from 2:45–3:15 P.M. every Monday, Wednesday, and Friday. This goal is stated positively, is specific, and has a deadline. You can observe or measure its completion.

You should make sure the goals you set are realistic. A teacher who sets the goal of collaborating with regular classroom teachers three times a week must be sure that he or she has the planning time to do so and that the other teachers are willing and able to meet at this time. In other words, you should make sure this is a reasonable expectation.

One other suggestion about goals may assist you. Timm (1987) believes that goals should be *written,* not merely verbalized. He contends that spoken words are more like wishes and that sometimes wishes come true, but not as often as goals do.

■ ■ Activity
Rewrite the following goals to include the three criteria (positive, deadline, specific).

1. I want to have more relaxation time.
2. I will not miss deadlines for turning in materials orders.
3. I will analyze how much time I spend on work, family, leisure, community activities, health, and fitness. ■ ■

Next, you should prioritize the goals into three categories or lists: (a) essential (must do), (b) desire but not essential (should do), and (c) good but may be delayed (can do). Then, work on the first list of goals, going to the second and third lists only if you achieve the first list. You may want to prioritize categories for long-term (yearly or monthly) goals as well as for more immediate (weekly or daily) goals. For example, Ms. Greenwood developed a daily list to help accomplish her priorities for the day (see Figure 14.2).

My priorities for the day of _____ week of _____ .

List 1 — Must Do

1. Attend faculty meeting — 8:00 A.M.
2. Complete grade cards
3. Report for bus duty — 3:30 P.M.
4. Pick up cleaning

List 2 — Should Do

1. Call supervisor
2. Call Mrs. Valdez about scheduling a conference
3. Talk to guidance counselor

List 3 — Can Do

1. Check with media specialist about a videotape
2. Clean out vertical files

Figure 14.2
Priority List

You may delegate the responsibility for certain tasks to others in the school setting: students, teaching assistants, volunteers, or secretaries. You may do the same thing at home with family members. We realize that sometimes it is difficult to turn over control or responsibility to others, but when the long-term effects are realized (e.g., improved student performance or more effective use of your time) we think you'll agree it's worth it.

You may delegate responsibilities such as paperwork and nonteaching duties to teaching assistants, volunteers, and students (Weiskopf, 1980). For example, Mr. Johnson, a high school teacher, rotated responsibility for taking attendance and making announcements among the students in his homeroom. Each week Ms. Dubinski, a teacher at an elementary school, selected a very important person (VIP) from her resource room to take announcements to the office and to other teachers. Mr. Kerchev involved his middle school students in changing seasonal bulletin boards and asked his teaching assistant to assume responsibility for posting announcements, information, and important dates and deadlines.

You should develop an action plan to help achieve your goals. Break your goals down into small, attainable segments. For example, set aside a specific time period each day to work on IEPs. Block out a period of time each evening to relax, talk with friends, or spend time with family members. This step is crucial to the success of the preceding steps and the effective utilization of time.

Cohen and Hart-Hester (1987) suggest the following to help teachers accomplish necessary work as quickly as possible and with as little stress as possible. First, make a list of tasks and rank them according to their importance and deadlines. Check off the items as they are accomplished. Second, design a work area that is free from distractions and isolated from others. Third, develop forms for recording information about observations, meetings, and conferences. In this way, you need only fill in essential information in designated areas on the form. Haynes (1987) suggests the use of a conference planner. Each morning, list the names of people you need to contact that day, such as the principal, mainstream teachers, guidance counselors, parents, and program supervisor. Each time you think of something you need to ask that person, jot it down on a form such as the contact planning form that appears in Figure 14.3. Then, when you see or talk to that individual or you make a trip to the office, you are ready with your questions and comments. Fourth, perform tasks that require similar materials and information at one sitting. This eliminates having to assemble the same materials two or three times for different tasks and encourages maximum use of time and resources.

You can designate certain times of the day or certain days of the week for contacts with parents and teachers, testing, correspondence, lesson planning, monitoring student records, and

Name:	Mr. Godfrey 1. Early dismissal 2. Faculty meeting (Check date & time)
Name:	Dr. Delgado 1. In-service (How long is my presentation?) 2. 3-year evaluations (Need info. from district) 3. Jerry's bus schedule (Any progress?)
Name:	Nancy Berry 1. Conference (Set day & time) 2. Judy's behavior contract (Check) 3. Staffing for Richard (Can she attend?)
Name:	Jane 1. Car pool (Can't drive Wednesday) 2. PTA meeting (7:00 or 7:30?) 3. Field trip (Permission slips)

Figure 14.3
Contact Planning Form

Key: Mr. Godfrey (principal)
Dr. Delgado (director of special education)
Nancy Berry (third grade teacher)
Jane Roden (fifth grade teacher)

preparation of materials. For example, you can set aside 10 minutes before lunch and 10 minutes at the end of the day to return correspondence to parents, teachers, and administration instead of trying to respond to each memo or letter the minute you receive it or putting it in a pile and forgetting to respond at all.

Cook and Leffingwell (1982) suggest alloting a day to do paperwork while someone else assumes responsibility for the classroom routines. Teachers who must participate in IEP meetings or who need to write IEPs may be able to request a substitute for all or part of a day. If you feel this would be valuable, check with your principal to determine the policy in your school or district.

Timm (1987) recommends that you handle each piece of paper only once. He suggests using four options: (a) act on it now, (b) file it for future action, (c) refer it to another person, or (d) throw it away. This eliminates clutter and saves you time.

Instructional Time Management. Significant time pressures and responsibilities may be placed upon teachers during actual instructional time with students. Because teachers are aware of the importance of providing feedback and evaluative comments (oral and written), they impose a great deal of pressure upon themselves. Whether working in resource settings, self-contained classrooms, or regular classrooms, teachers of students with special needs strive to individually instruct and evaluate students. In order to effectively accomplish this with as little stress as possible, implement procedures to decrease stress and pressure and yet maintain a level of excellence in the classroom.

Cohen and Hart-Hester (1987) suggest that teachers designate specific days each week for students to check their own work or that they can appoint a student assistant to correct the work of other students. They further suggest a priority system for grading assignments, in which you grade tests and initial learning activities but allow student assistants to check practice and review sheets.

You may use peer tutoring and cooperative learning, as described in Chapter Eleven, to increase student instructional time and active involvement with the curriculum. Both elementary and secondary settings are conducive to this arrangement. In a supervisory role, you may oversee many students at the same time. For example, after receiving direct instruction from you, students working on an employability skills unit may work with partners to develop a list of questions that an employer might ask during an interview. In the regular classroom, you may supervise groups of students (regular and special

☐ Important Points

1. Stress may lead to burnout, which is a loss of idealism, energy, and purpose due to work-related variables.
2. The symptoms of stress or burnout may include boredom, emotional exhaustion, and fatigue.
3. Surveys and inventories are frequently used to determine the causes of teacher stress.
4. Common stress factors of special education teachers fall into the categories of time management, behavior problems of students, interpersonal relations, and role expectations.
5. Symptoms of poor time management include uncontrolled rushing, chronic vacillation between unpleasant alternatives, fatigue or listlessness with many slack hours

of nonproductive activity, constantly missed deadlines, insufficient time for rest or personal relationships, and the sense of being overwhelmed by demands and details.

6. Steps in the effective management of time are analysis, goal setting, prioritization, delegation, and action.
7. Goals should be positive and specific, and they should have a deadline.
8. Goals may be prioritized into three categories: essential (must do), desire but not essential (should do), and good but may be delayed (can do).
9. Instructional time may be managed with peer tutoring, cooperative learning, and enlisting student assistance.

---

education) as they collaborate on solving math problems. Assigning students to partners or groups is an effective instructional procedure for students from different cultural groups and frees you to provide direct teaching to those who need it.

■ ■ Activity
Go back and examine the time analysis you completed earlier in the chapter. Write three goals to complete within the next 3 months. Prioritize your goals and explain what strategies you will use to accomplish them. ■ ■

Behavior Problems
As you can see from the results of the research on teacher burnout, working with students who have special needs can be stressful. When you are confronted with students who refuse to comply with your request, question your authority, or swear at you, it is natural to feel stress. Many students with special needs exhibit these behav-

iors and no matter the number of years experience, such behaviors can lead to stress. However, some measures may help decrease the number of stressful encounters.

Many potential behavior problems may be prevented by the instructional decisions you make. If you select appropriate and motivational materials, present organized and motivational lessons, actively involve the students, and present structured routines and procedures, you can avert many behavior problems. These techniques are thoroughly discussed in other chapters, so we do not repeat them here. Unfortunately, not all behavior problems can be prevented or resolved with instructional decisions. To reduce stress when dealing with behavior problems, teachers must make wise decisions concerning their management options.

Selecting Rules
Rules are evidenced everywhere. In society, there are formal rules, or laws, and informal

rules, or social codes. Formal laws help maintain order, so, unlike in the days of the old West, disputes are not resolved by meeting on Main Street at high noon. Social codes are informal rules that vary from culture to culture. In many non-Western cultures, children learn that making eye contact with authority figures such as teachers is impolite. Unfortunately, not making eye contact is a sign of disrespect in the social code of many teachers.

Rules let students know what you expect. Students react differently during independent seatwork in a class where the teacher expects talking in a low voice and in a class where the teacher expects total silence. Two effective ways for you to identify class rules are to make a list of your behavioral expectations ahead of time and to check if there are any schoolwide rules (Sprick, 1985). A quick check of the list of schoolwide rules will let you know what behaviors the administrators and other teachers feel are necessary for maintaining order.

Once you define your expectations, you should establish rules. Following are some guidelines:

1. *Allow the students to give input concerning the rules.* Helping to select rules gives students a sense of being a part of the decision-making process and often makes them feel more responsible for following the rules. Sprick (1981) suggests that if you wish for students to design their own rules, you should post temporary ones for the first 3 or 4 days, until students become familiar with the routines.

2. *Base rules on acceptable behaviors.* In deciding the rules, keep in mind the behaviors that are expected in the mainstream setting. It may be acceptable for a student to complete work standing at a table in a special education setting, but this behavior may be totally unacceptable in a mainstreamed one. In many school districts, there are districtwide rules expected of all students. If this is the case, incorporate these rules into your system. Other consid-

erations for deciding which behaviors to include in rules are whether the behavior interferes with the student's learning, the student's personal safety, the preservation of property, and the teacher's teaching (Canter, 1979). For example, talking without permission may interfere with a student's learning and teacher's teaching, so you may select "Raise your hand if you have something to say" as a rule.

3. *State rules positively.* Positive rule statements lead to a positive atmosphere in the classroom and clue the students into appropriate behavior. "Speak politely to others by saying *thank you* and *please*" is a much better rule than "Don't shout at others." The first rule suggests an appropriate behavior, while the latter just warns the students not to shout.

4. *Select only about five or six rules.* A rule cannot be invented for every slight infraction that happens in the class. In addition, the more rules you have, the more difficult it is to consistently enforce them (Jensen, Sloan, & Young, 1988).

5. *Select rules for both academic and social behaviors.* Rules usually deal with academic behaviors, such as "Complete all assignments," and social behaviors, such as "Keep hands and feet to yourself." Research shows that it is important to focus on academic behaviors and that often such a focus, especially if the rules are reinforced, leads to improved conduct (Ayllon, Layman, & Burke, 1972; Ayllon & Roberts, 1974).

6. *Relate rules to specific behaviors and yet, at the same time, be general enough to cover many classes of that behavior.* A rule such as "Be kind to others" is general, so that it can cover many classes of behaviors, including "Say nice things to other students" and "Keep your hands to yourself." Thus, the use of a general rule reduces the number of rules needed. However, at the same time, the students may not understand what is

meant by the rule if no specific behavior is identified. This problem may be solved by listing examples of specific behaviors next to the rule or by discussing and role-playing the specific behaviors.

7. *Change rules when necessary.* If being unprepared for class is a problem for your third period class, then this behavior should become a new rule. If students are completing all work, then it may be time to remove the rule that deals with completing all assignments. This does not mean that students no longer have to complete the work, but since everyone is remembering it, a written rule is no longer necessary.

8. *Relate rules to IEP objectives.* For many students with special needs, behavior as well as academic objectives are written on the individualized education program. These objectives may be added to the rules for each individual student as individual goals, or if many students have similar objectives, these behaviors may become part of the group list of rules.

9. *If possible, consider cultural differences.* In the African-American culture, mental, emotional, and physical activities are integrated (Gay, 1975), so children from this culture may be on task even though they are not sitting quietly in their seats. For Hispanic students, the pace of work is often slower, and being "on time" is viewed as having little value (Briganti, 1989). Thus, you may want to incorporate such factors into rule selection. For example, perhaps a better rule than "Work quietly at your seat," is "Do your work quietly."

■ ■ Activity
Meet with a peer and list five or six rules you might use in your class. ■ ■

Teaching Rules
Once rules are selected, the next step is to teach and discuss them frequently. Every morning or at the beginning of each class period, particularly at the beginning of the school year, the class rules should be discussed, demonstrated, and for younger children, practiced. Adding a rationale to an explanation of the rules during the discussion is particularly effective for older students, who often are motivated if reasons for having rules are discussed (Morgan & Jenson, 1988).

The following techniques from concept teaching procedures adapted from the Direct Instruction procedures (Engelmann & Carnine, 1982) are suggested for teaching of rules. They include defining or describing the relevant attributes of the behavior, modeling examples and nonexamples, and asking students to discriminate between them (Morgan & Jenson, 1988). For example, with the stay-on-task rule, define what "stay on task" means for the students (e.g., "Stay on task means you write or listen or read when you work"). Next, give positive examples (e.g., "When you are doing a math paper, you are on task if you are writing down the problems, figuring out the answers, or thinking about how to solve the problem") and negative or nonexamples (e.g., "You are not on task if you are looking out the window, thinking about the beach, or talking to a neighbor"). Then, model different examples and nonexamples of on-task behaviors and ask the students to identify and explain why the behavior is an example or not an example of on-task behavior. In response to this question, a student may say, "You are on task because you are looking at the math book" or "You are not on task because you are looking around the room." Next, have students model the appropriate or inappropriate behavior, and have others identify whether the students are displaying on-task behaviors. During the role-playing activity, the students are not only practicing the rule, but also learning to evaluate behaviors.

Post the rules in the room or in individual notebooks to help students remember them. Many adolescents write the rules on a sheet of paper to keep in their notebooks. One creative student teacher incorporated the rules into a class constitution to parody the United States Constitution.

Prompting Rules

Having rules does not mean students will automatically follow them immediately. Students often need prompts to internalize or perform behaviors independently (Rosenshine, 1990). Prompts are ways to remind students to follow the rules. For example, use of verbal prompts such as "Remember, raise your hand" or visual prompts such as a finger over the lip usually prevents talk-outs from occurring. The visual prompt of standing near the whispering students often stops the off-task behavior. Other prompts include sharing expectations, praising students who are following the rules, and issuing either warning or choice statements.

Sharing Expectations. Sharing expectations is a way to explain to students what rules are in effect or what behaviors you expect for that particular activity (Sprick, 1985). Rules often vary, depending on whether the activity is to be completed by individuals or by small groups. As noted in Chapter Seven, stating the behavioral rules for a lesson is especially effective for students with problem behaviors (Borg & Ascione, 1982; Emmer, Evertson, & Anderson, 1980; Englert, 1984; Evertson & Emmer, 1982).

An example of sharing expectations about behaviors appears in these sample instructions given to secondary students: "Today, we begin our study of the Roman Empire. As we are discussing the beginning of Roman civilization, please remember to listen to others' ideas without interruptions, to copy the notes from the board, and to participate in the discussion." With many elementary students, you must share your expectations before academic and nonacademic activities. For example, "Bernice, remember, when we stand in line, we keep our hands to ourselves, we face the door, and we do not talk."

Peer Modeling. Peer modeling may also serve as a prompt for following rules (Alberto & Troutman, 1990). To use peer modeling, praise students who are following the rule by identifying specific behaviors (e.g., "Good, Jason, you are standing quietly in line") and ignore the student who is not (e.g., ignore Rashonda). Then, when the student displays the appropriate behavior, praise him or her (e.g., "Good, Rashonda, that's the way to stand quietly in line").

Positive Repetition. Positive repetition is similar to peer modeling in that you first tune in to positive behaviors of the students who are following the rules. At the same time, however, you repeat the directions or instructions you gave (Canter & Associates, 1986). For example, if Jane, a middle school student, is refusing to follow your directions to take out her sentence writing book and turn to page 45, ignore Jane and say to Ramone, "Thank you, Ramone. I can see you have your sentence writing book out. I appreciate your turning to page 45, Towanda. This side of the room is ready to begin."

Praising other students instead of tuning in to the inappropriate behavior of a student is difficult even for seasoned teachers. The natural reaction to this stress-producing situation is to focus on the deviant behavior immediately instead of praising the students who are following the rules. Deviant behaviors can make teachers fearful that their authority is being questioned. Yet, being positive as a first step is frequently sufficient to stop inappropriate behavior. In addition, praising teaches students that teacher attention, often a powerful motivator (Alberto & Troutman, 1990), may be secured through appropriate behaviors instead of inappropriate behaviors.

Issuing Warning and Choice Statements. We recommend the use of warning and choice statements only after you have tried to change the behavior by positively attending to the appropriate behaviors of other students. If after praising others, a student is still not following the rule, you may want to use a warning or choice statement. A warning statement alerts the student to the rule infraction. For example, "You are forgetting our rule to listen to others, Sam. This is a warning" lets Sam know that he needs to display appropriate behavior immediately. Warning statements are often used with younger children.

With a choice statement, you present the appropriate behavior that relates to the rule and some sort of unpleasant option to the student; for example, "Sally, you are breaking rule 4. Either remember to raise your hand (rule) or leave the group (option). It is your choice."

Once you issue a choice statement, give the student an opportunity to think about the choice. Move out of the student's vicinity to avoid a direct confrontation and continue with other activities. That way, a student can save face and even mumble nasty things out of your hearing range. (Or, at least, you can pretend not to hear it.) Be certain to always acknowledge an appropriate choice in some way, such as "I see you've made a good choice, Sally. Thank you."

An advantage of the use of choice statements is that they place responsibility for the actions with the student. In the previous example, if Sally comes back and blames you for her problems, an appropriate reply is "No, Sally, I gave you a choice and you decided to leave the group." Choice statements help students with special needs realize that they are responsible for their own behaviors. Choice statements are also effective with students from various cultural backgrounds. Grossman (1984) suggests nonauthoritarian methods when disciplining Hispanic adolescents, who due to the patriarchal society of their culture may have problems taking commands from female teachers.

In issuing choice or warning statements, you should remain calm and speak in a quiet, firm voice. You should also lower your voice at the end of a warning statement. Moreover, you should be aware of nonverbal behaviors, such as eye contact. When issuing a warning statement, many teachers point a finger at the student, which is often a clue to the student that he or she is upsetting the teacher. Hands resting at the side usually convey an air of confidence.

The type of prompt given often depends on the type of behavior, the time of the year, and student characteristics. It is not possible to administer a choice statement for behaviors that are physically detrimental to a particular student, other students, the teacher, or school property. Sally cannot be given a choice if she is hitting Jim. You must stop her immediately and send her to the time-out area or refer her to the dean of students or the principal. Frequently, more prompts are given at the beginning of the year, until students become familiar with the rules. Often, students who display severe behaviors or who are expected to adjust to the mainstream setting are given fewer reminders.

■ ■ Activity

Find two other students to participate in this activity with you. One will be the student and one will be the observer. The observer is to evaluate your use of a choice statement by marking with X under *yes* or *no* for each statement on the following checklist. The student is telling you that he is not going to do his math (disobeying the rule to follow teacher directions) and is trying to involve you in a confrontation. Use a choice statement.

Observer Checklist

	Yes	No
1. Did the teacher remain calm?		
2. Did the teacher speak in a firm, quiet voice?		
3. Did the teacher maintain eye contact?		
4. Did the teacher use her or his hands appropriately?		
5. Did the teacher state the appropriate behavior and the option in the choice statement?		
6. Did the teacher repeat the choice idea by saying either it is your choice or it is your decision?		
7. Did the teacher give the student some time to think about it?		
8. Did the teacher acknowledge selection of the appropriate choice?		

Now, change roles so that everyone gets a chance to be the teacher. ■ ■

Enforcing Rules

The next step is to decide what you are going to do when students follow rules and when they do not. You may want to use specific praise or positive attention intermittently to call attention to students who are following the rules and then award certificates or free time at the end of the week based on particular criteria.

Specific praise statements identify the praiseworthy aspects of students' behaviors. When using a specific praise statement, include a description of the specific behavior the student is demonstrating and the student's name, for example, "I like the way you are working quietly, Terrie" for the young student and "Thank you, Josh. I appreciate the quiet work" for the adolescent. For many adolescents, positive public praise from a teacher is unpleasant or embarrassing, as they don't want to be singled out from their peers (Sprick, 1985). Thus, you may want to praise adolescents in private or praise the group effort instead of individuals. This is also true for many Native Americans, who prefer a quiet and private type of specific praise (Pepper, 1976).

Positive attention involves interacting with students in a positive manner. A pat on a student's shoulder or a greeting as a student enters the room is a positive attention behavior. However, you must be aware of the responses of different cultural groups to such positive attention. In some cultures, a pat on the shoulder or a personal greeting is not viewed positively, such as in the Asian-American culture, which emphasizes a more formal school atmosphere (Grossman, 1990).

Specific praise and positive attention may be interwoven into your daily routine, as neither is time consuming. Attending to a student with the raised hand and ignoring the one shouting out requires no extra time. Stopping at secondary students' desks to compliment them for staying on task during independent practice activities is appropriate for students who enjoy being praised or singled out for teacher attention in private (Sprick, 1985). Specific praise and positive attention are particularly effective for Hispanic students, whose culture typically endorses a dependency on the approval of others (Grossman, 1984).

Some students, especially those with severe behavior disorders, have a difficult time accepting specific praise and positive attention (Sprick, 1985). It is highly likely that this type of student may respond with "I don't care what you think" to a positive statement. It is best to remain calm and just ignore that comment, as it was precipitated by your praise statement, and perhaps counter with "I'm sorry you don't, but I still think you are doing good work. All of your problems are correct." Then, examine the effect of the statement on behavior. If the behavior improves, the feedback worked, no matter what the student said. Do not be discouraged, but continue with the positive comments. Sprick (1985) states, "Every student needs to learn that he has enough self-worth to accept recognition from someone else" (p. 44).

If all students obeyed the rules all of the time, teachers would not identify behavior problems of students as a stress factor. Stress occurs when a student, even after prompting, continues to break the rules.

What are your options to decrease inappropriate behaviors? Usually, the option is (a) withholding something the student likes or (b) presenting the student with something he or she doesn't like. Many teachers withhold points, privileges, or free time from students who do not follow the rules, while others write referrals or require students to eat lunch alone. Canter (1979) recommends a hierarchy of consequences, such as writing the student's name on the board for the first rule infraction, withdrawing 5 minutes of recess time for the next, and referring the student to the principal for the third. He further states that a severe rule infraction (e.g., a fight) warrants an immediate severe punishment, such as referral to the principal.

Whatever consequence you use, remember to remain calm and to follow through. Some students try to talk teachers out of the consequence, such as "Oh, Mr. Jones, please don't send me to the principal's office. I'll do my work now." A teacher who does not follow through at this time is only teaching students that they can wait to do their work until the teacher threatens to take them to the office and then they can talk the teacher out of taking them there. You need to follow through with the consequence, or your effort just becomes a threat.

In addition to following through with consequences, consistency is a prime consideration in enforcing rules. If "Raise your hand to speak" is a rule, then all students should have to follow it. Be careful not to fall into the trap of giving attention to a student who is shouting out because that student happens to be blurting out the correct answer. Consistency allows students to learn that there are expectations in your class and consequences for not following them.

Finally, remember to provide appropriate feedback. For example, Mr. Anderson gave his secondary students the following feedback at the end of fifth period: "Most of today's class went well. All of you followed directions, copying the notes from the board, but I had to prompt you to not interrupt when someone was talking. Let's work on this during tomorrow's class."

In Table 14.1, we present the management decisions made by an elementary and secondary special education teacher in the areas we have just described. We wish we could assure you that now, after reading this section, you will have no management problems. If only it would be possible to provide management solutions like recipes. Take one-half cup of positive praise and all problem behaviors will sift out of the class. Most students with mild disabilities have had many years to develop inappropriate behaviors, and a mere 6 weeks or even a year will not "cure"

Table 14.1
Sample Management Decisions

Elementary Plan	Secondary Plan

• *Select Rules*
  1. Follow directions.
  2. Be kind to others (say *thank you, please;* keep your hands to yourself).
  3. Raise your hand.
  4. Stay on task.
• *Teach Rules*
Present all rules the first day.
Then, role-play a rule a day for the first week.
• *Prompt Rules*
Use peer modeling, positive repetition, and warning.
Share your expectations before each activity.
• *Enforce Rules*
Provide specific praise, stickers, or certificates.
Provide loss of privileges, time-out, or referrals.
Give feedback at the end of each lesson.
	• *Select Rules*
	  1. Be prepared for class.
	  2. Be in the area when the bell rings.
	  3. Be respectful of others' property.
	  4. Use appropriate school language.
	  5. Follow teacher directions and instructions.
	  6. Complete all assignments.
	• *Teach Rules*
	Discuss the need for rules and present some temporary rules.
	Monday of the second week, have the students create their own rules with input.
	Discuss rules when inappropriate behavior becomes a problem.
	• *Prompt Rules*
	Provide positive repetition with the group.
	Provide choices.
	Share your expectations.
	• *Enforce Rules*
	Use specific praise, or provide positive attention, free time, or a homework pass.
	Subtract points from the conduct grade, or provide time-out or referral.
	Give feedback at the end of the period for each group.

☐ Important Points

1. Many potential behavior problems may be prevented by the selection of appropriate and motivational materials; the presentation of organized and motivational lessons, that actively involve the students; and the incorporation of structured routines and procedures.

2. Guidelines for establishing effective rules are to incorporate student input, to base rules on acceptable behaviors, to state rules positively, to select only about five or six rules, to relate to both academic and social behaviors, to make rules specific, to change rules when necessary, to relate rules to IEP objectives, and to consider cultural differences.

3. Teaching rules requires defining or describing the important attributes of the behavior, as well as modeling examples and nonexamples and asking students to discriminate between them.

4. Prompts are used to remind students to follow the rules.

5. Prompts include the procedures of sharing expectations, peer modeling, positive repetition, and issuing warning or choice statements.

6. In sharing expectations, teachers should notify the students of the behaviors expected.

7. In peer modeling, teachers should praise appropriate behavior, ignore a student displaying inappropriate behavior, and eventually praise that student once the behavior changes.

8. In positive repetition, teachers should praise the appropriate behaviors by calling attention to the instructions they are following.

9. Specific praise and positive attention may be used for students who follow the rules, while withholding privileges or presenting something unpleasant may be used for students who do not follow the rules.

10. Teachers must be consistent in enforcing rules and in following through when students do not follow rules.

---

them. However, rules and consistent implementation of them should make your interactions with students less stressful.

■ ■ Activity

Examine the decisions made for the two levels presented in Table 14.1. Under each heading, specify the procedures that you plan to use to help you alleviate the stress caused by problem behaviors. ■ ■

Interpersonal Concerns

Various interpersonal concerns are related to stress and lack of job satisfaction among teachers of students with special needs. Some of these are poor staff relations, insufficient opportunities for professional growth, administrative ineffectiveness (Garland, 1981), hassles with administration, and lack of recognition (Lawrenson & McKinnon, 1980). Teacher stress appears to be inversely related to the amount of on-the-job administrative, supervisory, and peer support that teachers receive (Fimian, 1986). In other words, the greater the degree of support, the lower the stress levels of teachers.

In a study on social support and stress, Fimian (1986) reported that the stress levels of teachers who did not receive supervisory support were higher than the levels of those who did. Teachers reported that administrators' and supervisors' unavailability, inadequate communication skills, and lack of support increased their stress levels (Holifield, 1981).

Peer support, another interpersonal concern, also seems to be related to teacher stress levels. Fimian (1986) found that teachers who did not receive support from coworkers reported significantly higher levels of stress than did those receiving support. Zabel and Zabel (1982) found that special education teachers who received external support from administrators, other teachers, and parents were less emotionally exhausted and reported fewer feelings of depersonalization than did teachers who did not receive support. Finally, many dissatisfied teachers reported frustration with being isolated from their peers (Shaw, Bensky, Dixon, & Bonneau, 1980).

You may want to utilize various techniques to increase the level of support that you have at school. In this section, we provide suggestions for securing and maintaining support from administrators, supervisors, and coworkers.

Support from Supervisors and Administrators

Unlike regular education teachers, special education teachers are often responsible to more than one supervisor. You may be assigned to a school where you work with a building administrator, the principal. In addition, you may also be responsible to the school district's director of special education or a program supervisor. This means that you may have at least two supervisors with whom you must communicate and work, and whom you must look to for support. If you are assigned to more than one school or you travel extensively as part of your work, you will have even more supervisors with whom to interact. This makes it essential to learn how to work effectively with supervisors and to know how to secure supervisory support.

Supervisors may be more supportive when you make them aware that you (a) provide direct service to students, (b) consult with regular education teachers, (c) work with students with

special needs in mainstream settings, (d) perform required administrative duties (e.g., participate in staffings and preparation of IEPs), (e) communicate with parents, and (f) grow professionally through in-service education. As you clarify your roles, you should show how supervisory support will enhance the district's special education program, the school's functioning, and the students' progress. The cooperation of your supervisor in facilitating your efforts also reflects positively on that supervisor.

For example, Mr. Rudolph, a teacher of an elementary resource room asked his program supervisor if the district's special education office would fund his attendance at a 2-day session to learn about a new math curriculum. He offered to present it to other teachers upon his return. Then, he asked his principal if he could have a substitute for the 2 days and offered to present the new program to the rest of the faculty and help them implement some of the techniques with his students who were mainstreamed in their classes. He clearly communicated his needs to his supervisors and demonstrated that many positive effects would be realized by others. Both his program supervisor and his principal willingly approved his request.

■ ■ Activity

Choose a partner to assume the role of your principal or supervisor. Role-play a situation in which you (the special education teacher) are trying to secure your supervisor's support for you to visit a model whole language program in the district. Now, switch roles and role play a different situation. ■ ■

As a special education teacher, you need to communicate positive events to your supervisors. Then, if you have a particular need or problem, your supervisors may be better informed and more willing to listen. Consider the following examples.

- Working collaboratively with a fifth grade teacher, Mrs. Farmer shared with her supervisor a copy of the newspaper that the students in the fifth grade class had developed. Her students had interviewed the school principal and several of the faculty and staff members. Mr. Proferes, a teacher of a primary pull-out program, regularly sent his students to see the principal when they accomplished something special or achieved a goal. The principal was delighted to visit with students who had come to the office with an achievement instead of a problem. This type of recognition may be accompanied by a commendation referral (see Figure 14.4), which specifies how the student will be recognized or rewarded.

- The job placement specialist at a high school called his supervisor to report that a student who had been a problem in the school system for many years was going to graduate and would continue working for the employer with whom he had been placed earlier that year.

Commendation Referral

DATE: _____

TEACHER: _____

NAME OF STUDENT: _____

REASON FOR COMMENDATION:

_____

_____

_____

Recommended Action (Please check):

_____ Interview student

_____ Call or send a letter to parents

_____ Make out an award certificate

_____ Announce on intercom

_____ Mention in PTA Newsletter

_____ Other: (Please specify.) _____

Figure 14.4
Positive Referral

As a special education teacher, you may keep your program supervisors and school administrators informed about your students' progress, the success of your collaborative efforts with regular education teachers, and your work with parents. You may share test scores, students' grades or report cards, and samples of your students' work. One elementary school principal was pleased when the special education teacher showed him samples of stories that had been written by his students. A secondary school principal was impressed with the efforts of students who role-played for him what they would do when they interviewed for a job. It is important for special education teachers to share positive experiences and to keep supervisors informed about their programs. In this way, supervisors and building administrators can give recognition to special education teachers for their achievements and contributions at district staff meetings and school faculty meetings. Additionally, Greer and Wethered (1984) suggest the use of newsletters and announcements to promote public awareness of teachers' accomplishments.

Inviting supervisors and school administrators to your classroom or to the regular classroom to see mainstreamed students keeps supervisors involved and informed. Supervisors may view your effectiveness firsthand, and sometimes, they notice program or classroom needs, such as a lack of materials or equipment and inadequate space. Through observation, supervisors may gain appreciation for the demands being placed upon you and recognition of your program's needs.

Remember, you can exercise more control over the amount and type of support that you receive from supervisors and administrators if you take a proactive role in regard to your interactions. You should interact positively, keep supervisors well informed, and clearly express your needs to increase the level of supervisory support that you receive.

Support from Coworkers

It is important for you to avoid isolation from other staff members (Weiskopf, 1980). When you make your supervisors aware of the need for social support, they may then facilitate supportive efforts of the teachers in your school.

Support Groups. Farber (1984) found that the most promising approach to stress reduction for teachers is social support. Teacher support groups are effective in reducing isolation, encouraging collegiality, renewing commitment, and promoting a sense of professionalism (Walley & Stokes, 1981).

Fimian (1986) reports that teachers are more likely to receive support from peers than from supervisors. If this is the case, then special educators may benefit from the establishment of peer support groups. Support groups are informal groups of people who meet on a regular basis to provide personal support to coworkers who are trying to improve their teaching; share expertise; and discuss problems, successes, and concerns. Factors that may influence the makeup of support groups include (a) common need, (b) existing groupings, (c) high school and middle/junior high feeder schools, (d) geographical proximity, and (e) time schedules (Hutchins et al., 1984). Unless a support group is composed of teachers in the same school where the principal has allotted in-school time for the members to meet, the group will have to meet after school. In an effort to encourage the formation of peer support groups, some school districts award in-service points to members who participate in these groups. The group members send a copy of their agenda and the minutes of their meetings to the district office to receive their points. Support groups that have met with success may have done so because their members had a common need, received support in implementing something new, and developed professionally.

Effective support groups start promptly, stop on time, have a set agenda, and allocate a certain number of minutes to successes, problems, solutions, new issues, and goals. Special education teachers who participate as members of support groups may be recognized for this involvement at school district meetings.

Students at the preservice level can develop support groups with other students during their special education teacher training. By sharing successes and concerns and solving problems as a group, they can ease their transition from the role of student to teacher, and they are more likely to participate in support groups as teachers. Raiser (1987) reports success with monthly meetings of university faculty members and preservice, first-year, and veteran special education teachers who meet for the purpose of generating solutions to problems. Between monthly meetings, the university facilitator is available for phone calls at specifically designated times.

One school district involved the members of its local Council for Exceptional Children (CEC) chapter in working with new special education teachers through a collaborative partnership program. A new teacher and a veteran teacher were teamed up as partners for the school year.

■ ■ Activity

Part 1. Form a support group of six to nine members. Develop an agenda. Discuss the successes, problems, and concerns you are having in your course work, teaching, or some other aspect of your program. Brainstorm some solutions and make some recommendations. Implement some or all of the recommendations and call another support group meeting.

Part 2. Think of a hypothetical situation in a special education classroom. Call a meeting of your support group. Discuss the situation and develop some solutions. List the advantages of discussing a problem like this one in a group as opposed to solving it on your own. ■ ■

Peer Coaching. In addition to participating as a member of a support group, special education teachers can work with other teachers through peer coaching. Teachers can work in a supportive arrangement with coaching partners who observe and confer with them about the implementation of techniques and strategies in their classrooms. Peer coaching prevents the isolation that impedes the improvement of teaching skills and student learning (Leggett & Hoyle, 1987). Coaching can facilitate and encourage a mutually supportive and nonthreatening relationship.

Peer coaching initially involves a discussion and planning phase, in which the coaching partners decide what they are going to work on. For example, Mr. Beaty may ask his peer coach to work with him on the use of specific academic praise. The next phase includes observation, at which time the partners decide exactly what behaviors to observe. Mr. Beaty may ask his peer coach to observe him as he teaches a lesson and to determine how often he provides specific ac-

---

☐ Important Points

1. Among the interpersonal concerns related to teacher stress is lack of recognition and support.
2. Suggestions for gaining the support of supervisors and administrators include interacting positively, keeping them informed, and communicating needs.
3. Two ways to secure support and recognition are to develop social support groups and to participate in peer coaching.
4. Support groups are informal groups of people who meet on a regular basis to pro-

vide personal support to coworkers who are trying to improve their teaching; share expertise; and discuss problems, successes, and concerns.
5. Peer coaching is a supportive arrangement between teachers, or coaching partners, who observe and confer with each other for the purpose of improving their teaching skills.

ademic praise to his students. The final phase involves feedback. During this phase, the partners share information about what was observed (Joyce & Showers, 1987). At this stage, Mr. Beaty and the coach would talk about the use of specific academic praise during the lesson.

Peer coaching provides supportive, individual assistance as teachers try out new skills (Leggett & Hoyle, 1987). Coaching involves working with colleagues in a supportive manner and appears to be a viable alternative for reducing stress.

■ ■ Activity
Audiotape yourself teaching a lesson. Choose a partner to work with as a peer coach. Ask your partner to listen to and count the number of specific praise comments. Discuss your impressions of the lesson along with the observations of your peer coach. Now, switch roles and have your partner teach a lesson. Do you think you can improve your teaching skills through coaching? In what ways? ■ ■

Role Expectations
Teachers bring with them a set of expectations that often center around being liked, helpful, and in control (Morse, 1981; Pickardt, 1978). Many of these normal expectations must be adapted when working with students with special needs. Noncompliant, angry students who make slow progress are not likely to fulfill these expectations. "Being in control" may mean enjoying an hour when Gus does not have a tantrum or eventually replacing shorter periods of chaos with longer, productive teaching times. "Being helpful" may mean that Jennifer completes 65% of the math problems correctly with your tutoring instead of the usual 60%. "Being liked" may mean that Jason no longer uses a four-letter word to describe you. As Morse (1981) says when talking about how the normal expectations of teachers fit into the education of special students, "One has to get one's satisfaction from knowing we are doing the

right thing to help, though the change may be too delayed to give us the desired feedback" (p. 2).

Mathews (1980) identified certain self-punishing expectations that are related to burnout. Some of these irrational ideas are:

1. The idea that it is a dire necessity for a teacher to be loved or appreciated by every student.
2. The idea that one must always enjoy the favor of one's supervisor.
3. The idea that one must be thoroughly competent and successful in doing one's job if one is to consider oneself worthwhile.
4. The idea that one's unhappiness is caused by the students or the institution and that one has little or no ability to control one's emotional reactions.
5. The idea that there is invariably a right, precise, and perfect solution to human problems and that it is catastrophic if the solution is not found. (p. 5)

The sources of stress dealing with expectations are usually measured in burnout studies by asking teachers to complete a role questionnaire dealing with role ambiguity and role conflict constructs (Crane & Iwanicki, 1986). Both constructs have been found to relate to burnout.

Role Ambiguity
Role ambiguity is a confusion about the scope and specific responsibilities of the job. The information is insufficient to allow the individual to carry out assigned responsibilities (Fimian & Blanton, 1986). "I know exactly what is expected of me"; "Clear, planned goals exist for my job"; and "I feel certain about how much authority I have" are sample items found on the role questionnaire measuring role ambiguity (Crane & Iwanicki, 1986, p. 26).

One suggestion to deal with role ambiguity is for administrators to develop clear teacher job descriptions (Schwab & Iwanicki, 1982). During an interview with the principal or other administrator, you should ask specific questions to determine if there are clear role descriptions (see Table 14.2). You may also ask to examine the handbook dealing with district procedures and guidelines. A knowledge that goals, discipline policy, and mainstreaming policies are not clearly defined should lead to a realization that it may be difficult to carry out assigned duties. In this case, you should ask more questions and seek clarification on vague items.

Role Conflict

Role conflict results in a discrepancy between a teacher's perception of the job and the perceptions of significant others. Possible role conflict situations occur when responsibilities are specified but there is a lack of resources or skills to execute them or when schoolwide or district-wide policies and rules are in conflict with the teacher's rules and policies (Fimian & Blanton, 1986). Some sample items found on a role questionnaire measuring role conflict are "I have to work on unnecessary things"; "I receive incompatible requests from two or more people"; and "I have to buck a rule or policy in order to carry

out an assignment" (Crane & Iwanicki, 1986, p. 26).

One suggestion for dealing with role conflict is to identify variables that are within your control. Jones (1987) recommends knowing the difference between stressful work features that are controllable and modifiable and those that are inherent to the workplace. Beasley, Myette, and Serna (1983) asked administrators to examine the feasibility of changing certain stress-producing factors identified by special and regular education teachers. The administrators marked the following identified stressors as impossible to change: class size, more pay, pay for additional work, more breaks during the year rather than the summer only, a 4-day week, and a few unrestricted leave days. However, administrators felt increased parent support, discipline support, more teacher assistants, and positive feedback were factors amenable to change.

■ ■ Activity

Examine the list of factors that administrators identified as impossible to change and interview two teachers who have taught for at least 3 years. Ask them to identify what factors they would like to see changed and which they feel they could change. ■ ■

Table 14.2
Suggested Interview Questions

1. Are any extra duties connected with the job?
2. Is there a provision for release time to write IEPs and annual reviews?
3. What is the discipline policy in terms of sending students to the office?
4. Is there a schoolwide discipline plan?
5. Are there any school committee responsiblities?
6. How many students are likely to be in the class?
7. What do you think I should accomplish within the year?
8. Is an aide assigned to the class? If so, for how many hours?
9. What is the school's position with regard to mainstreaming?

Another suggestion for dealing with role conflict is to examine the congruence between the school's philosophy and yours. Zabel, Boomer, and King (1984) warn that teachers who are unable to develop some degree of congruence may be expected to suffer stress leading to burnout. If you like to teach academic skills, you undoubtedly will not be satisfied with a job where only affective or social skills are taught. If you enjoy teaching students, you probably will not be satisfied with a situation where you work only with regular education teachers. For this reason, you need to identify your philosophy concerning goals (e.g., to mainstream all students), instructional techniques (e.g., to teach using peer

☐ Important Points

1. Role ambiguity results when teachers do not know what they are expected to do.
2. Asking questions during an interview and checking district or county procedures are two ways to handle ambiguity concerns.
3. Role conflict results when teachers disagree with what they are expected to do.
4. Suggestions for handling role conflict include identifying variables that are within a teacher's control and examining the congruence between philosophies.

---

tutoring techniques), curriculum content (e.g., to teach social skills mainly), management techniques (e.g., to use reality therapy with student contracts), and relationships with parents, administrators, and regular educators (e.g., to use parent volunteers, to team teach with the regular educator, to use the administrator as a discipline resource).

Once you are aware of your philosophy, you may find a tour of the school building helpful in determining the philosophical match. The materials, bulletin boards, and physical layout of the classroom often provide clues to the schoolwide philosophy. If *Reading Mastery, Distar Mathematics,* and *Spelling with Morphographs* texts are on the shelves, there is a poster with rules and consequences on the bulletin board, and there are many parent volunteers in the room, it is safe to assume that the school philosophy involves direct teaching as the preferred instructional technique, teaching of basic skills as the curriculum content, assertive discipline as the management system, and active parent involvement. If instead, your philosophy includes whole language as the preferred instructional technique, teaching of thinking skills and strategies as the curriculum content, token systems as the management system, and parent involvement only through parent conferences, there is a definite lack of congruence and a possible source of stress.

In conclusion, you must resolve both role ambiguity and conflict in order to reduce stress. To paraphrase a saying from Reinhold Niebuhr (1943), "Give me the serenity to accept the things I cannot change, the courage to change the things I can, and the wisdom to know the difference."

■ ■ Activity
Identify your philosophy concerning goals, instructional techniques, curriculum preferences, management techniques, and preferred relationships with parents, administrators, and regular educators. Look back at the classroom described in the preceding text (*Reading Mastery* materials and so on). Does your philosophy match? ■ ■

Personal Solutions
As long as stress-producing factors exist in special education, you will be faced with the threat of stress and potential burnout. Ultimately, you must develop and implement personal solutions for coping with potential burnout.

Relaxation
Relaxation usually involves practicing tension regimentation or visual imagery. To use muscle tensing as a means of relaxation, find a quiet area, close your eyes, and breathe slowly and deeply. As you are breathing deeply, tighten different muscle groups, hold the tightness for 8 seconds, and then release. The muscle groups in the feet, legs, abdomen, chest, neck, face, hands, and arms are first tensed and then relaxed. Once all

of the muscle groups are tensed and relaxed, search for more tenseness and relax those muscles.

To use visual imagery, think of a relaxing or positive situation (e.g., being in a favorite room) or setting (e.g., relaxing on the beach watching the ocean). Now, elaborate on the images (e.g., looking around that favorite room or feeling the ocean breeze blowing softly). Soon, the positive images replace the feelings of stress. At this time, you may also focus on a word that is associated with or synonymous with relaxation, such as *serenity*. Schloss, Sedlak, Wiggins, and Ramsey (1983) found that teachers who were trained in relaxation along with systematic desensitization techniques were able to reduce the stress associated with aggression management of adolescents with severe behavior disorders.

Compartmentalized Thinking

Another personal management strategy, compartmentalized thinking, involves a separation between work-related and personal events. Put simply, it involves leaving school problems at school and learning to enjoy vacations or weekends free of school concerns. When asked how she escaped burnout, one very effective teacher of adolescents with severe problem behaviors replied, "I care about my students when I am with them, but I do not talk about any of them or their problems when I get home." It would appear that this teacher has learned to compartmentalize her thinking.

Detached Concern

A related personal management strategy, detached concern, provides a balance between involvement and nonattachment. Potter (1987) describes this strategy in a story about the Nobel Prize-winning nun, Mother Theresa. When asked by a reporter how she was able to work with sick children who would die in spite of her efforts, she replied, "We love them while they are here." Mother Theresa loved and cared for the children, which shows concern, and yet, she let them go when they died, which shows detach-

ment. Similarly, teachers show detached concern when they work hard with students in school (concern), helping them reach their potentials and yet let them go at the end of the day (detachment) without dwelling on the things over which they have no control.

Personal Time

Assigning some time in the day for oneself is another way to alleviate stress. Alschuler (1984) suggests activities, such as sitting in the park on the way home from school or soaking in a hot tub after a long day, or developing a positive addiction, such as jogging or exercising. Bradfield and Fones (1985) found that teachers with less stress tended to exercise more than those with a high degree of stress. For other teachers, an entertaining movie, a good book, or a nice dinner may help relieve stress (Fimian, 1986).

Cognitive Restructuring

Cognitive restructuring involves altering the way you think about situations in order to alter negative emotional reactions (Casteel & Matthews, 1984). A teacher who focuses on the one weakness instead of the many strengths in the principal's evaluation is demonstrating a thinking process that produces negative emotions. The focus should be redirected to the many positive comments. Thought halting is another technique to alter negative emotional reactions (Cautela & Groden, 1978). In thought halting, simply say, "stop" or create a picture of a stop sign whenever a negative thought presents itself. A final technique to guide your thoughts in a positive direction is that of thinking powerfully, suggested by Potter (1987) in her telling of the Zen Story, *The Muddy Road.*

> Two monks were walking along a muddy road when they came upon a beautiful woman unable to cross the road without getting her silk shoes muddy. Without saying a word, the first monk picked up the woman and carried her across the road, leaving her on the

☐ Important Points

1. Teachers must develop and implement personal solutions for coping with stress.
2. Personal management strategies include relaxation, compartmentalized thinking, detached concern, attention to personal time, and cogitive restructuring.
3. Relaxation techniques include tension regimentation (tightening and relaxing the muscles) and visual imagery (visualizing positive and relaxing situations).
4. Compartmentalized thinking is the separation between work-related and personal events.
5. Detached concern is the balance of involvement and nonattachment.
6. Attention to personal time involves assigning some time during the day for activities such as walking, jogging, seeing a movie, going to dinner, or soaking in a hot tub.
7. Cognitive restructuring involves changing the way you think about something to change your negative reaction to it.

---

other side. Then the two monks continued walking without talking until the end of the day. When they reached their destination, the second monk said, "You know monks are to avoid women, why did you pick up that woman this morning?" The first monk replied, "I left her on the side of the road. Are you still carrying her?" (p. 66)

This story reminds us not to continually dwell on our worries, frustrations, and problems. Potter believes that if you think powerless thoughts, you will be depressed, frustrated, and angry. If you think powerful thoughts, you will feel positive, confident, and energized.

■ ■ Activity

Practice using relaxation techniques. Utilize both the muscle-tensing routine and the visual imagery techniques described in the chapter. Tell how you felt before and after using these methods of stress reduction. ■ ■

Summary

In this chapter, we examined causes and symptoms of stress and presented some suggestions to alleviate it. The common factors of stress were grouped into the following categories: time demands, behavior or discipline problems, interpersonal concerns, and unclear role expectations.

Excessive time demands include such factors as inadequate preparation time, clerical work, deadlines, and overwhelming workload. Special educators who cannot handle time constraints frequently enter meetings late, miss deadlines, and feel as though they are drowning in a sea of paper. Time analysis, goal setting, prioritization, delegation, and organizational action were discussed as solutions for time management problems.

The discussion of excessive time demands was followed by a discussion of the stress caused by student behavior problems and concerns about discipline. You may prevent many problem behaviors by making wise instructional decisions concerning materials, lesson presentation, motivational techniques, and the routines and procedures. In the rest of the section, we described how to select, teach, prompt, and enforce rules. Guidelines for establishing effective rules include incorporating student input, basing rules on acceptable behaviors, stating rules positively, making rules specific, changing rules when necessary, and relating rules to IEP objectives.

We presented stressors categorized as interpersonal concerns, such as lack of supervisory and administrative support. We suggested ways to improve communication with supervisors and administrators, ways to form social and support groups, and ways to use peer coaching to resolve stress due to interpersonal concerns. Support groups are informal groups of people who meet on a regular basis to provide personal support to coworkers. Peer coaching is a supportive arrangement between teachers who observe and confer with each other for the purpose of improving their teaching skills.

In the next section, we dealt with role ambiguity and role conflict and their relationship to stress. Role ambiguity is a confusion about the responsibilities of the job, and role conflict is a discrepancy between perceptions of teachers and others.

In the last section, we dealt with personal solutions to stress. Ultimately, *you* must take control of stress by implementing techniques such as those provided in this chapter.

Appendix A
Ethnic Groups

In this appendix, we furnish some background information regarding the immigrations of various ethnic groups to the United States. Our purpose in including this appendix is to heighten your awareness of the history of the various cultural groups that comprise the population of our country. We follow with some information concerning each group in today's society.

African-Americans

African-Americans have a history different from that of most immigrants, as for the most part, they did not have a choice about settling in the United States. The first Africans to reach the Americas were explorers. Diego El Negro was a member of Christopher Columbus's crew, and Estevanico, a Moor, arrived in America in 1529 and explored present-day New Mexico and Arizona (Banks, 1987). Africans also helped establish St. Augustine, Florida.

The first Africans to settle in the United States came in 1619 as indentured servants, which meant they eventually earned their freedom. For economic reasons, some colonists decided to replace black indentured servants with slaves, as slaves were bound to the master forever. Separated from families and homelands, the slaves developed a new culture from their African heritage and experience in the new land (Gollnick & Chinn, 1990). The black church became the cornerstone of the black heritage (Ghent, 1988). In the North, slaves often worked as laborers, house servants, and skilled artisans, and many of them later purchased their freedom. In the South, slaves frequently worked as farm hands on large plantations. After the Civil War, African-Americans eventually migrated to northern cities to obtain industrial jobs. They frequently congregated in ethnic groups in the cities.

Today, African-American communities can be found isolated in numerous northern, eastern, and western cities (Banks, 1987; Gollnick & Chinn, 1990). The racial ideology of Anglo-American culture tends to hinder the assimilation of African-Americans into the mainstream (Gollnick & Chinn, 1990). Although there currently is a large middle class, the number of African-Americans at the poverty level is still very high (Gollnick & Chinn, 1990).

According to Edelman (1987) black children compared to white children are:

> twice as likely to
> die in the first year of life
> live in substandard housing
> have no parent employed
> three times as likely to
> live in a female-headed family
> be in foster care
> four times as likely to
> be murdered before one year of age
> or as a teenager be incarcerated between fifteen and nineteen; and
> five times as likely to
> be dependent on welfare. (p. 5)

Even though the achievement scores in math and reading of African-Americans have increased (Ascher, 1987), according to many black professionals (Wilson, 1989), racism in many public schools takes the "form of low expectations and low demands on African-American students" (p. 138). African-American students are currently overrepresented in vocational and general tracks and underrepresented in the academic (Ascher, 1987).

Asian and Pacific Americans (APA)

Asian and Pacific Americans living in the United States represent twenty-nine distinct ethnic groups with many within-group differences (D. Chan, 1987). The three largest groups are Chinese, Japanese, and Filipino. The newest groups are Indochinese, represented mostly by Vietnamese, Cambodians, and Laotians.

The three largest groups migrated to the United States for economic reasons, while the Indochinese came due to the ending of the Vietnam War and the establishment of communist governments in the region. In the 1800s, the Chinese came to work the railroads and to supply a cheap labor force to the developing western states. According to Banks (1987), "Almost single-handedly, the Chinese labor force built the Pacific portion of the transcontinental railroad" (p. 420). A majority were Cantonese, from Southern China or Gwongtung Province (D. Chan, 1987). When Chinese immigration was severely limited by the U.S. government, Japanese immigrants replaced the labor void in the West. The largest number of Japanese immigrants arrived between 1891 and 1924 (Banks, 1987). When Japanese immigration was severely limited, plantation owners in Hawaii and large-farm owners on the West Coast turned to the Philippines for cheap labor.

The U.S. government supported immigration of the Indochinese beginning in 1975 by establishing refugee camps to assist in the transition to American life (Banks, 1987). The first wave included the baby-lift children who came to live with foster parents, whereas the second wave, from 1978 to 1981, included the boat people who many times had to wait a long period in refugee camps for resettlement and frequently led chaotic lives while trying to survive (Leung, 1989). During the stay in the refugee camps, many youth did not attend schools, as most refugee camps did not have schools (Grossman, 1990). These immigrants were resettled into various states, but they are currently moving to urban centers where other Asian-Americans are located (Leung, 1989).

Two thirds of all Asian-Americans live in Hawaii, California, and New York (Ascher, 1987). Many live in ethnic communities in urban centers such as Chinatown in San Francisco. There are many wage earners in Asian-American families, and many Asian-Americans work more hours per week than members of any other group (Ascher, 1987). Although many of the earlier immigrants are currently middle class, newer immigrants are poorer. Sixty-five percent of the Vietnamese, 76% of the Laotians, and 82% of the Cambodians live below the poverty line (Chinn & Plata, 1987).

As a group, Asians are frequently pointed out as the "model minority" (Ascher, 1987, p. 9). More than a proportional number appear in the gifted category of exceptional education (Chan & Kitano, 1987) and have attained "high achievement records in mathematics and science and attend college at a rate disproportionately higher than other groups" (Gollnick & Chinn, 1990, p. 99). However, Asian-Americans for whom English is not the primary language are often assigned to lower academic tracks (Ascher, 1987).

Hispanics

Basically, four distinct groups comprise the Hispanic population: Central Americans, Cuban-Americans, Mexican-Americans, and Puerto Ricans. The population is concentrated in the nine states of Arizona, California, Colorado, Florida, Illinois, New Mexico, New Jersey, New York, and Texas (Dew, 1984). A high concentration of Cubans live in Florida; Puerto Ricans, in Illinois, New Jersey, and New York; and Mexican-Americans in California and Texas (Orum, 1986). In fact, in the state of Texas, 34% of school children and approximately half of all kindergarten children are Mexican-Americans (Hyland, 1989).

The pattern of and reasons for immigration of the various groups differed. Many Mexican-Americans remained in the United States after the Mexican-American War, which ceded Texas and other states of the Southwest to the United States. Of the 80,000 Mexicans who lived in the territory ceded to the United States in 1848, only 3,000 moved to the Mexican side of the border after the war (Banks, 1987). Even though many of the Mexicans owned land at the time, various United States laws stripped the Mexicans of land ownership (Banks, 1987). Thus, by the turn of the century, Mexicans were made foreigners within their original homeland (Banks, 1987) and an oppressed minority (Gollnick & Chinn, 1990). Other Mexicans came to America to seek jobs. Between 1910 and 1930, one million Mexican immigrants were needed for agricultural labor in the Southwest. However, when the Great Depression hit in 1929, more than 64,000 Mexican aliens were returned to Mexico. Since then, large numbers of undocumented Mexicans have entered the United States as farm laborers.

The Puerto Ricans also migrated to the United States for economic reasons. In 1917, Puerto Ricans became citizens of the United States. Puerto Ricans began migrating to the United States in significant numbers between World War I and World War II. When the United States economy is booming, Puerto Rican migration usually increases, but it decreases when the economy is bad (Banks, 1987). Many Puerto Ricans find jobs in the blue-collar and service areas (Banks, 1987).

The Cubans migrated to the United States in two waves. The first came for political reasons to escape the Castro revolution of 1959. These immigrants were often from the middle and upper classes. In 1980, the second wave of Cubans entered the United States via a boatlift from Mariel. These immigrants were often single males and blue-collar workers. Less than 5% of these immigrants committed serious crimes or suffered mental or physical problems (Banks, 1987).

Most Hispanics live in urban areas in racially isolated neighborhoods. Seventy-one percent live in homes with females as head of the household, and 38.7% live at the poverty level, according to the 1984 census (Valero-Figueira, 1988). The 1984 census also recorded 13% below the poverty level for Cubans, 42% for Puerto Ricans, and 24% for Mexican-Americans (Hyland, 1989). The school dropout rate of Hispanics (about 40%) is higher than that for either white Americans (14%) or African-Americans (25%) (Yates, 1989). Many Mexican-Americans fail to go beyond sixth grade (Hyland, 1989).

Native Americans

The Native American culture is very diverse. There are 2,200 different languages and various occupations, from agriculture to hunting and fishing (Banks, 1987). The Native American population includes the American Indians, Eskimos, and Aleuts. There are many similarities in the beliefs held by various tribes (Banks, 1987). The Native American culture values and shares a deep respect and reverence for the earth and other living things. Indians believed people could use the earth as long as they treated it with respect and that no human could own the earth (Banks, 1987). The Indian culture as a whole also believed in the dignity of the individual and a respect for individual rights. The leaders in most tribes other than the Incas had little authority over their followers. Behaviors were limited by the tribal council (Banks, 1987). Thus, the signing of a treaty by the chief did not necessarily mean that everyone in the tribe would abide by the signature.

In the early days, a routine pattern of relationship existed between the American Indians and the Europeans (Banks, 1987). First, a trading relationship was formed, where the Indians supplied the Europeans with furs. This was followed by the Indians fighting other Indians to reach fur-producing animals. When the fur trade was depleted, the whites wanted the Indian land. The Indians fought and lost, signing treaties that were frequently dissolved by the whites. The Indians were moved farther west to new lands. Eventually, the Native Americans were forced into segregation from the Anglo-American culture, as they were moved into reservations, typically far from their historical geographical locations (Gollnick & Chinn, 1990).

Currently, most American Indians live on reservations in twenty states. Harrington (1984) reports that poverty is extreme, life expectancy is 20 years less than the expectancy for whites, and unemployment rates are high. The Native American dropout rate is as high as 55% (Gollnick & Chinn, 1990). American Indians are significantly underrepresented in science, mathematics, and technology-related careers (Gollnick & Chinn, 1990). Recently, tribes are attempting to attain the full benefits of United States citizenship, fighting in the courts to uphold the terms of many of the treaties. They are a unique minority group, as the tribes frequently own land with many rich resources (Banks, 1987).

Information Sources

We list the following sources of information for students who wish to learn more about various multicultural groups.

1. Tribal councils, such as the *Navajo Tribal Council*, Window Rock, AZ, or the *Zuni Tribal Council*, Zuni People, NM.

2. Culture and language study centers, such as *Alaska Native Language Center*, Fairbanks, AK; *Language and Intercultural Research Center*, Brigham Young University, Provo, UT; or *Information Center on Children's Cultures*, 331 E. 38th St., New York, NY 10016.

3. *National Association for Bilingual Education*, Room 405, 1201 16th St., NW, Washington, DC 20036.

4. *National Clearinghouse for Bilingual Education*, 11501 Georgia Ave., Suite 100, Wheaton, MD 20902.

5. *Center for Applied Linguistics*, 1118 222 St., NW, Washington, DC 20037.

6. *Bureau of Indian Affairs*, Department of Interior, Superintendent of Documents, U.S. Government Printing Office, Washington, DC 20402.

7. *The American Indian Museum of Natural History*, Central Park West & 79th St., New York, NY 10024.

8. *National Museum of the American Indian, A Smithsonian Institution*, Broadway at 155th St., New York, NY 10032.

9. *Trends and Issues in Urban and Minority Education*, 1987 (Trends and Issues Series No. 6) ($3.00 a copy). ERIC Clearinghouse on Urban Education, Box 40, Teachers College, Columbia University, New York, NY 10027.

10. *News Digest* (#9): *"Minority Issues in Special Education: A Portrait of the Future."* Free copies can be requested by contacting the National Information Center for Children and Youth with Handicaps, 7926 Jones Branch Dr., Suite 1100, McLean, VA 22101; (703) 893-6061.

11. *The Council for Exceptional Children*, Publications Department, 1920 Association Dr., Reston, VA 22091, has many books available concerning students with special needs from various cultural backgrounds.

Appendix B
Software for Survival
by Eileen Pracek

Developing a list of recommended software for you and the children or adolescents you teach is an awesome task. To be useful, such a list must take into consideration (a) the various types and models of computers which you might encounter, (b) the many ways software can be used as a tool to support and enhance curriculum, and (c) the many sources of software which might be tapped for student and teacher use, including free and inexpensive programs. Above all, the list must take into account the rapidly evolving, always changing nature of the technology media.

For example, as this list is being compiled, the Macintosh has made a serious attempt to become the school computer of choice for the Apple product line while IBM, Tandy, and Apple are bringing more total curriculum software support into schools through networking. Hypermedia has opened up a whole new world of options as teachers create rich, multimedia learning environments by linking software and hardware with available media such as videotape, videodisc, and 35 mm film.

Also, it is impossible to create such a list without demonstrating some personal preferences as to how computers should be used in the classroom. This list demonstrates a preference for the use of computers as a tool and encourages you to take full advantage of the multisensory environ-

Eileen Pracek is project coordinator for FDLRS/TECH, a specialized center in the FDLRS (Florida Diagnostic Learning Resources System) network.

ment possible with the computer. In addition, this list may assist you in using the computer to reach students through a variety of interests and abilities, including art and music, and to consider the full capabilities of the computer as a tool for assisting students with higher level thinking and problem solving skills.

Key for Identification of Levels:
- R = Readiness (Kindergarten)
- P = Primary (First–Third Grade)
- I = Intermediate (Fourth–Sixth Grade)
- M = Middle (Sixth–Eighth Grade)
- S = Secondary (Ninth–Twelfth Grade)
- A = Adult

All-Purpose Tools

You and your students will find many ways to use programs which allow you to create professional looking products which meet a variety of classroom needs. These tools help you and your students to reinforce specific subject matter through computer-generated games or products. Each of these programs has some feature which allows for creating or entering one's own data.

The Print Shop—Broderbund (Apple, MS-DOS, Commodore, Macintosh)
For many years this program has proved invaluable to both teachers and students for creating banners, signs, cards for all occasions, covers for

reports, awards and weekly monthly calendars. Hundreds of graphics are available both commercially and in the public domain. (P–A)

The Children's Writing and Publishing Center — The Learning Company (Apple, MS-DOS)
An easy-to-use but sophisticated desktop publishing program which allows students and teachers to mix text and graphics to create professional looking reports and newsletters. With its built-in processor, it readily supports process writing and whole language activities. (P–A)

Certificates and More — Mindscape/SVE (Apple, MS-DOS)
With this versatile utility, teachers and students can create certificates for all occasions from the templates provided, or design original ones. The program will also generate such items as game boards, calendars, charts, checklists and number lines. (P–A)

Crossword Magic — Mindscape (Apple, MS-DOS, Commodore)
This program creates crossword puzzles which may be worked on the screen, printed, and/or saved to disk. Teachers and students enter the words, write the clues, and edit the format for the interconnecting words arranged by the computer. (I–A)

The Game Show — Advanced Ideas (Apple, MS-DOS, Commodore)
A classic which uses the TV game show Password's format to reinforce vocabulary and thinking skills. One or two students, or two teams of students can compete to solve the mystery word. Teachers and students can create their own games. Additional subject disks are also available. (I–A)

Word Processors

For students who have difficulty writing, learning to use a word processor may be considered a basic skill. For computer-using teachers, the word processor is an indispensable tool for cre-

ating classroom materials. Although new programs and new versions of old programs continue to appear, here are some which teachers have consistently recommended.

Appleworks — Claris (Apple)
This integrated word processor, database, and spreadsheet has been widely used by students in grades 7–12 to create professional looking documents, and by teachers for all types of tasks needed to manage student information and grades, develop curriculum materials, and prepare classroom budgets. (I–A)

Dr. Peet's TalkWriter — Hartley (Apple)
This talking program takes young learners from letter recognition to simple word processing. The introductory disk has large, screen-size letters and sings all menus and commands, as well as the ABC Song. Requires the Echo speech synthesizer. (R–P)

FrEdWriter — Public Domain (Apple)
This public domain word processor was developed specifically for educational use and may be freely copied. It allows teachers to create writing (or other curricular) activities through the use of on-screen prompts. A number of student activities are also available, as is a Spanish version. (P–A)

Listen to Learn — IBM
This is a talking word processor for the IBM which may be used by elementary students. It requires a speech adaptor for 3.5 inch or an Echo IBM PC or other compatible speech synthesizer and appropriate adaptor for 5.25 inch version. (R–I)

Magic Slate II — Sunburst (Apple)
Available in 20-, 40-, or 80-column format, this word processor for the Apple series grows with the students. The 20-column version features large letters, a picture menu, and simple commands. The 40- and 80-column versions offer more features and typestyles. The program includes an excellent teacher's guide. (P–A)

Microsoft Works 2.0 — Microsoft — (Macintosh)
This easy-to-use, integrated program offers a word processing, database, spreadsheet, desktop publishing, and telecommunications (with a modem). The word processor includes such features as newspaper-type column formatting, different fonts, page preview and a spelling checker. (I–A)

Word Processing for Kids — Public Domain (IBM)
This program was designed to teach students how to use a word processor. It explains the function of various keys and invites students to write and print their own stories. (P–I)

Curriculum Support

Although the quality of programs available to support and enhance curriculum continues to improve, the quantity is mind boggling. Here is a sampling of programs which address those academic areas with which students with special needs continue to have difficulty. For effective use, these programs must be matched to student levels and interests, and curriculum needs. You need to choose from these lists carefully and preview the programs to be sure they match the needs of your students.

Mathematics
Bake and Taste — Mindplay (Apple, MS-DOS)
A tasty way for students to learn to use fractions for measuring, this program also has them reading for detail, following directions, and problem solving as they organize, measure and bake desserts for company. This is an excellent program for cooperative learning for students in grades 1–9. (P–M)

Box Solves Story Problems — SVE (Apple)
A multimedia package in which Box solves perplexing word problems by applying math skills and some secrets which include reading, visualizing, noting clue words, and focusing on questions and important facts. Filmstrips provide an excellent tutorial in problem-solving skills. (I–M)

Clock — Hartley (Apple, MS-DOS)
An easy-to-use program for students who are learning to tell time. Students select the appropriate level from hour, half-hour, quarter-hour, 5-minute, or 1-minute intervals for exercises. They can manipulate the hands of an on-screen clock or type in the time to see it displayed on a digital clock. (P–M)

DLM Math Fluency Program Series — DLM (Apple)
A well-researched series that helps students learn automatic math fact recall by way of a structured, systematic development of ability which must come prior to customary drill and practice activities. The program requires regular 10-minute sessions which include built-in periodic assessment, instruction of nonfluent facts, and practice of fluent facts. (P–M)

Hands-On Math Series — Ventura Educational Systems (Apple, MS-DOS, Macintosh)
These programs combine the use of concrete materials for teaching math concepts with the use of the computer. Students can explore math with the use of rods, counters, tiles, chips, tangrams, and a geoboard in the electronic playground, or choose a specific manipulative which has exercises related to it. (P–S)

Homework Helper: Math Word Problems — Spinnaker (Apple, MS-DOS, Commodore)
This program provides tutorials and practice on solving the categories of word problems commonly found in pre-Algebra or Algebra I curricula. It teaches a step-by-step method for translating English sentences into mathematical equations. (M–S)

How the West Was One + Three × Four — Sunburst (Apple, MS-DOS)
A motivating game environment for students to review and practice order of operations and learn the significance of parentheses in arithmetic expression. The program adjusts to the student's skill entry level and provides hints to improve their problem-solving skills by suggesting game strategies. (I–S)

Math Blaster Plus—Davidson (Apple, MS-DOS)
Students can increase speed and accuracy with this highly motivating program. The program has four different learning activities which cover more than 600 facts in addition, subtraction, multiplication, division, fractions, decimals, and percents. It includes an easy-to-use editor and student record keeping. (P–S)

Math Concepts I and II—Hartley (Apple, MS-DOS)
Level I helps students learn and practice such concepts as before and after, odd and even, more or less, smallest to largest, less than and greater than, and regrouping. Level II works on such concepts as rounding, prime numbers, place value, greatest common factor and least common multiple. (I–S)

Math Shop Series—Scholastic (Apple, MS-DOS, Macintosh)
Set in shopping malls, these programs have students practice math skills in a real world setting as they complete transactions in different stores. Programs adjust to students' skill levels and include *Math Shop Jr.* (Grades 1–4), *Math Shop* (4–8), *Algebra Shop, Weights and Measures, Fractions and Decimals.* (I–S)

Mechanics of Word Problems—The Ellen Nelson Learning Library (Apple, MS-DOS)
Students learn the six-step method for solving word problems and practice problem solving with addition, subtraction, multiplication, and division. The program uses "clue" words to help students identify the type of math operation to use. (I–S)

Money—Gamco (Apple, MS-DOS, Commodore)
Students can select problems at various levels to count money, decide what they can purchase with a given amount of money, determine the least number of coins needed to make a transaction and how much change should be given. Helpful for teaching "transition to real world" skills. (I–S)

Zero in on Zero—DLM (Apple, MS-DOS)
Available for addition and subtraction or multiplication and division, these programs help students work problems containing one or more zeros. Two levels of guided help are available when students give incorrect responses. The program prints worksheets with problems in vertical or horizontal format. (P–S)

Language Arts

Breakthrough to Language—Creative Learning (Apple)
Using a multisensory approach, this program teaches early reading skills. Students select responses on the Touch Window in response to spoken directions from the Echo speech synthesizer as they proceed through well-sequenced instruction. Eight word packs in various categories are available. (R–S)

Capitalization—Hartley (Apple)
This program introduces the basic rules of capitalization for such topics as proper personal names, titles, days of the week, months, and holidays and provides mastery tests for the items on a second disk. Most students can operate the program independently. The program keeps student records and may be modified. (P–S)

Core Reading and Vocabulary Development—Educational Activities (Apple, MS-DOS)
Designed for the older student who is a beginning reader, the program begins with 35 basic words and progresses to over 200 words through various activities. An optional speech component pronounces featured words for each lesson. A Spanish version is available. (M–A)

Diascriptive Language Arts—Educational Activities (Apple, MS-DOS)
This tutorial program diagnoses, prescribes, and develops skills in such areas as sentence mechanics, sentence sense, nouns, verbs, adjectives, and pronouns. Students with a 3.5 reading level can work through 36 progressive developmental programs to improve skills and concepts. (M–A)

Explor-a-Series—William K. Bradford—(Apple, MS-DOS, Macintosh)
These programs engage students with colorful, animated stories in a variety of content areas. The programs empower students to create their own stories by easily manipulating characters, objects, backgrounds, and text. Students become excited participants in the reading and writing process. (P–M)

Kittens, Kids, and a Frog—Hartley (Apple, MS-DOS)
Eighteen animal stories are included with questions designed to develop factual and inferential comprehension for elementary students. *Chariots, Cougars, and Kings* and *New Kid on the Block* continue to build on comprehension skills and appeal to older students. (P–I)

Monsters & Make-Believe—Pelican Software (Apple, MS-DOS, Macintosh)
This program, and any of the others from Pelican, stimulate and challenge students to create characters based on a specific theme and then write about their creation. A Spanish version and a talking version are available for the Apple. These programs are exciting additions to whole language units. (P–M)

Poetry Express—Mindscape (Apple)
This program helps students learn poetry forms. It gives them the basic formula for each style and guides them line-by-line through the process of creating verse in diamente, cinquain, limerick, haiku, sijo, rhyme, tanks, and lists and litanies. Students refine skills as they develop themes and create moods. (I–S)

Punctuation Put-On—Sunburst (Apple, MS-DOS)
Students practice placing punctuation marks in short passages in a game-like setting. The teacher controls punctuation options and may add new passages. Students may make judgments about using not-so-common punctuation marks. (I–S)

Reader Rabbit—The Learning Company (Apple, MS-DOS, Commodore)
A highly motivating program which focuses on three-letter words with a consonant-vowel-consonant pattern. Students sort words and move them onto a conveyor belt, label boxes marked with pictures, and load words into train cars as they practice phonetic reading skills. (P–I)

Reading Realities—Teacher Support Software (Apple, MS-DOS)
A "whole language" package which engages secondary students in real reading and therapeutic writing. This well-researched program guides students to think about ways other students have coped with teen problems and encourages them to problem-solve and write their own reactions to the situations presented. Reading level ranges from 2 through 6. (P–M)

Term Paper Writer—Personal Choice Software (Apple, MS-DOS, Commodore)
A multipurpose program to guide students in writing and formatting a term paper. It includes a notetaker, outliner, writer, footnotes, and bibliography compiler. It inserts footnotes on appropriate pages and automatically compiles a bibliography from notes. Works well as a cooperative learning activity. (M–S)

Who, What, Where, When, Why—Hartley (Apple, MS-DOS)
This classic helps build reading comprehension by providing sequenced practice on these critical concepts. Easy-to-read screens, helpful feedback, lessons which can be modified, and a management system make this a consistently valuable program. (P–S)

Word Attack!—Davidson (Apple, MS-DOS)
Students reading at a third grade level or above build vocabulary through a series of activities which include learning words and definitions, choosing definitions in a multiple choice format, completing sentences and playing a fast-paced arcade game for reinforcement. Content may be modified. (P–S)

Social Studies

Black Americans—Hartley (Apple, MS-DOS)
Students study and learn facts about some of our most influential black Americans in this program, which is one in the challenging *Medalistas-Series.* Content and point values can be modified in this series of programs, which includes such topics as presidents, women in history, and states. (M–S)

Choices, Choices Series—Tom Synder Productions (Apple, MS-DOS)
These simulations help students develop the skills and awareness they need to make wise choices. Students explore good and bad behavior as they work in groups with the teacher to set goals, consider consequences, make a decision, and realize consequences. This program, and others from Tom Synder, may be used effectively in a classroom with only one computer. (P–I)

Conversations with Great Americans Series—Focus Media (Apple)
Students look at history through the eyes of the people who lived it as they interview the men and women who shaped America's past. The program encourages students to explore various areas of personal interest as they interact with the characters who appear to come alive on the screen. (I–S)

Lollipop Dragon's World of Maps and Globes—SVE (Apple)
With four activities the Lollipop Dragon teaches young students to find their way around maps and globes. Students can create and print maps. The software supplements the four filmstrips which focus on reading scale and symbols, defining directions, recognizing different kinds of maps, and creating a map. (P–I)

Oregon Trail—MECC (Apple, MS-DOS)
In this classic students use their information-gathering and decision-making skills to travel safely across the United States by wagon train in 1848. Written at a fourth grade reading level, this simulation encourages students to talk to people they meet, hunt for food, overcome obstacles, and use map skills. (I–S)

PC Globe—PC Globe (MS-DOS)
This tool provides a computerized world atlas and database which features instant profiles and comparisons of 177 countries. The atlas includes world, continent, and country maps. The database categories include population, health statistics, economic data, national leaders, and tourist attractions. A computerized USA atlas and database is also available. (M–S)

See the USA—CompuTeach (Apple, MS-DOS)
Students learn the states and capitals as they travel across the country. A geography quiz game offers several options including famous places and people. Although the program requires students to spell out names of states and capitals, it offers aids. A USA puzzle and map are included. (P–M)

Social Studies Explorer Series—Mindscape (Apple, MS-DOS)
The adventure format of this series allows students to explore and identify a historical *Event in the American History Set,* and identify the state or country they're visiting in the *World Geography Set.* Students experience the spirit of discovery as they learn curriculum and develop problem-solving skills. (M–S)

Stickybear Town Builder—Weekly Reader (Apple, Commodore)
Students create their own towns and use them to learn about map symbols, distances, and directions. They can drive a purple car to as many places as possible before running out of gas, or play a hide-and-seek activity. The program shows objects as they look from an aerial perspective. (P–I)

USA Geograph—MECC (Apple)
This allows students to view the entire United States, individual states, or regions with 30 maps and manipulate 80 categories of information in the database. Database information can be viewed and printed. Maps can be printed in color with an Imagewriter II printer and a color ribbon. (I–S)

Where in the World Is Carmen San Diego?—
Broderbund (Apple, MS-DOS, Commodore)
Students explore great cities of the world as they pursue Carmen and her band of thieves who have stolen the Statue of Liberty's torch. With 10 suspects, 30 cities, and 1,000 clues, students cooperate to take notes, use references, read for meaning, and sharpen decision-making skills. One of a series. (I–S)

Science

Audubon Wildlife Adventure Series—Advanced Ideas (Apple, MS-DOS)
These programs challenge students to become involved in environmental concerns as they track a grizzly bear through Yellowstone Park, catch wildlife poachers, track a whale migrating from Alaska to Baja California, and uncover the secrets of the mysterious shark. (I–S)

The Body System Series—Marshware (Apple)
These programs use creative activities and colorful graphics to help students learn about what happens to the food we eat in the digestive system, how air gets to the lungs in the respiratory system, the functions of the heart and the importance of keeping it healthy, and the intricacies of bones and muscles. (I–S)

Car Builder—Weekly Reader (Apple)
Students design, construct, refine and test the cars they build on the screen, and print their creation. The program includes wind tunnel and test track simulations to test the aerodynamics, racing, and fuel capabilities of the cars. A favorite of students interested in any aspect of cars. (I–S)

Colortrope—HRM (Apple, MS-DOS)
This program uses colored gels and crystal spheres to help students explore the basic principles of light and color. The monitor becomes a light source which students use to investigate how the screen produces the colors we see and how we can change those colors with filters. (I–M)

Operation Frog—Scholastic (Apple)
In this simulation, students dissect a frog. The program encourages students to apply scientific principles of logical analysis and synthesis as they learn biology and anatomy. (I–S)

Learn About Animals—Sunburst (Apple, MS-DOS)
Young students learn about animal life as they place animals in their homes, find their parents, count their babies, identify their way of moving, measure them and compare sizes, creatively explore their worlds, and write stories about their discoveries. They can create animals and print out animal masks for play. (P–I)

Science Toolkit Plus Series—Broderbund (Apple, MS-DOS)
Students use this series of programs which include probes and on-screen tools to perform computer-aided science experiments. The master module includes light and temperature probes, an experiment guide and teacher's manual. Other modules offer additional probes for studying speed and motion, harmonic and wave motion, and the human body. (M–S)

Software Publishers

Advanced Ideas, Inc.
2902 San Pablo Avenue
Berkeley, CA 94702
(415) 526-9100

Big Red Computer Club
423 Norfolk Avenue
Norfolk, NE 68701
(402) 379-4680

Broderbund Software
PO Box 12947
San Rafael, CA 94913-2947
1-800-521-6263

Claris
PO Box 526
Santa Clara, CA 95052
(408) 727-8227

CompuTeach
78 Olive Street
New Haven, CT 06511
1-800-44-TEACH or (203) 777-7738

Creative Learning, Inc.
PO Box 829
North San Juan, CA 95960
(916) 292-3001

DLM
PO Box 4000
One DLM Park
Allen, TX 75002
1-800-527-4747

Educational Activities, Inc.
PO Box 392
Freeport, NY 11520
1-800-645-3739

Focus Media
839 Stewart Avenue
PO Box 865
Garden City, NY 11530
1-800-645-8989

Gamco Industries, Inc.
Box 310J5
Big Spring, TX 79721
1-800-351-1404

Hartley Courseware, Inc.
PO Box 419
Dimondale, MI 48821
1-800-247-1380

HRM Software
Room Z1 01 02 03 04 05
175 Tompkins Avenue
Pleasantville, NY 10570-9973
1-800-431-2050

IBM
PC Software Department 999
One Culver Road
Dayton, NJ 08810
1-800-IBM-2468, ext. 999

MarshWare
PO Box 8082
Shawnee Mission, KS 66208
1-800-821-3303

MCE
1800 South 35th Street
Galesburg, MI 49053
1-800-421-4157

MECC
3490 Lexington Avenue North
St. Paul, MN 55126
1-800-228-3504 or (612) 481-3500

Mediagenic
3885 Bohannon Drive
Menlo Park, CA 94025
(415) 329-0800

Microsoft Corporation
16011 NE 36th Way
Box 97017
Redmond, WA 98073-9718
(206) 882-8080

Mindplay
Department C4
Unit 350, PO Box 36491
Tucson, AZ 85740
1-800-221-7911

Mindscape/SVE
Dept. D
1345 W. Diversey Parkway
Chicago, IL 60614
1-800-829-1900

PC Globe, Inc.
4700 South McClintock
Tempe, AZ 85282
(602) 730-9000

Pelican Software, Inc.
21000 Nordhoff Street
Chatsworth, CA 91311
1-800-247-4641

San Diego County Office of Education
FrEd, TEC Center
6401 Linda Vista Road
San Diego, CA 92111

Spinnaker Software Corp.
201 Broadway
Cambridge, MA 02139
1-800-826-0706

Sunburst Communications
101 Castleton Street
Pleasantville, NY 10570-3498
1-800-628-8897

SVE
Department VR
1345 Diversey Parkway
Chicago, IL 60614-1299
1-800-829-1900

Teacher Support Software
1035 NW 57th Street
Gainesville, FL 32605
1-800-228-2871 or (904) 332-6404

The Learning Company
6493 Kaiser Drive
Fremont, CA 94555
1-800-852-2255

Ventura Educational Systems
3440 Brokenhill Street
Newbury Park, CA 91320
1-800-336-1022

Weekly Reader Software
Optimum Resource, Inc.
10 Station Place
Norfolk, CT 06058
1-800-327-1473

William K. Bradford Publishing Co.
310 School Street
Acton, MA 01720
1-800-421-2009

References

Aaronson, S. (1975). Notetaking improvement: A combined auditory, functional, and psychological approach. *Journal of Reading, 19,* 8–12.

Abramowitz, J. (1979). *American history,* (5th ed.). Chicago, IL: Follett.

Adamson, D. R., Matthews, P., & Schuller, J. (1990). Promising programs to bridge the resource room to regular classroom gap. *Teaching Exceptional Children, 22*(2), 74–78.

Adelman, H. S., & Taylor, L. (1982). Enhancing the motivation and skills needed to overcome interpersonal problems. *Learning Disabilities Quarterly, 5,* 438–446.

Adelman, H. S., & Taylor, L. (1983). Enhancing motivation for overcoming learning and behavior problems. *Journal of Learning Disabilities, 16,* 384–392.

Alberto, P. A., & Troutman, A. C. (1990). *Applied behavior analysis for teachers* (3rd ed.). Columbus, OH: Merrill/Macmillan.

Albion, F. M. (1980, April). *Development and implementation of self-monitoring/self-instruction procedures in the classroom.* Paper presented at The Council for Exceptional Children's 58th annual international conference, Philadelphia.

Algozzine, B., & Maheady, L. (1986). When all else fails, teach? *Exceptional Children, 52*(6), 487–488.

Algozzine, B., Maheady, L., Sacca, K. C., O'Shea, L., & O'Shea, D. (1990). Sometimes patent medicine works: A reply to Braaten, Kauffman, Polsgrove, and Nelson. *Exceptional Children, 56*(6), 552–557.

Allen, V. L. (1976). The helping relationship and socialization of children: Some perspectives on tutoring. In V. L. Allen (Ed.) *Children as teachers: Theory and research on tutoring.* New York: Academic Press.

Alley, G. R., & Deshler, D. D. (1979). *Teaching students with learning problems.* (3rd ed.). Columbus, OH: Merrill/Macmillan.

Alley, G. R., Deshler, D. D., Clark, F. L., Schumaker, J. B. & Warner, M. M. (1983). Learning disabilities in adolescent and young adult populations: Research implications (part II). *Focus on Exceptional Children, 15*(9), 1–14.

Alschuler, A. S. (1984). Causes, consequences, and cures: A summary. In A. S. Alschuler, J. Carl, R. Leslie, I. Schweiger, & D. Unistal. *Teacher burnout.* Washington, DC: National Education Association.

Alschuler, A. S., Carl, J., Leslie, R., Schweiger, L., & Unistal, D. (1980). *Teacher burnout. Analysis and action series.* (ERIC Document Reproduction Service No. ED 201 640)

Altwerger, B., Edelsky, C., & Flores, B. M. (1987). Whole language: What's new. *The Reading Teacher, 41*(2), 144–152.

Alvermann, D. E. (1983). Putting the textbook in its place—Your students' hands. *Academic Therapy, 18*(3), 345–351.

Anderson, L., Evertson, C., & Brophy, J. (1979). An experimental study of effective teaching in first grade reading groups. *Elementary School Journal, 79,* 193–223.

Anderson, M. A. (1985). Cooperative group tasks and their relationship to peer acceptance and cooperation. *Journal of Learning Disabilities, 18*(2), 83–88.

Anderson, R. C., & Pearson, P. D. (1984). A schema-theoretic view of basic processes in reading. In P. D. Pearson (Ed.), *Handbook of reading research* (pp. 255–291). NY: Longman.

Anderson, T. H., & Armbruster, B. B. (1980). *Studying.* Technical Report No. 155, Arlington, VA. (ERIC Document Reproduction Service No. ED 181 427)

Anderson, T. H., & Armbruster, B. B. (1984). Studying. In P. D. Pearson (Ed.), *Handbook of reading research* (pp. 657–679). New York: Longman.

Anderson-Inman, L. (1986). Bridging the gap: Student-centered strategies for promoting the transfer of learning. *Exceptional Children,* 52(6), 562–572.

Annis, L., & Davis, J. K. (1978). Study techniques: Comparing their effectiveness. *The American Biology Teacher,* pp. 108–110.

Archer, A., & Gleason, M. (1989). *Skills for school success.* North Billerica, MA: Curriculum Associates.

Archer, A. L., & Isaacson, S. L. (1990). Teaching others how to teach strategies. *Teacher Education and Special Education,* 13(2), 63–72.

Argyle, M. (1975). The syntaxes of bodily communication. In J. Benthall & T. Polhemus (Eds.), *The body as a medium of expression* (pp. 143–161). New York: E. P. Dutton.

Armbruster, B. B., & Anderson, T. H. (1981). *Content area textbooks* (Reading Education Report No. 23). Urbana: University of Illinois, Center for the Study of Reading.

Aronson, E. (1978). *The jigsaw classroom.* Beverly Hills, CA: Sage.

Ascher, C. (1987). *Trends and issues in urban and minority education,* 1987. New York: ERIC Clearinghouse on Urban Education.

Atkinson, R. C. (1975). Mnemotechnics in second-language learning. *American Psychologist, 30,* 821–828.

Au, K. H., Scheu, J. A., Kawakami, A. J., & Herman, P. A. (1990). Assessment and accountability in a whole literacy curriculum. *The Reading Teacher, 43*(8), 574–581.

Ausubel, D. P. (1968). *Educational psychology: A cognitive view.* New York: Holt, Rinehart, & Winston.

Ausubel, D. P., & Robinson, F. G. (1969). *School learning: An introduction to educational psychology.* New York: Holt, Rinehart, & Winston.

Ayllon, T., & Roberts, M. D. (1974). Eliminating discipline problems by strengthening academic performance. *Journal of Applied Behavior Analysis, 7,* 71–76.

Ayllon, T., Layman, D., & Burke, S. (1972). Disruptive behavior and reinforcement of academic performance, *The Psychological Record, 22,* 315–322.

Babcock, N. L., & Pryzwansky, W. B. (1983). Models of consultation: Preferences of education professionals at five stages of service. *Journal of School Psychology, 21,* 356–359.

Baca, L. M., & Cervantes, H. T. (1989). *The bilingual special education interface* (2nd ed.). Columbus, OH: Merrill/Macmillan.

Bailis, P., & Hunter, M. (1985, August). Do your words get them to think? *Learning,* p. 43.

Baker, G. C. (1983). *Planning and organizing for multicultural instruction.* Reading, MA: Addison-Wesley.

Baker, L., & Brown, A. L. (1980). *Metacognitive skills and reading* (Technical Report No. 188). Urbana: University of Illinois, Center for the Study of Reading.

Bakewell, D., McConnell, S. R., Ysseldyke, J. E., & Christenson, S. L. (1988). *Teacher stress and student achievement for mildly handicapped students.* (Research Report No. 13). Minneapolis: University of Minnesota, Instructional Alternatives Project.

Balajthy, E. (1989). The printout: Holistic approaches to reading. *The Reading Teacher, 42*(4), 324.

Bandura, A. (1977). *Social learning theory.* Englewood Cliffs, NJ: Prentice-Hall.

Banks, J. A. (1987). *Teaching strategies for ethnic students* (4th ed.). Boston: Allyn & Bacon.

Barker, L. L. (1971). *Listening behavior.* Englewood Cliffs, NJ: Prentice-Hall.

Barron, R. F. (1969). The use of vocabulary as an advance organizer. In H. L. Herber & P. L. Sanders (Eds.), *Research on reading in the content area: First-year report.* Syracuse, NY: University Press.

Baskwill, J., & Whitman, P. (1988). *New direction-evaluation: Whole language, whole child.* NY: Scholastic.

Bauman, J. (1986). Effects of rewritten content textbook passages on middle grade students' comprehension of main ideas: Making the inconsiderate considerate. *Journal of Reading Behavior, 18*(1), 1–21.

Bauwens, J., Hourcade, J. J., & Friend, M. (1989). Cooperative teaching: A model for general and special education integration. *Remedial and Special Education, 10*(2), 17–22.

Baxter, J. (1970). Interpersonal spacing in natural settings. *Sociometry, 33*, 44.

Bayes, M., & Neill, T. K. (1978). Problems for paraprofessionals in mental health services. *Administration in Mental Health, 6*, 133–146.

Beale, A., & Beers, C. S. (1982). What do you say to parents after you say hello? *Teaching Exceptional Children, 15*(1), 34–39.

Beaseley, C. R., Myette, B. M., & Serna, B. (1983, April). *On the job stress and burnout: Contributing factors and environmental alternatives in educational settings.* Paper presented at the Annual Meeting of the American Educational Research Association, Montreal.

Bellezza, F. S. (1983). Mnemonic-device instruction with adults. In M. Pressley & J. R. Levin (Eds.), *Cognitive strategy research: Psychological foundations* (pp. 51–73). New York: Springer-Verlag.

Belpre, P. (1973). *Once in Puerto Rico.* NY: Wame.

Benavides, A. (1989). High-risk predictors and prereferral screening for language-minority students. In A. A. Ortiz & B. A. Ramirez (Eds.), *Schools and the culturally diverse exceptional student: Promising practices and future directions* (pp. 19–31). Reston, VA: The Council for Exceptional Children.

Bender, W. N. (1984). Daily grading in mainstream classes. *The Directive Teacher, 6*(2), 4–7.

Benz, M. R., & Halpern, A. S. (1986). Vocational preparation for high school students with mild disabilities: A statewide study of administrator, teacher, and parent perceptions. *Career Development of Exceptional Individuals, 9*, 3–15.

Berdine, W. H., & Cegelka, P. T. (1980). *Teaching the trainable retarded.* Columbus, OH: Merrill/Macmillan.

Bergan, J. R. (1977). *Behavioral consultation.* Columbus, OH: Merrill/Macmillan.

Berliner, D. C. (1984). The half-full glass: A review of research on teaching. In P. L. Hosford (Ed.), *Using what we know about teaching* (pp. 51–77). Alexandria, VA: Association for Supervision and Curriculum Development.

Berliner, D. (1982). '82 issue: Should teachers be expected to learn and use direct instruction? *Association of Curriculum and Development Update, 24*, 5.

Berry, E. (1983). The unit process. In W. J. Stewart (Ed.), *Unit teaching: Perspectives & prospects* (pp. 3–14). Saratoga, CA: R & E Publishers.

Bickel, W. E., & Bickel, D. D. (1986). Effective schools, classrooms, and instruction: Implications for special education. *Exceptional Children, 52*(6), 489–500.

Bigge, J. (1988). *Curriculum-based instruction for special education students.* Mountain View, CA: Mayfield.

Biklen, D., & Zollers, N. (1986). The focus of advocacy in the LD field. *Journal of Learning Disabilities, 19*, 579–586.

Binder, C., Haughton, E., & Eyk, D. V. (1990). Increasing endurance by building fluency: Precision teaching attention span. *Teaching Exceptional Children, 22*(3) 24–27.

Birdseye, T. (1990). *A song of stars.* New York: Holiday House.

Bittle, R. (1975). Improving parent-teacher communication through recorded telephone messages. *Journal of Educational Research, 69*, 87–95.

Blackburn, J. E., & Powell, W. C. (1976). *One at a time all at once: The creative teacher's guide to individualized instruction without anarchy.* Glenview, IL: Scott Foresman.

Blanchard, J. S. (1985). What to tell students about underlining . . . and why. *Journal of Reading,* 199–203.

Blase, J. J. (1986). A qualitative analysis of sources of teacher stress: Consequences for performance. *American Educational Research Journal, 23,* 13–40.

Bode, B. A. (1989). Dialogue journal writing. *The Reading Teacher, 42*(8), 568–571.

Boomer, L. W. (1982). The paraprofessional: A valued resource for special children and teachers. *Teaching Exceptional Children, 14,* 194–197.

Borg, W., & Ascione, F. (1982). Classroom management in elementary mainstreaming classrooms. *Journal of Educational Psychology, 71*(6), 733–750.

Bos, C. S., & Vaughn, S. (1988). *Strategies for teaching students with learning and behavior problems.* Boston: Allyn & Bacon.

Bott, D. A. (1990). In J. Salvia & C. Hughes, *Curriculum-based assessment: Testing what is taught* (pp. 270–294). New York: Macmillan.

Boyer, E. L. (1987). Early schooling and the nation's future. *Educational Leadership, 44*(6), 4–6.

Boyer, J. (1985). Yes, they can learn. In J. M. Newman (Ed.), *Whole language: Theory in use* (pp. 163–168). Portsmouth, NH: Heinemann Educational Books.

Bradfield, R. H., & Fones, D. M. (1985). Special teacher stress: Its product and prevention. Special Report. *Academic Therapy, 21*(1), 91–97.

Bragstad, B. J., & Stumpf, S. M. (1987). *A guidebook for teaching study skills and motivation.* Boston: Allyn & Bacon.

Bridge, C. A., Winograd, P. N., & Haley, D. (1983). Using predictable materials vs. pre-primers to teach beginning sight words. *The Reading Teacher, 36*(9), 884–891.

Brigance, A. (1977). *Brigance Diagnostic Inventory of Basic Skills.* North Billerica, MA: Curriculum Associates.

Brigance, A. (1981). *Brigance Diagnostic Inventory of Essential Skills.* North Billerica, MA: Curriculum Associates.

Brigance, A. (1983). *Brigance Diagnostic Comprehensive Inventory of Basic Skills Student Booklet.* North Billerica, MA: Curriculum Associates.

Briganti, M. (1989). *An ESE teacher's guide for working with the limited English proficient student.* Orlando, FL: Orange County Public Schools.

Brolin, D. E. (Ed.). (1989). *Life-centered career education: A competency-based approach.* Reston, VA: The Council for Exceptional Children.

Bromley, K. D. (1989). Buddy journals: Invitations to participate in literature. *The Reading Teacher, 43*(2), 112–121.

Brophy, J. E. (1979). Teacher behavior and its effects. *Journal of Educational Psychology, 71*(6), 733–750.

Brophy, J. E. (1980). *Recent research on teaching.* East Lansing, MI: Institute for Research on Teaching, Michigan State University.

Brophy, J. E., & Evertson, C. (1977). Teacher behaviors and student learning in second and third grades. In G. D. Borich (Ed.), *The appraisal of teaching: Concepts and process* (pp. 117–139). Reading, MA: Addison-Wesley.

Brophy, J. E., & Good, T. L. (1986). Teacher behavior and student achievement. In M. L. Wittrock (Ed.), *Handbook of research on teaching* (3rd ed.) (pp. 328–375). New York: Macmillan.

Brown, A. L., & Palincsar, A. S. (1982). Inducing strategic learning from texts by means of informed, self-control training. *Topics in Learning and Learning Disabilities, 2*(1), 1–17.

Brown, T. J. (1986). *Teaching minorities more effectively: A model for educators.* Lanham, MD: University Press of America.

Bryan, T., Donahue, M., & Pearl, R. (1981). Learning disabled children's peer interactions during a small-group problem-solving task. *Learning Disability Quarterly, 4*(1), 13–22.

Bryant, B. (1984). A word from the coach. *Bits and Pieces, 1*(1), p. 5.

Budoff, M., Thormann, M. J., & Gras, A. (1984). *Microcomputers in special education: An introduction to instructional applications.* Cambridge, MA: Brookline Books.

Bulgren, J. (1986). *Concept diagrams* (Research Report). Lawrence: University of Kansas Institute for Research in Learning Disabilities.

Burnette, J. (1987). *Adapting instructional materials for mainstreamed students.* Washington, DC: Office of Special Education Programs, United States Department of Education.

Burns, P. C. (1980). *Assessment and correction of language arts difficulties.* Columbus, OH: Merrill/Macmillan.

Burns, P. C., & Broman, B. L. (1983). *The language arts in childhood education* (5th ed.). Chicago: Rand McNally.

Burns, P. C., & Roe, B. (1985). *Informal reading inventory* (2nd ed.). Boston: Houghton Mifflin.

Burns, R. W. (1972). *New approaches to behavioral objectives.* Dubuque, IA: William C. Brown.

Butler, S., Magliocca, L., Torres, L., & Lee, W. (1984). Grading the mainstreamed student: A decision-making model for modification. *The Directive Teacher, 6*(2), 6–7.

Byars, B. (1974). *Summer of the swans.* New York: Avon.

Cain, E. J. (1984). The challenge of technology: Educating the exceptional child for the world of tomorrow. *Teaching Exceptional Children, 16*(4), 239–241.

Calkins, L. M. (1986). *The art of teaching writing.* Portsmouth, NH: Heinemann Educational Books.

Canter, L. (1979). Competency-based to discipline—It's assertive. *Thrust for Educational Leadership, 8,* 11–13.

Canter, L. (1986). Assertive discipline. Los Angeles, CA; Canter & Associates.

Canter, L., & Associates. (1986). *Assertive discipline videotape No. 2: Implementing assertive discipline in the classroom.* Santa Monica, CA: Canter & Associates.

Caplan, G. (1970). *The theory and practice of mental health consultation.* New York: Basic Books.

Carnine, D. (1989). Teaching complex content to learning disabled students: The role of technology. *Exceptional Children, 55*(6), 524–533.

Carnine, D. W., & Engelmann, S. (1981). *Corrective mathematics.* Chicago: Science Research Associates.

Carnine, D., Silbert, J., & Kameenui, E. J. (1990). *Direct instruction reading* (2nd ed.). Columbus, OH: Merrill/Macmillan.

Cartledge, G., & Milburn, J. F. (1978). The case for teaching social skills in the classroom. *Review of Educational Research, 1,* 133–156.

Cartledge, G., & Milburn, J. F. (Eds.). (1986). *Teaching social skills to children.* Elmsford, NY: Pergamon.

Cashen, V. M., & Leicht, K. L. (1970). Role of the isolation effect in a formal education setting. *Journal of Educational Psychology, 61*(6), 484–486.

Casteel, J. F., & Mathews, D. B. (1984). *Burnout prevention program: A must for staff development.* Paper presented at the Annual National Conference of the National Council of States for Inservice Education, Orlando. (ERIC Document Reproduction Service No. ED 253 501)

Castenada, A. (1976). Cultural democracy and the needs of Mexican-American children. In R. L. Jones (Ed.), *Mainstreaming and the minority child* (pp. 181–194). Reston, VA: The Council for Exceptional Children.

Cautela, J. R., & Groden, J. (1978). *Relaxation: A comprehensive manual for adults, children, and children with special needs.* Champaign, IL: Research Press.

Chalfant, J. C., & Pysh, M. V. (1981, November). Teacher assistance teams: A model for within-building problem solving. *Counterpoint,* pp. 1–4.

Chalfant, J. C., Pysh, M. V., & Moultrie, R. (1979). Teacher assistance teams: A model for within-building based problem solving. *Learning Disabilities Quarterly, 2,* 85–96.

Chambers, J. A., & Sprecher, J. W. (1983). *Computer-assisted instruction: Its use in the classroom.* Englewood Cliffs, NJ: Prentice-Hall.

Chan, D. M. (1987). Curriculum development for limited-English-proficient exceptional Chinese children. In M. K. Kitano & P. C.

Chinn (Eds.), *Exceptional Asian children and youth* (pp. 61–69). Reston, VA: The Council for Exceptional Children.

Chan, K. S., & Kitano, M. K. (1987). Demographic characteristics of exceptional Asian students. In M. K. Kitano & P. C. Chinn (Eds.), *Exceptional Asian children and youth* (pp. 1–11). Reston, VA: The Council for Exceptional Children.

Chan, L. K., & Cole, P. G. (1986). The effects of comprehension-monitoring training on the reading competence of learning-disabled and regular class students. *Remedial and Special Education, 7*(4), 33–40.

Chan, S. (1987). Parents of exceptional Asian children. In M. K. Kitano & P. C. Chinn (Eds.), *Exceptional Asian children and youth* (pp. 36–53). Reston, VA: The Council for Exceptional Children.

Chapman, J. E., & Heward, W. L. (1982). Improving parent-teacher communication through recorded telephone messages. *Teaching Exceptional Children, 49*(1), 79–82.

Cherniss, C. (1980). *Staff burnout: Job stress in the human services.* Beverly Hills, CA: Sage.

Chesler, B. (1982, July-August). ACLD committee survey on LD adults. *ACLD Newsbrief, 145,* 1, 5.

Chiang, B. (1986). Modifying public domain software for use by the learning disabled student. *Journal of Learning Disabilities, 19*(5), 315–317.

Chiang, B., Thorpe, H. W., & Darch, C. B. (1980). Effects of cross-age tutoring on word-recognition performance of learning disabled students. *Learning Disabilities Quarterly, 3*(4), 11–17.

Chinn, P. C., & Plata, M. (1987). Perspectives and educational implications of southeast Asian students. In M. K. Kitano & P. C. Chinn (Eds.), *Exceptional Asian children and youth* (pp. 12–28). Reston, VA: The Council for Exceptional Children.

Chisholm, D. P. (1988). Concerns respecting the regular education initiative. *Journal of Learning Disabilities, 21*(8), 487–492.

Christenson, S. L., Thurlow, M. L., & Ysseldyke, J. E. (1987). *Instructional effectiveness: Implications for effective instruction of handicapped students* (Monograph No. 4). Minneapolis, MN: University of Minnesota, Instructional Alternatives Project.

Christenson, S. L., Ysseldyke, J. E., & Thurlow, M. L. (1989). Critical instructional factors for students with mild handicaps: An integrative review. *Remedial and Special Education 10*(5), 21–29.

Clark, G. M. (1979). *Career education for the handicapped child in the elementary classroom.* Denver, CO: Love Publishing.

Clark, G. M. (1980). Career preparation for handicapped adolescents: A matter of appropriate education. *Exceptional Education Quarterly, 1*(2), 11–17.

Clark, G. M., & Kolstoe, O. P. (1990). *Career development and transition education for adolescents with disabilities.* Boston: Allyn & Bacon.

Clymer, T., & Fenn, T. (1979). *Reading 720 rainbow edition.* Lexington, MA: Ginn.

Cobb, J. A., & Hops, H. (1973). Effects of academic survival skill training on low-achieving first graders. *The Journal of Educational Research, 67,* 108–113.

Cohen, A. D., Kirk, J. C., & Dickson, W. P. (1972). *Guidebook for tutors with an emphasis on teaching minority children.* Stanford, CA: Stanford University Committee on Linguistics.

Cohen, S. B. (1983). Assigning report card grades to the mainstreamed child. *Teaching Exceptional Children, 15*(2), 86–89.

Cohen, S. B. (1986). Teaching new material. *Teaching Exceptional Children, 19*(1), 50–51.

Cohen, S. B., & Hart-Hester, S. (1987). Time management strategies. *Teaching Exceptional Children, 20*(1), 56–57.

Coker, H., Medley, D., & Soar, R. (1980). How valid are expert opinions about effective teaching? *Phi Delta Kappan, 62,* 131–134.

Coleman, J. M., Pullis, M. E., & Minnett, A. M. (1987). Studying mildly handicapped children's adjustment to mainstreaming: A systemic approach. *Remedial and Special Education, 8*(6), 19–30.

Collins, A., & Smith, E. E. (1980). *Teaching the process of reading comprehension* (Technical Report No. 182). Center for the Study of Reading, Urbana, IL: University of Illinois.

Collins, M., Carnine, D., & Gersten, R. (1987). Elaborated corrective feedback and the acquisition of reasoning skills: A study of computer-assisted instruction. *Exceptional Children, 54*(3), 254–262.

Conger, J. C., & Keane, S. P. (1981). Social skills intervention in the treatment of isolated or withdrawn children. *Psychological Bulletin, 90,* 478–493.

Conoley, J. C., & Conoley, C. W. (1988). Useful theories in school-based consultation. *Remedial and Special Education, 9,* 14–28.

Cook, J. M., & Leffingwell, R. J. (1982). Stressors and remediation techniques for special educators. *Exceptional Children, 49*(1), 54–59.

Cooper, A. (1981). Learning centers: What they are and aren't. *Academic Therapy, 16*(5), 527–31.

Cosden, M., Pearl, R., & Bryan, T. H. (1985). The effects of cooperative and individual goal structures in LD and nondisabled students. *Exceptional Children, 52*(2), 103–114.

Council for Exceptional Children Delegate Assembly. (1983). Code of ethics and standards for professional practice. *Exceptional Children, 50,* 8–12.

Cox, V. F., & Platt, J. M. (1986). *Read with expression books.* Unpublished educational materials.

Cox, V. F., & Platt, J. M. (1985). *Dolch word books.* Unpublished educational materials.

Crane, S. J., & Iwanicki, E. F. (1986). Perceived role conflict, role ambiguity, and burnout among special education teachers. *Remedial and Special Education, 7*(2), 24–31.

Crisis Prevention Institute. (1983). *CPI workshop materials.* Milwaukee, WI: Author.

Crocker, M. (1983). Creating a vertical file. In J. Newman (Ed.), *Whole language: Translating theory into practice* (pp. 150–161). Halifax, N.S., Canada: Dalhousie Univ.

Cummings, R. W., & Maddux, C. D. (1987). Self-administration and scoring errors of learning-disabled and nonlearning-disabled students on two forms of the self-directed search. *Exceptional Children, 54,* 167–170.

Cummins, J. (1989). A theoretical framework for bilingual special education. *Exceptional Children, 56*(2), 111–120.

Curtis, M. J., & Meyers, J. (1988). Consultation: A foundation for alternative services in the schools. In J. L. Graden, J. E. Zins, & M. J. Curtis (Eds.), *Alternative educational delivery systems: Enhancing instructional options for all students* (pp. 35–48). Washington, DC: National Association for School Psychologists.

D'Alonzo, B. J. (1983). *Educating adolescents with learning and behavior problems.* Austin, TX: Pro-Ed.

D'Alonzo, B. J., D'Alonzo, R. L., & Mauser, A. J. (1979). Developing resource rooms for the handicapped. *Teaching Exceptional Children, 11,* 91–96.

Darch, C. & Gersten, R. (1986). Direction-setting activities in reading comprehension: A comparison of two approaches. *Learning Disabilities Quarterly, 9*(3), 235–243.

Davis, A., & Clark, E. (1981, October). *High-yield study skills instruction.* Paper presented at the annual meeting of the Plains Regional Conference of the International Reading Association, Des Moines. (ERIC Document Reproduction Service No. ED 208 372)

Day, J. D. (1980). *Training summarization skills: A comparison of teaching methods.* Doctoral dissertation, University of Illinois, Urbana.

DBS Corporation. (1987). *1986 elementary and secondary civil rights survey: National summaries.* Department of Education Office for Civil Rights, Washington, DC, Contract No. 300–86–0062.

deBettencourt, L. U. (1987). How to develop parent relationships. *Teaching Exceptional Children, 19*(2), 26–27.

Delquadri, J., Greenwood, C. R., Whorton, D., Carta, J. J., & Hall, R. V. (1986). Classwide peer tutoring. *Exceptional Children, 52*(6), 535–542.

Demi (1990). *The empty pot.* New York: Henry Holt.

Deno, E. (1970). Special education as developmental capital. *Exceptional Children, 37,* 229–237.

Deno, F., Marston, D., Mirkin, P., Lowry, L., Sindelar, P., & Jenkins, J. (1982). *The use of standard tasks to measure achievement in reading, spelling and written expression: A normative developmental study* (Research Report No. 87). Minneapolis, MN: University of Minnesota, Institute for Research on Learning Disabilities.

Deno, S. L. (1985). Curriculum-based measurement: The emerging alternative. *Exceptional Children, 52*(3), 219–232.

Deno, S. L. (1987). Curriculum-based measurement. *Teaching Exceptional Children, 20*(1), 41–42.

Deno, S. L., Marston, D., & Mirkin, P. (1982). Valid measurement procedures for continuous evaluation of written expression. *Exceptional Children, 48,* 368–371.

Deno, S. L., Mirkin, P., & Chiang, B. (1982). Identifying valid measures of reading. *Exceptional Children, 49,* 36–45.

Deno, S. L., Mirkin, P., & Wesson, C. (1984). How to write effective data based IEPs. *Teaching Exceptional Children, 16*(2), 99–104.

de Paola, T. (1983). *The legend of the bluebonnet: An old tale of Texas.* New York: G. P. Putnam's Sons.

DeRegniers, B. (1985). *Jack and the beanstalk.* New York: Atheneum.

Desberg, P., & Taylor, J. H. (1986). *Essentials of task analysis.* Lanham, MD: University Press of America.

Deshler, D. D., & Graham, S. (1979). *Tape recording educational materials for secondary handicapped students.* The Council for Exceptional Children.

Deshler, D. D., & Schumaker, J. (1986). Learning strategies: An instructional alternative for low-achieving adolescents. *Exceptional Children, 52*(6), 483–490.

Deshler, D. D., & Schumaker, J. B. (1988). An instructional model for teaching students how to learn. In J. L. Graden, J. E. Zins, & M. L. Curtis (Eds.), *Alternative educational delivery systems: Enhancing instructional options for all students* (pp. 391–411). Washington, DC: National Association of School Psychologists.

Deshler, D. D., Schumaker, J. B., Alley, G. R., Warner, M. M., & Clark, F. L. (1982). Learning disabilities in adolescents and young adult populations: Research implications (part I). *Focus on Exceptional Children, 15*(1), 1–12.

Devine, T. G. (1981). *Teaching study skills.* Boston: Allyn & Bacon.

Devin-Sheehan, L., & Allen, V. L. (1976). Implementing tutoring programs: Some alternatives for practitioners and researchers. In V. L. Allen (Ed.), *Children as teachers: Theory and research on tutoring* (pp. 253–268). New York: Academic Press.

Devries, D. L., & Slavin, R. E. (1978). Teams-games-tournaments (TGT): Review of ten classroom experiments. *Journal of Research and Development in Education, 12,* 28–38.

Dew, N. (1984). The exceptional bilingual child: Demography. In P. C. Chinn (Ed.), *Education of culturally and linguistically different exceptional children* (pp. 1–41). Reston, VA: The Council for Exceptional Children.

Duffey, J. B., Salvia, J., Tucker, J., & Ysseldyke, J. (1981). Nonbiased assessment: A need for operationalism. *Exceptional Children, 47*(6), 427–434.

Duffy, G. G., Roehler, L. R., Meloth, M. S., Putnam, J., & Wesselman, R. (1986). The relationship between explicit verbal explanations during reading-skill instruction and student awareness and achievement: A study of reading teacher effects. *Reading Research Quarterly, 21*(3), 237–252.

Duffy, G., Roehler, L., & Rackliff, G. (1986). How teachers' instructional talk influences students' understanding of lesson content. *Elementary School Journal, 87*(1), 3–16.

Duke, D., Showers, B., & Imber, M. (1980). Teachers and shared decision making: The costs and benefits of involvement. *Educational Administration Quarterly, 16,* 93–106.

Dunn, L. M., & Markwardt, F. C. (1970). *Peabody Individual Achievement Test*. Circle Pines, MN: American Guidance Service.

Eaton, M. D. (1978). Data decisions and evaluation. In N. G. Haring, T. C. Lovitt, M. D. Eaton, & C. L. Hansen (Eds.), *The fourth R: Research in the classroom* (pp. 167–90). Columbus, OH: Merrill/Macmillan.

Echevarria-Ratleff, J., & Graf, V. R. (1988). California bilingual special education model sites (1984–1986): Programs and research. In A. A. Ortiz & B. A. Ramirez (Eds.), *Schools and the culturally diverse exceptional student: Promising practices and future directions* (pp. 104–112). Reston, VA: The Council for Exceptional Children.

Edelman, M. W. (1987). *Families in peril: An agenda for social change*. Cambridge, MA: Harvard University Press.

Edelwich, J., & Brodsky, A. (1980). *Book: Burnout: Stages of disillusionment in the helping professions*. New York: Human Sciences Press.

Edgar, E. (1987). Secondary programs in special education: Are many of them justifiable? *Exceptional Children, 53*, 555–561.

Eisen, L. (1986). Regular software for special ed. kids? Yes! *Classroom Computer Learning, 7*(2), 26–28.

Eiserman, W. D. (1988). Three types of peer tutoring: Effects on the attitudes of students with learning disabilities and their regular class peers. *Journal of Learning Disabilities 21*(4), 223–229.

Ekwall, E. E. (1985). *Locating and correcting reading difficulties* (4th ed.). Columbus, OH: Merrill/Macmillan.

Ellis, E. S. (1989). A metacognitive intervention for increasing class participation. *Learning Disabilities Focus, 5*(1), 36–46.

Emmer, E. T., Evertson, C., & Anderson, L. (1980). Effective classroom management at the beginning of the school year. *The Elementary School Journal, 80*, 219–231.

Enell, N. (1984, April). *A cost comparison of planning special education individualized education programs (IEPs) with and without computer as-*sistance. Paper presented at the annual meeting of the American Educational Research Association, New Orleans, LA.

Engelhardt, J. M. (1977). Analysis of children's computational errors: A qualitative approach. *British Journal of Educational Psychology, 47,* 149–154.

Engelmann, S., Becker, W. C., Hanner, S., & Johnson, G. (1980). *Corrective reading program*. Chicago: Science Research Associates.

Engelmann, S., & Bruner, E. C. (1974). *Distar Reading I* (2nd ed.). Chicago: Science Research Associates.

Engelmann, S., & Bruner, E. C. (1988). *Reading mastery: Distar Reading I*. Chicago: Science Research Associates.

Engelmann, S., & Bruner, E. C. (1988). *Reading mastery: Distar Reading II*. Chicago, IL: Science Research Associates.

Engelmann, S., & Bruner, E. C. (1988). *Reading mastery: Fast cycle*. Chicago, IL: Science Research Associates.

Engelmann, S., & Carnine, D. W. (1972). *DISTAR arithmetic level III*. Chicago, IL: Science Research Associates.

Engelmann, S., & Carnine, D. W. (1975). *DISTAR arithmetic level I* (2nd ed.). Chicago, IL: Science Research Associates.

Engelmann, S., & Carnine, D. W. (1976). *DISTAR arithmetic level II* (2nd ed.). Chicago, IL: Science Research Associates.

Engelmann, S., & Carnine, D. (1982). *Theory of instruction: Principles and applications*. New York: Irvington Publishers.

Engelmann, S., & Hanner, S. (1988). *Reading mastery III*. Chicago, IL: Science Research Associates.

Engelmann, S., & Hanner, S. (1988). *Reading mastery IV*. Chicago, IL: Science Research Associates.

Engelmann, S., Hanner, S., & Haddox, P. (1989). *Corrective reading: Comprehension*. Chicago, IL: Science Research Associates.

Engelmann, S., Meyer, L., Johnson, G., & Carnine, L. (1988). *Corrective reading: Decoding*. Chicago, IL: Science Research Associates.

Engelmann, S., Osborn, J., & Hanner, S. (1978). *Corrective reading.* Chicago, IL: Science Research Associates.

Engelmann, S., Osborn, J., Osborn, S., & Zoref, L. (1988). *Reading mastery V.* Chicago, IL: Science Research Associates.

Engelmann, S., Osborn, J., Osborn, S., & Zoref, L. (1988). *Reading mastery VI.* Chicago, IL: Science Research Associates.

Englert, C. S. (1983). Measuring special education teacher effectiveness. *Exceptional Children, 50*(3), 247–254.

Englert, C. S. (1984). Effective direct instruction practices in special education settings. *Remedial and Special Education, 5*(2), 38–47.

Englert, C. S., & Thomas, C. C. (1982). Management of task involvement in special education classrooms: Implications for teacher preparation. *Teacher Education and Special Education, 5*(1), 3–10.

ERIC Digest. (1988, September.) *Social integration of handicapped students: Cooperative goal structuring, Brief T1.* Reston, VA: The Council for Exceptional Children.

Evans, S. S. (1980). The consultant role of the resource teacher. *Exceptional Children, 46,* 402–404.

Evans, S. S., & Evans, W. H. (1986). Training needs of special education paraprofessionals: Results of a survey conducted by a community college. *New Directions, 1,* 4–6.

Evans, S. S., Evans, W. H., & Mercer, C. E. (1986). *Assessment for instruction.* Boston: Allyn & Bacon.

Evertson, C. (1982). Differences in instructional activities in higher- and lower-achieving junior high English and mathematics classrooms. *Elementary School Journal, 82,* 329–351.

Evertson, C., & Emmer, E. (1982). Effective management at the beginning of the school year in junior high classes. *Journal of Educational Psychology, 74,* 485–498.

Fagan, W. T. (1989). Empowered students; empowered teachers. *The Reading Teacher, 42*(8), 568–571.

Farber, L. A. (1984). Stress and burnout in suburban teachers. *Journal of Educational Research, 77,* 325–331.

Farr, R. F. (1989). A response from Robert Farr. In K. S. Jongsma (Ed.). Questions & answers: Portfolio assessment. *The Reading Teacher, 43*(3), 264–265.

Farris, P. (1989, Fall). From basal reader to whole language: Transition tactics. *Reading Horizons,* pp. 23–29.

Fasold, R., & Wolfram, W. (1975). Some linguistic features of Negro dialect. In D. Stroller (Ed.), *Black American English: Its ways in the schools and in literature.* New York: Dell.

FDLRS (Florida Diagnostic and Learning Resource System). (1982). *Communication skills materials.* Daytona Beach, FL: Author.

Fimian, M. J. (1986). Social support and occupational stress in special education. *Exceptional Children, 52*(5), 436–446.

Fimian, M. J. & Blanton, L. P. (1986). Variables related to stress and burnout in special-education teacher trainees and first-year teachers. *Teacher Education and Special Education, 9*(1), 9–21.

Fimian, M. J., & Santoro, T. M. (1983). Sources and manifestations of occupational stress as reported by full-time special education teachers. *Exceptional Children, 49*(6), 540–545.

Fisher, C., Berliner, D., Filby, N., Marliave, R., Cahen, L., & Dishaw, M. (1980). Teaching behaviors, academic learning time, and student achievement: An overview. In C. Denham & A. Lieberman (Eds.), *Time to learn* (pp. 7–32). Washington, DC: National Institute of Education.

Flake-Hobson, C., & Swick, K. J. (1984). Communication strategies for parents and teachers, or how to say what you mean. In M. L. & E. M. Nesselroad (Eds.), *Working with parents of handicapped children: A book of readings for school personnel* (pp. 141–149). Lanham, MD: University Press of America.

Flavell, J. (1976). Metacognitive aspects of problem solving. In L. B. Resnick (Ed.), *The nature of intelligence.* Hillsdale, NJ: Erlbaum.

Flood, J., & Lapp, D. (1989). Reporting reading progress: A comparison portfolio for parents. *The Reading Teacher, 42*(7), 508–514.

Florida Performance Measurement System (FPMS)—Domains: Knowledge base of the Florida Performance Measurement System (1984). Tallahassee, FL: Florida Coalition for the Development of a Performance Measurement System, Office of Teacher Education, Certification and Inservice Staff Development.

Ford, B. A., & Jones, C. (1990). Ethnic feelings book: Created by students with developmental handicaps. *Teaching Exceptional Children, 22*(4), 36–39.

Foster, S. L., & Ritchey, W. L. (1979). Issues in assessment of social competence in children. *Journal of Applied Behavior Analysis, 12,* 625–638.

Fountain Valley Teacher Support System in Reading. (1971). Huntington Beach, CA: Richard L. Zweig.

Fowler, R. L., & Barker, A. S. (1974). Effectiveness of highlighting for retention of text material. *Journal of Applied Psychology, 59,* 358–364.

Fradd, S., & Hallman, C. L. (1983). Implications of psychological and educational research for assessment and instruction of culturally and linguistically different students. *Learning Disability Quarterly, 6*(4), 468–478.

Frank, A. R., Keith, T. Z., & Steil, D. A. (1988). Training needs of special education professionals. *Exceptional Children, 55*(3), 253–258.

Frederick, W. C., & Walberg, H. J. (1980). Learning as a function of time. *The Journal of Educational Research, 73,* 183–194.

Friend, M. (1988). Putting consultation into context: Historical and contemporary perspectives. *Remedial and Special Education, 9*(6), 7–13.

Frith, G. H., & Armstrong, S. W. (1986). Self-monitoring for behavior-disordered students. *Behavioral Disorders, 18*(2), 144–148.

Frith, G. H., & Lindsey, J. D. (1980). Paraprofessional roles in mainstreaming multihandicapped students. *Education Unlimited, 2,* 17–21.

Frith, G. H., & Lindsey, J. D. (1982). Certification, training, and other programming variables affecting special education and the paraprofessional concept. *Journal of Special Education, 16,* 229–236.

Frith, G. H., Lindsey, J. D., & Edwards, R. (1981). A noncategorical approach for serving exceptional children of low-incidence exceptionalities in rural areas. *Education, 101,* 276–278.

Frith, G. H., & Mims, A. (1985, Spring). Burnout among special education paraprofessionals. *Teaching Exceptional Children,* pp. 225–227.

Fuchs, L. S., & Deno, S. (1981). *The relationship between curriculum-based mastery measures and standardized achievement tests in reading* (Research Report No. 57), Minneapolis, MN: University of Minnesota Institute for Research on Learning Disabilities.

Fuchs, L. S., Fuchs, D., & Hamlett, C. L. (1989). Effects of alternative goal structures within curriculum-based measurement. *Exceptional Children, 55*(5), 429–438.

Fuchs, L., Hamlett, C., & Fuchs, D. (1988). *Improving data-based instruction through computer technology: Description of software: Year 3.* Unpublished manuscript, Vanderbilt University, Peabody College, Nashville, TN.

Fullan, M. (1982). *The meaning of educational change.* New York: Teacher's College Press.

Fullan, M., & Pomfret, A. (1977). Research on curriculum and instruction implementation. *Review of Educational Research, 47,* 335–397.

Gable, R. A., Young, C. C., & Hendrickson, M. J. (1987). Content of special education teacher preparation: Are we headed in the right direction? *Teacher Education and Special Education, 10*(3), 135–139.

Gajar, A. H. (1977). Characteristics and classification of educable mentally retarded, learning disabled, and emotionally disturbed students (Doctoral dissertation, University of Virginia). *Dissertation Abstracts International* (University Microfilms No. 77–28, 644)

Galbo, J. J. (1983). Teacher anxiety and student achievement. *Educational Research Quarterly, 7,* 44–49.

Galdone, P. (1970). *The three little pigs.* New York: Seabury Press.

Galdone, P. (1973). *The three billy goats gruff.* New York: Seabury Press.

Gall, M., Ward, B., Berliner, D., Chaen, L., Winne, P., Elashoff, J., & Stanton, G. (1978). Effects of questioning techniques and recitation on student learning. *American Education Research Journal, 15*(2), 175–199.

Gallagher, P. A. (1979). *Teaching students with behavior disorders: Techniques for classroom instruction.* Denver: Love Publishing.

Gallagher, P. A. (1988). *Teaching students with behavior disorders: Techniques and activities for classroom instruction* (2nd ed.). Denver: Love Publishing.

Garcia, S. B. (1984). *Effects of student characteristics, school programs and organization on decision making for the placement of Hispanic students in classes for the learning disabled.* Unpublished doctoral dissertation, The University of Texas, Austin, TX.

Garland, V. E. (1981). *Organizational and individual burnout factors: Interviews of teachers formerly in an urban public school district.* Unpublished doctoral dissertation, University of Connecticut, Storrs, CT.

Garner, R., & Kraus, C. (1982). Good and poor comprehension differences in knowing and regulating reading behaviors. *Educational Research Quarterly, 6,* 5–12.

Gartner, A., & Lipsky, D. K. (1989). *The yoke of special education: How to break it.* Rochester, NY: National Center on Education and the Economy.

Gay, G. (1975, October). Cultural differences important in the education of Black children, *Momentum,* pp. 30–33.

Gelzheiser, L. M., Shepherd, M. J., & Wozniak, R. H. (1986). The development of instruction to induce skill transfer. *Exceptional Children, 53*(2), 125–129.

George, J. C. (1987). *Water Sky.* New York: Harper & Row.

George, P. (1986). Teaching handicapped children with attention problems: Teacher verbal strategies make a difference. *Teaching Exceptional Children, 18*(3), 173–175.

George, P. S. (1983). *Time management for teachers.* Paper presented at the annual meeting of the National Middle School Association, Chicago, IL.

Gersten, R. (1985). Direct instruction with special education students: A review of evaluation research. *Journal of Special Education, 19*(1), 41–58.

Gersten, R., & Carnine, D. (1984). Direct instruction mathematics: A longitudinal evaluation of low-income elementary school students. *Elementary School Journal, 84*(4), 395–407.

Gersten, R., Carnine, D., & Woodward, J. (1987). Direct instruction research: The third decade. *Remedial and Special Education 8*(6), 48–56.

Gersten, R., & Maggs, A. (1982). Teaching the general case to moderately retarded children: Evaluation of a five-year project. *Analysis and Intervention in Developmental Disabilities, 2,* 329–343.

Gersten, R., Woodward, J., & Darch, C. (1986). Direct instruction: A research-based approach to curriculum design and teaching. *Exceptional Children, 53*(1), 17–31.

Gettinger, M., & Fayne, H. (1982). Classroom behaviors during small group instruction and learning performance in learning-disabled and nondisabled children. *Journal of Educational Research, 75*(3), 182–187.

Ghent, J., (1988, December 19). Julius Lester: Controversial Black convert to Judaism. *The Oakland Tribune,* pp. 1–2.

Gillet, J., & Temple, C. (1982). *Understanding reading problems: Assessment and instruction.* Boston: Little, Brown.

Gillet, P. (1981). Career education for exceptional children and youth. *Of work and worth: Career education for the handicapped.* Salt Lake City, UT: Olympus.

Gilliam, H. V., & Van Den Berg, S. (1980). Different levels of eye contact: Effects on black and white college students. *Urban Education, 15*(1), 83–92.

Gitter, A. G., Black, H., & Mostofsky, D. (1972). Race and sex in the perception of emotion. *Journal of Social Issues, 28,* 63–78.

Glatthorn, A. A. (1990). Cooperative professional development: Facilitating the growth of the special education teacher and the classroom teacher. *Remedial and Special Education, 11*(3), 29–50.

Gleason, M. M. (1988). Study skills: Teaching study strategies. *Teaching Exceptional Children, 20*(3), 52–53.

Glynn, S. M. (1978). Capturing readers' attention by means of typographical cueing strategies. *Educational Technology, 18,* 7–12.

Goldstein, A. P., Sprafkin, R. P., Gershaw, N. J., & Klein, P. (1980). *Skillstreaming the adolescent: A structured approach to teaching prosocial skills.* Champaign, IL: Research Press.

Goldstein, H. (1972). Construction of a social learning curriculum. In E. L. Meyen, G. A. Vergason, & R. J. Whelan (Eds.), (1972). *Strategies for teaching exceptional children.* Denver, CO: Love Publishing.

Goldstein, M. J. (1986). Curriculum: The keystone for special education planning. *Teaching Exceptional Children, 18*(3), 220–225.

Gollnick, D. M., & Chinn, P. C. (1990). *Multicultural education in a pluralistic society* (3rd ed.). Columbus, OH: Merrill/Macmillan.

Gollnick, D. M., Sadker, M. P., & Sadker, D. M. (1982). Beyond the Dick and Jane syndrome: Confronting sex bias in instructional materials. In M. P. Sadker & D. M. Sadker (Eds.), *Sex equity handbook for schools* (pp. 60–90). New York: Longman.

Good, T., & Brophy, J. (1984). *Looking in classrooms* (3rd ed.) New York: Harper & Row.

Good, T. L., & Grouws, D. A. (1979). The Missouri mathematics effectiveness project. *Journal of Educational Psychology, 71,* 355–362.

Goodman, K. S., & Goodman, Y. M. (1983). Reading and writing relationships: Pragmatic functions. *Language Arts, 60,* 590–599.

Goodman, K. S., Goodman, Y. M., & Hood, W. J. (1989). *The whole language evaluation book.* Portsmouth, NH: Irwin Publishing.

Goodman, L. (1985). The effective schools movement and special education. *Teaching Exceptional Children, 17*(2), 102–105.

Goodman, Y. M. (1985). Kidwatching: Observing children in the classroom. In A. Jaggar & M. T. Smith-Burke (Eds.), *Observing the language learner* (pp. 9–19). Newark, DE: International Reading Association.

Goodman, Y. M., & Burke, C. L. (1972). *Reading miscue inventory: Manual of procedures for diagnosis and evaluation.* New York: Macmillan.

Goodman, Y. M., & Burke, C. (1980). *Reading strategies: Focus on comprehension.* New York: Holt, Rinehart, & Winston.

Goodman, Y. M., & Goodman, K. S. (1979). Learning to read is natural. In L. B. Resnick & P. A. Weaver (Eds.), *Theory and practice of early reading* (Vol. 1, pp. 137–154). Hillsdale, NJ: Erlbaum.

Gottlieb, J., Semmel, M. I., & Veldman, D. J. (1978). Correlates of social status among mainstreamed mentally retarded children. *Journal of Educational Psychology, 70,* 396–405.

Graden, J. L., Casey, A., & Christenson, S. L. (1985). Implementing a prereferral intervention system. Part I: The model. *Exceptional Children, 51,* 377–384.

Graham, S. (1985). Teaching basic academic skills to learning-disabled students: A model of the teaching-learning process. *Journal of Learning Disabilities, 18*(9), 528–534.

Grant, C. A., & Sleeter, C. E. (1989). *Turning on learning: Five approaches for multicultural plans for race, class, gender, and disability.* Columbus, OH: Merrill/Macmillan.

Graves, D., & Stuart, V. (1985). *Write from the start.* New York: New American Library.

Great Falls Public Schools. (1981). *Great Falls precision teaching training manual* (5th ed). Great Falls, MT: Author.

Greenwood, C. R., Delquadri, J., & Hall, R. V. (1984). Opportunity to respond and student academic performance. In W. L. Heward, T. E. Heron, J. Trap-Porter, & D. S. Hill (Eds.), *Focus on behavior analysis in education* (pp. 58–88). Columbus, OH: Merrill/Macmillan.

Greenwood, C. R., Dinwiddie, G., Terry, B., Wade, L., Stanley, S., Thibadeau, S., & Delquadri, J. (1984). Teacher-versus-peer-mediated instruction: An ecobehavioral analysis of achievement outcomes. *Journal of Applied Behavior Analysis, 17,* 521–538.

Greer, J. G., & Wethered, C. E. (1984). Learned helplessness: A piece of the burnout puzzle. *Exceptional Children, 50*(6), 524–530.

Gregory, R. P., Hackney, C., & Gregory, N. M. (1982). Corrective reading programs: An evaluation. *British Journal of Educational Psychology, 52,* 33–50.

Gresham, F. M., & Elliott, S. N. (1984). Assessment and classification of children's social skills: A review of methods and issues. *School Psychology Review, 13,* 292–301.

Gresham, F. M., & Elliott, S. N. (1990). *The social skills rating system.* Circle Pines, MN: American Guidance Service.

Grossman, H. (1984). *Educating Hispanic students: Cultural implications for instruction, classroom management, counseling, and assessment.* Springfield, IL: Charles C Thomas.

Grossman, H. (1990). *Trouble-free teaching: Solutions to behavior problems in the classroom.* Mountain View, CA: Mayfield.

Guess, D., Smith, J., & Ensminger, E. (1977). The role of nonprofessional persons in teaching language skills to mentally retarded children. *Exceptional Children, 37,* 447–453.

Gunderson, L., & Shapiro, J. (1988). Whole language instruction: Writing in first grade. *The Reading Teacher, 41*(4), 430–440.

Haight, S. H. (1985). Special education teacher consultant: Idealism versus realism. *Exceptional Children, 50,* 507–515.

Hale, J. E. (1981). Black children: Their roots, culture, and learning styles. *Young Children, 36*(20), 37–50.

Hall, G. E., & Hord, S. M. (1984). *Change in schools: Facilitating the process* (p. 60). Albany: State University of New York Press.

Hall, R. V., Delquadri, J., Greenwood, C. R., & Thurston, L. (1982). The importance of opportunity to respond in children's academic success. In E. Edgar, N. Haring, J. Jenkins, & C. Pious (Eds.), *Mentally handicapped children: Education and training* (pp. 107–140). Baltimore: University Park Press.

Hallahan, D. P., Kauffman, J. M., Lloyd, J. W., & McKinney, J. D. (1988). Questions about the regular education initiative. *Journal of Learning Disabilities, 21*(1), 3–5.

Hallahan, D. P., Keller, C. E., McKinney, J. D., Lloyd, J. W., & Bryan, T. (1988). Examining the research base of the regular education initiative: Efficacy studies and the adaptive learning environments model. *Journal of Learning Disabilities, 21*(1), 19–35, 55.

Halpern, A. S., Close, D. W., & Nelson, D. J. (1986). *On my own: The impact of semi-independent living programs for adults with mental retardation.* Baltimore, MD: Paul H. Brookes.

Hannah, G. G. (1982). *Classroom spaces and places.* Belmont, CA: Pitman Learning.

Haring, N., & Eaton, M. (1978). Systematic instructional procedures: An instructional hierarchy. In N. Haring, T. Lovitt, M. Eaton, & C. Hansen (Eds.), *The fourth R: Research in the classroom* (pp. 23–40). Columbus, OH: Merrill/Macmillan.

Haring, N. G., & Gentry, N. D. (1976). Direct and individualized instructional procedures. In N. G. Haring & R. L. Schiefelbusch (Eds.), *Teaching special children* (pp. 77–111). New York: McGraw-Hill.

Haring, N. G., Lovitt, T. C., Eaton, M. D., & Hansen, C. L. (1978). *The fourth R: Research in the classroom.* Columbus, OH: Merrill/Macmillan.

Harrington, M. (1984). *The new American poverty.* New York: Holt, Rinehart, & Winston.

Harrington, R. G., & Mitchelson, D. (1987). Special education paraprofessionals: How effective are they? *New Directions, 3–4.*

Harris, K. R., & Graham, S. (1985). Improving learning-disabled students' composition skills: A self-control strategy training approach. *Learning Disability Quarterly, 8,* 27–36.

Harste, J. (1984). *Language stories and literacy lessons.* Portsmouth, NH: Heinemann Educational Books.

Hasazi, G., Gordon, L., & Roe, C. (1985). Factors associated with the employment status of handicapped youth exiting high school from 1979 to 1983. *Exceptional Children, 51,* 455–469.

Hasselbring, T. S., & Hamlett, C. L. (1983). *AIMSTAR.* Portland, OR: ASIEP Education.

Hawisher, M. F., & Calhoun, M. L. (1978). *The resource room: An educational asset for children with special needs.* Columbus, OH: Merrill/Macmillan.

Hayek, R. A. (1987). The teacher assistance team: A prereferral support system. *Focus on Exceptional Children. 20*(1), 1–7.

Hayes, M. L. (1985). Materials for the resource room. *Academic Therapy, 20*(3), 289–297.

Haynes, M. E. (1987). *Personal time management.* Los Altos, CA: Crisp Publications.

Hazel, J. S., Schumaker, J. B., Sherman, J. A., & Sheldon-Wildgen, J. (1981). *ASSET: A social-skills program for adolescents.* Champaign, IL: Research Press.

Hazel, J. S., Schumaker, J. B., Sherman, J. A., & Sheldon-Wildgen, J. (1983). Social skills training with court-adjudicated youths. *Social Skills Training for Children and Youth, 5,* 117–187.

Heffren, M., & Diviaio, L. (1989). *A resource manual for the development and evaluation of special programs for exceptional students, Volume V-D: Techniques of precision teaching, Part 1: Training manual.* Tallahassee, FL: Bureau of Education for Exceptional Students.

Heinich, R., Molenda, M., & Russell, J. D. (1989). *Instructional media and the new technologies of instruction.* New York: Macmillan.

Heit, S. B. (1980). *Gameboards for everyone.* Carthage, IL: Good Apple.

Heller, K. A., Holtzman, W. H., & Messick, S. (1982). *Placing children in special education: A strategy for equity.*

Henk, W. A., Helfeldt, J. P., & Platt, J. M. (1986). Alternative approaches to reading instruction for learning disabled students. *Teaching Exceptional Children, 18*(3), 202–206. Washington, DC: National Academy Press.

Hepworth, D. H., & Larsen, J. A. (1990). *Direct social work practice: Theory and skills* (3rd ed.). Homewood, IL: The Dorsey Press.

Herald-Taylor, G. (1987). How to use predictable books for K–2 language arts instruction. *The Reading Teacher, 40*(7), 656–663.

Heron, T. E., & Kimball, W. H. (1988). Gaining perspective with the educational consultation research base: Ecological considerations and further recommendations. *Remedial and Special Education, 9*(6), 21–28.

Herr, C. M. (1988). Strategies for gaining information. *Teaching Exceptional Children, 20*(3), 53–55.

Herrmann, B. A. (1988). Two approaches for helping poor readers. *The Reading Teacher, 42*(1), 25–28.

Hillard, A. (1976). *Alternatives to IQ testing: An approach to the identification of gifted minority children.* Sacramento, CA: Final report to the California State Department of Education.

Hillard, A. G. (1980). Cultural diversity and special education. *Exceptional Children, 46,* 584–588.

Hiller, J. H., Fisher, L., & Kaess, J. (1969). A computer investigation of verbal characteristics of effective classroom lecturing. *American Educational Research Journal, 6,* 661–675.

Hittleman, D. R. (1983). *Developmental reading, K–8.* Boston: Houghton Mifflin.

Hoffer, A. R., Johnson, M. L., Leinwald, S. J., Lodholz, R. D., Musser, G. R., & Thoburn, T. (1991). *Teacher's edition: Mathematics in action.* New York: Macmillan/McGraw-Hill School Publishing Company.

Hoffer, K. H. (1983). Assessment and instruction of reading skills: Results with Mexican-American students. *Learning Disabilities Quarterly 6*(4), 458–467.

Holifield, J. R. (1981). An analysis of junior high/middle school teachers' perceptions of factors affecting teacher job stress and principals' perceptions of ways to alleviate or manage teacher stress (Doctoral dissertation, Ball State University, 1981). *Dissertation Abstracts International, 42,* 1401A.

Hops, H., & Greenwood, C. R. (1981). Social skills deficits. In E. J. Mash & L. G. Terdal (Eds.), *Behavioral assessment of childhood disorders.* New York: Guilford Press.

Howell, K. W., & Kaplan, J. S. (1980). *Diagnosing basic skills: A handbook for deciding what to teach.* Columbus, OH: Merrill/Macmillan.

Howell, K. W., & Morehead, M. K. (1987). *Curriculum-based evaluation for special and remedial education.* Columbus, OH: Merrill/Macmillan.

Huck, S. W., Cormier, W. H., & Bounds, W. C. (1974). *Reading statistics and research.* New York: Harper & Row.

Hudson, T. (1982). The effects of induced schemata on the "short circuit" in L2 reading: Nondecoding factors in L2 reading performance. *Language Learning, 32,* 1–31.

Huefner, D. S. (1988). The consulting teacher model: Risks and opportunities. *Exceptional Children, 54*(5), 403–414.

Hughes, C. A., Ruhl, K. L., & Peterson, S. K. (1988). Promising practices: Teaching self-management skills. *Teaching Exceptional Children, 20*(2), 70–72.

Hutchins, C. L., Everson, S., Ewy, R., Marzano, R., Chapman, H., & Kessler, B. (1984–85). Coaching: A powerful strategy for improving staff development and inservice education. *Noteworthy,* Winter.

Hyland, C. R. (1989). What we know about the fastest-growing minority population: Hispanic-Americans. *Educational Horizons,* 131–135.

Hymes, L., & Hymes, J. L. (1972). Oodles of noodles. In B. Martin, & P. Brogan (Eds.), *Sounds around the clock* (p. 480). New York: Holt, Rinehart, & Winston.

Idol, L. (1986). *Collaborative School Consultation* (Report of the National Task Force on School Consultation). Reston, VA: Teacher Education Division, The Council for Exceptional Children.

Idol, L. (1988). A rationale and guidelines for establishing a special education consultation program. *Remedial and Special Education Program, 9*(6), 48–62.

Idol, L., Paolucci-Whitcomb, P., & Nevin, A. (1986). *Collaborative consultation.* Rockville, MD: Aspen.

Idol, L., & West, J. F. (1987). Consultation in special education (Part II): Training and practice. *Journal of Learning Disabilities, 20*(8), 474–494.

Idol-Maestas, L. (1983). Special educator's consultation handbook. Rockville, MD: Aspen.

Idol-Maestas, L., & Ritter, S. (1985). A follow-up study of resource/consulting teachers. *Teacher Education and Special Education, 8,* 121–131.

Idstein, P., & Jenkins, J. R. (1972). Underlining versus repetitive reading. *Journal of Educational Research, 65,* pp. 321–323.

Jackson, G., & Cosca, C. (1974). The inequality of educational opportunity in the Southwest: An observational study of ethnically mixed classrooms. *American Educational Research Journal, 11,* 219–229.

Jenkins, J. R., & Mayhall, W. F. (1976). Development and evaluation of a resource teacher program. *Exceptional Children, 41,* 21–30.

Jenkins, J. R., Pious, C. G., & Jewell, M. (1990). Special education and the regular education initiative: Basic assumptions. *Exceptional Children, 56*(6), 479–491.

Jensen, W. R., Sloan, H. N., & Young, K. R. (1988). *Applied behavior analysis in education: A structured teaching approach* (2nd ed.). Englewood Cliffs, NJ: Prentice-Hall.

Johnson, D., & Wen, S. (1976). Effects of correct and extraneous markings under time limits on reading comprehension. *Psychology in the Schools, 13,* 454–456.

Johnson, D. W., & Johnson, R. T. (1980). Integrating handicapped children into the mainstream. *Exceptional Children, 47,* 90–98.

Johnson, D. W., & Johnson, R. T. (1986). Mainstreaming and cooperative learning strategies. *Exceptional Children, 52*(6), 553–561.

Johnson, D. W., Johnson, R. T., & Maruyama, G. (1983). Interdependence and interpersonal attraction among heterogeneous and homogeneous individuals: A theoretical formulation and meta-analysis of the research. *Review of Educational Research, 53,* 5–54.

Johnson, D. W., Johnson, R. T., Warring, D., & Maruyama, G. (1986). Different cooperative learning procedures and cross-handicap relationships. *Exceptional Children, 53*(3), 247–252.

Johnson, K. R. (1971). Black kinetics: Some nonverbal communication patterns in the Black culture. *Florida Reporter,* Spring/Fall, *57,* 17–20.

Johnson, L. J., Pugach, M. C., & Hammitte, D. J. (1988). Barriers to effective special education consultation. *Remedial and Special Education, 9*(6), 41–47.

Johnson, M. J. (1987). American Indian parents of handicapped children. In M. J. Johnson & B. A. Ramirez (Eds.), *American Indian exceptional children and youth* (pp. 6–7). Reston, VA: Council for Exceptional Children.

Jones, J. (1987). *Identification of topics for an inservice training program for special education professionals on the control of burnout.* (ERIC Document Reproduction Service No. ED 287 805)

Jones, R. L., Gottlieb, J., Guskin, S., & Yoshida, R. K. (1978). Evaluating mainstreaming programs: Models, caveats, considerations, and guidelines. *Exceptional Children, 44*(8), 588–603.

Jongsma, K. S. (1989). Questions and answers: Portfolio assessment. *Reading Teacher, 43*(3), 264–265.

Joyce, B. R., & Showers, B. (1983). *Power in staff development through research on training.* Alexandria, VA: Association for Supervision and Curriculum Development.

Joyce, B. R., & Showers, B. (1987). Low-cost arrangements for peer coaching. *Journal of Staff Development, 8*(1), 22–24.

Kahan, E. H. (1981). Aides in special education—A boon for students and teachers. *Teaching Exceptional Children, 55*(3), 101–105.

Kaplan, S. N., Kaplan, J. B., Madsen, S. K., & Taylor, B. K. (1973). *Change for children: Ideas and activities for individualizing learning.* Pacific Palisades, CA: Goodyear.

Karlsen, B., Madden, R., & Gardner, F. (1977). *Stanford Diagnostic Reading Test.* New York: Harcourt Brace Jovanovich.

Kauffman, J. M., Gerber, M. M., & Semmel, M. I. (1988). Arguable assumptions underlying the regular education initiative. *Journal of Learning Disabilities, 21*(1), 6–11.

Kellogg, S. (1984). *Paul Bunyan: A tall tale.* New York: William Morrow.

Kelly, E. J. (1979). *Elementary school social studies instruction: A basic approach.* Denver: Love Publishing.

Kerman, S. (1982). *Teacher expectations and student achievement. Workshop handout:* TESA Training.

Kerr, M. M., & Nelson, C. M. (1989). *Strategies for managing behavior problems in the classroom* (2nd ed.). Columbus, OH: Merrill/Macmillan.

Kinnison, L. R., Hayes, C., & Accord, J. (1981). Evaluating student progress in mainstream classes. *Teaching Exceptional Children, 13*(3), 97–99.

Kitano, M. K. (1987). Gifted and talented Asian children. In M. K. Kitano & P. C. Chinn (Eds.), *Exceptional Asian children and youth* (pp. 1–11). Reston, VA: The Council for Exceptional Children.

Kokaska, C. J. (1980). A curriculum model for career education. In G. M. Clark & W. J. White (Eds.), *Career education for the handi-*

capped: Current perspectives for teachers (pp. 35–41). Boothwyn, PA: Educational Resources Center.

Kokaska, C. J., & Brolin, D. E. (1985). *Career education for handicapped individuals* (2nd ed.). Columbus, OH: Merrill/Macmillan.

Koorland, M. A., Keel, M. C., and Ueberhorst, P. (1990). Setting aims for precision learning. *Teaching Exceptional Children, 22*(3), 64–68.

Krivacska, J. J. (1986). Selection of the IEP management systems. *Computers in the Schools, 3*(3–4), 91–95.

Kroth, R. (1987). Parent involvement considerations. In M. J. Johnson & B. A. Ramirez (Eds.), *American Indian exceptional children and youth.* Reston, VA: The Council for Exceptional Children (p. 5).

Kulik, C. L., Kulik, J., & Schwalb, B. J. (1983). College programs for high-risk and disadvantaged students: A meta-analysis of findings. In C. E. Weinstein, E. T. Goetz, & P. A. Alexander (Eds.), *Learning and study strategies: Issues in assessment, instruction, and evaluation* (pp. 1–9). San Diego: Academic Press.

Kyriacou, C., & Sutcliffe, J. (1978). A model of teacher stress. *Educational Studies, 4*(1), 1–6.

Lado, R. (1964). *Language teaching: A scientific approach.* New York: McGraw-Hill.

Lambie, R. A. (1980). A systematic approach for changing materials, instruction, and assignments to meet individual needs. *Focus on Exceptional Children, 12*(1), 1–12.

Lamme, L. L. (1989). Authorship: A key facet of whole language. *The Reading Teacher, 42*(9), 704–711.

Langer, J. (1984). Examining background knowledge and text comprehension. *Reading Research Quarterly, 19,* 468–481.

Lawrenson, G., & McKinnon, A. (1980). *Attrition, burnout, and job satisfactions of teachers of the emotionally disabled.* Paper presented at a topical conference of the Council for Exceptional Children, Minneapolis. (ERIC Document Reproduction Service No. ED 195 104)

Lawrenson, G., & McKinnon, A. (1982). A survey of classroom teachers of the emotionally disturbed: Attrition and burnout factors. *Behavioral Disorders, 8,* 41–49.

Lazerson, D. B., Foster, H. L., Brow, S. I., & Hummel, J. W. (1988). The effectiveness of cross-age tutoring with truant, junior high students with learning disabilities. *Journal of Learning Disabilities, 21*(4), 253–255.

Leggett, D., & Hoyle, S. (1987). Peer coaching: One district's experience in using teachers as staff developers. *Journal of Staff Development, 8*(1), 16–20.

Leigh, J. E. (1980). Whole-language approaches: Premises and possibilities. *Learning Disability Quarterly, 3*(4), 62–92.

Leinhardt, G., Zigmond, N., & Cooley, W. (1981). Reading instruction and its effects. *American Education Research Journal, 18*(3), 343–361.

Lenz, B. K., Alley, G., & Schumaker, J. (1987). Activating the inactive learner: Advance organizers in the secondary content classroom. *Learning Disabilities Quarterly, 10*(1), 53–67.

Lenz, B. K., Clark, F. C., Deshler, D. D., & Schumaker, J. B. (1988). *The strategies instructional approach.* (Preservice Training Package). Lawrence, KS: University of Kansas Institute for Research in Learning Disabilities.

Lerner, J. (1985). *Learning disabilities: Theories, diagnosis, and teaching strategies.* Boston: Houghton Mifflin.

Leslie, L. & Caldwell, J. (1990). *Qualitative reading inventory.* Glenview, IL: Scott, Foresman.

Leung, B. (1987). Psychoeducational assessment of Asian students. In M. K. Kitano & P. C. Chinn (Eds.), *Exceptional Asian children and youth* (pp. 29–35). Reston, VA: The Council for Exceptional Children.

Leung, E. K. (1989). Cultural and acculturational commonalities and diversities among Asian Americans: Identification and programming considerations. In A. A. Ortiz & B. A. Ramirez (Eds.), *Schools and the culturally diverse exceptional student: Promising practices and future directions* (second printing, pp. 86–95). Reston, VA: The Council for Exceptional Children.

Levin, J. R. (1985). Educational applications of mnemonic pictures: Possibilities beyond your wildest imagination. In A. A. Sheikh (Ed.), *Imagery in education: Imagery in the educational process.* (pp. 63–87). Farmingdale, NY: Baywood.

Lewis, E. R., & Lewis, H. P. (1965). An analysis of errors in the formation of manuscript letters by first grade children. *American Educational Research Journal, 2,* 25–35.

Lewis, R. B., & Doorlag, D. H. (1991). *Teaching special students in the mainstream* (3rd ed.). New York: Merrill/Macmillan.

Lieberman, L. M. (1985). Special education and regular education: A merger made in heaven. *Exceptional Children, 51,* 513–516.

Lilly, M. S. (1987). Lack of focus on special education in literature on educational reform. *Exceptional Children, 53*(4), 325–326.

Lilly, M. S., & Givens-Ogle, L. B. (1981). Teacher consultation: Present, past, & future. *Behavioral Disorders, 6*(2), 73–77.

Lindsey, J. D. (1983). Paraprofessionals in learning disabilities. *Journal of Learning Disabilities, 16,* 467–472.

Lindsley, O. R. (1990). Precision teaching: By teachers for children. *Teaching Exceptional Children, 22*(3), 10–15.

Lippitt, P. (1976). Learning through cross-age helping: Why & how. In V. L. Allen (Ed.) *Children as teachers: Theory and research on tutoring* (pp. 157–168). New York: Academic Press.

Litt, M. D., & Turk, D. C. (1985). Sources of stress and dissatisfaction in experienced high school teachers. *Journal of Educational Research, 78,* 178–185.

Little, J. W. (1982). Norms of collegiality and experimentation: Workplace conditions of school success. *American Educational Research Journal, 19,* 325–340.

Lloyd, J. W. (1988). Direct academic intervention in learning disabilities. In M. Wang, M. Reynolds, & H. Walberg, (Eds.), *Handbook of special education research & practices Vol. 2* (pp. 345–366). New York: Pergamon.

Lloyd, J., Cullinan, D., Heins, E. D., & Epstein, M. H. (1980). Direct instruction: Effects on oral and written language comprehension. *Learning Disabilities Quarterly, 3*(4), 70–76.

Lovitt, D. L., & Harris, M. B. (1987). Important skills for adults with mental retardation: The client's point of view. *Mental Retardation, 25,* 351–356.

Mack, C. (1988). Celebrating cultural diversity calendar. *Teaching Exceptional Children, 21*(1), 40–43.

Madaus, G. F., Kellaghan, T., & Schwab, R. L. (1989). *Teach them well: An introduction to education.* New York: Harper & Row.

Madden, N. A., & Slavin, R. E. (1983). Effects of cooperative learning on the social acceptance of mainstreamed academically handicapped students. *Journal of Special Education, 17*(1), 171–182.

Maddux, C. D. (1986). Issues and concerns in special education microcomputing. *Computers in the Schools, 3*(3–4), 1–19.

Maheady, L., & Harper, G. F. (1987). A classwide peer-tutoring program to improve the spelling test performance of low income, third- and fourth-grade students. *Education and Treatment of Children, 10,* 120–133.

Maheady, L., Sacca, M. K., & Harper, G. F. (1987). Classwide student tutoring teams: The effects of peer-mediated instruction on the academic performance of secondary mainstreamed students. *Journal of Special Education, 21*(3), 107–121.

Maheady, L., Sacca, M. K., & Harper, G. F. (1988). Classwide peer tutoring with mildly handicapped high school students. *Exceptional Children, 55*(1), 52–59.

Maheady, L., Towne, R., Algozzine, B., Mercer, J., & Ysseldyke, J. (1983). Minority overrepresentation: A case for alternative practices prior to referral. *Learning Disability Quarterly, 6*(4), 448–457.

Maher, C. A. (1982). Behavioral effects of using conduct problem adolescents as cross-age tutors. *Psychology in the Schools, 19,* 360–364.

Maher, C. A. (1984). Handicapped adolescents as cross-age tutors: Program description and evaluation. *Exceptional Children, 51*(1), 56–63.

Male, M. (1988). *Special magic: Computers, classroom strategies, and exceptional students.* Mountain View, CA: Mayfield.

Mandoli, M., Mandoli, P., & McLaughlin, T. F. (1982). Effects of same-age peer tutoring on the spelling performance of a mainstreamed elementary LD student. *Learning Disability Quarterly, 5*(2), 185–189.

Marion, R. L. (1981). *Educators, parents, and exceptional children.* Rockville, MD: Aspen.

Markwardt, F. C. (1989). *Peabody Individual Achievement Test-Revised.* Circle Pines, MN: American Guidance Service.

Marston, D., Fuchs, L., & Deno, S. L. (1985). Measuring pupil progress: A comparison of standardized achievement tests and curriculum-based measures. *Diagnostique, 11,* 77–90.

Marston, D., & Magnusson, D. (1985). Implementing curriculum-based measurement in special and regular education settings. *Exceptional Children, 52*(3), 266–276.

Martin, B. (1970). *Brown bear, brown bear.* New York: Holt, Rinehart, & Winston.

Martin, J. B. (1970). *Fire! fire! said Mrs. McGuire.* New York: Holt, Rinehart, & Winston.

Maslach, C., & Jackson, S. E. (1979). *Burnout: The cost of caring.* Englewood Cliffs, NJ: Prentice-Hall.

Maslach, C., & Jackson, S. E. (1986). *Maslach burnout inventory manual* (2nd ed.). Palo Alto, CA: Consulting Psychologists Press.

Masters, L. F., & Mori, A. A. (1986). *Teaching secondary students with mild learning and behavior problems: Methods, materials, strategies.* Rockville, MD: Aspen.

Mastropieri, M. A. (1988). Using the keyword method. *Teaching Exceptional Children, 20*(2), 4–8.

Mastropieri, M. A., Scruggs, T. E., & Levin, J. R. (1986a). Direct vs. mnemonic instruction: Relative benefits for exceptional learners. *Journal of Special Education, 20*(3), 299–308.

Mastropieri, M. A., Scruggs, T. E., & Levin, J. R. (1986b). Maximizing what exceptional students can learn: A review of keyword and other mnemonic strategy research. *Remedial and Special Education, 6*(2), 39–45.

Mastropieri, M. A., Scruggs, T. E., Levin, J. R., Gaffney, J., & McLoone, B. (1985). Mnemonic vocabulary instruction for learning-disabled students. *Learning Disability Quarterly, 8,* 57–63.

Mathews, D. B. (1980). *The prevention of teacher burnout through stress management.* (ERIC Document Reproduction Service No. ED 213 693)

Mathews, D. B. (1984). *The Mathews burnout scales.* Orangeburg, SC: South Carolina State College.

Mathews, D. B. (1985). *Prevention of teacher burnout: The challenge of the future.* Paper presented at the annual meeting of Teacher Educators, Las Vegas, NV.

Matson, J. L., Rotatori, A. F., & Helsel, W. J. (1988). Development of a rating scale to measure social skills in children: The Matson evaluation of social skills with youngsters (MESSY). *Behavior Research and Therapy, 21,* 335–340.

May, L. J., & Hood, V. R. (1973). *Basic arithmetic skill evaluation.* Salem, OR: Media Research Associates.

McBride, J. W., & Forgnone, C. (1985). Emphasis of instruction provided LD, EH, and EMR students in categorical and cross-categorical resource programs. *Journal of Research and Development in Education, 18,* 50–54.

McCarney, S. B. (1986). Preferred types of communication indicated by parents and teachers of emotionally disturbed students. *Behavioral Disorders, 11*(2), 118–123.

McCarthy, B. (1987). *The 4MAT system.* Barrington, IL: Excel.

McCutcheon, G. (1980). How do elementary school teachers plan their courses? *Elementary School Journal, 81,* 4–23.

McGill, D., & Pearce, J. K. (1982). British families. In M. Giodrick, J. K. Pearce, & J. Giordano (Eds.), *Ethnicity in family therapy* (pp. 457–482). NY: Guilford Press.

McHardy, R. J. (1983). Stress among teachers of the gifted, teachers of the handicapped, and regular classroom teachers. (Doctoral dissertation, Columbia University, 1982). *Dissertation Abstracts International, 43,* 3881A.

McKeachie, W. J. (1974). The decline and fall of the laws of learning. *Educational Researchers, 3,* 7–11.

McKenzie, R. G., & Houk, C. S. (1986). Use of paraprofessionals in the resource room. *Exceptional Children, 53*(1), 41–45.

McKinney, J. D., & Hocutt, A. M. (1982). Public school involvement of parents of learning disabled and average achievers. *Exceptional Education Quarterly, 3*(2), 64–73.

McKinney, J. D., & Hocutt, A. M. (1988). The need for policy analysis in evaluating the regular education initiative. *Journal of Learning Disabilities, 21*(1), 12–18.

McKnab, P. A., & Mehring, T. A. (1984). *Attrition in special education: Rates and reasons.* Paper presented at the annual convention of the Council for Exceptional Children, Washington, DC.

McNutt, G. (1984). A holistic approach to language arts instruction in the resource room. *Learning Disabilities Quarterly, 7*(4), 315–320.

McPhie, W. E. (1983). The teaching unit: What makes it tick? In W. J. Stewart (Ed.), *Unit teaching: Perspectives and prospects* (pp. 51–57). Saratoga, CA: R & E Publishers.

McWhirter, A. M. (1990). Whole language in the middle school. *The Reading Teacher, 43*(8), 562–567.

Medley, D. M. (1979). The effectiveness of teachers: In P. L. Peterson & H. J. Walberg (Eds.), *Research on teaching: Concepts, findings, and implications* (pp. 11–27). Berkeley, CA: McCutchan.

Mehrabian, A. (1969). Significance of posture and position in the communication of attitude and status relationships. *Psychological Bulletin, 71,* 359–372.

Melaragno, R. J. (1976). In V. L. Allen (Ed.) *Children as teachers: Theory and research on tutoring* (pp. 189–198). New York: Academic.

Mendez, P. (1989). *The black snowman.* New York: Scholastic.

Mercer, C. D. (1987). *Students with learning disabilities* (3rd ed.). Columbus, OH: Merrill/Macmillan.

Mercer, C. D., & Mercer, A. R. (1989). *Teaching students with learning problems* (3rd ed). Columbus, OH: Merrill/Macmillan.

Mercer, C. D., Mercer, A. R., & Bott, D. A. (1984). *Self-correcting learning materials for the classroom.* Columbus, OH: Merrill/Macmillan.

Meyen, E. L. (1981). *Developing instructional units for the regular and special teacher* (3rd ed.). Dubuque, IA: Wm. C. Brown.

Meyen, E. L. (1986). A perspective on computing and special education. *Computers in the Schools, 3*(3–4), 11–19.

Meyen, E. L., & White, W. J. (1980). Career education and P.L. 94-142: Some views. In G. M. Clark & W. J. White (Eds.), *Career education for the handicapped: Current perspectives for teachers* (pp. 119–125). Boothwyn, PA: Educational Resources Center.

Meyer, L. A. (1984). Long-term academic effects of the direct instruction project Follow-Through. *The Elementary School Journal, 84*(4), 380–394.

Meyer, L. A. (1986). Strategies for correcting students' wrong responses. *Elementary School Journal, 87*(2), 227–241.

Meyer, L. A., Gersten, R. M., & Gutken, J. (1983). Direct instruction: A project Follow-Through success story in an inner-city school. *The Elementary School Journal, 84*(2), 241–252.

Michelson, L., & Wood, R. (1980). Behavioral assessment and training of children's social skills. *Progress in behavioral modification* (Vol. 9). New York: Academic Press.

Mickelson, J. M. (1983). The evolving concept of general method. In W. J. Stewart (Ed.), *Unit teaching: Perspectives & prospects* (pp. 15–26). Saratoga, CA: R & E Publishers.

Midgett, J., Olson, J., & Hornbeck, D. (1985, Winter). Comprehension games: Yes! yes! *Florida Media Quarterly, 10*(2), 13–14.

Minner, S., Beane, A., & Prater, G. (1986). Try telephone answering machines. *Teaching Exceptional Children, 19*(1), 62–63.

Minner, S., Prater, G., & Beane, A. (1989). Alternative methods of communicating with parents. *Academic Therapy, 24*(5), 619–624.

Mintz, A. L. (1979). *Teacher planning: A simulation study.* Unpublished doctoral dissertation, Syracuse University, Syracuse, NY.

Mithaug, D., Horiuchi, C., & Fanning, P. (1985). A report of the Colorado statewide follow-up survey of special education students. *Exceptional Children, 51*, 397–404.

Moran, M. (1980). *An investigation of the demands on oral language skills of learning disabled students in secondary classrooms* (Research Report No. 1). Lawrence, KS: University of Kansas Institute for Research in Learning Disabilities.

Morgan, D. P., & Jenson, W. R. (1988). *Teaching behaviorally disordered students: Preferred practices.* Columbus, OH: Merrill/Macmillan.

Morgan, L. (ed.) (1988). *Langston Hughes: He believed humor would help defeat bigotry and fear.* Seattle: Turman.

Morris, D. (1967). *The naked ape.* New York: McGraw-Hill.

Morse, W. C. (1981). Adults and adolescents. *Iowa Perspective, 8*–10.

Moskowitz, G., & Hayman, J. L. (1976). Success strategies of inner-city teachers: A yearlong study. *Journal of Educational Research, 69*, 283–289.

Mossip, J. (1985). It makes you feel needed: Students as teachers. In J. M. Newman (Ed.). *Whole language: Theory in use* (pp. 131–136). Portsmouth, NH: Heinemann Educational Books.

Moyer, B., & Dardig, M. (1978). Practical task analysis for special educators. *Teaching Exceptional Children, 10*, 16–18.

Muessig, R. H. (1983). Bridging the gap between textbook teaching and unit teaching. In W. J. Stewart (Ed.), *Unit teaching: Perspectives and prospects* (pp. 65–72). Saratoga, CA: R & E Publishers.

Murphy, M. D., & Brown, A. L. (1975). Incidental learning in preschool children as a function of level of cognitive analysis. *Journal of Experimental Child Psychology, 19*, 509–523.

Naslund, R., Thorpe, L., & Lefever, D. (1978). *SRA achievement series.* Chicago, IL: Science Research Associates.

The national career development guidance and counseling guidelines: High schools. (1988). Washington, DC: National Occupational Information Coordinating Committee.

National Committee on Excellence in Education. (1983). *A nation at risk: The imperative for educational reform.* Washington, DC: Government Printing Office.

Nelson, C. M., & Stevens, K. B. (1981). An accountable model for mainstreaming behaviorally disordered children, *Behavioral Disorders, 6*(2), 82–91.

Newcomer, P. (1986). *Standardized Reading Inventory.* Austin, TX: Pro-Ed.

Newland, T. E. (1932). An analytical study of the development of illegibilities in handwriting from the lower grades to adulthood. *Journal of Educational Research, 26*, 249–258.

Newman, J. M. (Ed.). (1985). *Whole language: Theory in use.* Portsmouth, NH: Heinemann Educational Books.

Newman, J. M., & Church, S. M. (1990). Commentary: Myths of whole language. *The Reading Teacher, 44*(1), 20–27.

New Mexico/Albuquerque Public Schools Center for Parent Involvement. (1979). Albuquerque, NM: University of New Mexico/Albuquerque Public Schools Center for Parent Involvement.

Nichols, R. G., & Stevens, L. A. (1957). *Are you listening?* New York: McGraw-Hill.

Niebuhr, R. (1943). *Serenity prayer.* Prayer written for service in Congregational church in Heath, Massachusetts, *Monthly Bulletin:* Federal Council of Churches.

Niemiec, R., Samson, G., Weinstein, T., & Walberg, H. J. (1987). The effects of computer-based instruction in elementary schools: A quantitative synthesis. *Journal of Research on Computing in Education 20*(2), 85–103.

Oberg, C., Muret-Wagstaff, S., Moore, S., & Cummings, B. (1983). *A cross-cultural assessment of maternal-child interaction: Link to health and development.* Paper presented at the Hmong Conference II: The Hmong in transition, Minneapolis, MN. (ERIC Document Reproduction Service No. ED 243 995)

Ogle, D. M. (1986). K-W-L: A teaching model that develops active reading of expository text. *The Reading Teacher, 39,* 564–570.

Olion, L. (1989). Enhancing the involvement of Black parents of adolescents with handicaps. In A. A. Ortiz & B. A. Ramirez (Eds.), *Schools and the culturally diverse exceptional students: Promising practices and future directions* (second printing, pp. 96–103). Reston, VA: The Council for Exceptional Children.

Olson, J. (1982a). Self-management. In B. Algozzine (Ed.), *Problem behavior management: Educator's resource service* (pp. 2:52–2:57, Unit 2). Rockville, MD: Aspen.

Olson, J. (1982b). Treatment perspectives: Peer tutoring, Unit 2. In B. Algozzine (Ed.), *Problem behavior management* (pp. 40–44). Rockville, MD: Aspen.

Olson, J. (1987). Spoken language. In C. Mercer, *Students with learning disabilities,* (3rd ed.) (pp. 298–333). Columbus, OH: Merrill/Macmillan.

Olson, J. (1989). Managing life in the classroom: Dealing with the nitty gritty. *Academic Therapy, 24*(5), 545–554.

Olson, M. W. (1980, February). *Pattern guides: An alternative for content teachers.* Paper presented at the annual meeting of the southwest regional conference of the International Reading Association, Albuquerque, NM.

Orange County Public Schools. (1986). *Orange County curriculum guide.* Orlando, FL: Author.

Ortiz, A. A. (1989). *Factors to consider when adapting materials for ESE/LEP students.*

Handicapped Minority Research Institute, Department of Special Education, University of Texas, Austin, TX.

Ortiz, A. A., & Garcia, S. B. (1989). A preferral process for preventing inappropriate referrals of Hispanic students to special education. In A. A. Ortiz & B. A. Ramirez (Eds.), *Schools and the culturally diverse exceptional student: Promising practices and future directions* (second printing, pp. 6–18). Reston, VA: The Council for Exceptional Children.

Ortiz, A. A., & Polyzoi, E. (1989). Language assessment of Hispanic learning disabled and speech and language handicapped students: Research in progress. In A. A. Ortiz & B. A. Ramirez (Eds.), *Schools and the culturally diverse exceptional student: Promising practices and future directions* (second printing, pp. 32–44). Reston, VA: The Council for Exceptional Children.

Ortiz, A. A., & Yates, J. R. (1989). Characteristics of learning disabled, mentally retarded, and speech-language Hispanic students at initial evaluation and reevaluation. In A. A. Ortiz & B. A. Ramirez (Eds.), *Schools and the culturally diverse exceptional student: Promising practices and future directions* (second printing, pp. 51–62). Reston, VA: The Council for Exceptional Children.

Orum, L. (1986). *The education of Hispanics: Status and implications.* Washington, DC: National Council of La Raza.

Osborne, S. S., Kosiewicz, M. M., Crumley, E. B., & Lee, C. (1987). It worked in my classroom. *Teaching Exceptional Children, 19*(2), 66–69.

O'Shea, L., & O'Shea, D. (1988). Using repeated readings. *Teaching Exceptional Children, 20*(2), 26–29.

O'Shea, L. J., Sindelar, P. T., & O'Shea, D. J. (1985). The effects of repeated readings and attentional cues on reading fluency and comprehension. *Journal of Reading Behavior, 17,* 129–141.

Palincsar, A. S. (1982). *Improving the reading comprehension of junior high students through reciprocal teaching of comprehension-monitoring strategies.* Unpublished doctoral dissertation, University of Illinois, Urbana.

Palincsar, A. S. (1986a). Metacognitive strategy instruction. *Exceptional Children, 53*(2), 118–124.

Palincsar, A. S. (1986b). The role of dialogue in scaffolded instruction. *Educational Psychologist, 21,* 73–98.

Palincsar, A. S., & Brown, A. L. (1984). The reciprocal teaching of comprehension fostering and comprehension monitoring activities. *Cognition and Instruction, 1,* 117–175.

Palincsar, A. S., & Brown, A. L. (1986). Interactive teaching to promote independent learning from text. *The Reading Teacher, 39*(8), 771–777.

Palincsar, A. S., & Brown, A. L. (1987). Enhancing instructional time through attention to metacognition. *Journal of Learning Disabilities, 20*(2), 66–75.

Palincsar, A. S., & Brown, A. L. (1988). Teaching and practicing thinking skills to promote comprehension in the context of group problem solving. *Remedial and Special Education, 9*(1), 53–59.

Palincsar, A. S., & Brown, A. L. (1989). Instruction for self-regulated reading. In L. B. Resnick & L. E. Klopfer (Eds.), *Toward the thinking curriculum: Current cognitive research: 1989 ASCD yearbook* (pp. 19–39). Alexandria, VA: Association for Supervision and Curriculum Development.

Palmer, U. (1975). The value and training of paraprofessionals. *Journal of Rehabilitation of the Deaf, 8,* 3–9.

Papert, S. (1980). *Mindstorms.* New York: Basic Books.

Paris, S. G. (1988). Models and metaphors of learning strategies. In C. E. Weinstein, E. T. Goetz, & P. A. Alexander (Eds.), *Learning and study strategies: Issues in assessment, instruction, and evaluation* (pp. 299–321). San Diego: Academic Press.

Paris, S. G., & Cross, D. R. (1983). Ordinary learning: Pragmatic connections among children's beliefs, motives, and actions. In J. Dis-anz, G. L. Disanz, & R. Kail (Eds.), *Learning in children* (pp. 137–169). New York: Springer-Verlag.

Paris, S. G., Lipson, M. Y., Jacobs, J., Oka, E., Debritto, A. M., & Cross, D. (1982, April). *Metacognition and reading comprehension.* Symposium conducted at the annual meeting of the International Reading Association, Chicago, IL.

Paris, S. G., Newman, R., & McVey, K. (1982). Learning the functional significance of mnemonic actions: A microgenetic study of strategy acquisition. *Journal of Experimental Child Psychology, 34,* 490–509.

Paris, S. G. & Oka, E. R. (1986). Self-regulated learning among exceptional children. *Exceptional Children, 53*(2), 103–108.

Pascal, F. (1983–1989). *Sweet valley high series.* New York: Bantam.

Patton, J., & Braithwaite, R. L. (1984). Obstacles to the participation of black parents in the educational programs of their handicapped children. *Centering Teacher Education, 1*(2), 34–37.

Pauk, W. (1984). *How to study in college.* Boston: Houghton Mifflin.

Pearson, P. D. (1982). Asking questions about stories. *Occasional Paper, No. 15.* Columbus, OH: Ginn.

Pearson, P. D., & Johnson, D. (1978). *Teaching reading comprehension.* New York: Holt, Rinehart, & Winston.

Pepper, F. C. (1976). Teaching the American Indian child in mainstream settings. In R. L. Jones (Ed.), *Mainstream settings and the minority child* (pp. 133–158). Reston, VA: The Council for Exceptional Children.

Peterson, N. L. (1987). *Early intervention for handicapped and at-risk children: An introduction to early childhood-special education.* Denver, CO: Love Publishing.

Peterson, S. K., Scott, J., & Sroka, K. (1990). Using the language experience approach with precision. *Exceptional Children, 22*(3), 28–31.

Phillips, V., & McCullough, L. (1990). Consultation-based programming: Instituting the collaborative ethic in schools. *Exceptional Children, 56*(4), 291–304.

Pickett, A. L. (1988). *A training program for paraprofessionals working in special education and related services.* New York: National Resource Center for Paraprofessionals in Special Education, New Careers Training Laboratory, City University of New York.

Pickhardt, D. E. (1978). Fear in school: How students make teachers afraid. *Educational Leadership, 36*(2), 107–112.

Pikulski, J. J. (1989). The assessment of reading: A time for change. *The Reading Teacher, 43*(1), 80–81.

Platt, J. M. (1987). Increasing the independence of learning-disabled adolescents through self-detection of errors. *Ideas in Education, 4*(1), 17–23.

Platt, J. M., & Olson, J. (1990). Why teachers are leaving special education: Implications for preservice and inservice educators. *Teacher Education and Special Education, 13*(3–4), 192–196.

Platt, J. M., & Williams, K. (1988). Preservice and inservice teachers' reading comprehension skills and their metacognitive awareness of processing of text. *Eighth Yearbook of the American Reading Forum.* Sarasota, FL: American Reading Forum.

Polloway, E. A., Epstein, M. H., Polloway, C. H., Patton, J. R., & Ball, D. W. (1986). Corrective reading program: An analysis of effectiveness with learning disabled and mentally retarded students. *Remedial and Special Education, 7*(4), 41–47.

Polloway, E. A., Patton, J. R., Payne, J. S., & Payne, R. A. (1989). *Strategies for teaching learners with special needs* (4th ed.). Columbus, OH: Merrill/Macmillan.

Poplin, M. S. (1984). Toward an holistic view of persons with learning disabilities. *Learning Disability Quarterly, 7*(4), 290–294.

Potter, B. A. (1987). *Preventing job burnout.* Los Altos, CA: Crisp Publications.

Powers, D. A. (1986). Evaluating software for use by mentally handicapped learners. *Computers in the Schools, 3*(3–4), 41–49.

Putnam, J. W., Rynders, J. E., Johnson, R. T., & Johnson, D. W. (1989). Collaborative skill instruction for promoting positive interactions between mentally handicapped and nonhandicapped children. *Exceptional Children, 55*(6), 550–558.

Pressley, M., Borkowski, J. G., & O'Sullivan, J. T. (1984). Memory strategy instruction is made of this: Metamemory and durable strategy use. *Educational Psychologist, 1,* 94–107.

Pressley, M., Symons, S., Snyder, B. L., & Cariglia-Bull, T. (1989). Strategy instruction research comes of age. *Learning Disability Quarterly, 12*(1), 16–31.

Pryzwansky, W. B. (1974). A reconsideration of the consultation model for delivery of school-based psychological services. *American Journal of Orthopsychiatry, 44,* 579–583.

Pryzwansky, W. B., & White, G. W. (1983). The influence of consultee characteristics on preferences for consultation approaches. *Professional Psychology: Research and Practice, 14,* 651–657.

Pugach, M. (1987). The national education reports and special education: Implications for teacher education. *Exceptional Children, 53*(4), 308–314.

Pugach, M. C., & Johnson, L. J. (1988). Rethinking the relationship between consultation and collaborative problem solving. *Focus on Exceptional Children, 21*(4), 1–14.

Pugach, M. C., & Johnson, L. J. (1989). The challenge of implementing collaboration between general and special education. *Exceptional Children, 56*(3), 232–235.

Raiser, L. (1987). A teacher support network. *Teaching Exceptional Children, 19*(3), 48–49.

Ramirez, B. A. (1988). Culturally and linguistically diverse children. *Teaching Exceptional Children, 20*(4), 45–46.

Rathjen, D. P. (1984). Social skills training for children: Innovations and consumer guidelines. *School Psychology Review, 13,* 292–301.

Raygor, A. L. (1970). *Study skills test: Form A.* New York: McGraw-Hill.

Reichard, C. L. (1979). *Project RETOOL report.* Reston, VA: The Council for Exceptional Children, Teacher Education Division.

Reid, E. (1986). Practicing effective instruction: The exemplary center for reading instruction approach. *Exceptional Children, 52*(6), 510–517.

Reynolds, M. C., & Wang, M. C. (1983). Restructuring "special" school programs: A position paper. *Policy Studies Review, 2*(1), 189–212.

Reynolds, M. C., Wang, M. C., & Walberg, H. J. (1987). The necessary restructuring of special and regular education. *Exceptional Children, 53*(5), 391–398.

Rhodes, L. K. (1981). I can read: Predictable books as resources for reading and writing instruction. *The Reading Teacher, 34*(5), 511–518.

Rhodes, L. K., & Dudley-Marling, C. (1988). *Readers and writers make a difference: A holistic approach to teaching learning disabled and remedial students.* Portsmouth, NH: Heinemann Educational Books.

Rhodes, L. K., & Shannon, J. L. (1982). Psycholinguistic principles in operation in a primary learning disabilities classroom. *Topics in Learning and Learning Disability 1*(4), 1–10.

Rich, H. L., & Ross, S. M. (1989). Student's time on learning tasks in special education. *Exceptional Child, 55*(6), 508–515.

Rickards, J. P., & August, G. J. (1975). Generative underlining strategies in prose recall. *Journal of Educational Psychology, 67,* 860–865.

Rieth, H. J., & Frick, T. W. (1982). *An analysis of academic learning time in special education service delivery systems: Initial report on classroom process variables.* Technical report. Bloomington, IN: Center for Innovation in Teaching the Handicapped, Indiana University.

Rieth, H. J., & Frick, T. W. (1983). *An analysis of the academic learning time provided to mildly handicapped students in different service delivery systems.* Bloomington, IN: Center for Innovation in Teaching the Handicapped, Indiana University.

Rieth, H. J., Polsgrove, L., Okolo, C., Bahr, C., & Eckert, R. (1987). An analysis of the secondary special education classroom ecology with implications for teacher training. *Teacher Education and Special Education, 10*(3), 113–119.

Rivera, D., & Smith, D. (1988). Using a demonstration strategy to teach midschool students with learning disabilities how to compute long division. *Journal of Learning Disabilities, 21*(2), 77–81.

Roberds-Baxter, S. (1984). The parent connection: Enhancing the affective component of parent conferences. *Teaching Exceptional Children, 17*(1), 55–58.

Robinson, F. P. (1961). *Effective study* (rev. ed.). New York: Harper & Row.

Robinson, H. A. (1975). *Teaching reading and study strategies: The content areas.* Boston: Allyn & Bacon.

Roblyer, M. D. (1988). The effectiveness of microcomputers in education: A review of the research for 1980–1987. *T.H.E. Journal, 16*(2), 85–89.

Roblyer, M. D. (1989). *Making the most of microcomputers in the classroom.* Tallahassee, FL: Florida Department of Education.

Roblyer, M. D., Castine, W. H., & King, F. J. (1988). *Assessing the impact of computer-based instruction: A review of recent research.* New York: Haworth Press.

Rose, S. R. (1983). Promoting social competence in children: A classroom approach to social and cognitive skill training. *Social Skills Training for Children and Youth, 5,* 43–59.

Rosenberg, M. S. (1986). Maximizing the effectiveness of structured classroom management programs: Implementing rule-review procedures with disruptive and distractible students. *Behavioral Disorders, 11*(4), 239–248.

Rosenholtz, S. (1985). Effective schools: Interpreting the evidence. *American Journal of Education, 92,* 352–389.

Rosenholtz, S., Bassler, O., & Hoover-Dempsey, C. (1985). *Organizational conditions of teacher learning.* (NIE-G-83-0041). Urbana, IL: University of Illinois.

Rosenshine, B. (1980). How time is spent in elementary classrooms. In C. Denham & A. Lieberman (Eds.), *Time to learn*. Washington, DC: National Institute of Education.

Rosenshine, B. (1983). Teaching functions in instructional programs. *Elementary School Journal, 83*, 335–351.

Rosenshine, B. (1986). Synthesis of research on explicit teaching. *Educational Leadership, 43*(7), 60–69.

Rosenshine, B. (1990). *Scaffolds for teaching content-specific higher-level skills*. Unpublished manuscript, The University of Illinois at Urbana.

Rosenshine, B., & Stevens, R. (1986). Teaching functions. In M. Wittrock (Ed.), *Third handbook of research on teaching* (pp. 376–391). New York: Macmillan.

Roser, N. L., Hoffman, J. V., & Farest, C. (1990). Language, literature, and at-risk children. *Reading Teacher, 43*,(8), 554–561.

Rowe, M. B. (1974). Wait time and rewards as instructional variables, their influence on language, logic, and rate control: Part 1: Wait time. *Journal of Research in Science Teaching, 11*, 81–94.

Rubinstein, F. D. (1989). *ACT: Adolescent competence training*. Westport, CT: Franklin Learning Systems.

Ruiz, N. T. (1989). An optimal learning environment for Rosemary. *Exceptional Child, 56*(2), 130–144.

Rusch, F. R., & DeStefano, L. (1989). Transition from school to work: Strategies for young adults with disabilities. *Interchange, 9*, 1–2.

Rutter, M., Maughan, B., Mortimore, P., & Ouston, J. (1979). *Fifteen thousand hours: Secondary schools and their effects on children*. Cambridge, MA: Harvard University Press.

Salend, S. J. (1984). Factors contributing to the development of successful mainstreaming programs. *Exceptional Children, 50*(5), 409–419.

Salend, S. J., & Allen, E. M. (1985). A comparison of self-managed and externally managed response cost systems on learning disabled children. *Journal of School Psychology, 23*, 59–67.

Salend, S. J., & Washin, B. (1988). Team-assisted individualization with handicapped adjudicated youth. *Exceptional Children, 55*(2), 174–180.

Salvia, J., & Hughes, C. (1990). *Curriculum-based assessment: Testing what is taught*. New York: Macmillan.

Salvia, J., & Ysseldyke, J. E. (1988). *Assessment in special and remedial education* (4th ed.). Boston: Houghton-Mifflin.

Sargent, L. R. (1981). Resource teacher time utilization: An observational study. *Exceptional Children, 47*(6), 420–426.

Saville-Troike, M. (1976). *Foundations for teaching English as a second language: Theory and method for multicultural education*. Englewood Cliffs, NJ: Prentice-Hall.

Scardamalia, M., & Bereiter, C. (1985a). Helping students become better writers. *School Administrator, 42*(4), 16–26.

Scardamalia, M., & Bereiter, C. (1985b). In B. Rosenshine (Ed.), *Scaffolds for teaching content-specific higher level skills*. Unpublished manuscript, University of Illinois, Urbana, IL.

Schein, E. H. (1969). *Process consultation: Its role in organization development*. Reading, MA: Addison-Wesley.

Schloss, P. J., & Schloss, C. N. (1987). A critical review of social skills research in mental retardation. In R. P. Barrett & J. L. Matson (Eds.), *Advances in developmental disorders*. Greenwich, CT: JAI Press.

Schloss, P. J., Schloss, C. N., & Harris, L. (1984). A multiple baseline analysis of an interpersonal skills training program for depressed youth. *Behavior Disorders, 9*, 182–188.

Schloss, P. J., & Sedlak, R. A. (1986). *Instructional methods for students with learning and behavior problems*. Boston: Allyn & Bacon.

Schloss, P. J., Sedlak, R. A., Wiggins, E. D., & Ramsey, D. (1983). Stress reduction for professionals working with aggressive adolescents. *Exceptional Children, 49*(4), 349–354.

Schniedewind, N., & Salend, S. J. (1987). Cooperative learning works. *Teaching Exceptional Children, 19*(2), 22–25.

Schuler, L., Ogulthorpe, R. T., & Eiserman, W. D. (1987). The effects of reverse-role tutoring on the social acceptance of students with behavioral disorders. *Behavioral Disorders, 13*(1), 35–44.

Schumaker, J. (1989). The heart of strategy instruction. *Strategram: Strategies intervention model, 1*(4). Kansas City, KS: The University of Kansas Institute for Research in Learning Disabilities, pp. 1–5.

Schumaker, J. B., & Deshler, D. D. (1984). Setting demand variables: A major factor in program planning for the LD adolescent. *Topics in Language Disorders, 4,* 22–40.

Schumaker, J. B., & Deshler, D. D. (1988). Implementing the regular education initiative in secondary schools: A different ball game. *Journal of Learning Disabilities, 21*(1), 36–42.

Schumaker, J. B., Hazel, J. S., & Pederson, G. S. (1988). *Social skills for daily living.* Circle Pines, MN: American Guidance Service.

Schumaker, J. B., Nolan, S. M., & Deshler, D. D. (1985). *The error monitoring strategy.* Lawrence, KA: The University of Kansas.

Schumaker, J. B., Pederson, G., Hazel, J. S., & Meyen, E. (1983). Selecting a social skills curriculum for mildly handicapped secondary students. *Focus on Exceptional Children, 16*(4), 1–16.

Shumaker, J. B., & Sheldon, J. (1985). *Learning strategies curriculum: The sentence writing strategy, instructor's manual.* Lawrence, KA: The University of Kansas.

Schwab, R. L., & Iwanicki, E. F. (1982). Perceived role conflict, role ambiguity, and teacher burnout. *Educational Administration Quarterly, 18*(1), 60–74.

Scibior, O. (1985). Learning to spell. In J. M. Newman (Ed.), *Whole language: Theory in use* (pp. 83–90). Portsmouth, NH: Heinemann Educational Books.

Scruggs, T. E., & Mastropieri, M. A. (1984). Improving memory for facts: The "keyword" method. *Academic Therapy, 20*(2), 159–166.

Scruggs, T. E., & Mastropieri, M. A. (1986). Academic characteristics of behaviorally disordered and learning-disabled students. *Behavioral Disorders, 11*(3), 184–190.

Scruggs, T. E., Mastropieri, M. A., Levin, J. R., & Gaffney, J. S. (1985). Facilitating the acquisition of science facts in learning-disabled students. *American Educational Research Journal, 22,* 575–586.

Scruggs, T. E., Mastropieri, M. A., & Richter, L. (1985). Peer tutoring with behaviorally disordered students: Social and academic benefits. *Behavioral Disorders, 10*(4), 283–294.

Scruggs, T. E., Mastropieri, M. A., Veit, D. T., & Ogulthorpe, R. T. (1986). Behaviorally disordered students as tutors: Effects on social behavior. *Behavioral Disorders, 12*(11), 36–44.

Scruggs, T. E., & Richter, L. (1986). Tutoring learning disabled students: A critical review. *Learning Disability Quarterly, 9*(1), 2–14.

Serebrin, W. (1985). Andrew and Molly: Writers and context in concert. In J. M. Newman (Ed.), *Whole language: Theory in use* (pp. 45–54). Portsmouth, NH: Heinemann Educational Books.

Seuss, D. (1940). *Horton hatches the egg.* New York: Random House.

Shade, B. J. (1979). *Racial preferences in psychological differentiation: An alternative explanation to group differences.* (ERIC Document Reproduction Service No. ED 179 672)

Sharp, Q. (Ed.). (1989). *Evaluation-whole language checklists for evaluating your children for grades K to 6.* New York: Scholastic.

Shaw, S., Bensky, J., Dixon, B., & Bonneau, R. (1980). *Preventing teacher burnout: Suggestions for efficiently meeting PL 94-142 mandates and providing for staff survival.* Paper presented at the 58th annual international convention of the Council for Exceptional Children, Philadelphia. (ERIC Document Reproduction Service No. ED 187 048)

Shinn, M., & Marson, D. (1985). Differentiating mildly handicapped, low achieving, and regular education students: A curriculum-based approach. *RASE, 6*(2), 31–38.

Short, E. J., & Ryan, E. B. (1984). Metacognitive differences between skilled and less-skilled readers: Remediating deficits through grammar and attribution training. *Journal of Educational Psychology, 76*, 225–235.

Sibley, S. (1986). *A meta-analysis of school consultation research.* Unpublished doctoral dissertation, Texas Women's University, Denton, TX.

Siegel, M. A., & Crawford, K. A. (1983). Two-year follow-up study of discrimination learning by mentally retarded children. *American Journal of Mental Deficiency, 88*(1), 76–78.

Silbert, J., Carnine, D., & Stein, M. (1990). *Direct instruction mathematics* (2nd ed.). Columbus, OH: Merrill/Macmillan.

Silver Burdett Spelling Teacher Resource Book 4, Unit 6 (developed by J. D'Andrea Hunt). Morriston, NJ: Silver Burdett Co., 1986.

Simpson, R. L. (1982). *Conferencing parents of exceptional children.* Rockville, MD: Aspen.

Sinclair, R. L., & Ghory, W. J. (1987). *Reaching marginal students: A primary concern for school renewal.* Chicago: McCutchan.

Sindelar, P. T. (1987). Increasing reading fluency. *Teaching Exceptional Children, 19*(2), 59–60.

Sindelar, P., Espin, C., Smith, M., & Harriman, N. (1990). A comparison of more and less effective special education teachers in elementary-level programs. *Teacher Education and Special Education, 13*(1), 9–16.

Sindelar, P., Smith, M., Harriman, N., Hale, R., & Wilson, R. (1986). Teacher effectiveness in special education programs. *Journal of Special Education, 20*(2), 195–207.

Singer, H. J., McNeil, D., & Furse, L. (1984). Relationship between curricular scope and reading achievement in elementary schools. *Reading Teacher, 37*, 608–612.

Sisley, B. (1983). Timely tips: Time management for the administration. *Physical Educator, 40*, 75–77.

Slavin, R. E. (1984). Team-assisted individualization: Cooperative learning and individualized instruction in the mainstreamed classroom. *Remedial and Special Education, 5*(6), 33–42.

Slavin, R. E. (1985). Cooperative learning: Applying contact theory in desegregated schools. *Journal of Social Issues, 41*(3), 45–62.

Slavin, R. E. (1988a). Cooperative learning and student achievement. *Educational Leadership, 46*(2), 31–33.

Slavin, R. E. (1988b). *Student team learning: An overview and practical guide* (2nd ed.). Washington, DC: National Education Association.

Slavin, R. E., Leavey, M., & Madden, N. A. (1984). Combining cooperative learning and individualized instruction: Effects on student mathematics achievement, attitudes, and behaviors. *Elementary School Journal, 84*, 409–22.

Slavin, R. E., & Oickle, E. (1981). Effects of cooperative learning teams on student achievement and race relations: Treatment by race interactions. *Sociology of Education, 54*, 174–80.

Slavin, R. E., Stevens, R. J., & Madden, N. A. (1988). Accommodating student diversity in reading and writing instruction: A cooperative learning approach. *Remedial and Special Education, 9*(1), 60–66.

Smith-Davis, J., Burke, P. J., & Noel, M. (1984). *Personnel to educate. The handicapped in America: Supply and demand from a programmatic viewpoint.* College Park, MD: University of Maryland, Institute for Study of Exceptional Children and Youth.

Smith, L., & Cotten, M. (1980). Effect of lesson vagueness and discontinuity on student achievement and attitudes. *Journal of Educational Psychology, 72*, 670–675.

Smith, L. R., & Land, M. (1980). Student perception of teacher clarity in mathematics. *Journal of Research in Mathematics Education, 11*, 137–146.

Soldier, L. L. (1989). Language learning of Native American students. *Educational Leadership, 46*(5), 74–75.

Sonnenschein, P. (1981). Parents and professionals: An uneasy relationship. *Teaching Exceptional Children, 14*(2), 62–65.

Spache, G. D., & Spache, E. B. (1977). *Reading in the elementary school.* Boston: Allyn & Bacon.

Sperry, A. (1940). *Call it courage.* New York: Macmillan.

Spier, P. (1977). *Noah's ark* (translated from Jacobus Revius). Garden City, NY: Doubleday.

Spizzirri, L. (1985). *An educational coloring book of southeast Indians.* Medinah, IL: Spizzirri.

Sprick, R. S. (1981). *The solution book: A guide to classroom discipline.* Chicago: Science Research Associates.

Sprick, R. S. (1985). *Discipline in the secondary classroom: A problem-by-problem survival guide.* West Nyack, NY: The Center for Applied Research in Education.

Squires, D. A., Huitt, W. G., & Segars, J. K. (1983). *Effective schools and classrooms: A research-based perspective.* Alexandria, VA: Association for Supervision and Curriculum Development.

Staab, C. F. (1990). Teacher mediation in one whole literacy classroom. *The Reading Teacher, 43*(8), 548–553.

Stahl, S. A., & Miller, P. D. (1989). Whole language and language experience for beginning reading: A quantitative research synthesis. *Review of Educational Research, 59* (1), 87–116.

Stainback, S., & Stainback, W. (1985). The merger of special and regular education: Can it be done? *Exceptional Children, 51,* 517–521.

Stainback, W., & Stainback, S. (1984). A rationale for the merger of special and regular education. *Exceptional Children, 51*(2), 102–111.

Stallings, J. (1975). Implementation and child effects of teaching practices in Follow-Through classrooms. *Monographs of the Society for Research in Child Development, 40*(7–8), Serial No. 163.

Stallings, J. (1980). Allocated academic learning time revisited, or beyond time on-task. *Educational Researcher, 9,* 11–16.

Stallings, J., Needels, M., & Staybrook, N. (1979). *The teaching of basic reading skills in secondary schools.* Phase II and Phase III. Menlo Park, CA: S.R.I. International.

Stamm, J. M. (1980). Teacher competencies: Recommendations for personnel preparation. *Teacher Education and Special Education, 3*(1), 52–57.

Stanley, S. O., & Greenwood, C. R. (1983). How much "opportunity to respond" does the minority disadvantaged student receive in school? *Exceptional Children, 49,* 370–373.

Stebbins, L., St. Pierre, R. G., Proper, E. L., Anderson, R. B., & Cerba, T. R. (1977). *Education as experimentation: A planned variation model* (Vols. 4 A–D). Cambridge, MA: ABT Associates.

Stein, C. L'E., & Goldman, J. (1980). Beginning reading instruction for children with minimal brain dysfunction. *Journal of Learning Disability, 13*(4), 52–55.

Stein, J. (1984). Microcomputer uses to promote physical proficiency and motor development of students with handicapped conditions. *Physical Educator, 41*(1), 40–42.

Stephens, T. M. (1980). *Technical information: Social behavior assessment.* Columbus, OH: Cedars Press.

Stephens, T. M., Blackhurst, A. E., & Magliocca, L. A. (1988). *Teaching mainstreamed students* (2nd ed.). New York: Pergamon.

Steptoe, J. (1987). *Mufaro's beautiful daughters.* New York: Lothrop, Lee, & Shepard.

Stevens, R., & Rosenshine, B. (1981). Advances in research on teaching. *Exceptional Education Quarterly, 2*(1), 1–10.

Stevenson, R. L. (1883). *Treasure island.* New York: Grosset & Dunlap.

Stokes, T. F., & Baer, D. M. (1977). An implicit technology of generalization. *Journal of Applied Behavior Analysis, 10,* 349–367.

Strickland, D. S., & Morrow, L. M. (1988). Creating a print-rich environment. *The Reading Teacher, 42*(3), 156–157.

Strickland, D. S., & Morrow, L. M. (1989). Emerging readers and writers: Interactive experiences with storybook reading. *The Reading Teacher, 42*(4), 322–323.

Strickland, D. S., & Morrow, L. M. (1990). Emerging readers and writers: Integrating the emergent literacy curriculum with themes. *The Reading Teacher, 43*(8), 604–605.

Sugai, G., & Maheady, L. (1988). Cultural diversity and individual assessment for behavior disorders. *Teaching Exceptional Children, 2*(1), 28–31.

Swanson, H. L. (1989). Strategy instruction: Overview of principles and procedures. *Learning Disability Quarterly, 12*(1), 3–15.

Swedo, J. (1987, Fall). Effective teaching strategies for handicapped limited-English-proficient students. *Bilingual Special Education Newsletter,* pp. 1–5.

Syzmandera, C. (1976). *Sound Foundations Program II.* Allen, TX: Developmental Learning Materials.

Syzmandera, C. (1981). Troll Listening Lab. Nahwah, NJ: Troll Associates.

Tarver, S. G. (1986). Cognitive behavior modification, direct instruction and holistic approaches to the education of students with learning disabilities. *Journal of Learning Disabilities, 19*(6), 368–375.

Taylor, B. M., & Beach, R. W. (1984). The effects of text structure instruction on middle-grade students' comprehension and production of expository text. *Reading Research Quarterly,* 19, 134–146.

Taylor, R. L. (1984). *Assessment of exceptional students: Educational and psychological procedures.* Englewood Cliffs, NJ: Prentice-Hall.

Taylor, S. E. (1964). *Listening.* Washington, DC: National Education Association.

Teacher Education Division, Council for Exceptional Children. (1987). The regular education initiative. *Journal of Learning Disabilities, 20*(5), 289–293.

Tharp, R. (1975). The triadic model of consultation. In C. Parker (Ed.), *Psychological consultation in the schools: Helping teachers meet special needs* (pp. 133–151). Reston, VA: The Council for Exceptional Children.

Tharp, R. G., & Wetzel, R. J. (1969). *Behavior modification in the natural environment.* New York: Academic Press.

Thomas, W. R. (1984). *Occupational stress among special education teachers.* Paper presented at the annual convention of the Council for Exceptional Children, Washington, DC.

Thormann, J. (1982). *Public school use of computers in special education: Results of a statewide survey.* Unpublished doctoral dissertation, University of Oregon, Eugene.

Thormann, J. (1985). *Computer use in special education: Results of a statewide survey.* Quincy, MA: Massachusetts Dept. of Education, Division of Special Education.

Thormann, J., Gersten, R., Moore, L., & Morvant, M. (1986). Microcomputers in special education classrooms: Themes from research and implications for practice. *Computers in the Schools, 3*(3–4), 97–109.

Thurlow, M., Christenson, S., & Ysseldyke, J. (1987). *School effectiveness: Implications of effective instruction for handicapped students* (Monograph No. 3). Minneapolis, MN: Instructional Alternative Project, University of Minnesota.

Thurston, L. P., & White, W. J. (1990, March). Life survival skills for mildly handicapped students in high school. Paper presented at the American Council on Rural Special Education Annual Conference, Tucson, AZ.

Tiedt, P. L., & Tiedt, I. M. (1986). *Multicultural teaching.* Boston: Allyn & Bacon.

Timm, P. R. (1987). *Successful self-management.* Los Altos, CA: Crisp Publications.

Tindal, G. (1987). Graphing performance. *Teaching Exceptional Children, 20*(1), 44–46.

Tindal, G. A., & Marston, D. B. (1990). *Classroom-based assessment: Evaluating instructional outcomes.* Columbus, OH: Merrill/Macmillan.

Tobin, K. (1987). The role of wait time in higher cognitive level learning. *Review of Educational Research, 57*(1), 69–95.

Tolan, S. S. (1978). *Grandpa and me.* New York: Charles Scribner's Sons.

Toliver, M. (1990). Try it, you'll like it: Whole language. *The Reading Teacher, 43*(4), 348–349.

Torgesen, J. K. (1977). Memorization processes in reading disabled children. *Journal of Educational Psychology,* 69, 571–578.

Torgesen, J. K. (1982). The learning disabled child as an inactive learner: Educational implications. *Topics in Learning and Learning Disabilities, 2*(1), 45–52.

Trachtenburg, P., & Ferruggia, A. (1989). Big books from little voices: Reaching high-risk beginning readers. *The Reading Teacher, 42*(4), 284–289.

Trent, S. (1989). Much to do about nothing. *Journal of Learning Disabilities, 22*(1), 23–25, 45.

Troutman, A. P., & White, J. A. (1988). *The micro goes to school: Instructional applications of microcomputer technology.* Pacific Grove, CA: Brooks/Cole.

Truett, C., & Gillespie, L. (1984). *Choosing educational software.* Littleton, CO: Libraries Unlimited.

Tunnell, M. O., & Jacobs, J. S. (1989). Using "real" books: Research findings on literature-based reading instruction. *The Reading Teacher, 42*(7), 470–477.

Turnbull, A. P., Strickland, B. B., & Brantley, J. C. (1982). *Developing and implementing individualized education programs.* Columbus, OH: Merrill/Macmillan.

Turnbull, A. P., & Turnbull, H. R. (1986). *Families, professionals, and exceptionality: A special partnership.* Columbus, OH: Merrill/Macmillan.

Turnbull, A. P., Winton, P. J., Blacher, J. B., & Salkind, N. (1983). Mainstreaming in the kindergarten classroom: Perspectives of parents of handicapped and nonhandicapped children. *Journal of the Division of Early Childhood, 6,* 14–20.

Unia, S. (1985). From sunny days to green onions: On journal writing. In J. M. Newman (Ed.), *Whole language: Theory in use* (pp. 65–72). Portsmouth, NH: Heinemann Educational Books.

Uthe-Reyno, M. G., & McKinnon, D. L. J. (1989). Teacher's modeling encourages learning in Indian students. *Education Horizons, 67*(4), 163–165.

Valencia, S. (1990). A portfolio approach to classroom reading assessment: The whys, whats, and hows. *The Reading Teacher, 43*(4), 338–340.

Valero-Figueira, E. (1988). Hispanic children. *Teaching Exceptional Children, 20*(40), 47–48.

VanDijk, T. A. (1979). *Macrostructure.* Hillsdale, NJ: Erlbaum.

Veit, D. T., Scruggs, T. E., & Mastropieri, M. A. (1986). Extended mnemonic instruction with learning disabled students. *Journal of Educational Psychology, 78,* 300–308.

Viorst, J. (1972). *Alexander and the terrible, horrible, no-good, very bad day.* New York: Atheneum.

Waksman, S. A. (1985). *The Waksman social skills rating scale—aggressive and passive.* Portland, OR: ASIEP Education.

Walker, B. L. (1988). *Basic English grammar* (2nd ed.). Baltimore: Media Materials.

Walker, H. M., & Hops, H. (1976). Increasing academic achievement by reinforcing direct academic performance and/or facilitating nonacademic responses. *Journal of Educational Psychology, 68,* 218–225.

Walker, H. M., McConnel, S., Holmes, D., Todis, B., Walker, J., & Goldern, N. (1983). *The Walker social skills curriculum.* Austin, TX: Pro-Ed.

Walker, J. L. (1987). Language and curriculum development for American Indian handicapped children. In M. J. Johnson & B. A. Ramirez (Eds.), *American Indian exceptional children and youth* (pp. 17–23). Reston, VA: The Council for Exceptional Children.

Walker, J. L. (1988). Young American Indian children. *Teaching Exceptional Children, 20*(4), 50–51.

Walker, S. (1981). *Structuring the learning environment for minority handicapped students.* Washington, DC: National Alliance of Black School Educators, Special Education Programs.

Wallace, G., & Kauffman, J. M. (1986). *Teaching students with learning and behavior problems* (3rd ed.). Columbus, OH: Merrill/Macmillan.

Wallace, W. P. (1965). Review of the historical, empirical, and theoretical status of the Von-Restorff phenomenon. *Psychological Bulletin, 63,* 410–424.

Walley, W. V., & Stokes, J. P. (1981, January). *Self-help support groups for teachers under stress.*

Paper presented at the annual meeting of the American Psychological Association, Los Angeles.

Wang, M. C., & Reynolds, M. C. (1985) Avoiding the "catch 22" in special education reform. *Exceptional Children, 52,* 497–502.

Wang, M. C., Reynolds, M. C., & Walberg, H. J. (1986). Rethinking special education. *Educational Leadership, 44*(1), 26–31.

Washington, V. M., & Miller-Jones, D. (1989). Teacher interactions with nonstandard English speakers during reading instruction. *Contemporary Educational Psychology, 14,* 280–312.

Watson, D. L., Northcutt, L., & Rydele, L. (1989). Teaching bilingual students successfully. *Educational Leadership, 46*(5), 59–61.

Watson, O. M. (1970). Proxemic behavior: A cross-cultural study. *The Hague.* The Hague: Mouton.

Webb, N. M. (1985). Verbal interaction and learning in peer-directed groups. *Theory into Practice, 24*(1), 32–39.

Wei, T. T. D. (1980). *Vietnamese refuge students: A handbook for school personnel* (2nd ed.). (ERIC Document Reproduction Service No. ED 208 109)

Weinstein, C. S. (1981). Classroom design as an external condition for learning. *Educational Technology, 21*(8), 12–19.

Weinstein, C. E., Goetz, E. T., & Alexander, P. A. (1988). *Learning and study strategies: Issues in assessment, instruction, and evaluation.* San Diego: Academic Press.

Weiskopf, P. E. (1980). Burnout among teachers of exceptional children. *Exceptional Children, 47*(1), 18–23.

Weitzman, L. J., & Rizzo, D. (1974). *Biased textbooks: A research perspective.* Washington, DC: Resource Center on Sex Roles in Education.

Welch, M., Judge, T., Anderson, J., Bray, J., Child, B., & Franke, L. (1990). COOP: A tool for implementing prereferral consultation. *Teaching Exceptional Children, 22*(2), 30–31.

Wells, G. (1981). *Learning through interaction.* Cambridge, MA: Cambridge University Press.

Wesson, C. L. (1987). Increasing efficiency. *Teaching Exceptional Children, 20*(1), 46–47.

West, J. F., & Brown, P. A. (1987). State departments of education policies on consultation in special education: The state of the states. *Remedial and Special Education, 8,* 45–51.

West, J. F., & Cannon, G. S. (1988). Essential collaborative consultation competencies for regular and special educators. *Journal of Learning Disabilities, 21*(1), 56–63.

West, R. P., Young, K. R., & Spooner, F. (1990). Precision teaching: An introduction. *Teaching Exceptional Children, 22*(3), 4–9.

West, R. P., Young, K. R., West, W. J., Johnson, J. I., & Freston, C. W. (1985). *AC-CEL: An artificial intelligence system for student performance evaluation and instructional decision making.* Sarasota, FL: Precision Teaching Materials and Associates.

White, O. R. (1980). *Precision teaching workshop.* Orlando, FL.

White, O. R., & Haring, N. G. (1976). *Exceptional teaching.* Columbus, OH: Merrill/Macmillan.

White, O. R., & Haring, N. (1980). *Exceptional teaching* (2nd ed.). Columbus, OH: Merrill/Macmillan.

White, O. R., & Liberty, K. A. (1976). Evaluation and measurement. In N. G. Haring & R. Schiefelbusch (Eds.), *Teaching special children* (pp. 31–71). New York: McGraw-Hill.

White, W. J. (1985). The validity of occupational skills in career education: Fact or fantasy? *Career Development for Exceptional Children, 6,* 51–60.

White, W. J., Alley, G. R., Deshler, D. D., Schumaker, J. B., Warner, M. M., & Clark, F. L. (1982). Are there learning disabilities after high school? *Exceptional Children, 49,* 273–274.

Wicklund, L. K. (1989). Shared poetry: A whole language experience adapted for remedial readers. *The Reading Teacher, 42*(7), 478–481.

Wiig, E., & Semel, E. (1984). *Language assessment and intervention for the learning disabled.* (2nd ed.). Columbus, OH: Merrill/Macmillan.

Will, M. (1984). Bridges from school to work life. *Interchange,* June 2–6.

Will, M. C. (1986). Educating children with learning problems: A shared responsibility. *Exceptional Children, 51*(5), 411–416.

Willig, A., & Swedo, J. (1987, April). *Improving teaching strategies for exceptional Hispanic limited English proficient students: An exploratory study of task engagement and teaching strategies.* Paper presented at the annual meeting of the American Educational Research Association, Washington, DC.

Wilson, A. B. (1989). Theory into practice: An effective program for urban youth. *Educational Horizons, 67,* 136–144.

Wilson, L., Cone, T., Bradley, C., & Reese, J. (1986). The characteristics of learning disabled and other handicapped students referred for evaluation in the state of Iowa. *Journal of Learning Disabilities, 19*(9), 553–557.

Wilson, R. (1987). Direct observation of academic learning time. *Teaching Exceptional Children, 19*(2), 13–17.

Winters, P. (1976). *The bear and the fly.* New York: Crown.

Winton, P., & Turnbull, A. P. (1981). Parent involvement as viewed by parents of preschool handicapped children. *Topics in Early Childhood Special Education, 1*(3), 11–19.

Wohlge, N. (1983). Keeping communication clear. In O. Miramontes (Ed.), Application of research and theory in the classroom, (p. 538). *Learning Disability Quarterly, 6*(4), 535–542.

Wolf, D. P. (1989). Portfolio assessment: Sampling student work. *Educational Leadership, 46*(7), 35–39.

Wolf, M. M. (1978). Social validity: The case for subjective measurement or how applied behavior analysis is finding its heart. *Journal of Applied Behavioral Analysis, 11,* 103–214.

Women on Words and Images. (1975). *Dick and Jane as victims: Sex stereotyping in children's readers.* Princeton, NJ: author.

Wong, B. Y. (1986). Metacognition and special education: A review of a view. *The Journal of Special Education, 20*(1), 9–29.

Wong, B. Y., & Jones, W. (1982). Increasing metacomprehension in learning-disabled and normally-achieving students through self-questioning training. *Learning Disability Quarterly, 5,* 228–240.

Wong, B. Y., Wong, R., & LaMare, L. (1982). The effects of knowledge of criterion-task on comprehension and recall in normally achieving and learning-disabled children. *Journal of Educational Research, 76,* 119–126.

Wood, J. W., & Wooley, J. A. (1986). Adapting textbooks. *Clearing House, 59*(7), 332–35.

Woodcock, R. W. (1967). *The Peabody-Chicago-Detroit reading project—A report of the second-year results.* (ERIC Document Service No. ED 017 413)

Woodcock, R. W. (1981). *Woodcock reading mastery tests.* Circle Pines, MN: American Guidance Service.

Yates, J. R. (1989). Demography as it affects special education. In A. A. Ortiz & B. A. Ramirez (Eds.), *Schools and the culturally diverse exceptional student: Promising practices and future directions* (second printing, pp. 1–5). Reston, VA: The Council for Exceptional Children.

Yee, L. Y. (1988). Asian children. *Teaching Exceptional Children, 20*(4), 49–50.

Young, J. (1983, July). *Improving communications with parents of black students.* Presentation at National Conference and Training Workshops on the Exceptional Black Child, Atlanta, GA.

Ysseldyke, J. E., & Algozzine, B. (1990). *Introduction to special education.* Boston: Houghton Mifflin.

Ysseldyke, J. E., Algozzine, B., Richey, L., & Graden, J. (1982). Declaring students eligible for learning disability services: Why bother with the data? *Learning Disability Quarterly, 5,* 37–44.

Zabel, R. H., Boomer, L., & King, T. (1984). A model of stress and burnout among teachers of behaviorally disordered students. *Behavioral Disorders, 9*(3), 215–221.

Zabel, R. H., & Zabel, M. K. (1982). Factors in burnout among teachers of exceptional children. *Exceptional Children, 49*(3), 261–263.

Zaragoza, N. (1987). Process writing for high-risk and learning-disabled students. *Reading Research and Instruction, 26*(4), 290–301.

Zigmond, N., & Thorton, H. (1985). Follow-up of postsecondary age learning-disabled graduates and drop-outs. *Learning Disability Research, 1,* 50–55.

Author Index

Subject Index

MAF. *See* Materials Analysis Form
Magic Slate II, 406
Main ideas, 271
Mainstreaming, 12, 15
 cooperative learning and, 300
 monitoring progress and, 116–120
Maintenance level, 73, 123
Mapping, 275, 278, 289
Marginal gloss technique, 132, 133
Marking systems, audiotapes and, 136
Maslach Burnout Inventory (MBI), 377
Mastery aims, 64–65, 69–71, 73, 74
 appropriateness of skills and, 72
 computers and, 330
 graphing and, 92
Mastery learning, 229, 230
Mastery monitoring, 104–109, 110, 119
Materials. *See* Instructional materials
Materials Analysis Form (MAF), 128,
  129–130
Math
 curriculum-based measurement and, 77
 errors in, 57–58
Math Blaster Plus, 408
Math Concepts I and II, 408
Mathematics in Action, 62, 63
Math Shop Series, 408
MBI (*Maslach Burnout Inventory*), 377
Mechanics of Word Problems, 408
Memory strategies, 281–285
Mental health consultation, 155, 157, 192
Metacognition, 246–251, 265
Microsoft Works 2.0 -Microsoft, 407
Minority representation, 6. *See also* Culturally
  diverse students
 literature and, 124–126, 128
Miscue analysis, 80–81, 84
Mnemonic strategies, 281–282, 285, 289
Modeling, 211–213, 228. *See also* Guided
  practice
 direct instruction and, 233–234
 note taking and, 274
 peer tutoring and, 297
 social skills training and, 369–370, 372
 strategic instruction and, 260
 student involvement and, 216
Money, 408
Monsters & Make-Believe, 409
Motivation
 computers and, 330

instructional materials and, 122, 128
instructional techniques and, 201–205, 210
printed materials and, 135
reciprocal teaching and, 254
study skills and, 269–270
whole language approach and, 312
Multicultural literature, 124–126, 128

National Committee on Excellence in Education
  (1983), 47
Native Americans, 403–404
 literature for, 124
Naturalistic observation, 366
No-chance days, 92
Nonverbal skills, 178–179, 180, 182, 193
Notes and newsletters, 188–190
Note taking, 167, 272–274

Objectives
 cooperative learning and, 305
 criterion-referenced tests and, 64–65
 identification of, 72
 mastery monitoring and, 105, 106
 peer tutoring and, 295
 short term, 35–36
 unit method and, 238, 239, 243
Observations, written, 106, 109
Off-task talk, 200
OLE (Optimal Learning Environment Curriculum
  Guide), 315
Open-ended questioning, 182
Operation Frog, 411
Optimal Learning Environment (OLE) Curriculum
  Guide, 315
Oregon Trail, 410
Organization
 databases and, 344, 345
 data collection and, 112
 information and, 282–285
 instructional materials and, 127
 learning centers and, 146
 note taking and, 273
 printed materials and, 134–135
 Skills for School Success program and, 262
 study skills and, 281
Orientation activities, 49–52
Outlines, 283–285, 287
Outlining, 273
Output channels, 68–69
Overhead transparencies, computerized, 340